BRINGING CULTURAL DIVERSITY TO FEMINIST PSYCHOLOGY

Bringing Cultural Diversity to Feminist Psychology

THEORY, RESEARCH, AND PRACTICE

edited by Hope Landrine

American Psychological Association

Washington, D C

First printing September 1995
Second printing May 1996

Published by
American Psychological Association
750 First Street, NE
Washington, DC 20002

Copies may be ordered from
APA Order Department
P.O. Box 2710
Hyattsville, MD 20784

Typeset in Goudy by PRO-Image Corporation, Techna-Type Div., York, PA

Printer: Data Reproductions Corp., Rochester Hills, MI
Cover Designer: Supon Design Group, Washington, DC
Cover Illustrator: Debra E. Riffe, La Jolla, CA
Technical/Production Editor: Susan Bedford

Library of Congress Cataloging-in-Publication Data
Bringing cultural diversity to feminist psychology : theory, research,
    and practice / edited by Hope Landrine.
        p.   cm.
    Includes bibliographical references and index.
    ISBN 1-55798-292-9 (acid-free paper)
    1. Feminist psychology   2. Multiculturalism—Psychological
aspects.   I. Landrine, Hope, 1954–
BF201.4..B75   1955
150'.82—dc20   95-18570
                                                         CIP

British Library Cataloguing-in-Publication Data
A CIP record is available from the British Library

Printed in the United States of America

*For my mother Sarah, my sisters Faith, Caryl, and Felicia,
and for bell hooks, whose books continue to challenge and inspire me.*

CONTENTS

CONTRIBUTORS

Mimi Acosta is a child psychologist in Seattle with faculty appointments in the departments of psychiatry and psychology at the University of Washington. She also conducts a part-time private practice specializing in assessment and treatment of traumatized children. Dr. Acosta provides training in play therapy and assessment of children with special needs to graduate students and postdoctoral fellows.

Betty M. Bayer, a social psychologist, is at Hobart and William Smith Colleges. She has published articles in social psychology and critiques of sociobiology. She is currently studying social psychology's construction of gender in small group research, and the development of social psychology's laboratory practices, including the relation between experimenters and machines.

Laura S. Brown is a feminist therapist in private practice and a clinical professor of psychology at the University of Washington. She has written extensively on feminist therapy, ethics, and practice, as well as on the integration of anti-domination strategies into the continuum of feminist psychology.

Ana Mari Cauce is associate professor and director of clinical training in the Department of Psychology, University of Washington. She received her PhD in clinical/community psychology at Yale University in 1984. Dr. Cauce's research has focused primarily on factors that influence the socioemotional and adaptive functioning of ethnic minority adolescents and "at-risk" adolescents, such as runaway and homeless youths. She also has interests in social policy affecting children and families, especially children and families of color. She has provided services to several local and national panels and advisory boards.

Sandra Bennett Choney is an assistant professor of counseling psychology at the University of Oklahoma, where she earned her PhD in 1991. She has been involved in American Indian education since the late 1970s. Her most recent research interests include racial attitude formation in American Indian and White cultures and the effects of these attitudes on mental health. Other research interests include the effects of certain social influence variables in counseling American Indians.

Gloria Cowan, a professor of psychology at California State University, San Bernardino, has conducted research and published articles on attitudes toward pornography regulation, dominance and exploitation in X-rated videocassettes, and gender and survival in "slasher" films. She also has conducted research on racism and sexism in interracial pornography and the types of themes in pornography seen as degrading and dehumanizing. She participated in a national conference, Speech, Equality, and Harm: Feminist Legal Perspectives on Pornography and Hate Propaganda.

Michael G. Garko is an assistant professor in the Department of Communication at the University of South Florida and a communication consultant specializing in corporate communication and survey research. He received his PhD in communication theory and research from Florida State University in 1988. In addition to his research on feminist issues, Dr. Garko has published in the areas of social influence and persuasion within organizational settings, medical communication, communication education, and corporate social performance. He has received a number of awards for his achievements in teaching and research.

Angela B. Ginorio is director of the Northwest Center for Research on Women, and assistant professor in Women Studies with adjunct appointments in Psychology and American Ethnic Studies at the University of Washington. She received her BA and MA from the University of Puerto Rico and her PhD from Fordham University. Her work focuses on equity issues for women in science and education, ethnicity and feminism, and sexual harassment. The Association of American Colleges published her recent monograph, *Warming the Climate for Women in Academic Science* (1995).

Lorraine Gutiérrez is associate professor of social work and psychology at the University of Michigan. Her research, practice, and teaching are focused on multicultural theory and practice. One of her major interests is how ethnic and gender identity affect women's life choices. She is currently coauthoring a book with Edith Lewis on empowering Women of Color.

Diane F. Halpern is a professor of psychology at California State University, San Bernardino. She is the author of several books on gender and cognition, including *Sex Differences in Cognitive Abilities* (2nd ed.), *Thought and Knowledge: An Introduction to Critical Thinking* (3rd ed.), and *Changing College Classrooms: The Challenge of Educating Students for the 21st Century*. Dr. Halpern has won numerous awards for her teaching and research, including the California State University (state-wide) Outstanding Professor Award and the Outstanding Alumna Award from the University of Cincinnati.

Calliope Haritos is a doctoral student in developmental psychology at the Graduate School and University Center of City University of New York. She is conducting research on bilingual memory in children.

Nancy M. Henley, professor of psychology at the University of California, Los Angeles, is the coauthor of *Language and Sex: Difference and Dominance* (with Barrie Thorne, 1975) and *Language, Gender, and Society* (with Barrie Thorne and Cheris Kramarae, 1983). She is also the author of several journal articles and book chapters on language, nonverbal communication, gender, and power.

Nicole E. Holland is a doctoral student in social-personality psychology at the Graduate School and University Center of City University of New York. Her dissertation research addresses issues of race and ethnicity in higher education.

Amy James is a doctoral student in counseling psychology at the University of Wisconsin—Madison. She has an MA and an MED in counseling and secondary guidance from Teachers College, Columbia University, and a BS in education from Cornell University.

Elizabeth Kelly is a doctoral student in developmental psychology at the Graduate School and University Center of City University of New York. Her dissertation research focuses on gender and communication issues in the development of children.

Ellen B. Kimmel is a professor in the Psychological and Social Foundations Department of the University of South Florida and holds a joint appointment in psychology. She served on APA's first Committee on Women, was president of Division 35, and continues to be active in women's issues. In 1978 she was president of the Southeastern Psychological Association. Dr. Kimmel is a Fellow of APA's Divisions 35 and 9 and of the American Psychological Society and the American Association of Applied and Preventative Psychology. She and coauthor Michael Garko have collaborated on a series of gender studies combining psychology and communication.

Elizabeth A. Klonoff, a clinical and health psychologist, received her PhD in clinical psychology from the University of Oregon in 1977. She was the director of the Behavioral Medicine Clinic at University Hospitals of Cleveland, Case Western Reserve University Medical School (1979–1988) and is currently professor of psychology and executive director of the Behavioral Health Institute at California State University, San Bernardino. In addition to teaching and acting as director of the Institute, she conducts several grant-supported projects on sexism, racism, and health. Dr. Klonoff has published widely on culture and gender diversity in health behavior and behavioral medicine. Her articles have appeared in *Journal of the American Medical Association*, *Preventive Medicine*, *Psychology of Women Quarterly*, *Journal of Black Psychology*, and *Health Psychology*.

Teresa D. LaFromboise is an associate professor of counseling psychology at the University of Wisconsin. She received her PhD from the University of Oklahoma in 1980 and has been involved in American Indian education and mental health since 1971. Her current research is on the cultural adaptation of social skills training interventions for health promotions with American Indian youth. She also is interested in social influence variables in the counseling psychology process with American Indian clients.

Bernice Lott, a UCLA PhD, is a professor of psychology and women's studies at the University of Rhode Island. She teaches social psychology and has published in the areas of interpersonal attraction, sexist discrimination, sexual harassment, and the social construction of gender. In 1988 she received her university's Award for Scholarly Excellence, and she served as president of APA Division 35 in 1990–1991. Her book *Women's Lives: Themes and Variations in Gender Learning* is in its second edition (Brooks/Cole, 1994), and a new book, *The Social Psychology of Interpersonal Discrimination*, coedited with Diane Maluso, is in press (Guilford).

Shari E. Miles is the Fellowship Program director and a research associate with the Women's Research and Education Institute, and a doctoral candidate in the Department of Psychology at Howard University. Her research interests include racial identity development and reproductive health issues.

Jill G. Morawski is a professor of psychology at Wesleyan University. Her interests in theory extend to gender studies and to the history of science. In addition to writing articles in these areas, she edited *The Rise of Experimentation in American Psychology* (Yale, 1988) and authored *Feminist Psychology: Practices of a Liminal Science* (University of Michigan, in press).

Michele A. Paludi is Principal of Michele Paludi & Associates, Consultants in Sexual Harassment, and offers education and training in issues related to sexual harassment at schools, colleges, and other organizations. She was a member of Governor Cuomo's Task Force on Sexual Harassment, and she serves as an expert witness for academic and court proceedings involving sexual harassment. Dr. Paludi is the author of nine books on sexual harassment, psychology of women, and gender. *Ivory Power: Sexual Harassment on Campus* (SUNY Press, 1990) was the 1992 recipient of the Gustavus Myers Center Award for the Outsanding Book on Human Rights in the United States.

Natalie Porter is associate professor and chief psychologist in the Division of Child and Adolescent Psychiatry, University of New Mexico School of Medicine. She directs Programs for Children and Adolescents, an outpatient mental health program. Dr. Porter is coeditor of *Feminist Ethics in Psychotherapy*, with Hannah Lerman, and she has written several articles on feminist and multicultural training issues. She is past president of Division 35 of the APA.

Pamela Trotman Reid, professor of developmental psychology, is currently acting associate provost and dean of academic affairs at the Graduate School and University Center of the City University of New York. Her publications attempt to illuminate the dynamics of class, ethnicity, and gender, particularly for children and women. Her recent research focuses on stress related to poverty. She is a fellow of the APA and the American Psychological Society, and a past president of Division 35 of the APA.

Maria P. P. Root is a clinical psychologist in private practice in Seattle, Washington, and clinical associate professor of psychology and associate professor of ethnic studies at the University of Washington. Her interests include the mental health of minorities and women, and race relations. Her last two edited books are *Racially Mixed People in America* (Sage, 1992) and *Racially Mixed People in the New Millenium* (Sage, in press). She is a consultant to the National Research Center on Asian American Mental Health.

Paulette Running Wolf is a doctoral student in counseling psychology at the University of Wisconsin-Madison. She received her MEd in school counseling from Western Washington University in 1987 and has worked extensively in tribal communities in the areas of adolescent health and substance abuse prevention.

Judyth Scott is currently a project associate for the Behavioral Health Institute at California State University, San Bernardino. She received her BA in sociology from California State University, San Bernardino in 1993. In her capacity as project associate, Judyth conducts tobacco-control research and has coauthored articles on gender and cultural diversity in health behavior.

Veronica G. Thomas is professor and chair in the Department of Human Development and Psychoeducational Studies at Howard University. Her research interests include midlife development, gender roles, the psychology of African American women, well-being and coping in African American families, and career aspirations of women and minorities. Thomas has published numerous articles and book chapters in these areas. Her work has appeared in journals such as *Journal of the National Medical Association, Sex Roles, Journal of Multicultural Counseling and Development, Journal of Social Psychology, Psychological Reports,* and *Adolescence.*

Rhoda K. Unger is a professor of psychology and director of the honors program at Montclair State University. She received a PhD in experimental psychology from Harvard University. Most of her research has been on the psychology of women and the social construction of gender. She is past president of Division 35 of the APA and the first recipient of its Carolyn Wood Sherif Award. Her recent publications include a special issue of the *Psychology of Women Quarterly* on gender and culture, coedited with Janis Sanchez-Hucles (December 1993) and a textbook *Women and Gender: A Feminist Psychology,* coauthored with Mary Crawford (1992; 2nd ed. in press).

FOREWORD

It is an honor and a pleasure to have been asked to write the Foreword for this outstanding book. This book deals directly with the most challenging issues within feminist psychology, raises urgent and necessary questions about the situation of "woman" in cultures, large or small, and attempts to provide some preliminary, testable answers. The contributors to this book address issues that are vital to the continued health and vitality of feminist psychology. They ask us to consider the impact that serious attention to women's ethnicity, and recognition of the reality of our multiculturalism, will have on the research questions we ask, who we study, where we search for answers, how we ask our questions, our process and analyses, our theories of gender, our conceptions of power, and our practice as teachers, counselors, therapists, administrators, consultants, and social activists.

My pride in this book has two personal sources beyond that of being a small part of the brilliant group of scholars whose contributions comprise it. Hope Landrine, the book's editor and "mother," is one of my former graduate students, and it is with awe and delight that I watch her continuing growth as a feminist theorist and researcher. This book also is an indirect product of a goal I set when I first became president of the Psychology of Women Division (Division 35) of the American Psychological Association: to encourage ethnic diversity in our leadership and, as a primary focus of our activities, our research, teaching, and practice. I urged the division's members to take seriously the words we had carefully and clearly drafted for our membership brochure: "Division 35 provides a forum for the development of a comprehensive and multi-cultural approach to understanding the psychological and social realities of women." In practicing feminist psychology, these words were only sometimes reflected in our work, and this was especially true of those of us who were not women of color.

European American feminist women had been focusing so intently on our position and experiences relative to European American men that many had simply not considered the cultural limitations of this focus. They were not hearing the articulate voices of women of color talking about positions and experiences relative to other women as well as to men. It was primarily the feminists who had been excluded from theory, research, training, and positions of leadership who spoke directly and pointedly to the reality of this exclusion and to its consequences for feminist scholarship and practice.

Hurtado (1989) reminded White middle-class women of their position of privilege within contemporary United States society and of the "economic and social benefits attached to [their] roles" as "the lovers, mothers, and partners (however unequal) of [W]hite men" (p. 842). If White women are subordinated through seduction but women of color are subordinated through rejection, "these groups of women have different political responses and skills" (p. 843), and women of color are oppressed "not only by members of their own group but by [W]hites of both genders" (p. 839). Thus, Hurtado argued, "the definition of woman is constructed differently for [W]hite women and women of Color" (p. 845). In their introduction to a special issue of *Sex Roles* on gender and ethnicity, Reid and Comas-Diaz (1990) documented the failure of gender research to include race and ethnic concerns. Espin (1991) argued, as have others, that if feminist psychology is not a psychology for all women, then it is not really feminist, and we can add that it is also not really psychology.

To take seriously our understanding of gender as a social construction means that it is essential to place ourselves and the women (and men) we work with, study, theorize about, assist, and teach in positions relevant to ethnicity, time and place, social class, sexuality, age, and so on. This is not an addition to the feminist psychology we practice but a fundamental requirement of our perspective. Inclusion of all women and recognition of diversity are not really options; otherwise, our feminist psychology will grow pale and inconsequential. There can be no feminist psychology (indeed, no valid psychology) without attending to variation among persons in culture (i.e., in background, language, values, norms, aspirations, special problems, barriers to goal achievement, etc.). It is only by acknowledging and studying variations that commonalities can be discerned and understood, enabling feminist strategies for achieving equal status among people to be proposed and pursued.

The scope of the chapters in this book is impressive, covering areas of interest to developmental, social, clinical, and general psychologists. Each author explores ways of attending to diversity and multiculturalism to enrich our thinking, research, and practice. The contributors share the common objective of keeping feminist psychology robust, meaningful, and useful as we further our understanding of women's lives, challenge patriarchal stereotypes, institutions, and power inequities, and move toward the achievement of personal, social, and political conditions that will contribute positively to the skills, health, and joy of all women.

BERNICE LOTT
University of Rhode Island

REFERENCES

Espin, O. M. (1991, August) *Ethnicity, race and class and the future of feminist psychology*. Paper presented at the 99th Annual Convention of the American Psychological Association, San Francisco.

Hurtado, A. (1989). Relating to privilege: Seduction and rejection in the subordination of white women and women of color. *Signs, 14,* 833–855.

Reid, P. T., & Comas-Diaz, L. (1990). Gender and ethnicity: Perspectives on dual status. *Sex Roles, 22,* 397–408.

PREFACE

In the past decade, feminist psychologists have shown increasing interest in the diversity of women's experiences and have begun to emphasize the need to integrate data on race, social class, and cultural differences into the mainstream of research and theory (Anthias & Yuval-Davis, 1983; Cole, 1986; Fine, 1985; Kahn & Jean, 1983; B. L. Lott, 1991). There also has been an increase in research on specific groups of women of color, resulting in new, challenging data and theory on Latina women (e.g., Amaro & Russo, 1987; Mirande & Enriquez, 1979), Native American women (e.g., Blackwood, 1984; Greene, 1980; Medicine, 1978), Asian American women (e.g., Fujitomi & Wong, 1981; J. T. Lott & Pian, 1979), and African American women (e.g., Matson, 1983; Murray & Scott, 1981; Smith & Stewart, 1983), as well as on poor women (e.g., Belle, 1990; Dill, 1983).

Unfortunately, despite such data and calls for their integration into the mainstream of feminist psychology, a White, middle-class focus nonetheless still characterizes many textbooks on the psychology of women and many articles in feminist psychological journals (Brown, Goodwin, Hall, & Jackson-Lowman, 1985; Thomas & Miles, chapter 13 in this book). Thus, even though women of color constitute most of the women in the world and are steadily increasing in the United States, data on such women usually receive a perfunctory treatment that reflects and perpetuates their marginal status in feminist psychology.

To begin to address this problem, Bernice Lott, president of the American Psychological Association's (APA's) Division 35 (1990–1991), appointed the task force on cultural diversity in feminist psychology and appointed me to chair that task force. The charge of the task force was to begin the process of bringing cultural diversity into the mainstream of feminist psychological research, theory, practice, and advocacy. To meet such a challenge, I gathered a large group of women from across the nation and from many ethnic groups. Among other goals (see the Appendix), the task force wished to gather data and theory on women of color into a single book that could serve as a resource for students, practitioners, and scholars. This book represents the most tangible fruits of those efforts. It can be a valuable resource not only for psychologists but also for other mental health professionals, for sociologists and other social scientists, and for scholars in women's studies and in ethnic studies.

This book is groundbreaking in feminist psychology because it is the first book to address issues of cultural diversity in feminist psychology as a whole—in theory, specific areas of research, and practice. Because it is the first effort, it provides much yet also omits some important topics. For example, although the book provides chapters on ethnicity and feminist therapy and on culture and gender socialization, it simultaneously lacks chapters on ethnicity and battering, culture and the sexual abuse of girls, ethnicity and rape, culture and women's sexuality, intimacy, susceptibility to influence, leadership, and so on. The absence of these chapters reflects the neglect of culture in feminist psychology. Because of such neglect, there is only a handful of feminist scholars who have done research on these important topics from a multicultural perspective. In addition to their own professional responsibilities, those women are overwhelmed by their roles as earnest or token representatives of cultural diversity on countless national, regional, and university committees and on journal editorial boards. When asked to contribute scholarly chapters on ethnicity and rape or culture and battering to this book, they responded that they simply did not have time. When reading this book, one can focus either on the absence of these chapters or on what the book provides. My hope is that readers will focus primarily on what this book provides but also consider assisting us in making future editions more inclusive and superior by contacting me and contributing chapters on the topics that have been omitted. This book is the first but not the final effort to bring cultural diversity to the foreground of feminist psychology. As such, it is an ongoing process. Future books will change and improve as feminist psychology becomes more inclusive, as more feminist psychologists devote their attention to issues of diversity, and as more radical voices choose to be heard in books like this one.

The chapters in this book differ significantly from each other in length, focus, perspective, writing style, and the kind of information presented. This diversity reflects not only differences in the data available on specific topics but also cultural (positional) differences among the authors. The authors here represent African Americans (from vastly different geographical regions and cultural backgrounds), European Americans (from a diversity of cultures), Asian Americans (from different cultures), Latinas (from different Latino cultures) and Native Americans (from different tribes). Each author brings her own cultural perspective, values, and concerns to her chapter and focuses on the issues that she chose as the most relevant to address. As editor, I could have (and the editors at the APA could have) severely edited these chapters in an all too common, Procrustean effort to render them similar despite the limbs lost. That kind of editing, known as "white-washing" among scholars of color (hooks, 1992), is one of the many ways that feminist psychology excludes diversity (viz., by voicing-over the voices of women of color). Neither I nor APA's editors and reviewers have white-washed these chapters because this is perhaps the most fundamental level at which cultural diversity in feminist psychology needs to begin. Reviewers and editors of feminist journals and of books like this one must begin to accept the differences in perspectives among women of different cultures and allow views to be heard without editing the "baby out with the bath water." Women of color complain incessantly about the cultural biases of reviewers and editors who transform what they never understood into something the author never wrote, thereby excluding the diversity we ostensibly seek to achieve (hooks, 1990).

In contrast, each chapter here focuses on the issues deemed most relevant by its authors, and offers its own conclusions and suggestions for feminist psychology. Those differ significantly from chapter to chapter and do not necessarily agree with one another, and readers may not agree with all of them. Likewise, when reading this book, one may wonder how chapters that differ so vastly in perspective could be grouped together into a single topical section. That diversity is precisely the point.

HOPE LANDRINE
Rancho Cucamonga, California

REFERENCES

Amaro, H., & Russo, N. F. (1987). Hispanic women and mental health: Contemporary issues in research and practice [Special issue] *Psychology of Women Quarterly, 11*(4).

Anthias, F., & Yuval-Davis, N. (1983). Contextualizing feminism: Gender, ethnic, and class divisions. *Feminist Review, 15*, 62–75.

Belle, D. (1990). Poverty and women's mental health. *American Psychologist, 45*, 385–389.

Blackwood, E. (1984). Sexuality and gender in certain Native American tribes: The case of cross-gender females. *Signs, 10*, 27–42.

Brown, A., Goodwin, B. J., Hall, B. A., & Jackson-Lowman, H. A. (1985). Review of psychology of women textbooks: Focus on the Afro-American woman. *Psychology of Women Quarterly, 9*, 29–38.

Cole, J. B. (1986). *All American women: Lines that divide, ties that bind.* New York: Free Press.

Dill, B. T. (1983). Race, class, and gender: Prospects for an all-inclusive sisterhood. *Feminist Studies, 9,* 131–150.

Fine, M. (1985). Reflections on a feminist psychology of women. *Psychology of Women Quarterly, 9,* 167–183.

Fujitomi, I., & Wong, D. (1981). The new Asian-American woman. In J. S. Cox (Ed.), *Female psychology: The emerging self* (pp. 213–248). New York: St. Martin's Press.

Greene, R. (1980). Native American women. *Signs, 6,* 248–267.

hooks, b. (1990). *Yearning: Race, gender and cultural politics.* Boston: Gloria Watkins/South End Press.

hooks, b. (1992). *Black Looks: Race and representation.* Boston: Gloria Watkins/ South End Press.

Kahn, A., & Jean, P. (1983). Integration and elimination or separation and redefinition: The future of the psychology of women. *Signs, 8,* 659–671.

Lott, B. L. (1991). Dual natures or learned behavior: The challenge to feminist psychology. In R. Hare-Mustin & J. Marecek (Eds.), *Making a difference* (pp. 65–101). New Haven, CT: Yale University Press.

Lott, J. T., & Pian, C. (1979). *Beyond stereotypes and statistics: Emergence of Asian and Pacific American women.* Washington, DC: Organization of Pan-Asian American Women.

Matson, M. R. (1983). Black women's sex roles: The social context for a new ideology. *Journal of Social Issues, 39,* 79–100.

Medicine, B. (1978). *The Native American woman: A perspective.* Las Cruces: New Mexico State University Press.

Mirande, A., & Enriquez, E. (1979). *La Chicana: The Mexican-American woman.* Chicago: University of Chicago Press.

Murray, S. R., & Scott, P. B. (Eds.). (1981). A special issue on Black women. *Psychology of Women Quarterly, 6*(3).

Smith, A., & Stewart, A. J. (1983). Racism and sexism in Black women's lives (Special issue). *Journal of Social Trends, 39*(3).

ACKNOWLEDGMENTS

To accomplish the work that went into achieving the goals of the Cultural Diversity Task Force (see the Appendix), which included the publication of this book, many women devoted considerable time and effort to the challenges we faced. Although many of these task force participants did not write chapters for this book, their contributions in other ways were invaluable. Deepest thanks to the following for their work for the Cultural Diversity Task Force: Rosalie Ackerman, Mimi Acosta, Martha Banks, Betty Bayer, Lula Beatty, Mary Kay Biaggio, Michele Boyer, Laura Brown, Mary L. Brown, Alice Brown-Collins, Ana Mari Cauce, Lillian Comas-Díaz, Gloria Cowan, Darlene DeFour, Linda Dyer, Michael Garko, Carol Gilligan, Angela Ginorio, Lorraine Gutiérrez, Diane Halpern, Calliope Haritos, Nancy Henley, Christine Ho, Nicole Holland, Elizabeth Kelly, Ellen Kimmel, Elizabeth Klonoff, Teresa LaFromboise, Bernice Lott, Andrea Marino, Shari Miles, Jill Morawski, Kelly Morton, Michele Paludi, Martha Pearse, Natalie Porter, Pam Reid, Rosemarie Roberts, Maria Root, Anna Maria Tedesco, Veronica Thomas, Ethel Tobach, Deborah Tolman, Judith Worell, and Karen Wyche

Special thanks also to Bernice Lott for creating and supporting the task force; to Ethel Tobach for her support and advice; to Cheryl Travis for her work to see this book published as the first in an exciting series from Division 35; to the many outside reviewers and APA editors who participated in making this book possible; and to authors who, despite their schedules and responsibilities, wrote the chapters.

1

INTRODUCTION: CULTURAL DIVERSITY, CONTEXTUALISM, AND FEMINIST PSYCHOLOGY

HOPE LANDRINE

In recent years, psychology as a whole and feminist psychology in particular have focused greater attention on cultural diversity and on the need to integrate such diversity into teaching, theory, research, and practice. There has been an enormous increase in the past 10 years in publications reporting ethnic differences on a variety of behaviors relevant to feminist, social, clinical, health, and developmental psychology (Dana, 1993; Goodchilds, 1991; Jones, 1991; Sue, 1991). Although the sheer amount of data on ethnic differences continues to mount, theories regarding those differences have not. Instead, research on ethnic differences remains strikingly atheoretical relative to research on all other topics, including research on gender differences (Jones, 1991). Typically, researchers simply investigate the extent to which ethnic groups differ on some scale or behavior without predicting the nature and direction of those differences and without presenting a theoretical model of why such differences should or would exist. The ensuing ethnic differences are then reported without

1

meaningful theoretical explanation, or with simplistic speculations about the cultures of others (Jones, 1991; Sue, 1991). Reporting ethnic differences without theoretical explanation belittles culture and simultaneously exploits it as a commodity for publication purposes and career advancement in the zeitgeist of multiculturalism. Reporting ethnic differences with speculative remarks about the cultures of others derides and dismisses culture, and it simultaneously re-"discovers" exotic "natives" and "primitives" whose "difference" maintains the very social arrangements ostensibly challenged by the focus on diversity (hooks, 1992).

Thus, the evidence on ethnic differences continues to mount, and most psychologists take it for granted (rightfully so) that this evidence has important implications for their knowledge and interventions. Simultaneously and nonetheless, however, explanations for the differences have not been forthcoming, and the absence of such theoretical models reflects and perpetuates the marginal status of culture in psychology. Indeed, unlike all other topics in the discipline, ethnicity alone remains without theory: There is no general theory of the relation between culture and behavior; there is no unified model of cultural differences; there is no framework for psychologists to use to make sense of the multitude of ethnic differences in the literature (Jones, 1991), and that may be precisely why integrating data on diversity into research, teaching, and practice remains difficult.

The challenge for psychology in this increasingly multicultural society and the major problem that psychologists in the next century must solve is to develop an explicit, theoretical framework through which sociocultural variables and differences will be rendered coherent. I see this as the most important problem for psychology in a multicultural society for three reasons. First, the model through which psychologists understand cultural variables will shape the structure and content of research on cultural diversity for decades to come, just as the implicit, deficit model[1] has in the past. Second, the model through which psychologists understand cultural differences will define the place of culture in psychology and will either justify its current relegation to the periphery or place it squarely in the center of the science. Finally, like the implicit, deficit model before it, the model psychology develops for understanding cultural differences likewise will play a major role in public attitudes toward minorities and in the perception, status, and the treatment of people of color in American society.

Thus, psychology as a whole and feminist psychology in particular need a model for understanding cultural variables, a theory of the relationship between culture and behavior that neither romanticizes cultures nor renders difference deviance. In this chapter I argue that contextualistic

---

[1]The term *deficit model* refers to the tendency to interpret ethnic differences as deficits, deviances, pathologies, and problems within minorities (see Jones, 1991).

behaviorism is one such possible model for psychology as a whole and specifically for feminist psychology. This is because contextualism provides a simple but radical model not only for understanding culture and ethnicity but also for understanding gender. First, I describe the concept and understanding of "behavior" that dominates modern psychology and other social sciences and highlight the manner in which this way of thinking about behavior has hampered the understanding of ethnicity. That approach is then contrasted with the contextualistic approach, and the advantages of the latter are emphasized. Finally, I summarize the manner in which the chapters in this book argue for and indeed demonstrate the benefits of contextualism.

TWO WAYS OF DEFINING *BEHAVIOR*

There are two ways that one can think about behavior, and both stem from the two radically different definitions of the word *behavior* that B. F. Skinner offered in his classic 1938 book, *Behavior of Organisms*. The first way that one can think about and understand the term *behavior* has been called *mechanistic* (Biglan, Glasgow, & Singer, 1990; Hayes & Hayes, 1992; Morris, 1988; Pepper, 1942), and this view dominates psychology as well as several other disciplines.

Mechanistic Behaviorism

The mechanistic way of conceptualizing behavior is based on Skinner's (1938) definition of behavior as "the movement of an organism or of its parts" (p. 6). Here, behavior is defined as superficial, mechanical movements, and the name for a behavior is based on the precise features of those movements. For example, reading a newspaper is a movement with specific features and therefore is a type of behavior. Not looking someone in the eye is a movement with specific features and is another type of behavior. Being aggressive or being passive likewise are both highly specific sequences of mechanical movements and are additional types of behavior. Behavior is defined and labeled in terms of the precise features of superficial mechanical movements irrespective of the context in which such movements occur. Reading a newspaper is a type of behavior and is the same type of behavior irrespective of the political, social, or cultural context in which it appears. Thus, picking up a newspaper and reading it while riding the subway on one's way to work, and picking up a newspaper and reading it in the middle of a serious discussion with one's significant other on a topic one does not want to hear about are the same behavior, regardless of these different contexts. Certainly, different contingencies surround these two episodes of reading the newspaper; the episodes have different causes or motives and most would agree with that. Nonetheless, the behavior or operant[2] is "reading the newspaper" in both cases. The essence of mechanistic behaviorism then is the assumption that movements have a meaning and a label, and have one and the same meaning and label, regardless of the context in which they are exhibited.

This mechanistic view of behavior dominates psychology, feminist psychology, and most other social sciences, irrespective of whether scholars and clinicians consider themselves to be behaviorists or to have a behavioral theoretical orientation. When researchers study aggression or aggressive behavior, they define that operant as a specific set of superficial, mechanical movements abstracted from their context. When they study depression or depressive behavior, achievement behavior, passive behavior, leadership behavior, risky sexual behavior, or any other behavior, researchers typically mean specific constellations of superficial, mechanical movements that have a label regardless of their context. The name for these various movements is assumed to be inherent in the movements themselves. Behaviors are assumed to have one and only one label and meaning that they carry with them like designer luggage across time, race, ethnicity, gender, social class, age, and international borders.

When one defines and understands behavior as superficial–mechanical movements with an inherent meaning irrespective of context, one produces a multitude of types or categories of behavior out there in the world. This way of thinking produces a social world filled with a multitude of behavioral types—of behavioral shoes that everyone everywhere can and does walk in. From this perspective, then, any person of any culture or ethnicity who engages in the specific set of movements is by definition engaging in the "same behavior" regardless of its different sociocultural contexts. When an African American woman does not look a person in the eye, an Asian American woman does not look a person in the eye, and a European American woman does not look a person in the eye, they are all necessarily engaging in precisely the same behavior. When African American, Asian American, Native American, and European American women make self-belittling remarks, they are all engaging in the same behavior, a priori. Because they are understood as engaging in the same behavior regardless of their different sociocultural contexts, they can be compared; one can compare women of different ethnic groups and ask if they differ in the frequency or prevalence of a specific behavior. The answer often is affirmative.

Implications of Mechanistic Behaviorism

This way of conceptualizing and defining behavior has several serious consequences and implications for understanding culture and ethnic

---

[2]Operants are movements or behaviors that are voluntarily exhibited, as opposed to respondents, which are movements or behaviors that are involuntary (e.g., blinking and other reflexes).

groups. First, the only reason that researchers can compare ethnic groups at all is that they have defined *behavior* as inherently meaningful, superficial, context-free movements. Behavior has to be removed from its sociocultural context and defined and labeled independent of that context in order for people of different ethnic groups—people from different sociocultural and historical contexts—to be compared. All data on ethnic differences in feminist psychology, women's studies, sociology, psychology, public health, and several other disciplines is this kind of data. Evidence of differences in the frequency and prevalence of superficial mechanical movements believed to have the same meaning irrespective of their sociocultural, political, and historical context constitutes knowledge of cultural diversity and of gender differences as well. The first serious consequence of the mechanistic view of behavior then is that it makes ethnic comparisons—and gender comparisons—possible.

In addition, by defining and understanding behavior as movements irrespective of context, the mechanistic view relegates culture and context to the periphery and renders them superfluous. The sociocultural, historical, and political context is not an integral part of the label for and definition of behavior but is instead something outside of it, something surrounding it. Thus, for example, gender stratification (i.e., the sociocultural context of women's powerlessness relative to men) is not part of the label researchers attribute to women's behavior but is instead understood as being outside of women's behavior, as a larger setting in which women's behavior occurs. Movements labeled *dependent*, for example, when engaged in by women or by men, are understood as the same behavior with the same label and meaning, and women's powerlessness does not alter that label for those movements. Women and men can be compared and women "discovered" to engage in dependent behaviors more frequently. Likewise, cultural contexts are not part of the definition and label of the behavior of people of color but instead are understood as being outside of it.

Thus, the mechanistic view creates a bifurcated world of types of behavior on the one hand, and sociocultural contexts from which they can be differentiated on the other. The context is not part of behavior but is instead understood as a place, as a mere setting in which behavior occurs. The context is viewed as a setting that impinges on behavior like a mechanistic force, changing the intensity, frequency, and probability of a behavior, but not the name and meaning of it. When researchers speak of "understanding behavior in its context" (something most endeavor to do), they mean that they invoke the ostensible forces of the context post hoc to explain the frequency or intensity of a behavior understood as exhibited within that context; the context and its forces nonetheless are conceptualized as being outside of and impinging on behavior and are not part of the name for it. The second serious consequence of the mechanistic view of behavior then is that it relegates the sociocultural, historical, and political context to the periphery of human action by making said context fully independent of the name for or meaning of the type of behavior viewed as merely occurring within it.

Finally, the third consequence of this view is that it creates, it produces ethnic differences and, indeed, gender differences as well. Race, ethnicity, culture, and gender are the most robust and complex of social, cultural, political, and historical contexts. When one defines *behavior* as mechanistic movements irrespective of these contexts, ethnic and gender differences in behavior so defined necessarily are found and exist only by virtue of that definition.

In summary, the mechanistic view of behavior manufactures the ethnic and gender "differences" that it struggles incessantly to explain. This ongoing production of a hierarchy of behavioral differences[3] reproduces and reinforces existing social hierarchies and thus perpetuates the very social arrangements purported to be challenged by the focus on differences. People of color and women are invited and encouraged to speak and write about their differences in a celebration of diversity because the ensuing hierarchy of difference maintains their low statuses. As bell hooks (1990) put it, "[the new] unprecedented support among scholars and intellectuals for the inclusion of [diversity] is a 'celebration' that fails to ask who is sponsoring the party and who is extending the invitations" (pp. 54–55). Diversity, in the current vernacular, is yet another "bandwagon" construct, Mednick's (1989) term for regressive, political constructs in psychological garb that masquerade as liberal, political change.

Thus, the bifurcated world created by the mechanistic behaviorism that dominates social science has not advanced the analysis of gender and culture. Instead, it has reduced the complex, chaotic contexts and positions of gender and culture to superficial, context-free behavioral differences that reinforce racist, patriarchal, and capitalist ideology.

Contextualistic Behaviorism

The alternative way of thinking about behavior has been called *contextualistic behaviorism* or *contextualism* (Biglan et al., 1990; Hayes & Hayes, 1992; Morris, 1988; Rosnow & Georgoudi, 1986). This way of thinking is based on the alternative definition of the term *behavior* that Skinner gave in his 1938 book, and indeed, it appeared on the same page as the mechanistic definition. The alternative definition he gave was that behavior refers to "an organism . . . having commerce with the world" (Skinner,

---

[3]The differences researchers discover typically reveal that ethnic minorities, women, the poor, and other subordinate groups have a higher prevalence of behaviors understood to be deviant, pathological, less functional, less healthy, less normal, and the like. Differences discovered always produce a psychological hierarchy in which the Other occupies a lower status than the dominant group. This psychological hierarchy of difference matches and reinforces existing social hierarchies.

1938, p. 6). In this definition, behavior is a meaningful exchange with, in, and by virtue of a context. Behavior and its context are a single unit. The operant is not a superficial–mechanical movement irrespective of context but a highly specific act-in-context. The context is therefore part of the name for the behavior, for the act-in-context. Consequently, from this perspective, a movement does not have a single label and meaning but several different labels and meanings, depending on the context in which it appears, because that context is part of what the behavior-in-context is called.

For example, from a contextualistic perspective, picking up a newspaper and reading it on the subway on one's way to work, and picking up a newspaper and reading it when one's significant other raises a topic that one does not want to hear about are *not* the same behavior; they are not both "reading the newspaper" because their contexts are different. The first behavior is "killing time on the subway" or "avoiding the potentially hostile strangers on the subway by not looking at them and pretending to be busy," where the context is part of the name of the behavior. The second behavior is "ignoring one's partner" or "letting one's partner know that one does not want to have this conversation," where the context is again part of the name of the behavior. When defined contextually, these are two different behaviors despite the similarity of the superficial–mechanical movements entailed. These two acts-in-context are responses to (elicited by) different stimuli, are maintained by different consequences, and elicit different responses from others. Thus, most people probably would not respond with anger at their significant other for picking up a newspaper and reading it on the subway on her or his way to work. However, most people probably would respond with some anger at a significant other who picks up a newspaper and reads it in the middle of a serious conversation; picks up a newspaper and reads it at the table during a holiday dinner; picks up a newspaper and reads in in synagogue or church; or picks up a newspaper and reads it while making love. In the psychology of people's everyday lives, they do not label and understand behavior as superficial movements. Instead, people think contextually; they use the context to tell them what the behavior is, what it means, and how to respond. Thus, most people would reject the idea that a partner who picked up a newspaper and started reading it in the middle of a serious discussion was simply, merely "reading the newspaper," and indeed would insist that the behavior was everything but that.

The assumptions of contextualistic behaviorism can now be made explicit. First, from this perspective, behaviors have no inherent label or meaning, no matter how obvious, there-on-the-surface, self-evident, and inherent in superficial–mechanical movements such a label and meaning may appear to be. Instead, the label for a behavior is to be discovered empirically through a careful analysis of the context in which the behavior occurs, with this context as part of the behavior's name. Silence can be "respect for my teachers," "avoiding being hit by my violent husband," or "distrust of outsiders," depending on the social, cultural, and historical context in which the superficial movement "silence" occurs. Not looking someone in the eye can be "showing respect for my elders," "ignoring the speaker," "paying close attention to the speaker," or "avoidance of the Navajo monster 'He-who-kills-with-his-eyes'," depending on the cultural, historical, and political context of the individual who does not look others in the eye. The name for a behavior is to be discovered empirically by analyzing the context, and the name is given (not by the movement but) in its context.

Finally, the third and most important assumption of contextualism is that superficially similar mechanical movements appearing in different contexts are not the same behavior. They are different behaviors, unless an empirical analysis of their discriminative stimuli, correlates, and contingencies indicates otherwise. As radical as this latter view may seem at first, it has ample empirical support. For example, studies have shown that even among White American couples and families of the 1980s of the United States, whether a movement is labeled as hitting, helping, aggression, or affection is contingent, not on the act, but on the structure and form of the relationship in which it occurs, on the context. These labels and meanings are socially constructed and negotiated in relationships. The manner in which these labels are applied to specific movements does not generalize across relationships of various types, such that these labels are by and large independent of the movements themselves (see Gergen & Gergen, 1983; Greenblat, 1983; Harre, 1981; Kayser, Swinger, & Cohen, 1984; Lasswell & Lasswell, 1976; Mummendey, Bonewasser, Loschper, & Lenneweber, 1982; Tedeschi, 1984). Such data suggest that people appear to understand behavior contextually; psychologists' ability to predict and understand behavior, and feminist psychologists' understanding of such gender-related behaviors as aggression, hitting, and helping, can be facilitated by a similar contextual approach.

Implications of Contextualism

The implications of this view for culture are clear. From this perspective, ethnic groups (as well as women and men) engaged in similar superficial movements must be assumed to be engaged in different behaviors, because their sociocultural contexts are different. Ethnic minority groups therefore cannot be compared with European Americans or with each other because there is no common behavior on which to compare them. Ethnic groups (and women and men) cannot be compared unless researchers can demonstrate empirically that the context of the movements, and so the label and meaning of the behavior, is the same. This perspective assumes that there are no ethnic (or even gender) differences in behavior. What researchers have understood to be ethnic or gender differences in the frequency or intensity of a decontextualized, superficial movement are not ethnic or gender differences at all; they are different acts in different contexts.

CONTEXTUALISTIC ANALYSIS AND INTERVENTION: TWO EXAMPLES

How can researchers conduct research or therapists perform clinical work from this perspective? Although somewhat more time-consuming, one can approach behavior contextually by following these four steps. First, begin with the assumption that, when one is observing members of cultures other than one's own, one does not know what kind of behavior one is observing. One does not know what it is called or what it means; one assumes that what the behavior is called and means is an empirical question. Second, examine the sociocultural context of the behavior and gather as much information as possible about the antecedents, contingencies, and correlates of the behavior in that context. Third, use the context to define and label the behavior under investigation as a specific act-in-context. Finally, manipulate and modify the contingencies of the context to create change. I next provide two brief examples of this process to elucidate these points.

Example 1: Gender × Ethnic Differences in Unprotected Anal Intercourse

Recent studies have shown that the prevalence of AIDS among young Latinas is significantly higher than for other Gender × Ethnic groups (e.g., Mays & Cochran, 1988). Other studies (e.g., Singer et al., 1990) have shown that this ethnic difference is in part a function of differences in the frequency of engaging in unprotected anal intercourse (with intravenous drug abusers in particular). This risky sexual behavior appears to be frequent among young, unmarried, heterosexual Latinas, but infrequent among heterosexual women of other ethnic groups. Researchers who have reported this Ethnic × Gender difference in behavior among heterosexual women did not predict such findings and offered no theoretical model of why these differences should or would be found.

The standard, mechanistic–behavioral approach to reducing AIDS among this population would be to define the problematic behavior to be modified in this case as unprotected anal intercourse. By the term *unprotected anal intercourse* one would mean a highly specific sequence of movements that anyone anywhere can engage in, with these movements presumed to have the same label and meaning irrespective of their sociocultural context. In the absence of a theoretical model of the unpredicted ethnic difference in behavior so defined, researchers have resorted to a deficit model in which they have suggested that young Latinas are deficient in information about the risks entailed in this sexual behavior and therefore require culturally tailored AIDS education (e.g., Mays & Cochran, 1988). Yet, other studies have shown that young Latinas are well aware of how AIDS is transmitted. Singer et al. (1990), for example, found that Latinos knew as much about the transmission of AIDS as other ethnic groups. Although Latinos did hold the additional erroneous belief that AIDS could be transmitted through casual contact, they nonetheless knew that unprotected vaginal or anal intercourse with anyone, and with intravenous drug abusers in particular, was dangerous and was a means of transmitting AIDS. They were not deficient in AIDS information.

If the problem is not a lack of information about AIDS transmission, the solution is not to send health educators to Latino communities to provide such information in a culturally sensitive manner. Where, then, does one go from here? How do researchers intervene to change behavior and to save lives by so doing? The traditional, mechanistic–behavioral approach (a) has produced titillating ethnic differences that cannot be explained; (b) has manufactured exotic "primitives" whose cultural "difference" is readily translated as a (sexual) "deviance" that reinforces existing social arrangements and racist ideology; and (c) has left researchers and educators without a way to intervene.

The alternative approach, the contextual approach, begins with the assumption that the name for this behavior is to be discovered empirically through a careful analysis of its context and of its highly contextual contingencies. The first step is to discover what the behavior-in-context is and what it means by observing the behavior and its correlates and consequences, as well as by talking informally to the young Latinas who engage in it. Arguello (1993) and her colleagues at the Center for the Study of Latino Health in Los Angeles did precisely that. What they found was that these young unmarried Latinas (many of whom were gang members) were engaging in anal intercourse in order to maintain their virginity. As unmarried, Roman Catholic, Mexican American women, they wanted to be (and men demanded that they be) virgins when they finally got married, but their boyfriends were demanding intercourse. Anal intercourse was a solution to these contradictory Gender × Culture demands; it was a way to have intercourse with, yet still remain a virgin for, boyfriends who demanded both in a Culture × Gender × Age × Class context (working-class gang community) where the consequences of failing to meet men's sexual demands are aversive. Condoms were not used because condoms were conceptualized as a means of birth control and birth control is not an issue when intercourse is anal.

When contextually defined, when understood as an act-in-context, the behavior here is not unprotected anal intercourse except in the most superficial way of thinking about complex human beings. For these particular Latinas, the behavior was "trying to maintain virginity for, but still have intercourse with, men who are demanding both," and that surely is not the behavior gay men engage in when the exhibit similar, superficial, mechanical movements. Comparisons across groups on superficially similar movements cannot be made because the acts-in-context are different behaviors and have different meanings. The contingencies that control the behavior also differ for different groups. For these particular Latinas, the contingency was the aversive consequences of losing one's virginity before one is married in a cultural context where women's virginity is valued and the Virgin Mary is a powerful symbol. For these specific Latinas, the consequence of losing one's virginity before marriage was that one may render oneself un-marry-able and bring shame on one's family. That contingency was viewed by Arguello's (1993) sample as more aversive than the possibility of contracting AIDS.

When viewed in its context, there is no need to attribute information deficits to these Latinas. Instead, by defining the behavior contextually as "trying to maintain virginity for and simultaneously have intercourse with men who demand both," the culturally specific contingencies that elicit and maintain this behavior-in-context are obvious, as are several contextualistic and culturally specific interventions entailing manipulating those contingencies. At the simple level, the intervention can stress the need to use condoms without addressing the act-in-context. At a more fundamental level, the intervention must be a feminist one that addresses virginity, the sexual double standard, and young Latinos' control of Latinas' sexuality. Arguello (1993) and her colleagues began doing that in a series of feminist workshops on Virginity as Social Control, Virginity as Oppression, and Who Owns Latinas' Bodies? These workshops are led by feminist, Latina health educators who, like Arguello, are former gang members and so are not only well attended and effective but popular in the community. This intervention has a far greater potential to succeed than a standard AIDS education intervention and is extraordinarily effective according to Arguello's preliminary data.

Feminist workshops on the concept of virginity as a way to reduce AIDS among Latinas occurred to these researchers only because they defined behavior contextually. Such an intervention would be irrelevant to gay men because the act-in-context that they engage in may be superficially similar to, but nonetheless is totally unrelated to, the act-in-context of these Latinas.

Example 2: Gender × Ethnic Differences in Cigarette Smoking Among Adolescents

Cigarette smoking is still one of the most preventable causes of illness and death in the United States. Data indicate that 80–90% of children and adolescents have smoked at least one cigarette, that 20–40% of them are regular smokers, and that smoking as a child or adolescent is the best predictor of being a chronic, regular smoker as an adult (Klonoff, Fritz, Landrine, Riddle, & Tully-Payne, 1994; Landrine, Klonoff, & Fritz, 1994; Landrine, Richardson, Klonoff, & Flay, 1994). Consequently, interventions designed to prevent smoking are typically directed toward children and adolescents (Landrine, Klonoff, et al., 1994). Ethnic, gender, and Gender × Ethnicity differences in the prevalence of cigarette smoking among children and adolescents have been found in which smoking is lowest among ethnic minority boys and girls (who also have a later onset of smoking than European Americans) and highest among European American girls, while steadily decreasing among European American boys. Indeed, despite the plethora of smoking prevention programs in elementary, middle, and high schools, smoking appears to be increasing among European American girls and teenagers alone (Lynch & Bonnie, 1994).

This Gender × Ethnic difference in cigarette smoking was not predicted by the various researchers who have reported it, and little theoretical explanation for why European American girls would smoke more than other groups has been offered. Thus, a way to intervene to decrease and prevent smoking among these girls (a Gender × Culture-Specific program) does not suggest itself. As previously, this is because the behavior has been defined and understood as the superficial, mechanical, decontextualized movement "smoking," a movement presumed to have the same label and meaning irrespective of the context in which it appears. Smoking is understood as a type of behavior that girls and boys of any ethnicity can and do engage in, and therefore unpredicted Gender × Ethnic differences in behavior so defined have emerged.

The alternative, contextualistic approach is to empirically discover the label for and meaning of this behavior by observing the correlates and consequences of it for the European American girls who engage in it, in their context. Those contextual correlates and consequences can then be modified in a Gender × Culture intervention. Using this approach, Camp, Klesges, and Relyea (1993) discovered that European American girls who smoked also were engaged in chronic, perpetual dieting, were obsessed with their weight and physical appearance, and smoked to reduce and control their appetites, eating, and subsequent weight. Their nonsmoking cohorts, as well as ethnic minority girls and boys and European American boys, did not share these weight concerns and so did not smoke; those who did smoke did not do so for weight reduction and were not on diets.

When approached contextually, the behavior here is not "smoking," except in the most superficial understanding of these European American girls and teenagers. Instead, the behavior is "one more self-destructive way to keep my weight down." The contingencies maintaining this act-in-context are loss of male attention and affection in response to girls' weight and loss of self-esteem, name-calling, belittling, distancing, ostracism, and other negative responses to girls' obesity in the cultural context of European American teenagers, their parents, their role models, and their culture's messages. These contingencies are viewed as more aversive (in that context) than the destructive health consequences of smoking.

Although Camp et al. (1993) did not suggest a new, Gender × Ethnicity-Specific intervention for these girls, such an intervention is obvious. The intervention must be a purely feminist one that focuses on complex issues about weight among European American girls and women and on the self-destructive things that they do (dieting, self-starvation, vomiting, smoking) to control their weight. Such an intervention is likely to be more successful for this specific Gender × Ethnic group than the standard educational intervention that teaches children to resist peer pressure to smoke. This is because peers are only a variable when the behavior is "trying to fit in with my peers and look cool," and that is not the behavior that these girls (or that ethnic minority boys and girls) engage in when smoking (Landrine, Richardson, et al., 1994). Likewise, exercise, something that is not included in standard smoking prevention programs for adolescents, also must be discussed and encouraged as a healthy means of controlling weight, provided that the European American girls in question are actually overweight. This new intervention would be irrelevant to ethnic minority girls and boys who smoke, as well as to European American boys who smoke, because the act-in-context differs for these groups.

Advantages of Contextualism

Rather than obstructing social scientists' understanding of and ability to predict and modify behavior, contextualism facilitates new and deeper understandings and new, more effective interventions. In addition, by defining behavior contextually, social scientists do not manufacture politically functional ethnic and gender differences that can be exploited to maintain the status quo; they do not produce a hierarchy of behavioral difference that justifies existing social hierarchies, and they do not discover primitives whose existence maintains their masters' positions. Contextualism, then, is one possible model for understanding culture and gender. Contextualism argues that the relationship between behavior and its context is a simple one in which culture and context are an essential part of the behavior of all people. The view that the appropriate label for and meaning of behavior is to be found in its sociocultural context is one that has the potential to advance the understanding of all behavior, especially of behavior in various ethnic and gender contexts.

The suggestion that the label for and meaning of a behavior depend on its sociocultural context does not mean that a variety of behaviors do not exist in certain contexts or cultures. I am not suggesting that anal intercourse and cigarette smoking do not exist in certain cultures. Rather, the point is that understanding and interventions are advanced and improved more by viewing smoking and anal intercourse as acts-in-context than by approaching these behaviors mechanistically. Certainly, both the mechanistic and the contextual approach to behavior are viable. However, the mechanistic approach examines the mere surface structure, the grammar of behavior, and simultaneously serves regressive political purposes. The contextual approach examines the deep structure, the syntax of behavior, and thereby challenges ideological representations and exploitation of diversity.

CONTEXTUALISM AND THE CHAPTERS IN THIS BOOK

This book is divided into four major sections that address (a) culture and feminist theory and methodology in psychology, (b) culture and feminist advocacy and practice in psychology, (c) the psychology of four specific ethnic groups of women, and (d) cultural diversity in specific, feminist research topics. Each chapter in this book provides data on women's diversity, data that are by and large anomalous insofar as they fail to fit neatly into current conclusions regarding gender differences. In light of that, the major question raised by this book is, Can such anomalous data be integrated into the existing paradigm of feminist psychology and women's studies?

For example, a plethora of studies indicate that the extended, sociocentric experience of the self (and its ethic of care) is the most prevalent way of experiencing the self among people of color (Heelas & Locke, 1981; Landrine, 1992; Shweder & Bourne, 1982). Specifically, data suggest that the extended or sociocentric self characterizes the experiences of Asian American men and women (e.g., DeVos, 1985; Marsella, DeVos, & Hsu, 1985), Native American men and women (e.g., Strauss, 1977), Latino men and women (e.g., Gaines, 1982), and African American men and women in particular (Haraway, 1986; Nobles, 1976; Stack, 1986). Can these data be integrated into a feminist psychology that regards the sociocentric self and its morality as inherently "womanly" experiences that stem from women's unique, early interactions with mothers (e.g., Bordo, 1986, 1990; Chodorow, 1978; Flax, 1986, 1990; Gilligan, 1977; Lykes, 1985)? Can such anomalous data be sprinkled like an exotic spice on textbooks and articles without radically changing the flavor of the assumptions, the issues and styles defined as women's, and therefore the agenda beneath?

The chapters in this book suggest that the answer to these questions is no and yes, depending on the direction that feminist psychology takes in the future. One direction is to retain the paradigmatic assumption that gender by and large can be understood without reference to context and that feminist psychology's knowledge therefore is knowledge of gender per se. If psychologists choose to persist in that belief, then the answers provided by the chapters here are negative; the answer is "no, cultural diversity cannot be integrated into feminist psychology." This is because, to persist in the belief that knowledge that is based almost solely on studies of middle-class, European American women and men is knowledge of gender, while readily admitting that women of color are cultural products, is to render culture exotic, superfluous, and relevant to people of color alone. To persist with such an assumption is to continue the implicit belief that European American cultures are not relevant to the behavior of European Americans. In the context of such beliefs, women and men of color can be understood only as exceptions to feminist psychology's knowledge of gender, and the chapters in this book are relegated to the status of mere footnotes in a basic White text.

Alternatively, feminists can modify their beliefs. Their paradigmatic assumption can be changed to the view that gender cannot be understood without reference to context. To give this assumption more than the perfunctory nod that it has been afforded, to regard it with a seriousness currently lacking, is to render European American cultures powerful, problematic contexts requiring analysis. Feminists have not yet done so; they have not begun to analyze the role of European American cultures in the gender behavior of European American women and men. The failure to do so is the best empirical evidence that the purpose of focusing on cultural diversity at present is not to analyze and reveal culture in behavior but to manufacture politically functional "differences."

Thus, for example, articles increasingly offer hypotheses regarding the role of the culturally specific values and beliefs of minorities in minority behavior, but similar analyses for European American samples are not conducted, even though the plethora of scales assessing values and politics were standardized on them. Acculturation and ethnic identity scales are increasingly used as measures of cultural context in studies of people of color, but middle-class European American samples are rarely required to complete these as well, although such scales for them exist (e.g., Helms, 1990). Similarly, feminist researchers have begun to address the role of poverty in the behavior of poor women, but have they ever analyzed the role of financial security and privilege in that of others? Indeed, Camp et al. (1993) failed to analyze, expose, and render problematic the middle-class European American values, beliefs, and cultural practices surrounding gender and weight that lead young White girls to smoke, vomit, and starve themselves, even though such an analysis was appropriate. Exotic, problematic cultural differences specific to middle-class European Americans are hidden or neglected in favor of a focus on the differences of people of color. European American values of individualism, autonomy, control, and a belief in rights, liberty, the self, self-fulfillment, opposites, and progress have yet to fully be analyzed as the lathe of European American gender, gender differences, and gender politics.

Despite vigorous protests to the contrary, then, feminist researchers do not yet believe that context is truly relevant to understanding gender, for if they did, the European American contexts that characterize most samples would be addressed as the source of their differences from people of color. Likewise, feminist researchers do not yet believe that culture is an integral part of behavior, for if they did, the abundance of studies of gender among European Americans would explore the relevant, explanatory cultural beliefs and practices entailed. Indeed, if feminists truly believed that culture and context were relevant to gender, studies of European American women and men would analyze the extent to which being Jewish, Irish, Italian, or Greek accounts for the variance found within White samples. Consequently, feminist psychologists have yet to relinquish the paradigmatic assumption that they deny embracing, viz., that European American gender is gender per se.

Thus, to bring cultural diversity to feminist psychology requires not only a focus on the cultures of others but a focus on European American cultures. As long as "cultural diversity" means "how those minorities are different" (from whom?), diversity discourse eloquently eludes addressing, yet quietly maintains, existing social arrangements. Until the focus on culture regards European American cultures as being as salient and in need of analysis as the cultures of others, cultural diversity belittles culture while exploiting it. Culture will be regarded with dignity and the sociology of knowledge altered only when European American cultures are treated like all others. As bell hooks (1990) put it,

> [cultural diversity] is always an issue of Otherness that is not white; it is black, brown, yellow, red, purple even [and thereby is] a discourse on race that perpetuates racial domination.... Few ... scholars are being awarded grants to investigate and study all aspects of white culture from a standpoint of "difference"; doesn't this indicate just how tightly the colonizer/colonized paradigm continues to frame the discourse on race and the "Other"? (pp. 54–55)

Alternatively, then, the chapters in this book also suggest that, "yes, culture can be integrated into feminist psychology," but if and only if all cultures are subjected to a similar analysis, the diversity of cultures of European Americans (lumped together as "White") first and foremost. Thus, the chapters here present differences between European Americans and people of color and indicate that gender for White, middle-class American women and men is so inextricably interwoven with their racial, ethnic, and class privilege and practices that it appears not to be. Although these chapters are guilty of focusing on the "other," they nonetheless unveil the primacy of European American cultures in ostensible gender; they unmask "the culture of gender" (Stack, 1986) and demonstrate that what has been presumed to be gender and gender difference is merely gender in and by virtue of a specific context. What has been understood as a main effect for gender is a Gender × European-American culture interaction effect.

This book's message is not that culture is an additional variable that demarcates the local limits of otherwise universal gender-related principles and gender differences. This book's message is not that culture is an additional, moderating variable whose inclusion will allow researchers to account for a larger percentage of the variance in human behavior. Rather, the message of this book is simply that culture is us, it is each of us, and thus only it can be known, revealed, and discovered in social science. These chapters challenge researchers to understand that European American culture is the structure and content of feminist psychology and is the only thing that is discovered and revealed in feminist data, constructs, therapies, and theories on gender. By challenging researchers to understand feminist data in this manner, each chapter, in its own way, argues for and demonstrates the benefits of contextualism as a philosophy of science for a multicultural feminist psychology.

REFERENCES

Arguello, M. (1993, February). *Developing outreach programs for AIDS prevention with Latino youth.* Paper presented at the Institute for Health Promotion and Disease Prevention Research, University of Southern California Medical School, Los Angeles.

Biglan, A., Glasgow, R. E., & Singer, G. (1990). The need for a science of larger social units: A contextual approach. *Behavior Therapy, 21,* 195–215.

Bordo, S. (1986). The Cartesian masculinization of thought. *Signs, 11,* 439–456.

Bordo, S. (1990). Feminism, postmodernism, and gender skepticism. In L. J. Nicholson (Ed.), *Feminism/postmodernism* (pp. 133–156). New York: Routledge & Kegan Paul.

Camp, D. E., Klesges, R. C., & Relyea, G. (1993). The relationship between body weight concerns and adolescent smoking. *Health Psychology, 12,* 24–32.

Chodorow, N. (1978). *The reproduction of mothering: Psychoanalysis and the sociology of gender.* Berkeley: University of California Press.

Dana, R. H. (1993). *Multicultural assessment perspectives for professional psychology.* New York: Allyn & Bacon.

DeVos, G. (1985). Dimensions of the self in Japanese culture. In A. J. Marsella, G. DeVos, & F. Hsu (Eds.), *Culture and the self: Asian and western perspectives* (pp. 141–184). New York: Tavistock.

Flax, J. (1986). Gender as a social problem: In and for feminist theory. *Amerikastudien/American Studies, 31,* 193–213.

Flax, J. (1990). Postmodernism and gender relations in feminist theory. In L. J. Nicholson (Ed.), *Feminism/postmodernism* (pp. 39–62). New York: Routledge & Kegan Paul.

Gaines, A. (1982). Cultural definitions, behavior and the "person" in American psychiatry. In A. J. Marsella & G. M. White (Eds.), *Cultural conceptions of mental health and therapy* (pp. 167–192). London: Reidel.

Gergen, K., & Gergen, M. (1983). The social construction of helping relationships. In J. D. Fisher, A. Nadler, & B. DePaulo (Eds.), *New directions in helping* (Vol. 1). San Diego, CA: Academic Press.

Gilligan, C. (1977). In a different voice: Women's conception of the self and of morality. *Harvard Educational Review, 47,* 481–517.

Goodchilds, J. D. (1992). *Psychological perspectives on human diversity in America.* Washington, DC: American Psychological Association.

Greenblat, C. S. (1983). A hit is a hit is a hit . . . or is it? In R. Finnkelhor, R. Gelles, & M. Straus (Eds.), *The dark side of family violence research,* Beverly Hills, CA: Sage.

Haraway, D. (1986). The curious coincidence of feminine and African moralities: Challenges for feminist theory. In E. Kittay & D. Meyers (Eds.), *Women and morality.* Totowa, NJ: Rowman & Allenheld.

Harre, R. (1981). Expressive aspects of descriptions of others. In C. Antaki (Ed.), *The psychology of ordinary explanations.* San Diego, CA: Academic Press.

Hayes, S. C., & Hayes, L. J. (1992). Some clinical implications of contextualistic behaviorism. *Behavior Therapy, 23,* 225–249.

Heelas, P., & Locke, A. (1981). *Indigenous psychologies: The anthropology of the self.* San Diego, CA: Academic Press.

Helms, J. E. (1990). *Black and white racial identity.* New York: Greenwood.

hooks, b. (1990). *Yearning: Race, gender, and cultural politics.* Boston: Gloria Watkins/South End Press.

hooks, b. (1992). Eating the other. In b. hooks, *Black looks: Race and representation* (pp. 21–39). Boston: Gloria Watkins/South End Press.

Jones, J. M. (1991). Psychological models of race: What have they been and what should they be? In J. Goodchilds (Ed.), *Psychological perspectives on human diversity in America* (pp. 3–46). Washington, DC: American Psychological Association.

Kayser, E., Swinger, T., & Cohen, R. (1984). Laypersons' conceptions of social relationships. *Journal of Social and Personal Relationships, 1,* 433–458.

Klonoff, E. A., Fritz, J. M., Landrine, H., Riddle, R. W., & Tully-Payne, L. (1994). The problem and sociocultural context of single cigarette sales. *Journal of the American Medical Association, 271,* 618–620.

Landrine, H. (1992). Clinical implications of cultural differences: The referential v. the indexical self. *Clinical Psychology Review, 12,* 401–415.

Landrine, H., Klonoff, E. A., & Fritz, J. M. (1994). Preventing cigarette sales to minors: The need for contextual, sociocultural analysis. *Preventive Medicine, 23,* 322–327.

Landrine, H., Richardson, J. L., Klonoff, E. A., & Flay, B. (1994). Cultural diversity in the predictors of adolescent cigarette smoking: The relative influence of peers. *Journal of Behavioral Medicine, 17,* 331–346.

Lasswell, T., & Lasswell, M. (1976). I love you but I'm not in love with you. *Journal of Marriage and Family Counseling, 38,* 211–224.

Lynch, B. S., & Bonnie, R. J. (Eds., 1994). *Growing up tobacco free: Preventing nicotine addiction in children and youths.* Washington, DC: Institute of Medicine, National Academy Press.

Lykes, M. B. (1985). Gender and individualistic v. collectivist bases for notions of self. *Journal of Personality, 53,* 356–383.

Marsella, A. J., DeVos, G., & Hsu, F. (1985). *Culture and self: Asian and western perspectives.* New York: Tavistock.

Mays, V. M., & Cochran, S. D. (1988). Issues in the perception of AIDS risk and risk reduction activities by Black and Hispanic/Latina women. *American Psychologist, 43,* 949–957.

Mednick, M. (1989). On the politics of psychological constructs: Stop the bandwagon, I want to get off. *American Psychologist, 44,* 1118–1123.

Morris, E. K. (1988). Contextualism: The world view of behavior analysis. *Journal of Experimental Child Psychology, 46,* 289–323.

Mummendey, A., Bonewasser, M., Loschper, G., & Lenneweber, V. (1982). It is always somebody else who is aggressive. *Zeitschrift fur Sozialpsychologie, 13,* 341–355.

Nobles, W. W. (1976). Extended self: Rethinking the so-called "Negro" self concept. *Journal of Black Psychology, 2,* 2–8.

Pepper, S. C. (1942). *World hypotheses: A study in evidence.* Berkeley: University of California Press.

Rosnow, R. L., & Georgoudi, M. (1986). *Contextualism and understanding in behavioral science.* New York: Praeger.

Shweder, R., & Bourne, E. J. (1982). Does the concept of the "person" vary cross-culturally? In A. J. Marsella & G. M. White (Eds.), *Cultural conceptions of mental health and therapy* (pp. 97–137). London: Reidel.

Singer, M., Candida, F., Davison, L., Burke, G., Castillo, Z., Scanlon, K., & Rivera, M. (1990). SIDA: The economic, social and cultural context of AIDS among Latinos. *Medical Anthropology Quarterly, 4,* 72–114.

Skinner, B. F. (1938). *Behavior of organisms.* New York: Appleton-Century-Crofts.

Stack, C. (1986). The culture of gender: Women and men of color. *Signs, 11*, 321–324.

Strauss, A. S. (1977). Northern Cheyenne ethnopsychology. *Ethos, 5*, 326–357.

Sue, S. (1991). Ethnicity and culture in psychological research and practice. In J. Goodchilds (Ed.), *Psychological perspectives on human diversity in America* (pp. 47–86). Washington, DC: American Psychological Association.

Tedeschi, T. (1984). A social psychological interpretation of human aggression. In A. Mummendey (Ed.), *Social psychology of aggression.* Berlin: Springer-Verlag.

I

CULTURAL DIVERSITY IN THEORY AND METHODOLOGY IN FEMINIST PSYCHOLOGY

INTRODUCTION

Chapter 1 of this book described how psychology's mechanistic understanding of behavior has rendered culture and context superfluous to the analysis of human action and has manufactured ethnic and gender differences. Chapter 1 also presented an alternative, contextualistic model of behavior and demonstrated the advantages of that approach. Contextualism (i.e., the view that behavior and its sociocultural context form a single unit), it was argued, is a more appropriate philosophy of science than is mechanism, particularly for multicultural feminist psychology.

The chapters in this section focus on cultural diversity in theory and methodology in feminist psychology. In chapter 2, "Ethnic Diversity in the Experience of Feminism," Ellen Kimmel and Michael Garko present their study of women's ethnic differences and similarities in the experience of feminism—in becoming and being a feminist. In addition, however, this chapter illustrates the process of conducting feminist research from a multicultural perspective and highlights the subtle manner in which cultural contexts inform the research process.

In chapter 3, "Cultural Diversity and Methodology in Feminist Psychology," Hope Landrine, Elizabeth Klonoff, and Alice Brown-Collins ask whether traditional, empiricist methods are sufficient for investigating women's diversity and then conclude from an empirical investigation that they are not. In the process, Landrine et al. challenge the concept of "observation" itself. They argue that objective observation is a cultural projection, that what European Americans "observe" others to be doing is merely what that behavior would mean and be called if they were engaged in it, if it occurred in their sociocultural context. They present an interesting, empirical investigation in which they demonstrate that women from different sociocultural backgrounds do not interpret the words in simple questionnaires in the same way and that their different, context-saturated interpretations alter their responses to questionnaires. They conclude that in standard methodologies it is assumed that women research participants share a single cultural context, that this assumption is problematic, and that different methodologies are needed to study women from a diversity of cultures. Chapters 2 and 3 demonstrate that *sociocultural contexts shape the structure and content of research.*

In chapter 4, "Cognitive Gender Differences," Diane Halpern demonstrates that the evidence for gender differences in verbal, mathematical, and visual–spatial ability stems from studies of European American, middle-class samples who have average levels of cognitive functioning. When other ethnic groups are included in such analyses and a wider range of skills is assessed (the very low and the very high range of functioning), these differences are challenged and often reversed. Importantly, data on people of color render biological explanations for cognitive gender differences suspicious at best. For example, if (purported) male superiority (higher scores) in mathematics is the product of male biology, Halpern asks, then why are the men in question overwhelmingly Asian rather than Black or Latino? Unless one wishes to suggest that Black and Latino men are less biologically male than Asian men, achievement in mathematics— by women or men—seems to be a question of reinforcement and opportunity within specific sociocultural contexts rather than an issue of biology. Halpern reveals how the sociocultural context of middle-class European Americans has produced ostensible cognitive gender differences and highlights the dangers of using monocultural samples who represent the middle range of skills, income, and the like, in gender research. Such samples represent a serious methodological issue.

In chapter 5, "Socialization of Girls," Pam Reid, Calliope Haritos, Elizabeth Kelly, and Nicole Holland similarly demonstrate that knowledge of gender socialization stems from studies of middle-class European American samples. In addition, Reid et al. illustrate the methodological flaws, limitations, and cultural biases in these studies and highlight the need for more complex methodologies and multicultural theories to investigate and understand gender socialization among girls from different sociocultural contexts.

Finally, in chapter 6, "Stirring Trouble and Making Theory," Jill Morawski and Betty Bayer discuss the difficulties of bringing diversity to feminist psychological theory. They argue that the two typical approaches to diversity are part of the problem feminist psychologists seek to solve. Specifically, perfunctory remarks about ethnic exceptions to feminist findings on the one hand, and treating ethnicity as an "additional" variable on the other, both reproduce the set of social relations they purport to challenge. Morawski and Bayer offer and describe a challenging alternative model and process for bringing diversity to theory: reflexivity. By simultaneously applying this model in their chapter, they challenge readers to consider doing theory in a radically different manner. In the process, Morawski and Bayer highlight some of the advantages of postmodernist theory as one possible framework through which multiculturalism in feminist theory and analysis might be achieved. Although prevalent in research in other disciplines within women's studies, postmodernist discourse is rarely used in feminist psychology's studies. Thus, the language at first may seem difficult and obscure. Readers are encouraged to read this chapter slowly and to stick with it. This is because postmodernist views are increasingly important in feminist analysis and thereby must be considered, and because Morawski and Bayer's analysis is worthy of attention and careful reflection.

The six chapters in this section present a few of the many methodological and theoretical issues in feminist psychology. The chapters differ in perspective, length, analysis, and language but have in common the conclusion that *a European American sociocultural context has structured and informed feminist psychology's methodologies, concepts, and theories and has produced monocultural gender differences and principles.* These chapters challenge feminist psychologists to change those theories and methodologies to bring diversity to feminist psychology.

2

ETHNIC DIVERSITY IN THE EXPERIENCE OF FEMINISM: AN EXISTENTIAL–PHENOMENOLOGICAL APPROACH

ELLEN B. KIMMEL and MICHAEL G. GARKO

What does feminism mean to feminists? Research to answer that question has been emergent and represents an ongoing effort to define, in a more comprehensive way, feminism as it is lived by those who label themselves feminists. Kimmel (1989) reported the first results of this kind of research in her presidential address to Division 35 (Psychology of Women) of the American Psychological Association (APA). In that study, fellows of the division were asked to write narratives about the experience of feminism using an existential–phenomenological protocol of probes to defined lived experience. The women who participated were almost all White and middle class. Although the study yielded important data on the experience of feminism, it was nonetheless limited by the ethnicity and social class of the participants.

Both authors contributed equally to this project. We would like to acknowledge the tenacious efforts of Gina Besosa in assisting us with the thematic analysis for this study.

If it is true that there is a core experience of feminism, then that should generalize across women of many ethnic groups as well as across their diversity of contexts. If this is not so, then such a finding itself is important and would preclude assumptions and generalizations about feminists that serve only to alienate groups and keep them ignorant of each other. Thus, it is imperative that various groups speak independently of their experience of feminism.

In the current study we attempted to add to and complement the previous study (Kimmel, 1989). We invited Women of Color to report, in their own words, the meaning of feminism as they have lived it. This existential–phenomenological approach may illuminate meanings that guide attitudes and behaviors and reveal common and differing realities between women of color and their White feminist sisters.

A FUNNY THING HAPPENED ON THE WAY TO COLLECTING OUR DATA

Although it is not traditional to detail the trials and tribulations in carrying out research, our experience warrants a discussion here and is germane to the cultural diversity issues involved. On receiving the request from Hope Landrine to conduct a replication of the original study with Women of Color, we blithely proceeded. We located all the original materials, the cover letter sent to fellows of Division 35, the demographic data sheet, and the protocol of probes to yield descriptions of the experience of feminism. The next task, finding participants who were similar in education (scholars), age, and class to the original group, was more challenging. We decided to review issues of the previous 5 years of feminist and ethnic minority journals in which psychologists (or social scientists) published research on girls and Women of Color. We suspected that individuals producing research on girls and Women of Color were likely to have political beliefs that feminists would share, might identify themselves as such, and might be Women of Color themselves. We also restricted the list to names we interpreted as women's. Because this method was far from precise, we added a sheet after the revised letter (explaining the genesis of this study) that allowed the recipients to indicate their reasons for not participating, including (a) they were White "majority" persons; (b) they did not consider themselves to be feminists; and (c) they simply chose not to participate (no reason specified).

As we anticipated, we received a number of returns with the first reason listed; some of these White women indicated that they had given the material to a Woman of Color colleague and supplied us with her name and address. Several others returned the material and indicated that they did not consider themselves feminists, and a few others were eliminated because they were men. As expected, many packages were returned with addressee unknown. What we never expected was that only a handful of individuals would actually answer the protocol and that they would write on the questionnaire despite our request that they use separate sheets (to avoid our influencing the length of their response).

In our combined 26 or more years of gathering data, this was the first time either of us had ever "given a party and no one showed up." Remembering a discussion one of us had heard at an Association for Women in Psychology (AWP) meeting about ways to gain the research participation of Women of Color, we realized that Women of Color were not waiting around to give White women answers to their questions. What the speaker at the AWP reported was that the use of networks and social exchanges (e.g., "I help you in this way, you help me in that . . .") is far more effective. For example, a face-to-face, personal interaction with a colleague or friend in which there is trust and a connection is the most likely avenue for reaching African American women.

Given that our intended participants were scholars and likely to be academically based, we also analyzed their situations. If White women 15 years ago were appointed to every committee as token females, today Women of Color are even further stretched. The demands on them for service in and out of the university community, for mentoring Women (and Men) of Color, for speaking at every conference, and for continuing to carry out extensive family roles while still trying to publish and otherwise "pass muster" as a faculty member, are backbreaking. The last priority for their time, even if they were highly interested, might be answering a set of open-ended, time-consuming, and potentially thought- and emotionally provoking probes about something personal, even conflictual, requested by a stranger.

We informed Hope Landrine (who is an African American) that we had gotten few answers to our questionnaires and asked for suggestions for modifying it. She suggested (without knowing what had happened) that we restructure the questionnaire so that respondents could write their answers directly on it rather than on separate sheets. She said that the demand to type on separate sheets was too high and that Women of Color might complete the questionnaire on receipt if they could write their answers under the questions as they read them; this was less time-consuming. She also suggested that our cover letter was too long and that Women of Color would be more open to a letter that quickly got to the point. Finally, she suggested that we indicate in the cover letter how Women of Color might benefit from completing the questionnaire. With the detailed feedback Landrine provided by reading and responding to the original package, we rewrote the cover letter and changed the format and language of the demographic and protocol sheets. We made these changes in the letter and in the questionnaire. Finally, Landrine suggested that we add the term *womanism* to the term *feminism* because some African American feminists might think of themselves as the former rather than the latter. We further suggested that if they were interested in the issue of gender equity, they might respond regardless of whether either label was adopted. The second mailing included individuals on the original list who had not responded, along with new names from personal networks and the Women's Program Office of the APA. The second mailing was more productive.

We describe this experience because we believe that it is relevant to our study and to issues of cultural diversity. What we learned from this is that feminist psychology may need to do more than add Women of Color to samples to bring cultural diversity to its data (see also Goodwin, 1991, and Wallston, 1981). Feminist psychologists also may need to bring diversity to their methods for collecting data, because obtaining data from diverse groups of women may require culturally appropriate (and different) approaches; colleagues of color may need to be consulted on possible ways to do this.

THE STUDY

To explore the meaning of feminism for Women of Color, we adopted the existential–phenomenological perspective used by Kimmel (1989).[1]

Method

Participants

From a review of all issues for the previous 5 years of 11 primarily feminist journals,[2] we located 147 female authors who had conducted research on girls and Women of Color. Thirty-one colleagues were added to the 147 names generated, resulting in a total of 178 women who were mailed the package. As described earlier, this yielded few responses. The second mailing of 141 revised packages was more fruitful and yielded a sufficient response so that the thematic analysis could be performed;[3] a

---

[1]This approach is grounded in the work of Giorgi (e.g., 1981), Hawes (1977), James (1918), Luijpen and Koren (1987), Misiak and Sexton (1973), Solomon (1980), Valle, King, and Halling (1989), and von Eckartsberg (1986).

[2]The 11 journals reviewed were *Psychology of Women Quarterly, Sex Roles, Women and Therapy, Journal on Black Psychology, Child Welfare, Signs, International Journal of Women's Studies, Feminist Studies, Frontiers, Women's Studies Quarterly,* and *Gender and History.* Selection of journals was limited to those available in our university's library for the 5 consecutive years 1986–1991.

[3]Note that this method does not require a representative sample, only enough individuals who can articulate the experience until themes are "exhausted" (see the section on the analysis). Researchers (e.g., Langellier & Hall, 1989) using the method interviewed as few as 4 participants. In our case, we analyzed as few as 6 to as many as 15 responses for the various probes.

total of 84 questionnaires (56.9%) were returned. However, of these, only 17 were usable.[4] The respondents ranged in age from 36 to 66 years (average 46), were mainly academicians (all but 2) and mainly psychologists (2 were in African literature; 1 of these also was in culture studies). All but 5 were African Americans; of the 5, 2 were Asian Americans, 2 Hispanic Americans, and 1 was American Indian.

Instruments

Cover Letter. A cover letter described the purpose of the study and the method, requested participation, and promised anonymity.

Demographic Data Sheet. A separate sheet asked for information on specialization in psychology, sex, race, ethnic group, age, and date of first employment as a professional.

Experience Questionnaire. Seven open-ended questions constituted the problem of participants' experience of feminism. First, each person was asked to describe what she meant by the term *feminism* and then to discuss when she first described herself as a feminist. Next was a general question about the experience of feminism, and participants were asked to describe a particular time of awareness of being a feminist and whether it was a positive or negative experience. The impact of feminism on four aspects of their lives (employment, family relationships, personal relationships, and spiritual life) was solicited in further questions. An additional probe asked when in their daily lives they were most and least aware of being a feminist. Finally, they were asked to assess whether or not and how their experiences of feminism changed over time.

Procedure

In the early winter of 1991, the 178 identified scholars were mailed a package containing a letter requesting participation, a questionnaire on their experience of feminism, and a demographic data sheet. A second mailing of 141 packages, modified somewhat, was sent to nonrespondents in April.

Thematic Analysis. Two independent scorers followed the procedure developed by Jones (1984) to analyze narrative data, with slight revision to accommodate the fact that our material was not generated by face-to-face interviews. Briefly, the initial step was to "bracket" responses into units, determined to be a change of subject (Dapkus, 1985), and to list these in order. Lines were drawn to connect units with similar wording or ideas, and these were grouped and numbered. Subsequently, each group was named using the actual wording of the participants whenever possible.

---

[4]There were a variety of reasons why some respondents did not provide data for this study: (a) wrong gender (*n* = 4), (b) incorrect mailing address (*n* = 24), (c) wrong race (*n* = 27), (d) not a feminist (*n* = 5), and (e) chose not to participate (*n* = 7).

The themes for the first participant's responses to a question, the second participant's response to that question, and so on, were analyzed until two responses (protocols) were analyzed past the last new theme (Jones, 1984). At this point, the themes were grouped, and narrative summaries in the respondent's own words were developed in the order of most to least frequent themes. These steps were carried out for responses to all questions.

Reliability. Reliability was calculated by the percentage of agreement between raters for both major and subthematic units. The percentage of agreement ranged from 88% to 95% ($m = 91.5\%$).

Results

Table 1 shows the major themes offered to the question, "Describe what you mean by the term feminism and/or womanism," and the frequency of each response. Ten respondents wrote about their reactions to the term *feminist* and their identification with that label. One wrote that she was not a feminist because feminist research and literature is as unrelated to her as is work written by White males. Feminism, for her, connoted a struggle to advance only the status of White women. Another woman who had no objection to being labeled a feminist nonetheless preferred the term *womanist.* For her, African feminism was acceptable because it combined African with feminist concerns and had about the same meaning as womanism. Another, who considered herself a feminist and accepted the

TABLE 1
Major Themes of Participants' Responses to Question 1: Describe what you mean by the term feminism (&/or womanist)?

Theme	Frequency
Label or identification*	10
Beliefs of feminism*	10
Own beliefs and commitments*	8
Perspective	6
Race and gender*	4
Change	2
Definitions*	1
Meaning	1
Images	1
Stratification*	1
Sex as class	1
Differences*	1
Not minority women	1
Eliminating oppression*	1
University system	1

*Responses or themes that also emerged from the previous White sample (Kimmel, 1989).

term, wrote that she was not knowledgeable about womanism despite being African American. Another respondent wrote that she was a feminist but did not like the term because of its historical basis. Six respondents stated that they considered themselves to be feminists.

Ten respondents wrote about feminist beliefs, including recognizing inequities between genders and working to change them; protecting the human rights of women and women having equal access in the workplace, education, and social recognition; the right of human beings to control their own life; eradicating all inequalities on the basis of sex, race, class, age, sexual preference, and so on, that impede the full realization of human potential; protecting and preserving the environment; eradicating war; respecting women; equal treatment; equal choice; equal rights; viewing women as equal rather than inferior; women having access to the same goods and privileges as men and having the same right to develop themselves based on desires and abilities; being able to make own choices; equality and fairness for women; women and men constituting different classes that differ in power, prestige, and privilege; people being politically, socially, and economically equal regardless of gender; and eliminating oppression on the basis of gender, race and class.

Eight respondents wrote more specifically about their own beliefs and commitments. Their concerns included women's issues within the context of racial and ethnic concerns; women's rights to pursue their potential; living and working according to the principles of equality and freedom for all human beings; recognizing the oppression of women in terms of power status as unacceptable and having a personal commitment to social change; believing gay and lesbian rights to be a part of feminist beliefs; believing feminist politics to be valid; confronting male domination and transforming one's relationships while moving toward mutual responsibility, respect, and value; a consciousness about promoting equality; and advocating women's interests, concerns, and rights vis-à-vis men's because equality does not exist between men and women. Another woman described her meaning of feminism as including rethinking women's roles; an awareness of female traits as being valuable ones; going beyond female–male dichotomies; addressing differences in nonoppressive ways; opportunities to share standpoints and to expose myths about women; going beyond female issues to improving the quality of life for all; changing all forms of oppression; raising men's and women's levels of consciousness; and women, especially Black women, making significant contributions toward affecting women's oppression.

Six respondents began their essays by describing exactly what they thought feminism is: a sociocultural, historical way or perspective for evaluating and developing initiatives; a political philosophy; a political movement; a political theory; a method of analysis and criticism or methodology;

an attitude and belief transferred into behavior; a way of life; an ideology; a political position; a psychological viewpoint; a movement; and a social and political agenda.

Four women made distinctions between race and gender issues in response to this question. One described her feeling of having a double minority status as a Mexican American and a woman. Another wrote that she did not translate "feminist" to mean "White." Another wrote that it was often difficult for her to determine whether the disparate treatment she received was attributable to her race or to her gender. The other wrote that feminism should include people of different racial backgrounds, although it is often limited to gender; for her, gender implied heterogeneity, not homogeneity.

Two women wrote about a change in attitude. One changed because she still saw large numbers of women being treated unequally. The other's attitude has changed over time as she came to see feminism as a philosophy of the White middle class that no longer included her.

One woman wrote a specific definition of womanist as "a Black feminist who loves herself, [is] committed to the emancipation of women and the liberation of males and females from all forms of oppression and [is] dedicated to the wholeness of a people." Another wrote that she "chose to make meaning of life through our gender's world view." Another wrote that feminism "conjures up images of White women, more or less middle class, privileged, protesting their 'ghetto' status as wives and mothers trapped in suburban houses."

One respondent wrote that the simple proposition of feminism is as follows: "Women and men constitute two different classes of people." She explained that the term *class* implies that women and men differ in power, privilege, and prestige, and that the unequal distribution of power, privilege, and prestige is universal, structural, transhistorical, planned, and purposeful. That is, it constitutes a stratification from which the more powerful male group benefits and so seeks to maintain. This respondent also wrote that feminism assumes that the sociological difference between the sexes, namely, power, causes any psychological difference.

One respondent wrote that although feminists strive to enhance the position of women in general, she did not perceive any concerted effort to improve the lot of minority women. Another respondent wrote about the university system as a dominant White male organization, particularly in upper administration, in which women have a long way to go.

In response to Question 2 ("When did you first describe yourself as a feminist [womanist]?"), most women responded in terms of a year or era, particularly the 1970s (see Table 2). Five named their teens. Five women distinguished between conscious and unconscious feminist thoughts and feelings. These women wrote that they had feminist feelings all or most of their lives, but did not label them until college, after exploring feminism,

TABLE 2
Major Themes of Participants' Responses to Question 2: When did you first describe yourself as a feminist (womanist)?

Theme	Frequency
Year*	7
Era	6
Concerns and issues	6
Consciousness*	5
Preference	5
Feminist insights	4
Label*	4
Read feminist literature	3
Age*	2
Lifelong	2
Meaning of terms	2
Friend	1
Event	1
Marriage	1
Membership	1
Black women	1
Against grain	1

*Responses or themes that also emerged from the previous White sample (Kimmel, 1989).

reading feminist literature, and realizing that the issues discussed were part of their lives already. Some less frequent responses were specific ages (such as 6 and 18); through a friendship with a feminist whom she liked and listened to after marriage when she did not want to lose her identity with her married name; and following a specific historical event (i.e., the Poor People's March on Washington, DC).

One respondent wrote that she saw feminist ideology as being a gut sense of what is humane. Three women named particular authors[5] they had read whose writings helped them to identify themselves as feminists.

Of the five women who discussed their preference for terms (feminist or womanist), the responses varied: One said she could work with both and did not see them as oppositional; another preferred the term *humanist*; another expressed that the term *womanist* fulfilled her needs; another liked the term *feminist*; and another identified with neither term. One wrote that she "likes the term feminist because it captures a history of women's efforts for liberation" but that "womanist is important in presenting a Black women's critique of the limitations of feminism," although "womanist does not sufficiently address the gender tensions in the African-American community." Another, although she was a Division 35 member, wrote that the

---

[5]Jean Baker Miller, Mary McCarthy, Betty Friedan, Robin Morgan, Mary Daly, Shulamith Firestone, Charlotte Perkins Gilman, Elizabeth Gould Davis, Margaret Mead, Kate Millett, Andrea Dworkin, Michelle Wallace, and Alice Walker.

women's movement is typically "led by White women who see women (themselves) as recent arrivals in the workplace." Black women "have always had to balance wage earning and child care," and it "goes against the grain to hear privileged White women complain of these hardships (balancing act) as though they invented motherhood and working."

Several of the respondents took this opportunity to express their concerns and identify issues. Two wrote about facing gender and racial issues and being committed to the fight against racism and sexism in social, political, religious, and educational institutions. Although only one woman expressed a specific concern with the rights of Black women, 3 others wrote about inequities that are based on gender. The suffering of women and children during the 1960s and wanting the same rights and privileges as men were mentioned. One said that she was concerned with the welfare of all. One respondent recalled being told as a child that she "could not do certain things/activities because she was a girl and 'girls do not do such things.'" Another reported that she realized in high school how little choice her mother had and how extra hard she would have to work to break that mold because her father had planned for his sons to go to college, but did not make such plans for his daughters.

In response to Question 3 ("Describe the experience of being a feminist [womanist]"), issues of race were salient: "My experience as a Black feminist working with White feminists is bad"; "the gender dimension of race poses problems among Black people that are not addressed and plague the Black community"; "As a Black woman I have been able to bring together all dimensions of my struggles with a deeper understanding of total resistance"; and "Quietly accepting the many race/gender based inequalities is impossible, so it is easy to get attacked by and from several quarters." Another respondent wrote that feminism had not been part of her struggle; rather, fighting racism was her experience. She was saddened to experience women who considered themselves to be feminists relating to Women of Color in racist ways. (See Table 3.)

Sexism was the second most recurrent topic: disdain for sexism; "am always alert to racist or sexist behavior or language to which I respond immediately"; "I see gender based injustices as they relate to women as well as understand that males are also constricted by gender based socialization"; and "I have grown in my reaction to the external sexist world and feel much more in control and capable and confident on when, how and who to challenge."

Two respondents cited intellectual growth as part of their experience: "My intelligence has increased exponentially"; "I see not only differently but also more with this consciousness"; and "I experienced tremendous intellectual and political growth and development during the past two decades." Two respondents wrote about social change in terms of being committed to it and stated that feminism was the beginning of social change.

TABLE 3
Major Themes of Participants' Responses to Question 3: Describe your experience of being a feminist (womanist)

Theme	Frequency
Black or White	6
Sexism*	4
Intellectual growth	2
Social change*	2
Support	2
Liberating	2
Self-disgust	1
Crazy	1
Difficulty with men*	1
Difficulty with women*	1
Loathing	1
Anger	1
Marriage	2
Unnatural	1
Uncomfortable	1
Painful	1
Opportunity	1
Attached	1
Acceptance	1
Work more useful	1
Morally right	1
Disillusionment	1
Hopelessness	1
Depriving	1
Frustrating	1
Punished	1
Conflict	1
Troubling	1
Difficult	1
Competition	1
Good	1
Want it	1
Increase it	1
Empathy	1
Friendships	1
Working hard	1
Political growth or development	1
Value own experience	1
Commonalities with other women*	1
Not know how	1
Ostracized in school	1
Radical feminist consciousness*	1
Way of seeing or being*	1
Criticized or questioned	1
Unremovable lense*	1
Men	1
Outspoken	1
Gravitate	1
Fitting in with movement*	1
Empowering	1
Part of self or nature	1

*Responses or themes that also emerged from the previous White sample (Kimmel, 1989).

Appreciating women's support of each other and finding support in the literature, especially support from mentors, was mentioned. Two respondents called their experiences liberating: awareness of not being "strange"; "that other women shared the same beliefs and aspirations"; and "being liberated by becoming much more aware of the interlocking systems of oppression." Two women commented on marriage: "accepting the terms of my marriage then or now is impossible" and "marrying outside my ethnic subgroup to a man who would not be threatened by my career goals but would also be supportive seems impossible."

Experiences of feminism were talked about in many additional ways: as an opportunity to relate with other female feminists in deeper and meaningful ways; gaining empathy for women's experiences; having a great dislike for women competing against other women for men; appreciating men who understand sexist behavior and reject traditional women's roles; being outspoken about issues of inequality and defending own beliefs; and having female students who assume she is feminist and gravitating toward her. Also, one woman described her experience of being ostracized during graduate school for taking the position that feminism was too exclusionary for not considering the standpoints of Black women, other Women of Color, class differences, race differences, and the idea that the issues are greater than "just women." Others described themselves as "theoretically approving and supportive but have trouble finding where she fits in as a single professional African American woman"; "learning to value own experience and recognize and appreciate the commonalities with other women"; and "working extra hard in everything." Another wrote that it was difficult but empowering, whereas another wrote that lots of her deepest personal friendships developed through feminist work with other women.

One respondent wrote at length about her experience as a radical feminist. She called feminism "a most unnatural act" and an uncomfortable position; she described her radical feminist consciousness as "a depriving, frustrating, troubling, difficult, frightening, anxiety-provoking, burning, horrible yet uplifting way of seeing/being." Although she experienced this consciousness as horrible, and had loathing and disgust for just about everyone and everything, she felt it was morally right. She viewed this as good, wanting it and choosing to increase it by reading and attending lectures. She made the analogy that being a feminist was "like wearing a pair of contact lenses that cannot be removed and that make it possible for one to see disease in everyone and everything including oneself." She became disgusted by her own desires and began to hate her boyfriend, hate her father, and feel crushing, irreversible guilt about her relationship with her mother. She wrote that she "went crazy the way that radical feminists do go crazy" and that she no longer knew how to touch others, have sex, and express feelings because she criticized and questioned everything from a feminist perspective.

In response to Question 4 ("Think about an experience, a particular event or period in your life, when you were especially aware of being a feminist. Describe it. Was it a positive or negative experience for you?"), most respondents who clearly indicated whether the experience was positive or negative wrote that negative experiences were related to hiring (see Table 4). One woman described her department's low salaries, and how women did not apply because the salary would be less than they were currently making. The men in her department made more than their female supervisor, and the supervisor subsequently quit her job. This negative experience was made positive when the respondent documented misbehavior and filed a sexism charge for which the departmental chairperson was removed. Another respondent wrote about interviewing for the presidency of a small Black college. Many of the questions from the male trustees revolved around her feminist activities, implying that she would

TABLE 4

Major Themes of Participants' Responses to Question 4: Think about an experience, a particular event, or a period in your life when you were especially aware of being a feminist. Describe it. Was it a positive or negative experience for you?

Theme	Frequency
Hiring	4
At work	3
Lack of female role models	1
Rape reports	1
Inequities in power and privilege*	1
Inequities in tenure, promotion, or treatment*	1
Job activities	1
Money	1
After divorce	1
Self-expression	1
Sexism charge	1
Childrearing	1
New job	1
Learned	1
Positive and negative varies*	1
Constant	1
Can't choose time	1
Clash	1
Chose truth	1
In college*	1
Launched project	1
Identity	1
Work as clinician	1
Patriarchal domination	1
Sorting racism and sexism	1

*Responses or themes that also emerged from the previous White sample (Kimmel, 1989).

be more interested in gender matters than racial issues if she were chosen to lead the college. One White female interviewer pointed out that if the respondent were male, no such questions would be asked. The respondent wrote that this was her first major encounter with sexism from her Black brothers and it still hurts to remember it. When her male counterpart got the position, she wrote to congratulate him by saying, "I'm sure the best man won." Another respondent simply stated that While male candidates are preferred over Blacks and women for faculty positions. Another respondent wrote about an incident in which she fought to have her department hire another Woman of Color. The Black men were against her and said she was not qualified and lacked credentials. The respondent realized that they wanted a man and that that implicated her as a scholar.

Three women wrote about negative experiences in the workplace generally. One said that the absolute worst, ongoing experience was trying to work productively, introduce nontraditional, non-male-oriented, non-White American viewpoints, and to be recognized and promoted for her work within her department. Another woman wrote about a professional meeting where the argument was over replacing the word *history* with *heritage*. Later, when the same people were discussing how to obtain diversity on editorial boards, they felt that one Black and one Latino would be sufficient. The respondent felt that she was operating on feminist principles when she pointed out the contradictions, although she doubted that she changed their opinions. From this experience, she learned not to confuse feminism with her understanding of racial equality. The other explicitly negative experience at work as a woman came from an academic administrator over men. Although she felt that her position was the most demanding, she received the lowest salary. She also felt that getting her recommendations accepted entailed more than the required documentation and ingenuity on her part.

Other negative experiences included men making more money for the same position despite poorer credentials; realizing that there are inequities in tenure, promotion, and treatment between women and men in university positions; and pointing out the lack of female role models. One respondent wrote about her job activities as director of a training program for women. Although the male professors she worked with were nice, competent men, they were "very male." She found the experience frightening and painful because she felt that she was betraying students when she showed support for her colleagues. There was a clash of philosophies between her and her colleagues over what a professor's work should be. Her "survival" relied on her abandoning feminist students who were questioning the training they received while "swallowing it whole" for nonfeminist students. She eventually lost her job because her colleagues were more powerful than she. She chose to be true to herself, her feminist beliefs, and the students. She looked for a job where she could be herself and where feminist pedagogy was respected. She then felt that she was in "heavier" in her new position educating women about women's realities. Two other non-work-related negative experiences were cited: realizing the inequities in power and privilege between her parents and an incident in which a female rape victim was identified and the men who gang-raped her were not.

Several women noted positive experiences. One wrote that she wanted to learn more about womaness after her divorce. Those learning experiences led her to new forms of self-expression, and she eventually established her own organization. One respondent wrote about how feminism had affected the way she was raising her son, in that her feminist ideals allowed her to guide him through life as a person rather than as a male person. Because of this, he had a clear perspective of how valuable women are as people rather that being incompetent or sexual commodities. Other positive experiences were described earlier.

One woman wrote that she was aware of being a feminist every waking moment of every day for the past 20 years; it was constant. She wrote that perhaps less radical feminists could choose a time, but she could not. For her, whether a situation was positive or negative varied and was contingent on how many other feminists were present and on the behavior she engaged in in response. Another respondent wrote that her awareness came in college when her high school friends were all marrying; her parents expected her to do the same and were surprised at her persistence in wanting a career. Another wrote that, in response to local community Black women, she launched a project that commenced a decade-long effort to write the history of Black women. Working with women from all walks of life and seeing their commitment to the project as a means of empowerment cemented her own identity as a feminist. One respondent wrote about her work as a clinician in a women's center. The issues she saw being brought up in group therapy and peer consultation included incest survival, spouse abuse, adolescent pregnancy, abortion, workplace struggles, sexual harassment, and many other relational issues peculiar to women. This respondent was aware of her feminism during her experience as a Roman Catholic nun. She felt that she was keenly attuned to unfair patriarchal domination in institutional religions, especially Catholicism. Roman Catholic women who are militant are not so by nature, she believed, but out of desperation. Finally, one respondent wrote about trying for years to discover and sort out elements of racism and sexism. She tried to go beyond superficial, personality, petty "stuff," and tended to do it with everything. This formidable enterprise kept her busy studying history, laws and lawmakers, women and their strengths and weaknesses and views, and so on.

In response to Question 5 ("How has being a feminist affected employment, family, personal relationships, and spiritual life?"), 5 respondents noted little or no effect on their employment overall, whereas 3 specifically noted that they either had no problem getting jobs or were successful at keeping jobs (see Table 5). One woman wrote that she probably would have been invited to join a faculty if she had had more mainstream and less feminist ideas, but she would not have wanted to stay in a sexist, racist department anyway. One woman who said she had no problem getting jobs felt that promotions had been hampered or limited, but indicated that her feminism had not stopped promotions. For one, the effect had been negligible until this year, when her ability to articulate feminist ideals, point out discrepancies, and practice in a woman-centered institution had helped to parlay a promotion and raise.

Several respondents noted positive effects stemming from their feminist perspective. Richer exchanges with colleagues, good peer support, mentoring, and getting along well with others were some of the benefits. One wrote that coworkers knew her beliefs about race and gender and did not go out of their way to antagonize her. One wrote about being goal oriented, not letting obstacles get in her way, and working until the job was complete even if it meant time away from her home and family. Another wrote that there had been some effect but that her work stood on its own merits. Being a feminist, for one respondent, helped her to identify sexism as the villain instead of using self-blame when she was treated poorly. Similarly, another respondent wrote that she was more aware of the inequities in the treatment of women and men. This respondent felt that in most businesses, men are given more money, more latitude to grow, and more respect. She found it difficult to accept this and even more difficult to fight it without massive support.

One respondent who said feminism had had a great effect on her employment wrote that her feminist views often contrasted with the norms and behaviors in the world of work and in substantive approaches to research. These contrasting views often led to conflict with male colleagues. She wrote, "It has been noted that 'I am no Shirley Violet'—this is a nice way to avoid the 'B' word [bitch]—in spite of behavioral patterns that clearly show male collegaues to have similar or more aggressive behaviors."

Although one respondent's feminism had caused her to concentrate her work in women's studies, another applied an African feminist perspective to her teaching, writing, and research in literature. The texts that she selected had to reflect a feminist and African American view. She introduced students to Zora Neale Hurston, Willa Cather, and Sylvia Plath in her American literature course and used a woman's perspective when visiting male writers. Her students, she noted, wanted her to teach only Hemingway, Faulkner, and Fitzgerald and accused her of teaching only feminist and Black literature rather than "American" literature.

With regard to family relationships, 5 respondents explicitly stated that there had been no effect. One respondent wrote that her relationships

TABLE 5

Major Themes of Participants' Responses to Question 5: What effect has your being a feminist had on work, family, and personal relationships, and spiritual life?

Work		Family Relationships		Personal Relationships		Spiritual Life	
Theme	Frequency	Theme	Frequency	Theme	Frequency	Theme	Frequency
Get along well*	2	No effect*	4	None*	1	None*	3
Richer exchanges	1	Admires me	3	More demands on men	1	Don't know what spiritual experience is	3
Good peer support*	1	Family adores me	1	Don't play traditional role	1	Feminism reaffirms aetheism	3
Mentoring	1	More open	1	Why she's still unmarried	1	Perceived God beyond sexual identity	2
Respect for all job levels	1	Less judgmental	1	Deeper relation with men and women*	1	Reject institutional patriarchal religion	1
No problem getting jobs*	1	Less "enmeshed" with others' business	1	Deeper relation with other feminists*	1	Church materials depict a male God	1
Will limit promotions*	1	Husband supports women's rights	1	Deep friendships	1	Sexism in Black Baptist churches	1
Not inhibit promotion	1	Awareness of role differences	1	Friends are also feminists	1	No longer attend	1
Identify sexism	1	Relatives are feminists	1	Feel and talk like a womanist	1	Men wrote Bible	1
Awareness of male and female inequities	1	Feminism is ingrained in me	1	Liberating	1	Women excluded	1
Job in women's studies	1			Still growing	1	Passages create unworthy feeling	1
No effect*	1			Self not strange	1	Greater bonding with other women*	1
				Shared beliefs and aspirations	1	Spiritually oriented*	1
				Torn between beliefs and actions	1	Church was part of childhood	1
				Shaped life*	1	Churchgoing versus spirituality	1
				Choose humanist friends	1	Passages that comfort	1
				Superficial relations with nonfeminists	1	Understand Mary and other women differently	1

*Responses or themes that also emerged from the previous White sample (Kimmel, 1989).

had been better than most because the level of consciousness of her family and friends regarding "feminist issues" has increased notably. Some others wrote about their familial relationships in broad terms. One respondent wrote that family members adored her because she managed to obtain her doctorate despite being Black and from a welfare family; they admired her, respected her, and listened to her. Another respondent felt that her female relatives always had been feminists, although they would not call themselves such. Another said that the men in her family were sensitive to women's rights and would never make sexist remarks in her presence, making for better family relationships. On the other hand, one wrote that family members had difficulty interacting with her because of differences in beliefs. She feels that "all people, including gays and lesbians, are equal and should be treated as such; my family's definition does not include gays and lesbians."

Several spoke about their husbands and marriages. One complained that her husband resisted feminist ideology, whereas another reported the opposite. Another wrote that she met her husband at a professional conference and that they shared similar interests. However, her husband, who considered himself a liberal, asked to have the term *feminism* defined at every conference they attended. She believed that he felt threatened by feminism. When he wished to "punish" her, he called her independent, which he equated with feminist. She felt that his comments really meant that she could buy whatever she wanted but that he would not contribute. She told her husband that, in her next existence, she would be a man. One respondent said she became angry with herself because it was difficult to let go of "wifely duties," but then felt abused when she had to perform those duties as well as take care of her professional work and personal needs.

Two respondents also wrote about their daughters: One wrote that her daughters (aged 9 and 13) were feminists, and the other wrote that she taught her daughters to think for themselves, work for their goals, and be responsible for themselves. This respondent also said she became impatient with her mother because she was very dependent and had a traditional outlook on life and women's roles.

Several additional comments were that feminism had affected their family relationships by: being clearer in her expectations; having greater awareness of gender role differences; and being more open, less judgmental, and less "enmeshed" with others' business. One respondent said, "feminism has brought about lots of arguments and frustrations from early on about the unequal power and limits placed on me, but not my brothers, based on gender."

Regarding friendships, 6 respondents wrote that they selected male and female friends on the basis of their humanist, or feminist, outlooks and that the deepest friendships had grown from work with other feminists.

They chose friends who were independent like themselves, because otherwise it was a strain to tolerate, change, or inform nonfeminist friends. Several respondents distinguished between relationships with other feminists, characterized as deepened, versus nonfeminists, characterized by a day-to-day superficial chatter. One woman noted that her low tolerance for nonfeminists meant that she had an extraordinarily small number of friends.

Five women commented directly about the effects their feminism had had on relationships, ranging from selection of partners and friends to putting more demands on male relationships. As a result of her feminism, one said she did not play traditional roles and attributed her unmarried status to that choice. Another respondent wrote at length about feminism's effects on her relationship to herself and others and stated that there has been no greater impact than that of her radical feminism. For her, feminism dictated what she liked to do, where she liked to go, how she related to others, and what forms of relationships she would take part in and with whom. The greatest impact has been on her sexuality: She grew up "heterosexual like everyone else, had boyfriends, and wanted and intended to marry." Her radical feminism later destroyed that, making it difficult to relate to men. Over time, she became a lesbian and felt that she had always valued her female friends more than her male friends, had more intimate, meaningful friendships with women, and felt that her occasional attraction to her female friends was a pretty ordinary experience for straight women. As she began to appreciate women more, her radical feminist consciousness was a revolution in her life; it changed her mind and all of her behavior. After 10 years, she made an intellectual and emotional decision to be a lesbian. The dissonance stopped, and the content and structure of her relationships became consistent with her politics and values. She wrote that she could not go back to being straight anymore than she could lose her feminist consciousness.

One respondent wrote that her earliest recollection of herself was as a feminist and that feminist values and perspectives had shaped her entire life. Another woman, who "feels and talks like a womanist," said that she was still growing. At times, she was torn between her beliefs and actions. One woman commented that she was not aware of any impact feminism had had and that she did not speak overtly as a feminist. However, when she did speak and write, it was usually in harmony with the ideals of protection of women's rights, equal access in work, and education and social institutions.

Regarding spiritual lives, several women commented directly on their spirituality by saying, "I consider myself to be a spiritually oriented person," "I am very spiritual, but not always observant person," or "I am not very spiritually oriented." Two women said that their feminism had had no effect on their spiritual lives, and another wrote that although her spiritual life had opened tremendously, she did not see it as being related to her feminist perspective quite so much. Another wrote that she did not know what the question meant, did not know what a spiritual experience is, and did not imagine she had ever had one. This respondent described herself as a "born-again atheist (and proud of it)"; her atheism began as a college sophomore after she took courses in comparative religion and history of religious beliefs. She stated that her feminism reaffirmed her atheism.

Two respondents commented on bonding; one felt greater bonding with other women, whereas another felt bonds with the Earth and nature. Women's roles and inequalities were mentioned by several respondents. One wrote that she viewed the role of Mary and other women in the Bible in a totally different light and now rejected institutional and patriarchal religion. Another wrote that certain convictions regarding women in the Roman Catholic church were what led her to leave the religious life. This respondent did not grow up Catholic and was therefore not culturally Catholic. She was aware of feminist groups within the Catholic church, but did not take part in them because she did not feel strongly about their issues. She noted her support of choice in reproductive issues even though she did not make political alliances on the basis of that belief. Another woman wrote that she no longer attended church because of the problems with sexism in Black Baptist churches. Another woman expounded on the issue of sexism in the church by noting features that bother her, which she is working to alleviate. She told the story of her participation as a steward, which is typically a male position. Her church got a new minister who habitually referred to women as "sugar" and "honey." She asked him to refrain from addressing her in that manner, and he replied that he would try but that other women liked it. She retorted that such language is still sexist and asked him if he had such endearing terms for men. Another respondent wrote that "church readings glorify a male God, men wrote the Bible, and that books on women were excluded from the Bible." She had to "carefully weed out and select passages which comfort her from those which make her feel unworthy simply because she is not a man." Although churchgoing was a part of her childhood spirituality, as an adult she found it extremely difficult to reconcile the religious part of spirituality (church activities) with the spiritual part of spirituality.

One respondent wrote that she was a strong advocate of women's equality in spiritual matters, such as the church, and that she did not believe God is a man; rather, she learned to perceive God beyond a gender identity. Another wrote that traditional spiritual experiences are male focused and had turned her off to organized religion. She found it limiting and unacceptable; thus, she was more open than most people to "alternative" experiences of spirituality. She also commented that it had taken her "much time to explore more woman-affirming spiritual modes."

Regarding Question 6 ("In your daily life now, when are you most or least aware of being a feminist?"), 4 respondents were most aware of their feminism at work (see Table 6). One described work as an environment in which women were solicitous, helpful. and friendly to men simply because they were men or in which some departments got things done more quickly and efficiently because their department heads were men. Another wrote that she was acutely aware of power relations and how they got played out in the work environment. She said that meetings were microcosms of social dynamics that reminded her on a daily basis of how women are devalued and mistreated in subtle and not-so-subtle ways. Another respondent specifically named the university and national professional circles as the settings in which she was most aware.

Two respondents wrote that they were always aware of their feminism: all the time, for every waking moment of every day, there were no degrees to this, no continuum of awareness, always most aware; it was part of the personality. Two respondents named incidences of sexism in situations in which sexist attitudes or behaviors occurred or encountering oppressive acts toward women. Two other respondents said that they were most aware in their research or in the classroom.

TABLE 6

Major Themes of Participants' Responses to Question 6: In your daily life now, when are you most aware of being a womanist/feminist? Least aware?

Theme	Frequency
Most aware	
At work*	4
Always*	2
Sexism	2
Research and teaching	2
Work with other women	1
In relationships*	1
At home*	1
Questionnaire	1
Racist men	1
Least aware	
At home*	3
With other feminists	1
Ethnicity/gender	1
With other women	1
Shopping	1
Leisure activities	1
No gender conflicts	1
Usually	1

*Responses or themes that also emerged from the previous White sample (Kimmel, 1989).

Other situations in which the women were most aware of their feminism included the following: when working with other women; in relationships; at home when she was conscious of wanting to rid herself of the pressures of housework; and when she confronted condescending, racist men while she was going about basic daily functions. One woman stated that she became aware only when she was asked to fill out questionnaires such as this one.

Three respondents were least aware of their feminism while at home, where it is natural, with a husband who was also feminist. One respondent wrote that her ethnic identity was far more pervasive than her gender. One wrote that when she was with other feminists, it seemed most natural and she did not think about it so much. Another was least aware in her personal life, especially with female friends; she belonged to three groups that were exclusively female. Another wrote that it was ironic that she was least aware when shopping for clothes, cosmetics, and the like. One woman said she was least aware in leisure activities. Another wrote that she was least aware in contexts in which there was little or no conflict that arose because of gender.

Regarding Question 7 ("Has your experience of feminism changed over time? If so, how?"), many respondents wrote about how their feminism had changed, but only two of these themes were repeated by more than one person (see Table 7). Five women explicitly stated that their ideas of feminism had changed, and only one said that it had not. She wrote, "I do not believe it has. I have never been very aggressive about it. I just act and speak in ways that convey my feelings to others." Two women wrote about inclusion. One of them said that the term no longer included her and that she had noted that research and publications by "feminists" were as unrelated to her experiences and realities as that conducted or published by White men. The other wrote that the term had become more inclusive for her, because she had come to respect homemakers and accept them as feminists. Two respondents wrote that their feminism had grown deeper: "It has deepened. I don't feel the need to constantly challenge anymore." "It is deeper, more pervasive, more integrated."

Other respondents wrote specifically about changes, although there were no recurrent themes. Some of these included "stronger in my convictions about a feminist perspective, more outspoken without feeling angry—it has grown and continues to grow deeper, it is more extreme, reading feminist literature has helped." One elaborated that she moved from denying feminism to identifying as a womanist and not being too uncomfortable with the term *feminist*. At first it meant being pro-woman; later it meant being pro-human—it is essential to being herself, and she could not have allowed herself to be who she is were it not for a feminist awareness of reality (i.e., the world, herself, professional pursuits). Her views had

TABLE 7
Major Themes of Participants' Responses to Question 7: Has your
experience of feminism changed over time? If so, how?

Theme	Frequency
Change*	7
Convictions	2
Outspoken	2
Deeper	1
Inclusion	1
Anger	1
Grown	1
More extreme	1
Joy–pain	1
Appreciation of women*	1
Cultural diversity	1
Hopeful	1
Inclusion	1
Unrelated	1
Literature	1
Not aggressive	1
Act and speak	1
Identify*	1
Meaning	1
Deeper	1
More pervasive	1
More integrated*	1
Essential to self*	1
Rights	1
Stronger*	1
Teaching and research	1
Support	1
Reaction to sexism	1
Value	1
Commonalities	1
Enabled decision	1
Oppression	1
Acknowledge other standpoints	1
Challenge	1

*Responses or themes that also emerged from the previous White sample (Kimmel, 1989).

grown stronger, and the biggest impact on her outlook began after she started teaching and conducting research in a university.

One respondent wrote about the persistent pain and increasing joy of this consciousness. The joy, which grew consistently with her appreciation for and fascination with women, was low initially but was now as high as the pain. This same respondent felt that, with cultural diversity being "in," the receptivity to people to color resulted in a new involvement with feminist work. Now that she was hopeful that her perspective would have an ear, she wanted to work with White feminists again, and she rejoined the groups that she dropped out of in the 1980s.

One respondent noted that she grew more conscious of women's rights and that growing up Black made her more conscious of her rights, so it was not a difficult leap for her to make the association with race and gender. Another respondent wrote that she found support in literature and from other women with similar perspectives, especially mentors. She grew in her reaction to the external sexist world in that she felt much more in control, capable, and confident on when, how, and whom to challenge. She learned to value her own experience as a woman and to recognize and appreciate the commonalities with other women. Another respondent wrote about feminism as enabling her to make the decision to leave the convent, which was a major change. One other respondent wrote that she found it encouraging to observe the impact feminism had had on women's oppression and that is was "refreshing that feminism is beginning to recognize the interlocking and intertwining aspects of oppression, thus moving beyond an additive, prioritizing, or olympic sense of oppression." She also found it "refreshing that feminism is beginning to acknowledge the standpoints of Black women and others."

OVERALL COMPARISON OF THE EXPERIENCE OF FEMINISM FOR WOMEN OF COLOR WITH THAT OF WHITE WOMEN

Do different groups of women have a similar experience of feminism? Our data suggest that they do, to a substantial degree. An examination of the tables showing the frequency of the themes of experience shows that the Women of Color and White women shared a number of themes. Although the proportion of the themes was small, the narratives of the Women of Color and White women were comparable in that there was much similarity between the nature of the experiences that the two groups of women described in their narratives.

In addition, both groups talked about the myriad ways their lives had been changed by and infused with their feminism. Having deeper friendships, possessing selective friendships on the basis of shared beliefs about gender, having "war stories" about work, raising feminist daughters and sons, and experiencing supportive and antagonistic relationships with husbands and lovers were among some of the ways in which feminism influenced the day-to-day existence of Women of Color and White women. Finally, both groups of women reported that their awareness of feminism was greater at work and was generally more positive than negative.

Along with the similarities, there were some important differences between the Women of Color and the White women. For example, the narratives of the Women of Color contained greater elaboration about reported conscious content. In other words, the Women of Color gave "thicker" overall descriptions of their experiences of feminism. These thicker descriptions stemmed from the larger number of stories that the Women of Color offered in their responses to the questions they were asked. This inclination by Women of Color to provide richer descriptions was particularly reflected in their narratives about race and the intersection of race and gender. Not surprisingly, race emerged as a far more salient theme for Women of Color than for White women (see also Reid, 1989). Moreover, Women of Color wrote more passionately about the tension between gender and race issues and the women's movement than did White women.

One of the most striking differences between the Women of Color and the White women's narratives was their reaction to the question about the impact of feminism on their spiritual lives. With only one exception, the Women of Color articulated strong feelings about their spiritual life and its relationship to feminism. By contrast, the White women essentially did not respond to the item on spirituality. A few indicated that they did not know what spirituality was.

In summary, Women of Color and White women shared similar themes of experience and offered comparable narratives in terms of the nature of their feminist experiences. However, compared with the narratives of the White women, the descriptions of the Women of Color were richer in detail and more passionately expressed, especially regarding the relationship between spirituality and feminism. Predictably, Women of Color also were more deeply concerned about race and the relationship between race and gender as embodied in the women's movement.

CONCLUSION

The purpose of this study was to further the understanding of feminism as it is experienced by feminist Women of Color. To accomplish this, we adopted an existential–phenomenological perspective and asked Women of Color to report their consciousness of this phenomenon. Our primary assumption was that feminism is not just an ideology or just a set of behaviors but it is a phenomenon (see also Wallston, 1986) that is dialogically derived. It is experienced and exists in the consciousness of feminists. It has meaning in relationship to others, and the meaning evolves and is manifested as they communicate with others and the world. We also wished to compare the experiences of feminism for Women of Color with those of White women.

It appears that feminism can be labeled a phenomenon that entails a thick, experiential component that may underlie objective descriptions of feminism and of feminist behaviors and attitudes. Feminism also appears to be meaningful for Women of Color as well as White women.

We found both shared and distinct meanings in the reports about the phenomenon. Commonalities were most evident in the paragraphs constructed from the themes the analysis identified. Some remarkable differences in reported meanings also were apparent, which supports the assertion that the women's movement is not a homogeneous, monolithic "thing," but is comprised of feminists who imbue different meanings to their and others' experiences as feminists (Hare-Mustin & Maracek, 1988). Women of Color may be harder to locate and entice to participate, but those who took the time to write seemed passionate and unambivalent about their experience. They found the task viable, which we interpret to mean that the method was indeed congruent with the thing that it was designed to illuminate.

REFERENCES

Dapkus, S. (1985). A thematic analysis of the experience of time. *Journal of Personality and Social Psychology, 49*, 408–419.

Giorgi, A. (1981). On the relationship among the psychologist's fallacy, psychologism, and the phenomenological reduction. *Journal of Phenomenological Psychology, 12*, 75–86.

Goodwin, B. J. (1991, August). *Inclusion in the curriculum: Psychology as a case study.* Paper presented at the 99th Annual Convention of the American Psychological Association, San Francisco.

Hare-Mustin, R. T., & Maracek, J. (1988). The meaning of difference: Gender theory, post-modernism, and psychology. *American Psychologist, 43*, 455–464.

Hawes, L. C. (1977). Toward a hermeneutic phenomenology of communication. *Communication Quarterly, 25*(3), 30–41.

James, W. (1918). *The principles of psychology.* New York: Holt.

Jones, C. S. (1984). *Training manual for thematizing interview protocols phenomenologically.* Unpublished manuscript (Tech. Rep. No. 1). University of Tennessee, Phenomenological Psychology Research Group.

Kimmel, E. B. (1989). The experience of feminism. *Psychology of Women Quarterly, 13*, 133–148.

Kruger, D. (1979). *An introduction to phenomenological psychology.* Pittsburgh, PA: Duquesne University Press.

Langellier, K. M., & Hall, D. L. (1989). Interviewing women: A phenomenological approach to feminist communication research. In K. Carter & C. Spitzach (Eds.), *Doing research on women's communication: Perspectives on theory and method.* Norwood, NJ: Ablex.

Luijpen, W. A., & Koren, H. J. (1987). *A first introduction to existential phenomenology*. Pittsburgh, PA: Duquesne University Press.

Misiak, H., & Sexton, V. S. (1973). *Phenomenological, existential, and humanistic psychologies: A historical survey*. New York: Grune & Stratton.

Reid, P. (1989, March). *All the Blacks are men and all the women are White*. Paper presented at the Meeting of the Southeastern Psychological Association, New Orleans, LA.

Solomon, R. C. (1980). General introduction: What is phenomenology? In R. C. Solomon (Ed.), *Phenomenology and existentialism* (pp. 1–41). Lanham, MD: University Press of America.

Valle, R. S., King, M., & Halling, S. (1989). An introduction to existential-phenomenological thought in psychology. In R.S. Valle & S. Halling (Eds.), *Existential-phenomenological perspectives in psychology* (pp. 3–16). New York: Plenum.

von Eckartsberg, R. (1986). *Life-world experience: Existential-phenomenological research approaches in psychology*. Lanham, MD: University Press of America.

Wallston, B. S. (1981). What are the questions in psychology of women? A feminist approach to research. *Psychology of Women Quarterly, 5*, 597–617.

Wallston, B. S. (1986, March). *What's in a name revisited: Psychology of women versus feminist psychology or feminist psychology. Evolution of psychology of women*. Paper presented at the meeting of the Association for Women in Psychology, Oakland, CA.

3

CULTURAL DIVERSITY AND METHODOLOGY IN FEMINIST PSYCHOLOGY: CRITIQUE, PROPOSAL, EMPIRICAL EXAMPLE

HOPE LANDRINE, ELIZABETH A. KLONOFF, and
ALICE BROWN-COLLINS

In this chapter[1] we advocate for a revision of the methodology used in feminist psychological research on the grounds that cultural diversity in feminist psychology cannot be achieved without methodological change. First, we review the feminist challenge to traditional, empiricist methods; present a cultural critique of those methods; and discuss the need for a revised method to address cultural differences. We then outline a revised method and present the results of a simple study as an example of the need for and benefits of the revised methodology.

---

[1]This chapter is an expanded version of an article by Landrine, Klonoff, and Brown-Collins (1992) that appeared in *Psychology of Women Quarterly*, Vol. 16, pp. 145–163. Adapted with permission of Cambridge University Press.

THE FEMINIST CRITIQUE OF METHODOLOGY

In recent years, many have questioned the appropriateness of using traditional research methodologies in feminist psychological research. Many have argued that traditional research practices are embedded in a context of gender stratification and so recapitulate patriarchal forms of relation. The most obvious recapitulation is the traditional experimental method in which participants are the subordinates in a hierarchical relationship and are regarded as objects to be manipulated until they satisfy the needs of powerful, emotionally detached, omniscient, deceiving experimenters (McHugh, Koeske, & Frieze, 1986; Morawski, 1985; Wallston & Grady, 1985). Additional recapitulations are the devaluation of experience and of the subjective (Morawski, 1985; Wittig, 1985), as well as the removal of behavior from its context for the sake of (highly valued) "control" (Crawford & Maracek, 1989; Fine, 1985; Hoffnung, 1985).

In light of these concerns, many feminist psychologists have suggested that this methodology needs to be changed to a more person-centered, feminist, constructionist one (Lykes & Stewart, 1986; Wittig, 1985). In the revised methodology, one would attend to women's subjective experiences (Wallston, 1981); investigate the intentions and subjective meanings of research participants (Wittig, 1985); regard the research participant as "the primary interpreter of his or her experience" (Crawford & Marecek, 1989, p. 159); and regard the researcher's observations as merely one of several possible constructions or interpretations of behavior (Wittig, 1985). Thus, many have advocated a feminist methodology characterized by a combination of traditional objective (quantitative and controlled) and nontraditional subjective (qualitative and descriptive) methods (Crawford & Marecek, 1989; DuBois, 1983; Fine, 1985; Unger, 1981; Wallston, 1981).

Despite these concerns and advocacy for a revised methodology, there has been little movement in the direction suggested (Crawford & Marecek, 1989). This resistance to a more person-centered methodology might be understood as a reflection of feminist psychologists' sociopolitical context as marginal persons in psychology: Feminist conformity to traditional forms of research may be an attempt to compensate for the nontraditional, deviant, and marginal content of the research (Morawski, 1991). Feminist psychologists may feel that they must demonstrate that they are legitimate scientists conducting legitimate research (as the ruling class of men in the discipline has defined legitimacy) before feeling that they have "the right" to challenge the definition of legitimacy itself (Flax, 1990; Morawski, 1991). Alternatively, feminist psychologists' concern that methodological deviance can be used as a rationalization for the further marginalization of feminist research is a valid one, and thus many conform to the traditional method with the hope that such conformity will lead their work to have an impact on the discipline as a whole.

A CULTURAL CRITIQUE OF METHODOLOGY

Feminist psychologists' concern about the extent to which research practices mirror patriarchal forms of relation is only one of several reasons to consider revising traditional methodology. Culture and cultural differences, and feminist psychologists' need to investigate and integrate those, are alternative, equally compelling yet neglected reasons for revision. Traditional research practices also are embedded in a context of race, class, and ethnic stratification and thereby recapitulate racist, classist, and ethnocentric forms of relation. Among the recapitulations of race and class stratification is the tendency to refer to research participants as "subjects," a term denoting vassals and serfs owned and governed by a superior class of masters and rulers. These subjects labor without compensation for experimenter-rulers who capture and use them to secure or improve their own status. These captive subjects are often the students of experimenter-professors who control their grades and degrees. Thus, students are frequently the peons of professors and are held in servitude to labor as subjects, not for pay but for their eventual manumission: their graduation. This system of peonage is most obvious in departments that require students to labor as subjects for a specific number of hours in order to obtain their degrees.

An additional recapitulation of national and international race and ethnic relations is the tendency to regard European Americans as "people" (i.e., as acultural, universal prototypes of humanity) and to regard all other ethnic groups as "subcultures" or non-"people." Thus, studies of gender differences and socialization that are based solely on European American women and men are regarded as revealing generalizable facts about gender per se—facts about people; however, similar studies that are based solely on African American women and men are regarded as revealing non-generalizable facts about African Americans alone. Consequently, for studies of gender that are based solely on a sample of European Americans, feminist psychologists' commitment to experimental rigor does not lead them to insist on a African American control group; yet, gender studies that are based solely on African Americans are often viewed as poorly designed (as methodologically deficient) in the absence of a European American control group. Finally, even the assumption that experimenter-outsiders should and can observe and accurately interpret the behavior and practices of subject-others can be viewed as a recapitulation of the legacy of North American, intercultural contact and as subsequently plagued by the arrogance, lack of concern for others, and misinterpretations that such contact continues to entail.

This recapitulation of ethnic and class relations can be removed from the methodology:

1. Feminist psychologists can refer to human research participants as such and cease the use of the term *subjects*.
2. Feminist psychologists could pay research participants for
   their labor.
3. The American Psychological Association's (APA's) Ethical
   Principles might include the statement that servitude as a
   research participant shall not be a contingency for receiving
   a degree or for a grade in a course (e.g., for extra credit). No
   matter how "educational" the researcher believes the experience of servitude to be, such arrangements decrease the vol-
   untary nature of participation and thereby constitute uneth-
   ical treatment of participants.[2]
4. Feminist psychologists might assume that their interpretations (i.e., objective observations) of the behavior of research
   participants may differ significantly from the participants'
   meanings and intentions.
5. Feminist psychologists can regard studies that are based on
   African American, Latino, European American, Asian American, or Native American women and men as equally culturally saturated.
6. Feminist psychologists can define the presence of multiple
   control groups of people of color and of European Americans
   as the prototype of rigorous, experimental design

In addition to these suggestions, we agree with the position that feminist psychology must adopt a revised methodology that consists of traditional and of more person-centered approaches. Our reason for echoing
that view, however, stems from our understanding of the role of culture in
behavior.

THE ROLE OF CULTURE IN BEHAVIOR

One definition of culture is that it is an intersubjective, shared, unconscious pool of information, categories, and set of decision rules that tell
its members how to perceive, comprehend, label, and understand (how to
process) the input of the world (Goodenough, 1964, 1969, 1970).[3] Culture
provides the information and rules upon which people make the automatic,
implicit inferences that are synonymous with perception (D'Andrade,
1981). Perception (observation) is not a passive process of taking in what

---

[2]This suggestion was incorporated in the most recent version of APA's (1992) Ethical Principles.
[3]Certainly, a culture is more than this; it is also a context of laws, religion, art, and so on (see
Harris, 1980). The definition used here emphasizes the cognitive aspects of culture to highlight
specific epistemological quandaries.

is before us, but an active process of "going beyond the information given" to our senses (Bruner, 1957) to a culture that tells us how to label and interpret what we have seen, felt, and experienced. In this sense, culture is more of a cognitive than a behavioral variable (Shore, 1991; Schweder & LeVine, 1984). Cultural differences are not primarily differences in behavior but differences in the meanings (automatically, unconsciously) attributed and attached to the "same" behaviors. Culture can be regarded as the unwritten social and psychological dictionary[4] that each person has memorized and repressed and through which each person unwittingly interprets themselves and others. People each take their own culture's definitions for granted as "the way things are," as "what everybody knows," and so experience their culturally determined interpretations as objective observations of a reality available to all.

For example, imagine that you have invited a woman to dinner and she responded by saying, "Uh uh." What did she say? What did you observe? How do you label and understand her behavior? If she is a European American, she said no, and her behavior should be labeled as a refusal. If she is a Fijian, she said yes, and her behavior should be labeled as acceptance. This is because, in the dictionary that constitutes Fijian culture, the definition of and meaning attributed to the sound "uh uh" is consent (this difference in cultural definitions of the trivial sound "uh uh" created several nontrivial, difficult and amusing encounters for a student of the first author, who worked in Fiji). If she is a Japanese American, she probably said "maybe" because, within the norms of *enryo*, invitations are to be rejected once out of politeness and concern for the invitor and then accepted or rejected "for real" only after they have been extended again.

What, then, did she say: no, yes, or maybe? The answer is that what she said (her behavior's meaning and label) depends on the cultural context to which she belongs, and its interpretation is contingent on the culture to which the interpretor belongs. The answer is that the label for and meaning of her behavior is neither a shadow cast naturally by the behavior nor a face attached to it, but the culturally constituted, instantaneous attribution of an interpreting observer. The answer is that the label (meaning) that one attributes to behavior is a projection of what that behavior would mean and would be called if one engaged in it (if it occurred in one's own sociocultural context), irrespective of whether the interpretor is African American, European American, Latino, Asian American, or Native American. Thus, one does not observe but interprets, and those interpretations can be seriously mistaken. For example, a European American researcher might erroneously conclude that "uh uh" from a Fijian Ameri-

---

[4]The meanings and definitions contained in each culture's dictionary are provided by the powerful members of each culture. These definitions are sometimes challenged by the subordinate members of the culture.

can means "no"; that an African American who raises his or her voice feels anger; or that an Asian American who is silent is passive. The cultural projections that constitute these observations often then result in stereotypes (grounded in one's experience) of Asian Americans as clannish (i.e., they reject invitations) and of African Americans as hostile (i.e., they get angry quickly). Such stereotypes are confirmed by further observations until they finally result in what everyone would agree is rejection and hostility among ethnic groups. Ethnic stereotypes are descriptions of what others' behavior would be called and would mean if one engaged in it, if it occurred in one's own sociocultural context; they result from interpreting the behavior of people from one culture through the dictionary, or context, of another.

If culture can be understood as a dictionary behind the perception, observation, experience, and understanding of European Americans and of people of color alike, then every word people use (e.g., "flirting") to describe what they have observed, as well as to think about and remember their experiences of themselves and others is culturally constituted: Each word is a description of an interaction in their own specific sociohistorical and cultural context; an attribution of motivation that reflects their culture's theory of motives in that context; and a moral evaluation that is grounded in their culture's values. In each word people use to observe and describe the behavior of others and of themselves, the whole of their culture flashes for a moment. Culture, in this sense, is like a hologram; the whole of one's culture is contained in each word used, and the entirety of these words, their definitions, and the rules for their application constitute one's culture. When one adds to this the fact that the cultural dictionary of European Americans differs significantly from that of people of color and that the cultural dictionaries of various ethnic minority groups differ from each other, questions regarding feminist psychologists' observations of women and men, and regarding the content and form of research in a culturally diverse feminist psychology, become salient.

Culture and Method: What Do the Data Mean?

If the dictionaries through which people comprehend words and behaviors differ significantly across cultures, then how does one decide what behavior means? Do African American and European American women who raise their voices in an experiment engage in the same behavior? If so, what behavior is it and how does one label and interpret it—as anger or as enthusiasm? Are Japanese American, Chinese American, African American, and European American women who sit quietly and do not voice an opinion in a situation engaging in the same behavior? If so, what should the researcher call that behavior? Were they conforming to the Japanese norm of *enryo* or to the Chinese norm of *jang*? Were they being passive, and nonassertive or simply nonchalant and "chilled"? How does the researcher decide what she or he has observed and what does the researcher do if the label she or he uses to tally and report on participants' behavior does not match the label that research participants choose? Which culture's dictionary do researchers use to operationalize and then observe and study behaviors such as assertiveness, passivity, depression, helplessness, altruism, affection, hostility, conformity, aggression, dependency, and attraction? On whose dictionary do researchers rely to decide which persons will be labeled and understood as a "family," a "mother," a "couple"? How do researchers justify using one culture's dictionary, rather than that of another, to operationalize behaviors, emotions, and relationships, and what kind of data—of knowledge—results from so doing?

Do women of various ethnic and cultural groups who complete the Bem Sex-Role Inventory, the Personal Attributes Questionnaire, the Minnesota Multiphasic Personality Inventory, or the Beck Depression Inventory complete the same questionnaires? Do the words and phrases in such instruments carry the same meaning across cultures? If not, then what does it mean when the scores of women from diverse ethnic groups differ significantly on these instruments? Did they respond differently to the same stimuli or respond similarly to phenomenologically different stimuli?

These questions highlight the culturally constituted, interpretive nature of researchers' observations, instruments, data, and knowledge and underscore the need to investigate what behavior and stimuli mean to research participants. Qualitative and person-centered approaches are then prerequisites for a culturally diverse and culture-sensitive feminist psychology. In the absence of such approaches, feminist psychological research involving women of color will continue to yield stereotypes masqueraded as scientific evidence. This is because, as long as research is structured by a European American cultural dictionary for operationalizing and understanding behavior, data on women of color necessarily remain merely descriptions of what their behavior would mean if European American women had engaged in it. "Differences" found are then stereotypes—sophisticated, empirically grounded, but stereotypes nonetheless. Interpretive, experience-centered approaches must be integrated with traditional methodology, not only because traditional methods recapitulate gender, race, class, and ethnic stratification but also because the goal of a culturally diverse feminist psychology cannot be achieved without them.

Etic and Emic Method and Data

Including person-centered, qualitative approaches in research need not be at the expense of experimental rigor and thus does not necessarily raise the specter of the further marginalization of feminist psychological research. Rather, such approaches can be integrated with traditional ones by adopting the methodology that characterizes research in anthropology and cross-cultural psychology. These disciplines approach their subject matter with a two-fold methodology that is based on the distinction between *etic data* and *emic data* (Pike, 1967).

The term *etic* roughly refers to the outsider's (the researcher's) perspective and includes the researcher's observations, tallies of the frequency of specific behaviors, and scores on the researcher's instruments. These data and their collection tend to be standardized, quantified, and well controlled. However, behavior is consciously and purposefully operationalized and interpreted through the researcher's own cultural dictionary, categories, and definitions. Thus, etic approaches "have as their hallmark the elevation of observers [researchers] to the status of ultimate judges of the categories and concepts used in descriptions and analyses. . . . [These categories are not] necessarily real, meaningful and appropriate from the native's [the research participant's] point of view" (Harris, 1980, p. 32). Etic data consist of the mechanistic movements described in chapter 1.

Emic, on the other hand, roughly refers to the insiders' (the research participants') perspective and includes the participants' descriptions, definitions, categorizations, and explanations of their behavior's meaning and function; it involves categories and labels that may differ from those of the researcher.[5] These data and their collection tend to be nonstandardized and qualitative, usually consisting of open-ended interviews and comments and reflections offered by research participants at any time, under any conditions. Emic approaches "have as their hallmark the elevation of the native informant to the status of ultimate judge of the adequacy of the observer's descriptions and analyses. The test of [the success of emic approaches] is their ability to generate statements that the native accepts as real, meaningful, or appropriate" (Harris, 1980, p. 32).[6] Thus, emic data are the contextualistic descriptions of behavior described in chapter 1. "Truth" is understood as both the emic and etic data, or as the emic data alone, but not as the etic data alone.[7]

---

[5]The terms *etic* and *emic* are not synonymous with *objective* and *subjective*, respectively, because neither etic nor emic accounts of behavior are a "view from nowhere," the perspective of no one in particular (i.e., objective). Instead, both are a view from a specific locale. Likewise, *etic* and *emic* are not synonymous with *behavioral* and *mental*, respectively, because psychology is replete with etic accounts of others' thoughts, wishes, and desires.

[6]Pike (1967) argued that good emic research would be acceptable to the native informants and judged by them to be accurate. This implies that manuscripts should be submitted to research participants for approval of the researcher's labels, categories, and interpretations of their behavior and that manuscripts should be revised until the natives find them to be acceptable, accurate renderings of their behavior.

[7]Pike (1967) believed that only emic data constitute "truth" and saw etic data and approaches as necessary, preliminary evils that provide "access into the system" (Pike, 1967, p. 38). Pike (1967) believed that the "initial etic description [should be] gradually refined, and . . . ultimately . . . replaced by one which is totally emic" (pp. 38–39). In contrast to this view, most researchers in cross-cultural psychology take both etic and emic data to be equally acceptable sides of the coin of "truth."

Researchers in cross-cultural psychology tend to collect both etic and emic data to guard against ethnocentric misinterpretations and ensuing stereotypes of ethnic groups. For example, from an etic perspective, many Southeast Asian American women burn their children's chest and arms, and this is labeled as child abuse. From an emic perspective, these women are using folk cures (e.g., "cupping" and "burning") for colds that are standardized and accepted in their cultures, just as dispensing aspirin or chicken soup would be for a European American with a sick child; emically, their behavior is observed and labeled not as abusive but as nurturing (Schreiner, 1981).

There are good reasons for generalizing the emic and etic methodology of anthropology and cross-cultural psychology to feminist research. This methodology permits feminist psychologists to examine women's experiences and meanings in a manner consistent with feminist principles while nonetheless retaining a traditional experimental approach. This method also is accepted in at least one other specialization within psychology (i.e., cross-cultural) and so is unlikely to lead to the further marginalization of feminist research. Most importantly, the terminology used to describe the two approaches (etic vs. emic) is less sexist than the current gendered terminology in which qualitative, flexible, "soft" methodologies are regarded as "feminist" (women's) and quantitative, controlled, detached, "hard" methodologies are labeled as "masculinist" (men's). This tendency to gender methodology in part led Peplau and Conrad (1989) to reject the idea of a "feminist method" as "simplistic and misguided" and to insist that feminist research be characterized by its feminism rather than by soft methods.

In adapting the emic and etic integrative approach, one might regard the investigator as the outsider in all studies, including those in which the researcher's gender, ethnicity, and social class match those of the research participants. What participants mean by their behavior and how they interpret stimuli may vary considerably within as well as between ethnic groups, and these meanings are likely to play a role in behavior and responses. Emic data collected from racially homogeneous samples may decrease the percentage of etic variance currently attributed to error and lead to improved behavioral prediction. This is particularly important because racially homogeneous samples of European Americans (of "Whites") contain a diversity of ethnic and cultural groups (e.g., Italians, Greeks, Poles, Jews), as do racially homogeneous samples of African Americans. Assessing the ethnicity of European Americans and collecting emic data on them may improve the understanding of the variance found within European American samples and assist the discipline in transcending its tendency to erroneously equate putative "race" with culture and ethnicity. When racially diverse samples of women and men participate in research, careful collection of emic data is even more crucial for the reasons detailed earlier.

EMPIRICAL EXAMPLE

To demonstrate the importance of the issue of cultural interpretation and meaning raised here, as well as the benefits of the integrative methodology, we ran a simple experiment with an ethnically diverse sample of women. We began with the assumption that the words and phrases in feminist psychological (as well as all other) instruments do not carry the same meaning across cultures. We hypothesized that African American, European American, Latina, and Asian American women would interpret words and phrases differently and that these definitions would in part determine their responses. For the purpose of a simple demonstration, we used seven items from the Bem Sex-Role Inventory (Bem, 1974) and structured the questions and instructions in a manner matching that inventory.

Method

Participants

One hundred thirty-eight undergraduate women (aged 17–57 years, $M = 23.4$, $SD = 7.31$) participated. Seventy-one were European American, and 67 were Women of Color (35 African Americans, 13 Latinas, and 19 Asian Americans).

Procedure

The questionnaire consisted of seven gender-stereotypic phrases: "I make decisions easily"; "I am sensitive to the needs of others"; "I am feminine"; "I am assertive"; "I am independent"; "I have leadership abilities"; and "I am passive." Participants were asked to describe their own personality traits by attributing these phrases to themselves using Likert scales that ranged from 1 (never or almost never true of me) to 7 (always or almost always true of me). Each of the phrases was followed by several possible definitions. Participants were instructed to first rate themselves on the attribute and to then circle the definition that best matched what they had in mind when they rated themselves. They also were instructed to leave the definition blank if none of the choices was similar to what they had interpreted the phrase to mean.

In this design, the ratings that the women gave themselves on the items were etic data. Women of different ethnic groups can be compared for similarities or differences in attributing gender-stereotypic terms to themselves (with the assumption that these terms carried a single meaning), and the ensuing data thereby represent ethnic differences or similarities in gender role stereotypes. The definitions the women had in mind when rating themselves were emic data. Women of different ethnic groups can be compared on their interpretation of the phrases, and the relationship between their emic interpretations and the etic self-ratings can be explored.

Results

Etic Data: European American Women Versus Women of Color

A multivariate analysis of variance (MANOVA) was run to determine whether the self-ratings given by European American women and Women of Color differed. The MANOVA was not significant (TSQ = 5.24), $F(7, 130) = 0.72$, indicating that these two groups of women did not differ in their self-ratings on the composite of the items. The MANOVA was followed by ANOVAs (see Table 1) and none of those were significant. From an etic perspective, this suggests that European American women and women of color did not rate themselves differently on any of the gender-stereotypic phrases.

Emic Data: European American Women Versus Women of Color

The next question was whether the two groups had the same definitions in mind when they rated themselves. To answer this, we conducted a series of chi-square analyses to compare the number of Women of Color and of European American women who chose various definitions. Significant differences were found between European American women and Women of Color in their definitions of *passive, assertive,* and *feminine,* as well as in who the woman had in mind when rating herself as *sensitive* to the needs of others. These results are shown in Table 2.

While "laid back and easy going" was the most frequent definition of *passive* chosen by European American women (and probably does not match what feminist researchers' mean by the term), it was the least fre-

TABLE 1
ANOVA of Mean Self-Ratings

Phrase and item	European American women ($n = 71$)	Women of Color ($n = 67$)	SS	$F(1, 136)$	p
I make decisions easily	4.31	4.19	0.46	0.24	—
I am sensitive to others	5.48	5.31	0.94	0.70	—
I am feminine	5.42	5.25	0.98	0.64	—
I am assertive	4.62	4.89	2.62	1.60	—
I am independent	5.34	5.45	0.42	0.30	—
I have leadership abilities	5.03	5.07	0.74	0.50	—
I am passive	3.08	2.76	3.60	2.04	—

Note. ANOVA = analysis of variance.

TABLE 2
Definitions Used by European American Women and Women of Color

Phrase and definition	European American women		Women of Color		Total	
	n	%	n	%	n	%
Passive[a]						
1. Don't say what I really think	18	26.5	28	43.1	46	34.6
2. Let people take advantage of me	16	23.5	14	21.5	30	22.6
3. Agree with others when I shouldn't	11	16.2	14	21.5	25	18.8
4. Am laid back/easy-going	23	33.8	9	19.8	32	24.1
Total	68	100	65	100	133	100
Assertive[b]						
1. Say whatever's on my mind	13	19.1	22	35.5	35	26.9
2. Stand up for myself	32	47.1	19	30.6	51	39.2
3. Express myself well	18	26.5	10	16.1	28	21.5
4. Am aggressive	5	7.4	11	17.7	16	12.3
Total	68	100	62	100	130	100
Feminine[c]						
1. Physical appearance and clothes	8	11.3	10	14.9	18	13.0
2. Traits and personality	10	14.1	20	29.9	30	21.7
3. Both above equally	53	74.6	37	55.2	90	65.2
Total	71	100	67	100	138	100
Sensitive to whom[d]						
1. Significant others	9	12.7	22	32.8	31	22.5
2. People in general	62	87.3	45	67.2	107	77.5
Total	71	100	67	100	138	100

Note. [a]$\chi^2 = 8.73, p < .05.$ [b]$\chi^2 = 9.92, p < .05.$ [c]$\chi^2 = 6.29, p < .05.$ [d]$\chi^2 = 8.04, p < .005.$

quent chosen by Women of Color, who tended to define *passive* as not saying what one really thinks. Likewise, European American women were most likely to define *assertive* as "standing up" for themselves or as expressing themselves well, whereas Women of Color were most likely to define it as openly saying what is on their minds; for Women of Color, assertive and passive were opposite terms, but for European American women, the terms appeared to be unrelated. Although both European American women and women of color defined *feminine* as a combination of traits and physical characteristics, women of color were more likely to define it as traits alone. Women of color also were more likely than European American women to have specific relationships in mind (as opposed to people in general) when they rated themselves as sensitive to the needs of others.

Thus, although European American women and women of color did not rate themselves differently on these gender-related terms, they also did not interpret the terms in the same manner. From an etic perspective, these two groups did not differ significantly, but from an emic perspective they did. The cultural differences in how these women interpreted the phrases are interesting in their own right[8] and support the hypothesis. Yet, these differences could be dismissed as trivial if they bore no relationship to how women rated themselves on the items in question.

Emic X Etic: European American Women Versus Women of Color

To assess the relationship between ratings women gave themselves and the meaning they had in mind when they did so, we ran a series of one-way analyses of variance (ANOVAs) with post hoc *t* tests, with the definition women had in mind as the grouping variable and the rating they gave themselves as the dependent variable for each gender phrase. These analyses were run separately for Women of Color and for European American women. These analyses for European American women are shown in Table 3.

As shown in Table 3, the definition that a European American woman had in mind was strongly related to the rating she gave herself on assertive, independent, leadership abilities, sensitive, and whosensitive. European American women who defined *assertive* as standing up for themselves (Definition 2) rated themselves as significantly more assertive than those who had any of the other definitions in mind. European American women who defined *independent* in financial terms (Definition 1), compared with those who defined it in psychological terms (e.g., "I have my own opinions"; Definition 2) rated themselves significantly higher. European American women who construed leadership abilities as the desire to be a leader, compared with those who interpreted it as potential (Definition 1) or actual behavior (Definition 3), rated themselves higher on leadership abilities. European American women who interpreted *sensitive* as doing what others demand (Definition 2) rated themselves as significantly less sensitive than those who had other definitions in mind. Women who were thinking of people in general (Definition 2), compared with those who were thinking about their own personal relationships (whosensitive) rated themselves as being significantly less sensitive to the needs of others.

Thus, for some of these well-known gender-related terms, how a European American woman rated herself was at least in part contingent on

---

[8]For example, a sociopolitical context in which femininity is defined as the physical characteristics of European American women denies Women of Color the possibility of defining themselves as feminine. This may in part explain their tendency to define *feminine* in personality as opposed to physical terms. Likewise, the cultures of many people of color understand the self as defined and "indexed" by the specific relationships through which one has or is a self at all, whereas European Americans understand the self as an individual unit possessing cross-situational and longitudinal traits such as sensitivity (see Landrine, 1992). This may explain why Women of Color thought of themselves as sensitive to the needs of a specific other ("sensitive" within the context of a specific relationship), whereas European American women understood being sensitive as a stable trait describing not an interaction but themselves. European American cultural constructs and assumptions, like those of the cultures of people of color, played a role in how words were understood.

TABLE 3
Analysis of Variance of Self-Ratings × Definition Used for European
American Women

Phrase and definition	n	M	SS	F	p
Passive			7.07	1.48	—
1. Don't say what I really think	18	3.48			
2. Let people take advantage of me	16	3.00			
3. Agree with others when I shouldn't	11	3.17			
4. Am laid back/easy-going	23	2.63			
Assertive			19.85	4.13	<.01[a]
1. Say whatever's on my mind	13	4.38			
2. Stand up for myself	32	5.39			
3. Express myself well	18	4.44			
4. Am aggressive	5	3.40			
Independent			17.77	5.41	<.01[b]
1. Care for self financially	14	5.63			
2. Have own point of view	48	4.34			
3. Don't need people	4	5.00			
4. Don't care what others think of me	3	5.25			
Make decisions easily			4.43	0.62	—
1. Decisions about people	5	4.22			
2. Decisions about money, work, school	8	4.38			
3. Make minor decisions	8	4.25			
4. Make major and minor decisions	50	5.20			
Define easily			6.41	1.51	—
1. Quickly	29	4.64			
2. On my own	4	4.03			
3. Both	36	4.75			
Feminine			4.46	1.97	—
1. Physical appearance and clothes	8	5.42			
2. Traits and personality	10	5.00			
3. Both above equally	53	6.00			
Leadership ability			23.85	9.73	<.01[c]
1. Potential to be	46	4.81			
2. Want to be	7	6.00			
3. Am leader now	17	4.14			
Sensitive			8.93	3.19	<.05[d]
1. Understand others' point of view	33	5.58			
2. Do what others demand	9	4.56			
3. Care about other people	27	5.67			
Sensitive to whom			6.79	4.94	<.05[e]
1. Significant others	9	5.59			
2. People in general	62	4.67			

Note. [a]Post hoc tests on assertive; Definition 1 vs. 2, $p < .05$; Definition 2 vs. 3, $p < .01$; Definition 2 vs. 4, $p < .01$.
[b]Post hoc tests on independent; Definition 1 vs. 2, $p < .01$.
[c]Post hoc tests on leadership ability; Definition 1 vs. 2, $p < .01$; Definition 2 vs. 3, $p < .01$.
[d]Post hoc tests on sensitive; Definition 1 vs. 2, $p < .05$; Definition 2 vs. 3, $p < .02$.
[e]Post hoc tests on sensitive to whom; Definition 1 vs. 2, $p < .05$.

how she had interpreted the term. Similar analyses for Women of Color are presented in Table 4.

As shown in Table 4, the definition that a Woman of Color had in mind was related to how she rated herself on passive, independent, sensitive, and whosensitive. Women of Color who defined *passive* as "laid back and easy-going" (Definition 4) rated themselves as less passive than those who defined it as "letting others take advantage of me" (Definition 2); those who defined passive as "going along with others when I shouldn't" (Definition 3) rated themselves as being significantly more passive than those using other definitions. Women of Color who defined *independent* as "I don't care what other people think of me" (Definition 4) rated themselves lower than those who used the other definitions. Women who defined *sensitive* as doing what others demand (Definition 2) rated themselves as being less sensitive to the needs of others than those choosing the other two definitions. Women who had their own relationships (Definition 1) rather than people in general (Definition 2) in mind rated themselves as being significantly more sensitive to the needs of others.

The hypothesized differences in interpretation of simple experimental stimuli (emic variance) was supported, as was the hypothesis that these interpretations would be related to etic behavior (self-ratings).

Etic Data: All Ethnic Cells

The next question was whether European American, African American, Latina, and Asian American women would differ in the ratings they gave themselves on the adjectives. To assess this, we ran a MANOVA using all four ethnic cells. This MANOVA was not significant (L ratio = 0.823), $F(21, 365) = 1.22$, indicating that these four groups of women did not differ in the ratings they gave themselves on the overall package of phrases. The MANOVA was followed by a series of ANOVAs (one for each phrase), and six of these seven ANOVAs also were not significant. The exception was on the item "I am passive," on which African American women rated themselves as being significantly less passive than all other groups, $F(3, 133) = 3.19$, $p < .05$. From an etic perspective, these data suggest that these four ethnic groups of women did not, on the whole, differ in the ratings they gave themselves on the items.

Emic Data: All Ethnic Cells

To assess the extent to which the four groups of women differed on the definitions they had in mind when rating themselves, we ran a series of chi-squares. Differences emerged only for the definition of assertive and for whom women had in mind when rating themselves as being sensitive to the needs of others (i.e., whosensitive). Latinas and Asian American women were most likely to define *assertive* as "saying whatever is on my

TABLE 4
Analysis of Variance of Self-Ratings × Definition Used for Women of Color

Phrase and definition	n	M	SS	F	p
Passive			26.27	5.44	<.01[a]
1. Don't say what I really think	28	3.14			
2. Let people take advantage of me	14	2.43			
3. Agree with others when I shouldn't	14	3.78			
4. Am laid back/easy-going	9	1.86			
Assertive			7.02	1.65	—
1. Say whatever's on my mind	22	4.91			
2. Stand up for myself	19	5.00			
3. Express myself well	10	5.40			
4. Am aggressive	11	4.27			
Independent			15.13	3.62	<.02[b]
1. Care for self financially	19	4.91			
2. Have own point of view	38	6.00			
3. Don't need people	3	5.26			
4. Don't care what others think of me	1	3.33			
Make decisions easily			3.36	0.78	—
1. Decisions about people	2	4.29			
2. Decisions about money, work, school	9	4.11			
3. Make minor decisions	3	4.33			
4. Make major and minor decisions	52	3.00			
Define easily			2.66	0.91	—
1. Quickly	27	4.15			
2. On my own	11	4.07			
3. Both	29	4.64			
Feminine			2.91	0.75	—
1. Physical appearance and clothes	10	5.10			
2. Traits and personality	20	4.90			
3. Both above equally	37	5.43			
Leadership ability			8.08	2.46	—
1. Potential to be	36	4.78			
2. Want to be	7	5.00			
3. Am leader now	22	5.55			
Sensitive			10.61	4.82	<.01[c]
1. Understand others' point of view	34	5.48			
2. Do what others demand	7	4.14			
3. Care about other people	25	5.41			
Sensitive to whom			8.03	7.21	<.01[d]
1. Significant others	22	5.56			
2. People in general	45	4.82			

Note. [a]Post hoc tests on passive; Definition 1 vs. 4, $p < .01$; Definition 3 vs. 4, $p < .01$; Definition 2 vs. 3, $p < .02$.
[b]Post hoc tests on independent; Definition 1 vs. 4, $p < .01$; Definition 2 vs. 4, $p < .06$; Definition 3 vs. 4, $p < .01$.
[c]Post hoc tests on sensitive; Definition 1 vs. 2, $p < .01$; Definition 2 vs. 3, $p < .01$.
[d]Post hoc tests on sensitive to whom; Definition 1 vs. 2, $p < .01$.

mind openly," European American women were most likely to define it as "standing up" for myself, and African American women were most likely to define it as "saying what's on my mind" or "aggressive" ($\chi^2 = 22.33$, $p < .005$). Likewise, African American, Latina, and Asian American women were more likely than European American women to have a specific relationship in mind (rather than people in general) when they rated themselves as being sensitive to the needs of others ($\chi^2 = 8.58$, df = 3, $p < .05$). The failure to find differences on any of the other phrases might have been a function of the small number of women in the four ethnicity cells. Further analyses (Emic × Etic) to assess the relationship between objective self-ratings and subjective definitions across the four ethnic groups could not be conducted in light of the extremely small Ethnicity × Definition cell *ns*. We did notice, however, that African American women were more likely than all of the other groups of women to cross out the definitions provided and write in their own definitions. Such behavior on the part of research participants (ordinarily not reported by researchers who simply delete the troublesome people in question) underscores the point of this chapter.

Discussion

The study presented here was a simple one in which simple stimuli were used to demonstrate cultural differences in the interpretation of words and highlight the necessity of collecting both etic and emic data. Similar studies can be conducted using any psychological instrument, and they must raise questions about the meaning of ethnic differences or similarities reported in the literature. The same can be said for gender differences on any psychological test or scale, because researchers may suspect that women and men's different definitions (and so perceptions and interpretations) at least in part predict their different scores or behaviors. Gender differences, to whatever extent these exist (and there are questions about that; see Lott, 1991), like cultural differences, may reside more in the realm of meaning, interpretation, and perception (these are rooted in contextual differences) than in the realm of behavior. Thus, asking women and men about their interpretations or definitions of their own behavior (like asking members of different ethnic groups) has the potential to shed a long overdue emic light on etic data and advance understanding. Similar studies collecting etic and emic data could be run to assess ethnic and gender differences in observations of behavior (in perceptions of and labels attributed to the "same" acts), and would further underscore the cultural- and gender-constituted, interpretive nature of research. To some extent, such studies already exist, but they have failed to lead researchers to reject the rhetoric and so the value of the traditional methodology.

Three levels of interpretation enter into research and these cast aspersions on the rhetoric of the "objectivity" of the traditional method: The first level is that of the research participants who interpret and reinterpret the stimuli, the researcher's behavior, and their own behavior during the study. These interpretations are powerful variables in how research participants behave (Antaki, 1981; Miller, 1984; Sabini & Silver, 1981) and are at least in part culturally determined, as our study suggests. The second level is that of the researcher who interprets and labels the participants' behavior and test scores, where these interpretations may bear little resemblance to the former ones. Researchers' interpretations also are culturally and historically determined and situated and are therefore embedded in their values, context, power, privilege, and gender (Collins & Pinch, 1982; Knorr, Krohn, & Whitely, 1980; Latour & Woolgar, 1979). Researchers' interpretations of participants' behavior also are influenced by the gender and the other status attributes of the participant, as implied by the plethora of studies on the devaluation of women's competence and on salience and solo effects on appraisals. The third level is the researcher's interpretation of the data from such experiments. These data are mute (Feyerabend, 1976) and do not speak for or against any hypothesis. What is taken to be the voice of data is the voice of the researcher's interpretation of them. Such interpretations differ significantly, as indicated by ongoing debates over the meaning of data that some choose to interpret as indicative of the biological determination of etic–behavioral differences between the sexes and ethnic groups.

Thus, the traditional psychological experiment never has yielded or entailed objective observations or brute behavioral data; rather, it always has entailed and yielded *interpretations of interpretations of interpretations* (Rabinow & Sullivan, 1979), each level of which is in part culturally determined and situated. Although feminist psychologists have not, in the past, felt compelled by such arguments to bring more experience-centered methods to their research, they may be compelled now to do so by the increase in the numbers and the diversity of Women of Color in the population. If Women of Color and European American women do not even interpret experimental stimuli similarly, then a method that permits researchers to assess women's interpretations is crucial to a culturally diverse feminist psychology, and indeed to feminist science and knowledge as a whole. If feminist psychological knowledge is based on studies whose operational definitions come from the cultural dictionary of European American women of privileged social class, then knowledge of gender is confounded by class and culture; a change in method will afford the opportunity to separate these three effects, as well as to understand Women of Color, not as deviants from European American, middle-class women, but as themselves.

Did the European American women differ from the Women of Color in this study in their self-ratings? If our answer to this question is yes, or even yes and no, then the complexity and diversity of women's behavior, the role of culture in it, and the need for alternative methods to assess these is clear.

SUMMARY AND CONCLUSIONS

In summary, we believe that feminist research can be characterized by rigorous experimental and sensitive person-centered methodologies. We also believe that a culturally diverse feminist psychology inevitably may be contingent on such a methodology. We offer several suggestions for the treatment of research participants, for the interpretation of data from ethnically homogeneous samples, and for an etic–emic integrative methodology as possible means to that end. We recommend replication of our methodology with alternative stimuli and of our study with a larger sample of women from a diversity of ethnic groups and social classes to clarify the generalizability of these findings. We also recommend that feminist manuscripts involving women research participants be submitted to those participants for approval of the researcher's interpretations, labels, and constructions of their behavior and revised until participants view them as accurate renderings. This emic quality control of etic constructions will inform researchers of the extent to which women "out there" agree with what researchers say about them and has the potential to make researchers accountable to their ostensible constituents. Such feedback also may entail alternative hypotheses and interpretations unavailable to those who occupy researchers' privileged status. Finally, such a move toward bringing the emic to feminist psychological research has the potential to disrupt the hierarchical power relations between researcher and participants in a manner consistent with feminist ethics.

REFERENCES

American Psychological Association. (1992). Ethical principles of psychologists and code of conduct. *American Psychologist, 47,* 1597–1611.

Antaki, C. (1981). *The psychology of ordinary explanations.* San Diego, CA: Academic Press.

Bem, S. L. (1974). The measurement of psychological androgyny. *Journal of Consulting and Clinical Psychology, 42,* 155–162.

Bruner, J. S. (1957). Going beyond the information given. In *Contemporary approaches to cognition.* Cambridge, MA: Harvard University Press.

Collins, H. M., & Pinch, T. J. (1982). *Frames of meaning: The social construction of extraordinary science.* London: Routledge & Kegan Paul.

Crawford, M., & Marecek, J. (1989). Psychology reconstructs the female. *Psychology of Women Quarterly, 13,* 147–165.

D'Andrade, R. (1981). The cultural part of cognition. *Cognitive Science, 5,* 179–195.

DuBois, B. (1983). Passionate scholarship: Notes on values, knowing, and method in feminist social science. In G. Bowles & R. D. Klein (Eds.), *Theories of women's studies* (pp. 105–115). London: Routledge & Kegan Paul.

Feyerabend, P. (1976). *Against method: Outline of an anarchist theory of knowledge.* New York: Humanities Press.

Fine, M. (1985). Reflections on a feminist psychology of women. *Psychology of Women Quarterly, 9,* 167–183.

Flax, J. (1990). Postmodernism and gender relations in feminist theory. In L. J. Nicholson (Ed.), *Feminism/postmodernism* (pp. 39–62). London: Routledge & Kegan Paul.

Goodenough, W. H. (1964). Cultural anthropology and linguistics. In D. Hymes (Ed.), *Language in culture and society* (pp. 36–39). New York: Harper & Row.

Goodenough, W. H. (1969). Frontiers of cultural anthropology. *Proceedings of the American Philosophical Society, 113,* 329–335.

Goodenough, W. H. (1970). *Descriptions and comparison in cultural anthropology.* Chicago: Aldine.

Harris, M. (1980). *Cultural materialism: The struggle for a science of culture.* New York: Vintage Books.

Hoffnung, M. (1985). Feminist transformation: Teaching experimental psychology. *Feminist Teacher, 2,* 31–35.

Knorr, K. D., Krohn, R., & Whitley, R. (1980). *The social process of scientific investigation.* Dordrecht, The Netherlands: Reidel.

Landrine, H. (1992). Clinical implications of cultural differences: The referential vs. the indexical self. *Clinical Psychology Review, 12,* 401–415.

Latour, B., & Woolgar, S. (1979). *Laboratory life: The social construction of scientific facts.* Beverly Hills, CA: Sage.

Lott, B. L. (1991). Dual natures or learned behaviors: The challenge to feminist psychology. In R. T. Hare-Mustin & J. Marecek (Eds.), *Making a difference: Psychology and the construction of gender* (pp. 65–101). New Haven, CT: Yale University Press.

Lykes, M. B., & Stewart, A. J. (1986). Evaluating the feminist challenge to research in personality and social psychology. *Psychology of Women Quarterly, 10,* 393–412.

McHugh, M. D., Koeske, R. D., & Frieze, I. H. (1986). Issues to consider in conducting nonsexist psychological research. *American Psychologist, 41,* 879–890.

Miller, J. G. (1984). Culture and the development of everyday social explanation. *Journal of Personality and Social Psychology, 46,* 961–978.

Morawski, J. G. (1985). The measurement of masculinity and femininity: Engendering categorical realities. *Journal of Personality, 53,* 196–223.

Morawski, J. G. (1991). Toward the unimagined: Feminism and epistemology in psychology. In R. T. Hare-Mustin & J. Marecek (Eds.), *Making a difference* (pp. 150–183). New Haven, CT: Yale University Press.

Peplau, L. A., & Conrad, E. (1989). Beyond non-sexist research: The perils of feminist methods in psychology. *Psychology of Women Quarterly, 13,* 379–400.

Pike, K. (1967). *Language in relation to a unified theory of the structure of human behavior* (2nd ed.). The Hague, The Netherlands: Mouton.

Rabinow, P., & Sullivan, W. M. (1979). *Interpretive social science.* Berkeley, CA: University of California Press.

Sabini, J., & Silver, M. (1981). Introspection and causal accounts. *Journal of Personality and Social Psychology, 40,* 171–179.

Schreiner, D. (1981, September). *Southeast Asian folk healing practices or child abuse?* Paper presented at the Indochinese Health Care Conference, Eugene, OR.

Shore, B. (1991). Twice born, once conceived: Meaning construction and cultural cognition. *American Anthropologist, 93,* 9–27.

Shweder, R., & LeVine, R. A. (1984). *Culture theory.* Cambridge, MA: Cambridge University Press.

Unger, R. K. (1981). Sex as a social reality: Field and laboratory research. *Psychology of Women Quarterly, 5,* 645–653.

Wallston, B. (1981). What are the questions in psychology of women? A feminist approach to research. *Psychology of Women Quarterly, 5,* 597–617.

Wallston, B., & Grady, K. E. (1985). Integrating the feminist critique and the crisis in social psychology: Another look at research methods. In V. O'Leary, R. K. Unger, & B. Wallston (Eds.), *Women, gender and social psychology* (pp. 7–35). Hillsdale, NJ: Erlbaum.

Wittig, M. A. (1985). Metatheoretical dilemmas in the psychology of gender. *American Psychologist, 40,* 800–811.

4

COGNITIVE GENDER DIFFERENCES: WHY DIVERSITY IS A CRITICAL RESEARCH ISSUE

DIANE F. HALPERN

Reports of research on cognitive gender differences have made front page news in virtually all major newspapers over the past several years. The prestigious "above the fold" section of the front page has been used, for example, for headlines reporting that few girls are among the most mathematically gifted youth (Benbow, 1988), that women's fine motor and cognitive performance vary over the menstrual cycle (Hampson & Kimura, 1988), that toddlers' toy preferences are mediated by prenatal sex hormones (Berenbaum & Hines, 1992), and that females and males use different parts of their brains when they think (Begley, 1995). It seems that editors must believe that news of sex differences, like sex itself, sells. The effect of sensationalized news coverage on public opinion is difficult to assess, but it is certain that the popular press provides a distorted view of what psychologists know and do not know about cognitive gender differences.

It is easy to dismiss the "sound bite" and simplistic coverage given to complex issues by the popular press and other media, but a reasoned analysis of the original research also reveals serious flaws in the empirical literature. One of the greatest problems in interpreting and generalizing results from these studies involves the way participants are selected for psychological studies of human cognition, the branch of psychology concerned with the way people think, learn, and remember.

CONTROVERSIES AND POLITICAL AGENDAS

The many questions about cognitive gender differences are among the most controversial issues in contemporary psychology. Whether, when, and how much women and men differ in thinking abilities is a charged topic that has sparked stormy debates and tens of thousands of journal and text pages. The reason for the acrimony is apparent: If psychologists were to decide that women and men differ in their cognitive abilities, then these results could be used to justify discrimination, affirmative action based on gender, or both. For this reason, many people (especially feminists) are suspicious of any research that supports the notion that women and men are different in any way that is not directly related to their reproductive roles. They are justifiably concerned that if differences are emphasized, then the greater number of similarities between women and men will go unnoticed.

For many, the questions of similarities and differences in the cognitive abilities of women and men are highly emotional. There is a modal response to any research that examines questions pertaining to gender similarities and differences that goes something like this: (a) There are no differences; any differences that are found are attributable to flaws in the experimental design, researcher bias, or both. If this explanation should fail, then a second argument is offered. (b) If differences are found, they are too small in magnitude to be of any practical importance. However, with an increasing number of large effect sizes being reported (e.g., effect sizes greater than 1 SD such as the female advantage in verbal fluency reported by Hines, 1990, and similar size effects favoring males on mental rotation tasks as reported by Masters & Sanders, 1993), a third response is given. (c) If large differences are found, they are caused solely by gender-differentiated rearing practices. This line of reasoning is frequently offered by those who are legitimately concerned with the chilling possibility that gender differences research could be and has been misused (Halpern, 1994; Hare-Mustin & Maracek, 1994). One reason that diverse subject pools are needed in interpreting findings of cognitive gender differences concerns the "tug" between biological and psychosocial explanations of these differences. If psychologists find that cognitive differences are influenced by other variables such as socioeconomic status or level of education, then the interactive effects of both biology and environmental variables must be considered in understanding why and how these differences arise.

DIFFERENCES ARE NOT DEFICIENCIES

There is an unstated assumption by those who are opposed to gender differences research. The tacit assumption is that every time a difference is found, there is a "winner" and a "loser." However, gender differences research is not a "zero sum game," and what does it really mean to say that there are gender differences with respct to some variable? There is nothing inherent in this conclusion to suggest that either women or men have "better" abilities overall. Inherent in this reasoning is a fallacy that I have called *the women have less fallacy*. It refers to the mistaken and often unspoken fear that if the "truth" were known, women would be found to be "less"—less smart, less strong, or less of whatever society values—than men (Halpern, 1992).

Differences do not imply deficiencies. Few would argue against the idea that women and men have different genitals, and most agree that it would be ludicrous to argue which gender has the better genitals. Yet, when the topic is cognitive abilities, there is a rush to assume that whenever differences are found, it is the woman who will have less ability. The reasons for this concern are grounded in the way data have historically been interpreted. It was less than 100 years ago when scientists "discovered" that women had inferior brains and that if women engaged in weighty thoughts, then the blood that was needed for normal menstruation would be used in thinking with unfortunate biological consequences (cited in Gould, 1978).

The fact that research has been used to justify discrimination and support the prevailing social view is precisely why sound empirical research is needed. If researchers find that society consistently values those traits that are associated with being a man and devalues those traits that are associated with being a woman, then the fault lies in the society in which researchers are participants, not in the research that demonstrates that there are gender differences. Consider a similar example from another domain to clarify this point. It is well-known that people with light-colored skin are at a greater risk for skin cancer than people of color. Yet, I have never heard anyone interpret this as evidence that white skin is pathological or "less good" than dark skin or that this research must be wrong. Similarly, researchers know that men die an average of approximately 6 years earlier than women (Halpern & Coren, 1991), yet I know of no researcher who has concluded that being a man is a life-threatening handicap and no one who has insisted that the research results must be wrong or biased by experimenter expectations. Data of these sort show that there are group differences; it is society that decides when differences are deficiencies and it is society that can change the way these value judgments are made.

It is *because* of the politicized nature of gender differences research and the very real possibility that results will be misused that careful empirical research is needed. This point was made eloquently by Eagly (1987, 1995). Carefully controlled research on the ways in which women and men are different and are similar does not create gender role stereotypes or discrimination. These social ills exist in the absence of data-based research. The only way to debunk myths about the ways in which women and men differ is by empirically demonstrating that they are myths. It is important to realize that silence does not rebut stereotypes and that ignorance does not promote equality. Feminists have more to lose by censorship, even self-imposed censorship, than they have to gain.

DIVERSITY IN COGNITIVE GENDER RESEARCH

It is interesting that the mountains of research that have been conducted in both the traditional and nontraditional modes have failed to consider the fact that the world is diverse. All of the psychological theories about how, why, and when women and men differ in their thinking abilities pertain to all females and all males. Yet, most of the research designed to answer questions about gender differences in cognitive abilities has used students, especially college students, as their respondents. Researchers cannot legitimately generalize to all women and men from such a biased sample. Researchers know very little about the cognitive skills of the vast majority of the population. Do the cognitive gender differences that are found with college-bound high school seniors (e.g., from data from the Scholastic Aptitude Test [SAT]) appear among high school dropouts? What about cognitive gender differences for the majority of adults who never serve as research participants (e.g., mechanics, postal employees, homemakers, janitors, secretaries, and Third World people)? If there are gender cognitive differences that are related to either biologically mediated mechanisms, social construction, or the interaction between them, then such differences should be found in the entire diversity of the population. In other words, if the differences are caused by some variable that is directly related to femaleness and maleness, then cognitive gender differences should be found in women and men of various ages, socioeconomic classes, countries, education levels, and across the entire range of human diversity. Despite this requirement, researchers have ignored most of the world in their studies. The information that is needed before reaching any meaningful conclusion about cognitive gender differences is missing from the research literature.

HOW FAILURE TO CONSIDER DIVERSITY LEADS TO BIAS

There are numerous examples of the way failures to consider diversity has led to biased and erroneous conclusions. Consider, for instance, the following examples.

Example 1: The Problems With Meta-Analysis

Meta-analysis has been hailed as a "methodological revolution" (Eagly, 1986, p. 162). As readers probably know, meta-analysis is a statistical method for synthesizing and quantifying experimental results from multiple studies (Hyde & Linn, 1986). It involves the computation of a directional effect size statistic (d) that can be used as a standard of comparison. d is computed by subtracting the mean of one group (e.g., men) from the mean of another group (e.g., women) and dividing this mean distance score by the pooled standard deviation. Mathematically, this is

$$d = \frac{M \text{ (women)} - M \text{ (men)}}{SD}.$$

Thus, d is a measure of effect size that is quantified in standard deviation units. If $d = -1$, then the mean of the women's group is 1 SD below the mean of the men's group. Similarly, a positive d value indicates that women score higher than men on whatever is being measured, and a negative d value indicates that men score higher than women on whatever is being measured (assuming that the mean for the men is subtracted from the mean for the women). d values can be aggregated across studies to yield a single number summarizing any number of independent studies.

Although meta-analysis has many desirable properties (i.e., it is based on the results of several studies rather than just a few), it is subject to many of the same problems that plague traditional research analyses. The greatest problem is that although it provides an effect size statistic, it cannot answer the most fundamental research question: When does an effect size become large enough to be meaningful or important? Cohen (1969) suggested that .2 SD units is a small effect size, .5 SD is a medium effect size, and .8 SD is a large effect size. However, there is no valid rationale for accepting these guidelines, and, like all difficult questions, a better answer is that it depends on what is being assessed and the values of the researcher. An effect size of .2 can mean thousands of lives saved if the research concerns drug effects on some dread disease. Thus, *small* is not synonymous with *unimportant*. Furthermore, Riefer (1991) found that more than 58% of all effect size statistics published in the contemporary literature in psychology (including developmental psychology, memory and cognition, and perception) are less than .2. If one were to accept Cohen's heuristic that .2 is a small effect size, then one must also accept the fact that most of psychology deals with small effects.

There has been a great flurry of meta-analytic reviews in the gender differences literature in the past 5 years (e.g., Hyde, Fennema, & Lamon, 1990; Masters & Sanders, 1993). Yet, few of them have addressed the fact that most of the studies that are included in meta-analyses have involved restricted samples and yet have made generalizations about all women and all men.

Consider, for example, an extensive meta-analytic review of the literature on gender differences in verbal ability (Hyde & Linn, 1988). The researchers divided experiments on the basis of the participants' age and type of verbal ability assessed—all tests, vocabulary tests, and tests of reading comprehension. They found differences that depended on the type of test and the participants' age, with virtually no gender differences in vocabulary ($d = .02$), reading comprehension ($d = .03$), essay writing ($d = .09$), and the Verbal portion of the SAT ($d = -.03$, with the negative value indicating that men tend to score higher); differences were found, however, in anagrams ($d = .22$), general and mixed verbal abilities ($d = .20$), analogies ($d = -.16$, indicating a male advantage), and speech production ($d = .33$). When the mean of all of the effect sizes was computed, the overall d value was .11. They concluded from these results that "gender differences in verbal ability no longer exist" (Hyde & Linn, 1988, p. 53). I do not believe that this conclusion is supported by their own data. The 165 studies that they reviewed showed no gender differences for some verbal abilities, small differences for others (with some results favoring men), and moderately large differences for at least one component of verbal ability. It makes little sense to conclude from this mixed pattern of results that, overall, there are no differences. More important, however, the literature on which the meta-analysis was based was highly biased by the nature of the participants included in the studies.

The majority of the researchers who have addressed the question of cognitive gender differences studied a narrow range of participants. Virtually all of the studies involve students, and beyond 9th or 10th grade, these samples become increasingly unrepresentative of the population of all males and females in the United States (or other industrialized countries). The size of the gender differences effect in verbal abilities would be much larger if the experiments that were included in the meta-analysis had involved more participants from the low end of the abilities distribution—a group that is rarely included in gender differences research. The largest verbal ability effects are found in areas of stuttering (Skinner & Shelton, 1985), dyslexia, and other extreme forms of reading disabilities (Bannatyne, 1976; Sutaria, 1985), with males exhibiting more of these problems than females. In addition, men are substantially overrepresented in certain categories of mental retardation (e.g., Coren, 1990). If more of the studies included in the meta-analysis had included samples selected from the low end of the distribution, the overall effect size favoring women would have been much larger. Gender ratios are highly disparate in the low end of the verbal abilities distribution, and the systematic exclusion of low-ability participants has led researchers to conclude that the female verbal advantage is smaller than it actually is. Furthermore, large differences favoring women ($d = 1.2!$) have been found on tests of associational (finding synonyms) and generational fluency (naming words that begin with a particular letter; Hines, 1990). The largest differences favoring males occur with moving stimuli, another research paradigm that is rarely used (Law, Pellegrino, & Hunt, 1993). Relatively few studies have included these tests that show the largest between-gender differences. Thus, it is more accurate to conclude that gender differences are sometimes large, sometimes small, and sometimes nonexistent, and that the size of the difference depends on how verbal ability is assessed and who serves as the participants. Thus, any meta-analysis is only as good as the studies that it summarizes. As long as the research literature is based on a narrow selection of participants and assessment procedures, the results of any analysis will be biased.

Example 2: The Problem of Null Results

It is difficult to estimate the number of studies of cognitive gender differences that have failed to show any statistically significant differences between the women and men. The problem with null results is that they are difficult to interpret. Unfortunately, studies that show null results cannot be used to "cancel" studies that show statistically significant differences. There are many ways to obtain null results in any study. A low power design (e.g., too few participants) can virtually ensure that significant differences will not be found even if large differences do exist. Furthermore, plain old sloppy research can be the cause of null results.

Consider the problem of null results in a less politicized area. Suppose that a researcher read that 50 studies were conducted on the effect of a certain drug on blood pressure and that half of them showed that the drug causes a dangerous increase in blood pressure, whereas half showed no effect of the drug on blood pressure. Would that researcher feel confident in concluding that the drug does not affect blood pressure? Most people can understand that the null cannot be used to cancel the drug studies that found differences especially when the significant results are all found in the same direction (i.e., increase). Yet, when the topic is gender differences, many people believe that null results should be given equal weight to studies that find differences. A more fruitful approach is to examine those studies that showed differences and those that did not to see how the two types of studies differ. Similarly, reports of cognitive gender differences should be examined to determine the circumstances under which differences do and do not appear.

Example 3: Biological Theories of Cognitive Gender Differences

There is a large class of theories that posits that biological indexes and correlates of gender are the origin of cognitive gender differences. These theories concern variables such as prenatal hormones, maturation rate, brain organization and structure, and hormones available at puberty. (See Halpern, 1992, in press-a, for a review of these theories.) Some of these theories specifically concern the possibility that the male brain (on the average) is organized most optimally for good visual–spatial ability (e.g., Levy, 1976; McGlone, 1980). The strength of the data in support of these hypotheses is varied. Yet, they all share a common weakness: The biology of femaleness and maleness is the same the world over, yet the gender differences that are found in cognition are not universal.

In the United States, more than two thirds of the bachelor's degrees and 80% of the doctorates in mathematics are earned by Asian and White men (Steen, 1987). If biological variables are involved in determining mathematical ability (or any other ability), their effects are much too small to account for gender differences of this magnitude. Nor can such biological variables explain the scarcity of men from other ethnic groups in higher mathematics. There are no theories arguing that African American men or Hispanic men differ from White and Asian men in their biological indicators of sex (e.g., concentrations of sex hormones, gonads, genitals, brain structures). If researchers would take a broader, more culturally diverse view, they would see that the success in mathematics is related to Gender × Ethnicity interactions and not to the main effect of sex per se.

Similarly, research that supports the notion that men are better in higher mathematics than women is based on data from Western industrialized nations. The International Mathematics Olympiad, for example, is a mathematics competition that involves the most mathematically gifted individuals from many countries. When one looks at Western industrialized countries, one finds that virtually all of the participants are men, yet when one examines the composition as a function of gender of the team from China, one finds that Chinese teams have contained several women who have been gold and silver award winners (Stanley, 1990). The conclusion that there is a "universal" absence of women from international mathematics competition is obviously shown to be wrong when one includes data from non-Western countries. Thus, even though some of the gender differences with regard to quantitative ability are found in other countries, the size of the gender effects varies across countries. It is clearly not a biologically fixed ability that is tied to the biological correlates or causes of one's sex.

Example 4: Main Effects and Interactions

One of the principal problems with relying on data collected from a narrow range of the population is that results that really may be interactions appear as main effects. Suppose, for example, that virtually all of the researchers on mathematical ability had students as their participants. (This should not be too hard to imagine because it is true.) In general, students are either children (preschool through 12th grade) or adults in their late teens or 20s. Only a small percentage of undergraduates are in their 30s or older.

One of the largest gender differences is found on the Mathematics section of the SATs. Since the late 1960s, men have scored an average of 46–47 points higher than women (National Education Association, 1989). Of course, such data do not indicate why there is a consistent difference of this magnitude, a critical question that cannot be addressed in this chapter because it requires a careful analysis of massive amounts of data. Putting aside the problem of why there are such large differences, consider the fact that it exists.

A descriptive conclusion is that women are scoring much lower than men on a standardized test that is used, in part, to determine eligibility for higher education. In the language of data analysis, this means that there is a "main effect" for gender. That is, the gender of the test taker makes a difference, on the average, in how well test takers score on this test. Unfortunately, because test takers tend to be relatively homogenous, important interactions are masked. I doubt, for example, that mathematical gender differences of this magnitude or of any magnitude would be found among middle-age and older adults. Unfortunately, there are not enough data to support the Gender × Age interaction that I am suggesting. Similarly, the majority of those who plan to attend college tend to be of middle and higher socioeconomic status. In fact, there is some evidence that men who take the SATs are from a higher socioeconomic class than women (Ramist & Arbeiter, 1986). It seems likely that Sex × Socioeconomic Status interactions also would be found if the appropriate data were collected. Other interactions also are likely. One obtains a much different picture of cognitive gender differences when low socioeconomic status participants are included in research than when they are excluded, again suggesting that it is the interaction of other variables (class and age) with gender that are the most important mediators of results that appear as main effects for gender.

Example 5: The Changing Nature of Populations

Consider again data from the SATs to illustrate the importance of diversity in the kinds of results researchers obtain. Other examples are possible, but the SATs are well-known and widely used and are therefore convenient for making several points. Consider the data shown in Figure 1, which depicts average scores for women and men on the Verbal portion of the SATs since 1967.

As shown in Figure 1, it appears that women have "lost" verbal ability over time relative to men. Part of this "apparent decline" can be explained by considering the differential dropout rates for girls and boys in junior and senior high school. Prior to 1980, girls dropped out of secondary school at higher rates than boys, with gender differences in dropout rates narrowing throughout the 1970s (Center for Education Statistics, 1987a). Currently, the dropout rate for students who enrolled as high school sophomores is 18.2% for men and 14.6% for women (Center for Education Statistics, 1987b). The inclusion in testing of a greater proportion of below-average girls and fewer below-average boys over the past several decades

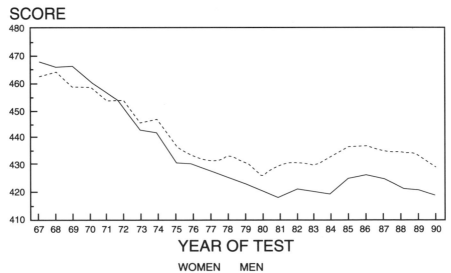

Figure 1. Scholastic Aptitude Test Scores–Verbal for college-bound high school seniors: 1967–1990. From Halpern (1992). Reprinted with permission of the publisher.

has diminished the female advantage on the Verbal portion of the SATs. Once again, failure to include data from groups other than current students can be misleading, and what may appear as a loss for women can be explained as a function of the changing nature of the high school population.

Example 6: Poverty as a Diversity Issue

It is well-known that a disproportionate number of families living below the poverty level are composed of people of color (U.S. Bureau of the Census, 1990). Families headed by women also are disproportionately overrepresented among the poor. Thus, the weight of poverty in America tends to be borne largely by minority groups and women. Harold L. Hodgkinson, a demographer (cited in National Research Council, 1989), made this point succinctly when he noted that "every day in America, 40 teenage girls give birth to their third child" (p. 19). Given this fact, is it any wonder that researchers find that people of color and women in general tend to perform more poorly on standardized tests of ability or achievement? Men score an average of approximately 50 points higher than women on the SAT (National Education Association, 1989). The difference in scores between African Americans and White students is close to 200 points. (The mean score in 1989 was 737 for African Americans and 935 for White students; "How Students Fare," 1989, p. 6c). When these data are considered separately from the covariance among gender, race, and poverty, they seem ominous. Yet, when one adds the fact that 50% of African American children are growing up in households whose income is below the poverty level, these numbers seem to say less about gender and race than they do about the crushing effects of poverty on standardized tests of scholastic achievement. When poverty is considered as a diversity issue, the main effects of ethnicity and the Gender × Ethnicity interaction are further modified and explained. The relative absence of the poor from psychological studies of cognitive gender differences has led researchers to overestimate the effect of gender on indicators of cognitive performance.

KNOWLEDGE AS EMPOWERMENT

How can data such as these be interpreted and used? I do not believe that researchers should eliminate tests that show these discrepancies or downplay their importance. Quite the contrary. The needs of women or ethnic minority groups are not served by suppressing these data. Rather, researchers need to know that these discrepancies exist if they are ever to address or redress them. One does not improve the condition of women and minorities by pretending that there are no differences. There are some tests that show large gender differences (such as the SATs, as described earlier). It is important that researchers continue the many debates about when, where, and why these differences are found, but researchers cannot have these debates unless they examine the many variables that affect these data. It is not the purpose of this chapter to provide pat answers to these questions. Instead, my purpose is to ensure that readers ask and consider these questions every time these issues are discussed, every time there is a front page news story about gender differences, and every time value judgments are made about the nature of gender differences research.

RECOMMENDATIONS AND CAVEATS FOR THOSE CONCERNED WITH DIVERSITY

If you are concerned that the psychology we study is genuinely a psychology of all people, then keep the following recommendations in mind when you are planning, reading, and interpreting research (Halpern, in press-b):

1. Are the appropriate generalizations being made? For example, are inferences being made about all women and all men when only college students were subjects?

2. Are main effects being moderated by unidentified interactions? For example, is the main effect of gender or ethnicity really the effect of socioeconomic status on gender or ethnicity? Would the effects of gender, for example, change if different age groups had been included as subjects? What other variables are confounded with gender and ethnicity? For example, African Americans in the United States take fewer college preparatory courses in high school than White students. Given the confounding of these variables, would at least part of the differences that are found be attributable to differential course-taking patterns?

3. Were the hypotheses clearly stated before the data were collected? Is there a plausible and falsifiable theory that can explain these data? Have the critical experiments been conducted that would allow the proposed theory to be found false? Have you considered ways in which experimenter bias could be responsible for the obtained results?

4. Were tests of significance followed with effect size statistics? How does the obtained effect size compare with others in the literature? How were decisions about the importance of an effect size determined? Were results that were not in accord with the researcher's worldview labeled as "small" and those that were in accord with the researcher's world-

view described as "large" when they were, in fact, quite similar in size?

5. Were there enough participants in the study to be representative of the population from which they were sampled? Small samples yield inaccurate estimates of what is true in the population and large samples virtually assure statistical significance. Have you considered the way sample size could have affected the results?

6. Are different levels of evidence being used for results that either support or fail to support the researcher's hypothesis? For example, do studies that show significant relationships have more statistical power (e.g., larger sample size or more sensitive measurement) than studies that fail to show significant relationships?

7. Are meta-analyses based on studies that have involved a wide range of participants? For example, would the conclusions change if there had been more studies that included participants from the low end of the ability distribution, or if a different measure had been used?

8. Are you careful to scrutinize your own willingness to accept evidence to determine whether it has been tainted by personal bias? Are you able to maintain an open mind even when the results do not support your favored hypothesis?

9. Do you understand why null results cannot be used to cancel studies that show significant relationships?

10. Are you careful to distinguish between research results and interpretations of research results? For example, the finding that women and men show different patterns of scores on the SATs does not necessarily mean that there are gender ability differences. All it does mean is at this time and with this test, there are "on the average" between-gender differences. Results of this sort indicate nothing about the cause of the differences.

11. Do you avoid and require others to avoid stereotypic generalizations? For example, are you consciously correcting the mistaken belief that because differences are sometimes found between groups on the average, this does not mean that all the members of one group are different from all the members of another group?

12. Have you maintained an amiable skepticism? Do you scrutinize new research carefully and require independent replications before you are willing to place too much faith in the findings?

13. Are there changes in the nature of the population or the instrument that could be mediating results that look like changes over time?

It is likely that media headlines reporting cognitive gender differences will continue to be published because the general public is fascinated with this topic. Cultural and other types of diversity are rarely addressed in this area of research, yet results are inappropriately generalized to all females and all males. The next time you read or hear about such a study, will you remember to ask the critical questions that were just posed? We live in a diverse and complex world. The type of answer one gets to questions about the ways in which the genders differ with regard to cognitive abilities will depend on a host of other variables that include ethnicity, age, socioeconomic status, native language, educational level, life experiences, nutrition, and the biology of femaleness and maleness. There can be no simple gender effects for complicated questions.

REFERENCES

Bannatyne, A. (1976). *Language, reading, and learning disabilities: Psychology, neuropsychology, diagnosis, and remediation.* Springfield, IL: Charles C Thomas.

Begley, S. (1995, March 27). Gray matters. *Newsweek*, 48–54.

Benbow, C. P. (1988). Sex differences in mathematical reasoning ability in intellectually talented preadolescents: Their nature, effects, and possible causes. *Behavioral and Brain Sciences, 11*, 169–232.

Berenbaum, S. A., & Hines, M. (1992). Early androgens are related to childhood sex-typed toy preferences. *Psychological Science, 3*, 203–206.

Center for Education Statistics. (1987a). *Digest of education statistics: 1987.* Washington, DC: U.S. Government Printing Office.

Center for Education Statistics. (1987b). *The condition of education: 1987.* Washington, DC: U.S. Government Printing Office.

Cohen, J. (1969). *Statistical power analysis for the behavioral sciences.* San Diego, CA: Academic Press.

Coren, S. (Ed.). (1990). *Left-handedness: Behavioral implications and anomalies.* Amsterdam: North-Holland.

Eagly, A. H. (1986). Some meta-analytic approaches to examining the validity of gender-difference research. In J. S. Hyde & M. C. Linn (Eds.), *The psychology of gender: Advances through meta-analysis* (pp. 159–177). Baltimore: Johns Hopkins University Press.

Eagly, A. H. (1987). *Sex differences in social behavior: A social-role interpretation.* Hillsdale, NJ: Erlbaum.

Eagly, A. H. (1995). The science and politics of comparing women and men. *American Psychologist, 50*, 145–158.

Gould, J. S. (1978). Women's brains. *Natural History, 87,* 44–50.

Halpern, D. F. (1992). *Sex differences in cognitive abilities* (2nd ed.). Hillsdale, NJ: Erlbaum.

Halpern, D. F. (1994). Stereotypes, science, censorship and the study of sex differences. *Feminism & Psychology, 4,* 523–530.

Halpern, D. F. (in press-a). Psychological and psychobiological perspectives on sex differences in cognition [Special double issue]. *Learning and Individual Differences.*

Halpern, D. F. (in press-b). *Thought and knowledge: An introduction to critical thinking* (3rd ed.). Hillsdale, NJ: Erlbaum.

Halpern, D. F., & Coren, S. (1991). Handedness and life span. *New England Journal of Medicine, 324,* 998.

Hampson, E., & Kimura, D. (1988). Reciprocal effects of hormonal fluctuations on human motor and perceptual-spatial skills. *Behavioral Neuroscience, 102,* 456–495.

Hare-Mustin, R. T., & Maracek, J. (1994). Asking the right questions: Feminist psychology and sex differences. *Feminism & Psychology, 4,* 531–537.

Hines, M. (1990). Gonadal hormones and human cognitive development. In J. Balthazart (Ed.), *Hormones, brain and behavior in vertebrates: 1. Sexual differentiation, neuroanatomical aspects, neurotransmitters and neuropeptides* (pp. 51–63). Basel, Switzerland: Karger.

How students fare on SAT, ACT tests (1989, January 17). *USA Today,* p. 6c.

Hyde, J. S., Fennema, E., & Lamon, S. J. (1990). Gender differences in mathematical performance: A meta-analysis. *Psychological Bulletin, 107,* 139–155.

Hyde, J. S., & Linn, M. C. (Eds.). (1986). *The psychology of gender: Advances through meta-analysis.* Baltimore: Johns Hopkins University Press.

Hyde, J. S., & Linn, M. C. (1988). Gender differences in verbal ability: A meta-analysis. *Psychological Bulletin, 104,* 53–69.

Law, D., Pellegrino, J. W., & Hunt, E. B. (1993). Comparing the tortoise and the hare: Gender differences and experience in dynamic spatial reasoning tasks. *Psychological Science, 4,* 35–41.

Levy, J. (1976). Cerebral lateralization and spatial ability. *Behavior Genetics, 6,* 171–188.

Masters, M. S., & Sanders, B. (1993). Is the gender difference in mental rotation disappearing? *Behavior Genetics, 23,* 337–341.

McGlone, J. (1980). Sex differences in human brain asymmetry: A critical survey. *Behavioral and Brain Sciences, 3,* 215–227.

National Education Association. (1989). *The NEA 1989 almanac of higher education.* Washington, DC: Author.

National Research Council. (1989). *Everybody counts: A report to the nation on the future of mathematics education.* Washington, DC: National Academy Press.

Ramist, L., & Arbeiter, S. (1986). *Profiles, college-bound seniors, 1985.* New York: College Entrance Examination Board.

Riefer, D. (1991). *Effect size statistics*. Unpublished manuscript, California State University, San Bernardino.

Skinner, P. H., & Shelton, R. L. (1985). *Speech, language, and hearing: Normal processes and disorders* (2nd ed.). New York: Wiley.

Stanley, J. (1990, January 10). We need to know why women falter in math [Letter to the editor]. *Chronicle of Higher Education*, p. B4.

Steen, L. A. (1987). Mathematics education: A predictor of scientific competitiveness. *Science, 237*, 251–252.

Sutaria, S. D. (1985). *Specific learning disabilities: Nature and needs*. Springfield, IL: Charles C Thomas.

Task Force on Women, Minorities, and the Handicapped in Science and Technology. (1988, September). *Changing America: The new face of science and education*. Washington, DC: Author.

U.S. Bureau of the Census. (1990). *Statistical abstracts of the United States, 1989* (109th ed.). Washington, DC: U.S. Government Printing Office.

5

SOCIALIZATION OF GIRLS: ISSUES OF ETHNICITY IN GENDER DEVELOPMENT

PAMELA TROTMAN REID, CALLIOPE HARITOS, ELIZABETH KELLY, and NICOLE E. HOLLAND

Socialization is the process through which children acquire the behavior considered appropriate by the groups to which they relate (i.e., their family, community, and the larger society). Researchers who focus on the psychology of women have been particularly interested in illuminating this process with respect to gender. They have noted that girls, as well as boys, are expected to develop attitudes and behaviors that fit societal norms for their gender designation; that parents, teachers, and other societal agents foster gender-typed behavior; and that children themselves adopt gender-stereotypic characteristics at very early ages (Ruble, 1988).

Despite considerable research in recent years on the topic of socialization and gender, major questions remain unanswered regarding the psychological assumptions underlying these investigations. For example, What are the actual gender-type beliefs of a changing society? How strong a consensus is there among the various segments of society regarding appropriate gender behavior as it pertains to girls? To what extent do the biological commonalities of gender allow generalizability across race, social class, and varying ethnicity?

These questions involve a number of research issues that we attempt to address in this chapter. However, the issue of paramount importance is the need for the recognition of diverse perspectives and experiences, particularly those of ethnic minorities, as we try to uncover the processes involved in becoming a woman in American society. Addressing this issue appears a formidable task as we consider demographic data that indicate increasingly larger proportions of the U.S. population are represented by ethnic minority groups.

Although no one argues or doubts that these diverse groups often hold different assumptions, family styles, and gender expectations, there seems to be no great urge by psychologists to reflect this reality in studies that purport to assess social behavior (Reid, 1993). Indeed, our concern stems from the fact that research on gender socialization has been focused overwhelmingly, and almost exclusively, on White middle-class populations, based on their assumptions, and embedded with their expectations. Although a few studies have included girls from other ethnic communities (e.g., Nelson-LeGall, 1990; Reid, Tate, & Berman, 1989), such inclusions are more often the exception than the rule.

There are many reasons to consider the existing body of research on gender socialization extremely limited, if not totally flawed. These reasons stem from theoretical concerns, methodological problems, and issues of bias in assumptions and conclusions (see chapters 3 and 4 of this book; Reid, 1988, 1993). We strongly support theoretical formulations that specify the conditions and circumstances for which propositions are to be used. Sound methodology demands the consideration of all relevant information before clear conclusions may be drawn. Research assumptions that are based on one segment of society cannot remain the rule if researchers accept the heterogeneity of society in general and American society in particular. Thus, researchers cannot continue to investigate a major social process and ignore persistent factors such as ethnic background and social class.

We believe that the factors of ethnicity and social class represent critical influences on socialization and that the omission of these in the developmental research, particularly in the area of gender socialization, must be corrected. We suggest that questions may, and in fact *must*, be raised about the generalizability of the body of research findings on gender socialization. To thoroughly examine this issue of generalizability, it appears necessary (a) to question the relevance of psychological theories of gender socialization to issues of ethnicity; (b) to examine how ethnic issues in socialization are handled by current research strategies; and (c) to determine what impact will result from the inclusion of ethnic issues in the study of gender socialization on developmental psychology. In this chapter, we attempt to conduct such examinations. Specifically, we examine diversity through a focus on the socialization of girls from diverse ethnic American backgrounds. We address the overall and particular expectations with which girls who are ethnic minorities are reared, the forces that operate to shape their expectations, and the methodological issues that seem useful for the study of different ethnic populations.

ADDRESSING ETHNICITY IN DEVELOPMENTAL THEORIES

The socialization of girls has been approached from a number of theoretical perspectives. These include psychoanalytic, social learning, cognitive–developmental, and gender schema theory. Each of these perspectives attempts to the address questions such as what factors operate to produce the manifestation of characteristically female behavior; what process leads girls to accept this behavior as their own; and how does the development of girls differ from that of boys. Note that most theorists have not seriously questioned that there is "female behavior" or that girls can be easily distinguished from boys on the basis of it. Because the assumption of the existence of female behavior is pervasive throughout society, perhaps it should not be surprising that theories seem to focus on revealing its development on the basis of a single "representative" population. As we briefly review each of the major theoretical approaches, we examine its potential for addressing ethnicity and consider how likely it is that the potential will be met.

Psychoanalytic Theory

Psychoanalytic theory suggests that the development of gender-typed behavior is attributable to a child's identification with an adult model, namely, a parent (Bronfenbrenner, 1960). The process of identification is viewed by psychoanalytic proponents as critical to all socialization, because it entails a child's acceptance of an adult's value or belief system (Langer, 1969). For a girl, this process involves identifying with her mother, accepting the feminine role, and rejecting the masculine one. Thus, the role is defined for each girl by the woman with whom she has close, even intimate, connections. This explanation may be congruent with a variety of female experiences across social class and ethnic lines; however, in practice, researchers have adopted norms that assume family structures and behavior that do not necessarily describe how many ethnic communities operate (Harrison, Wilson, Pine & Chan, 1990). For example, in African American families, multiple generations of women often share in childcare duties (Tolson & Wilson, 1990; Wilson, Tolson, & Hinton, 1990). Thus, the assumption of a single female role model falls apart.

Although the psychoanalytic assumption of a nuclear family structure may be incompatible with reality for many girls, particularly problematic is this assumption that a child has one model and one set of values. In today's world of single parents, lesbian and gay parents, blended families resulting from divorce and remarriage, and multigenerational families, nuclear families are no longer the norm (Katz, 1987). Additionally, economic necessities and changing expectations have led most mothers to join the labor force, which means that many children may experience multiple female caregivers outside the family. With the possibilities of no male models, multiple female models, and contradictory values, it is unclear how psychoanalytic theory can predict which gender behavior a girl will accept or reject.

Social Learning Theory

Social learning theorists explain the development of gender behavior as a process of cumulative experience that depends on factors such as social expectations; differential reinforcement of behavior by parents, peers, and teachers; and imitation of same-sex models. Gender roles, as they exist in society, are said to induce gender differences because they are behaviorally confirmed (Eagly, 1987). In other words, girls are rewarded or positively recognized for behaving in ways consistent with group-held norms; they also are punished or ignored for inconsistent gender behavior. Block (1983) found that White middle-class parents were more likely to strictly supervise their daughters and to encourage help seeking and dependency. Boys, on the other hand, were more likely to be left alone by parents during play and encouraged to be independent. Experiences of this nature are seen as shaping female responses and characteristics over time.

Social learning theory is flexible enough that it appears to be applicable to minority groups. In the abstract, experiences common to each ethnic group or social class segment determine what should be expected from the females in that group. However, as with other theories, there have been few empirical attempts to demonstrate the relevance of different cultural practices to girls' behavior. Thus, the recognition that gender-appropriate behavior for females in one cultural group may be considered gender inappropriate in another has been relatively unexamined. Indeed, the search for similar gender-type behavior from one culture to another may mislead researchers by examining that behavior out of its social context.

Cognitive–Developmental Theory

The cognitive–developmental perspective of socialization focuses on children's mental processing of information available to them in their world. Understanding of gender follows similarly. According to cognitive–developmental theory, a child's interpretations and subsequent use of gender depends on his or her ability to understand and categorize observable gender behavior and characteristics (Ruble, 1988). Children initially distinguish between the sexes on a purely physical basis (Kohlberg, 1966). As they interact with others, they learn about female and male roles by observing the association of physical attributes, activities, and traits linked to female and male gender categories. An associative network, which corresponds to the gender norms of the child's culture, is subsequently established, whereby the child assumes that all individuals labeled as female and male will possess the characteristics associated with these categories (Serbin & Sprafkin, 1986).

Cognitive theorists have discussed the child's need for self-categorization as a girl or boy and observations of gender-stereotypic behavior of women and men in society (Kohlberg, 1966). However, cognitive researchers have not typically demonstrated the linkage of actual observations to gender understanding and self-categorization. Such an issue is critical to the acceptance of the cognitive proposal for gender socialization, particularly when considering its applicability to ethnic or cultural minorities. In addition to the failure of cognitive theorists to address differences in experiences, in observations, and in interpretations of gender roles attributable to ethnic and social class background, they, like other theorists, have frequently not attended to clarifying the definition of female and male roles beyond the assumptions accepted by White middle-class Americans.

Gender Schema Theory

Gender schema theory is perhaps the most useful of theories for explaining the development of gender behavior in girls and women of color. Differences in individual experiences, observations, and interpretations can be clearly viewed as subject to ethnic and social class background in particular, as well as to the culture or society in general. The linkage of an individual's observations of gender roles as they exist in society to that individual's understanding of gender and self-categorization is evident from various explanations of gender schematicity or consistency (Bem, 1983; Martin & Halverson, 1981).

Gender schema theorists have generally attempted to explain the development of gender behavior by combining cognitive and behavioral factors. Therefore, gender behavior is said to result from an individual's generalized readiness to process information on the basis of sex-linked associations. These associations constitute gender schemas (Bem, 1981). Gender schemas, then, may be described as cognitive structures consisting of children's knowledge and attitudes about gender-related issues. In addition, they may include self-defining characteristics relevant to gender

(Martin & Halverson, 1981). According to Bem (1981), the degree to which a girl may be considered gender typed depends on that girl's socialization history. Her history includes her preferences, skills, personal attributes, behavior, and the self-concept that she acquired during childhood. To the extent that her history or experience is consistent with the culture's definition of femaleness, she will be highly gender appropriate or consistent in her gender schema. The extent of strong feminine gender schema will also be a function of the importance placed on a gender dichotomy by her culture.

Bem (1983, 1993) reasoned that in a culture in which gender-differentiated practices are nonexistent, the distribution of activities and roles by sex must be interpreted as a reflection of biology. However, in a society with strongly gender-differentiated activities, it is not possible to restrict explanations to biology alone. Indeed, gender schema theorists acknowledge that cultural factors, individual and familial differences, and societal expectations can influence the specific manifestations of gender interpretations. Bem (1983) suggested that children whose parents have provided them with alternative schemas for interpreting sex-linked associations can build up a resistance to cultural norms. This resistance allows them to be gender aschematic in a gender schematic society. Therefore, families who hold beliefs about gender-related issues that vary with the cultural beliefs, for whatever reason—be it class or ethnicity—may produce children who also will not fit the societal norms in their gender interpretations.

STUDYING GENDER AND ETHNIC ISSUES

In evaluating gender and ethnic issues in children's socialization, researchers have typically focused their attention only on one dimension: either gender or ethnicity. Studies of gender development have, in the main, derived findings on the basis of samples of exclusively, or at least primarily, White middle-class samples (e.g., Serbin & Sprafkin, 1986; Stern & Karraker, 1989). Rarely have studies of gender development considered children of color.

There also has been little attention given to gender in studies of ethnic identity and ethnic socialization. Indeed, although we can cite some exceptions (Reid et al.,1989; Reid & Trotter, 1993; Romer & Cherry, 1980; Zalk & Katz, 1978), studies of children that include both gender and ethnic issues are rare. For this reason, much of what is presumed to be true about children from ethnic communities has been, at best, only extrapolations of observations of adult members of those groups. Even among Euro-American groups, researchers have been content to assume that they can make generalizations from one group to another. The validity of this assumption has yet to be tested. Thus, there is an increasing need for researchers who focus on people of color to clarify the commonalities and draw more clearly the lines of distinction for assumptions about gender and for other issues as well.

African American Families and Gender

Members of African American families have traditionally been exposed to undifferentiated, blended gender role models (Allen & Majidi-Ahi, 1989; Gibbs, 1989). Although few empirical data exist, observers suggest that African American women are aggressive, independent, self-confident, and sexually assertive (Lewis, 1975; Reid, 1982, 1988). Much of the literature on African American women and men focuses on their failure to conform to existing White gender norms (see chapter 13 in this book). For example, researchers have examined high rates of absence of a male head of household, female family status, and the existence of extended family networks (Stack, 1974; Staples, 1988; Tanner, 1974). However, research conducted specifically on gender socialization has been difficult to identify. Indeed, the differences that exist between African American girls and boys have not been fully explicated, and studies of their development of gender knowledge and attitudes are either nonexistent or rare.

Asian American Families and Gender

Family traditions and values are known to hold much importance among the various Asian American populations. Huang and Ying (1989) pointed out, for example, that Chinese Americans are more conservative in their sexual values and in their attitudes toward the role of women. Yet, Asian American women have the highest labor force participation rate of any group of women (Simpson & Yinger, 1985). Because Asian Americans have for so long fit the role of the "model minority" (i.e., not openly challenging majority notions or stereotypes), few researchers have examined the family practices or expectations for girls qua girls. Of the little research that exists, the majority examines adult experiences (e.g., see chapter 12 in this book; also see Lott, 1990; True, 1990).

Native American Families

John (1988) pointed out that "little is known about gender roles among Native Americans" (p. 350). However, John did cite research to suggest that Native American women are more concerned with interpersonal relationships and the men with material matters. LaFromboise, Heyle, and Ozer (1990) also described the various roles Native American women may hold in the family and in the tribe. They demonstrated that no single description is sufficient to characterize the female role in Native American communities. Yet, LaFromboise et al. did not make clear how Native American women come to adopt one role or another and other research on Native American populations has not focused attention on gender concerns (see chapter 10 in this book).

Latin American Families

With research on Puerto Rican, Mexican American, and other Latino families, one again finds that children have been generally excluded from gender investigations. Although some of the gender-based expectations that predominate among adult Latin American populations have been described (e.g., Espin, 1987; Sanchez-Ayendez, 1988; also see chapter 11 in this book), the question of how these are developed or encouraged in children awaits illumination. It is known that Latinas are expected to demonstrate spirituality and to conduct themselves in a virtuous manner; nevertheless, they often express power in domestic situations (Comas-Díaz, 1987). How do these messages become encoded and translated by children? The studies on gender development seem not to recognize the many forms and beliefs that families in the United States adopt.

Methodology in the Study of Ethnicity and Gender

Repeatedly, researchers have been forced to recognize the dearth of information in the study of ethnicity and gender. An examination of methodological issues also supports this contention. Even a recently compiled handbook of tests and measures used for gender role research (Beere, 1990) included no measures developed to investigate the combined effects of gender and ethnicity. Because we know of no measures to examine the combined factors, we propose instead to look at the methodological strategies that researchers have used to evaluate gender socialization and to examine the degree to which these strategies are sensitive to ethnicity.

Research that supports the socialization theories discussed earlier use a variety of methodological strategies. In this section, we review the major types of measures used to evaluate the cultural forces and sources of societal expectations (e.g., parents, peers, schools, media). We then examine the methods used to evaluate children and their developing gender roles.

Evaluating Parental Attitudes and Beliefs

Cultural expectations about gender roles are closely related to the attitudes and stereotypes about gender that are prevalent in the general society. Because the study of gender stereotypes and attitudes began with adults, researchers frequently evaluate parents as the providers of children's cultural and gender milieu. For example, how parents' beliefs about gender roles socialize their children was examined by Stern and Karraker's (1989) look at the gender stereotyping of infants in a review of gender-labeling studies.

Self-Report Questionnaires. One of the most frequently used strategies for assessing parents' attitudes is the self-report questionnaire. These measures of gender stereotypes typically use descriptions of behavior, personality traits, or occupations and provide a scale to rate them as masculine or feminine. Alternatively, parents are asked to respond with level of agreement to statements about gender roles. The problems with measuring either expectations or stereotypes through self-report techniques includes bias and ambiguity. In addition, self-report scales (a) are susceptible to social approval bias, whether consciously or not; (b) produce other response bias sets; and (c) use terms that are often not clearly defined, thus causing respondents to be uncertain of what they are being asked (Beere, 1990). Questions of validity also may be raised with respect to self-report scales. The relationship between scale scores and behavior is usually not addressed, and scales developed on one population are often used with another. This last issue is one that we find most troublesome and most common among scales of gender stereotyping. Some examples of scales normed using primarily White college students and applied to many other segments of the general population are Bem's (1974) Adjective Checklist, the Bias in Attitudes Survey (Jean & Reynolds, 1980), and the Beliefs about Women Scale (cited in Beere, 1990).

Direct Observation. Another approach to assessing parents' beliefs about gender roles is direct observation of their interactions with and treatment of their children. The behaviors measured in such observations include frequency and quality of directives, frequency of physical contact, response to aggressive behavior, and frequency of punishment and encouragement. Observational methods also may pose problems of bias. First, parents are likely to be very conscious of their behavior and may perform to what they believe are the examiner's standards. Second, each study will often have a slightly different definition of a category for classifying behavior so that comparisons among studies lead to inaccurate conclusions. Third, the laboratory setting or interview situation itself may elicit atypical behavior from both the parents and child.

Although observation of behavior may appear to be immune from the charge of inappropriate group comparison, it is not. Definitions of categories, the selection of behavior for observation, and the interpretation given to what was observed are all compounded by the experimenter's own values and assumptions. Because these assumptions are rarely examined, it is unusual to learn what conclusions might result from an alternative value system. For example, low-income African American girls, as well as boys, are typically taught to defend and protect themselves, particularly against peer physical aggression (Lewis, 1975). Their self-assertive behavior may be viewed as aggressive compared with the behavior of middle-class White girls and boys who are encouraged to consider other responses or to turn to adults for assistance.

Evaluating Media Influences

The examination of cultural expectations about gender roles has led researchers to consider media, as well as parental, influences on children. Thus, a variety of methods have been used in attempts to determine what messages are being sent, how these messages are interpreted, and what impact they have on children's understanding of gender. The Personal Attributes Questionnaire was used by Dambrot, Reep, and Bell (1988) to measure college students' ratings of themselves and TV characters. Children's reactions to sex-typed toys in TV commercials were assessed by observing their toy choices after viewing the commercial (Ruble, Balaban, & Cooper, 1981). Finally, the Scale for Sexism in the Media (Pingree, Hawkins, Butler, & Paisley, 1976) has been used to assess advertisements in magazines. None of these studies or measures, however, take into account ethnic variations. Thus, once more, feminist psychologists are prevented from seeing a fuller picture of how ethnic and cultural diversity may interact with gender.

Evaluating Gender Understanding in Children

Although studies of gender role behavior in adults typically favor the use of self-report instruments, those used with children often have relied on measures of children's preferences for games, toys, peers, and activities (Beere, 1990). These studies have depended on an initial stereotyping of behavior, games, occupations, and personality traits in order for the researchers to categorize the children's preferences. In scoring sex-stereotyping measures, ratings are either assigned to individuals or to items. We suggest that, for the most part, it is distressingly unclear whether the findings obtained reflect the extent to which the children are aware of prevailing stereotypes or the extent to which a particular stereotype is held by them (Beere, 1990).

Researchers have recently moved toward adopting self-report scales for children. Some examples include the Adolescent Sex Role Inventory (T. Thomas & Robinson, 1981), the Children's Sex Role Self-Concept Inventory (Kurdek & Siesky, 1980), the Children's Androgyny Scale (Ritchie, Villiger, & Duignan, 1977), and the Children's Personal Attributes Questionnaire (Hall & Halberstadt, 1980). These measures are certainly subject to the same biases discussed earlier. It also is possible, as

Beere (1990) suggested, that young children are not reliable reporters, even when reporting information about their own preferences and traits.

As with evaluations of parents and media, tests used with children were not designed with norms for ethnic populations. Nevertheless, researchers have used them with children from a variety of social class and ethnic backgrounds. Thus, the possibility of bias may result from a lack of consistency among different ethnic groups. That is, the behavior accepted as correctly classified as feminine or masculine for one group may in fact be incorrectly classified for another population.

INCLUSION AND IMPACT OF ETHNIC ISSUES

We have developed the proposition that the socialization of ethnic minority American girls may differ from that of White American girls because of a variety of factors, including differences in family practices and expectations. For example, although girls and women in White American families have traditionally been socialized to be passive, dependent, conforming, expressive, and sexually receptive, African American women have been found to behave independently and to expect more egalitarian relationships (Lewis, 1975; Reid, 1982, 1984). On the other hand, Latinas, including Puerto Rican and Mexican American women, appear to be extremely submissive and indulgent toward men (Inclan & Herron, 1989; Shorris, 1992; Sowell, 1981). Chinese American women similarly appear to be submissive in public; however, they are vocal and demanding in private (Huang & Ying, 1989).

Which of these groups represents the "American ideal," or the norm? Our response is all of them and none of them. All, because every American group must be included and represented in Americans' image and none, because one, alone, is not adequate to convey the complexity of developing gender behavior in the context of family and community. To demonstrate how researchers may consider the interaction of gender and ethnicity, we have selected an exemplar: achievement behavior. Achievement was selected because it is considered particularly important in the majority culture and has been clearly marked by gender distinctions.

Achievement and Girls of Color

The term *achievement*, in the developmental literature, refers to academic success. It has been found to be influenced by a child's abilities, interests, expectancies of success, personality characteristics, and social environment (Dweck, 1975). Psychologists have demonstrated the relationship of gender to each of these important factors. For example, both societal and personal expectations of success are typically lower for girls than boys (Entwisle & Baker, 1983). Other factors that have been linked to a girl's feelings of discomfort with academic success include teacher expectancy and the responses of male peers (Borrow, 1966; Diener & Dweck, 1977; Mahony, 1983).

Effects of Gender Expectations

As the influence of gender is illuminated, one might strongly suspect that racial factors also could result in differing expectations and that the combined impact of race and gender could be particularly devastating if both expectations were negative. The few studies that have considered this possibility seem to support this speculation. For example, Rubovitz and Maehr (1973) found that intelligent Black girls greatly disconfirmed teachers' expectancies about Black children and about girls; thus, they received less attention than any other race or gender group. Similarly, Nelson-LeGall (1990) found that as Black girls advanced through school, they received less attention from teachers.

The effect of societal expectations on girls' achievement continues during adolescence, during which girls still face the dilemma of "playing dumb" to gain affection or demonstrate competency and risk the loss of approval by their peers. For example, gender expectations make math and careers in math appear incongruent with the female role. Girls have been found to modify their nontraditional choices to make them more appropriate and consistent with acceptable feminine roles (Hollinger, 1983). Girls who took math for 4 years in high school were reported to experience more conflict between their roles as females and achievement as opposed to girls who took the least math in high school (Sherman, 1982). Again, we suspect that gender issues may be heightened by racial factors. In one study that examined this possibility, it was reported that Black women experienced little encouragement and academic preparation to pursue math and science courses in school (Hall & Post-Kammer, 1987).

Children's expectancies of success also are affected by their definitions of achievement as well as their interpretations of success and failure, each of which appear to be gender based and acquired from a sex-stereotypic society. Duda (1985) found that White girls defined achievement as effort and preferred success that involved social comparisons. White boys defined success in terms of ability. White girls also explained failure as low ability, whereas boys attributed the lack of success to low effort (Dweck & Repucci, 1973; Nicholls, 1975).

These expectations may not hold for girls from families with African American, Asian, Latino, or Native American backgrounds. Consider that girls from African American families have models of mothers who have traditionally been employed outside the home. During the era when White college women were struggling with the choice of career or family, this was a nonissue for Black college women (Reid, 1988). Recent studies further indicate that Black and Latin American mothers hold higher expectations for their daughters than White American mothers (Stevenson, Chen, & Uttal, 1990).

Career Stereotypes and Aspirations

Children are quite cognizant of the occupational stereotypes that presently exist in society. They have been found to be knowledgeable of such stereotypes as early as preschool with little variability by middle childhood (Barry, 1980; Eisenberg, Wolchik, Hernandez, & Pasternack, 1985; Miller & Stanford, 1987; Nadelman, 1974; Signorella, 1987). It also is clear that boys and girls learn different things about careers. Boys have been found to recognize their roles as varied and show a wide range of adult goals, such as doctor, pilot, and firefighter. Girls, on the other hand, were found to view their roles as circumscribed and fixed. They saw themselves as mothers, teachers, or nurses (Beuf, 1974).

Career expectations also appear to be bound by class and race. Given the economic realities for children in many African American and Latino families, it appears difficult and unlikely for girls from poor ethnic families to achieve high social statuses. In fact, this conclusion is supported by a survey that demonstrated that although Black men from diverse family backgrounds achieved high professional status, Black women with equivalent achievements typically came from middle-class families (Reid & Robinson, 1985).

Kerckhoff (1972) reported that although lower class White girls were more traditionally feminine and more likely to become housewives, middle-class White girls were more career oriented and had more flexible definitions of the "female role." Black girls also were found to be traditional in their career choices (Frost & Diamond, 1979). Indeed, role attitudes and aspirations of girls have been reported to correlate significantly with those of their mothers (Meyer, 1980; V. G. Thomas & Shields, 1987). When researchers assessed the aspirations of Anglo, Latino, and African American children, only Black girls were found to choose "housekeeper" as a career. Still, we must wonder whether such a choice represents career foreclosure by the girls themselves or whether it is the result of the limited exposure to career alternatives for girls of color.

SUMMARY AND SUGGESTIONS

Research on the socialization of girls has been examined relative to the factors of ethnic and racial diversity. We have found that, in the main, little attention has been given to these issues in theories or methods. When researchers have examined gender socialization, they have not included girls of color. Similarly, when ethnicity has been a central focus of investigation, it has been treated as only incidentally coinciding with gender. Although we have not discussed it, social class also is understudied.

We have underscored the lack of attention given to the combined issues of gender and ethnicity by indicating specific populations neglected by researchers. Furthermore, we have used the specific area of achievement to illustrate how socialization in both roles are important determinants of children's behavior. Through our examination of the literature, we have attempted to raise the awareness of researchers who focus on gender issues to the need for attention to the influence of culture and ethnicity among girls.

Finally, we offer three general suggestions for correcting and improving the psychological approach to the study of gender socialization. First, researchers should examine closely the traditional assumptions that dominate gender research. These assumptions include stereotypes fostered and controlled by the American majority culture. The tendency to misapply and overgeneralize based on these assumptions is one that should be resisted. Second, researchers should adopt strategies that will reveal interactive, not only simple, effects. Although psychology as a discipline encourages parsimony in theoretical explanations, approaches designed to understand the complexity of human behavior are sorely needed. Indeed, strategies to uncover the interactions among gender, ethnicity, and class are ultimately necessary for a realistic worldview. Third, researchers should prepare themselves for the study of a variety of people. The need to develop new explanations and theories on the basis of the multiplicity of cultural backgrounds and experiences found represented in urban areas of the United States is a growing demand. Researchers must learn that it is sometimes essential to reject or limit the use of explanations that do not fit all people rather than to reject or limit the people who do not appear to fit their explanations.

REFERENCES

Allen, L., & Majidi-Ahi, S. (1989). Black American children. In J. T. Gibbs, L. N. Huang, & Associates (Eds.), *Children of color: Psychological interventions with minority youth* (pp. 148–178). San Francisco: Jossey-Bass.

Barry, R. J. (1980). Stereotyping of sex role in preschoolers in relation to age, family structure, and parental sexism. *Sex Roles, 6,* 795–806.

Beere, C. A. (1990). *Gender roles: A handbook of tests and measures.* New York: Greenwood Press.

Bem, S. (1974). *Bem's Adjective Checklist.* Palo Alto, CA: Consulting Psychologists Press.

Bem, S. L. (1981). Gender schema theory: A cognitive account of sex typing. *Psychological Review, 88,* 354–364.

Bem, S. L. (1983). Gender schema theory and its implications for child development: Raising gender aschematic children in a gender schematic society. *Signs, 8,* 598–616.

Bem, S. L. (1993). *The lenses of gender: Transforming the debate on sexual inequality.* New Haven, CT: Yale University Press.

Beuf, A. (1974). Doctor, lawyer, household drudge. *Journal of Communications, 24,* 142–145.

Block, J. H. (1983). Differential premises arising from differential socialization of the sexes: Some conjectures. *Child Development, 54,* 1335–1354.

Borrow, H. (1966). Development of occupational motives and roles. In L. W. Hoffman & M. C. Hoffman (Eds.), *Review of child development research* (pp. 373–422). New York: Russell Sage Foundation.

Bronfenbrenner, U. (1960). Freudian theories of identification and their derivatives. *Child Development, 31,* 15–40.

Comas-Díaz, L. (1987). Feminist therapy with Mainland Puerto Rican women. *Psychology of Women Quarterly, 11,* 461–474.

Dambrot, F. H., Reep, D. C., & Bell, D. (1988). Television sex roles in the 1980s: Do viewers' sex and sex role orientation change the picture? *Sex Roles, 19,* 387–401.

Diener, C. I., & Dweck, C. S. (1977). *An analysis of learned helplessness: Ongoing changes in performance, strategy and achievement cognition following failure.* Unpublished manuscript, University of Illinois, Urbana-Champaign.

Duda, J. L. (1985). Goals and achievement orientation of Anglo and Mexican American adolescents in sports and the classroom. *International Journal of Intercultural Relations, 9,* 131–150.

Dweck, C. S. (1975). The role of expectations and attributions in the alleviation of learned helplessness. *Journal of Personality and Social Psychology, 31,* 674–685.

Dweck, C. S., & Repucci, N. D. (1973). Learned helplessness and reinforcement responsibility in children. *Journal of Personality and Social Psychology, 25,* 109–116.

Eagly, A. H. (1987). *Sex differences in social behavior: A social role interpretation.* Hillsdale, NJ: Erlbaum.

Eisenberg, N., Wolchik, S.A., Hernandez, R., & Pasternack, J. F. (1985). Parental socialization of young children's play: A short term longitudinal study. *Child Development, 56,* 1506–1513.

Entwisle, D. R., & Baker, D. B. (1983). Gender and young childrens' expectations for performance in arithmetic. *Developmental Psychology, 19,* 200–209.

Espin, O. (1987). Psychological impact of migration on Latinas: Implications for psychotherapeutic practice. *Psychology of Women Quarterly, 11,* 489–504.

Frost, F., & Diamond, E. E. (1979). Ethnic and sex differences in occupational stereotyping by elementary school children. *Journal of Vocational Behavior, 15,* 43–54.

Gibbs, J. T. (1989). Black American adolescents. In J. T. Gibbs, L. N. Huang, & Associates, *Children of color: Psychological interventions with minority youth* (pp. 179–223). San Francisco, CA: Jossey-Bass.

Hall, E. R., & Post-Kammer, P. (1987). Black mathematics and science majors: Why so few? *Career Development Quarterly, 35,* 206–219.

Hall, J. A., & Halberstadt, A. G. (1980). Masculinity and femininity in children: Development of the Children's Personal Attributes Questionnaire. *Developmental Psychology, 16,* 270–280.

Harrison, A. O., Wilson, M. N., Pine, C. J., & Chan, S. Q. (1990). Family ecologies of ethnic minority children. *Child Development, 61,* 347–362.

Hollinger, C. L. (1983). Counseling the gifted and talented female adolescent: The relationship between social self esteem and traits of instrumentality and expressiveness. *Gifted Child Quarterly, 27,* 157–161.

Huang, L. N., & Ying, Y. W. (1989). Chinese American children and adolescents. In J. T. Gibbs, L. N. Huang, & Associates (Eds.), *Children of color: Psychological interventions with minority youth* (pp. 30–66). San Francisco: Jossey-Bass.

Inclan, J. E., & Herron, D. G. (1989). Puerto Rican adolescents. In J. T. Gibbs, L. N. Huang, & Associates (Eds.), *Children of color: Psychological interventions with minority youth.* San Francisco: Jossey-Bass.

Jean, P., & Reynolds, C. (1980). Development of Bias in Attitudes Survey: A sex role questionnaire. *Journal of Psychology, 104,* 269–277.

John, R. (1988). The Native American family. In C. H. Mindel, R. W. Habenstein, & R. Wright, Jr. (Eds.), *Ethnic families in America: Patterns and variations* (pp. 325–363). New York: Elsevier.

Katz, P. A. (1987). Variations in family constellation: Effects on gender schemata. *New Directions for Child Development, 38,* 39–56.

Kerckhoff, A. C. (1972). *Socialization and social class.* Englewood Cliffs, NJ: Prentice Hall.

Kohlberg, L. (1966). A cognitive-developmental analysis of children's sex role concepts and attitudes. In E. Maccoby (Ed.), *The development of sex differences* (pp. 82–173). Stanford, CA: Stanford University Press.

Kurdek, L. A., & Siesky, A. E. (1980). Sex role self-concepts of single divorced parents and their children. *Journal of Divorce, 3,* 249–261.

LaFromboise, T. D., Heyle, A. M., & Ozer, E. J. (1990). Changing and diverse roles of Native American women [Special issue]. *Sex Roles, 22,* 455–476.

Langer, J. (1969). *Theories of development.* New York: Holt, Rinehart & Winston.

Lewis, D. K. (1975). The Black family: Socialization and sex roles. *Phylon, 36,* 221–237.

Lott, J. T. (1990). A portrait of Asian and Pacific American women. In S. Rix (Ed.), *The American woman 1990–91* (pp. 258–264). New York: Norton.

Mahony, P. (1983). How Alice's chin really came to be pressed against her foot: Sexist processes of interaction in mixed sex classrooms. *Women's Studies International Forum, 6,* 107–115.

Martin, C. L., & Halverson, C. F. (1981). A schematic processing model of sex typing and stereotyping in children. *Child Development, 52,* 1119–1134.

Meyer, B. (1980). The development of girls' sex-role attitudes. *Child Development, 51,* 508–514.

Miller, M. J., & Stanford, J. T. (1987). Early occupation restriction: An examination of elementary school children's expression of vocational preferences. *Journal of Employment Counseling, 24,* 115–121.

Nadelman, L. (1974). Sex identity in American children: Memory, knowledge, and preference tasks. *Developmental Psychology, 10,* 413–417.

Nelson-LeGall, S. (1990). Academic achievement orientation and help-seeking behavior in early adolescent girls. *Journal of Early Adolescence, 10,* 176–190.

Nicholls, J. G. (1975). Causal attributions and other achievement related cognition: Effects of task outcomes, attainment value, and sex. *Journal of Personality and Social Psychology, 31,* 379–389.

Pingree, S., Hawkins, R. P., Butler, M., & Paisley, W. (1976). A scale for sexism. *Journal of Communication, 26,* 193–200.

Reid, P. T. (1982). Socialization of black female children. In P. W. Berman & E. R. Ramey (Eds.), *Women: A developmental perspective* (pp. 137–156). Washington, DC: National Institutes of Health.

Reid, P. T. (1984). Feminism vs. minority group identity: Not for Black women only. *Sex Roles, 10,* 247–255.

Reid, P. T. (1988). Racism and sexism: Comparisons and conflicts. In P. A. Katz & D. Taylor (Eds.), *Eliminating racism* (pp. 203–221). New York: Plenum.

Reid, P. T. (1993). Poor women in psychological research: Shut up and shut out. *Psychology of Women Quarterly, 17,* 133–150.

Reid, P. T., & Robinson, W. L. (1985). Professional Black men and women: Attainment of terminal academic degrees. *Psychological Reports, 56,* 547–555.

Reid, P. T., Tate, C. S., & Berman, P. W. (1989). Preschool children's self presentations in situations with infants: Effects of sex and race. *Child Development, 60,* 710–714.

Reid, P. T., & Trotter, K. H. (1993). Children's self presentations with infants: Age, race and gender effects. *Sex Roles, 29,* 171–181.

Ritchie, J., Villiger, J., & Duignan, P. (1977). Sex role differentiation in children: A preliminary investigation. *Australian and New Zealand Journal of Sociology, 13,* 142–145.

Romer, N., & Cherry, D. (1980). Ethnic and social class differences in children's sex-role concepts. *Sex Roles, 6,* 245–262.

Ruble, D. N. (1988). Sex-role development. In M. H. Bornstein & M. E. Lamb (Eds.), *Developmental psychology: An advanced textbook* (2nd ed., pp. 411–460). Hillsdale, NJ: Erlbaum.

Ruble, D. N., Balaban, T., & Cooper, J. (1981). Gender constancy and the effects of sex-typed televised toy commercials. *Child Development, 52,* 667–673.

Rubovitz, P. C., & Maehr, M. L. (1973). Pygmalion black and white. *Journal of Personality and Social Psychology, 23,* 210–218.

Sanchez-Ayendez, M. (1988). Puerto Rican elderly women: The cultural dimension of social support networks. *Women and Health, 14,* 239–252.

Serbin, L., & Sprafkin, C. (1986). The salience of gender and the process of sex typing in three-to-seven year old children. *Child Development, 57,* 1188–1199.

Sherman, J. A. (1982). Mathematics, the critical filter: A look at some residues. *Psychology of Women Quarterly, 6,* 428–444.

Shorris, E. (1992). *Latinos: A biography of the people.* New York: Norton.

Signorella, M. L. (1987). Gender schemata: Individual differences and context effects. *New Directions for Child Development, 38,* 23–35.

Simpson, G. E., & Yinger, I. M. (1985). *Racial and cultural minorities: An analysis of prejudice and discrimination* (5th ed.). New York: Plenum.

Sowell, T. (1981). *Ethnic America: A history.* New York: Basic Books.

Stack, C. B. (1974). Sex roles and survival strategies in an urban Black community. In M. Z. Rosaldo & L. Lamphere (Eds.), *Women, culture, and society* (pp. 113–128). Stanford, CA: Stanford University Press.

Staples, J. (1988). The Black American family. In C. H. Mindel, R. W. Habenstein, & R. Wright (Eds.), *Ethnic families in America: Patterns and variations* (pp. 303–324). New York: Elsevier.

Stern, M., & Karraker, K. (1989). Sex stereotyping of infants: A review of gender labeling studies. *Sex Roles, 20,* 501–522.

Stevenson, H. W., Chen, C., & Uttal, D. H. (1990). Beliefs and achievement: A study of Black, White, and Hispanic children. *Child Development, 60,* 508–523.

Tanner, H. (1974). Matrifocality in Indonesia and Africa among black Americans. In M. Z. Rosaldo & L. Lamphere (Eds.), *Women, culture, and society* (pp. 129–156). Stanford, CA: Stanford University Press.

Thomas, T., & Robinson, M. (1981). Development of a measure of androgyny for adolescents. *Journal of Early Adolescence, 1,* 195–209.

Thomas, V. G., & Shields, L. C. (1987). Gender influences on work values of black adolescents. *Adolescence, 22,* 37–43.

Tolson, T. F., & Wilson, M. N. (1990). The impact of two- and three-generational Black family structure on perceived family climate [Special issue: Minority children]. *Child Development, 61,* 416–428.

True, R. H. (1990). Psychotherapeutic issues with Asian American women [Special issue: Gender and ethnicity]. *Sex Roles, 22,* 477–486.

Wilson, M. N., Tolson, T. F., & Hinton, I. D. (1990). Flexibility and sharing of childcare duties in Black families [Special issue: Gender and ethnicity]. *Sex Roles, 22*, 409–425.

Zalk, S. R., & Katz, P. A. (1978). Gender attitudes in children. *Sex Roles, 4*, 349–357.

6

STIRRING TROUBLE AND MAKING THEORY

JILL G. MORAWSKI and BETTY M. BAYER

The trouble with culturally diverse theory in feminist psychology is that everything is trouble. We begin with a paradox: Feminist thinking in the social sciences (and of critical thought in general) has generated provocative and trenchant analyses that simultaneously render the most basic tools, language, and even the very institution of science problematic. Over the past 25 years, feminist and critical psychologists have uncovered the androcentric axes structuring what is taken to be "psychology" and what psychologists aspire to when we make "theory." They have uncovered unsettling components that comprised our traditional categories of "woman" and "gender." Such critical scrutiny has revealed troublesome implications that arise from studying cultural diversity, including problems with the

From the outset, our task to approach the possibility of cultural diverse theory in psychology posed plentiful troubles, and we soon discovered that we could do nothing less than make trouble. Later, we encountered Judith Butler's mapping of gender trouble and are indebted to her extensive analyses. We also thank Melanie Killen, Hope Landrine, Roslyn Mendelson, Scott Plous, and Robert Steele for their critical readings and suggestions. Preparation of this chapter was supported in part by a Social Sciences and Humanities Research Council of Canada Postdoctoral Fellowship awarded to Betty M. Bayer.

notions of race, class, and diversity itself. And, to add paradox to paradox, even the newer correctives to the totalizing nature of these categories are creating havoc as some feminist scholars have identified nontrivial, if latent, problems with these "postmodern," "interpretive" and "relativist" alternatives to the conventional perspective.

Such impasses in knowledge production are not accidental: The gateway to theories of knowing has not been locked by the workings of happenstance, but by pervasive and long-standing social and political conditions (Kahn & Yoder, 1989; Morawski, 1988). A sense of impasse has been one paradoxical outcome of the success of feminist work. For instance, some of the few feminist scholars who have achieved substantial recognition within academia have done so, in part, by devising abstracted, dense, and universalizing theories. In other words, they have advanced by undertaking the abstract theorizing common to androcentric science rather than engaging feminist activism or pedagogy. Similarly, many feminist researchers have worked to recover and privilege "women's experience." Yet, all too frequently their efforts have resulted in the reification of the categories that sustain oppressive relations; thus, research on women's experience tends to "repeat our litany of woe, a repetition of clichés and stereotypes about victims and heroines" (Marks, 1985, p. 105). From these paradoxes and impasses, one may sense that everything is trouble in the making of culturally diverse theories. Nevertheless, in following this step, we must be mindful that (a) some troubles may be the accompaniments of feminist psychologists' successes in countering the conventions of a sexist world and, at the same time, (b) some troubles may derive from long-standing and recurrent resistances to feminism.

We also must be mindful of the fact that although the successes of feminist inquiry may be paradoxical, they are not necessarily tautological; we need not end where we began—with exclusive and oppressive worldviews. In trying to envision how we might create more inclusive theories (meaning that the theories are grounded in sociohistorical meanings of race, class, gender, and ethnicity), we are inevitably engaged in an historical dialectic with past theoretical constructions. As feminist psychologists we are in a liminal space—that place in ritualized passage betwixt and between what has been assumed to be real and possible, however problematic those assumptions, and what awaits our imaginative envisioning (Morawski, 1994).

This chapter is an adventure in and through such thresholds of liminality, an excursion aspiring to inspire metamorphoses of theory making. We discuss problematic areas of contemporary theory work and some specific places of liminality to reconfigure not only categories and constructs but also scientific practice itself. We also discuss several strategies for shifting from a practice of problematics—paradoxes and impassess—to a practice of possibilities.

MAKING CATEGORICAL REALITIES

It is not that psychology has failed historically to incorporate the concepts of race, class, gender, and sexual orientation, but rather that it has constituted them through a set of premises that exclude and privilege. Part of the critical work of theory making involves relinquishing the hold that traditional, empiricist paradigms have on these concepts. This work proceeds first by understanding how conventional concepts serve a particular social order. As such, it entails interrogation of psychology's theoretical commitment to certain definitions of gender, ethnicity, race, and class; in such interrogations, we ask who and what has benefited from these definitions. It also requires an examination of the extent to which these definitions construe social relations as hierarchical, relatively static, and universal. In doing this kind of critical work, we must, as Haraway (1989) remarked, "look always through the lenses ground on the stones of the complex histories of gender and race in the constructions of modern sciences" (p. 8). We must always consider what cultural productions are enabled or restricted (or disabled) by scientific practice, as well as how these cultural productions inscribe on scientific studies of race, class, and gender varying subjectivities and varying relations of power.

Analyses of the dominant concepts of psychological theory and method accommodate the workings of a particular social order, one manifest in the partisan values of liberalism, individualism, and capitalism (Cushman, 1990; Danziger, 1990; Graebner, 1981; Harris, 1984; Sampson, 1978). Thus, for instance, contemporary conceptualizations of cognition reaffirm notions of autonomous individuals and obscure the problems of economics and social structure by emphasizing mental conditions over material ones (Sampson, 1981). The relation between psychological concepts and politics is not one way. Critical inquiry has shown how epistemology and methodology in social science also govern cultural conditions in such a way as to streamline diversity into a uniform cultural production of presupposed universal consequence. As Rose (1990) wrote, "psychological knowledge and techniques . . . forge new alignments between the rationales and techniques of power and the values and ethics of democratic societies" (p. 4). It is in the light of such an interactive and culturally specific production that an understanding begins to emerge of the psychological concept of gender as systematically interlocked with racism, classism, and sexism (hooks, 1990). Class, race, gender, and ethnicity are thus socially constructed markers of already-marked psychological consequence as much as they are psychologically constructed markers of marked social consequence. Either way, they signify existing relations of power.

These critical inquiries must delve below the surface features of exclusions or inclusions and go beyond mere attempts to reconceptualize or correct biases in what are often taken to be otherwise worthy empirical enterprises. Feminist and nonfeminist critics alike take psychology's treatment of race, gender, class, and ethnicity to be a much more epistemologically entrenched and complicated affair. For example, from early psychological research on mental traits to the subsequent research on prejudice and discrimination and, later, to research on race or ethnic relations, it has been shown that empiricism, contrary to claims of objective knowledge making, has never been situated outside of political or social influence (Samelson, 1978). In another case, a trend analysis of developmental research on African American children found the research to be sensitive to various social movements of different historical moments. However, at the same time, that research was found to be insensitive to how psychology's reigning paradigm set up the preconditions for comparative studies in which the standard ideal remains White and middle class. Without critical reflection, the research also has promoted "person-blame interpretations of social problems" (McLloyd & Randolph, 1986, p. 91). These cases indicate that sensitivity toward or mere inclusion of underrepresented social groups does not guarantee the eradication of bias, social myths, or hierarchical assumptions. Based on an individual–society dichotomy (which itself is filtered through the enmeshed workings of liberalism, individualism, and capitalism), psychological theory and practice allows "even radical analyses to be pressed into the service of existing social relations, thereby reinforcing and perpetuating them" (Henriques, 1984, p. 60). Thus, social psychological studies, intended to replace sexist and racist biological theories, remain anchored to constraining or otherwise problematic assumptions. For instance, social psychological theorists have tended to first identify racial or ethnic relations in terms of problems (e.g., prejudice and discrimination) and then to locate their causes in the irrational thought (or cognitions) of an individual. By reducing analysis of the social to the level of the individual, social psychology joins cognitive psychology in the erasure of social relations and material conditions (Henriques, 1984; Lopes, 1991; Sampson, 1981).

A similar case can be made for research on sex and gender. Initial research focused on sex and mental traits but was replaced later by a focus on personality traits, social roles, and gender cognitions (schemas). This shift, although signaling a move toward gender as a "social category imposed on a sexed body" (Scott, 1986, p. 1056), nevertheless leaves basically undisturbed both psychology's prevailing empirical paradigm with its emphasis on the existence of differences and evaluation (ranking) of those differences. Likewise, remaining even after this shift to gender as a social category are cultural presuppositions about men and women (Hare-Mustin & Marecek, 1990; Morawski, 1987; Unger, 1989). Although attending to ethnicity, class, race, and gender in psychological theory may displace psychology's reliance on White, middle-class norms, such efforts rarely disrupt empiricism's "prediscursive structure" of hierarchically organized, foundational, and oppositional categories (Butler, 1990a). Rather, the regulatory functions of epistemology and methodology transform these dynamic and fluid social meanings into static, bounded, and foundational social categories. The use of such social categorization then makes them appear to be social givens, to be "natural" rather than "social" constructions.

Two suggested models for more inclusive research elucidate how moves toward inclusive theory, in failing to extend their analyses to the paradigm itself, reach similar theoretical dead-ends. In the first model, identity components and forms of oppression are analyzed additively. This model operates with the assumptions that race and class and gender function independently of one another and that their separate or distinct effects can be combined through addition (or separated through subtraction). The attempt to add diverse components of identity and oppression, however, often functions to erase from view the very women it purportedly seeks to embrace. With such an additive model, "proposals to include 'different' viewpoints amount to keeping race and class peripheral to feminist inquiry even while seeming to attend to them" (Spelman, 1988, p. 167). That is, non-White and non-middle-class women are simply added to preexisting theories. One result of this building-block approach to studying cultural diversity is that the all-too-often White, middle-class norms are left intact. In this theory revision, psychological phenomena are presumed to be context free rather than context dependent. A second consequence of this approach is that of treating race, class, and sexual orientation as additive qualities of oppression. The assumption here is that the same psychological phenomena vary only by degree for women of different social groups. In other words, endeavors to make visible and to include in theory those people previously made invisible and excluded may be founded on specious premises when we do not centrally locate, race, class, and gender in our feminist theories. For example, most studies of women and eating disorders have relied on young, White, and middle-class norms. When Black women are studied, which has been rarely the case, they are compared to this norm, and conclusions are drawn about how their race "buffers" them from the American cultural ideal of hyperslender women. By contrast, research focusing on African American and Jamaican women has revealed that they do not see their race as protecting them from such cultural ideals of female bodies. Instead, they use different strategies both to negotiate the meanings of multiple (sometimes opposing) body-image ideals and to regulate their body size (Obiechina & Bayer, 1994). Here, we can see how stepping outside of comparative analyses leads to a much different understanding of Black women and their bodies and may suggest ways to rethink how questions about body-image and eating disorders are studied.

In the second model, various components of gender, race, and class are combined interactively or multiplicatively; that model is structured to compare Black, middle-, and lower-class women with White middle- and lower-class women (e.g., Reid & Comas-Díaz, 1990; Smith & Stewart, 1983). Although this approach seems to offer a theoretical improvement over the additive model, it renders such social groupings essential and fixed. Black, middle-class, heterosexual women, for example, become almost a unitary class, and the approach produces a durable and singular understanding of all women fitting that description. Furthermore, such multiplicative identities pose the possibility of infinite forms (i.e., factoring in other categories such as religion or health status or whatever suggests the need to create a new class). Multiplying and mixing social categories, in the end, sows the seeds of its own destruction, for "if the analyses were taken far enough, even these names would begin to show the ragged edges for their own limits are unitary determinations" (Spivak, 1987, p. 114). The dialectic of determinate and indeterminate relations at the intersections of race, gender, and class are turned into static, definitive, and fixed boundaries. In so doing, relations are made into objects and variables, ever more amenable to dissection. When race, class, and gender are objectified in this way, psychological theory denies ways in which they enter "into the research process itself—into the selection of a problem, into the methodology . . . and [into] the relationship with those we are researching" (Edwards, 1990, p. 482). Psychological theory and method alike thus work together to flatten and to homogenize both the innumerable dimensions of gender, race, and class, and the relations among them. It returns researchers to an ironic homogeny of heterogeneous types. The kind of self or subjectivity that this approach constructs is (despite its multiple determinations) no less individualistic or essentialist than that found in nonintegrative theories.

Neither model helps to counter or rework those social relations that have served as the standard or normative order in psychological theory and research. Indeed, it can be argued that such adjustments to psychology's prevailing logical empiricist paradigm may, contrary to a researcher's intention, simply underscore the centrality of a White, middle-class psychology (Zinn, Cannon, Higginbotham, & Dill, 1986). By keeping this social group at its core, "other" social groups continue to be relegated to the periphery of theory and research or to be treated as a "special case." One can see, then, how the underlying assumptions of psychology's positivist paradigm, in both the additive or multiplicative–interactive models, function to perpetuate the status quo. That is, "Whiteness" is not only left unexamined, but its centrality is now maintained by the inclusion of non-White, non-middle-class women. Two main problems follow from these kinds of limited alterations to psychology's traditional paradigm. First, the seemingly monolithic politics of the paradigm place such diverse representations at the margins or periphery before they are even brought into an epistemological discourse. The paradigm thereby reinscribes the central position of White, middle-class representations (e.g., Gordon, 1985; King,

1988). Being *brought* into a discourse from the outset signals a marginality that functions to keep the center central. Second, questions about Whiteness and about the presumed centrality of this social category are often ignored. That is, the meaning of being White, middle-class, and heterosexual, and of the privileges that come with this social position are left untheorized and unexamined (see Frankenberg, 1993). Predetermined positionings of selves as marginal, as "other," leave uninterrogated the center—traditionally White ethnicity—and thereby "redoubles" its hegemony "by naturalizing it" (hooks, 1990, p. 171; see also Christian, 1989a). The theoretical work to be done, then, involves a deconstruction of what researchers have for so long constructed as the "center," in addition to refashioning central theoretical constructions. This does not mean that we simply replace the center with what it constitutes as marginal, but, as Spivak (1987) argued, that we seek to displace the center through the agency of positioning themselves within it and making knowable the center's marginal politics. Such a move requires that we accept "theory" as comprising cultural histories and theoretical stability as an interest in reproducing those same cultural histories (Spivak, 1987). As Butler (1990a) stated, this is problematic: "The question is not: what meaning does that inscription carry within it, but what cultural apparatus arranges this meeting between instrument and body, what interventions into this ritualistic repetition are possible?" (p. 146).

In combination, these feminist critiques present far-reaching challenges to theory making, ones that can be usefully extended to psychology. As we have attempted to point out in our discussion of the additive or interactive approaches to making theory and research culturally diverse, psychologists' tools of knowledge production can never be assumed to be politically neutral. Rather, they must be scrutinized for ways in which they function to reproduce hierarchical social relations among women of differing races, classes, ethnicities, and sexual orientation. We must also see how our traditional approaches direct us toward individual-centered psychological theories instead of toward the historical, social, and cultural contingencies of psychological phenomena, as well as ways of seeing and thinking about our everyday lives. Similarly, psychologists' routine investigative practices need be examined for how our theorizing, research designs, questions, and writing style impose limitations on a multicultural psychology. We must consider how these "tools of the trade" can arrange the inclusion of forgotten and ignored "others," of voices silenced by assumptions of a universal psychological subject and subjectivity. We also need to move back several steps to ask ourselves about the very categories of race, class, ethnicity, and sexual orientation that we take to be "natural" givens rather than cultural constructions. Similarly, it seems that we need to confront our equation of these social categories with cultural reality and of multiple categories with cultural diversity. Unraveling the meanings of these categories therefore is as key to culturally diverse psychological theories as is an examination of how conventional uses of these categories might function to preserve rather than alter dominant–subordinate-type relations that are based on race, class, gender, ethnicity, and sexual relations. Taking cultural diversity seriously, then, will mean that psychologists must undertake theory making with difficult questions.

With full recognition that the difficulties and troubles that accompany any effort to revise or re-create the ways and means of culturally diverse psychological theories will not be remedied completely by a single theoretical swoop, we offer what we take to be crucial considerations for a revision of theory making. The most basic of these considerations, and the one from which the others follow, is that of changing our view of theory itself. Contrary to seeing theory as the glue that holds scientific variables together in some meaningful way or as the logic behind scientific hypotheses, we suggest that theory be understood as *practice* (and science as the practice of theory and knowledge making). By shifting to a view of theory as practice, the theory becomes characterized by action and reflection that is situated culturally and historically. As a result, when psychologists produce theory, they simultaneously create possibilities for selves, relations, and social actions.

Yet, the practice is perforce of a double nature: at the same time that it is to *direct* the ways of theory making, it must also *intervene* in those established and disciplined practices of psychological theory. It must, in all senses, break ground. Butler (1990a), in her writing on gender and sexuality, envisioned strategic intervention as "parodic practices in which the original, the authentic, and the real are themselves constituted as effects" (p. 146). That is, she posited intervention that "reengage[s] and reconsolidate[s] the very distinction between a privileged and naturalized . . . configuration and one that appears as derived, phantasmatic, and mimetic—a failed copy, as it were" (Butler, 1990a, p. 146). This means, as Butler suggested, that constructions of "fundamental locales" of identity are shown to be "uninhabitable" and therefore are observed as "political structures" (Butler, 1990a, 146–147). Following Butler's ideas, one might envision practice in terms of habitable locales. That is, our practice might well begin with the lived conditions of race, gender, class, and ethnicity (cf. hooks, 1990), with how our social relations, in many ways, structure their locales of identity, be they habitable or uninhabitable. Taking theory as practice and grounding this practice in the everyday world of social relations and psychological experiences is all part of making knowledge situated.

Although feminist theory in psychology has taken a first step toward such a view (with its emphasis on gender as a process of social interaction and not just an attribute, role, or ascribed quality), many feminist theorists do not regard this move as commensurate with theoretical diversity. Two examples illustrate how new theoretical understandings follow from situating knowledge within the context of social–cultural relations. Viewing oppression and subordination as arising not from attributes or traits but from disparate histories of social relations, Hurtado (1989), for example, analyzed the relationship between White women and Women of Color, including its conflict and tension, within the framework of their dissimilar historical relations to White men. Directing her attention to different forms of oppression rather than degrees of oppression, Hurtado elucidated White women's oppression in terms of subordination through "seduction" and Women of Color's oppression in terms of subordination through "rejection." Class is seen as mediating the "rewards of seduction" and the "sanctions of rejection" (Hurtado, 1989, p. 844). Hurtado's analysis disrupts a number of traditional fronts in psychology. Gender identity becomes understood as a historical construction of diverse and variable social relations, even though it remains "the marking mechanism through which subordination . . . is maintained" (Hurtado, 1989, p. 845). Dichotomized categories, such as public–private, visibility–invisibility, and silence–speech, simply do not hold up under the analytic weight of diverse histories of social relations. Also, once the dichotomies are dissolved, assumptions of universal, transhistorical, and abstract categories also begin to crumble, for they are constructed with and sustained through these bipolar categories.

These elaborations of the intricate relations among gender, ethnicity, and class were also made evident by Prell (1990). Her social and historical analysis of Jewish stereotypes showed how multifaceted understandings can spring forth when researchers break away from studies of differences between bounded categories. In looking at stereotypes for the Jewish mother (selfless giver) and "Jewish American princess" (self-focused consumer), Prell located the social origin of these stereotypes not in relations between women but in relations between Jewish men and American culture, which are then projected onto women. Stereotypes of Jewish women thus symbolize "the conflicts experienced by Jewish men as they negotiate their difference from and continuity with American culture" (Prell, 1990, p. 249). These stereotypes represent, as Prell noted, symbolic expressions of Jewish men's wishes and fears. Although Prell did extend her analysis far enough to take into account the production of the particular symbolic expressions, her approach of "reading" culture reveals the embeddedness of cultural constructions (Jewish) within other cultural constructions (American). Relations among ethnicity, class, and gender are thus shown to be a diverse complex of multiple, ongoing cultural histories.

Both of these studies demonstrate the possibility of moving beyond the staid and stymied places of theory making to cultural and historical sites of action and agency, where there are many diverse social and cultural relations. They also illustrate the theoretical benefits to be derived from pressing beyond simple and fixed social categories. In these cases, identity becomes refashioned as the result of complex social relations that are always undergoing revision in historically and culturally meaningful ways. Within these new theoretical sites, locales are diversified across, within, and without race, gender, ethnicity, and class. Within these locales, diversity prevails in historical, shifting, and dynamic meanings. Simple social–cultural categories of identity, social relations, or both are replaced by an elaboration of their interconnectedness. The hollowness of simple social–cultural categories of identity, social relations, or both is thereby made evident. Making theory in this way thus at once intervenes in psychology's conventional individual-centered theories and its ahistorical treatment of social relations.

Having stirred a few troubles with traditional conceptualizations of race, class, gender, culture, and diversity, we turn now to the terrain on which these troubles arose: social science at the boundaries of theory, method, and social relations. Our purpose here is to extend the ideas of theory as practice and knowledge as situated by exploring the social relations and practices of doing scientific work. This means that we examine how psychologists are inevitably a part of knowledge-making endeavors and how knowledge producers and the tools they use also need to be understood in historical and cultural terms.

DISTURBING BOUNDARIES IN THE SCIENCES

A dissection of problematic categories in psychology is not possible without deeper reflection on epistemological matters, on beliefs about the form and acquisition of valid knowledge. In fact, the predominant approach of feminist psychologists—that of adopting an empiricist episteme—eventually raised several crucial questions about empiricism. Feminist-empiricist psychologists initially located sexist practices not in epistemology (i.e., in the theories of knowledge) but in methodology, and they believed that the construction of nonsexist science required simply that bias be eliminated from empirical methods. Yet, in correcting these biases, feminist empiricists actually transgressed the epistemic boundaries of empiricism. For instance, in suggesting that sound (nonsexist) science would result from including more women in the scientific community, they violated the empiricist tenet that attributes of the observer are irrelevant to objective observation. Also, in occasionally admitting that science mirrors human values (in this case, sexist values), they compromised the empiricist conception of an objective fact that stands apart from any value. Finally, in describing science as a self-contained rule system, feminist empiricists overlooked the unfortunate fact that conforming to conventional methods, however sanitized of androcentric tendencies, often meant conforming to institutional practices that not only perpetuate sexism but also reject, blunt, or erase feminist scientific accomplishments (Fine & Gordon, 1990; Morawski, 1990; Parlee, 1991).

Several alternatives to empiricist epistemology have emerged in feminist science. Three of these alternatives are readily identifiable (Harding, 1986): standpoint feminism, radical relativism, and postmodern feminism. *Standpoint feminism* argues that material conditions of observers (the concrete and specific conditions in which they live and work) do affect scientific observation and that because of the specific conditions of their subordinate position in society, women make better observers. Women make better observers because they are more able to detect features of the physical and social world that members of more privileged groups (i.e., men) are unable to see.

Radical relativism ensues from the claim that all knowledge statements are constituted relative to the observer's position and, hence, knowledge is relative only to some time or place. However, the actual existence of any radically relativist feminist science (outside of "straw-man" portrayals of relativists by its opponents) needs to be further investigated.

Postmodern feminism is premised on the possibilities for developing scientific knowledge on an anti-foundationalist philosophy, on abandoning any claims to abstract or universal foundations to knowledge. This stance has been known more recently by the trademark "postmodern," with its claims that no fixed or transhistorical foundations of knowledge exist.

Of the three alternative epistemologies, postmodernism is most suited to addressing some of the difficulties that attend the search for culturally diverse theory or theoretical practice. In showing how all foundations of or guidelines for generating knowledge are the result of historically specific interests and ambitions, postmodernist inquiries compare favorably with feminist studies demonstrating how Western knowledge has been constituted through hierarchical gender relations, and how that knowledge serves to maintain those inequitable arrangements. The postmodern exposure of the idea of human agency as a legacy of a fantasy (dating back at least to the Enlightenment period) about independent, autonomous, and rational knowers corresponds to feminist investigations of the masculine orientation that undergirds the social sciences. Postmodernists further posit that human subjectivity is partial, fragmented, and multiple and is the product of local historical conditions in much the same way as feminist scholars have suggested that subjectivity is gendered in fragmentary, contradictory, and historically specific ways. Postmodern philosophies reconceptualize the search for knowledge as local, partial and tentative, and thus share with feminist scholars a refusal to blindly adopt traditional epistemologies (Flax, 1990; Fraser & Nicholson, 1990).

Postmodern or antifoundational philosophies offer a paradigm of social criticism that is congenial to feminist criticism, but they do not provide the solution to generating feminist theory. Despite the rejection of grand theory and metanarratives, these philosophies have tended to preserve certain essential premises about epistemology that, for instance, emphasize master theories and underappreciate concrete or lived experiences (Fraser & Nicholson, 1990; Skinner, 1985). More specifically, postmodern work tends to reproduce the transcendent and rational theorizer while constructing the "other" as partial and fractured (Hartstock, 1990). Such tendencies raise questions: Should those who remain outside positions of power not be suspicious of this epistemological move? Or, as Hartstock (1990) asked,

> Why is it that just at the moment when so many of us who have been silenced begin to demand the right to name ourselves, to act as subjects rather than objects of history, that just then the concept of subjecthood becomes problematic? Just when we are forming our own theories about the world, uncertainty emerges about whether the world can be theorized. (pp. 163–164; see also Christian, 1989b)

Postmodernism falters on another account: It fails to recognize the relatively stable macrostructures of power in society. Postmodern theorizing cannot accommodate the dominant axes that stratify power according to gender, race, and class. Systematic forms of social power are denied by postmodern theorists such as Foucault. Just as postmodernism denies or overlooks these social arrangements, it provides no legitimate means to envision an alternative social order. These conditions led Latour (1991) to define postmodernism as "a disappointed form of modernism. It shares with its enemy all its features but hope" (p. 17). The postmodern option, then, can lead feminist theorizing to yet another dead-end. And it will do so as long as feminist theorists construe their epistemological choices in simple or binary oppositions and thus remain "imprisoned by the alternatives imposed by Enlightenment thought and postmodernism," which insist that "either one must adopt the perspective of the transcendental and disembodied voice of 'reason' or one must abandon the goal of accurate and systematic knowledge of the world" (Hartstock, 1987, p. 17).

Other choices do remain possible, especially if feminists acknowledge the social, and thus socially strategic, nature of knowledge production, and if they remain vigilant about the inevitable consequences of continuing to adhere to oppositional and binary systems of knowledge (Addelson, 1983). A fuller array of choices emerges once we abandon the old schemas about the form and function of knowledge, particularly scientific knowledge. One set of alternative choices is emerging from recent work in social studies of science. Over the past two decades, the field of science studies has shown how science as practiced is remarkably different from science as recorded: These studies have demonstrated that what scientists do in their everyday activities is not what is recorded in either conventional scientific texts, histories of science, or philosophical models. In other words, "the whole edifice of epistemology, all the clichés about scientific method, about what it is to be a scientist, the paraphernalia of Science, was constructed out of science-made, out of science-past, never out of science in the making, science now" (Latour, 1991, p. 7). Such illustrated distinctions between mythic science and science as actually practiced open the way for rethinking those very practices. In particular, they open the way for reconsidering how science is made and, in turn, makes the world.

Taken together, the critical unpacking of theoretical categories, feminist objectives for new knowledge and politics, critical writings by members of oppressed groups, and radically different understandings of science multiply and transform the possibilities for theoretical action. Taken together, these movements demand that all boundaries, from the old demarcations between what is taken to be nature and culture to those between purportedly contesting epistemologies, need to be reconsidered. Taken together, these movements are essentially renegotiations of knowledge making that are at once transgressive, radical, and utopian. Although the specifics of such renegotiations cannot be fully spelled out here, some sense of the project can be conveyed through examples of such boundary reworking. For example, Haraway (1985) framed some of these possibilities in the form of a manifesto that links science studies, Marxist studies, and feminism. She invoked the image of a cyborg, an entity that is half human and half machine, to describe the dissolution of boundaries between machine and organism, human and animal, imagination and material reality, and physical and nonphysical entities. The boundary transgressions and "potent fusions" symbolically embodied in the cyborg myth help one to see not only how progressive intellectuals themselves remain caught in dualist thinking (especially when that thinking is about science and technology), but also how other visions of the world are possible. Although a cyborg world elicits immediate thoughts about the ultimate dangers of political domination and technological determinism, it also affords the opportunity to think creatively: "From another perspective, a cyborg world might be about lived social and bodily realities in which people are not afraid of their joint kinship with animals and machines, not afraid of permanently partial identities and contradictory standpoints" (Haraway, 1985, p. 72).

Another locus of boundary reworking occurring in science studies also has implications ranging far beyond science. Woolgar (1988b) identified several crucial boundaries produced through and sustained by scientific practices. These established and honored divides are neither stable nor certain and, for that reason, some of them constitute "methodological horrors" for scientists. For instance, presumed dualism of "representation" and the "object" to be represented raise horrors about the relation between the two. Although in science it is presupposed that objects in the world ultimately determine the (scientific) representations of those objects, in actuality representations can influence those very objects—their form, properties, and dynamics. Yet, to acknowledge this mutuality between objects in the world and representations of them threatens the conventional understanding of science itself. Scientists routinely seek not to acknowledge these multivalent dynamics but to cover over or manage them; in analyzing these management strategies, science studies researchers have unsettled another presumed boundary: the demarcation between science and all other human activities. The findings from science studies suggest that science proceeds with the same human resources and skills as do nonscientific activities. These studies suggest "that there is no essential difference between science and other forms of knowledge production; that there is nothing intrinsically special about 'the scientific method'" (Woolgar, 1988b, p. 12).

Dismantling the boundaries of science and nonscience, the demarcations between science and other everyday practices, has substantial implications for making theory, scientific claims, social policy, and politics. However, this particular boundary dissolution has even more radical implications because it reveals yet more obdurate dualisms that sustain science and nonscience alike. For example, Latour (1991) identified a historically constituted divide between what is taken to be "human" and "nonhuman." Originating in the 17th century, the dichotomy between human (with political representation) and nonhuman (with scientific representation) has underwritten a "political constitution of truth" that is more inclusive than a political consitution as it is conventionally understood, because the former deals with both human and nonhuman representation. A political constitution of truth "also distributes powers, will, rights to speak, and checks and balances. It decides on the crucial distribution of competence; for instance, matter has or does not have will; God speaks only to the heart and not of politics" (Latour, 1991, p. 13). Divisions between human–nonhuman, political–scientific, and social–natural serve the creation of "two separate parliaments, one hidden for things, the other open for citizens" (Latour, 1991, p. 15). A related divide in this political world also concerns agency, in this case the agents of representation "which mediate the world and its representations" (Woolgar, 1988b, p. 101). That is, Woolgar located in scientific practice a moral order that sustains representation; in this moral order, agents (scientists) are considered passive in the sense that they are thought to be incapable of affecting the form of the world, yet they are considered active in that they are understood as responsible for the representations they furnish. This drama of moral responsibility is difficult to see because agency is complex and obscured in scientific practices. For Woolgar (1988b), the task was even more challenging because it "is not just to understand the moral order which sustains the ideology of representation, but to seek ways of changing it" (p. 105).

The reworking of such boundaries through science studies has parallels in feminist studies, particularly in the work of Women of Color. For example, Dill (1987) identified several conventional markers that structure conventional research on Black women, including the oppositional play between concepts of femininity and Black women, class and culture, and autonomy and caring. Beyond these operational, oppositional confusions that recur in the research, Black women who engage in intellectual activities confront additional problems. Collins (1989) indicated how Black feminist theorists are expected to subscribe to a hegemonic epistemology that denigrates their identity as Black women. By recovering this identity in its historical specificity, Collins explored an alternative epistemological framework, one that dislodges the boundaries between self and knowledge production and between experience and what is taken to be a valid representation of that experience. From another perspective, Christian (1989b) opposed the "race for theory" because of its reinvention of an authoritative monolithism that excludes Women of Color; she called for reflexive work that would place Women of Color as subjects *and* agents of inquiry. By refusing the problematic boundaries between agent and representation, however refashioned in contemporary theorizing, Christian (1989a) forced hard questions to be asked: "To whom are we accountable? And what social relations are in/scribing us?" (p. 74).

PRACTICING POSSIBILITIES: IDENTITY, REFLEXIVITY, AND AFFINITY

The impasses in (feminist) empiricism, and the paradoxes that abound in feminist theorizing generally, complicate developing a culturally diverse psychological theory. The recent history of North American feminism records recurring, troubling divides. Although some feminists have called for a final resolution of these political and theoretical schisms (Alcoff, 1988), others have suggested that such a resolution is either impossible or undesirable (Snitow, 1990). Given the problems and possibilities recalled in this chapter, we stand among the latter group of feminist thinkers. We hold that no simple correction will mend the problems, but that unresolved tensions can be a generative force of unknown potential for strategic action. They can stimulate the reconceptualization of identity, social relations, and activism as they constitute the processes and products of knowledge making. In particular, they enable reconceptualizations that take gender, race, and class to be located in the social relations of knowledge making as well as in the social relations of other lived experiences. Feminists must make these new configurations with clear recognition of their dual ambitions in continuing "an *anti-sexist* project, which involves challenging and deconstructing phallocentric discourses; and in a positive project of constructing and developing alternative models, methods, procedures, discourses, etc." (Gross, 1986, p. 195).

Reconfiguring identity, social relations, and activist accomplishments, then, form "not a true discourse, nor a mere objective or scientific account. It could be appropriately seen, rather, as a *strategy*, a local, specific intervention with definite political, even if provisional aims and goals" (Gross, 1986, p. 196). This revising involves destabilizing and shifting the narrative field of conventional knowledge, rather than inventing an entirely different narrative (Haraway, 1986). It requires nothing more or less than working locally and tactically to name and revise identities, social relations, and intellectual practices. Above all, it demands awareness of one's engagement in the project. That is, whenever feminists introduce their identity (their subjectivity), they interrupt the taken-for-granted separations between the object and subject of knowledge. Whenever feminists make subjectivity the focus of their inquiry, they further tamper with the normative order of constituting truth. And whenever feminists suggest that identity (of observers and the observed alike) involves fictions, concealments, and multiplicities, they really make trouble (Braidotti, 1986; Butler, 1990b). In each of these instances, self-awareness or reflexivity is acknowledged.

In the construction of new theory, reflexivity becomes significant not only as a general property of all theory (i.e., theories are always reflexive either in intentional or inadvertent forms) but also as central to the very process of theory building. That is, ceasing to take identity (subjectivity) for granted goes well beyond mere explication of the analyst's personal values. Simple efforts at value clarification or the naming of certain attributes of the analyst-scientist, in the end, avert confronting reflexivity. Those efforts either assume that there is some simple correspondence between intellectual discourse and its producer (i.e., feminist texts are related to female authors, sexist texts to male authors) or pretend that any correspondence between discourse and producers can be eliminated (by proclaiming feminist values, the author thereby becomes more objective). Such remedial strategies, reliant as they are on common sense and stereotypes, merely expose superficial features of identity and its relation to scientific representations. The irony in this is that these same superficial features may serve to restrain further exploration because with them comes the belief that some meaningful semblance of reflexivity has been realized.

Taking subjectivity more seriously means taking reflexivity more seriously. Reflexivity is most generally defined as "a turning back on oneself, a form of self-awareness" (Lawson, 1985, p. 9). Reflexivity is the self-referential character of theory and "an aspect of all social science, since any statement which holds that humans act or believe in particular ways under particular circumstances refers as much to the social scientist as to anyone else" (Gruenberg, 1978, p. 322). Viewed from a larger perspective, reflexivity concerns the very relations between object (reality) and agents' representations (observers' accounts of reality); it refers to that back-and-forth process whereby making sense of an account of reality depends on preexisting knowledge of what that account refers to and vice versa (Ashmore, 1989; Woolgar, 1988a). Thus, reflexivity undermines the assumed independence of representation and object (that was discussed earlier) because "the character of representation, as perceived by the actor, changes to accommodate the perceived nature of underlying reality and the latter simultaneously changes to accommodate the former" (Woolgar, 1988b, p. 33).

Once this broader presence of reflexivity is acknowledged, the awareness of analyst and the awareness of object are seen to be bound together. Self-regard and other-regard are interdependent. With these acknowledgements, we return to Christian's (1989a) question: "To whom are we accountable? And what social relations are inscribing us?" (p. 74). Feminists also can join Woolgar in the task of discovering (and redefining) the moral order of the self that exists in the constitution of truth statements. And as Snitow (1990) suggested, each of these undertakings requires "an internal as well as external struggle about goals and tactics" (p. 29). In summary, reflexivity concerns the analyst's lived relations in a collective enterprise, locating agency and moral responsibility, and continual attention to the shifting social and moral order of representation.

Two experiments illustrate the task of reflexive work and the unstable relations of self-regard and other-regard that must be examined in theory construction and research. Linden (1990) conducted an ethnographic study of Holocaust survivors in which she, the analyst, was reflexively positioned within the study (and within the final written account). Linden (1990) challenged ethnographic dualisms of subject and object, self and other, and historically specific events and transhistorical knowledge "by inscribing myself in the text, as a partner in dialogue or as an active commentator on 'native' discourses" (p. 6). Linden wove her account of survivors' accounts of their lives with her changing accounts of those accounts over the years. The weaving was not of disparate strands, for Linden attended to the mutual interdependence of tellers and creators of accounts. In particular, Linden (1990) reflected on her earlier bewilderment over one of her interviewee's decision to join the resistance and thus further risk her life during the war years:

> The limitations of my lived experience—and hence, of my imagination—are reflected in the fact that I didn't understand the force of her words, and perhaps I still do not. Now as I reread my interpretation of her decision to join the underground, my own hypostatized meanings

of resistance are reflected back to me. I feel as though I am staring into a mirror at my own image. (p. 17)

Linden revealed how ethnographic subjects are constructed through multiple levels of social relations, varied positionings of self and other, and inscription techniques that are structured by culture and historical resources, including language and epistemic rules. Her intersubjective writing also indicated the indexicality of representation—the continual shifts of meaning and interpretation over time. These interpretative shifts are as dependent on the interrogator and her relation to the participants as they are on the participant's particular framework.

A second experiment dealt with the textual interplay of other-regard and self-regard in psychological articles. Morawski and Steele (1991) examined a selection of psychological writings for the implicit construals of femininity and masculinity that sustained the accounts being given in these writings. Most of the texts that were sampled contained representations of males as self, agent, analyst, masterful, rational, and female as other, subject, dependent, and bad. However, in the feminist psychological writings, these dichotomies of self–other, agent–subject were fractured, and multiple selves were empowered in different social relations. While demonstrating an inadvertent form of reflexive practice, however, Morawski and Steele resisted reflexivity. In depicting how pervasive cultural relations of power (in this case, gender relations) help sustain scientific discourse, Morawski and Steele actually relied on conventions of scientific discourse. Not only did the study depend on the traditional structure of theoretical debate in psychology (between contesting and opposing positions, between the masculine and feminine), but it maintained the persona of the passive analyst: "We have written of others and disclosed little of ourselves, and rarely been in doubt. Like the good experimenter, we have kept our distance and avoided personal involvement" (Morawski & Steele, 1991, p. 128). Like good experimenters, Morawski and Steele also took responsibility for their representations, but not for the character of the world (Woolgar, 1988b). Although the authors acknowledged the fragility of their textual representations, they pushed the exploration of reflexivity no further: Their selves and their world remained in a safety box. Had the authors gone further, had they pursued additional reflexive work, they might have gone beyond exposing their own dependence on discursive practices. They also might have confronted their reluctance either to transgress these discursive practices or to examine more closely the political and moral axes on which these practices are structured. Such confrontations might have meant getting experimental in the truest sense of the word, that is, it might have meant writing in an unorthodox way (e.g., use of poems, pictures, fiction). Or it might have meant getting personal (e.g., talk of promotions, fears, their own relationship). In the end, however, these alternative practices might have meant not getting published.

Inclusive psychological theory will require investigation of the social relations that enable subject and object, self and other, and object and representation. It will require much different experiments with identity and reflexivity, perhaps even many false starts and failed attempts. Our successes, however, probably will be readily identifiable more by successive changes to the way we write and think about identity than by some absolute measure of the goodness of our reflexive efforts. To say this, however, does not assuage us of our own reflexive responsibility in the writing of this chapter. Our conclusions can serve as a practice field for exploring these responsibilities.

Conclusion 1

How, then, do we reflexively locate ourselves in the proposals we offer of feminist strategies toward realizing culturally diverse, psychological theory? We envision our reflexive efforts through Haraway's (1985) idea of affinity projects or groups ("related not by blood but by choice, the appeal of one chemical nuclear group for another, avidity," p. 72). Although our work is in the local context of knowledge production, and our representations are shaped by our nationalities, and by the local contours of ourselves as feminists, White, women, academics, mothers, and colleagues, our affinity project as a "response through coalition, not identity" (p. 73) seeks to subvert or alter our own partial locations. We share an affinity with those who endeavor to disrupt the hegemonic hold of science as traditionally practiced and hence to change the political conditions that structure our social relations. To accomplish this end, our affinity project has moved along diverse avenues of intellectual thought. Shortcomings and all, we take our work to be an affinity project wherein reflexivity comes to mean, in this case, a marshaling of agencies to a political end of creating theoretical perturbations.

Conclusion 2

In trying to enter personally into this discourse to turn theory back on itself, I, Betty, find myself confronted with specific questions about practicing reflexivity that are making a little trouble of their own. For example, by placing my personal reckoning at the conclusion of our chapter, is it therefore an afterthought, an epilogue to the main text? And, if so, does this mean that the main text is depersonalized (cf. Miller, 1991)? Do I signal either my central or my marginal relation to the main text by having some final personal say? By positioning reflective writing at the end, have

I paradoxically donned the robes of traditional discourse in my efforts to shed them? Does my language of "center" or "margin" perpetuate or resist tradition? And, do these personal disclosures reflexively involve theory or do they just exist alongside theory work?

For me, personal appraisal, as one form of reflexive practice, not only raises those questions, but it also presents me with a bit of conundrum. Whatever I choose to include, disclose, gloss over, or exclude rests with me and my demands of myself as one of the authors (and not from readers or authors whose texts I have drawn on). To acknowledge such conditions is to realize that reflexive practice is also about the personal responsibility I assume in writing these words, in fashioning my relationship to theory, and especially my relationship to culturally diverse theoretical work. Reflexive practice involves, but is not limited to, the relations between me and theory, between my personal authorial voice and theory's authorial voice. Miller (1991) called this the "double challenge" (i.e., the problem of "recast[ing] the subject's relation to itself and to authority, the authority *in* theory" (p. 21). But this challenge prompts an additional consideration: To whom am I writing these personal words? To Jill? To the theorists in this chapter? To readers? To myself? To everyone?

One way to look at these relations is by examining what is concealed and what revealed when I adopt the traditional discursive practice of theory making. Such an authorial voice, for example, serves not only to distance me from the theories I discuss but also to conceal my very work of selecting, interpreting, and positioning the theories I have drawn on. That voice conveys nothing about the relation between me and these theories because I have not made this relationship known. And, in a curious twist of events, I remain masked by the traditional position assumed by theorists—posing either as a medium through which these texts speak or as a mediator who negotiates the ways and means of making culturally diverse feminist theory (an authorial position whichever way one looks at it). On this front, I have not been as disruptive as I set out to be. While engaged in this process of working out a way to make possible the practice of culturally diverse feminist psychology, I find myself merely sketching the contours of how I (seeking to be more than a interlocutor, a commentator, or interpreter) engage the personal in the practice of theory. For it may be that only through reflexive work on our relations to culturally diverse feminist theories that we will begin to change our social relations of practice, and this would indeed be the most stirring trouble we could introduce to theory making.

Conclusion 3

One of the troubles less thoroughly stirred than others in this chapter is that of reflexivity: the quandary of the subject's identity (researcher's subjectivity) in representations of reality. Reflexivity sometimes proves to be an odd ingredient in a study of culture because it appears to demand emphasis on individual identity in the study of an ostensibly collective phenomena. In this concoction, the identity of "we," the authors, is positioned in a distinctly conventional way; "we" are an authorial third-person plural voice. But that positioning is rent with complications, not the least of which is a problem of the multiple positioning I, Jill, assume: In the third-person collective voice of this chapter's coauthor; in a separate third-person plural voice created with the coauthor of another article, Robert Steele; and in my own textual voice referenced by several recent publications.

The matter of positioning these authorial voices is complicated even further if the status of psychology's literary style is considered, especially its clarion renunciation of the subjective or personal. My multiple voices, although faint sounds against an orchestrated positivist science, in some (perhaps ironic) ways conform to the profession's constraints on discursive practices. And to complicate matters again, my writings also transpire in a culture of feminist scholarship, with its own literary and discursive standards. As Miller (1991) recalled, feminist works of the 1970s "were clearly fueled by taking the personal as a category of thought and gender as category of analysis" (p. 14). However, these initial motivations were followed by a "self-conscious depersonalization" in feminist writings of the 1980s as researchers refined feminist theories and established legitimate lines of inquiry. In other words, my complicated multiple voices conform, in varying degrees, to contemporary disciplinary standards.

Despite or perhaps because of such complex layering of authorial voices, and deference to disciplinary styles of writing, our chapter concludes (the first conclusion) with a commitment to affinities, to "coalition, not identity." By demanding attention to social relations, to coalitional affinities, the claim does establish a vantage point for speaking and writing somewhere between the social and the personal. Yet, such a capstone claim also saves me from fully confronting the multiple collective "we's" in which my "self" speaks. By displacing my "self" through attention to coalitions, I can proceed with the project of writing about cultural diversity while being a White, professional middle-class, faculty member at an elite university, and so forth. These reflections prompt a question: Does the first conclusion describe viable practices or a form of "passing"? As I contemplate this awkward and difficult question, I am compelled yet again to "get" theoretical, to use that very question as an illustration of how massive is the project of a reflexive psychology—the project of expanding theoretical practices to include the personal. Similarly, I am tempted to add another thoroughly theoretical comment on the multiplicity and fragmentation of identities in contemporary culture. These are not horrendous moves, but however promising, they do push us back into a textual position that evades or dislodges the "personal." These reflections prompt a second question: Why, when I try to "get" personal, do I seem to end up getting abstract? Is the personal held captive by discursive practices of theorizing? In the feminist psychology to come, or at least in my involvement with it, these two questions must be addressed.

REFERENCES

Addelson, K. P. (1983). The man of professional wisdom. In S. Harding & M. B. Hintikka (Eds.), *Discovering reality: Feminist perspectives on epistemology, metaphysics, methodology and philosophy of science* (pp. 165–186). Boston: Reidel.

Alcoff, L. (1988). Cultural feminism versus post-structuralism: The identity crisis in feminist theory. *Signs, 13,* 405–436.

Ashmore, M. (1989). *The reflexive thesis: Writing the sociology of scientific knowledge.* Chicago: University of Chicago Press.

Braidotti, R. (1986). Ethics revisited: Women and/in philosophy. In C. Pateman & E. Gross (Eds.), *Feminist challenges: Social and political theory* (pp. 44–60). Boston: Northeastern University Press.

Butler, J. (1990a). *Gender trouble: Feminism and the subversion of identity.* New York: Routledge & Kegan Paul.

Butler, J. (1990b). Gender trouble, feminist theory, and psychoanalytic discourse. In C. J. Nicholson (Ed.), *Feminism/postmodernism* (pp. 324–340). New York: Routledge & Kegan Paul.

Christian, B. (1989a). But what do we think we're doing anyway: The state of black feminist criticism(s) or my version of a little bit of history. In C. A. Wall (Ed.), *Changing our own words* (pp. 58–74). New Brunswick, NJ: Rutgers Univeristy Press.

Christian, B. (1989b). The race for theory. In L. Kaufman (Ed.), *Gender and theory: Dialogues on feminist criticism* (pp. 225–237). Oxford, England: Basil Blackwell.

Collins, P. (1989). The social construction of black feminist thought. *Signs, 14,* 745–773.

Cushman, P. (1990). Why the self is empty: Toward a historically situated psychology. *American Psychologist, 45,* 599–611.

Danziger, K. (1990). *Constructing the subject: Historical origins of psychological research.* Cambridge, England: Cambridge University Press.

Dill, B. T. (1987). The dialectics of black womanhood. In S. Harding (Ed.), *Feminism and methodology* (pp. 97–108). Bloomington: Indiana University Press.

Edwards, R. (1990). Connecting method and epistemology: A white woman interviewing black women. *Women's Studies International Forum, 13,* 477–490.

Fine, M., & Gordon, S. M. (1990). Feminist transformations of/despite psychology. In M. Crawford & M. Gentry (Eds.), *Gender and thought: Psychological perspectives* (pp. 146–174). New York: Springer-Verlag.

Flax, J. (1990). *Thinking fragments: Psychoanalysis, feminism, and postmodernism in the contemporary west.* Berkeley: University of California Press.

Frankenberg, R. (1993). *The social construction of whiteness: White women, race matters.* Minneapolis: University of Minnesota Press.

Fraser, W., & Nicholson, L. J. (1990). Social criticism without philosophy: An encounter between feminism and postmodernism. In L. J. Nicholson (Ed.), Feminism/postmodernism (pp. 19–38). New York: Routledge & Kegan Paul.

Gordon, E. W. (1985). Social science knowledge production and minority experiences. *Journal of Negro Education, 54,* 117–132.

Graebner, W. (1981). The unstable world of Benjamin Spock: Social engineering in a democratic culture, 1917–1950. *Journal of American History, 67,* 612–629.

Gross, E. (1986). What is feminist theory? In C. Pateman & E. Gross (Eds.), *Feminist challenges: Social and political theory* (pp. 190–204). Boston: Northeastern University Press.

Gruenberg, B. (1978). The problem of reflexivity in the sociology of science. *Philosophy of Social Science, 8,* 321–343.

Haraway, D. (1985). A manifesto for cyborgs: Science, technology, and socialist feminism in the 1980's. *Socialist Review, 15,* 65–107.

Haraway, D. (1986). Primatology is politics by other means. In R. Bleier (Ed.), *Feminist approaches to science* (pp. 77–118). Elmsford, NY: Pergamon Press.

Haraway, D. (1989). *Primate visions: Gender, race and nature in the world of modern science.* New York: Routledge & Kegan Paul.

Harding, S. (1986). The instability of the analytical categories of feminist theory. *Signs, 11,* 645–664.

Hare-Mustin, R., & Marecek, J. (Ed.). (1990). *Making a difference.* New Haven, CT: Yale University Press.

Harris, B. (1984). Give me a dozen healthy infants: John B. Watson's popular advice on childrearing, women and the family. In M. Lewin (Ed.), *In the shadow of the past: Psychology portrays the sexes* (pp. 126–154). New York: Columbia University Press.

Hartstock, N. C. M. (1987). The feminist standpoint: Developing the ground for a specifically feminist historical materialism. In S. Harding (Ed.), *Feminism and methodology* (pp. 157–180). Bloomington: Indiana University Press.

Hartstock, N. C. M. (1990). Foucault on power: A theory for women? In L. J. Nicholson (Ed.), *Feminism/post-modernism* (pp. 157–175). New York: Routledge & Kegan Paul.

Henriques, J. (1984). Social psychology and the politics of racism. In J. Henriques, W. Hollway, C. Urwin, C. Venn, & V. Walkerdine (Eds.), *Changing the subject: Psychology, social regulation and subjectivity.* London: Methuen.

hooks, b. (1990). *Yearning: Race, gender, and cultural politics.* Boston: South End Press.

Hurtado, A. (1989). Relating to privilege: Seduction and rejection in the surbordination of white women and women of color. *Signs, 14,* 833–855.

Kahn, A. S., & Yoder, J. D. (1989). The psychology of women and conservatism: Rediscovering social change. *Psychology of Women Quarterly, 13,* 417–432.

King, D. K. (1988). Multiple jeopardy, multiple consciousness: The context of a black feminist ideology. *Signs, 14,* 42–72.

Latour, B. (1991). The impact of science studies on political philosophy. *Science, Technology, and Human Values, 16,* 3–19.

Lawson, H. (1985). *Reflexivity: The post-modern predicament.* LaSalle, IL: Open Court.

Linden, R. (1990). *Threshold ethnography: Life histories as liminal texts.* Unpublished manuscript.

Lopes, L. L. (1991). The rhetoric of irrationality. *Theory and Psychology, 1,* 65–82.

Marks, E. (1985). Feminism's wake. *Boundary Two, 14,* 99–111.

McLloyd, V. C., & Randolph, S. M. (1986). Secular trends in the study of Afro-American children: A review of child development, 1936–1980. *Monographs of the Society for Research in Child Development, 211*(50, Serial No. 4–5).

Miller, N. K. (1991). *Getting personal: Feminist occasions and other autobiographical acts.* New York: Routledge & Kegan Paul.

Morawski, J. G. (1987). The troubled quest for masculinity, feminity and androgyny. *Review of Personality and Social Psychology, 7,* 44–69.

Morawski, J. G. (1988). Impasse in feminist thought? In M. M. Gergen (Ed.), *Feminist thought and the structure of knowledge* (pp. 182–194). New York: New York University Press.

Morawski, J. G. (1990). Toward the unimagined: Feminism and epistemology in psychology. In J. Maracek & R. Hare-Mustin (Eds.), *Making a difference: Psychology and the construction of gender* (pp. 150–188). New Haven, CT: Yale University Press.

Morawski, J. G. (1994). *Practicing feminisms, reconstructing psychology: Notes on a liminal science.* Ann Arbor: University of Michigan Press.

Morawski, J. G., & Steele, R. S. (1991). The one and the other: Textual analysis of masculine power and feminist empowerment. *Theory and Psychology, 1,* 107–131.

Obiechina, C. B., & Bayer, B. M. (1994, August). *Black women, their bodies and culture.* Poster presented at the 102nd Annual Convention of the American Psychological Association, Los Angeles.

Parlee, M. B. (1991). Happy birth-day to feminism and psychology. *Feminism and Psychology, 1,* 39–48.

Prell, R. (1990). Rage and representation: Jewish gender stereotypes in American culture. In F. Ginsburg & A. L. Tsing (Eds.), *Uncertain terms: Negotiating gender in American culture* (pp. 248–266). Boston: Beacon Press.

Reid, P. T., & Comas-Díaz, L. (1990). Gender and ethnicity. *Sex Roles, 22,* 397–408.

Rose, N. (1990). *Governing the soul: The shaping of the private self*. New York: Routledge & Kegan Paul.

Samelson, F. (1978). From "race psychology" to "studies in prejudice": Some observations on the thematic reversal in social psychology. *Journal of the History of the Behavioral Sciences, 14,* 265–278.

Sampson, E. E. (1978). Scientific paradigms and social values: Wanted—a scientific revolution. *Journal of Personality and Social Psychology, 36,* 1332–1343.

Sampson, E. E. (1981). Cognitive psychology as ideology. *American Psychologist, 26,* 730–743.

Scott, J. (1986). Gender: A useful category of historical analysis. *American Historical Review, 91,* 1053–1075.

Skinner, Q. (Ed.). (1985). *The return of grand theory in the human sciences*. Cambridge: Cambridge University Press.

Smith, A., & Stewart, A. J. (1983). Approaches to studying racism and sexism in black women's lives. *Journal of Social Issues, 39,* 1–15.

Snitow, A. (1990). A gender diary. In M. Hirsch & E. F. Keller (Eds.), *Conflicts in feminism* (pp. 9–43). New York: Routledge & Kegan Paul.

Spelman, E. V. (1988). *Inessential woman: Problems of exclusion in feminist thought*. Boston: Beacon Press.

Spivak, G. C. (1987). *In other worlds: Essays in cultural politics*. New York: Methuen.

Unger, R. K. (1989). Sex, gender, and epistemology. In M. Crawford & M. Gentry (Eds.), *Gender and thought* (pp. 17–35). New York: Springer-Verlag.

Woolgar, S. (Ed.). (1988a). *Knowledge and reflexivity* (pp. 17–35). Newbury Park, CA: Sage.

Woolgar, S. (1988b). *Science: The very idea*. New York: Tavistock.

Zinn, M. B., Cannon, L. W., Higginbotham, E., & Dill, B. T. (1986). The costs of exclusionary practices in women's studies. *Signs, 11,* 290–303.

II

CULTURAL DIVERSITY
IN FEMINIST PRACTICE
IN PSYCHOLOGY

INTRODUCTION

The chapters in this section address three of the many areas of feminist practice and advocacy: feminist therapy, the supervision and training of feminist-multicultural therapists, and feminist advocacy and policy regarding sexual harassment in colleges and universities.

In chapter 7, "Cultural Diversity in Feminist Therapy: Theory and Practice," Laura Brown discusses the middle-class, European American origins of feminist therapy and its implications for practice. She argues that many of the issues focused on by feminist therapists (e.g., learning to express anger, learning to forgive and relate to one's mother) are by and large culture bound and may be irrelevant to or inappropriate for many groups of Women of Color. She concludes that what feminist therapists have defined as "women's issues" are middle-class, European American women's issues alone. She challenges feminist therapists to move beyond speaking largely to each other about themselves and presents suggestions for increasing diversity in the theory and practice of feminist therapy.

In chapter 8, "Supervision of Psychotherapists: Integrating Anti-Racist, Feminist, and Multicultural Perspectives," Natalie Porter presents a model of clinical supervision that can assist current and future therapists in moving toward a feminist, multicultural therapy. Porter presents a detailed, step-by-step description of this process so that it can readily be adopted. One of the major desired outcomes of this therapy is that client, student therapist, and supervising therapist alike each engage in collective political action on an agenda of importance to women, people of color, or both.

Finally, in chapter 9, "Academic Sexual Harassment: From Theory and Research to Program Implementation," Michele Paludi and colleagues briefly discuss ethnic differences among victims of sexual harassment in universities. They note that Women of Color are more likely than European American women to be sexually harassed because of male academicians' racist beliefs regarding the sexuality of Women of Color and because Women of Color are even more powerless than European American women (e.g., relying on departmental assistantships to pay for school). This discussion is brief because of the dearth of studies on ethnicity and sexual harassment. They then turn their attention to concrete methods for reducing the sexual harassment of all women in university settings and present a culturally sensitive model for achieving such change.

The three chapters in this section address only a few of the many practice issues in feminist psychology. These chapters highlight how *a European American cultural context has informed feminist practice, policy, and advocacy* and challenge readers to bring cultural diversity to this important aspect of feminist work.

7

CULTURAL DIVERSITY IN FEMINIST THERAPY: THEORY AND PRACTICE

LAURA S. BROWN

Theories in psychotherapy are powerful tools for creating shared realities and directions for practice. The theory to which a therapist adheres prescribes not only the technique and approach used to make interventions, but also describes the nature of reality, normalcy, and psychopathology. Feminist therapy has tended to lack a theory specifically related to the practice of psychotherapy. Although this lack has begun to be addressed (Brabeck & Brown, in press; Brown, 1994) and attempts at theory development are starting to influence feminist practice, attention to theory has not been one of the strengths of feminist therapy.

However, such practice has not been entirely atheoretical. Rather, its theories have been political and sociological, derived from a feminist political analysis of the place of women and other oppressed groups in society.

This chapter is an expanded version of an article previously published by the author in *Women and Therapy*, Vol. 9, pp. 1–22.

My thanks to Miriam Vogel for invaluable assistance in preparing the final version of this chapter. My continuing appreciation to my colleagues in feminist therapy who have been models, sisters in struggle, and sources of support for the development of my thinking on this topic, particularly Jeanne Adleman, Anne Ganley, and Maria Root.

143

This analysis has leaned heavily on critiques of sexism in theories of personality and psychopathology (Brown & Ballou, 1992) and has, for the most part, been overlaid onto or woven into the psychotherapeutic theories ascribed to by a particular feminist therapist. The result has been a myriad of feminist therapies in practice that share certain core precepts but vary widely in their descriptions of normative human growth and development, pathology, and appropriate psychotherapeutic intervention strategies (Dutton-Douglas & Walker, 1988).

NEED FOR A UNIFIED THEORY OF FEMINIST THERAPY

In the past decade, some feminist therapists have begun to attempt development of a unified theory of feminist therapy that would allow us to expand our applications of practice by making our work more theoretically coherent. Without such a theory, feminist therapy has risked becoming stereotyped as simply a collection of women therapists working with women in certain identified areas such as violence, lesbianism, eating disorders, or women in transition. Without theory, it becomes difficult if not impossible to create feminist therapy applications and preventive interventions with men (Bograd, 1990), children, families (Luepnitz, 1988), and larger social systems. Thus, feminist therapists have begun to move toward the foundations of a theory, including the demarcation of the parameters of such a paradigm.

Hannah Lerman (1987) described the criteria that such a theory must meet in order to be a feminist theory of personality, psychopathology, and psychotherapy. The criterion proposed by Lerman (1987) that has proved to be the most problematic for the majority of theory builders in feminist therapy is that a feminist theory "encompasses the diversity and complexity of women and their lives" (p. 173). Underlying this phrase is the assumption that a genuinely feminist therapy is one that would resonate to the lives and realities of all women, not simply those with whom feminist therapy already has been practiced.

Similarly, I (Brown, 1994) commented on the problems that would be inherent in any attempt to create a theory of feminist therapy that failed to center diversity of knowledge and experience as core to feminist therapeutic theorizing. Yet, such emphasis on diversity, although applauded in feminist therapy circles, has not been widely practiced and continues to be an exception rather than a rule in the feminist therapy scholarly literature. Why has feminist therapy done poorly addressing the issue of cultural diversity? What can be done to create a more diverse feminist therapy theory and practice?

INATTENTION TO DIVERSITY IN THE ROOTS OF FEMINIST THERAPY

One main problem for those attempting to create a multicultural feminist therapy theory lies within the origins and intellectual heritage of feminist therapy theory and practice. Feminist therapy theory and practice have been developed almost entirely by and with White, European American women. Prior to the mid-1980s, there had been little in the literature about feminist therapy theory that directly addressed itself to, or was primarily written by, women who were from outside the dominant White and middle-class stratum of society. As a result, feminist therapy theory was deficient from the start by excluding, through acts of "benign neglect," the lives and realities of Women of Color, poor or working-class women, non-North American women, women older than 65 years of age, or women with disabilities.

Commonly cited landmark books from the early years of feminist therapy practice such as Miller (1976), Sturdivant (1980), and Greenspan (1983) appear to describe the realities of feminist therapy practice only with White women, with occasional passing references to the fact that Women of Color, women with disabilities, poor women, and others may bear even heavier burdens of oppression than do their White, able-bodied, and financially more secure sisters. The *Handbook of Feminist Therapy* (Rosewater & Walker, 1985), which reflects the contents of the first Advanced Feminist Therapy Institute, acknowledges the absence of Women of Color as either authors or subjects of discussion, although lesbians and (more superficially) women in poverty are addressed in that book (Rosewater & Walker, 1985). Dutton-Douglas and Walker's (1988) *Feminist psychotherapies* is similarly cursory in addressing diversity in feminist therapy practice, with one chapter focused on a combined discussion of Black and Latina women (Mays & Comas-Díaz, 1988). These last two books focus on applications of feminist therapy rather than theory. However, they accurately reflect the zeitgeist in which theory is being developed and present a picture of feminist therapy practice in the late 1980s that was centered on White, mostly middle- or upper-middle-class women.

Authors who have made explicit attempts to create feminist theories of female development, such as Eichenbaum and Orbach (1983), Chodorow (1979), Gilligan (1982), and Dinnerstein (1976), have similarly positioned the women that they are describing squarely in the family and social structures of White, Northern European and North American society. This also is the case for the highly influential Stone Center group of authors (Jordan, Kaplan, Miller, Stiver, & Surrey, 1992), who have built their theoretical constructions around Miller's (1976) original work and their own clinical observations of a primarily White client group. As Lorde

(1980) cogently noted, "when white women ignore their built-in privilege of whiteness and define woman in terms of their own experience alone, then Women of Color become 'Other,' the outsider whose experience and tradition is too alien to comprehend" (p. 117). When reading the feminist therapy literature, it frequently seems as if the lives of Women of Color have been too alien to comprehend and too far from sight to be included in the writings or perhaps the work and practice of most White feminist therapists.

To a large degree, this historical failure of feminist therapy theorists to address the lives of all women, and the consequent difficulties of meeting the "diversity and complexity" criterion, can be traced to the training of White feminist therapists in traditional systems and theories of personality and psychotherapy. Such systems are themselves highly culture bound. As a consequence, even the White feminist therapist who approaches her professional training determined to take a feminist perspective will be confronting a base of data and theory that is White, Western, heterosexual, and male. Most feminist therapists have been quick to identify the masculine biases inherent in other theories and the practices that are associated with such androcentrism. Many also have been able to cull out the heterosexist and homophobic biases of dominant cultural models. However, the subtle aspects of racist and classist assumptions appear to have been less visible and less salient to many White feminist therapists—as well as to many White women—who themselves have benefited from the privileges of race and (in many instances) class (Brown, 1990; Brown & Root, 1990; Greene, 1986; Kanuha, 1990).

RACISM IN MAINSTREAM SOCIAL AND BEHAVIORAL SCIENCES

In the social and behavioral sciences, racism and classism render people who are not members of dominant groups invisible and thus nonexistent for the purposes of understanding and describing human behavior. The three Black participants whose responses are thrown out of the data pool because they disturb the symmetry of the statistics, or the questions about class background that are never asked because of the powerful nonconscious assumption that Americans live in a classless society, typify the ways in which people who are non-White or non-middle-class disappear or become invisible to the science of psychology. This invisibility of Women of Color has been the case in the field of feminist therapy as well as when women's lives are being studied and addressed.

Specific coursework on working with people of color is scarce in graduate training programs in the mental health and behavioral science disciplines. When present, it is often an optional rather than core and required course of study. This marginalization of scholarship on people of color causes what appears to be an official seal of approval on the invisibility of these groups. Wyatt and Parham (1985), reporting on a survey of American Psychological Association-approved graduate programs and internships in clinical and counseling psychology, found that only a small minority of students had had any courses available in "culturally sensitive training." Most of what was available occurred at the internship level and was optional rather than required course work. Although programs accredited by both psychology and social work require "diversity" to be represented in the training of practitioners, this requirement is broadly interpreted and often operationalized as one lecture on working with "minorities" in a psychotherapy or assessment course.

Aside from its collusion with racism in White trainees, sending the message that anything related to diversity in the human population is of lesser value than other topics, this particular version of racism and classism also often has profound limiting impacts on the vision of Women of Color or poor women who enter professional training. The trainee from a non-dominant group is faced in many instances with the untenable choice of making the absence of multicultural training an issue, which can sometimes lead to the trainee being stigmatized as problematic. The risks to self, safety, and pursuit of the advanced degree or tenure that may develop when attempting to make visible such subtle, "civilized" racist or classist tactics are often too great for a graduate student or newly degreed faculty woman to tolerate. In learning not to comment, it also becomes possible to join with White culture in learning not to see these forms of oppression (Brown, 1987; Evans, 1985; Tyler, Sussewell, & Williams-McCoy, 1985). For a feminist therapist of color in training, the survival requirements may be even higher, because feminist perspectives are themselves still marginalized in many professional training settings and the available role models and mentors even fewer and harder to find. This sort of institutionalized and non-conscious bias, difficult to confront head-on, becomes one of the many invisible obstacles to the participation of Women of Color in the practice of feminist therapy.

The process of professional socialization, which is seen as central to graduate training in psychology (*Accreditation Handbook* of the American Psychological Association, 1987), also is a socialization into this narrow, all-White, and middle-class reality. In an academic culture in which it is still considered too risky to raise feminist questions, anti-racist or class-conscious feminism has even less room. As Jones (1985), paraphrasing Sue (1983), put it, "these conflicts [between the traditional values of the professions and new concerns regarding people of color] make it easier to confront the problems by recruiting and admitting increasing numbers of ethnic minority persons to the guild than to pitch battle on core values" (p. 454). Implied, but not stated, is that once people of color are recruited to the guild, a process of internal colonization will take place that results in allegiance to the White, Western values of the guild in question (viz., psychotherapy and behavioral science). The profession can then point to an increase in numbers, without making meaningful changes toward a more multicultural and diverse epistemology or methodology.

Again, this strategy of "add women of color and stir" (Espin & Gawelek, 1992) has been an unfortunate norm within feminist therapy. Attempts have been made by various groups of White feminist therapists to have more faces of color at the conference, but there has not been sufficient challenge by the White and middle-class women in the positions of power and leadership to Eurocentric norms of thinking and sources of data. Data on Women of Color, and experiences of practice with Women of Color, are set in a sort of parallel and separate track and are not construed as being of broad importance to the core of training and practice in feminist therapy.

Evans (1985), commenting on the training that graduate students in psychology receive to deliver services to people of color, noted that psychologists are often trained to have "a lack of hope and lack of optimism about Black people," which constitutes "the greatest impediments to the proper utilization of psychotherapy with them" (p. 459). She theorized that this lack of hope comes from "lack of 'the stuff' out of which conviction and hope are born, i.e., broad knowledge and appreciation of different cultures . . . and the histories of people showing their travail and their indomitability" (Evans, 1985, p. 459). In other words, lack of data and lack of awareness go hand in hand to create trained-in insensitivity to and ignorance of the broad spectrum of realities for people of color and other oppressed groups. A related problem within feminist therapy has been the assumption that an understanding of sexism will substitute for genuine multicultural literacy (Childs, 1990; Kanuha, 1990), leading to a similar outcome in terms of therapist education (or lack thereof) regarding diverse populations.

CHALLENGING EUROCENTRISM IN FEMINIST THERAPY THEORY AND PRACTICE

This almost hypnotic induction of therapists in training into a White, Western, and subtly racist worldview seems to act as the filter on the sensitivities of feminist therapists who are attempting to generate their own nonsexist, nonmasculinist data sources. Feminist therapy theory always has been one part sociology (i.e., a description of the external reality and social context) and one part phenomenology (i.e., the description of lived and felt internal reality as experienced from within the social context). The special contribution of feminist therapy has been to attempt to describe the interactive relationships of internal and external realities and to promulgate epistemologies and methodologies that would lend themselves to this interactive model of human growth and development (Brown, 1994). Through the filters of their original trainings, however, there has developed within feminist psychology and feminist practice a skewed vision of a social context of White women and a limited phenomenology of White women's experiences. In addition, feminist therapy theorists have tended to approach their understanding of behavior via linear models of causality, which limit their understandings of the variety of contextual factors that can influence the development of personality and that themselves may represent a Eurocentric mode of thinking that can be exclusionary to feminist therapists coming from other intellectual traditions (Greene, 1990; Kanuha, 1990; Lerner, 1988; Sears, 1990).

When one reviews research in feminist psychology, which has largely provided the base of empirical data from which White feminist therapists have constructed their visions of the external context and reality, one finds that such research has been conducted almost overwhelmingly by and with White women. The clichéd "White-male-middle-class-college-sophomore" research participant often has been replaced by his sister. When one speaks, for instance, of "female socialization" or "women's growth and development," terms used constantly in the feminist therapy literature as explanatory fictions, one is describing information on that process that has been gathered almost entirely from a White, middle-class, Western subject pool. Feminists in psychology insist on the importance of context (Parlee, 1979) and then seem to forget in practice that there are many contexts. Socialization to be a white, middle-class Jewish woman is not socialization to be a Black, middle-class Southern Baptist woman or to be a Southeast Asian female refugee in the United States (Greene, 1990; Ho, 1990; Siegel & Cole, 1991). Socialization into one age cohort's female gender role will be different from that experienced by another cohort, even holding all other demographic variables constant (Sang, Warshaw, & Smith, 1991). Whose socialization is being referred to when "female socialization" is cited as the source of X or Y problems described in samples of women?

One of the strengths of feminist psychology and feminist therapy is that it often uses as a heuristic the issues that arise from the life of the researcher, a core concept contained in the phrase, "the personal is political." Individual experience is construed as simply one unique version of a broader social phenomenon that has political meaning within the domain of patriarchal cultures. Thus, White feminists ask questions about menstruation and mothering; about the experience of being sexually harassed; about acquaintance rape or working in nontraditional careers; about being in a lesbian couple; about surviving an abusive relationship with a partner; or about being incestuously abused by one's father. The lack of diversity among those currently in the field of feminist psychology limited the scope of the questions asked to those most relevant to White feminist concerns. The word *personal* has consequently encompassed a narrow range of experiences and a noninclusive politic. This particular means of making the personal the political has obstructed the development of a more multicultural database. Although it can be argued that having multicultural literacy may be an ethical imperative for a feminist therapist (Brown, 1991; Kanuha, 1990), this ethic has not been consistently or even frequently applied to the scholarship in the field.

Likewise, there has been a tendency to overgeneralize from White women's experience in a literature that is more phenomenological than empirical. It is within this literature that the recent development of a rapprochement with psychodynamic theories such as Jungian analysis, object relations, and self psychology has occurred. Without being as overtly sexist and thus as offensive as orthodox psychoanalysis, the psychodynamic, intrapsychic theories offer intriguing hypotheses about the experience of internal reality, glimpses that have appeared useful to feminist theoreticians of personality such as Chodorow (1979), Eichenbaum and Orbach (1983), and Gilligan (1982). Yet, here too, the cradle and context of internal, phenomenological reality are White and Western. The psychodynamic theories offer potential strategies to investigate questions of intrapsychic difference on the basis of the experiences of race, class, culture, and so on, but as currently stated, they provide answers that are severely limited in their generalizability because they are culture bound and are thus likely to "pathologize" those who differ from an implied but rarely stated Eurocentric norm.

Also problematic in these theories are assumptions regarding the context that serves as a possible cause of intrapsychic phenomena. H. G. Lerner (1988), critiquing the feminist psychoanalytic theorists, pointed out that when they adopt the assumptions of psychodynamic theories regarding the centrality of mother–child relations, even when that relationship has been reframed into a properly feminist positive perspective, these authors have neglected to attend to the influence or presence of the father. Such models also tend to ignore the family and the cultural system in which a child develops, as well as the interplay of relationships among these factors. Although H. G. Lerner acknowledged the importance that these writers have had in bringing certain aspects of phenomenology to light, she pointed out that because psychodynamic thinking emphasizes the primacy of the mother as the shaper of personality, such theories subtly convey a metamessage of mother-blaming; this occurs even when the overt content is to value the mother–child relationship and honor the mother's role in the face of sexist reality. In other words, by reentering reality as mapped by psychodynamic thought, feminist theorists inevitably encounter sexism. What Lerner did not say is that by defining *mother* in racially and culturally particularistic manners, theorists also weave racism into their models. The phenomenology of the psychodynamic mother–child dyad does not, for instance, begin to describe the social context in which Black mothers and their daughters must deal with the interactive effects of racism and sexism (Greene, 1990). Nor does it describe the extended family systems of many families of color, immigrant families, and so on, in which the person in the role of "mother" may not always or ever be the biological female parent of a child.

The embrace of a psychodynamic framework of phenomenology that is based primarily in the available intrapsychically oriented theoretical systems moves feminist therapy theory development even further away from a multicultural perspective and places it more firmly in a White, Western mode. It leaves feminist therapy theoretically weakened by having feminist theorists stand, in the words of Rachel Hare-Mustin, on the shoulders of dead White men, the "fathers" of psychodynamic thought, rather than on the foundation of feminist scholarship. As feminist historian Gerda Lerner noted, this placement of an epistemological center in the paradigms of patriarchy impedes the development of feminist consciousness, which in turn moves the theory more toward patriarchal and exclusionary values (G. Lerner, 1993).

These questions and critiques are central and cannot be ignored by feminist therapy theorists who wish to describe the diversity and complexity of women's lives and wish to do so in a manner that avoids inadvertent re-creation of woman-blaming methodologies. Psychodynamic theoretical systems are phenomenological and thus descriptive of powerful yet unquantifiable and experiential data. Consequently, they are more seductive, and their racism or ethnocentrism more difficult to challenge, than theoretical systems oriented more toward observable external phenomena. Yet, because they are phenomenological, they also are clinically powerful explanatory fictions for many of the experiences of the White women writing these theories. This tends to lend to such theories a spurious but strongly felt validity that embeds them in the thinking of many White feminist therapists.

The work of the Stone Center authors (Jordan et al., 1992), for example, offers images of relationships between women that have a feeling of rightness to many White women. However, as Palladino and Stephenson (1990) pointed out, these models fail to describe the phenomenology of emotional intimacy between women in a way inclusive of the experiences of Women of Color. Because the Stone Center model has been so profoundly influential to the thinking of many currently practicing White feminist therapists, its exclusionary and Eurocentric biases are to some degree riskier to feminist practice than are the value embedded in the mainstream psychodynamic theories that the Stone Center authors criticize and reformulate.

Models of feminist therapy practice also contain assumptions about the goals for therapy and positive outcomes for women that are highly reflective of culture and class-bound norms. Several authors (Boyd, 1990; Childs, 1990; Comas-Díaz, 1987; Faunce, 1990; Sears, 1990) have pointed out that the methods and goals of feminist therapy as usually practiced may be inimical to the experiences, realities, and in some cases the survival capacities of women who do not participate in White or middle-class norms. These models of practice reflect the theories from which they derive in that they contain generic assumptions about what "women" (read: White women) need to be healthy and functional. For example, many White feminist therapists write about the importance for women of learning to express anger and be more assertive (Greenspan, 1983). However, there are a variety of cultural contexts in which this generic prescription may be inappropriate in either its goals, forms, or both. Such feminist prescriptions are White middle-class assumptions that obscure and make invisible that which may be needed by women of color for healthy functioning (Boyd, 1990).

TOWARD MULTICULTURAL FEMINIST THERAPY THEORY AND PRACTICE

Feminist therapy theorists must not make the error of being intellectually seduced by that which resonates for them, particularly if they are White women. Rather, the questions should be of how one could, in a consciously and deliberately anti-racist manner, draw on the models for theory building and development offered by both highly phenomenological, traditional theories of personality and psychotherapy as well as the database of empirical scholarship. This addition of the clarifying and enlarging lens of an anti-racist perspective to feminist analysis appears to be what will be necessary to develop a model that is both feminist and multicultural. An essential step toward a multicultural feminist therapy theory and practice would be the development of a multicultural, non-White and non-Western feminist database on the varieties of women's experiences. In other words, it is necessary that feminist theorists operate from a canon of scholarship that is diverse and multicultural in methodology and content. A feminist consciousness must inform the way in which research questions are framed and pursue the task of gathering information. At the same time, feminist theorists must consciously avoid the trap of assuming that one woman's context is constructed in a manner equivalent to another's. They must particularly guard against imposing their own personal contexts, whatever they may be, on the meanings and realities of women different from themselves. This caution particularly must be observed by White women, given that one of the pernicious effects of growing up as a member of the dominant cultural group is the tendency to construe Whiteness as the equivalent of expertise.

Additionally, by working from the feminist principle of respecting experience as it is defined by those who live it, feminist therapy theory and practice must cease to insist on the primacy of gender as the issue in the examination of the lives of poor women, women from non-Western cultures, and so on. Although gender is an important locus for the analysis of cultural matrices of power and dominance, it is not the sole variable of value for feminist scholarship and practice, nor does it operate in isolation from other diverse experiences of oppression. A number of authors (Kanuha, 1990; Lorde, 1980; Moraga & Anzaldua, 1981; Walker, 1983) have pointed out that for feminist Women of Color, the requirement that sexism be chosen as the "ultimate" oppression negates the validity of their internal realities. In keeping with this reality, feminist researchers and therapists must not assume that gender and gender membership will be the variable of most importance in all women's lives. Feminist research on developing a complete picture of all women's contexts must guard against that tendency. Although gender as an organizing variable is central to a feminist analysis and understanding of the data that are collected, it may not be central to the women who are studied in all cases.

Thus, questions regarding what it means to be socialized as women in a particular culture must include questions regarding the salience of gender as an organizing principle within that particular cultural milieu. Researchers can then also ask about the meaning of differences between cultural groups in the power of gender as a factor. The meanings given to the social expression and construction of women's biology must and will vary across time and place. Those differences in meaning must be sought out and described to constitute a scholarly foundation for feminist therapeutic practice. It also will be necessary to ask how various factors interact with one another to create different varieties of social context for women who may appear, from a White or middle-class-centered perspective, to be similar. For example, there are meaningful differences in the social construction of gender between people from different Asian backgrounds, yet these groups are commonly lumped together in studies of "Asian Americans." Similarly, Native American groups vary greatly from one another regarding the meanings of gender, yet available texts tend to assume one norm.

Some of these data are already available to feminist therapy theorists in the work of feminist anthropologists, sociologists, political scientists, and historians, as well as in the growing contributions of feminist therapists of color (Comas-Díaz & Greene, 1994). Such an interdisciplinary and culturally informed database is essential to the creation of a multicultural feminist therapy theory and practice. The need to expand what feminist therapy theorists construe as "legitimate" sources of data is particularly pressing because North American psychology as a whole has ignored culture as well as other social scientific traditions through its rigid overemphasis on the controlled, individual-focused, laboratory, and experimental paradigm for understanding human behavior. Bleier (1984) pointed out that feminist scholarship in the sociology of knowledge has had less impact on psychology and psychotherapy than anywhere else in the social sciences. Yet, to create a multicultural theory, one must ask questions about how knowledge is defined (Ballou, 1990). To define the knowledge of our sister feminist social scientists as central to the development of feminist therapy theories and practice would aid in breaking through the tyranny of psychology's "affinity for positivism," to borrow Bleier's terminology.

Simultaneous with this, feminist therapists must create theories of personality that reflect the internal realities that grow within women's diverse social and cultural contexts. Because models of psychopathology follow directly from theories of "normal" personality, the theories of what is normative must be explicitly attentive to diverse experiences of life, which may lead to equally multifaceted images of "normal." The cultural biases inherent in views of what constitutes pathology also must be examined. As Caplan (1991) pointed out, most current diagnostic categories take a dominant perspective and label as pathological that which troubles the dominant group (e.g., "hysterical" women or "paranoid" people of color), rather than labeling as pathology those behaviors of the dominant that might be distressing or dangerous to marginal and oppressed groups (e.g., rigid sexist, heterosexist, or racist biases). Feminist therapists must be extraordinarily wary of how and if they appropriate traditional diagnostic labels in their theoretical formulations, in particular to the potentials for racism as well as sexism inherent in certain diagnostic categories.

The intrapsychically oriented theories that have been attractive to some feminist therapists may offer one useful strategy for asking questions about women's diverse internal realities by describing methodologies for gaining access to internal phenomenologies. However, feminist therapists must push beyond the answers and models given by White European men such as Jung, Kohut, and Winnicott and ask how internal reality is shaped differently, to different meanings and symbologies, by diverse external experiences. Although phenomenology and introspection as tools of theory development have long fallen out of favor among North American psychologists, they may be the most effective methods available to feminist therapists for this task. In relying on them, as feminist therapists ultimately must in their practice, they will be asking women to define the unique experiences of being women in their particular social settings. Only then will feminist therapists begin to meet the criterion of a theory that is diverse and complex and feminist in its attribution of expert knowledge to persons other than the therapist.

In this, too, feminist therapists have resources already available in the body of historical and autobiographical nonfiction literature and womanist (to use Walker's, 1983, term) fiction that has grown dramatically in the past decade. Women of color have been vividly describing the experiences of being Black and female, Chinese American and female, Caribbean and female, Lebanese/Laguna Pueblo and female, and so on, for many years. Freud, when asked what women want, suggested (for lack of a better idea on his own part) that one turn to the poets. A similar course of action might be a first step for White feminist therapy theorists and practitioners who are asking "What do women of color want?" and "What is it like to live inside the experience of being a woman who is not White?" Consider, for example, the social and familial realities depicted in Morrison's (1987) novel *Beloved*. If one applies (as suggested by Chodorow, 1979) the concepts of projective identification as a core construct of the development of self and identity in an infant to the generations of women who might come from this family, then one can ask how personality might develop in the line of women descending from one who has killed one of her children to save that one from slavery. This sort of questioning about the psychological heritages of diverse groups as they have survived under oppression potentially leads to some new and startling notions about the nature of normalcy and pathology. At the least, such different questions will suggest that the notions of personality development, and thus the concepts about therapeutic intervention, must eventually come to reflect an intergenerational understanding of the meaning of being female and the development of identity, rather than limiting the focus to the life of the observed individual alone and in isolation. Greene's (1990) feminist therapy perspective on the Black mother–daughter relationship provides a glimpse of what the field of feminist therapy will need to do to answer such questions in a manner that will empower and heal.

White feminist therapists also must examine how cultural factors outside of the control of members of a particular group shape internal experience. Giddings's (1984) book title, *When and Where I Enter*, reflects the internal reality for Black women in America. This title comes from an African American author and activist of the 1890s, Anna Julia Cooper, who stated, "When and where I enter . . . then and there the whole race enters with me." What does it mean to the development of self to carry that knowledge and awareness, to be the embodiment of the symbolic representations in the collective psyche of the dominant as an "other"? Even if feminist therapy theorists search for an archetype, they cannot, as Bolen (1984) suggested, turn to a Jungian typology of Greek goddesses to comprehend this experience, because such a typology resides solely within a Eurocentric dominant culture that has framed this context and defined these particular goddess symbologies. Although feminist therapy theorists have asked these questions about generic "woman" in relationship to generic "man" and generic "patriarchal culture," their answers have in the past failed to describe experiences arising from realities in which White women are the dominant group or to explore the impact of that dominant status both on White women's personalities and those of people of color in relationship to White women.

One very practical aspect of any solution to the dilemma of exclusion in feminist therapy is that the ranks of feminist therapists must include significant numbers of Women of Color and significant numbers of therapists of any background who work with people of color, because such a presence changes the discourse. My own experience of theory building as a feminist therapist, and my reading of that process as experienced by other theory builders, is that the creation of theory takes the form of an extended conversation (often in writing) between colleagues about their work and their insights. If I am not interacting with feminist therapists of color, with culturally literate White feminist therapists, with clients of color, and with others who work with them, my "conversations" will remain limited in their scope and understanding and will likely be racist, classist, and otherwise exclusionary. This restricted pattern of interaction has characterized the community of White feminist therapists for the past two decades; they have spoken largely to themselves about themselves and similar others, and they have not done the necessary work of removing insidious barriers to the full participation of Women of Color as colleagues. Some therapists who are Women of Color and feminist in their theoretical perspectives have refused to identify with feminist therapy partly because it is racially and ethnically biased and partly because feminist political theory more generally has denied the importance of race and culture (Kanuha, 1990). It is both inappropriate and racist to assume that female therapists of color will want to join with White women in the development of feminist therapy theory to raise the consciousness of White feminist therapists; "it is not the duty of the oppressed to educate the oppressor" (Moschkovich, 1981, p. 79).

Consequently, White and middle-class feminist therapists need to take the initiative to identify barriers to full participation and remove them and to actively solicit the input of their colleagues from nondominant groups. White feminist therapists and their theories must proactively seek to be anti-racist and multicultural so as to demonstrate their relevance to Women of Color, non-North American women, and so on. The burden must not be placed on these colleagues to generate all of the knowledge and information about multicultural and anti-dominant epistemologies and methodologies. White and middle-class feminist therapists must themselves make such development of theory and practice central in their own work.

Perhaps one answer to the question often raised in feminist therapy organizations about where all the feminist therapists of color are is that they are reluctant to affiliate with these essentially White organizations unless and until White feminist therapists have demonstrated in concrete ways their commitment to valuing diversity and comprehending the lives of women like themselves. Making their theories diverse and complex on their own initiative is one such concrete commitment. Examining their styles of practice for structures that are inherently oppressive or exclusionary is another commitment that White feminist therapists also must make.

Ultimately, to change the current of affairs in which feminist therapy theory and practice are overly narrow and exclusionary, feminist therapy organizations and individual White feminist therapists also must examine the obstacles they have erected to block the full participation of women of color in feminist therapy. How have their efforts to be more multicultural been shaped? Have editors of books on feminist therapy allowed most chapters to be oriented toward White women and then fulfilled a "diversity" criterion or quota with a single ghettoized chapter on Women of Color? Have training programs that offer an emphasis on feminist therapy constructed curricula that are explicitly multicultural in an integrated and consistent manner? When feminist therapists write, do they use the term *woman* as isomorphic with *White woman*, or do they use appropriate ethnic identifiers for all groups? What models of therapy practice are described as "feminist therapy"? Are these models Eurocentric in their assumptions about communication, therapy goals, the interaction of therapist and client, and the nature of the frame and boundaries of therapy? Or, do their images of feminist therapy practice include a diversity drawn not only from other schools of psychotherapy but, more important, from diverse women's life experiences and input?

Barriers to a multicultural feminist therapy exist at all levels of theory and practice and consequently need to be addressed at all levels. I have proposed that an anti-racist perspective is a necessary ethic for feminist therapy (Brown, 1991). In doing so, I suggest that one manner in which to define the commitment of White feminist therapists to a multicultural theory and practice is to place the struggle to overcome their racism and the ethnocentrism of both their theory and practice as equal in value to their desire not to do violence to clients' boundaries in psychotherapy. There are a variety of ways to operationalize this ethic, and, if taken seriously, such an ethic will be transformative to feminist therapy.

CONCLUSION

What I am suggesting may seem monumental in scope, in that I am proposing that as a matter of ethics we no longer accept as exemplary of feminist therapy theory or practice any work that does not directly address matters of culture or that is inherently exclusionary of women from nondominant groups. However, this vision is both essential and exciting in its realization. If now, at the initial stages of theory building in feminist therapy, we as feminist theorists start with these new challenges to our old assumptions, we have the potential to develop theory that is not simply a woman-centered revision of what has already been written by the dominant culture of patriarchy in psychology. Rather, we have the opportunity to reenvision a broader reality and generate a deeper understanding of how human beings come to know themselves and how pain and dysfunction develop and can be healed. We can question the paradigms by which we understand interpersonal and intrapersonal processes and integrate the best of all disciplinary perspectives into our work. Should we miss this opportunity, we risk making feminist therapy yet another reaction against or rewriting of the concepts of orthodox psychoanalytic personality theory that have so imbued the Western social and behavioral sciences for the past century. To remain true to our own ethics, we have no choice but to plunge into the task so that a multicultural perspective becomes core and central to, rather than an addition to, feminist therapy theory and practice.

REFERENCES

American Psychological Association. (1987). *Accreditation handbook.* Washington, DC: Author.

Ballou, M. (1990). Approaching a feminist-principled paradigm in the construction of a personality theory. *Women and Therapy, 9,* 23–40.

Bleier, R. (1984). *Science and gender.* Elmsford, NY: Pergamon Press.

Bograd, M. (Ed.). (1990). *Feminist approaches for men in family therapy.* New York: Haworth Press.

Bolen, J. S. (1984). *Goddesses in every woman.* New York: Harper Colophon.

Boyd, J. (1990). Ethnic and cultural diversity: Keys to power. *Women and Therapy, 9,* 151–168.

Brabeck, M., & Brown, L. S. (in press). Theory in feminist practice. In N. Johnson & J. Worell (Eds.), *Education and training in feminist practice.* Washington, DC: American Psychological Association.

Brown, L. S. (1987, May). *Training issues for white feminist therapists working with women of color.* Paper presented at the advanced Feminist Therapy Institute, Woodstock, IL.

Brown, L. S. (1990). The meaning of a multicultural perspective for theory-building in feminist therapy. *Women and Therapy, 9,* 1–23.

Brown, L. S. (1991). Anti-racism as an ethical imperative: An example from feminist therapy. *Ethics and Behavior, 1,* 113–127.

Brown, L. S. (1994). *Subversive dialogues: Theory in feminist therapy.* New York: Basic Books.

Brown, L. S., & Ballou, M. (Eds.). (1992). *Personality and psychopathology: Feminist reappraisals.* New York: Guilford Press.

Brown, L. S., & Root, M. P. P. (Eds.). (1990). *Diversity and complexity in feminist therapy.* New York: Haworth Press.

Caplan, P. (1991). Delusional dominating personality disorder. *Feminism and Psychology, 1,* 171–174.

Childs, E. K. (1990). Therapy, feminist ethics and the community of color with particular emphasis on the treatment of Black women. In H. Lerman & N. Porter (Eds.), *Feminist ethics in psychotherapy* (pp. 195–203). New York: Springer.

Chodorow, N. (1979). *The reproduction of mothering.* Berkeley: University of California Press.

Comas-Díaz, L. (1987). Feminist therapy with mainland Puerto Rican women. *Psychology of Women Quarterly, 11,* 461–474.

Comas-Díaz, L., & Greene, B. (1994). *Mental health and women of color.* New York: Guilford Press.

Dinnerstein, D. (1976). *The mermaid and the minotaur.* New York: Harper Colophon.

Dutton-Douglas, M. A., & Walker, L. E. A. (Eds.). (1988). *Feminist psychotherapies: Integration of feminist and therapeutic systems.* Norword, NJ: Ablex.

Eichenbaum, L., & Orbach, S. (1983). *Understanding women: A feminist psychoanalytic approach.* New York: Basic Books.

Espin, O., & Gawelek, M. A. (1992). Women's diversity: Ethnicity, race, class, and gender in theories of feminist psychology. In L. S. Brown & M. Ballou (Eds.), *Personality and psychopathology: Feminist reappraisals* (pp. 88–110). New York: Guilford Press.

Evans, D. (1985). Psychotherapy and Black patients: Problems of training, trainees and trainers. *Psychotherapy: Theory, Research, Practice, and Training, 22,* 457–460.

Faunce, P. (1990). Women in poverty: Ethical dimensions in therapy. In H. Lerman & N. Porter (Eds.), *Feminist ethics in psychotherapy* (pp. 185–194). New York: Springer.

Giddings, P. (1984). *When and where I enter: The impact of Black women on race and sex in America.* New York: Morrow.

Gilligan, C. (1982). *In a different voice.* Cambridge, MA: Harvard University Press.

Greene, B. (1986). When the therapist is white and the patient is Black: Considerations for psychotherapy in the feminist heterosexual and lesbian communities. *Women and Therapy, 5,* 41–46.

Greene, B. (1990). What has gone before: The legacy of racism and sexism in the lives of Black mothers and daughters. *Women and Therapy, 9,* 207–230.

Greenspan, M. (1983). *A new approach to women and therapy*. New York: McGraw-Hill.

Ho, C. K. (1990). An analysis of domestic violence in Asian American communities: A multicultural approach to counseling. *Women and Therapy, 9*, 129–150.

Jones, J. M. (1985). The sociopolitical context of clinical training in psychology: The ethnic minority case. *Psychotherapy: Theory, Research, Practice, and Training, 22*, 453–456.

Jordan, J. V., Kaplan, A. G., Miller, J. B., Stiver, I., & Surrey, J. (1992). *Women's growth in connection: Writings from the Stone Center*. New York: Guilford Press.

Kanuha, V. (1990). The need for an integrated analysis of oppression in feminist therapy ethics. In H. Lerman & N. Porter (Eds.), *Feminist ethics in psychotherapy* (pp. 24–36). New York: Springer.

Lerman, H. (1987). *A mote in Freud's eye: From psychoanalysis to the psychology of women*. New York: Springer.

Lerner, G. (1993). *The creation of feminist consciousness*. New York: Oxford University Press.

Lerner, H. G. (1988). *Women in therapy*. Northvale, NJ: Aronson.

Lorde, A. (1980, April). *Age, race, class and sex: Women redefining difference*. Copeland Colloquium, Amherst College, Amherst, MA.

Luepnitz, D. (1988). *The family interpreted*. New York: Basic Books.

Mays, V., & Comas-Díaz, L. (1988). Feminist therapy with ethnic minority populations: A closer look at Blacks and Hispanics. In M. A. Dutton-Douglas & L. A. Walker (Eds.), *Feminist psychotherapies: Integration of therapeutic and feminist systems* (pp. 228–251). Norwood, NJ: Ablex.

Miller, J. B. (1976). *Toward a new psychology of women*. Boston: Beacon Press.

Moraga, C., & Anzaldua, G. (Eds.). (1981). *This bridge called my back: Writings by radical women of color*. Watertown, MA: Persephone Press.

Morrison, T. (1987). *Beloved*. New York: Knopf.

Moschkovich, J. (1981). "But I know you, American woman." In C. Moraga & G. Anzaldua (Eds.), *This bridge called my back: Writings by radical women of color* (pp. 79–84). Watertown, MA: Persephone Press.

Palladino, D., & Stephenson, Y. (1990). Perceptions of the sexual self: Their impact on relationships between lesbian and heterosexual women. *Women and Therapy, 9*, 231–254.

Parlee, M. B. (1979). Psychology and women. *Signs: Journal of Women in Culture and Society, 5*, 121–133.

Rosewater, L. B., & Walker, L. A. (Eds.). (1985). *Handbook of feminist therapy: Women's issues in psychotherapy*. New York: Springer.

Sang, B., Warshaw, J., & Smith, A. (Eds.). (1991). *Lesbians in mid-life: The creative transition*. San Francisco: Spinsters/Aunt Lute.

Sears, V. L. (1990). Ethnics in small minority communities. In H. Lerman & N. Porter (Eds.), *Feminist ethics in psychotherapy* (pp. 204–213). New York: Springer.

Siegel, R. J., & Cole, E. (1991). *Jewish women in therapy: Seen but not heard.* New York: Haworth Press.

Sturdivant, S. (1980). *Therapy with women.* New York: Springer.

Sue, S. (1983). Ethnic minority issues in psychology. *American Psychologist, 38,* 583–592.

Tyler, F. B., Sussewell, D. R., & Williams-McCoy, J. (1985). Ethnic validity in psychotherapy. *Psychotherapy: Theory, Research, Practice, and Training, 22,* 311–320.

Walker, A. (1983). *In search of our mothers' gardens: Womanist prose.* New York: Harcourt Brace Jovanovich.

Wyatt, G., & Parham, W. D. (1985). The inclusion of culturally sensitive course materials in graduate school and training programs. *Psychotherapy: Theory, Research, Practice, and Training, 22,* 461–468.

8

SUPERVISION OF PSYCHOTHERAPISTS: INTEGRATING ANTI-RACIST, FEMINIST, AND MULTICULTURAL PERSPECTIVES

NATALIE PORTER

Psychotherapy supervision teaches the application of the principles of psychology regarding human behavior and the change process. Traditionally, this process has been influenced by Western European culture. At best, it has operated from an ostensibly "color-blind" and "gender-blind" perspective that is tantamount to treating all clients as if they were White, western European men; at its worst, it has operated within racist and misogynistic assumptions. Psychotherapy theory and practice have been developed as if all psychotherapy clients shared the same life experiences, originated from the same socioeconomic background, and represented a homogeneous cultural worldview. Women and people of color have been raising their voices and pens to label these biases, which are inherent in most psychotherapy. Critiques have proliferated addressing the failure of psychotherapy to meet the needs of women and people of color. Therapy guidelines have been developed by both the APA Task Force on Sex Bias and Sex-Role Stereotyping (American Psychological Association [APA], 1975) and the APA Board of Ethnic Minority Affairs (1990). All guidelines address the dire need for educating therapists about these issues.

In spite of these guidelines, education and supervision pertaining to psychotherapy with ethnic minority or female clients remain limited and rarely are considered a priority in training programs. Courses that are offered usually are electives. They frequently involve preaching to the converted, because the students seeking culturally and gender-sensitive supervision and coursework are those already more aware of race, class, ethnicity, and gender issues. Supervision focusing on these issues must move into the mainstream of psychotherapy training and be required for all prospective clinicians. In this chapter I focus on a process of therapy supervision that attempts to integrate feminist, cross-cultural, and anti-racist perspectives in psychotherapy.

TRADITIONAL THERAPIES ARE INADEQUATE FOR WOMEN

Feminist theorists and clinicians have formally critiqued the use of traditional psychotherapies with women for more than two decades. These critiques include: (a) that traditional therapy not only did not help women but harmed them (Chesler, 1972); (b) that male developmental and psychological norms cannot be used to explain women's conditions (Rosewater & Walker, 1985); and (c) that traditional therapists were gender biased (Broverman, Broverman, Clarkson, Rosenkrantz, & Vogel, 1970; Fabrikant, 1974; Tanney & Birk, 1976), used gender stereotypes (Abramowitz, Abramowitz, Jackson, & Gomes, 1973; Miller, 1974), and lacked knowledge about the psychological, physiological, and sociological concerns of women (Bingham & House, 1973; Sherman, Koufacos, & Kenworthy, 1978).

TRADITIONAL THERAPIES ARE INADEQUATE FOR PEOPLE OF COLOR

The literature on the use of mental health services by various ethnic minority groups has shown clearly that traditional therapies frequently do not meet their needs. These groups often negatively experience therapy, are underrepresented in receiving services, and are overrepresented in early terminations (La Fromboise, 1988; President's Commission on Mental Health, 1978; Sue, 1988; Sue & Zane, 1987). McGoldrick (1982) blamed the medical model for increasing noncompliance, dissatisfaction with treatment, and treatment failure. Sue and Zane (1987) argued that most therapists are unable to provide culturally responsive treatment to their ethnic minority clients because they are either unfamiliar with the cultural backgrounds and lifestyles of their ethnic minority clients or lack the ability to translate this knowledge into specific therapeutic interventions.

Racial and ethnic stereotyping influence case conceptualizations, treatment objectives, and choices of interventions with ethnic minority clients at least as much as with female clients. What White therapists may consider "healthy" treatment outcomes may be viewed by ethnic minority clients as pressure to relinquish one's cultural values and assimilate into mainstream culture. Native American authors uniformly have expressed the concern that Western psychiatry interprets the mental health problems of Native American clients from a bias that pathologizes their traditional ways of life and influences the client to adopt behaviors that conflict with their cultural origins (Jilek-Aall, 1976; Trimble, 1982; Trimble & La Fromboise, 1985). La Fromboise (1988) indicted the use of European-American mental health traditions, which promote dualistic thinking over holistic and spiritual perspectives, individualistic behavior over family and group cohesiveness and community well-being, and intrapsychic over social causes of emotional problems.

Falicov (1982) outlined the social issues faced by Mexican Americans that mainstream therapists misidentify as family pathology. She described how immigrating families adapt family structures, including roles, rules, boundaries, and hierarchies, to acclimate to the pressures of acculturation. For example, behaviors that facilitate coping with the loss of extended family and friends may include developing closer ties among members of the nuclear family. This behavior is frequently labeled "enmeshment" by mainstream therapists. Furthermore, different cultural values regarding family that emphasize intergenerational family ties are often misinterpreted as enmeshment by therapists whose theoretical frameworks emphasize separation and individuation over family continuity and cohesiveness. Bradshaw (1988) described a similar process when Japanese clients are viewed as pathologically dependent because of the conflict between their cultural values of interdependence and familial and community loyalty with the Western ideals of independence and autonomy. She cited Masterson (1985) as the prime example of this form of ethnocentrism when he, in essence, diagnosed the Japanese as narcissistic because of their early childhood rearing, which featured parental indulgence and dependency rather than separation and individuation. Pinderhughes (1982) addressed a similar concern in African American families by pointing out that Black families often protect themselves from a hostile, dangerous environment by developing strong, impermeable family boundaries, which then are seen as pathological by mainstream mental health professionals who ignore the sociocultural context.

FEMINIST THEORIES AND THERAPIES ARE INADEQUATE FOR PEOPLE OF COLOR

Feminist writings have frequently been critiqued as irrelevant to Women of Color (hooks, 1981; Wallace, 1979) for lacking attention to racism and classism (Chrisman & Beal, 1985; Davis, 1983; Moraga & Anzaldua, 1983). Feminist therapies also have ignored Women of Color. Kanuha (1990) criticized feminist therapy theory for overlooking the impact of racism and classism on women of color and by forcing them to choose sexism as their "primary oppression." Previous chapters in this book have enumerated the ways in which feminist theories and therapies have failed Women of Color.

USING SUPERVISION TO INTEGRATE FEMINIST, ANTI-RACIST, AND CROSS-CULTURAL PERSPECTIVES IN PSYCHOTHERAPY

Principles of Supervision

Educational and supervisory processes are pivotal to any changes in the practice of psychotherapy. Supervision must begin to incorporate an understanding of the analysis of oppression (Kanuha, 1990), as well as greater breadth of information about gender and cross-cultural issues. Respect for diversity must become the cornerstone of psychotherapy supervision. Supervision may focus on many of the same content and process issues as traditional supervision but incorporate the feminist, anti-racist, and multicultural values and principles delineated throughout this book.

Process of Supervision

The supervisory process must facilitate the student's ability to become more sensitive to the issues described earlier. Porter (1985) described this supervisory process in detail. In summary, the supervisor must model the objectives to be passed on to the student. The supervisor must facilitate the trainee's examination of her or his biases, values, and behaviors that enhance or inhibit change in ethnic minority and female clients. The supervisor must assist the trainee in becoming aware of the impact of the social structure on the trainee's behavior as well as the client's behavior, including an analysis of how class, gender, and racial privilege has benefited the therapist. The supervisor must create a climate that will facilitate the exploration of these issues and must model greater equality and respect for the trainee in doing so. The supervisor must focus on using power constructively in supervision, including jointly establishing objectives and criteria for performance, developing mechanisms for feedback pertaining to both the performance of the trainee and the supervisor, and in handling trainee self-disclosures with respect and sensitivity.

A DEVELOPMENTAL SUPERVISION PROCESS

The process of supervision must integrate awareness, knowledge, and skills regarding feminist and cross-cultural therapy. The process must be effective (i.e., it must not overwhelm the student and inhibit learning). The supervisory process may be conceptualized as a developmental model, designed to facilitate supervisee growth and learning.

The supervisory sequence moves from a less threatening presentation of didactic and intellectual material to stages that require greater emotional involvement and self-examination. Four stages have been proposed. The goal is to progress through all four stages, which can occur only with sufficient time and commitment on the part of the student, supervisor, and program. The stages are fluid and continuous. Not every student will need to start with Stage 1.

Stage 1: Introducing an Anti-Racist, Feminist, Multicultural Perspective

The first stage is a case-by-case introduction of feminist, anti-racist, and cross-cultural principles. As the student presents therapy cases, the supervisor begins to supply alternative explanations to traditional formulations. The supervisor begins to offer a conceptual framework that takes into account the cultural or gender issues relevant to a case in an informational or didactic manner. The student is referred to the anthropological, sociological, or psychological literature regarding particular cultural or gender issues. Cultural and gender-sensitive formulations are compared and contrasted with traditional ones. The implications of each view for treatment are discussed. Universalist assumptions, that all human beings develop alike, are examined and compared with more culturally specific approaches (Tyler, Sussewell, & Williams-McCoy, 1985).

This stage is fairly directive and not unlike traditional supervision. It emphasizes relationship-building skills, the development of behaviors seen as "giving" (Sue & Zane, 1987), and the matching of interventions with the client's view of his or her problem. The supervisee would be asked to learn the relevant cultural or gender literature, just as he or she might go to the literature to develop an understanding of effective treatment strategies for behavioral or diagnostic entities, such as obsessive–compulsive behaviors or eating disorders. Questions that may be asked to guide the student include the following: What do you see as the major therapeutic issues for this client? How have you accounted for cultural, ethnic, social class, or gender issues in your formulation? What impact might they have? Cultural consultants are invited to supervision to share their expertise on particular cultural or gender issues. Their presence both facilitates greater in-depth exploration of these issues and models the supervisor's commitment to a continuous learning process.

Beginning the process by presenting specific topics in a structured format has several positive aspects. The objective approach allows the student to approach threatening material in a nonjudgmental, nonblaming fashion. The student may feel able to explore a new area without feeling overwhelmed and retreating into her or his own defenses. The supervisor and student have the opportunity to get to know one another and to create the climate necessary for self-examination. The student can evaluate whether she or he trusts the supervisor and is willing to take risks in the future.

Lack of information about specialized areas of psychotherapy is less difficult for individuals to admit than are one's own sexism and racism. Most individuals monitor, at least overtly, their expression of prejudices, stereotypes, and biases, recognizing their social unacceptability. Beginning with an information-based approach provides the student with a great deal of challenging information and data, but in a nonconfrontative manner. This may be the student's first exploration of this material, which may motivate more in-depth contemplation of the issues.

Case Example

A Mexican American woman trainee, who began with heightened awareness of her own cultural and gender background, tended to minimize differences between her cultural beliefs and practices and those of other ethnic minority groups. The supervisor felt she was overlooking important cultural issues when treating a traditional Native American family. The supervisor provided readings and a consultation from an Native American therapist. The supervisee remarked that these experiences not only changed her understanding of both the historical and contemporary role of Native Americans but prompted her to reexamine her own Mestiza heritage.

Stage 2: Exploring the Roots of Racism, Sexism, and Ethnocentrism in Society

Stage 1 focuses primarily on content issues that set the stage for exploring more abstract and general issues. In this stage, the supervisor begins to redirect the student from purely psychological, individualized, or ahistorical analyses of behavior toward an understanding of the role of cultural, historical, and environmental factors. Socialization and acculturation factors are stressed. Client problems are placed in a broader sociocultural framework. The supervisor assists the student in making connections between "symptoms" as adaptive or once-adaptive solutions to societal expectations or oppression rather than mere expression of internalized psychopathology. The student may begin by labeling the client with pejorative terms that emphasize the individual's pathology and lack of adaptation. The supervisor helps the student to place the behaviors exhibited by the client in a cultural, relational, and patriarchal context and to understand how the environment has precipitated and maintained these behaviors.

Readings that will increase the student's empathy with, and understanding of, particular gender and cultural issues are recommended. They may take the form of biographies or novels or journals rather than psychological literature. Guided imagery is helpful in having the student take on the role of the client and explore her or his world, relationships, worldview, history of oppression, and related feelings.

Case Example

A divorcing couple asked for family therapy to assist them in their difficulties with the children's acceptance of their divorce. The cotherapists began to feel angry at the mother, for they felt she was giving inconsistent messages to the children about her relationship with them. She had immigrated to the United States as an adolescent from a rural Asian community. She had married an Anglo man, had two children, and had returned to the university for an undergraduate degree. She was currently completing a graduate program in a professional school. Of concern to the therapists was her tendency to overcommit her time to the children and then have to back out to study. She would then feel guilty and go visit the children at their father's, an act identified by the therapists as creating confusion, because she adamantly stated she did not want to reunite. They labeled the mother as extremely dependent and as acting out her ambivalence destructively. The therapists viewed her more negatively than they viewed the father, although he encouraged the mother's visits and used violence against her.

In supervision, we explored alternative hypotheses. We explored the possibility that her "mixed messages" were more attributable to her own gender role socialization and her resulting guilt at not fulfilling her role as a wife and mother, as defined for a woman in her Asian cultural context. We examined why she was viewed as more unstable, because she was emotionally expressive, than her husband even though he had recently threatened her with a knife. We analyzed the opinion of her as dependent, in the context of her remarkable bilingual and bicultural transition from a rural island community in the Pacific to a professional woman and mother in an urban area in the United States. As the therapists began to alter

Stage 3: Exploring the Student's Internalized Racism and Sexism

This stage coincides with the exploration of the student's own feelings, attitudes, or countertransference issues. The student must examine her or his own internalized racist and sexist attitudes and their pervasive effect on the therapy process. This stage is crucial; we must all face our own sexism and racism and how they may lead to differing expectations, goals, and behaviors in therapy. Focusing on how the student's specific therapeutic interactions are the result of her or his perceptions of, biases about, and responses to women and ethnic minority groups is the most challenging, fragile, and potentially productive aspect of this supervision.

Reviewing actual therapy sessions through video or audiotapes is essential. The supervisor must observe verbal and nonverbal communication to assess whether (and how) the therapist subtly and unconsciously reinforces "traditional" gender or racial stereotypes, uses power unnecessarily and hierarchically, or condescends to accept the client. How do the therapist's own nonconscious attitudes interfere with therapy, and how are they conveyed to the client? In this stage, the focus is on making these attitudes, biases, assumptions, and beliefs of the therapist explicit, exploring how the therapist came to possess them, and how they aid or interfere with therapy.

Case Example

An advanced student was counseling a young woman whom she described as controlling and resistant in therapy. I asked her to explore the concept of "control," its usually derogatory connotation for women, the double binds of women wanting to be professionals or leaders, and our own internalized sexism regarding "controlling women." We began by examining the negative cultural connotation of the term when used to describe women and our own beliefs that "controlling" women are "nags" and "bitches." She expressed her own fear of being viewed in her own community as a controlling woman, especially as a highly educated, lesbian, African American woman. She felt her family and community kept her in line by shaming her for her assertiveness and her being "overeducated." She labeled women with similar backgrounds as being "pushy." The exploration of these issues by the student freed her from enough of her own internalized sexism to be able to explore these same issues with her client.

Stage 4: Adopting a Social Action, Collective Perspective

In this stage, the supervisor facilitates the student's examination of a more collective perspective about ethnic, racial, or gender issues. Students are aided in taking the systemic perspective—that social change must accompany individual change. The relationship of self-help, support, or therapy groups to collective action is explored. In supervision, I encourage students to find alternative or adjunctive healing routes for their clients and to locate resources that emphasize group participation and collective action.

This shift from an individual to collective perspective also must be encouraged in the student's life. I encourage students to develop groups that will enhance their collective action. Support groups, reading groups, practicum teams, and consciousness-raising groups are effective. I encourage participation in professional groups such as APA's Public Interest divisions. Supervisors must model this particular stage by participating themselves in collective and social action groups.

Case Example

The supervisee described in Stage 3 decided that she needed more support. We discussed her involvement in a lesbian support group. She became discouraged after a few weeks of attending it because of the absence of Women of Color and neglect of their issues. I supported her raising these concerns in the group. She did; resolution came through the group soliciting other Women of Color members and working for a balance in the issues discussed.

COMPONENTS OF SUPERVISION

Supervision cannot, and should not, replace didactic seminars in cross-cultural or feminist psychotherapy. Supervision should be adjunctive to the formal presentation of the psychological and mental health literature in these areas, just as it is with more traditional therapy topics. It is impossible to provide all relevant information in the framework of supervision. However, even in the supervisory context, conceptual and theoretical schemas should guide the process. Five conceptual strands from the cross-cultural and feminist literature have influenced my supervision and are woven throughout the supervisory process.

1. Supervision should translate awareness into action: cultural sensitivity is not enough

Sue and Zane (1987) proposed that two basic processes—credibility and giving—are necessary for effective treatment. The term *credibility* refers to the client's perception of the therapist as an effective and trustworthy helper. The underrepresentation of ethnic minority clients in the mental health system may reflect its lack of credibility. The term *giving* refers to the client's feeling that she or he has gained something from the therapy contact. Giving requires that abstract knowledge about a culture be translated into a plan for concrete and useful interventions. Both credibility and giving require that the therapist act, not merely "understand."

2. Supervision must examine when cultural formulations are appropriate and accurate

Lopez and Hernandez (1987), Montalvo and Gutierrez (1989), and Martinez (1994) described contexts in which the therapist may be misapplying cultural information, failing to provide proper care by maintaining stereotypic cultural beliefs. For example, when should psychotic symptomatology be overlooked in African Americans because hearing voices of a religious nature sometimes may be culturally appropriate (Lopez & Hernandez, 1987)? When should rigid marital roles be considered normative in Mexican American families, although the empirical data give evidence to the contrary (Cromwell & Ruiz, 1979; Zinn, 1980)? When should the same form of therapy be given to all clients of a particular ethnic minority background, rather than individualizing treatment to meet their specific needs? These factors must always be salient in one's treatment formulation.

3. Supervision must take an anti-racist position and a cross-cultural perspective

A cross-cultural perspective that does not take into account the history of oppression of people within the dominant culture is incomplete. Ethnic minority groups have suffered at the hands of mainstream society economically, socially, and culturally. The impact of this oppression must be analyzed as part of treatment. Feminist therapists have argued that nonsexist therapies are inadequate because they ignore women's status in society, assuming actual equality between men and women. Attending only to cross-cultural issues is the cultural equivalent to providing nonsexist therapies. Focusing merely on cultural aspects of a group of people without examining how the cultural components have been devalued, transformed, or co-opted by mainstream society is insufficient and may be harmful. It continues to focus on the individual and overlook the sociocultural contributions to mental health outcomes.

4. The supervisor should emphasize the process of ongoing therapist self-examination

The therapist must continually evaluate the therapy to ensure that the client's needs, not the therapist's needs, are the focus of attention. For example, just as a traditional Native American family must receive care that does not conflict with its holistic, spiritual values, the desires of an immigrant family to become more acculturated also must be respected.

5. Supervision should assist the therapist in understanding the social construction of mental health concepts

The ethnic validity model (Tyler et al., 1985) provides a nondeficit, nonblaming model for therapists to understand cross-cultural definitions of emotional well-being. This model proposes that the client must be recognized at both the individual and group level in a way that respects diversity, builds on a person's strengths, and does not systematically advantage or disadvantage any cultural group. The model identifies three types of interactions that can occur between a supervisor–supervisee or therapist–client because of their culture's socially constructed views of mental health. This model can be used to assist supervisees in understanding the relativity of their own worldviews.

CONCLUSIONS

Psychology graduate departments and internships need to commit to teach prospective therapists how to work effectively with clients from diverse cultural backgrounds. Certainly, this goal is the result of a lifelong process and cannot be taught in a few years of graduate school.

What can be taught, however, is a process—a process that begins with a commitment to see one's clients in the rich, complex, and varied context of their culture, their gender, and their world; to listen to clients' goals as they arise from this context; to refrain from imposing one's own values and biases on clients; and to seek out ways to understand behavior and intervene in a culturally competent fashion. Cultural and gender competence in psychotherapy must be as strong of a priority as all other competencies expected in graduate programs.

REFERENCES

Abramowitz, S. J., Abramowitz, C. V., Jackson, C., & Gomes, B. (1973). The politics of clinical judgements: What nonliberal examiners infer about women who do not stifle themselves. *Journal of Consulting and Clinical Psychology, 41*, 385–391.

American Psychological Association. (1975). Report of the Task Force on Sex Bias and Sex-Role Stereotyping in Psychotherapeutic Practice. *American Psychologist, 30*, 1169–1175.

American Psychological Association Board of Ethnic Minority Affairs. (1990). *Guidelines for therapy with ethnic minority clients.* Washington, DC: American Psychological Association.

Bingham, W. C., & House, E. W. (1973). Counselors view women and work: Accuracy of information. *Vocational Guidance Quarterly, 21,* 262–268.

Bradshaw, C. (1988, May). *A Japanese view of dependency: What can it contribute to feminist theory and therapy?* Paper presented at the Advanced Feminist Therapy Institute, Seattle, WA.

Broverman, I. K., Broverman, D. M., Clarkson, F., Rosenkrantz, P., & Vogel, S. R. (1970). Sex-role stereotypes and clinical judgements of mental health. *Journal of Consulting Psychology, 34,* 1–7.

Chesler, P. (1972). *Women and madness.* New York: Doubleday.

Chrisman, R., & Beal, F. M. (Eds.). (1985). Black women and feminism. *The Black Scholar, 16,* 1–64.

Cromwell, R. E., & Ruiz, R. A. (1979). The myth of macho dominance in decision-making within Mexican and Chicano families. *Hispanic Journal of Behavioral Sciences, 1,* 355–373.

Davis, A. Y. (1983). *Women, race, and class.* New York: Vintage Books.

Fabrikant, B. (1974). The psychotherapist and the female patient: Perceptions and change. In V. Franks & V. Burtle (Eds.), *Women and therapy* (pp. 83–109). New York: Brunner/Mazel.

Falicov, C. J. (1982). Mexican families. In M. McGoldrick, J. K. Pearce, & J. Giordano (Eds.), *Ethnicity and family therapy* (pp. 134–163). New York: Guilford Press.

hooks, b. (1981). *Ain't I a woman: Black women and feminism.* Boston: South End Press.

Jilek-Aall, L. (1976). The western psychiatrist and his non-western clientele. *Canadian Psychiatric Association Journal, 21,* 353–359.

Kanuha, V. (1990). The need for an integrated analysis of oppression in feminist therapy ethics. In H. Lerman & N. Porter (Eds.), *Feminist ethics in psychotherapy* (pp. 24–35). New York: Springer.

La Fromboise, T. (1988). American Indian mental health policy. *American Psychologist, 43,* 388–397.

Lopez, S., & Hernandez, P. (1987). When culture is considered in the evaluation and treatment of Hispanic patients. *Psychotherapy, 24,* 120–126.

Martinez, K. J. (1994). Cultural sensitivity in family therapy gone awry. *Hispanic Journal of Behavioral Sciences, 16,* 75–89.

Masterson, J. F. (1985). *The real self: A developmental, self, and object relations approach.* New York: Brunner/Mazel.

McGoldrick, M. (1982). Ethnicity and family therapy: An overview. In M. McGoldrick, J. K. Pearce, & J. Giordano (Eds.), *Ethnicity and family therapy* (pp. 3–30). New York: Guilford Press.

Miller, D. (1974). The influence of the patient's sex on clinical judgement. *Smith College Studies in Social Work, 44,* 89–100.

Montalvo, B., & Gutierrez, M. J. (1989). Nine assumptions for work with ethnic minority families. In G. W. Saba, B. M. Karrer, & K. V. Hardy (Eds.), *Minorities and family therapy* (pp. 35–52). Binghamton, NY: Haworth Press.

Moraga, C., & Anzaldua, G. (1983). *This bridge called my back: Writings by radical women of color.* New York: Kitchen Table: Women of Color Press.

Pinderhughes, E. (1982). Afro-American families and the victim system. In M. McGoldrick, J. K. Pearce, & J. Giordano (Eds.), *Ethnicity and family therapy* (pp 108–122). New York: Guilford Press.

Porter, N. (1985). New perspectives on therapy supervision. In L. B. Rosewater & L. E. A. Walker (Eds.), *Handbook of feminist therapy: Women's issues in psychotherapy* (pp. 332–343). New York: Springer.

President's Commission on Mental Health. (1978). *Report to the President.* Washington, DC: U.S. Government Printing Office.

Rosewater, L. B., & Walker, L. E. A. (Eds.). (1985). *Handbook of feminist therapy: Women's issues in psychotherapy.* New York: Springer.

Sherman, J. A., Koufacos, C., & Kenworthy, J. A. (1978). Therapists: Their attitudes and information about women. *Psychology of Women Quarterly, 2,* 299–313.

Sue, S. (1988). Psychotherapeutic services for ethnic minorities: Two decades of research findings. *American Psychologist, 43,* 301–308.

Sue, S., & Zane, N. (1987). The role of culture and cultural techniques in psychotherapy: A critique and reformulation. *American Psychologist, 42,* 37–45.

Tanney, M. F., & Birk, J. M. (1976). Women counselors for women clients? A review of the research. *Counseling Psychologist, 6,* 28–32.

Trimble, J. E. (1982). American Indian mental health and the role of training for prevention. In S. M. Manson (Ed.), *New directions in prevention among American Indians and Alaska native communities* (pp. 147–168). Portland, OR: Health Sciences University.

Trimble, J. E., & La Fromboise, T. (1985). American Indians and the counseling process: Culture, adaptation, and style. In P. Pederson (Ed.), *Handbook of cross-cultural mental health services* (pp. 127–134). Beverly Hills, CA: Sage.

Tyler, F. B., Sussewell, D. R., & Williams-McCoy, J. (1985). Ethnic validity in psychotherapy. *Psychotherapy, 22,* 311–320.

Wallace, M. (1979). *Black macho and the myth of the superwoman.* New York: Dial Press.

Zinn, M. B. (1980). Employment and education of Mexican-American women: The interplay of modernity and ethnicity in eight families. *Harvard Educational Review, 50,* 47–62.

9

ACADEMIC SEXUAL HARASSMENT: FROM THEORY AND RESEARCH TO PROGRAM IMPLEMENTATION

MICHELE A. PALUDI, DARLENE C. DeFOUR, ROSEMARIE ROBERTS,
ANNA MARIA TEDESCO, JACQUELINE BRATHWAITE, and
ANDREA MARINO

IN WOMEN'S OWN VOICES

Have I been overtly discriminated against? Possibly no. Have I been encouraged, helped, congratulated, received recognition, gotten a friendly hello, a solicitous "can I help you out?" The answer is no. Being a woman here just makes you be tougher, work harder, and hope if you get a 4.0 GPA [grade point average] someone will say, "You're good." Perhaps like a fellow student told me, 'you're only here to get a husband.' If that were true, I can think of easier, less painful and discouraging ways.

When people treated me differently in college because I was Black and female in things like counseling me on the choice of a major or making comments about my background or about Blacks, I wondered what was wrong with me.

Who was going to believe me? I was an undergraduate student and he was a famous professor. It was an unreal situation.

One professor in my major was constantly making comments about 'how cute I was' or 'how serious' or 'how motivated I seemed to be' after class or while I was studying in the library. Needless to say, I felt very uncomfortable and started wearing old jeans to his classes.

I . . . became quite skilled at glancing down department hallways to make sure he wasn't there before venturing forth, and pretending not to see him when we did cross paths. The whole experience has left me quite mistrustful of faculty in general and I still feel some trepidation when visiting the department.

The impact of this isolated incident on me has been enormous. It has changed my way of relating to the program. I used to think it could be a place of learning, mentoring, work and fun. Now, although there are still people there whom I trust and learn from, I am angry and insecure every time I'm in that building. I have heard that this professor has propositioned at least two other students, and I am silently furious. I've said nothing about this except to my husband. . . .

I expected the graduate experience to be different. I expected that my major advisor would be my mentor. I have received very little time. I have noticed that male students seem to develop different kinds of relationships with professors and get more help and support.
—Project on the Status and Education of Women (1978)

As these women's accounts affirm, sexual harassment in colleges and universities is a major barrier to women's professional development and a traumatic force that disrupts and damages their personal lives (Paludi, 1990). Women's performance in course work suffers, and many women drop out of school altogether. And stress reactions invariably follow sexual harassment, including depression, tension, anger and fear, insomnia, headaches, feelings of helplessness and embarassment, and decreased motivation (Koss, 1990; Rabinowitz, 1990). For ethnic minority women who have been sexually harassed, economic vulnerability is paramount. They may be dependent on financial aid to fund their education; they have loans more often than research or teaching assistantships (Blackwell, 1981; DeFour, 1990; Paludi, 1993).

Women feel powerless, not in control; afraid, not flattered, by sexual harassment. Their emotional and physical well-being resembles victims of other sexual abuses (i.e., rape, incest, and battering). Their behavior does not resemble "courtship behaviors." As Quina (1990) stated, rape and harassments are both sexual assaults which lie on a continuum of sexual exploitation, varying primarily in degree of physical intrusion and potential injury to the victim. On the least physically violent pole, this continuum begins with verbal assaults, including sexually offensive jokes or degrading comments. At the most violent pole are rape-murder and femicide. On this scale, sexual harassment and rape are relatively close together. In fact, many assaults now called harassment—those involving sexual contact—are legally the equivalent of rape. (p. 94)

As Koss (1990) suggested, experiencing academic sexual harassment transforms women into victims and changes their lives: "It is inevitable that once victimized, at minimum, one can never again feel quite as invulnerable" (p. 74). Koss (1990) offered the following passage from Eugene O'Neill's play, *A Long Day's Journey Into Night*, to capture the psychological impact of academic sexual harassment:

> None of us can help the things that Life has done to us.... They're done before you realize it, and once they're done they make you do other things until at last everything comes between you and what you would like to be, and you've lost your true self forever. (p. 73)

In this chapter, we (a) review the psychological literature that documents the impact of academic sexual harassment; (b) describe the sexual harassment of ethnic and racial minority women; (c) describe the differing perceptions of sexual harassment commonly held by women and men; and (d) offer suggestions for curtailing sexual harassment through the institution of college policies and panels to enforce them, training of faculty and graduate students, and educational campaigns to inform the academic community of the nature and severity of the problem. We begin with an overview of the definitions and incidence of academic sexual harassment.

DEFINITIONS AND INCIDENCE OF SEXUAL HARASSMENT

Sexual harassment takes many forms, from sexist remarks and covert physical contact (e.g., patting, brushing against someone) to blatant propositions and sexual assaults. Researchers have developed five categories to encompass the range of sexual harassment (e.g., Fitzgerald, 1990): gender harassment, seductive behavior, sexual bribery, sexual coercion, and sexual imposition. These levels of sexual harassment correlate with legal definitions of sexual harassment. *Gender harassment* consists of generalized sexist remarks and behavior not designed to elicit sexual cooperation but to convey insulting, degrading, or sexist attitudes about women. *Seductive behavior* is unwanted, inappropriate, and offensive sexual advances. *Sexual bribery* is the solicitation of sexual activity or other sex-linked behavior by promise of reward. *Sexual coercion* is the solicitation of sexual activity by threat of punishment, and *sexual imposition* includes gross sexual imposition, assault, and rape.

Sexual harassment is clearly prohibited within the college and university system as a form of sexual discrimination, under both Title IX of the 1972 Education Amendments (and, for employees, Title VII of the 1964 Civil Rights Act). The Equal Employment Opportunity Commission states in its Guidelines on Sex Discrimination:

> Unwelcome sexual advances, requests for sexual favors, and other verbal or physical conduct of a sexual nature constitute sexual harassment when (1) submission to such conduct is made either explicitly or implicitly a term or condition of an individual's employment, (2) submission to or rejection of such conduct by an individual is used as the basis for employment decisions affecting such individual, or (3) such conduct has the purpose or effect of substantially interfering with an individual's work performance or creating an intimidating, hostile, or offensive working environment. (p. 33)

Sexual harassment involves the confluence of authority (power) relations and sexuality (or sexism) in a culture stratified by sex. This power or authority is either formal or informal; it can be achieved or ascribed. Formal power is derived from a formal role (e.g., research supervisor, professor, graduate teaching assistant, mentor). Informal power is derived from men's sexual prerogative. Informal power thus suggests that men have a right to initiate sexual interactions or assert the primacy of women's gender role (or race, class, age, and sexual orientation) over her role as student. As Fitzgerald (1990) commented, "it is this prerogative, a sort of psychological *droit de seigneuer*, that accounts for the mystification that often leads women to misperceive and mislabel their experiences of harassment" (p. 38).

Zalk, Paludi, and Dederich (1991) further discussed informal and formal power issues:

> The bottom line in the relationship is POWER. The faculty member has it and the student does not. As intertwined as the faculty-student roles may be, and as much as one must exist for the other to exist, they are not equal collaborators. The student does not negotiate indeed, has nothing to negotiate with. . . .
>
> All the power lies with the faculty member—some of it real, concrete, and some of it is imagined or elusive. The bases of the faculty member's almost absolute power are varied and range from the entirely rational into broad areas of fantasy. Professors give grades, write recommendations for graduate schools, awards and the like, and can predispose colleagues' attitudes towards students. (pp. 102–103)

For certain student groups, professors are particularly powerful (Barickman, Paludi, & Rabinowitz, 1992). For example,

(a) women of color, especially those with "token" status;
(b) graduate students, whose future careers are often determined by their association with a particular faculty member;
(c) students in small colleges or small academic departments, where the number of faculty available to students is quite small;
(d) students in male-populated fields, e.g., engineering;
(e) students who are economically disadvantaged and work part-time or full-time while attending classes.

Thus, the structure of the academy interacts with psychological dynamics to increase women's vulnerability to all forms of sexual harassment. Professors' greatest power lies in the capacity to enhance or diminish students' self-esteem. This power can motivate students to learn course material or convince them to give up. The tone and content of the student–professor interaction is especially important. Is the student encouraged or put down? Do the faculty members use their knowledge to let students know how "stupid" they are or to challenge their thinking? As Zalk et al. (1991) pointed out, this is real power.

Dziech and Weiner (1984) reported that 30% of undergraduate women suffer sexual harassment from at least one of their instructors during their 4 years of college. When definitions of sexual harassment include sexist remarks and other forms of "gender harassment," the incidence rate in undergraduate populations nears 70% (Paludi, 1990). Research by Adams, Kottke, and Padgitt (1983) showed that 13% of the women students they surveyed said they had avoided taking a class or working with certain professors because of the risk of being subjected to sexual advances. A 1983 study conducted at Harvard University indicated that 15% of the graduate students and 12% of the undergraduate students who had been harassed by their professors changed their major or educational program because of the harassment. Wilson and Krauss (1983) reported that 9% of the female undergraduates in their study had been pinched, touched, or patted to the point of personal discomfort, whereas 17% of the women in the Adams et al. survey received verbal sexual advances, 14% received sexual invitations, 6% had been subjected to physical advances, and 2% received direct sexual bribes.

Bailey and Richards (1985) reported that of 246 women graduate students in their sample, 13% indicated they had been sexually harassed, 21% had not enrolled in a course to avoid such behavior and 16% indicated they had been directly assaulted. Bond (1988) reported that 75% of the 229 female members of Division 27 who responded to her survey experienced jokes with sexual themes during their graduate training, 69%

were subjected to sexist comments demeaning to women, and 58% of the women reported experiencing sexist remarks about their clothing, body, or sexual activities.

Research by Paludi, DeFour, and Roberts (1994) suggested that the incidence of academic sexual harassment of ethnic minority women is even greater than that reported with White women. Dziech and Weiner (1984) and DeFour (1990) suggested that ethnic minority women are more vulnerable to receiving sexual attention from professors. Ethnic minority women are subject to stereotypes about sex, viewed as mysterious, and less sure of themselves in academia. Thus, although all women students are vulnerable to some degree, male faculty tend to select those who are most vulnerable and needy. As Tong (1984) commented, "sexual harassers tend to take advantage of those whom they perceive as most vulnerable, and whether we care to face it or not, Black women enflesh the vulnerability of their people's slave past" (p. 165). Sexual harassment is thus a major form of victimization of women in higher education, even though it is still largely a "hidden issue" (as the Project on the Status and Education of Women called it in 1978).

PERCEPTIONS OF SEXUAL HARASSMENT: IMPACT OF SEX AND ETHNICITY

Dovan et al. (1987) reported that college women were more likely to label a male faculty member's harassment of a female student in terms of his abusing his power as a professor over the student instead of abusing his power as a man. They recognized sexual harassment as allowing professors to undermine students' positions in higher education. This finding supports the organizational model of harassment identified by Tangri, Burt, and Johnson (1982): Women were able to explain harassment as resulting from the opportunities presented by power and authority relations that derive from the hierarchical structure of academia.

Dovan et al. (1987) also reported that women's adherence to the organizational model promoted their empowerment. Women who espoused this explanatory model reported seeking redress for the victimization. Such a response would not be predicted from adherence to the sociocultural model: Women would not be likely to take interpersonally assertive action or to act on an expectation that the organization will help them resolve the issue. Women are much more likely than men to assign a central role to the college for preventing and dealing with all levels of sexual harassment. Because the research indicates that men attribute more responsibility to women victims of sexual harassment, men also would be likely to minimize the potential responsibility of college and university officials (Paludi,

1990). As male faculty reported in Fitzgerald, Weitzman, Gold, and Omerod's (1988) study,

> in a classroom setting it is entirely appropriate that personal and professional lives be separated. However, undergraduates doing honor's research and graduate students become junior colleagues; a close personal relationship is to be encouraged. It has been my observation that students, and some faculty, have little understanding of the extreme pressure a male professor can feel as the object of sexual interest of attractive women students. (p. 337)

Fitzgerald et al. (1988) found that male faculty members typically do not label their behavior as sexual harassment despite the fact they report they frequently engage in behaviors that meet the legal definition of sexual harassment. Male faculty members denied the inherent power differential between faculty and students, as well as the psychological power conferred by this differential. Kenig and Ryan (1986) reported that faculty men were less likely than faculty women to define sexual harassment as including jokes, teasing remarks of a sexual nature, and unwanted suggestive looks or gestures. In addition, female faculty were more likely than men to disapprove of romantic relationships between faculty and students. Male faculty typically view sexual harassment as a personal, not an organizational issue.

These data thus suggest that education is needed in men's perceptions of the misuse of power, their perceptions about women who have been harassed, and their attitudes toward sexual interactions. Another focus of such training lies in the politics involved in the mentor–protégé relationship. Typically, mentors and protégés do not have a common understanding of their relationship (DeFour, 1990; Paludi & DeFour, 1992). Consequently, students and faculty have substantially different definitions of mentor and protégé.

Fitzgerald et al. (1988) reported that male faculty members who participated in their study typically denied that there is an inherent power differential between students and faculty. Female students, however, recognize this power differential. Thus, educational programs are needed to deal with women's and men's understanding of the concept of harassment and the social meanings attributed to the behaviors that legally constitute harassment. However, the interpretation given to the professor's behavior by female students is not flattery or friendliness.

All of these experiences contribute to emotional and physical stress reactions. In recent years, the label *sexual harassment trauma syndrome* (Shullman, 1989) has been applied to the effects of sexual harassment on physical, emotional, interpersonal, and career aspects of women's lives. Sexual harassment victims may experience a second victimization when they attempt to deal with the situation through legal and institutional means.

Stereotypes about sexual harassment and women's victimization blame women for the harassment. These stereotypes center around the myths that sexual harassment is a form of seduction, that women secretly want to be sexually harassed, and that women do not tell the truth. As DeFour (1990) commented,

> the images and perceptions of women of color also increase their vulnerability to harassment. These images either portray the women as weak and thus unlikely to fight back if harassed, or they are perceived as very sexual and thus desiring sexual attention. Hispanic women have been described as hot-blooded. . . . Asian women have been described as . . . submissive. However, they are also viewed by some as the exotic sexpot who will cater to the whims of any man. (pp. 48–49)

The behaviors that legally constitute academic sexual harassment is just that, despite what the professor's intentions may be. It is the power differential and the woman's reaction to the behavior that are the critical variables.

IMPLICATIONS FOR EDUCATION AND POLICY

Several kinds of intervention may be instituted to challenge attitudes that perpetuate harassment. Biaggio, Watts, and Brownell (1990) and Barickman et al. (1992) suggested that key individuals within organizations can be targeted—residence hall advisors in dormitories, department chairs—for attendance at workshops at which they can be informed about the institutional policy and procedures dealing with harassment. In addition, new student orientations are another arena for disseminating information about institutional policies that prohibit sexual and gender harassment. Items relating to gender and sexual harassment can be placed on teaching evaluations.

Sandler (1988) also offered suggestions for meeting this goal, including (a) establishing a policy statement that makes it clear that differential treatment of professional women on campus will not be tolerated, (b) establishing a permanent committee to explore and report on professional climate issues, and (c) publishing an annual report on progress relating to women on campus.

Barickman et al. (1992) offered advice for counselors, advocates, and educators in the area of academic sexual harassment:

- Acknowledge women's courage by stating how difficult it is to label, report, and discuss sexual harassment.
- Encourage women to share their feelings and perceptions.
- Provide information to women about the incidence of academic sexual harassment. Also share with women the symp-

toms associated with the Sexual Harassment Trauma Syndrome.

- Assure women that they are not responsible for their victimization.
- Work with women in their search for the meaning in their victimization; support them while they mourn their losses.
- Work with women in monitoring their physical, emotional, academic, and interpersonal responses to academic sexual harassment.
- Provide a safe forum for women's expression of anger and resentment.
- Work with women on ways to validate themselves so as to feel empowered.
- A student, faculty, or staff peer counseling group can be an important resource for women who are understandably wary of the entire institution as a result of sexual harassment by a member of that institution.

Paludi and Barickman (1991) suggested the following educational interventions:

- Include information about academic sexual harassment in faculty and student orientation materials.
- Hold a "Sexual Harassment Awareness Week" and schedule programs around the issue of lesbian and gay harassment.
- Require that student leaders attend workshops on sexual harassment.
- Encourage sororities and fraternities to present programs on sexual harassment.
- Include information on sexual harassment in packets for transfer students.
- Report annually on sexual harassment.
- Encourage faculty to incorporate discussions of sexual harassment in their courses.

Paludi and Barickman (1991) also provided questions concerning academic sexual harassment for campuses to address. For example,

- Are there policies and effective procedures for dealing with academic sexual harassment? for workplace sexual harassment?
- Do the policies forbid peer harassment behaviors or is it limited to harassment by faculty, administrators, and other staff?
- Are the policies forbidding sexual harassment well publicized? Are they circulated periodically among students, staff, faculty, and administrators?

- How do individuals in your campus community learn whom they should see to discuss sexual harassment?
- Are there specific individuals to whom individuals can go for help with sexual harassment issues?
- Are remedies clear and commensurate with the level of violation?
- Does your campus have procedures to inform new faculty, staff, and students about sexual harassment?
- Does your campus have a task force or other structure that examines and reports annually on sexual harassment?
- Are there regular campus workshops on sexual harassment, including peer harassment?
- What services are available to individuals who have experienced sexual harassment?

Education and training must follow the development of an effective policy statement and grievance procedures (Paludi, 1993). Sexual harassment occurs in a context of institutional power. It is thus important that the means of resolving complaints of sexual harassment be distinct from the regular departmental and administrative hierarchies (Barickman et al., 1992).

It is important to note that similar to women's intentions to report a rape, intentions to report academic sexual harassment varies according to ethnic group membership (Paludi et al., 1994). Women with the fewest resources to cope with victimization (e.g., ethnic minority women, returning women, physically challenged women) carry the most severe burden of fear (Riger & Gordon, 1981). Special attention must be paid to providing a safe place in the college and university setting for ethnic minority women to report academic sexual harassment should they choose this option. Rowe (1990) noted that ethnic minority women want their complaints defined as they wish them to be defined. She reported that many Asian American women and African American women view unwelcome sexualized behavior as racism, not sexism, and want it dealt with in those terms. Consequently, Rowe recommended the availability of several options for reporting for women on the basis of their own definitions and explanatory models of sexual harassment.

CONCLUSION

As Mead (1978) argued, a new taboo is needed on campus that demands that faculty make new norms, not rely on masculine-biased definitions of success, career development, and sexuality. What is also needed is an ethic of care—and the restructuring of academic institutions so that caring can become a central and active value (Stimpson, 1989). This suggests changes in the present institutional structures that dominate the college and university system.

One important change needs to be in the mentor–protégé relationship, where women are protégés and men are mentors (Haring-Hidore & Paludi, 1989). Women have reported needing much different kinds of information from mentors than do men. For example, women report wanting their mentoring relationship to include psychosocial aspects (e.g., receiving advice, mostly from women) on personal problems, receiving information on dealing with role strain involved in combining a career and family life, and being assisted with personal development (Paludi & DeFour, 1992). Women place considerable emphasis on working with mentors who combine personal and professional roles and who are likely to affirm them as professionals as well as encourage and support their professional goals. Women indicate that this affirmation and encouragement typically come from female faculty members.

However, many mentoring relationships involve men as mentors and women as protégés. This common arrangement by which men are in positions of power within mentoring relationships (as mentors) and women are in more vulnerable positions (as protégés) suggests that possibility of sexuality and sex as significant and complex factors within such relationships (Haring-Hidore & Paludi, 1989). More women than men experience problems in mentoring relationships (e.g., of not being included in faculty members' professional networks and of not being encouraged in their field of study). This finding is consistent with the findings of Brooks and Haring-Hidore (1987). Furthermore, women are typically isolated from informal collegial contacts; they consequently receive less encouragement for their successes and are avoided by their male mentors. Clow and Paludi (1985) reported that male mentors were reluctant to mentor women because they believe women are not as dedicated to their careers as are men. Male mentors indicate that they perceive a woman apprenticing herself to work with them as requiring help, remedial assistance. Thus, women are described as "needing" mentoring. This raises a paradox in the mentoring literature (LaFrance, 1987): As women continue to get the mentoring they *need*, they will be perceived as *needing* the mentoring they get. Women's achievements may thus be explained by external, unstable causal factors (e.g., help from a senior man).

Mentors are seen as essential because they generate power. The introduction of sexuality and sex into mentoring relationships can have negative implications for achievement for female protégés. Women who are suspected of having "slept their way to the top" are castigated by others, sometimes unfairly when the accusation is false. Women who have sex with their mentors may be unjustly deprived of their achievements if the achievements did not depend on an unfair advantage gained by a sexual mentoring relationship. Whether it is fair or not, achievements made in sexual mentoring relationships may never boost protégés' careers and may, in fact, detract from their careers because of the stigma attached by others (Haring-Hidore & Paludi, 1989).

A feminist perspective on mentoring has stressed the reciprocal nature of mentoring relationships. Moore (1984), for example, advocated an emphasis on (wo)mentoring—women mentoring other women, which she contended is sharing of power, competence, self, and differences. As Hetherington and Barcelo (1985) stated,

> if we are truly concerned about equal access, each of us must look around and see if we are mentoring all women, including women of Color, on an equal basis. To move forward together, administrators must educate themselves about cultures unfamiliar to them, and they must explore their own biases. (p. 14)

Paludi et al. (1988) and DeFour (1991) described the importance of feminist female faculty to mentor female graduate students, especially considering the politics of cross-race and cross-sex mentor–protégé relationships. Networking mentoring programs for women in graduate school and female faculty is recommended. These programs would offer reciprocal models of psychosocial and vocational development that would empower women, not intimidate them. We also suggest extending the mentor–protégé relationship to include larger social networks. DeFour and Hirsch (1990) found that Black women in graduate programs benefit from relationships with other Black female peers and faculty from other academic departments. DeFour and Hirsch also reported that Black graduate students who were in integrated departments had higher grades, were better adjusted, and perceived themselves as making good progress in their graduate work. Furthermore, one social support variable for Black graduate students was out-of-school contact with Black faculty. As DeFour (1991) concluded, "the presence of ethnic minority faculty may serve as evidence to the student that they too can complete their education and become competent professionals" (p. 1).

Gilbert, Gallessich, and Evans (1983) suggested forming networks and support systems to lessen the isolation many women encounter in academic departments (especially feminist women, lesbian women, ethnic minority women, and physically challenged women). Moses (1989) noted that Black women who attempt to initiate a mentor–protégé relationship (as protégés) are perceived as "pushy" and "aggressive." To facilitate the development of mentor–protégé relationships for ethnic minority women, nonminority faculty need to be trained in the career psychology of minority students and to initiate the mentor–protégé relationship.

We also recommend retraining faculty, student affairs personnel, and administrators in empowering women and avoiding a "chilly climate" for them. A blueprint for such training was provided by Paludi and Steuernagel (1990) in their text, *Foundations for a Feminist Restructuring of the Academic Disciplines*, and by Hall and Sandler (1983) in their monograph, "Academic Mentoring for Women Students and Faculty: A New Look at an Old Way to Get Ahead."

REFERENCES

Adams, J., Kottke, J., & Padgitt, J. (1983). Sexual harassment of university students. *Journal of College Student Personnel, 24,* 484–490.

Bailey, N., & Richards, M. (1985, August). *Tarnishing the ivory tower: Sexual harassment in graduate training programs in psychology.* Paper presented at the 93rd Annual Convention of the American Psychological Association, Los Angeles.

Barickman, R. B., Paludi, M. A., & Rabinowitz, V. C. (1992). Sexual harassment of students: Victims of the college experience. In E. Viano (Ed.), *Victimology: An international perspective* (pp. 153–165). New York: Springer.

Biaggio, M. K., Watts, D., & Brownell, A. (1990). Addressing sexual harassment: Strategies for prevention and change. In M. A. Paludi (Ed.), *Ivory power: Sexual harassment on campus.* Albany: State University of New York Press.

Blackwell, J. E. (1981). *Mainstreaming outsiders: The production of black professionals.* Bayside, CA: General Hall.

Bond, M. (1988). Division 27 Sexual Harassment Survey: Definition, impact, and environmental context. *The Community Psychologist, 21,* 7–10.

Brooks, L., & Haring-Hildore, M. (1987). Mentoring in academe: A comparison of mentors' and proteges' perceived problems. *International Journal of Mentoring, 1,* 3–9.

Clow, C., & Paludi, M. A. (1985). *Mentoring: An intergenerational perspective.* Unpublished manuscript, Kent State University, Kent, OH.

DeFour, D. C. (1990). The interface of racism and sexism on college campuses. In M. A. Paludi (Ed.), *Ivory power: Sexual harassment on campus* (pp. 45–52). Albany: State University of New York Press.

DeFour, D. C. (1991). Issues in mentoring ethnic minority students. *Focus, 5,* 1–2.

DcFour, D. C., & Hirsch, B. J. (1990). The adaptation of Black graduate students: A social networks approach. *American Journal of Community Psychology, 18,* 489–505.

Dovan, J., Grossman, M., Kindermann, J., Matula, S., Paludi, M. A., & Scott, C. A. (1987, March). *College women's attitudes and attributions about sexual and gender harassment.* Symposium presented at the annual meeting of the Association for Women in Psychology, Bethesda, MD.

Dziech, B., & Weiner, L. (1984). *The lecherous professor.* Boston: Beacon Press.

Fitzgerald, L. F. (1990). Sexual harassment: The definition and measurement of a construct. In M. A. Paludi (Ed.), *Ivory power: Sexual harassment on campus* (pp. 21–44). Albany: State University of New York Press.

Fitzgerald, L. F., Weitzman, L., Gold, Y., & Omerod, M. (1988). Academic sexual harassment: Sex and denial in scholarly garb. *Psychology of Women Quarterly, 12,* 329–340.

Gilbert, L., Gallessich, J., & Evans, S. (1983). Sex of faculty role model and students' self-perceptions of competency. *Sex Roles, 9,* 597–607.

Hall, R., & Sandler, B. (1983). *Academic mentoring for women students and faculty: A new look at an old way to get ahead.* Washington, DC: Project on the Status and Education of Women.

Haring-Hidore, M., & Paludi, M. A. (1989). Sexuality and sex in mentoring and tutoring: Implications of opportunities and achievement. *Peabody Journal of Education, 64,* 164–172.

Hetherington, C., & Barcelo, R. (1985). Womentoring: A cross-cultural perspective. *Journal of the National Association of Women Deans, Administrators and Counselors, 48,* 12–15.

Kenig, S., & Ryan, J. (1986). Sex differences in levels of tolerance and attribution of blame for sexual harassment on a university campus. *Sex Roles, 15,* 535–549.

Koss, M. P. (1990). Changed lives: The psychological impact of sexual harassment. In M. A. Paludi (Ed.), *Ivory power: Sexual harassment on campus* (pp. 73–92). Albany: State University of New York Press.

LaFrance, M. (1987, July). *The paradox of mentoring.* Paper presented at the Interdisciplinary Congress on Women, Dublin, Ireland.

Mead, M. (1978). A proposal: We need taboos on sex at work. Reported in B. Dzeich & L. Weiner (1984). *The lecherous professor.* Boston: Beacon Press.

Moore, K. (1984). Careers in college and university administration: How are women affected? In A. Tinsley, C. Secord, & S. Kaplan (Eds.), *Women in higher education administration.* San Francisco: Jossey-Bass.

Moses, Y. (1988). *Black women in the academy.* Washington, DC: Project on the Status and Education of Women.

Paludi, M. A. (Ed.). (1990). *Ivory power: Sexual harassment on campus.* Albany: State University of New York Press.

Paludi, M. A. (1993). Ethnicity, sex, and sexual harassment. *Thought and Action: The National Education Association Higher Education Journal, 8,* 105–116.

Paludi, M. A., & Barickman, R. B. (1991). *Academic and workplace sexual harassment: A manual of resources.* Albany: State University of New York Press.

Paludi, M. A., & DeFour, D. C. (1992). The Mentoring Experiences Questionnaire. *Mentoring International, 6,* 19–23.

Paludi, M. A., DeFour, D. C., Banks, M., Fitzgerald, L. F., Corcoran, C., Dix, J., & Valian, V. (1988, March). *Surviving as a feminist scholar.* Paper presented at the annual meeting of the Association for Women in Psychology, Bethesda, MD.

Paludi, M. A., DeFour, D. C., & Roberts, R. (1994). *Academic sexual harassment of ethnic minority women.* Unpublished manuscript.

Paludi, M. A., & Steuernagel, G. (Eds.). (1990). *Foundations for a feminist restructuring of the academic disciplines.* New York: Haworth Press.

Project on the status and education of women. (1978). Sexual harassment: A hidden issue. Washington, DC: Association of American Colleges.

Rabinowitz, V. C. (1990). Coping with sexual harassment. In M. A. Paludi (Ed.), *Ivory power: Sexual harassment on campus* (pp. 101–118). Albany: State University of New York Press.

Quina, K. (1990). The victimizations of women. In M. A. Paludi (Ed.), *Ivory power: Sexual harassment on campus.* Albany: State University of New York Press.

Riger, S., & Gordon, M. (1981). The fear of rape: A study in social control. *Journal of Social Issues, 37,* 71–92.

Rowe, M. (1990). People who feel harassed need a complaint system with both formal and informal options. *Negotiation Journal, 6,* 1–9.

Sandler, B. (1988, April). *Sexual harassment: A new issue for institutions, or these are the times that try men's souls.* Paper presented at the Conference on Sexual Harassment on Campus, New York, NY.

Shullman, S. (1989, March). *The sexual harassment trauma syndrome.* Paper presented at the Association for Women in Psychology, Newport, RI.

Stimpson, C. (1989). Over-reaching: Sexual harassment and education. *Initiatives, 52,* 1–5.

Tangri, S., Burt, M., & Johnson, L. (1982). Sexual harassment at work: Three explanatory models. *Journal of Social Issues, 38,* 33–54.

Tong, R. (1984). *Women, sex, and the law.* Totowa, NJ: Rowman & Allanheld.

Wilson, K., & Krauss, L. (1983). Sexual harassment in the university. *Journal of College Student Personnel, 24,* 219–224.

Zalk, S. R., Paludi, M. A., & Dederich, J. (1991). Ivory power revisited: Women's consensual relationships with male faculty. In M. A. Paludi & R. B. Barickman *Academic and workplace sexual harassment: A manual of resources* (pp. 99–114). Albany: State University of New York Press.

III

THE PSYCHOLOGY OF WOMEN OF FOUR ETHNIC GROUPS

INTRODUCTION

The chapters in this section focus on the psychology of women of four ethnic groups: African, Asian, Latina, and Native American women. Each chapter provides a different "take," a different angle, from which the women of various ethnic groups can be understood and, together, the chapters highlight the need for interdisciplinary analyses when examining culture and gender.

In chapter 10, "American Indian Women in Psychological Practice," Teresa LaFromboise, Sandra Bennett, Paulette Running Wolf, and Amy James discuss the paucity of studies of Native American women. They focus primarily on clinical issues of Native American women from the perspective of the help seeker and help provider.

In chapter 11, "Psychological Issues for Latinas," Angela Ginorio, Lorraine Guiterrez, Ana Mari Cauce, and Mimi Acosta summarize what social scientists do and do not know about Latina women and girls, detail the nature of gender roles in various Latino communities, and challenge ethnocentric stereotypes and assumptions regarding those roles.

In chapter 12, "The Psychology of Asian American Women," Maria Root similarly summarizes the evidence on Asian American women. She also highlights the differences among various Asian American populations (e.g., Koreans, Chinese, Japanese) and describes how their different immigration and political histories in the United States have affected gender roles and relations within each community.

In chapter 13, "The Psychology of Black Women," Veronica Thomas and Shari Miles summarize the data that exist, and highlight the data that must be collected, to bring African American women into the mainstream of feminist psychology. The chapter includes an analysis of studies on African American women that have been published in the major feminist psychological journals, as well as a history and description of the purpose and progress of Division 35's Section on Black Women.

These four chapters provide a glimpse of a culturally diverse psychology of women and have implications for how courses are taught and research is conducted. The chapters are diverse and provide clinical (LaFromboise et al.), gender role (Ginorio et al.), and historical–sociological (Root) approaches to women of color, as well as an analysis of women of color within feminist psychology (Thomas & Miles). These differences highlight the many types of analyses available for understanding the psychology and status of women of color and challenge us to use multiple approaches and multiple discipline perspectives in bringing diversity to feminist psychology. Despite this diversity in perspective, the four chapters are united in the demonstration that specific sociocultural context shapes gender roles, gender socialization, and gender relations within that context and that these cannot be understood without taking such contexts into account.

10

AMERICAN INDIAN WOMEN AND PSYCHOLOGY

TERESA D. LaFROMBOISE, SANDRA BENNETT CHONEY, AMY JAMES, and PAULETTE R. RUNNING WOLF

The ways of Native American women who choose to follow the healing path include the following: the way of the daughter, the way of the householder, the way of the mother, the way of the teacher, and the way of the wise woman. Each of these ways toward spiritual development, or "disciplines that accord with the age of the aspirant and her duties within the sacred wheel of life" (Allen, 1991, p. 10), leads one to ever more specialized modes of work. We have accepted this developmental framework as a guide for the description of diverse American Indian[1] women's quest for mental health. Whether their well-being is deemed effective functioning, adaptation, and competence or living a peaceful (Hopi), artful

We thank the following women who provided research ideas listed in Exhibit 1: Elizabeth Todd Bazemore, Joan Saks Berman, Rebecca Crawford, Anna Latimer, Phyllis Old Dog Cross, Loye Ryan, Dolores BigFoot Sipes, and Pamela Jumper Thurman.
[1]The term *American Indian* refers to all North American native people, including Indians, Aleuts, Eskimos, and Metis. For brevity, the terms *American Indian*, *Native American*, and *native* are used interchangeably throughout this chapter to denote these varied peoples.

(Acoma), or beautiful (Navajo) life, the path each takes is guided by a commitment foremost to family and community and the universal Indian values of wisdom, intelligence, poise, tranquility, cooperation, unselfishness, responsibility, kindness, and protectiveness of all life forms (Trimble, 1981). From a developmental perspective, their roles are well defined from the cradle to the grave. The central theme is caring for others. Red Horse (1980) described the cycle of this role formation as being cared for, preparing to care for, and caring for. As American Indian women prepare to care for, they are trained in skills that will help them become self-sufficient and better care for others. In this chapter on American Indian women and psychology, we explore the cultural demands and cultural responses toward American Indian women as clients and as therapists and outline ways in which both work together to advance the well-being of the community.

A value of female children, particularly for matrilineal, matrilocal tribes was their ability to ensure the continuation of the clan or tribe. In 1639, a Jesuit missionary noted that the Hurons rejoiced more at the birth of a daughter than a son (Axtell, 1981). Puberty rights, varying in requirements and ritual from tribe to tribe, were the hallmark of an American Indian girl's entrance into adulthood. Young women were expected to follow new rules and take on new responsibilities (Niethammer, 1977). Although young adulthood was typically a time of marriage and child rearing, there were alternative roles that would also allow for the caring of others. Nonconformist gender roles and the free expression of sexuality were permitted (Anderson, 1985; Hamamsy, 1957; Medicine, 1980; Welch, 1987), and lesbians were accepted to varying degrees in a number of tribes (Allen, 1981; Blackwood, 1984; S. E. Jacobs, 1977).

The traditional roles and status of American Indian women were undermined by European colonizers who perceived American Indian women's conduct as subversive to their intended style of political, social, and religious order (LaFromboise, Heyle, & Ozer, 1990). Missionary activity resulted in the Christian conversion of many American Indian people. With the erosion of traditional religious practices, the valued spiritual role of women suffered. Additional changes in women's roles were the result of systematic attempts by the U.S. government to bring American Indian women's behavior more in line with that of White European women. The establishment of boarding schools and the Bureau of Indian Affairs field matron program are just two examples of this cultural imperialism (Bannan, 1984; Lomawaima, 1994). The resultant weakening of the extended family network and American Indian women's place within that network affected their child-rearing responsibilities.

The social status of American Indian women increased with age (Witt, 1974). Older women's experiences and wisdom were revered, and their opinions regarding tribal history, herbal medicine, and sacred matters were highly valued (Metoyer, 1979). Elder women's own perspectives on caring for others expanded so that their caretaking role extended beyond the immediate and extended family to the tribal community at large (Erikson, 1963; Hungry Wolf, 1980).

Contemporary American Indian women are advocating for the re-traditionalization of women's roles in Indian communities (Green, 1983) and the evolution of leadership roles in the dominant culture and tribal government ("Clinton Selects Deer," 1993; "Native Americans Gaining," 1992; "Natives Cheer Clinton Choice," 1993). Although interactions in the majority culture may provide greater economic and political opportunities, it may also be a source of conflict and stress (Barter & Barter, 1974; Boyce & Boyce, 1983). Many American Indian women striving to meet the demands of both worlds are able to successfully resolve this stress. A healthy balance of leadership and community activities, dual cultural involvement, and refinement of skills in often opposing contexts leading toward bicultural competence (LaFromboise, Coleman, & Gerton, 1993) results not only in stress reduction but in higher levels of functioning (Neumann, Mason, Chase, & Albaugh, 1991).

BEING CARED FOR: INDIAN WOMEN AS CLIENTS

Social Context

Feminist psychology converges with the practices of clinicians working with American Indian women on many levels. It is helpful to use a feminist framework to understand contemporary American Indian women in a social context. Historically, Indian people have suffered tremendous cultural, spiritual, social, emotional, and economic loss. These losses are intergenerational and continue to be expressed clinically in the lives of American Indian women today. These women come from diverse tribal nations spanning reservations and rural and urban communities. Their help-seeking patterns are unique, and the knowledge base from which clinical information about them may be gleaned is sparse.

Ravaged communities continue to reel from other types of sustained and profound losses such as spiritual practices, native language use, traditional educational methods, and clear social roles. The ripple effects of ongoing and often unresolved grieving also interfere with the functioning of traditional care-taking roles within the community. Consequently, disproportionate levels of violence, child abuse and neglect, and other symptoms of distressed families are on the rise and are becoming the norm in some communities. The disempowerment of Indian people also has manifested itself in alcoholism. The destructive and traumatic effects of alcoholism on Indian communities can be compared to the small pox epidemics during initial European contact (Roberts, 1992).

Forty-five percent of Indian households are headed by women (United States All Races [USAR] 24%), 42% of those women are under the age of 20 when they have their first child, and many never marry (Snipp & Aytac, 1990). Additionally, 32% of the entire American Indian population is under the age of 15 (USAR 23%; Indian Health Service, 1989). Trends in the evolving family structure noted by John (1988) and Mohatt, McDiarmid, and Montoya (1988) include a proliferation of single-parent families as well as interracial or blended families and increasing numbers of unmarried fathers. As the number of dependents increases, the role demands on American Indian women as caregivers expands exponentially. Their responsiveness to enlarged role demands is expected by family, partners, and the community.

Prolonged communitywide hardship also is evident when the percentage of the population below the poverty line ranges from 47% for the Navajo Indian Health Service (IHS) area to 20% for the California IHS area, compared with 12% of USAR (Young, 1991). Unemployment is consistently extremely high in Indian communities, and the rate has climbed as high as 80% in some areas. The limited opportunities for employment that do exist are further depleted as traditional occupations such as fishing and logging become threatened by tribal, state, and federal conservation efforts and technological advancement. Furthermore, there are limited resources to facilitate the development of entry into new careers and little economic development beyond gaming enterprises on reservations. These factors force reservation and rural families to make difficult decisions concerning staying and facing escalating poverty or leaving their communities in search of employment (G. Smith, 1993).

Most American Indian women who are employed are in their peak child-bearing years (49% of American Indian women in their 20s, 55% of American Indian women in their 30s). Forty-six percent of American Indian women living in metropolitan areas are employed (6% are unemployed; 27% are not in the labor force), and 37% of American Indian women in rural and reservation areas are employed (6% are unemployed; 57% are not in the labor force; Snipp & Aytac, 1990). Their employability is influenced not only by their lack of education and training but also by their racial and ethnic background. In general, American Indian people with less than a college education have unemployment rates markedly higher than those of the European American population. Only American Indian college graduates have unemployment rates comparable to the European American population as a whole (Snipp & Aytac, 1990).

As the values of the dominant culture infiltrate the Indian community, American Indian women also are faced with sexism, which appears in the form of sexual politics, sexual victimization, and social and emotional exploitation (Indian Health Service, 1991; Medicine, 1980; McCoy,

1992). Stress between the sexes may be exacerbated as opportunities for the employment of women in Indian country improve. American Indian women's employment satisfaction and pursuit of career goals often conflict with guilt over their own success while their partners' employment opportunities diminish. American Indian men are perhaps less likely to assist their working partners with routine household or child-care responsibilities than their European American counterparts because of clearly defined cultural gender roles. In recent years, many American Indian men have assumed an aloof posture in reaction to expectations for reciprocal involvement in family life while women work (A. C. Lewis & Hayes, 1991). Time constraints of employment or educational training prevent American Indian women from fully assuming traditional or extended family responsibilities or observing and participating in culturally valued practices.

Clinical Problems

The impact of the welfare culture and the aforementioned losses can be identified at the individual level by feelings of victimization attributable to racism and stereotyping, value conflicts, or confusion, isolation, and oppression. Unresolved grief over losses and effects of ongoing cultural genocide are often presented by clients in the form of chronic cycles of crisis and depression. Rising feelings of "hopelessness" experienced by female children, adolescents, and adults were documented by Blum, Harmon, Harris, Bergeisen, and Resnick (1992) and Long (1983). Thirty-eight percent of visits to IHS-supported outpatient reservation-based mental health services were attributed to depression, anxiety, and adjustment reactions. A random sample of patient caseloads at urban Indian health clinics showed that 60% of those seeking care presented themselves for mental health problems (Manson, Walker, & Kivlahan, 1987). Clare Brant, a Canadian Native psychiatrist, estimated that 44% of depressed American Indian clients are suffering from grief reactions (Timpson et al., 1988).

A recent report of the American Psychological Association (APA) indicated that the typical client seeking help from IHS service units, on or off reservations, is depressed or anxious, is experiencing situational crises such as domestic violence, disruption, or victimization, and has been or is now using drugs or alcohol (G. Jacobs, Dauphinais, Gross, & Guzman, 1991). Neligh (1988) described an IHS utilization pattern of depression, anxiety, cultural conflict, alcohol misuse, and suicide attempts. The problem categories American Indian women seek help from IHS facilities also include adult–child relationships, grief reactions, child management or abuse, and marital conflict (Fleming, 1989). Furthermore, the proportion of American Indian women seeking IHS treatment for violent behavior (e.g., battery, rape, sexual assault, or incest) was 38% in 1982. One survey reported that 80% of American Indian female clients at a regional psychiatric center serving a five-state area had experienced sexual assault (Old Dog Cross, 1982).

Many speculate that a primary issue for mental health maintenance of American Indian women today is a cycle of endless, unresolved grief and mourning (Horejsi, Craig, & Pablo, 1992; Manson, Shore, & Bloom, 1985; Topper & Curtis, 1987). Tragedies occur frequently in Indian communities. Injuries involving motor vehicle accidents, homicide, and suicide are listed among the leading causes of death among American Indians (Indian Health Service, 1989). More than one third of all American Indian deaths involve people under age 45—three times the rate of the general population (G. Campbell, 1989). Additionally, the impact of alcoholism on marriages and families and the culturally supported emphasis on endurance has instilled a pattern of behavior by which an American Indian woman's expression and processing of personal grief is delayed indefinitely to fulfill caretaking roles.

Nagel (1988) suggested that the cultural patterning and shaping of the grief and mourning experience can go awry. Disturbed grief and unresolved mourning occur when the bereaved person is unable to complete this process. For example, in one tribe, the Navajo, grief and loss rituals follow a pattern of mourning limited to 4 days, after which the mourner is expected to resume usual routines with no further expression of emotion concerning the loss (Miller & Schoenfeld, 1973).

The presentation of somatic complaints by American Indian women (especially those having large families) may be indicative of either deeper pathology or greater cultural acceptance of physical rather than emotional symptomatology. Many, if not most, of the problems that are presented in therapy involve comorbidity with alcohol and other drug consumption, generalized anxiety disorder, or posttraumatic stress disorder.

Adolescent American Indian girls are a particularly vulnerable population. American Indian girls who are sexually active use contraception at one half the rate of their White European American peers (Blum et al., 1992). As a result, the pregnancy rate among American Indian adolescents is higher than it is for adolescents of the dominant population. American Indian girls are six times more likely to be sexually abused than are American Indian boys (United States Congress, 1990).

The mental health of young American Indian women seems to be at greater risk than it is for young men. Manson et al. (1985) found that female boarding school students were more prone to depression than were male students. Beiser and Attneave (1982) discovered that American Indian girls have a higher outpatient treatment rate than American Indian boys. According to a 1989 Indian Adolescent Health Survey, 20% of young American Indian women had attempted suicide. Young American Indian women (most between 15 and 17 years old) made up 70% of all suicide-related hospitalizations (United States Congress, 1990).

The prevalence of female alcohol abuse is rapidly growing in some tribes and has been relatively high in others for some time (May, 1986). The death rate of Indian women from chronic liver disease and cirrhosis exceeds the rate of Indian, Black, Hispanic, Asian, and White males (*National Institute on Alcohol Abuse and Alcoholism Newsletter*, 1978). Sporadic and binge drinking occurs along with chronic consumption that may develop into alcohol dependence syndromes and alcoholic psychosis. Female alcoholism, especially among those of child-rearing age, has grave implications for the future of American Indian people. The incidence of fetal alcohol syndrome and fetal alcohol effect ranges from 1 in 552 births to 1 in 55 births depending on the tribe and area of residence (May, Hambaugh, Aase, & Samet, 1983).

Many physiological outcomes of mental and emotional stressors are documented in the *Indian Women's Health Care Consensus Statement* (Indian Health Service, 1991). Some of the leading causes of death for American Indian women noted in the consensus statement include heart disease, malignant neoplasms, accidents, cerebrovascular diseases, diabetes, chronic liver disease, and cirrhosis. Some tribes document five times the rate of the White population for diabetes (Indian Health Service, 1991). Recent studies have indicated that American Indian and Alaska Native women experience a much higher rate of cervical cancer, more than twice the rate of women of all other ethnic groups (Joe & Justice, 1992). For American Indian women, cervical cancer is diagnosed in later stages than other women, and they have a poorer survival rate than women of other ethnic groups.

The physical and emotional well-being of elder American Indian women has long been neglected. The need to address disease prevention and screening, financial problems, and isolation have been well articulated (Indian Health Service, 1991). The stress on elder American Indian women when substance abuse and family dysfunction exists should not be overlooked. Unfortunately, the care of elders even on reservations is increasingly becoming the responsibility of nursing homes (Manson & Calloway, 1988).

Many of the preventable physical illnesses noted earlier are a direct result of the neglect of self. Physical and emotional self-care is given low priority and rarely practiced. Adherence to a regular exercise routine or monitoring one's weight, for example, may be viewed as selfish or vain. The cultural emphasis on enduring may interfere with an American Indian woman's psychological and physiological well-being. However, there appears to be a resurgence of respect for spiritual self-care and with that an increase in the participation in spiritually based activities by American

Indian women of all walks of life. A challenge for clinicians will be to formulate culturally sensitive treatment plans that include all of these aspects of health across the life span.

Help-Seeking Patterns

As American Indian women face the challenges of their present-day lives, they may seek therapy to overcome personal or familial difficulties. The way they seek help differs from that expected of European American women. In general, Native American people are reluctant to seek Western professional therapeutic services. Ho (1987) suggested that a cultural emphasis on endurance and noninterference along with mistrust of non-Indian service providers may explain this hesitancy.

Indian people of all lifestyles seem to follow a predictable cultural pattern when accessing their support systems (R. Lewis, 1984). The extended family support system is the first helping source sought. Spiritual leaders and tribal community leaders are next, and, as a last resort, the mainstream health care system is approached for assistance.

Because there is great tolerance for the behavior of others, extremely negative and disruptive behaviors rarely or infrequently result in referrals by family members to outside agencies. In reservation communities, some referrals may occur only as a result of tribal court-ordered referrals (Willis, Dobrec, & BigFoot Sipes, 1992). Victims of abuse and their abusers are therefore not only unlikely to seek assistance, but rarely have adequate resources. This may leave women and their children in extremely vulnerable positions. Examples of accepted behavior may include young mothers giving Aid to Families With Dependent Children benefits to absent and nonsupportive fathers and elderly women tolerating maladaptive and often violent familial dysfunction (G. Jacobs et al., 1991). Although such frustrating client behaviors seem counterproductive and passive, they are often viewed as appropriate within tribal contexts.

As Indian people are exposed to a wider range of services offered by mental health providers and as more Indian people work in mental health service settings, attitudes toward such services have become more positive (Kahn, Lejero, Antone, Francisco, & Manuel, 1988). Growing caseloads and increasing numbers of referrals within traditional, reservation-based communities reflect this attitudinal change. However, little is known about the dropout rate in rural and reservation communities. Comparative studies over the course of the past decade with urban American Indian clients do indicate a decrease in the therapeutic dropout rate (O'Sullivan, Peterson, Cox, & Kirkeby, 1989; Sue, Allen, & Conway, 1978). Nonetheless, cultural barriers to help seeking still persist.

Knowledge Base

Informed reports of the clinical concerns of American Indian women can be found on the margins of the knowledge base of psychology. To determine the extent and emphasis of attention paid to these concerns by psychology, we conducted a literature review for the year 1992 within psychology and related fields (i.e., education, sociology, and anthropology). That literature was arranged into a two-dimensional model suggested by LaFromboise and Plake (1984). This model, or method, organizes information into three major categories or levels of analysis (psychological, sociological, and ethnological) and then further subdivides each category according to the focus of the research.

Table 1 depicts the result of this review of 78 publications available in 1992.[2] As one might expect, the bulk of the literature was found within the ethnological level of analysis. The social bases of behavior (e.g., culture, communications, ethnicity, sex roles, and legal processes) emerged as the primary foci of this ethnological work. Within the psychological level of analysis, there were only two publications focusing specifically on American Indian women in the biological area, five in the cognitive–affective area, seven in the social area, and two in the individual differences area. Thus, it may be concluded that individuals interested in accessing information with respect to American Indian women and psychology face a difficult task. Even with the assistance of computer-based search procedures, the availability of government-compiled statistics, and access to specialty publications on ethnic minorities, practitioners, researchers, and students may find more questions than answers concerning American Indian women and mental health.

This paucity of psychological literature suggests the need for the creation of new knowledge that could take many forms. Most frequently used paradigms for research with Indian people have focused on either "pathological," "genetically deprived," or "culturally deprived" models of investigation. However, these models tend to ignore the many strengths of Native American cultures. They focus on remediation rather than prevention, pathology rather than health, and victims rather than survivors. Note that these models have resulted in some useful information. Yet, many issues of American Indian women remain unexamined, and the strength and coping skills necessary for the maintenance of psychological health persist in being unexplored.

Women clinicians working in the Indian community have suggested specific research topics amenable to the discovery of variables associated with the success patterns of American Indian women instead of those that

---

[2]These works are noted in the reference list of this chapter by an asterisk.

TABLE 1
Categorization of Reviewed Literature

Level of analysis	Analysis of subject areas					
	Biological	Cognitive–affective	Social	Individual differences	Research methods	Total
Psychological	2	5	7	2	3	19
Sociological	3	2	11	2	1	19
Ethnological	2	1	25	10	2	40
All	7	8	43	14	6	78

look exclusively at successive degrees of failure or dysfunction. The extensive list of problems generated by these clinicians has been divided into seven areas or categories and is presented in Exhibit 1. Four areas are similar to those categories of client variables reviewed by Ponterotto and Casas (1991) and include sociopsychological developmental constructs, behaviors and social patterns, specific problems, and attitudes toward Indians. The categories of intervention evaluations, instrumentation research, and miscellaneous research/policy issues were added to complete a framework inclusive of the research problems nominated by the clinicians surveyed.

Although this presentation of research topics to expand the clinical knowledge base is lengthy, it does not encompass all issues relevant for evaluation. The creation of new knowledge should be pertinent to the needs of the people it purports to further describe.[3] Therefore, we not only encourage investigation of the strengths of American Indian women, we also encourage consultation with Indian communities themselves to provide guidance in generating knowledge that is pertinent and relevant to their mental health needs.

PREPARING TO CARE FOR: INDIAN WOMEN IN TRAINING

Community-Based Training

Women's mental health is essential to the well-being of future generations of Indian people. Therefore, there is urgent need for tribal-specific mental health training for all levels of practitioners to better prepare to care for American Indian women and their families. Relevant to this need

---

[3]For those who consider doing research within Indian communities, an examination of the advantages and pitfalls of participatory action research is recommended. See the work of various contributors to the special issue of the *American Indian and Alaska Native Mental Health Research* journal covering the misalliances in the Barrow alcohol study (Manson, 1989) as well as the research suggestions provided by R. A. Ryan (1980) and Trimble (1977).

EXHIBIT 1
Specific Problems in Need of Investigation Categorized by Area as Suggested by Female Clinicians

1. Sociopsychological developmental constructs that are products of past history, personal experiences, and sociocultural patterns
   Identity issues
   Racial/tribal/gender role identity development; motivation for self-identification and/or reclaiming "Indianness"; identity coping strategies
   Problems of daily living
   Low self-esteem; powerlessness; limited motivation; short- and long-term effects of boarding school attendance; transracial adoption; developmental disabilities related to fetal alcohol syndrome; eating disorders
   Coping and skills
   Stress management; codependency support; parenting skills; social skills
2. Behaviors and Social Patterns Associated With Specific Sociocultural Values, Attitudes, and Customs
   Relationship and role issues
   Changing roles of American Indian women; relationships between Indian women and men; developing and maintaining bicultural competence
3. Specific Problems That Need to Be Understood Within the "Indian" Context
   Affective problems
   Trauma; posttraumatic stress disorder; stress; depression; unresolved grief; affective disorders associated with physical health problems; stress associated with disease progression; suicide
   Substance abuse and related problems
   Substance abuse (including inhalants); fetal alcohol and inhalant abuse exposure in vitro; effects of living with addicted families
   Societal problems
   Sexual and domestic abuse; results of abuse and rape (i.e., promiscuity, sexual acting out); AIDS
4. European American Attitudes That Affect American Indian Clients
   Perceptions, attitudes, and behaviors of non-Indian service providers, educators, and peers toward Indians
5. Intervention Evaluations
   Program evaluation
   All interventions particularly intervention and prevention strategies for depression, substance abuse, and family violence
   Individual interventions
   Culturally relevant interventions with children; treatment dealing with the management of chronic pain and illness, especially for elderly women
6. Instrumentation Research
   Standardization of behavioral inventories; baselines for all research instruments (e.g., Minnesota Multiphasic Personality Inventory-2, Kiddie Schedule for Affective Disorder and Schizophrenia, Personality Inventory for Children)
7. Miscellaneous Research and Policy Issues
   Reinterpretation of anthropological findings from a psychological perspective; studies of the impact of fluctuating resources on mental health in reservation economies

is a recent increase in the number of American Indian women returning to school (some due, in part, to mandates of the welfare system). This return has often been hampered by low self-esteem and fears of educational institutions, relocation stressors, reduction in support networks, child care, and transportation needs. Despite the increase of psychology-related university extension courses on reservations, the emotional and economic costs of relocation and "reliving" unpleasant educational experiences inhibit many from seeking educational and career advancement in mental health. Indian-specific mental health training programs are almost nonexistent in Indian communities.

Although little has been written about the role and training of American Indian paraprofessionals, two projects that rely on paraprofessional support may serve as national models to address issues of training in service delivery in Indian mental health. Key characteristics of a Tohono O'odham (Papago) program include professional consultation with medicine men, adaptations of current mental health techniques, and the creation of an effective specialized approach to group treatment with adolescents in trouble with the law (Kahn et al., 1988; Kahn, Lewis, & Galvez, 1974). The second program, involving a collaboration between two Coast Salish Indian (Swinomish and Upper Skagit) tribes and a county mental health program, resulted in the formulation of a multifaceted mental health program (Swinomish Tribal Mental Health Project, 1991). This program is unique because it includes paraprofessional consultation with elder American Indian women and training that leads to a 2-year associate degree in human services with a specialization in tribal mental health. This latter program represents one way to address the barriers to continued postsecondary education for women in paraprofessional positions outlined previously.

University-Based Training

Many American Indian women have acquired 50–100 college-level credits through outreach courses and continuing education credits received during their many years of service in the field. Census data from 1990 (Taeuber, 1991) revealed that 34% of American Indian women have completed some postsecondary work. Unfortunately, the many paraprofessional women resist completing associate or bachelor degrees because of the issues cited earlier. These women are not being encouraged to seek postsecondary training. This waste of an experienced pool of potential graduate-level practitioners has long been overlooked. Accredited on-site training programs need to be created for advanced skills and confidence building to facilitate this group's professional and academic development. A model for this type of training can be taken from either training and social work programs cooperatively coordinated by tribal community colleges and 4-

year institutions across the nation. Active recruitment and scholarship programs for those who complete their bachelor's degree would help more American Indian women set graduate-level training as their ultimate educational goal.

With increased interest in postsecondary education, many American Indian women discover a natural and acceptable extension of traditional caretaking roles in the field of psychology and education. Since 1979, more American Indian women than men received bachelor's and master's degrees in psychology and education (Taeuber, 1991). Twice as many degrees in psychology are awarded to American Indian women at the bachelor and master's levels. However, almost twice as many American Indian men than American Indian women receive a doctoral degree in psychology, a vivid illustration of the gender-related barriers experienced by American Indian women.

The only Indian-specific psychology training opportunities currently available at the graduate level are as follows: master's and doctoral programs at the University of Utah and the University of North Dakota; a predoctoral traineeship at Dull Knife Memorial College in Lame Deer, Montana; and two APA-approved doctoral internship training sites at the University of Colorado Department of Psychiatry in Denver and the Southwest Consortium in Albuquerque, New Mexico. It is believed that these programs are better able than conventional psychology training programs to help trainees understand how diverse tribal communities are organized across distinct family, social, and political lines. Trainees gain facility in helping communities and families reorganize and revitalize themselves. Optimally, students in these specialized programs receive ample opportunities to gain experience in designing and executing interventions that facilitate community empowerment.

CARING FOR: INDIAN WOMEN AS CLINICIANS

Professional Roles

Wise Women

While "caring for," American Indian women play a prominent role in facilitating the development of spiritual, mental, and physical well-being within the community. Historically and contemporarily, holy women, clan mothers, and women elders provide instruction, education, and leadership to the Indian community.

Those who we call *wise women* are often referred to in the literature as traditional healers or medicine women (Allen, 1991). Wise women display creative powers and maintain a central position within Indian society.

The Sioux, for example, trace all of their spiritual and healing power back to White Buffalo Calf Woman (T. H. Lewis, 1990). As early as 1691, missionaries noted the impact of wise women on the beliefs of would-be converts (Le Clerq, cited in Axtell, 1981). However, following the subjugation of the various tribes, Indian people were afraid of retaliation by missionaries if they sought out traditional healing practices (Moran, 1988). This once-public aspect of American Indian healing went underground but continued to flourish under the direction of female and male traditional healers. Federal policy prohibiting spiritual and healing practices continued until the American Indian Religious Freedom Act was passed in 1978. Unfortunately, the spiritual aspects of tribal cultures continue to be co-opted, misused, misrepresented, and exploited by outsiders (A. Smith, 1991). For these reasons, many wise women are not forthcoming with details regarding healing practices.

It is well documented that Western psychotherapy and traditional healing practices can be effectively integrated in therapy with American Indian clients (LaFromboise, Trimble, & Mohatt, 1990). Cultural identity and spirituality may be essentially interwoven into beliefs about mental health and its treatment (T. H. Lewis, 1990; Locust, 1988). Wise women often serve as referral sources for Indian people struggling with multiple roles and methods of coping with the conflicting bicultural and multicultural demands of diverse Indian communities and the dominant culture. Fortunately, wise women also provide services to American Indian therapists in the form of consultation and supervision. Many clinicians today involve wise women in information gathering regarding diagnosis, culturally appropriate behavior, and treatment recommendations.

Paraprofessionals

With the introduction of Western medical practices, this valued role of American Indian women became relegated to that of assistants to psychiatrists and other medical professionals. For those who operated within the Western formalized service delivery system and functioned as culture brokers, advisors, and interpreters, their role definition evolved into titles such as community health representatives (CHRs) and mental health technicians (MHTs). They also assumed other essential social service and educational positions.

In response to the increasing need for mental health services on Indian reservations and the limited availability of professional service providers, the Office of Mental Health within the IHS was established in 1965 at the Navajo reservation headquarters. A program that involved training local tribal members to assist in providing community mental health services simultaneously occurred (Nelson, McCoy, Stetter, & Vanderwagen, 1992). This model was patterned after the CHR model that had demonstrated success in networking between clinic and community and providing home-based health maintenance, aftercare, referrals, and health education services. MHT positions were almost exclusively filled by American Indian women in keeping with their caretaking role. Even though this paraprofessional program was phased out in 1977, MHTs continue to be trained on the job to provide assistance in crisis management, individual counseling, interagency case management, and identification and consultation with tribal healers.

American Indian women also provide paraprofessional counseling services in other human service and education-related positions. Examples of these include the Indian child welfare assistant who promotes coordination of social services to families in distress; the Johnson O'Malley or Title V counselor who often engages in counseling and parent advocacy while arranging tutoring support; and the Head Start social service coordinator who assists in the early identification of parent–child needs.

American Indian women serving as paraprofessionals have earned respect from their communities. These communities bore witness to their life span development and their triumph over personal battles (with education, abuse, alcohol, or drugs). Having "walked through the fire," so to speak, many American Indian women paraprofessionals are seen through the eyes of the community as strong and courageous healing leaders. As such, they are able to address family and community issues that are normally "untouchable" by non-Indian professionals. Although one might expect progressive professional advancement on the part of American Indian paraprofessional counselors, American Indian women seldom formalize their occupational role through completion of postsecondary education.

Graduate-Level Professionals

Graduate-level American Indian professional women may form the stable core of American Indian families, provide professional services to both Indians and non-Indians alike, teach at postsecondary institutions, train others to work multiculturally, or conduct research related to the needs of their people. Yet, in attempting to determine simple issues such as the number of American Indian female graduate-level professionals in psychology, it is apparent that they also remain on the margins of human resource accounts. First, the primary source of such information, the *Handbook of Labor Statistics* (U.S. Department of Labor, 1992), displays statistics on American Indians, Alaskan Natives, and Asian Americans in a category called "other" because the numbers are so relatively small. Secondary published sources, such as the IHS's documentation series, report that there were only four American Indian women employed as psychologists in 1991 by the IHS. Most American Indian women who deliver mental health services through the IHS are social workers ($n = 22$), MHTs ($n = 30$), or other mental health professionals ($n = 18$; W. Douglas, personal communication, December 3, 1991).

The *Directory of Ethnic Minority Human Resources in Psychology* (American Psychological Association, 1990) provides another possible avenue for determining the number of American Indian women in psychology. This source indicated that in 1990 there were 22 American Indian women holding doctoral degrees and working in various facets of mental health. The APA 1991 membership survey reported 39 women out of 110 American Indian members (American Psychological Association, 1991). Unfortunately, these sources report on only those who hold membership in the APA and are limited by members' willingness to respond to surveys. The National Science Foundation's 1989 survey of doctorate recipients reported that 46 of the 137 Native Americans earning a doctorate degree in psychology were women.

It appears that graduates of psychology training programs are fairly evenly divided in their decision to take positions in applied or academic settings. Recently, the *American Indian and Alaska Native Professors Directory* (Center for Indian Education, 1993) reported 16 American Indian women in faculty positions related to psychology and counseling. All but 2 of these women live and work in the West or Midwestern areas of the country. These sources, incomplete as these may be, serve to accentuate the need to encourage more American Indian women to enter this particular disciplinary and professional arena.

Clinical Process

Spiritual Basis of Helping

Cahuilla wise women reflect a fundamental understanding (Modesto & Mount, 1980) shared by traditional Navajo (Benally, 1992) and Sioux (Lewis, 1990) holy women and men (i.e., spiritual and emotional health cannot be separated). Non-Indian therapists working with Native American clients have noted the critical need for understanding this emphasis on interdependence (Hammerschlag, 1988; Herring, 1990). Indian educators such as Jaimes (1982) emphasized spiritual unity among women and men from a traditional perspective. Clinicians working with American Indian populations have come to expect presentations surrounding spirituality from American Indian women from all walks of life and degrees of cultural involvement. Although it is neither appropriate nor necessary to know specific details of traditional ritual practices, a clinician's understanding of spiritual issues and ability to develop an open and supportive atmosphere, in which client presentations of spiritual issues may be discussed, will contribute to the therapeutic outcome (Red Horse, 1982).

Unfortunately, an understanding of the role of spirituality in mental and emotional health has come very slowly to Western psychology (Collins, Hurst, & Jacobson, 1987; Lannert, 1991) because there has been a certain historic hostility toward things spiritual in general and a suspicion of clients who are highly religious (Vaugn, 1991). Feminist psychologists such as Laird and Hartman (1988) emphasized the utility of ritual for women within the context of therapy. They posited that encouraging women to develop their personal rituals outside of therapy may facilitate healing and promote positive mental health. The wisdom of maintaining a healthy spiritual perspective promulgated by traditional American Indian teachings is gaining increasing acceptance in conventional psychology circles (Goodloe & Arreola, 1992; Sweeny & Witmer, 1991).

Ways of Communicating

There are traditional aspects of Indian communication that subtly affect the behavior of American Indian women in therapy and thus influence the helping process. Many American Indian women maintain an intense respect for the power of the spoken word. They are taught that words can be used to think, talk to oneself, inform, and move or reconcile with others. Words also can be used to insult, frighten, threaten, or conceal. Great care should be taken in the selection of words, and a clear understanding of the purpose for which they are used must be established (Morey & Gilliam, 1972; Murphy, 1970). For example, when a client is in the process of describing an event, she may tell the therapist as much as possible about the circumstances surrounding that event by means of fact, hearsay, or sensory impressions in order to be exact (Spencer, 1959). She may again establish her relatedness to an event by talking in great detail about the event, putting all the pieces in place except for the crucial one, and leaving the major point for the therapist to discern (see Hall, 1976). A client also may use disclaimers or references to her humbleness and limitations prior to expressing a well-thought-out opinion (L. Dauphinais, 1982).

Indirect communication is essential for the maintenance of the traditional practice of noninterference. "From earliest childhood Indian people are trained to regard absolute noninterference in interpersonal relations as decent and normal. They often react to even the mildest coercion . . . with bewilderment, disgust, and fear" (Wax & Thomas, 1961, p. 310). An American Indian female client may refrain from making any kind of direct suggestion in order not to appear manipulative or meddling (Goodtracks, 1973). Noninterference also is practiced by indirectly stating one's needs without directly asking for help. This allows the therapist freedom to decide whether to help the client with the need she has presented, provided the therapist has correctly interpreted the client's needs. Gentle probes by the client (another form of indirect communication) may be used to determine the limits of the relationship, which, in turn, has direct implications for perceptions of trustworthiness (Edgarton, 1965).

Relationship Development. These and other traditional ways of communicating affect the building and enhancement of the "helping" relationship with American Indian female clients. Unfortunately, most culture-specific information regarding the therapeutic alliance is anecdotal in nature. Whenever possible, information from empirical studies of the counseling process with American Indians is provided (see Sue and Zane, 1994, for a detailed review of the limited research with American Indians in this area). Unfortunately, gender was seldom taken into account in the design or interpretation of clinical process studies.

There are a number of other ways in which the relationship is enhanced through communality. One area of concern for clinicians working with American Indian women is the client's expectation or preference for an ethnically similar counselor. Studies on client preference for ethnic similarity in counseling with American Indians have yielded mixed results (Atkinson, 1983; P. Dauphinais, Dauphinais, & Row, 1981; Haviland, Horswill, O'Connell, & Dynneson, 1983; LaFromboise, Dauphinais, & Rowe, 1980; LaFromboise & Dixon, 1981). Some authors, however, suggest that these mixed results might be a function of methodology and are not necessarily indicative of different expectations or preferences. In particular, Bennett and BigFoot Sipes (1991), BigFoot Sipes, Dauphinais, La-Fromboise, Bennett, and Rowe (1992), and Bennett (1991) used similar methodologies to determine the preferences of American Indian clients across three age groups. Their findings suggest that developmental level and gender may influence preferences for counselors. American Indian female and male adult clients (Bennett, 1991) and college students (Bennett & BigFoot Sipes, 1991) were found to be less concerned about having an American Indian counselor than about characteristics such as level of education or attitudinal similarity. American Indian female secondary students preferred a female American Indian counselor who had attitudes and values similar to theirs, and male secondary school students most preferred an American Indian counselor of either sex whose personality was similar to their own (BigFoot Sipes et al., 1992).

In summary, one might assume that, for young American Indian women, the therapeutic relationship may be enhanced if the counselor is an American Indian woman. However, as these young women grow older and become less consumed with the task of developing a personal identity that includes "Indianness" as an integral part, there is a decreased need for the encouragement found in talking to another American Indian person who may have experienced similar life events. At the college level, their preferences concerning counseling become more like those of their male counterparts, and the therapeutic relationship is encouraged through the expression of similar attitudes and values by the counselor, regardless of the counselor's ethnicity (Bennett & BigFoot Sipes, 1991). Finally, as adults, when American Indian women are actually experiencing some mental health problem and actively seeking help for that problem, a more pragmatic approach is taken. At this time, the therapeutic relationship may be strengthened if the counselor is an older American Indian person who has more education than the American Indian client (Bennett, 1991).

In the initial stages of relationship formation, the therapist's attitudes and skills are also under scrutiny. Therapists must display flexibility, support, good will, and self-awareness to gain the trust and respect of American Indian female clients. Flexible therapists not only adapt their communication and interventions to fit the client, they also are open to the client's preferred extended length of sessions and can be understanding about last-minute rescheduling of appointments. Much has been written about "Indian time" in therapy, referring to adherence to appointments (Tafoya, 1989). Hopi people, who have no word for *time*, describe it as a subjective experience of duration or "becoming later" (Dell, 1980). This runs counter to the feminist position that counselors should model boundary maintenance and time management (Lerner, 1988b).

Therapists also are urged to relax their standards of goal attainment. An American Indian female client who does not accomplish a task or reach a goal may not be upset because she believes others will complete the task in due time (R. A. Lake, 1991). Furthermore, clinicians should consider allowing a third party such as a child or other family member or a friend or advocate to be present in the session and should be willing to work with American Indian female clients outside the office.

Structuring. Clinical relationships also can be enhanced by other therapist attributes and behavior. The term *structuring* refers to an interactional process between clinicians and clients in which they arrive at similar perceptions of the role of the therapist (see Jilek-Aall, 1976, for a comparison of Western and Indian role definitions of psychiatrists), a mutual understanding of what occurs during the helping process, and an agreement concerning relevant and reasonable outcome goals (Brammer, Shostrom, & Abrego, 1989). Structuring helps increase therapist and client similarity through shared understanding of the helping process.

One important aspect of structuring with American Indian women, raised in more traditional tribes such as those in the Southwest, is the tendency to interpret reality as a continuous flow of events that develop in relation to one another. Dell (1980) described the Hopi view of reality not as analyzing singular events but as "eventing." Eventing involves open-ended, emerging processes of analyzing and preparing for what is to come. Thus, when an issue previously deemed resolved is worked on again in therapy, the structure allows an open invitation to revisit that issue at any time. This may require the therapist to check in with the client on issues "resolved" in earlier sessions rather than dividing therapy work into "finished" and "unfinished" business (O. Baldwin, personal communication, February 18, 1993). In this area the ongoing nature of helping actually compliments Indian worldviews and suggests the importance of follow-up visits.

American Indian women frequently enter counseling suspending trust until the therapist proves that she or he is worthy of being trusted (LaFromboise & Dixon, 1981). Given current and historic distrust of members of the dominant culture as offering help yet taking away valuable aspects of American Indian women's lives (e.g., removing children from their homes to send them to boarding schools; terminating parental rights because of misperceptions of neglectful parenting), trust can be difficult to establish and easily destroyed. Trust is developed and maintained through a series of relationship interchanges in which a therapist's consistency, acceptance of client disclosures, and responsiveness to client needs are verified. Broken promises, hidden agendas, and covert adherence to stereotypic beliefs on the part of clinicians are behaviors to which American Indian women are especially sensitive. American Indian female clients may not directly seek evidence that a therapist might take advantage of their vulnerability but may engage in subtle testing to determine the therapist's trustworthiness (Edgarton, 1965). Therapists may experience a client's testing for trust by her requesting information, telling secrets, asking for a favor, putting herself down, inconveniencing the therapist, and questioning the therapist's motives (Fong & Cox, 1983). Once the trust issue becomes apparent, the counselor should first clarify the issue and then gently respond rather than ignore the test or label the client as defensive.

It is generally thought that therapists should initiate personal self-disclosures with American Indian clients in the spirit of openness and reciprocity during the information exchange process (Proctor, 1979). LaFromboise (1992) labeled the disclosure of personal information that may be similar to the client's experience as an *affinity attempt*. She found that when this attempt is not tainted with patronizing cultural content, it can have a positive therapeutic valence, suggesting the therapist's agreeableness, affiliation, and nurturance. Previous research with American Indian clients also has indicated that when cultural material of questionable content is included in the affinity attempt, as in, "My best friend during training was a Comanche," judgments of therapist insincerity often ensues (LaFromboise, Dauphinais, & Lujan, 1981). When appropriately used, counselor self-disclosures may not only reduce the role distance between the clinician and client, they may also help an American Indian woman develop additional perspectives she needs to address problem behaviors.

Nonverbal Behavior. Therapists working with American Indian women must be able to understand the client from her own frame of reference. This includes the structure of her life experiences and everything that surrounds and permeates accounts of her concerns. Attention to culturally distinct aspects of nonverbal behavior may facilitate assessments of the congruence between the client's verbal and nonverbal behavior. A frequently referenced nonverbal behavior of American Indian clients is the avoidance of direct eye contact during some kinds of interpersonal interactions. The sanction against visual contact may be the reason some American Indian clients prefer to sit side by side rather than face to face when they are sharing highly personal information (W. Freeman, personal communication, May 6, 1980). Generally, avoidance of direct eye contact is a sign of respect, not a reaction of guilt or shame. Aggressive touch in the form of a firm handshake is often considered rude. Therapists must be able to handle frequent pauses occurring during sessions to allow the client time to interpret a message or make a decision about past, present, or future responses. Furthermore, it has been hypothesized by American Indian therapists that appropriate personal space among Indians in interpersonal interactions might be greater than the 3- to 4-foot comfort zone indicated by adult middle-class Americans (Lecomte, Bernstein, & Dumont, 1981).

Counseling Responses. Therapist verbal responses such as probes, paraphrases, reflection, summarization, and clarification are commonly considered to be critical to the helping process. However, there is reason to believe that the effectiveness associated with particular response types or response patterns may be different for American Indian clients. For instance, a communication style emphasizing the use of paraphrasing and reflection of feeling was rated by American Indian participants as less effective than a directive style (P. Dauphinais et al., 1981). Also, the use of clarifications with American Indian respondents has been found to encourage more client elaboration than paraphrases and reflections and to result in the perception of the therapist as agreeable and nurturant (LaFromboise, 1992).

Unfortunately, nothing is known empirically about the likely effect of responses such as various types of probes, confrontation, interpretation, and information giving. In noncounseling situations, such as classroom interactions, the use of direct questioning with American Indian students is considered to be intrusive (Lujan, Kennan, Hill, & Long, 1979). Although the situation is far from clear, the available evidence seems to suggest that effective therapeutic communication with American Indian clients would involve the use of clarification and the avoidance of paraphrasing and reflection. It could also be inferred that closed questions, confrontation, and interpretation would be less effective than open questions, information giving, and summarization. Further research on the differential impact of various response classes in counseling situations is necessary to help clinicians intentionally select responses that are most appropriate and effective given Indian cultural and gender preferences.

Successful termination requires a smooth transition through the dissolution of the therapeutic relationship. This involves helping American Indian female clients overcome their anxiety about ending therapy. Termination also conveys action expectations and information about what may happen after therapy is over. Given the incredible amount of loss many American Indian women experience, therapists need to allow considerably more session time around impending termination (Dixon, 1989). Once this process has been worked through, it is crucial that the therapist convey to the client that the door remains open and that the client is welcome to occasionally check in for follow-up sessions. The helping relationship may continue as the therapist is invited to important community and family functions such as a graduation feast or wedding ceremony. The therapist may be given a gift as a sign of respect or gratitude for the help the client has received (Attneave, 1982). This act of sharing should be accepted without awkwardness and considered a special case for ethical practice.

Diagnostic Issues

Although individual level of acculturation is an initial and primary component in determining a culturally appropriate method of intervention for adult and adolescent American Indian women, a global and holistic assessment also should be included. Vraniak and Pickett (1993) discussed the challenge of establishing "systemic interconnectedness" that focuses on the client's cultural, sociological, psychological, and biological needs. Treating American Indian women from a psychological perspective without also addressing their biological, social, and cultural needs undermines positive therapeutic outcomes.

In light of the multiple losses and vulnerability to violence and sexual abuse already discussed, clinicians who work with American Indian women must consider the impact of trauma when assessing their mental health status (Root, 1992). This includes the impact of direct trauma and indirect trauma. When a loved one, or one with whom the client closely identifies, is hurt, an empathic reaction may result in indirect trauma. Despite popular stereotypes, American Indian women are vulnerable to both types of trauma.

Root (1992) asserted that when women attempt to reorganize their self-perceptions after some sort of trauma, they often do so in ways that seem psychopathological. These responses may include, but are not limited to, anxiety, depression, despair, and suicide. All of these responses may appear at elevated rates among American Indian women. Therapists experienced in working with American Indian women therefore tend to use the revised third edition of the *Diagnostic and Statistical Manual of Mental Disorders'* diagnosis of posttraumatic stress disorder rather than unipolar depression, anxiety, and the controversial borderline personality disorder when they are called on to make a diagnosis (J. Berman, A. Latimer, and P. Thurman, personal communication, October 15, 1992). Like Root, they recognized the limited utility of the posttraumatic stress disorder diagnosis in designing psychotherapy interventions because this diagnosis was based on male combat veterans. Nonetheless, American Indian women experience multiple kinds of trauma, each with its unique impact on various dimensions of their lives.

Any bizarre behavior may be considered to be culturally bound rather than indicative of real pathology. Because the spirit world is immediate and accessible to Indian people, a naive therapist may mistake culturally appropriate references to contact with deceased ancestors or communion with The Creator as evidence of delusions or hallucinations (Matchett, 1972). Vizenor (1984) discussed the possibility that the experiences of traditional healers may be misdiagnosed as schizophrenia. Gustafson (1976) described a reaction to the loss of power and realistic fear of extinction (which could be realistic given governmental attempts at cultural genocide) as potential material for a misdiagnosis of narcissistic personality disorder. The possibility of misdiagnosis, missed diagnosis, or both underscores the need for consultation with knowledgeable tribal community members.

Many standard diagnostic instruments may be unsuitable for assessing American Indian women (see Manson et al., 1987, for a non-gender-specific review of validation studies on commonly used instruments with Indian adults). The Cornell Medical Index may be invalid for Alaska Native women who engage in cooperative decision-making styles because they tend to endorse items that are meant to reveal feelings of inadequacy (Chance, 1962). The Minnesota Multiphasic Personality Inventory (MMPI) often yields elevations on the *F*, *Pd*, and *Sc* scales while failing to discriminate psychopathological variation (Dahlstrom, Lachar, & Dahlstrom, 1986; Pollack & Shore, 1980). The MMPI-2 may not provide greater diagnostic precision because its developers included only 77 American Indians from one tribe in the standardization sample. This sample was too small for validation of the instrument and too restricted for generalizability to diverse American Indian populations (P. Dauphinais & King, 1992). Manson (personal communication, October 11, 1990) contended that the Beck Depression Inventory yields false-positives for depression among American Indian adolescents. Manson and his colleagues (Ackerson, Dick, Manson, & Baron, 1990) instead recommended the Inventory to Diagnose Depression (Zimmerman, Corenthal, & Wilson, 1986). Finally, care must be taken not to minimize the extent of disturbance when working with American Indian women. For example, feelings of victimization ought not to be assumed to be solely the result of prejudice and discrimination.

Interventions

Individual. A survey of 40 mental health workers providing individual psychotherapy with American Indians indicated that the most frequently used individual interventions stem from cognitive, behavioral, and psychoanalytic theories. In this survey, cognitive–behavioral, Adlerian, client-centered, transactional analysis, rational–emotive, gestalt, and psychoeducational approaches were seldom selected. American Indian therapists tended to use behavioral and cognitive–behavioral approaches more often than did non-Indian therapists who were more likely to use psychoanalytic, client-centered, and gestalt approaches (Tangimana & McShane, 1990). These findings on theoretical preference of American Indian therapists are consistent with the earlier work of P. Dauphinais et al. (1981), which indicated American Indian clients prefer a directive style, in which the counselor responds in a rational, problem-solving way (including asking for and giving specific information) over the nondirective or client-centered approach, in which the counselor tends to restate and reflect the client's thoughts and feelings. The nondirective and client-centered approaches may act to decontextualize the problem, isolating the client from the reality of her family and community life. The available evidence at this time would seem to favor culturally sensitive psychoeducational approaches for many of the concerns commonly presented by American Indian women.

Family. One of feminist psychologists' criticisms of conventional systems family therapy is that it views the family as a self-contained unit without regard for the impact of society on the family and individual members of the family (Lerner, 1988a; Webb-Watson, 1988). Furthermore, feminist psychologists believe that society has an impact on the gender roles and coping mechanisms of family members (Avis, 1988; Laird & Hartman, 1988). Experienced psychotherapists have learned to consider both the impact of the dominant society as well as changes within Indian societies and their influence on extended and nuclear American Indian family units (Hoffman, 1980).

In most cases, an American Indian woman cannot be an entity isolated from culture and context. Her family and culture are inseparably linked to an understanding of her sense of self and her mental health. However, to work with her in the context of family therapy may be quite difficult. Family therapy is virtually unexplored in both actual practice and the scientific study of its effectiveness in the Indian community. Although Attneave (1969) noted its tremendous potential in the treatment of American Indian families in presentations of the network therapy she developed, few clinicians seem to be conducting therapy with American Indian families.

The reluctance to do so may be attributed to a number of factors not unlike those of other minority groups. For instance, the willing participation of all members of the family (particularly the men) is often difficult to obtain. This form of therapy is perceived by some as extremely intrusive and a violation of privacy. Unwilling family members believe that they need to protect the family system from both historically negative interventions by the dominant society and further disclosure of personal family history. Few mental health workers are trained in American Indian family therapy, and there are few guides in the professional literature.

Still, a clinician with a strong background in family systems can have a significant impact on the growth and insight of American Indian female clients. Individual as well as family therapy may be structured around the understanding of roles and expectations within the family of origin and the client's immediate family (Lerner, 1988a, 1988b). This understanding may help women redefine their positions and advocate for a more equitable distribution of responsibility within the extended family network.

Some tribal mental health programs such as the Swinomish/Upper Skagit (1991) provide brief family therapy from an eclectic systems approach. The integration of traditional and conventional therapeutic practices appears to be a major theme of the following exemplary models of American Indian family therapy. Topper and Curtis (1987) advocated a multidimensional approach to Navajo Indian family therapy that views the client from medical, psychological, socioeconomic, and cultural–historical perspectives. Their approach is not an attempt to duplicate the efforts of wise women and men but a way of organizing Western specialties to bridge the differences between the two approaches.

Tafoya (1989) combined traditional Indian therapeutic techniques with Western psychological models. Using a traditional story, he created a paradigm of the way American Indians conceptualize relationships, responsibilities, learning, and teaching. He identified these four areas as the core elements of family therapy. He also integrated these American Indian family systems into modified interventions stemming from conventional counseling practices.

Schact, Tafoya, and Mirabla (1989) developed a home-based family therapy approach for families who are unable or unwilling to use clinic-based services. Home-based services are particularly relevant in rural and reservation communities because of the barriers of distance, transportation difficulties, foreign settings, and stigma attached to mental health services. This model focuses on intervening with families at risk for losing a child because of social service intervention. Besides providing a collection of highly plausible interventions, distinct family types such as "fringe families" and "two-world families" are delineated and pertinent family therapy techniques suggested. This model is unique in identifying beliefs through traditional healing ceremonies that are collaboratively provided in the home by the therapist and a wise woman or man and redefine the home as a place of healing.

Group. Historically, many tribes' social and political structures were based on group interaction and consensus. Group activities for social, cultural, spiritual, and healing ceremonies focusing on community support and participation is still the driving force in many Indian communities. One of the first references on group work with Indian clients was a descriptive article about group therapy in two languages in an alcohol treatment facility (Wolman, 1970).

More recently, group therapy has emerged as an effective mode of psychotherapy in Indian country. Ashby, Gilchrist, and Miramontez (1988) developed a successful group treatment approach for sexually abused American Indian girls that creatively incorporated cultural activities, experiential activities, and cognitive restructuring. A promising movement in the use of groups with American Indian women, based on social learning theory, is social skills training groups. American Indian clinicians have developed effective structured groups such as American Indian parenting skills (BigFoot, 1989) and assertion training (LaFromboise, 1989).

Personal identity and boundary clarification are examples of group issues that can be successfully explored and validated in a group process experience. Edwards and Edwards (1984) pointed out the necessity of establishing appropriate group purposes, identifying individual participant goals and objectives, and structuring the group for goal attainment. Kahn et al. (1974) noted that participants in adolescent therapy groups on the Tohono O'odham (Papago) reservation tended to discuss and question topics presented in terms of a third person. Edwards and Edwards also stressed careful consideration and planning for termination, which may be crucial variables affecting the entire group experience.

As in family therapy, alcohol and other drug abuse (AODA) treatment programs have successfully adapted traditional methods of group psychotherapy to an interactive educational structure. AODA topics are sequenced in an educational format and routinely followed by structured group therapy. Talking circles, sweat lodges, and other culturally grounded spiritual group experiences also have been successfully incorporated into many treatment programs. Caution is suggested in using these forms of experiences if they are not part of a client's cultural history or available in her community for access.

Community. Community-based interventions are not new to Indian communities. Rather, historically, they have been an integral component of a highly specialized community system. Community interventions were strategically incorporated throughout traditional spiritual and cultural rituals and activities.

Today, some form of traditional community interventions are still being practiced. These are supplemented by annual seasonal activities such as encampments and powwows (Roberts, 1992). Many educational and skills training groups sponsored by tribal social and educational programs are designed to respond to community needs such as AIDS and violence prevention. Many of these programs began through the efforts of formal or informal community crisis teams that coalesced in response to community issues or problems such as accidents, suicide attempts, violence, and death. Members of these teams are usually well respected and able to provide appropriate intervention services.

A number of larger American Indian tribes have been able to respond to the identified problem of substance abuse by creating alcoholism and addiction treatment facilities in their communities. However, there are only a few substance abuse treatment programs across the country that focus on the needs of American Indian women and allow their children to accompany them into inpatient treatment. These programs are usually in an urban area. In recent years, shelters for abused women and the homeless have been developed on reservations. These programs are usually staffed by individuals from the community who have had similar experiences and are committed to community change. Curricula and other educational media such as the video "To Find Our Way—First Steps" (The Sacred Heart Center, 1991) that portray a realistic picture of substance abuse and domestic violence are emerging to enhance service delivery within these programs.

Another form of community intervention is local Indian Alcoholics Anonymous (AA) groups, which function in a slightly culturally modified manner. National Association of Native American Children of Alcoholics (NANACOA) groups provide annual conferences and local community-based training to address the needs of adult children of American Indian alcoholics. AA and NANACOA groups have been organized by Indian communities to begin the task of interrupting the identified intergenerational cycle of abuse and awakening hope in Indian communities across the nation. This is an important first step toward community mobilization and reformation.

A well-organized health care system can provide services within community guidelines and offer services acceptable to all levels of the community network (G. Jacobs et al., 1991). Community-based services are excellent referral sources, but case coordination is an absolute necessity given the variety of services that may be available. A note of caution is warranted to new clinicians: Although community or family based interventions are perhaps the most effective mode of intervention, it takes time to establish personal credibility and trust within the community and among the multitude of service providers. Therefore, new clinicians need to patiently build bridges by becoming acquainted with and offering assistance to other community service providers before bringing forth new ideas.

CONCLUSION

When considering the issues and concerns of contemporary American Indian women presented here, certain themes become apparent. First, although many continue to deny the persisting pressure placed on American Indians to adopt dominant culture mores, norms, and social practices at the expense of traditional Indian ways, these pressures have existed in the past and are evident in the present. Thus, the fact remains that American Indian women face the lasting effects of historical movements to absorb American Indian people into the dominant culture as well as more subtle and recent actions related to assimilation. These effects include the weakening of the extended family network and changes in gender roles, which place increased responsibilities on American Indian women. At the same time, there is a growing movement in Indian country toward retraditionalization of women's roles in communities accompanied by the sometimes discongruent evolution of American Indian women as leaders in the dominant culture and in tribal government.

Second, social problems such as unemployment, poverty, alcoholism, familial distress, and sexism severely affect American Indian women. These social problems often create clinical problems that would prompt most women to seek help. In many instances, American Indian women suffer multiple losses (e.g., death of family members due to accident or disease; loss of employment; and loss of self-esteem as a product of sexism, racism, or both), which places them in continuing cycles of grief and depression. However, for American Indian people somatic complaints are more acceptable than psychological complaints, and they are more tolerant of others' behavior. Thus, American Indian women are less likely than non-Indians to seek psychological assistance. Given this, providing American Indian women with acceptable ways of seeking mental health services becomes an important concern. The use of paraprofessionals (e.g., CHRs who are known and trusted in the community) to conduct community outreach activities presents one alternative approach.

Third, psychology provides a limited knowledge base concerning American Indian women. We could find only 19 psychological articles in the 1992 review of literature conducted for this chapter. Although these numbers are disturbing, it is even more disturbing that some of the literature derives its knowledge from studies founded on models that emphasize pathology or genetic and cultural deprivation. Obviously, little organized, published, psychological knowledge exists describing the ways in which

American Indian women function successfully in today's diverse society. In this age of instantaneous communication and technological advancement, it is sad that American Indian women in clinical practice must continue to rely on the traditional but limited method of relaying knowledge: "word of mouth." In rectifying this situation, researchers are encouraged to define research questions that attempt to determine the attributes of successful American Indian women, to explore the coping skills that contribute to the resilience of certain American Indian women in the face of hardship and loss, and to delineate situational variables that promote success, rather than failure, in American Indian women.

Fourth, with respect to mental health training concerns, it may be concluded that more use should be made of those wise women found in American Indian communities. They might be included in training workshops in which culturally appropriate behaviors, assessment and diagnosis, and treatment recommendations are discussed. Also, given the scarcity of American Indian professionals working in direct service with Indian people, paraprofessionals form the foundation of most mental health agencies servicing American Indian communities. These paraprofessionals must be specifically trained to provide culturally appropriate responses as well as psychologically sound treatment. All training programs are encouraged to incorporate American Indian mental health issues into core areas of their curriculum. Equally important, however, programs designed specifically to increase the numbers of American Indian women and men earning master's and doctoral degrees in applied psychology are essential to the improvement of mental health services in American Indian communities.

Finally, the clinical process for American Indian women must allow for a number of cultural considerations. The spiritual underpinnings of the Indian community that find spiritual and emotional health to be inseparable constructs must be respected in therapy. Traditional forms of communication that are indirect and sometimes tentative should be taken as culturally appropriate and not necessarily signs of resistance, defensiveness, or pathology. The clinician working with American Indian female clients must make herself or himself aware of the cultural demands the client may be experiencing and work in more directive, nonthreatening ways to build trust and to encourage the formation of a therapeutic alliance.

In summary, this chapter has explored some of the cultural demands placed on American Indian women and the responses of American Indian women as those cared for and those caring for. We have outlined the ways they all work together to advance the well-being of the community. We have suggested that American Indian women's lives are encircled by caring that is expressed in a variety of ways. These expressions range from being cared for as a daughter to caring for the spiritual well-being of the community as wise woman.

REFERENCES

Ackerson, L. M., Dick, R. W., Manson, S. M., & Baron, A. E. (1990). Properties of the Inventory to Diagnose Depression in American Indian adolescents. *Journal of the American Academy of Child and Adolescent Psychiatry, 29*, 601–607.

*Albers, P. (1989). Voices from within: Narrative writings of American Indian women. *Humanity and Society, 13*, 463–470.

*Albers, P., & Medicine, B. (1983). *The hidden half: Studies of Plains Indian women.* New York: University Press of America.

Allen, P. G. (1981). Lesbians in American Indian cultures. *Conditions, 7*, 67–87.

*Allen, P. G. (1986). *The sacred hoop.* Boston: Beacon Press.

*Allen, P. G. (1991). *Grandmothers of the light: A medicine woman's sourcebook.* Boston: Beacon Press.

*Almquist, E. M. (1984). Race and ethnicity in the lives of minority women. In J. Freeman (Ed.), *Women: A feminist perspective* (pp. 423–453). New York: Mayflower.

American Psychological Association. (1990). *Directory of ethnic minority professionals in psychology.* Washington, DC: Author.

American Psychological Association. (1991). *1989 APA directory survey, and new member updates for 1990 and 1991.* Washington, DC: Author.

*Amott, T., & Matthaei, J. (1991, November–December). Before the "trail of tears." *Ms. Magazine, 1*, p. 82.

Anderson, K. (1985). Commodity exchange and subordination: Montagnais-Naskapi and Huron women, 1600–1650. *Signs, 11*, 48–62.

*Antell, J. A. (1991). American Indian women activists (Doctoral dissertation, University of California, Berkeley, 1990). *Dissertation Abstracts International, 51*, 4283A.

*Ashby, M. R., Gilchrist, L. D., & Miramontez, A. (1988). Group treatment for sexually abused American Indian adolescents. *Social Work With Groups, 10*, 21–32.

Atkinson, D. R. (1983). Ethnic similarity in counseling psychology: A review of research. *The Counseling Psychologist, 11*, 79–92.

Attneave, C. L. (1969). Therapy in tribal settings and urban network intervention. *Family Process, 8*, 192–210.

Attneave, C. L. (1982). American Indians and Alaska Native families: Emigrants in their own homeland. In M. McGoldrick, J. Pearce, & J. Giordano (Eds.), *Ethnicity and family therapy* (pp. 55–83). New York: Guilford Press.

Avis, J. M. (1988). Deepening awareness: A private study guide to feminism and family therapy. In L. Braverman (Ed.), *A guide to feminist family therapy* (pp. 15–46). New York: Harrington Park.

Axtell, J. (1981). *The Indian peoples of Eastern America: A documentary history of the sexes*. New York: Oxford University Press.

*Baker, N. R. (1983). American Indian women in an urban setting (Doctoral dissertation, Ohio State University, 1982). *Dissertation Abstracts International, 43*, 3359A.

Bannan, H. M. (1984). *"True womanhood" on the reservation: Field matrons in the United States Indian Service*. Tucson: Southwest Institute for Research on Women, University of Arizona.

Barter, E. R., & Barter, J. T. (1974). Urban Indians and mental health problems. *Psychiatric Annals, 4*, 37–43.

Beiser, M., & Attneave, C. L. (1982). Mental health disorders among Native American children: Rates and risk periods for entering treatment. *American Journal of Psychiatry, 139*, 193–198.

Benally, H. J. (1992). Spiritual knowledge for a secular society: Traditional Navajo spirituality offers lessons for the nation. *Tribal College: Journal of American Indian Higher Education, 3*(4), 19–22.

*Bennett, S. K. (1991). American Indian client preferences for counselor attributes (Doctoral dissertation, University of Oklahoma, 1991). *Dissertation Abstracts International, 52*, 1257A.

*Bennett, S. K., & BigFoot Sipes, D. S. (1991). American Indian and White college student preference for counselor characteristics. *Journal of Counseling Psychology, 38*, 440–445.

*Bergman, R. L. (1974). Paraprofessionals in Indian mental health programs. *Psychiatric Annals, 4*, 76–84.

*Berman, J. R. S. (1989). A view from rainbow bridge: Feminist therapy meets changing woman. *Women and Therapy, 8*(4), 65–78.

BigFoot, D. S. (1989). Parent training for American Indian families. *Dissertation Abstracts International, 50*, 1562A. (University Microfilms No. AAC 8919982)

*BigFoot-Sipes, D., Dauphinais, P., LaFromboise, T., Bennett, S., & Rowe, W. (1992). American Indian secondary school students' preference for counselors. *Journal of Multicultural Counseling and Development, 20*, 113–122.

*Blackwood, E. (1984). Sexuality and gender in certain Native American tribes: The case of the cross-gender females. *Signs, 16*, 27–42.

Blum, R., Harmon, B., Harris, L., Bergeisen, L., & Resnick, M. (1992). American Indian-Alaska Native youth health. *Journal of the American Medical Association, 267*, 1637–1644.

Boyce, W., & Boyce, T. (1983). Acculturation and changes in health among Navajo boarding school students. *Social Science and Medicine, 17*, 219–226.

Brammer, L. M., Shostrom, E. L., & Abrego, P. J. (1989). *Therapeutic psychology: Fundamentals of counseling and psychotherapy* (5th ed.). Englewood Cliffs, NJ: Prentice Hall.

*Briggs, J. L. (1974). Eskimo women: Makers of men. In C. J. Matthiasson (Ed.), *Many sisters: Women in cross-cultural perspective* (pp. 261–304). New York: Free Press.

*Brown, J. K. (1975). Iroquois women: An ethnohistoric note. In R. R. Reiter (Ed.), *Toward an anthropology of women* (pp. 235–251). New York: Monthly Review.

*Buffalohead, P. K. (1986). Farmers, warriors, traders: A fresh look at Ojibway women. In R. L. Nichols (Ed.), *The American Indian: Past and present* (pp. 28–38). New York: Knopf.

*Bushnell, J. M. (1981). Northwest Coast American Indians' beliefs about childbirth. *Issues in Health Care of Women, 3,* 249–261.

*Campbell, B. C., Kimball, E. H., Helgerson, S. D., Alexander, I. L., & Goldberg, H. I. (1989, November–December). Using 1990 national MCH objectives to assess health status and risk in an American Indian community. *Public Health Reports, 104,* 627.

Campbell, G. (1989). The political epidemiology of infant mortality. *American Indian Culture and Research Journal, 13*(3/4), 1–20, 105–148.

Center for Indian Education. (1993). *American Indian and Alaska Native professors directory.* Tempe, AZ: Author.

Chance, N. (1962). Conceptual and methodological problems in cross-cultural health research. *American Journal of Public Health, 52,* 410–417.

Clinton selects Deer for Indian Affairs job. (1993, May 12). *Wisconsin State Journal,* Section A, p. 1.

Collins, J., Hurst, J., & Jacobson, J. (1987). The blind spot extended: Spirituality. *Journal of College Student Personnel, 28,* 274–276.

Dahlstrom, W. G., Lachar, D., & Dahlstrom, L. E. (1986). *MMPI patterns of American minorities.* Minneapolis: University of Minnesota.

Dauphinais, L. (1982). American Indian and Anglo perceptions of speaker, message structure, and message orientation (Doctoral dissertation, University of Oklahoma, 1981). *Dissertation Abstracts International, 42,* 2989A.

Dauphinais, P., & King, J. (1992). Psychological assessment with American Indian children. *Applied and Preventive Psychology, 1,* 97–110.

Dauphinais, P., Dauphinais, L., & Rowe, W. (1981). Effects of race and communication style on Indian perceptions of counselor effectiveness. *Counselor Education and Supervision, 21,* 72–80.

Dell, P. F. (1980). The Hopi family therapist and the Aristotelian parents. *Journal of Marital and Family Therapy, 6,* 123–130.

*Devens, C. A. (1987). Separate confrontations: Indian women and Christian missions, 1630–1900 (Doctoral dissertation, Rutgers—the State University of New Jersey, New Brunswick). *Dissertation Abstracts International, 47,* 245A.

*Dixon, J. K. (1989). *Group treatment for Native American women survivors of incest.* Billings, MT: Indian Health Service and Mental Health Program.

Edgarton, R. B. (1965). Some dimensions of disillusionment in culture contact. *Southwestern Journal of Anthropology, 21,* 231–243.

Edwards, E. D., & Edwards, M. E. (1984). Group work with American Indians. *Social Work With Groups, 7,* 7–21.

*Emmerich, L. E. (1988). "To respect and love and seek the ways of White women": Field matrons, the Office of Indian Affairs, and civilization policy 1890–38 (Doctoral dissertation, University of Maryland, College Park, 1987). *Dissertation Abstracts International, 48,* 2148A.

*Englander, M. J. (1986). Through their words: Tradition and the urban Indian woman's experience (Doctoral dissertation, University of California, Santa Barbara, 1985). *Dissertation Abstracts International, 46,* 3513A.

Erikson, E. H. (1963). *Childhood and society* (2nd ed.). New York: Norton.

*Ewers, J. C. (1965). Deadlier than the male. *American Heritage, 16*(4), 10–13.

*Ferguson, H. J. S. (1985). A study of the characteristics of American Indian professional women in Oklahoma (Doctoral dissertation, Ohio State University, 1985). *Dissertation Abstracts International, 46,* 1518A.

*Fleming, C. (1989, August). *Mental health treatment of American Indian women.* Paper presented at the 97th Annual Convention of the American Psychological Association, New Orleans, LA.

*Fleming, C., & Manson, S. (1990). Native American women. In R. Engs (Ed.), *Women: Alcohol and other drugs* (pp. 143–148). Dubuque, IA: Kendal/Hunt.

Fong, M. L., & Cox, B. G. (1983). Trust as an underlying dynamic in the counseling process: How clients test trust. *Personnel and Guidance Journal, 62,* 163–166.

*Foreman, C. R. (1976). *Indian women chiefs.* Washington, DC: Zenger.

*French, L. A. (1976). Social problems among Cherokee females: A study of cultural ambivalence and role identity. *American Journal of Psychoanalysis, 36,* 163–169.

*Galloway, I. N. (1987). Trends in the employment of minority women as administrators in Texas public schools: 1976–1981 (Doctoral dissertation, Texas Southern University, 1986). *Dissertation Abstracts International, 47,* 4250A.

*Galloway, M. E. (1987). *American Indian women in literature: Stereotypical characterizations of insufficient self-determination.* Paper presented at the 10th Annual American Indian Conference, Mankato, MN.

*Glenn, L. D. (1990). Health care communication between American Indian women and a White male doctor: A study of interaction at a public health facility (Doctoral dissertation, University of Oklahoma, 1990). *Dissertation Abstracts International, 51,* 1826A.

Goodloe, N. R., & Arreola, P. M. (1992). Spiritual health: Out of the closet. *Journal of Health Education, 23,* 193–226.

Goodtracks, J. C. (1973). Native American non-interference. *Social Work, 18,* 30–34.

*Green, R. (1976). The Pocahontas perplex: The image of Indian women in American culture. *The Massachusetts Review, 16,* 698–714.

*Green, R. (1980). Native American women. *Signs, 6,* 248–267.

*Green, R. (1983). *Native American women: A contextual bibliography.* Bloomington: Indiana University Press.

Gustafson, J. P. (1976). The group matrix on individual therapy with Plains Indian people. *Contemporary Psychoanalysis, 12,* 227–239.

Hall, E. T. (1976). *Beyond culture.* Garden City, NY: Doubleday.

Hamamsy, L. (1957). The role of women in a changing Navaho society. *American Anthropologist, 59,* 101–111.

Hammerschlag, C. (1988). *The dancing healers: A doctor's journey of healing with Native Americans.* New York: Harper & Row.

*Hanson, W. (1980). *The urban Indian* (Rep. No. RCO14193). San Francisco: San Francisco State University. (ERIC Document Reproduction Service No. ED 213 587)

*Harjo, J. (1991, July–August). Three generations of Native American women's birth experience. *Ms. Magazine, 2,* p. 28.

*Harris, M. B., Begay, C., & Page, P. (1989). Activities, family relationships and feelings about aging in a multicultural elderly sample. *International Journal of Aging and Human Development, 29,* 103–117.

*Haupt, C. M. (1984). The image of the American Indian female in the biographical literature and social studies textbooks of the elementary schools (Doctoral dissertation, Rutgers—the State University of New Jersey, New Brunswick, 1984). *Dissertation Abstracts International, 45,* 408A.

Haviland, M. G., Horswill, R. K., O'Connell, J. J., & Dynneson, V. V. (1983). Native American college students' preference for counselor race and sex and the likelihood of their use of a counseling center. *Journal of Counseling Psychology, 30,* 267–270.

Herring, R. (1990). Understanding Native American values: Process and content concerns for counselors. *Counseling and Values, 34,* 134–137.

Ho, M. K. (1987). *Family therapy with ethnic minorities.* Newbury Park, CA: Sage.

Hoffman, F. (1980). *The American Indian family: Strengths and stresses.* Isleta, NM: American Indian Social Research and Development Associates.

*Holmstrom, D. (1991). Walks with hope. *Christian Science Monitor, 83,* 11.

Horejsi, C., Craig, B., & Pablo, J. (1992). Reactions by Native American parents to child protection agencies: Cultural and community factors. *Child Welfare, 71,* 329–343.

*Horn, B. M. (1977). An ethnoscientific study to determine social and cultural factors affecting Native American Indian women during pregnancy (Doctoral dissertation, University of Washington, 1975). *Dissertation Abstracts International, 37,* 4397A.

*Howard-Pitney, B., LaFromboise, T., Basil, M., September, B., & Johnson, M. (1992). Psychological and social indicators of suicide ideation and suicide attempts in Zuni adolescents. *Journal of Consulting and Clinical Psychology, 60,* 473–476.

*Hungry Wolf, B. (1980). *The ways of my grandmothers.* New York: William Morrow.

Indian Health Service. (1989). *Indian Health Service: Trends in Indian health.* Washington, DC: U.S. Department of Health and Human Services.

*Indian Health Service. (1991). *Indian women's health care: Consensus statement.* Rockville, MD: U.S. Department of Health and Human Services.

Jacobs, G., Dauphinais, P., Gross, S., & Guzman, L. (1991). *American Psychological Association site visitation report.* Washington, DC: American Psychological Association.

Jacobs, S. E. (1977). Berdache: A brief review of the literature. *Colorado Anthropology, 1,* 25–40.

*Jaimes, M. (1982). Towards a new image of American Indian women. *Journal of American Indian Education, 22*(1), 18–32.

*Jenks, K. (1986). "Changing woman": The Navajo therapist goddess. *Psychological Perspectives, 17,* 202–221.

Jilek-Aall, L. (1976). The Western psychiatrist and his non-Western clientele. *Canadian Psychiatric Association Journal, 21,* 353–359.

Joe, J. R., & Justice, J. W. (1992). Introduction: Proceedings of the first national conference on cancer in Native Americans. *American Indian Culture and Research Journal, 16*(3), 9–20.

John, R. (1988). The Native American family. In C. H. Mindel, R. W. Habenstein, & R. Wright (Eds.), *Ethnic families in America: Patterns and variations* (pp. 325–363). New York: Elsevier.

Kahn, M. W., Lejero, L., Antone, M., Francisco, D., & Manuel, J. (1988). An indigenous community mental health service on the Tohono O'odham (Papago) Indian reservation: Seventeen years later. *American Journal of Community Psychology, 16,* 369–379.

Kahn, M. W., Lewis, J., & Galvez, E. (1974). An evaluation of a group therapy procedure with reservation adolescent Indians. *Psychotherapy: Theory, Research and Practice, 11,* 241–244.

*Kay, N. W. (1986). Food behaviors and obesity among urban American Indian women (Doctoral dissertation, Southern Methodist University, 1986). *Dissertation Abstracts International, 47,* 1790A.

*Kidwell, C. S. (1978). The power of women in three American Indian societies. *Journal of Ethnic Studies, 6*(3), 113–121.

*Klein, A. M. (1983). The Plains truth: The impact of colonialism on Indian women. *Dialectical Anthropology, 7,* 299–313.

*Krause, M. L. (1982). Indian professional women: Factors in vocational achievement (Doctoral dissertation, Arizona State University, 1982). *Dissertation Abstracts International, 43,* 367A.

*LaFromboise, T. D. (1989). *Circles of women: Professionalization training for American Indian women.* Newton, MA: Women's Educational Equity Act.

LaFromboise, T. D. (1992). An interpersonal analysis of affinity, clarification, and helpful responses with American Indians. *Professional Psychology: Research and Practice, 23,* 281–286.

LaFromboise, T. D., Coleman, H. C., & Gerton, J. (1993). Psychological impact of biculturalism: Evidence and theory. *Psychological Bulletin, 114,* 395–412.

LaFromboise, T. D., Dauphinais, P., & Lujan, P. (1981). Verbal indicators of insincerity as perceived by American Indians. *Journal of Non-White Concerns, 9,* 87–94.

LaFromboise, T. D., Dauphinais, P., & Rowe, W. (1980). Indian students' perceptions of positive helper attributes. *Journal of American Indian Education, 19,* 11–16.

LaFromboise, T. D., & Dixon, D. N. (1981). American Indian perception of trustworthiness in a counseling interview. *Journal of Counseling Psychology, 28,* 135–139.

*LaFromboise, T., & Fleming, C. (1990). Keeper of the fire: A profile of Carolyn Attneave. *Journal of Counseling and Development, 68,* 537–547.

*LaFromboise, T. D., Heyle, A. M., & Ozer, E. J. (1990). Changing and diverse roles of women in American Indian cultures. *Sex Roles, 22,* 455–476.

LaFromboise, T., & Plake, B. (1984). A model for the concept of culture in American Indian educational research. *White Cloud Journal, 3,* 44–52.

LaFromboise, T. D., Trimble, J. E., & Mohatt, G. (1990). Counseling intervention and American Indian tradition: An integrative approach. *The Counseling Psychologist, 18,* 628–654.

Laird, J., & Harman, A. (1988). Women, rituals, and family therapy. In L. Braverman (Ed.), *A guide to feminist family therapy* (pp. 157–173). New York: Harrington Park.

*Lake, M. G. (1991). *Native healer: Initiation into an ancient art* (pp. 79–107). Wheaton, IL: Quest Books.

Lake, R. A. (1991). Between myth and history: Enacting time in Native American protest rhetoric. *Quarterly Journal of Speech, 77,* 123–151.

*Lake, R. G., Jr. (1980). Chilula religion and ideology: A discussion of Native American humanistic concepts and processes. *Humboldt Journal of Social Relations, 7*(2), 113–137.

*Landes, R. (1971). *The Ojibwa woman.* New York: Norton.

Lannert, J. L. (1991). Resistance and countertransference issues with spiritual and religious clients. *Journal of Humanistic Psychology, 31,* 68–76.

*Leacock, E. (1980). Montagnais women and the Jesuit program for colonization. In M. Etienne & E. Leacock (Eds.), *Women and colonization: Anthropological perspectives* (pp. 25–42). New York: Praeger.

Lecomte, C., Bernstein, B. L., & Dumont, F. (1981). Counseling interactions as a function of spatial–environmental conditions. *Journal of Counseling Psychology, 28,* 536–539.

Lerner, H. G. (1988a). Is family systems theory really systemic? A feminist communication. In L. Braverman (Ed.), *A guide to feminist family therapy* (pp. 47–63). New York: Harrington Park.

Lerner, H. G. (1988b). *Women in therapy.* New York: Harper & Row.

Lewis, A. C., & Hayes, S. (1991). Multiculturalism and the school counseling curriculum. *Journal of Counseling and Development, 70,* 119–125.

*Lewis, O. (1941). Manly-hearted women among the Northern Piegan. *American Anthropologist, 43,* 173–187.

Lewis, R. (1984). The strengths of Indian families. *Proceedings of Indian child abuse conference.* Tulsa, OK: National Indian Child Abuse Center.

Lewis, T. H. (1990). *The medicine men: Oglala Sioux ceremony and healing.* Lincoln: University of Nebraska.

*Light, H. K., & Martin, R. E. (1986). American Indian families. *Journal of American Indian Education, 26*(1), 1–5.

Locust, C. (1988). Wounding the spirit: Discrimination and traditional American Indian belief systems. *Harvard Educational Review, 58,* 315–330.

Lomawaima, K. T. (1994). *They called it prairie light: The story of Chilocco Indian School.* Lincoln: University of Nebraska Press.

Long, K. A. (1983). The experience of repeated and traumatic loss among Crow Indian children. *American Journal of Orthopsychiatry, 53,* 116–126.

Lujan, P., Kennan, W. R., Hill, L. B., & Long, L. W. (1979, November). *Communication reticence of Native Americans in the classroom: A reconceptualization and approach.* Paper presented at the annual convention of the Speech Communication Association, San Antonio, TX.

*Lurie, N. O. (1972). Indian women: A legacy of freedom. In R. L. Lacopi & B. L. Fontana (Eds.), *Look to the mountaintop* (pp. 29–36). San Jose, CA: Gousha.

*Lynch, R. (1986). Women in Northern Paiute politics. *Signs, 11,* 352–366.

Manson, S. (Ed.). (1989). Misalliances in the Barrow alcohol study [Special issue]. *American Indian and Alaska Native Mental Health Research, 2*(3).

*Manson, S. M., Beals, J., Dick, R. W., & Duclos, C. (1989). Risk factors for suicide among Indian adolescents at a boarding school. *Public Health Reports, 104,* 609–614.

Manson, S. M., & Callaway, D. (1988). Health and aging among American Indians: Issues and challenges for the biobehavioral sciences. In S. M. Manson & N. Dinges (Eds.), *Behavioral health issues among American Indians and Alaska Natives* (pp. 160–210). Denver: University of Colorado Health Sciences Center.

Manson, S., Shore, J., & Bloom, J. (1985). The depressive experience in American Indian communities: A challenge for psychiatric theory and diagnosis. In A. Klienman & B. Goods (Eds.), *Culture and depression* (pp. 331–368). Berkeley: University of California.

Manson, S., Walker, R. D., & Kivlahan, D. R. (1987). Psychiatric assessment and treatment of American Indians and Alaska Natives. *Hospital and Community Psychiatry, 38,* 165–173.

*Matchett, W. F. (1972). Repeated hallucinatory experiences as a part of the mourning process among Hopi women. *Psychiatry, 35,* 185–194.

May, P. A. (1986). Alcohol and drug misuse prevention programs for American Indians: Needs and opportunities. *Journal of Studies on Alcohol, 47,* 187–195.

*May, P. A., Hambaugh, K. J., Aase, J. M., & Samet, J. M. (1983). Epidemiology of fetal alcohol syndrome among American Indians of the Southwest. *Social Biology, 30,* 374–387.

McCoy, M. (1992). Gender or ethnicity: What makes a difference? A study of women tribal leaders. *Women and Politics, 12*(3), 57–68.

Medicine, B. (1980). American Indian women: Spirituality and status. *Bread and Roses, 2*(1), 15–18.

*Medicine, B. (1981). The interaction of culture and sex roles in the schools. *Integrated Education, 19,* 28–37.

*Metcalf, A. (1976). From schoolgirl to mother: The effects of education on Navajo women. *Social Problems, 23,* 535–544.

*Metoyer, C. (1979). The Native American woman. In E. Snyder (Ed.), *The study of women: Enlarging perspectives on social reality* (pp. 329–335). New York: Harper & Row.

Miller, S. I., & Schoenfeld, L. (1973). Grief in the Navajo: Psychodynamics and culture. *Journal of Social Psychiatry, 19,* 187–191.

*Mittlefehldt, P. K. (1990). A politics of transformation: Women and story in American culture (Doctoral dissertation, University of Minnesota, 1989). *Dissertation Abstracts International, 50,* 3993A.

Modesto, R., & Mount, G. (1980). *Not for innocent ears: Spiritual traditions of a desert Cahuilla medicine woman.* Arcata, CA: Sweetlight Books.

Mohatt, G., McDiarmid, G., & Montoya, V. (1988). Societies, families, and change: The Alaskan example [Monograph]. *American Indian and Alaska Native Mental Health Research, 1,* 325–365.

*Moore, C. I. (1990). Struggle and commitment: The experience of older minority women in returning to higher education (Doctoral dissertation, University of Michigan, 1990). *Dissertation Abstracts International, 51,* 1135A.

Moran, B. (1988). *Stoney Creek Woman: The story of Mary John.* Vancouver: Tillacum.

Morey, S. M., & Gilliam, O. L. (Eds.). (1972). *Respect for life.* New York: Waldorf.

Murphy, M. N. (1970). Silence, the word, and Indian rhetoric. *College Composition and Communication, 21,* 356–363.

*Nagel, J. K. (1988). Unresolved grief and mourning in Navajo women. *American Indian and Alaska Native Mental Health Research, 2*(2), 32–40.

National Institute on Alcohol and Abuse and Alcoholism Newsletter. (1978, September 20). Information and feature service no. 51. Washington, DC: U.S. Department of Health, Education and Welfare.

National Science Foundation. (1989). *1989 survey of doctorate recipients.* Washington, DC: Author.

Native Americans gaining new electoral ambitions. (1992, October 21). *Christian Science Monitor,* p. 7.

Natives cheer Clinton choice: Tribal-rights supporter Deer selected to head Indian Affairs. (1993, May 13). *Anchorage Daily News, 48,* p. 133.

Neligh, G. (1988). Major mental disorders and behavior among American Indians and Alaska Natives [Monograph]. *American Indian and Alaska Native Mental Health Research, 1,* 116–150.

Nelson, S. H., McCoy, G., Stetter, M. & Vanderwagen, W. C. (1992). An overview of mental health services for American Indians and Alaska Natives in the 1990s. *Hospital and Community Psychiatry, 43,* 257–261.

Neumann, A. K., Mason, V., Chase, E., & Albaugh, B. (1991). Factors associated with success among Southern Cheyenne and Arapaho Indians. *Journal of Community Health, 16,* 103–115.

*Niethammer, C. (1977). *Daughters of the earth.* New York: Collier.

*Old Dog Cross, P. (1982). Sexual abuse: A new threat to the Native American woman: An overview. *Listening Post, 6*(2), 18.

O'Sullivan, M. J., Peterson, P. D., Cox, G. B., & Kirkeby, J. (1989). Ethnic populations: Community mental health services ten years later. *American Journal of Community Psychology, 17,* 17–30.

*Parezo, N. (1982). Navajo sandpaintings: The importance of sex roles in craft production. *American Indian Quarterly, 6,* 25–48.

Pollack, D., & Shore, J. H. (1980). Validity of the MMPI with Native Americans. *American Journal of Psychiatry, 137,* 946–950.

Ponterotto, J. G., & Casas, J. M. (1991). *Handbook of racial/ethnic minority counseling research.* Springfield, IL: Charles C Thomas.

*Powers, M. (1980). Menstruation and reproduction: An Oglala case. *Signs, 6,* 54–65.

*Powers, M. (1986). *Oglala women: Myth, ritual, and reality.* Chicago: University of Chicago Press.

Proctor, N. (1979, August). Providing services to American Indians: Interaction or interference? In F. Everett (Chair), *Training providers of services to American Indian children and families.* Symposium presented at the annual meeting of the American Psychological Association, New York.

Red Horse, J. G. (1980). Family structure and value orientation in American Indians. *Social Casework, 61,* 462–467.

Red Horse, J. (1982). Clinical strategies for American Indian families in crisis. *Urban and Social Change Review, 15*, 17–19.

Roberts, C. (1992). *Pow wow country*. Helena, MT: American and World Geographic.

Root, M. (1992). Reconstructing the impact of trauma on personality. In L. S. Brown & M. Ballou (Eds.), *Personality and psychopathology: Feminist reappraisals* (pp. 229–266). New York: Guilford Press.

*Roscoe, W. (1991). *The Zuni man-woman*. Albuquerque: University of New Mexico.

*Ryan, B. (1988). Kinaalda: The pathway to Navajo womanhood. *Winds of Change, 3*(3), 74–77.

Ryan, R. A. (1980). A community perspective for mental health research. *Social Casework, 61*, 507–511.

Sacred Heart Center (Producer), & Farrow, T. (Director). (1991). *To find our way: First steps* [Video]. Chatsworth, CA: AIMS Media.

*Sandefur, G. D., & McKinnell, T. (1986). American Indian intermarriage. *Social Science Research, 15*, 347–371.

*Sauceda, J. B. (1979). From the inner circle: The relation of the space occupied, past and present, by Southwest American Indian women to the Southwest Indo-Hispano women of yesteryear and today (Doctoral dissertation, University of Colorado, 1979). *Dissertation Abstracts International, 40*, 2203A.

Schacht, A. J., Tafoya, N., & Mirabla, K. (1989). Home-based therapy with American Indian families. *American Indian and Alaska Native Mental Health Research, 3*(2), 27–42.

*Schlegal, A. (1973). The adolescent socialization of the Hopi girl. *Ethnology, 12*, 449–462.

*Schlegal, A. (1977). Male and female in Hopi thought and action. In A. Schlegal (Ed.), *Sexual stratification: A cross-cultural view* (pp. 245–269). New York: Columbia University Press.

*Skye, F. D. (1989). A study of the effects of dance education on stress in college-age American Indian women (Doctoral dissertation, University of South Dakota, 1988). *Dissertation Abstracts International, 49*, 1706A.

Smith, A. (1991). For all those who were Indian in a former life. *Women of Power, 19*, 74–75.

Smith, G. (1993, August). A woman of the people. *Sports Illustrated, 78*, pp. 54–58, 60, 62–64.

*Snipp, C. M., & Aytac, I. A. (1990). The labor force participation of American Indian women. *Research in Human Capital and Development, 6*, 189–211.

*Snow, J. T., & Harris, M. B. (1989). Disordered eating in Southwestern Pueblo Indians and Hispanics. *Journal of Adolescence, 12*, 329–336.

*Solomon, G. W. (1991). Women of poverty: Health perceptions of southwestern Oklahoma women in two women, infant and children's nutrition programs

(Doctoral dissertation, University of Oklahoma Health Sciences Center, 1990). *Dissertation Abstracts International, 51*, 4302B.

Spencer, R. F. (1959). The North American Eskimo. *Bulletin of the Bureau of American Ethnology, 171*, 383.

*Steiner, S. (1968). *The new Indians.* New York: Dell.

Sue, S., Allen, D. B., & Conway, L. (1978). The responsiveness and equality of mental health care to Chicanos and Native Americans. *American Journal of Community Psychology, 6*, 137–146.

Sue, S., & Zane, N. (1994). Research on psychotherapy with culturally diverse populations. In S. Garfield & A. Bergin (Eds.), *Handbook of psychotherapy and behavior change* (pp. 783–819). New York: Wiley.

Sweeny, T., & Witmer, J. M. (1991). Beyond social interest: Striving toward optimum health and wellness. *Individual Psychology, 47*, 527–540.

Swinomish Tribal Mental Health Project. (1991). *A gathering of wisdoms: Tribal mental health. A cultural perspective.* Mount Vernon, WA: Veda Vangarde.

Taeuber, C. (Ed.). (1991). *Statistical handbook of women in America.* Phoenix, AZ: Orynx.

Tafoya, T. (1989). Circles and cedar: Native Americans and family therapy. *Minorities and family therapy* (pp. 71–9). Binghamton, NY: Haworth House.

Tangimana, M., & McShane, D. A. (1990, March). *Theoretical orientations and treatment modality preferences of degreed mental health providers working with American Indian clients.* Paper presented at the annual meeting of the Southwestern Psychological Association, Tucson, AZ.

Timpson, J., McKay, S., Kakegamic, S., Roundhead, D., Cohen, C., & Matewapit, G. (1988). Depression in a Native Canadian in Northwestern Ontario: Sadness, grief, or spiritual illness? *Canada's Mental Health, 36*, 5–8.

Topper, M. D., & Curtis, J. (1987). Extended family therapy: A clinical approach to the treatment of synergistic dual anomic depression among Navajo agency-town adolescents. *Journal of Community Psychology, 15*, 334–348.

Trimble, J. E. (1977). The sojourner in the American Indian community: Methodological issues and concerns. *Journal of Social Issues, 33*, 159–174.

Trimble, J. E. (1981). Value differentials and their importance in counseling American Indians. In P. Pedersen, J. Draguns, W. Lonner, & J. Trimble (Eds.), *Counseling across cultures* (pp. 203–226). Honolulu: University Press of Hawaii.

*Tsosie, R. (1988). Changing women: The cross-currents of American Indian feminine identity. *American Indian Culture and Research Journal, 18*(1), 1–37.

*Udall, L. (1977). *Me and mine: The life story of Helen Sekequaptewa.* Tucson: University of Arizona.

United States Department of Labor. (1992). *Handbook of labor statistics.* Washington, DC: Bureau of Labor Statistics.

United States Congress. (1990). *Indian Adolescent mental health* (Tech. Rep. No. OTA-H-446). Washington, DC: U.S. Government Printing Office.

Vaugn, F. (1991). Spiritual issues in psychotherapy. *Journal of Transpersonal Psychology, 23*, 105–119.

Vizenor, G. (1984). *The people named the Chippewa* (pp. 139–153). Minneapolis: University of Minnesota.

Vraniak, D. A., & Pickett, S. A. (1993). Improving interventions with ethnic minority children: Recurrent and recalcitrant challenges. In R. Kratchowill & R. Morris (Eds.), *The handbook of psychotherapy with children* (pp. 501–576). Needham Heights, MA: Allyn & Bacon.

*Wagner, J. K. (1972). An examination and description of acculturation of selected individual American Indian women in an urban area (Doctoral dissertation, New York University, 1972). *Dissertation Abstracts International, 33,* 1364B.

*Wagner, J. K. (1976). The role of intermarriage in the acculturation of selected urban American Indian women. *Anthropologica, 18,* 215–229.

*Watkins, F. E. (1942). Crafts and industries of the American Indian women of California and the Southwest (Doctoral dissertation, University of Southern California, 1942). *American Doctoral Dissertations,* W1942.

Wax, R. H., & Thomas, R. K. (1961). American Indians and White people. *Phylon, 22,* 305–317.

Webb-Watson, L. (1988). Women, family therapy, and larger systems. In L. Braverman (Ed.), *A guide to feminist family therapy* (pp. 145–156). New York: Harrington Park.

*Welch, D. S. (1986). Zitkala-Sa: An American Indian leader, 1876–1938 (Doctoral dissertation, University of Wyoming, 1985). *Dissertation Abstracts International, 46,* 2792A.

*Welch, D. (1987). American Indian women: Reaching beyond the myth. In C. Calloway (Ed.), *New directions in American Indian history* (pp. 31–48). Norman: University of Oklahoma.

*Whitehead, H. (1981). The bow and burden strap. In S. Ortner & H. Whitehead (Eds.), *Sexual meanings: The cultural construction of gender and sexuality* (pp. 80–115). Cambridge, England: Cambridge University Press.

Willis, D. J., Dobrec, A., & BigFoot Sipes, D. S. (1992). Treating American Indian victims of abuse and neglect. In L. Vargas & J. Koss-Chioino (Eds.), *Working with culture* (pp. 276–299). San Francisco: Jossey-Bass.

*Witt, S. H. (1974). Native women today: Sexism and the Indian woman. *Civil Rights Digest, 6*(3), 29–35.

*Wittstock, L. W. (1980). Native American women: Twilight of a long maidenhood. In B. Lindsay (Ed.), *Comparative perspectives of Third World women: The impact of race, sex, and class* (pp. 207–228). New York: Praeger.

Wolman, C. (1970). Group therapy in two languages, English and Navajo. *American Journal of Psychotherapy, 24,* 677–685.

Young, T. J. (1991). Suicide and homicide among Native Americans: Anomie or social learning? *Psychological Reports, 68,* 1137–1138.

*Zak, N. (1984). Sacred and legendary women of native America. *Wildfire, 1*(1), 12–15.

Zimmerman, M., Corenthal, C., & Wilson, S. (1986). A self-report scale to diagnose major depression. *Archives of General Psychiatry, 43,* 1076–1081.

11

PSYCHOLOGICAL ISSUES FOR LATINAS

ANGELA B. GINORIO, LORRAINE GUTIÉRREZ, ANA MARI CAUCE, and MIMI ACOSTA

Latinos, people of Latin American descent, are the fastest growing ethnic group in the United States, yet psychologists have only recently begun to conduct studies specifically focusing on this population. Psychological knowledge of the Latina population (e.g., women of Latin American descent) is even less developed. This dearth of information stems from the relative invisibility of Latinos, the challenges presented by their demographics, and the tendency of the discipline to ignore ethnic and gender differences. In this chapter, we review four topics that we consider to be of central importance to understanding Latinas in the United States and to their integration into the mainstream of feminist psychology. These are (a) the Latino family and extended family, (b) gender attitudes within the Latino community, (c) Latina education and work life, and (d) mental health issues of special significance to Latinas. We first provide a historical context for our understanding of today's Latina in the United States.

PEOPLE OF LATIN AMERICAN DESCENT

Although people of Latin American descent have lived in the United States for centuries, only within the past 20 years have there been efforts to create an overarching ethnic term. Latinos are a heterogeneous group that includes new immigrants and descendants of some of the original inhabitants of this continent, aliens and American citizens, English and Spanish speakers, people with different national origins, and those who identify closely with their ethnic heritage and those who do not. The development of this new ethnic category has resulted from increasing contacts between different Latino subgroups, a recognition by Latinos that political efforts could be more effective through coalitions between them, perceptions by non-Latinos of cultural and phenotypic similarities between Latino subgroups, and efforts by the U.S. government to move beyond purely racial categorizations of the population (Hayes-Bautista & Chapa, 1987; F. Padilla, 1985; Portes & Truelove, 1987).

Social science research on Latinos has come from both the immigrant and minority group perspectives. The immigrant perspective looks at how Latinos have entered this country, how well they have acculturated (changed their cultural practices), and how well they have assimilated (participated in larger society). Some indicators used to measure acculturation and assimilation include the adoption of new traditions, rates of intermarriage, and acceptance of dominant values. An understanding of the power and status of Latinos in relation to other groups is usually not a component of this perspective (Arce, 1982; Portes, Parker, & Cobas, 1980).

An understanding of Latinos from a minority perspective uses conflict analysis rather than culture as a focus. The minority perspective considers how the Latino subgroups have experienced racism and discrimination on the basis of national origin (Acuña, 1988; Portes et al., 1980) and racial phenotype (Rodríguez, 1989). Demographic statistics on the status of Latinos as well as recent social science knowledge support this perspective (Acuña, 1988; Y. Padilla, 1990). An analysis of census and other governmental statistics reveals that Latinos lag behind all other groups in terms of median years of education (10.3) and participation in higher education (9.2% have attended 4 years of college or more compared with 26% of the non-Hispanic population). Their median income was only slightly higher than that of African Americans, they were concentrated in the secondary labor market, and their rate of poverty was 26%, more than double the national average (Garcia & Montgomery, 1991; J. Moore & Pachon, 1985). Nonetheless, these summary statistics gloss over the diversity of the groups who share the Latino label, which include Mexican Americans, Puerto Ricans, Cubans, and Central and South Americans of various nationalities.

Mexican Americans

Mexican Americans make up 60% of the Latino population (Portes & Truelove, 1987). The original population of Mexican Americans did not enter the United States as immigrants but were conquered during the Mexican War. Mexican Americans have experienced centuries of colonial domination, oppression, and exploitation by Anglo-American society. In the Southwest, colonial domination has taken the form of school segregation, housing discrimination, political gerrymandering, job discrimination, and other direct forms of oppression (Acuña, 1988). Throughout the nation, Mexican Americans have been targets of prejudice, stereotypes, and discrimination (Acuña, 1988; Estrada, Garcia, Macias, & Maldonado, 1982). Although subsequent waves of Mexican immigrants have entered this country voluntarily, they have been subject to the discrimination that has restricted their alternatives in jobs, housing, and political participation. This experience of domination helps explain why it is that Mexican Americans have been present in American society for more than 150 years and yet have relatively little economic and political power (Acuña, 1988; Estrada et al., 1982).

Puerto Ricans

Puerto Ricans, who make up 15% of the Latino population, have a history similar to Mexican Americans in relation to the United States (J. Moore & Pachon, 1985). Puerto Rico was acquired by the United States at the end of the Spanish American War almost a century ago. In spite of the economic transformation of the island from a plantation to an industrial economy, the high rate of unemployment has contributed to large waves of Puerto Rican migration to the continent during the past 45 years. Racial and ethnic discrimination, the low average education and poor job skills of Puerto Rican migrants, and a declining manufacturing sector in the Northeast have contributed to the marginal economic position of this group. Of the three major Latino subgroups, Puerto Ricans are the most disadvantaged economically (J. Moore & Pachon, 1985; Nelson & Tienda, 1985; Portes & Truelove, 1987).

Cubans

Cubans, who make up 5% of the Latino population, present a different socioeconomic picture. Their demographic profile in terms of education and economic status mirrors the national averages (Portes & Truelove, 1987). This is largely a result of those who formed part of the "first wave" of Cuban immigration to Miami, Florida, which took place between 1959 and 1965. However, Cuban enclaves have existed in Key West and Tampa, Florida, since the turn of the century. The relative success of Cubans has been attributed to three factors: (a) the high average educational and professional status of the first wave of immigrants; (b) their status as political refugees, with resulting federal economic benefits and positive reception; and (c) the development of an ethnic enclave economy by the initial immigrants that has provided jobs and support for more recent waves of immigrants from less privileged backgrounds (Nelson & Tienda, 1985; Portes & Truelove, 1987). Although first-wave Cubans have achieved economically, Cuban Americans have more recently become targets of ethnic discrimination and stereotypes, including the perception that they are all involved in drug trafficking and organized crime. Such stereotypes, which have been especially strong in terms of Cubans who immigrated during the Mariel boatlift during the Carter administration, have played a role in political conflicts over issues such as bilingual education (Portes, 1984; Queralt, 1984).

Other Latinos

In discussions about Latinos, which typically focus on Mexican Americans, Puerto Ricans, or Cubans, other Latino groups are generally ignored. Little has been published about other Latinos, who are the second largest (20%) and most rapidly expanding Latino subgroup. This is a very heterogeneous grouping that includes Central American refugees (e.g., from El Salvador and Nicaragua), white-collar and professional workers from South America (e.g., from Argentina or Uruguay), and migrants pushed by economic conditions from the Caribbean (e.g., from Haiti and Puerto Rico). Depending on their job skills, education, and mode of entry, they can either resemble first-wave Cubans or the more economically disadvantaged Latino groups (Melville, 1988; Portes & Truelove, 1987).

Latinos can be considered a meaningful ethnic grouping only if they have characteristics in common that differentiate them from other groups (Tienda & Ortiz, 1986). For Latinos, these characteristics include a shared regional origin in Latin America, which contributes to certain similarities in language, religion, and cultural values (J. Moore & Pachon, 1985). These similarities, when perceived by others, have provided a means for identifying Latinos as an ethnic group and discriminating against them.

THE LATINO FAMILY IN THE 1990s

Almost any description of the Latino culture notes the importance of strong family values and family unity. As such, any attempt to summarize the present issues facing Latina women would be incomplete without men-tion of their families and the challenges that Latina women face when they are wives, mothers, or members of extended family structures.

Ask most people to describe the "typical" Latina woman and they will conjure up the image of a plump, poor, but good-hearted *mamá* at home tending the children, cooking a large meal of rice and beans for *papá's* arrival from work. However, the demographic changes of the 1970s and 1980s have to a large degree relegated this image to that of a stereotype. To the degree that she exists, she is not at all typical.

In 1989, 70% of all Latino families were categorized as married couples, but the numbers varied from 57% of Puerto Ricans to 77% of Cubans (U.S. Department of Commerce, Bureau of the Census, 1989). During the early 1980s, approximately 10% of Latina women between 30 and 40 had never married, and another 14% were separated or divorced. It is noteworthy that 28% of Latino births were to unmarried mothers, and 48% of all Latinas are in the labor force (Amaro & Felipe Russo, 1987). Because most of these figures are based on data collected in the early to mid-1980s, they probably underestimate the number of female-headed households and the number of working women among Latinas in the 1990s.

In fact, the only part of the Latina stereotype that still applies is that of a poor woman. Twenty-five percent of Latino families live in poverty, compared with less than 10% of the general population (deLeón Siantz, 1989). The lack of economic resources available to such families is magnified because Latino families are typically large. Poverty, large families, overcrowding, and discrimination have all been implicated in the heightened rates of depression found among Latina women compared with White women. These factors also contribute to the higher dropout rates and higher rates of substance use and abuse among Latino children (Padilla 1979; Ramírez, 1990).

Low socioeconomic status (SES) has been consistently associated with a host of risk factors, including chronic stress, unemployment, underemployment, and poor mental health. Poverty is also associated with biological factors such as prenatal and perinatal biological insults and poorer physical health, conditions that affect a disproportionate number of Latino children (Garcia Coll, 1990). Laosa (1981) pointed out that studies of Latino child rearing, parenting, or early development at times attribute to culture effects that may well correspond to SES. The effects of SES are so pervasive and so confounded with ethnicity in the United States that one of the difficulties involved in synthesizing knowledge about Latinas is separating cultural from economic influences.

Family Roles, Child Rearing, and Stereotypes

Most ethnographic studies of Latino family life emphasized the "machismo" of men and the passivity of women (Madsen, 1964; Rubel, 1966).

Even now the results of such studies and observations are readily generalized to include all Latino families, up to the present, despite methodological problems in the studies, limited sample sizes, and the substantial transformation in family life that has characterized the past 20 years. For example, in a recent review, Inclán and Herron (1990) described the Puerto Rican family as patriarchal and the role of the husband as provider and protector despite the fact that 44% of Puerto Rican families are female headed.

Some researchers (Ramírez & Arce, 1981; Williams, 1988) have noted that early work emphasizing the passivity of Latinas distorted existing role patterns. Even in so-called "traditional" Mexican American families, women held much power within the private sphere of the family. At present, working-class Mexican American women have been characterized as actively reshaping their roles in both the public and private spheres as many enter the workforce and strive to develop social identities that go beyond their roles as mothers or wives (Ramírez & Arce, 1981; Williams, 1988). Among the business or professional women, success in the workplace requires the maintenance and development of a separate identity. In an ethnographic study, Williams (1988) found that although the majority of business and professional women placed precedence on their family obligations and responsibilities, they also emphasized their independence and gained satisfaction from their careers. She asserted that Mexican American women are reshaping their roles while their husbands, when present, are adapting, albeit more reluctantly, to those changes.

Our experience suggests that this process of role transformation is especially characteristic of Latinas in second-generation households. Nonetheless, traditional values such as the primacy of the family and the importance of extended family and kin (e.g., *compadres* or godparents) appear to characterize even second- and third-generation Latino families. This strong family emphasis is aided by the value placed on affiliation and cooperation during child rearing and the traditional Latino value of *personalismo*, which stresses the importance of personal goodness and getting along with others over ability and individual success (Ramírez, 1990).

Empirical examinations of child-rearing attitudes and behaviors in Latino families also have suggested that they report being more protective of their children than do White or African American families and that Latino families are more child centered, placing greater emphasis on the mother–child relationship than on the spousal relationship (Durrett, O'Bryant, & Pennebaker, 1975; Ramírez, 1990). This latter value is often referred to as "marianismo." Marianismo is based on the Catholic ideal of the Virgin Mary, where emphasis is placed on the woman's role as mother. Durrett et al. (1975) also suggested that compared with low-SES White and African American families, low-SES Mexican American families are less authoritarian in their parenting and emphasize individual responsibility less than do White and African American families. However, by contrast, Bartz & Levine (1978) suggested that, at least during early development, Chicano parents appeared to place greater value on individual responsibility and autonomy and emphasized the children's early development of control over bodily functions (e.g., weaning, walking, talking). Indeed, a review of the few empirical studies that have been conducted on Latino child-rearing practices shows confusing and conflicting accounts. This is partly due to the small number of studies, the different methodologies used in each study, and differences between the Latino subgroups sampled.

It also is possible that the conflicting results could be due to the fact that Latino child-rearing practices may differ systematically with the developmental period under study. For example, studies of Chinese child-rearing practices suggest that Chinese parents tend to be very child centered during Years 1–6 and that during this period Chinese children are doted on. However, following this early period, Chinese parents become increasingly strict in their child rearing and place more demands and responsibilities on their children (Chen & Yang, 1986). Although similar research has yet to be conducted with Latino families, we think that Latino parents are less restrictive of their children during the early phases of development but become more so as their children, especially their daughters, enter puberty. Empirical studies that examine sex-specific Latino child-rearing practices throughout the developmental life span are clearly needed to explore this hypothesis and clarify some of the seemingly contradictory findings in the sparse literature.

Social Support and the Extended Family

In its simplest form, social support is that sense that others are available to help in times of need. Such support may be entirely emotional or may consist of monetary or other forms of tangible assistance. During the past decade, countless studies have been conducted that suggest that social support is an important social resource. It is also one of the few such resources that Latinos appear to have ready access to.

The Latino family, regardless of subgroup, has been described as extended, with multigenerational kin such as grandparents, aunts, uncles, and siblings typically maintaining close and frequent contact with each other. Close friends are often considered as part of this extended family network, with godparents or *compadres* playing key roles in providing support to mothers and their children. This extended family network has often been viewed as one of the central strengths of Latino families (García-Coll, 1990).

The few empirical studies that have been conducted suggest that extended family is a source of support for Latina mothers. For example, de Anda (1984) found that mothers were considered the most important and influential source of support for Spanish-speaking Latina (mostly married) mothers. For English-speaking Latina mothers under 20, their mothers provided them with the most support, whereas respondents over 20 identified their husbands as the most important source of support. However, mothers were still second in importance.

This availability of support from family members may be especially important in providing support for child rearing. deLeón Siantz (1989) found that social support accounted for close to 75% of the variance in whether migrant Mexican American mothers were accepting or rejecting of their children. The role of supportive relationships is also important throughout the life span of Latina women, as suggested by Sánchez-Ayéndez (1989) in her study of social support networks among Puerto Rican elderly women.

In summary, the extended familial networks of Latina women may offer substantial social support, and research suggests that this can be an important asset in buffering the negative effects of life stress (Cohen & Wills, 1985). Yet, research is sorely needed to better explicate the role that Latina grandmothers play in providing support to their daughters with children. Virtually no research has been conducted on the role that *compadres* play, and little is known about the role that friends play in the lives of Latina women who do and do not have children.

Indeed, given the dearth of research on the social networks of Latinas, we advise that extreme caution be taken before one assumes that social support is as plentiful for Latino families or Latina women, as has so often been suggested. A study by Wagner (1988) suggested that although second- and third-generation Chicanas were geographically closer to their extended networks than were White women, they also experienced more complications in such relationships. In addition, over time they came to rely more on friends than on family for social support. Factors such as immigration, rapid urbanization in rural regions with large Latino populations, and the acculturation process can disrupt extended family networks and isolate Latinas from a source of support that has traditionally been considered accessible. The need for further research on the social networks of Latinas is apparent.

GENDER ROLE ATTITUDES AND BEHAVIORS

Over the past two decades, gender role attitudes and related behaviors have become a major theme in family research. One major focus of these studies has been attitudes regarding gender norms and the delegation of roles and tasks within a marriage. Most studies have shown an overall shift in the population to more "modern" attitudes, which are approving of less gender segregation regarding roles, more egalitarian decision-making styles, and less rigid role expectations on the basis of gender (Scanzoni & Fox, 1980). In the general population, these more egalitarian attitudes have been found to be positively associated with female labor force participation and negatively associated with fertility, with the direction of causation not consistently clarified (Thornton, Alwin, & Camburn, 1983).

Research on gender role attitudes that has compared Latinos with others has shown that they are more likely to hold traditional attitudes regarding women's roles (Fischer, 1987; J. Moore & Pachón, 1985). Many of these differences, however, become less significant when education, age, class, or generation are controlled (Vásquez-Nuttall, Romero-García, & de León, 1987). Studies that have examined sex role traditionalism within the Latino population have indicated considerable diversity with respect to attitudes. Within Latino groups, less restrictive attitudes toward women have been found to be associated with acculturation (Kranau, Green, & Valencia-Weber, 1982; Vásquez-Nuttall et al., 1987), education (Kranau et al., 1982; Soto, 1983; Vásquez-Nuttall et al., 1987), marital status and age (Kranau et al., 1982), and labor force participation (Vásquez-Nuttall et al., 1987; Ybarra, 1982). Younger working women, with more education, for example, have been found to have more equalitarian attitudes toward women than their older, less educated counterparts. Studies that have examined the interaction of these variables have shown that education has a particularly strong effect on sex role attitudes. This trend is similar to that found within the general population, suggesting that the classic depiction of Latinas as endorsing a very traditional view of women's roles most accurately represents only a subgroup within the larger population.

Some of the research on the effects of gender role traditionalism among Latinos has focused on the relationship between traditional attitudes and behaviors and psychological functioning.

In their study of 278 Puerto Rican women living in the United States, Soto and Shaver (1982) investigated the effects of sex role traditionalism and assertiveness on psychiatric symptoms. They posited that more traditional women would be less assertive and that unassertiveness would be associated with poor mental and physical health. Unassertiveness was identified as a predictor because of its prevalence in Puerto Rican culture for both men and women and because it interferes with attempts to cope with an unsupportive and hostile environment. Path analyses found a direct effect of traditionalism on assertiveness and of assertiveness on symptoms. This suggests that traditionalism, to the degree that it influences assertiveness, may contribute to poorer functioning and that assertiveness training could have a positive impact on psychological functioning.

The literature that addresses the attitudes and behaviors of Latinas also has examined the possible influence of traditional gender role attitudes on reproductive behavior. Although birth rates in Latin America are declining, Latinas in the United States maintain higher fertility rates than do other ethnic groups (Darabi, Dryfoos, & Schwartz, 1986; Ortiz & Casas, 1990). This is particularly true of Mexican American women, for whom the high birth rate is associated with low rates of contraceptive use (Darati et al., 1986; Mays & Cochran, 1988).

The high fertility rates among Mexican American women have been attributed both to cultural values and barriers to health care. Early research suggested that gender role attitudes may have less influence on fertility preferences among Latina women than among White or African American women (Beckman, 1979). More recent studies of reproductive beliefs showed a more complex picture of the relationship between gender role attitudes and fertility. Traditional attitudes toward women affect contraceptive use only among more traditional Latinas (Ortiz & Casas, 1990), and Mexican American women who had more modern beliefs regarding women's roles preferred planned family size and contraceptive use (Amaro, 1988; Jorgenson & Adams, 1987). Further, a study comparing the views of clinic staff with that of their potential Latina consumers indicated that service providers persist in viewing Mexican American patients as holding traditional beliefs that prevent the use of contraceptives, even when this is not the case (Jorgensen & Adams, 1987). Such studies suggest that the effect of traditional gender role attitudes on the part of Latinas may be a less important predictor of Latina fertility than previously believed and may be modulated by factors such as the stereotypes of Latinas held by health care providers.

What is rarely discussed in the context of either gender role attitudes and behaviors or reproductive behavior is the sexuality of Latinas. With few exceptions (e.g., Espín, 1984), little has been published on this topic.

EDUCATION

Many of the 623,591 Latinas and Latinos ("1986 Minority Enroll-ment," 1988) attending college in 1986 overcame great odds against them. One in 10 Latinas and Latinos who enter grade school do not graduate from eighth grade; 4 out of 10 who enter ninth grade do not get a high school diploma. Of those entering college (less than half of all Latina and Latino high school graduates go on to college), only 25–40% will graduate depending on field of study and region of the country. Fifty-four percent of all Latinas and Latinos in college attend 2-year colleges; more than half of these in California.

To succeed, many Latinas and Latinos must overcome the obstacles of poor preparation, financial need, racism, classism, and isolation from an educational system that poorly supports cultural diversity (Farrell, 1984; Hayes-Bautista, Schunk, & Chapa, 1988) and that is also androcentric

(H. A. Moore, 1983). In a study of 1,000 Latina and Latino and White sixth-grade students, H. A. Moore reported that teachers differentiate among females of equal skills using leadership, independence, and assertiveness to judge future occupational success. This reward system disadvantaged Latinas for two reasons: First, teachers' expectations were shaped not only by success-related measures such as educational skills but by students' characteristics such as ethnicity and gender. In this case, Latinas who were assertive and independent were expected to be less successful than other less conforming students. Second, characteristics typically encouraged within the traditional Latina family are not valued by Anglocentric schools. Similar sources of tension between cultural background and educational climate were discussed by Vásquez-Nuttall and Romero-García (1989).

Perhaps this dynamic helps explain the finding reported in the American Association of University Women report *Shortchanging Girls, Shortchanging America* (1991), which focuses on the interaction of self-esteem and educational and career aspirations of a nationally stratified sample of 3,000 students between the ages of 9 and 15 years. This study provided comparisons among Black, Latina, and White girls, finding that Latina girls had the highest levels of self-esteem of all three groups in elementary school (68% were happy the way they were, compared with 65% of Black girls and 55% of White girls) but suffered a larger drop in self-esteem by high school than any of the other groups. When it is considered that those surveyed had not dropped out of school, these figures acquire greater significance.

What is not addressed in most of these reports is the responsibility that girls carry for child care and housekeeping in many Latina families, even among girls in grade school. In their 1984 report "Chicanas in California Postsecondary Education," Cohen, Chacón, Camarena, González, and Strover (1983) found that Latina women not only experienced institutional sexism, but also double standards traced back to cultural and familial expectations most evident in two areas: domestic work and parental support. Women have greater responsibility for domestic work, especially if they have children. Although parental support for the educational aims of all students was high, male students were more likely to report very high support, with mothers being perceived as more supportive than fathers by both genders.

Similar results were reported in a study of 45 Chicanas and Chicanos who had received PhD, JD, or MD degrees and who came from low-SES backgrounds (Gándara, 1982). In this sample, women ($n = 17$) reported that their mothers encouraged them to pursue nontraditional roles more than fathers did. This group of high-achieving Chicanas relied more heavily on the emotional support of the family than did Chicanos. And even though they were better students than Chicanos, these women received less support from nonfamilial sources than did the males. What might be equally important for these women is that none of them married early and none had children until their education was almost complete. That did not exempt them from feelings of conflict between their family of origin's expectations and school requirements.

Although low SES did not stop the group of Chicanos and Chicanas studied by Cohen et al. (1983) from going to college, Buriel and Sáenz (1980) reported that higher family income was the strongest predictor of college-bound behaviors by Chicana seniors in high school. These women scored high on the Masculine scale of the Bem Sex Role Inventory and were more bicultural than a similar group of non-college-bound women. For students who enter college right after high school, a better family income and a more masculine orientation might be good predictors of educational achievement. However, in a Houston sample of Chicana first-year college students, the greatest number of women were androgynous (32%), and only 12% could be categorized in the masculine group (Zeff, 1982). Interestingly, more younger women (19 years or less) were masculine (13%) than those 20 or older (9%).

In summary, Latinas receive less familial and institutional support for educational achievement than Latinos and are more likely to be burdened by societal gender role responsibilities. Those who do achieve tend to be unmarried and less gender stereotyped than their counterparts who do not attend college or attain graduate degrees. This pattern appears similar to that seen among samples of White women and men pursuing higher education.

Many Chicanas in college believe that Chicano males are threatened by their educational attainment (González, 1988), even though the males reported not feeling threatened. Students who reported the highest levels of perceived threat were also those most likely to be endogamous. Endogamy, or intragroup marriage or pairing, might be one of the manifestations of ethnic identification. There are a few reports on the importance of ethnic identification among college students. In their survey of 45 Latinas and Latinos attending two Ivy League colleges, Ethier and Deaux (1990) found that female students reported significantly higher importance of Hispanic group identity to their own self-concept, but this was not related to aspects of their cultural background such as languages spoken at home or number of Latina and Latino friends. This Hispanic identity also related strongly to their identity as a daughter ($r = .61$), while no correlation was found for the males in this sample.

The list of issues just discussed is not different from that presented in an earlier review of the literature by Vásquez (1982). Unfortunately, the barriers do not fall once a Latina graduates and enters the workforce.

WORK

For Latinas, like for all other populations, there is a high correlation between educational attainment and poverty rate. In 1988, a National Council of La Raza analysis showed that among female-headed households, 64% of those with less than 4 years of high school were living below the poverty level, whereas only 16% of those with some college fell into that category. Compared with the rest of the U.S. population, a larger proportion of Latina families are headed by women (23% of Latinas vs. 16% for the United States; Escutiá & Prieto, 1987).

However, educational attainment alone is not the only predictor of income. As de la Vina (1984) reported, even though Latina business graduates had higher grade point averages than White or Latino males, they received salary offers that were $7,000 lower than those of males and $1,000 lower than those of White females. Differences in salary were significant even after adjusting for other factors (age, years of experience, etc.). These data suggest that Latinas are discriminated against in salary decisions on the bases of both gender and ethnicity.

Although Latinos have higher labor force participation than White and Black men, Latinas have the lowest labor force participation. However, the participation is not equal among the major Latino groups in the United States. There are marked differences for both men and women in labor force participation, with Chicanos having the highest participation rate among males and Cuban women having the highest participation rate among females. For both genders, Puerto Ricans have the lowest participation rate. Relative to the population increase, however, Latina and Latino employment has decreased from 74% in 1978 to 72% in 1985.

LATINAS AND MENTAL HEALTH

Despite the heterogeneous character of the Latina population, they clearly represent a group "at risk" for high levels of psychosocial stress attributable to discrimination, cultural role conflicts, immigration trauma, language barriers, and lowered levels of financial, educational, and medical resources. For many Latinas, the stresses of poverty and lack of resources are often primary difficulties in the struggle to maintain personal and emotional stability. The additional burdens of difficult migration histories, acculturation, racial discrimination, and language barriers can be overwhelming. When compared with White American and English-speaking Mexican Americans, for example, Spanish-speaking Mexican immigrants endorsed significantly more depressive symptomatology (Vega, Warheit, & Meinhardt, 1984). Additionally, the immigrant Mexican women in this study displayed higher depression scores than did their male counterparts. Although higher rates of acute depression are sometimes reported for the immigrant versus nonimmigrant Latinas (Vega et al., 1984), other studies have shown that the U.S.-born Latinas report more depression than do immigrant Latinas (Karno et al., 1987). The conflicting research findings suggest that Latinas experience psychological stress, irrespective of levels of acculturation and achievement. For the highly acculturated Latina, stress can be generated through conflicts between cultural expectations and achievement in the White world as well as the continuing experience of discrimination (Amaro, Russo, & Johnson, 1987).

Despite the high risk of psychosocial stress, Latinas, like other people of color, significantly underutilize mental health services. Institutional barriers to services that have been well documented in the literature include language, transportation to mental health facilities, and lack of culturally relevant treatment. In addition to these significant institutional barriers, Latinas as a group appear to be reluctant to seek mental health services for other reasons. These reasons range from the perception that mental health services are only for the severely impaired, to cultural beliefs about the importance of enduring suffering, to the lack of knowledge about available services. Service providers suggest that Latinas often seem to seek institutional interventions only when the problem is critical and that consequently the help first sought is medical. Studies based on institutional usage often label this pattern of help seeking "somatization," without taking into account the possibility that the individual may have previously sought treatment from culturally sanctioned or informal sources. In addition, Latino clinicians (e.g., Vargas-Willis & Cervantes, 1987) reported that Latinas may present their problems in a culturally prescribed fashion so that the problems or symptoms are not readily apparent to the non-Latino therapist. Vague descriptions of culture-bound syndromes such as "nervios," for example, can be misconstrued as somatization or even hysteria. Such misinterpretations can lead to inappropriate diagnosis and treatment of the presenting problem and it is imperative then that professionals working with Latina women be knowledgeable about cultural symptomatology. Nervios, for example, is one of several culture-bound syndromes that has been documented in Mexico, Colombia, Nicaragua, Costa Rica, Puerto Rico, and among Latino populations in the southwestern United States, (Oquendo, Horwath, & Martinez, 1992). Latinas presenting with nervios often describe feeling that their body is "out of control" (shaking or restless), and they report headaches, mood changes, and eating disturbances. If questioned directly, Latinas will report that episodes of nervios are related to family conflict, personal loss, or a need for supportive caretaking, demonstrating an appropriate understanding of the psychogenic origin of the illness (Dresp, 1985). Although drug treatment is often unfortunately pursued, nervios is better conceptualized as culturally sanctioned help-seeking behavior that symbolizes the Latina's desire to reestablish intra- and interpersonal harmony (Boulette, 1976; Comas-Díaz & Duncan, 1985; Soto & Shaver, 1982). Thus somatization can be viewed as a coping strategy in situations in which assertiveness is expressed in the context of largely subordinate and supportive roles (Comas-Díaz, 1983).

Likewise, *susto*, or magical fright, is another of the "males naturales," or natural ills. It is a culture-bound syndrome that has been documented in many Latin American countries, but varies somewhat in specific symptomatology. Susto is most commonly described as the reaction to a traumatic event (Rubel, 1993).

The strength and relevance of the aforementioned cultural beliefs are subject to factors such as differences in social class, generational status, and education among Latinas. A common complaint registered against early research on health-related folk beliefs (Klein, 1978; Rubel, 1966) was the use of samples of largely low-income, rural Latinos with subsequent overgeneralization to all Latinas. In initial response to this overgeneralization, service providers working with Latino communities suggested that a linear relationship existed between acculturation and acceptance of health beliefs, with the less acculturated individual espousing traditional folk beliefs more strongly than highly acculturated individuals. Highly acculturated Latinos, in other words, were believed to be no different from White Americans in their acceptance of westernized diagnoses and treatments. A study by Castro, Furth, and Karlow (1984) noted key errors in this assumption. In examining the health beliefs of low-acculturated, bicultural, and high-acculturated Mexican American women, these researchers found that women from all three samples endorsed mild-to-moderate acceptance of selected health and folk beliefs such as the "hot–cold" theory of illness. Although all three groups of Mexican American women differed significantly from a fourth sample of White American women, there was no significant difference among the Mexican American women in their espousal of specific health beliefs. Mexican-born women from the low-acculturated to the high-acculturated presented a dual system of health beliefs, a varying mixture of folk and medical model beliefs. This study is valuable because it documents the reporting of standard, Western biomedical beliefs among low-acculturated Mexican-born women and because it provides evidence against the "whitewashing" of high-acculturated Mexican American women.

Work with Latina immigrants must include assessment of the migration trauma to be effective. It is important to consider the nature of premigration stressors because research suggests that high premigration stress is related to high acculturation stress after actual migration (Salgado de Snyder, 1987). Premigration stressors may include such experiences as separation from one's husband, children, or extended family; economic hardship; refugee status in other host countries; undocumented entry into the

United States; or trauma due to state-supported or terrorist violence. The impetus behind the migration decision (i.e., the individual's personal history, social–political environment, and economic status) affects the working through and resolution of the postmigration trauma (Espín, 1987). This resolution is thought to be a lifelong process (Garza-Guerrero, 1974) involving formation of a new "immigrant" identity and significant issues of grief, loss, and guilt. Additionally, Latina immigrants who have experienced political persecution or physical torture prior to migration can, predictably, display posttraumatic stress reactions in addition to the expected stress of migration. Latinas from Central or South America who have experienced such traumas are often reluctant to discuss these experiences with American therapists because they fear reactions of disbelief (Cienfuegos & Monelli, 1983). Lack of treatment of these trauma reactions can result in depression and the emergence of more serious pathology over time.

Cultural Considerations in Therapy

In working with Latina women, it is important to be cognizant of the cultural values that are relevant to the Latina experience. These include values such as *respeto*, *personalismo*, *familiarismo*, and *marianismo*. Although the strength and form of these values will vary across different Latino groups as well as across social class, acculturation, and generation, most Latinas hold these values in some form. *Respeto*, or respect, refers to valuing and acknowledging hierarchies that define an individual's proper place in society on the basis of age, gender, race, and class. For women, respeto dictates that behavior toward older individuals or toward most men should be characterized by a respectful, subordinate attitude. Direct assertive behavior or a confrontational manner, particularly that aimed at older men or parental figures, is not culturally supported. *Personalismo* represents a way of staying connected to one's world and involves highlighting the personal aspects of interactions. Personalismo, in the mental health setting, can manifest as the preference to conduct business on a personal basis (i.e., with individuals to whom there is a family connection). A Latina woman, for example, may express a strong preference for working with a therapist who has previously counseled another member of her family. Related to the concept of personalismo, *familiarismo* is a value that places the extended family at the center of one's experience. Characteristics of interdependence, family loyalty, and cooperation among extended family members are encouraged by familiarismo (Canino, 1982; Falicov, 1982). The prevalence and importance of *marianismo* among Latina women has been hotly debated, with some authors dismissing the concept as a stereotype (Gibson, 1983) and others viewing it as a code of behavior that exists and requires some change (Comas-Díaz & Duncan, 1985). Marianismo demands that women model themselves after the Virgin Mary and so see themselves as spiritually superior to men and as capable of enduring great suffering. In this context, sexual "purity" is idealized, and women are expected to engage in sex primarily for procreation. Marianismo also is a value that some Latina women interpret as placing one's children's needs before one's own.

Therapeutic intervention with Latino individuals must accommodate these cultural values. Therapists using a family therapy approach, for example, may find that "standard" family therapy techniques are met with solid resistance from Latino families. Rather than seeing the Latino family as pathological or "stuck," it is helpful for therapists to reconceptualize the purpose of the intervention and modify the technique to match the family's cultural values. A common goal, for instance, in family therapy is to encourage direct communication of feelings, needs, and opinions. Respeto may lead Latinas to feel that it is not acceptable to voice opinions that openly conflict with others who are relationally significant to them or in "authority" positions. One suggestion for addressing the cultural component in this dilemma, proposed by Comas-Díaz and Duncan (1985), is to preface the "I" statement with a phrase acknowledging the cultural value (e.g., "With all the respect that you deserve, I feel . . ."). This style may be appropriate for Latinas whose families are willing to participate in family therapy. But in those situations where the family is not willing to attend, even this qualified "I" statement could be perceived as too direct and be counterproductive.

In individual therapy with Latinas, it is useful to conceptualize a model of therapy that is based on empowerment. Empowerment, as defined by Comas-Díaz (1987), consists of helping Latinas to (a) acknowledge the deleterious effects of racism and sexism; (b) deal with feelings of anger and self-degradation imposed by their status as ethnic minorities; (c) perceive themselves as causal agents in achieving solutions to their problems; (d) understand the interplay between the external environment and their inner reality; and (e) perceive opportunities to change the responses from the wider society.

This proposed model does not prescribe a specific theoretical orientation, but to be successful it requires knowledge of and participation in the social and cultural issues that affect the lives of Latina women. One treatment center in California, for example, has included job-skills training and interviewing techniques with its counseling program as a way of effecting positive change in the economic status of low-income Latina women (Texidor del Portillo, 1988). In the experience of this center, short-term "real-life" goals have facilitated attitude change among Latinas, helping them nurture a sense of personal power. Action, in other words, can be the catalyst for personal change.

CONCLUSIONS

The pages that precede this section and the references that follow provide a broad overview of our current state of knowledge about psychological issues for Latinas in four areas: family, education, work, and mental health. We have focused our attention on these topics not only because of their significance in psychology and in our cultures, but also because a significant body of knowledge exists. Topics of interest not addressed in this chapter, but worthy of further attention, include the increased incidence of depression in the Latina population (Karno et al., 1987), the underutilization of inpatient mental health services by Latinas (Russo, Amaro, & Winter, 1987), the increase of HIV infection among Latinas (Amaro, 1988), the prevalence of violence in Latinas' lives (Ginorio & Reno, 1986), and, on a more positive note, coping and empowerment strategies of Latinas (Amaro et al., 1987).

We emphasize the need for professionals in psychology to integrate cultural variables into standard practice and research methodologies. For the Latina population, such variables would include migration history, acculturation, adherence to culturally determined gender roles, worldview, dominant language, acceptance of cultural values, and family position. In addition to recognition of the importance of cultural variables, we highlight the necessity of evaluating the interaction between SES and ethnicity when studying or working with Latinas. It is critical to avoid pathologizing and overgeneralizing a Latina's response to the stress of poverty, lack of education, prejudice, and institutionalized discrimination as stereotypic of her ethnic group. Service providers must educate themselves about the realistic concerns facing Latina clients to provide relevant, effective interventions. Continued research with specified groups of Latina women is clearly necessary to enhance the understanding of the needs, strengths, and future development of this population of women.

REFERENCES

Acuña, R. (1988). *Occupied America: A history of Chicanos.* New York: Harper & Row.

Amaro, H. (1988). Women in the Mexican American community: Religion, culture and reproductive attitudes and experiences. *Journal of Community Psychology, 16,* 6–20.

Amaro, H., & Russo, N. F. (1987). Hispanic women and mental health: An overview of contemporary issues in research and practice. *Psychology of Women Quarterly, 11,* 393–407.

Amaro, H., Russo, N. F., & Johnson, J. (1987). Family and work predictors of psychological well-being among Hispanic women professionals. *Psychology of Women Quarterly, 11,* 505–521.

American Association of University Women. (1991). *Shortchanging girls, shortchanging America.* (Special report prepared by Greenberg-Lake.) Washington, DC: Author.

Arce, C. (1982). A reconsideration of Chicano culture and identity. *Daedalus, 110,* 177–191.

Bartz, K. W., & Levine, E. S. (1978). Child rearing by black parents: A description and comparison to Anglo and Chicano parents. *Journal of Marriage and the Family, 40,* 709–719.

Beckman, L. (1979). The relationship between sex roles, fertility, and family size preferences. *Psychology of Women Quarterly, 4,* 43–60.

Boulette, T. R. (1976). Assertive training with low income Mexican American women. *Spanish Speaking Mental Health Research Center Monograph Series, 3,* 67–71.

Buriel, R., & Sáenz, E. (1980). Psychocultural characteristics of college-bound and noncollege-bound Chicanas. *Journal of Social Psychology, 110,* 245–251.

Canino, G. (1982). The Hispanic woman: Sociocultural influences on diagnoses and treatment. In R. Bercerra, M. Karno, & J. Escobar (Eds.), *Mental health and Hispanic Americans.* New York: Grune & Stratton.

Castro, F. G., Furth, P., & Karlow, H. (1984). The health beliefs of Mexican, Mexican American and Anglo American women. *Hispanic Journal of Behavioral Sciences, 6*(4), 365–383.

Chen, C., & Yang, D. (1986). The self image of Chinese-American adolescents: A cross-cultural comparison. *International Journal of Social Psychiatry, 32,* 19–26.

Cienfuegos, A., & Monelli, C. (1983). The testimony of political repression as a therapeutic instrument. *American Journal of Orthopsychiatry, 54,* 43–51.

Cohen, E. G., Chacón, M. A., Camarena, M. M., González, J. T., & Strover, S. (1983). Chicanas in California Postsecondary Education. *La Red/The Net* (Winter Suppl., No. 65).

Cohen, S., & Wills, T. A. (1985). Stress, social support and the buffering hypothesis. *Psychological Bulletin, 88,* 310–357.

Comas-Díaz, L. (1987). Feminist therapy with mainland Puerto Rican women. *Psychology of Women Quarterly, 11,* 461–474.

Comas-Díaz, L., & Duncan, J. W. (1985). The cultural context: A factor in assertiveness training with mainland Puerto Rican women. *Psychology of Women Quarterly, 9,* 463–475.

Darabi, K., Dryfoos, J., & Schwartz, D. (1986). Hispanic adolescent fertility. *Hispanic Journal of the Behavioral Sciences, 8,* 157–171.

de Anda, D. (1984). Informal support networks of hispanic mothers: A comparison across groups. *Journal of Social Service Research, 7*, 89–105.

de la Vina, L. (1984). A study of the educational and career experiences of Anglo and Hispanic college of business graduates. *Intercambios Femeniles: The National Network of Hispanic Women, 2*, 1–14.

deLeon Siantz, M. (1989, May). *A profile of the Hispanic population.* Paper presented at the meeting on the health care needs of the Hispanic population, University of California, San Francisco.

Dresp, C. W. (1985). *Nervios* as a culture bound syndrome among Puerto Rican women. *Smith College Studies in Social Work, 55*(2), 115–130.

Durrett, M. E., O'Bryant, S., & Pennebaker, J. W. (1975). Childrearing report of white, black, and Mexican-American families. *Developmental Psychology, 2*, 871.

Escutía, M. M., & Prieto, M. (1987, February). *Hispanics in the Work Force, Part 1.* Washington, DC: National Council of La Raza.

Espín, O. M. (1984). Cultural and historical influences on sexuality in Hispanic/Latina women. In C. Vance (Ed.), *Pleasure and danger: Exploring the female sexuality.* London: Routledge & Kegan Paul.

Espín, O. M. (1987). Psychological impact of immigration on Latinas: Implications for psychotherapeutic practice. *Psychology of Women Quarterly, 11*, 489–503.

Estrada, L., Garcia, C., Macias, R., & Maldonado, L. (1982). Chicanos in the United States: A history of exploitation and resistance. *Daedalus, 110*, 103–131.

Ethier, K., & Deaux, K. (1990). Hispanics in Ivy: Assessing identity and perceived threat. *Sex Roles, 22*(7/8), 427–440.

Falicov, C. J. (1982). Mexican families. In M. McGoldrick, J. K. Pearce, & J. Groidans (Eds.), *Ethnicity and family therapy* (pp. 134–163). New York: Guilford.

Farrell, C. S. (1984, March 21). Two-year colleges offer haven for many Hispanic students. *Chronicle of Higher Education*, pp. 1, 11.

Fischer, G. (1987). Hispanic and majority student attitudes toward forcible date rape as a function of differences in attitudes toward women. *Sex Roles, 17*, 93–101.

Gándara, P. (1982). Passing through the eye of the needle: High-achieving Chicanas. *Hispanic Journal of Behavioral Sciences, 4*, 167–179.

García-Coll, C. T. (1990). Developmental outcome of minority infants: A process-oriented look into our beginnings. *Child Development, 61*, 270–289.

García, J., & Montgomery, P. (1991). *The Hispanic population of the United States: March 1990.* (U.S. Department of Commerce, Bureau of the Census; Current Population Reports, Series P-25 No. 995). Washington, DC: U.S. Government Printing Office.

Garza-Guerrero, A. C. (1974). Culture shock: Its mourning and the vicissitudes of identity. *Journal of the American Psychoanalytic Association, 22*, 408–442.

Gibson, G. (1975, March 12). *The Mexican-American woman and mental health.* Paper presented at Our Lady of the Lake College.

Ginorio, A. B., & Reno, J. (1986). Violence in the lives of Latina women. In M. C. Burns (Ed.), *The speaking profits us: Violence in the lives of women of color/ El Decirlo nos Hace Bien a Nosotras: La Violenca en la Vida de las Mujeres de Color* (pp. 13–16 & 28–30). (Available from Center for the Prevention of Sexual and Domestic Violence, 1914 N. 34th, Ste. 105, Seattle, WA 98103)

González, J. T. (1988). Dilemmas of the high-achieving Chicana: The double-bind factor in male/female relationships. *Sex Roles, 18,* 367–380.

Hayes-Bautista, D., & Chapa, J. (1987). Latino terminology: Conceptual bases for standardized terminology. *American Journal of Public Health, 77,* 61–68.

Hayes-Bautista, D., Schunk, D., & Chapa, J. (1988). *The burden of support: Young Latinos in a changing society.* Stanford, CA: Stanford University Press.

Inclán, J. E., & Herron, D. G. (1990). Puerto Rican adolescents. In J. T. Gibbs & L. N. Huang (Eds.), *Children of color* (pp. 251–279). San Francisco: Jossey-Bass.

Jorgenson, S., & Adams, R. (1987). Family planning needs and behavior of Mexican American women: A study of health care professionals and their clientele. *Hispanic Journal of the Behavioral Sciences, 9,* 265–286.

Karno, M., Hough, R. L., Burnam, A., Escobar, J. I., Timbers, D. M., Santana, F., & Boyd, J. H. (1987). Lifetime prevalence of specific psychiatric disorders among Mexican-American and non-Hispanic whites in Los Angeles. *Archives of General Psychiatry, 44,* 695–701.

Klein, J. (1978). *Susto:* The anthropological study of the disease of adaption. *Social Science and Medicine, 12,* 23–28.

Kranau, E., Green, V., & Valencia-Weber, G. (1982). Acculturation and Hispanic women: Attitudes toward men, sex-role attribution, sex-role behavior, and demographics. *Hispanic Journal of the Behavioral Sciences, 4,* 21–40.

Laosa, L. M. (1981). Maternal behavior: Sociocultural diversity in mode of family interaction. In R. W. Henderson (Ed.), *Parent-child interaction: Theory, research, and prospects* (pp. 125–167). New York: Academic Press.

Madsen, W. (1964). *The Mexican Americans of South Texas.* New York: Holt, Rinehart & Winston.

Mays, V., & Cochran, S. (1988). Issues in the perception of AIDS risk and risk reduction activities by Black and Hispanic/Latina women. *American Psychologist, 43,* 949–957.

Melville, M. (1988). Hispanics: Race, class or ethnicity? *Journal of Ethnic Studies, 16,* 67–83.

Moore, H. A. (1983). Hispanic women: Schooling for conformity in public education. *Hispanic Journal of Behavioral Sciences, 5,* 45–63.

Moore, J., & Pachon, H. (1985). *Hispanics in the United States.* Englewood Cliffs, NJ: Prentice Hall.

Nelson, C., & Tienda, M. (1985). The structuring of Hispanic ethnicity: Historical and contemporary perspectives. *Ethnic and Racial Studies, 8,* 49–73.

1986 minority enrollment at 3,200 institutions of higher education. (1988). *Chronicle of Higher Education*, A20.

Oquendo, M., Horwath, E., & Martinez, A. (1992). *Ataques de nervios*: Proposed diagnostic criteria for a culture-specific syndrome. *Culture, Medicine, and Psychiatry, 16*, 367–376.

Ortiz, S., & Casas, J. (1990). Birth control and low-income Mexican-American women: The impact of three values. *Hispanic Journal of the Behavioral Sciences, 12*, 83–92.

Padilla, E. R. (1979). Inhalant, marijuana, and alcohol abuse among barrio children and adolescents. *International Journal of the Addictions, 14*, 943–964.

Padilla, F. (1985). *Latino ethnic consciousness: The case of Mexican Americans and Puerto Ricans in Chicago*. Notre Dame, IN: University of Notre Dame Press.

Padilla, Y. (1990). Social science theory on the Mexican-American experience. *Social Service Review, 64*, 261–275.

Portes, A. (1984). The rise of ethnicity: Determinants of ethnic perceptions among Cuban exiles in Miami. *American Sociological Review, 49*, 383–397.

Portes, A., & Truelove, C. (1987). Making sense of diversity: Recent research on Hispanic minorities in the United States. *Annual Review of Sociology, 13*, 359–385.

Portes, A., Parker, R., & Cobas, J. (1980). Assimilation or consciousness: Perceptions of U.S. society among recent Latin American immigrants to the United States. *Social Forces, 59*, 200–224.

Queralt, M. (1984). Understanding Cuban immigrants: A cultural perspective. *Social Work, 29*, 115–121.

Ramírez, O. (1990). Mexican American children and adolescents. In J. T. Gibbs & L. N. Huang (Eds.), *Children of color* (pp. 224–250). San Francisco: Jossey-Bass.

Ramírez, O., & Arce, C. H. (1981). The contemporary Chicano family: An empirically based review. In A. Baron, Jr. (Ed.), *Explorations in Chicano psychology*. New York: Praeger.

Rodríguez, C. (1989). *Puerto Ricans: Born in the U.S.A.* Boston: Unwin Hyman.

Rubel, A. (1966). *Across the tracks: Mexican-Americans in a Texas city*. Austin: University of Texas Press.

Rubel, A. J. (1993). The study of Latino folk illnesses. *Medical Anthropology, 15*, 209–213.

Russo, N. F., Amaro, H., & Winter, M. (1987). The use of inpatient mental health services by Hispanic women. *Psychology of Women Quarterly, 11*, 427–441.

Salgado de Snyder, V. N. (1987). Factors associated with acculturative stress and depressive symptomatology among married Mexican immigrant women. *Psychology of Women Quarterly, 11*, 475–488.

Sánchez-Ayéndez, M. (1989). Puerto Rican elderly women: The cultural dimension of social support networks. *Women and Health, 14*, 239–252.

Scanzoni & Fox (1980). Sex roles, family, and society: The seventies and beyond. *Journal of Marriage and the Family, 42,* 43–58.

Soto, E. (1983). Sex-role traditionalism and assertiveness in Puerto Rican women living in the United States. *Journal of Community Psychology, 11,* 346–354.

Soto, E., & Shaver, P. (1982). Sex-role traditionalism, assertiveness, and symptoms of Puerto Rican women living in the United States. *Hispanic Journal of the Behavioral Sciences, 4,* 1–19.

Texidor del Portillo, C. (1988). Poverty, self-concept, and health: Experience of Latinas. *Women & Health, 12,* 229–242.

Thornton, Alwin, & Camburn (1983). Causes and consequences of sex-role attitudes and attitude change. *American Sociological Review, 48,* 211–227.

Tienda, M., & Ortiz, V. (1986). Hispanicity and the 1980 census. *Social Science Quarterly, 67,* 3–20.

Vargas-Willis, G., & Cervantes, R. C. (1987). Consideration of psychological stress in the treatment of the Latina immigrant. *Hispanic Journal of Behavioral Sciences, 9*(3), 315–329.

Vásquez, M. (1982). Confronting barriers to the participation of Mexican American women in higher education. *Hispanic Journal of Behavioral Sciences, 4,* 147–165.

Vásquez-Nuttall, E., & Romero-García, Y. (1989). From home to school: Puerto Rican girls learn to be students in the United States. In Garcia-Coll, C. T., & Mattei, M. de L. (Eds.), *The psychosocial development of Puerto Rican women* (pp. 60–83). New York: Praeger.

Vásquez-Nuttall, E., Romero-García, I., & De León, B. (1987). Sex roles and perceptions of femininity and masculinity of Hispanic women: A review of the literature. *Psychology of Women Quarterly, 11,* 409–425.

Vega, W. A., Warheit, G. J., & Meinhardt, K. (1984). Marital disruption and the prevalence of depressive symptomatology among Anglos and Mexican Americans. *Journal of Marriage and Family, 46,* 817–824.

Wagner, R. M. (1988). Changes in the friend network during the first year of single parenthood for Mexican American and Anglo women. *Journal of Divorce, 11,* 89–109.

Williams, N. (1988). Role making among married Mexican American women: Issues of class and ethnicity. *Journal of Applied Behavioral Sciences, 24,* 203–217.

Women's Bureau. (1985). *The United Nations decade for women, 1976–1985: Employment in the United States.* Washington, DC: U.S. Department of Labor.

Ybarra, L. (1982). When wives work. *Journal of Marriage and the Family, 44,* 169–178.

Zeff, S. B. (1982). A cross-cultural study of Mexican American, Black American, and White American women at a large urban university. *Cross-Cultural Study of University Women, 4,* 245–261.

12

THE PSYCHOLOGY OF ASIAN AMERICAN WOMEN

MARIA P. P. ROOT

The racial legacy of Asian Americans in the United States has made the declaration of identity much like a competition between two mothers: race and nation (Thornton, 1992b). This tension creates a dynamic of change. However, the Asian American woman also must struggle with loyalty to a "third mother," gender, which has often rendered her a second-class citizen even within her own family.

Compared with only 20 years ago, the Asian American woman is less defined by the men in her life (i.e., her father, her partner, her sons, or by traditional familial roles). The Asian American woman cannot be characterized by a single description; she is represented by more than 30 different ethnic groups that vary in religious and philosophical orientations, matriarchal versus patriarchal organization, and language. She may be an immigrant, refugee, or American born, first generation or fifth generation.

Several colleagues contributed to the development of this chapter with interesting conversations and critiques of an earlier draft. I especially thank Carla Bradshaw, Connie Chan, Jean Lau Chin, Barbara Lui, Chalsa Loo, and Norman Mar.

In this chapter I provide an overview of the psychology of Asian American women, who make up approximately half of the 7.3 million Asian Americans in this country, a number that has doubled in the past decade (Homma-True, 1991). A history of U.S. legislation offers insight into the far-ranging impact of more than 100 years of legislation enacted to keep Asians from settling in this country and its impact on Asian American women today.

When the first chapter on the psychology of Asian American women was published in 1973 (Fujitomi & Wong, 1973), those authors observed that the average Asian American woman was modally represented by a Sansei (third-generation Japanese American) or first- or second-generation Chinese American. She is now likely to be Chinese, Filipino, Japanese, Korean, or Vietnamese. However, she also may be Laotian, Taiwanese, Thai, Samoan, Hmong, Chamarro, Burmese, Nepalese, or 1 of 20 other ethnicities that have distinct signatures. She may still be first generation, but she might also be fourth generation or more. She may have chosen to come to this country, as did many women who were here in 1973, but she may also be a refugee who fled political terror. If she is young and born in this country, she is increasingly likely to be of multiple ethnic and racial heritages (Root, in press), a "biracial baby boomer" (Root, 1992a), who reflects the high rates of intermarriage in the various Asian American communities (Kitano & Fujino, in press; Kitano, Yeung, Chai, & Hatanaka, 1984; Sung, 1990).

Unfortunately, there has been a shortage of Asian American female psychologists and still a shortage of Asian American female psychologists to serve as role models for training an emerging generation of Asian American female psychologists (Nagata, 1994) or therapists in mental health settings (Homma-True, 1990). Concomitantly, the psychological literature on Asian American women is also growing.

Much of what Chen observed in 1976 remains true: The issues that inform the psychology of Asian American women in the 1990s still revolve around the social hierarchy constructed by race, gender, and class. And, for Asians, culture also informs one's psychology; it organizes roles within the family and between individuals and society. These proscribed roles ultimately affect identity, self-esteem, behavior, and mental health, the subjects of traditional psychology. The cultural and political legacies that bring Asian Americans to this country are necessarily part of the historical variables that must be understood in constructing a culturally relative psychology of Asian American women. Whereas psychology has often tended to be ahistorical, Allen (1988) aptly observed that "the roots of oppression are to be found in the loss of tradition and memory because that loss is always accompanied by a loss of a positive sense of self" (pp. 14–15). Ironically, the discriminatory treatment and rejection of Asian Americans may have reinforced the various communities' clinging to cultural roots and traditions, which has allowed Asian Americans to survive with some strength.

Understanding of Asian American women also rests on recognizing the tensions and transformations in gender roles that take place between generations. These experiences differ by how and when one or one's family came to this country. Furthermore, psychologists must differentiate changes between generations that reflect positive evolution versus changes that may reflect reactions to racism in its many forms (e.g., exclusion, isolation, internment, psychological and physical violence).

Many Asian American women, whether first or fifth generation, struggle with conflicts between culturally proscribed, restrictive behaviors that are intended to serve the family and society as opposed to more individually oriented values and behaviors that recognize and expand the value of being female. They subsequently struggle with guilt, fear, and responsibility for themselves, their sisters, and their daughters. They are also fueled by a gratitude to their mothers for the hardships they incurred and by knowing that the hardships are no longer necessary in the current generation; this generation gap in what it means to be female creates tension for many Asian American women and their mothers (Takagi, 1988).

Separation from the patriarchy without rejection of the family or betrayal of the community is a tenuous accomplishment. The Asian American woman's identity is currently informed by many different stages and iterations of changing expectations of self in relationship to others, particularly fathers, brothers, husbands, and sons. Female Asian America simultaneously exists in many stages of identity development.

A HISTORY OF ASIAN IMMIGRATION TO AMERICA

U.S. immigration legislation from the mid-1800s through mid-1900s had a focused goal of excluding Asians from establishing themselves in this country. This legislation has affected patterns of gender ratios, settlement, organization, and commitment to cultural values. The immigration experiences have shaped self-esteem, retention or rejection of cultural values, mental health, "generation gaps," and relations between genders.

In this section I provide an overview of exclusionary legislation that shows its general impact on the formation of Asian America: the Chinese Exclusion Law of 1882, the Gentleman's Agreement (1908), the Barred Zone Act of 1917, the Cable Act (1922), the 1924 National Origins Law, the Tydings-McDuffie Act (1934), the 1945 War Brides Act, the 1964–1965 Immigration Act, and the 1979 Refugee Act. Ironically, the Immigration Law of 1965 has resulted in a tremendous influx of Asians and a dynamic growth of Asian America. S. Chan (1991) provided an excellent history of immigration legislation as it affected Asians. E. H. Kim and

Otani (1983) also provided an excellent brief outline, particularly as it affected Asian American women.

Capitalism grew out of the European ideology of manifest destiny that has used non-White people, particularly men, to accomplish the manual labor that establishes profit for "colonists" (S. Chan, 1991). Asian labor was imported to build railroads, to mine, to farm on the mainland, and to plant and harvest plantations in Hawaii; the request for laborers with promises of wealth were specifically made to strong, young men from working classes. The nature of the work for which laborers were imported, the differences in customs, and racism fed characterizations of Asian male laborers as inferior beings. This characterization of Asians as being less than fully human was subsequently used to justify legislation that deprived Asians of political rights and legal protection, keeping them marginal members of society at best and subhuman at worst.

The United States did not intend for Asian manual laborers to make a permanent home here. Overt exclusion and discrimination of Chinese at a state level (particularly in California, where the majority of Chinese resided through the 1900 census) and the national level culminated in the Chinese Exclusion Law of 1882. This law excluded all Chinese from immigration except merchants, students, teachers, and tourists. Because Japan was a rising military force, the exclusion of Japanese laborers and potential immigrants was accomplished more indirectly through the 1908 Gentleman's Agreement with Japan. Koreans were never directly targeted, although they were affected by U.S. immigration laws. Japan had administrative authority and legislation that controlled Korean emigration.

U.S. legislation became necessarily convoluted to limit, discourage, and exclude immigration of Filipinos who, as "wards" of the United States, could not be excluded by these previous legislations. The Tydings-McDuffie Act of 1934, integrally related to giving the Philippines its independence, actualized a change in the citizenship status of Filipinos, which subsequently allowed the United States to restrict immigration to 50 Filipinos a year.

Confusion over the racial identity of Asian Indians resulted in the most arbitrary criteria for exclusion, culiminating in the Barred Zone Act of 1917, which was affiliated with the 1917 Immigration Law. It excluded and limited immigration from particular geographic regions that included Asians, Asian Indians, and other dark-skinned people (Thornton, 1992a). (The reader is referred to S. Chan, 1991, for more details on this history.)

The impact of U.S. immigration legislation has had far-reaching implications that ultimately affected the stratification of Asian American societies. To preserve a cultural community, the basis of which in the homeland was kinship ties, and to decrease the isolation associated with a marginal status, many fraternal organizations formed that were nonexistent in the countries of origin alongside some familial clan associations. These organizations provided a "home away from home," and protection in many cases as anti-Asian violence increased (S. Chan, 1991). As Chan (1991) noted, "belonging to clubs was definitely not a habit they brought from the homeland where kinship formed the basis of virtually all aspects of social life, but they readily became joiners in the new World out of necessity" (p. 78).

Whereas several Asian American Studies scholars have suggested that the lack of Asian female emigrants can be attributed to "the patriarchal, patrilineal, and patrilocal nature of Chinese, Japanese, and Korean societies" (S. Chan, 1991, pp. 103–104), this is much like blaming the victim, in this case Asian male laborers. Immigration laws were designed to prevent Asian American communities from being established and immigrant workers from settling in this country. Without women, the thought was the laborers would return to their countries of origin.

Unfortunately, legislation attempting to exclude Asians and prohibit permanent settlement in the U.S. perpetuated some paternalistic and usury patterns toward Asian women by both the U.S. government and Asian men. The highly imbalanced sex ratios, the anti-miscegenation laws starting in 1860 (Yung, 1991), and a subservient role to men in Asian culture at that time relegated many Asian immigrant women to the role of sexual commodities (E. H. Kim & Otani, 1983).

The majority of the earliest immigrant Chinese and Japanese women were tricked or sold into sexual slavery (Ichioka, 1977). In 1860 and 1870, 85% and 71%, respectively, of the Chinese women in San Francisco were prostitutes (Yung, 1991). The Asian American woman's oppressed role in the U.S. was used to prove further the depravity and inferiority of Asians and to justify discriminatory practices.

Filipina immigrants did not have the history of being sold into prostitution as were their Chinese and Japanese predecessors for several reasons (E. H. Kim & Otani, 1983). At the time they started to immigrate the United States was making serious efforts to eradicate Chinese and Japanese prostitution. Furthermore, several cultural and historical factors decreased this likelihood. For example, Filipino culture still has remnants of a matriarchy as manifested in the bilateral nature of kinship. The religious basis of Catholicism for many immigrant Filipinos, the derivation of American values as one of its "wards," and the level of education of many Filipinas initially immigrating—one of the positive outcomes of U.S. intervention in the Philippines—most likely made a significant difference.

Many male laborers found it financially difficult, if not impossible, to return "home"; establishing a family was extremely difficult. The Chinese Exclusion Act of 1882, which allowed only the wives of Chinese merchants (who were few) to immigrate, coupled with antimiscegenation laws, would result in few women and a limited (9,000) first generation of American-born Chinese children around the turn of the century (S. Chan, 1991).

The imbalanced sex ratios and anti-miscegenation legislation led Japanese and Korean men to solicit "picture brides"; sometimes, families arranged marriages in their countries of origin. The Japanese government encouraged young women to go as picture brides to establish a foothold on the American continent through ownership of land (S. Chan, 1991). The arrangement of many of these marriages regardless of the woman's consent were a manifestation of patriarchal practices and reflection of marriage between families rather than solely between individuals. As C. K. Ho (1990) noted, the destiny of the Asian (Chinese, Japanese, Korean) woman is to be initially obedient and subservient to her father, then her husband, and in her later years her oldest son. However, this avenue of immigration for women and establishment of more permanent communities was halted by the Gentleman's Agreement, but not before some of the sex ratio imbalances had been narrowed and there were already 30,000 American-born Japanese children (S. Chan, 1991). Fewer Asian Indian, Korean, and Filipinas immigrated before World War II. The Korean population and the presence of Korean women was markedly larger after the Korean War. Asian Indian women were virtually not present until after World War II.

Further legislation was passed to prevent the establishment of Asian communities through marriage with American-born Asian residents. In 1922, the Cable Act ruled that any woman with U.S. citizenship who married an Asian would lose her citizenship; this law had particularly serious implications for U.S.-born Asian women who would not be allowed to regain citizenship (S. Chan, 1991).

The 1924 National Origins Law established quotas for immigrants outside of Europe and Canada and established conditions for deportation of aliens. The latter clause would be used by American husbands to threaten their international brides with deportation if the women threatened to leave them.

The presence of the U.S. military in the Pacific Rim resulted in a significant number of international brides of Asian ancestry married to U.S. servicemen, usually non-Asian, during and following the Korean War from Japan, Korea, and the Philippines (B.-L. C. Kim, 1977). Despite international marriages to U.S. citizens, U.S. immigration laws were still prohibitive of Asian wives and children of U.S. citizens immigrating until the 1945 War Brides Act. Subsequently, many adult children who are products of these unions have unusual family histories of immigration or movement between countries.

The countries of origin for the brides have shifted along with the shifts in U.S. military involvement. Initially, they were primarily from Japan in World War II and then from the Philippines and Korea during and since the Korean War. More recently, the spouses also have come from Southeast Asia since the Vietnam War.

The 1965 Immigration Act removed barriers to Asian immigration. Subsequently, the majority of Asians who currently reside in the United States have been here post-1965. Thus, there is a juxtaposition of Asian Americans rooted in the United States for several generations and many immigrant Asian Americans. This factor creates even greater diversity in the Asian American community and potentially revitalizes aspects of Asian culture in those who have been here longer. Ironically, the United States' attempt to exclude Asians from immigration and identification as Americans perpetuated a strong affinity that Asian Americans and immigrants retained for their homeland.

In previous decades, only a small number of Asian Americans voiced discontent and laid claim to rights, because of the small numbers of Asians, the economic class status (and lack of power) of the groups from which the initial voices were raised, and fears of the recriminations that have historically followed increased Asian presence in America (e.g., Asian hate crimes and anti-Asian legislation, such as Japanese American internment). However, the significant increase in the numbers of Asian Americans in the past two decades has increased the likelihood that a critical mass could speak out.

FROM ORIENTAL TO ASIAN AMERICAN

Many young Asian Americans coalesced their power during and subsequent to the Third World student strike at San Francisco State University in November 1968 (Omi, 1988). The San Francisco State student strike extended the consciousness-raising and self-empowerment of the civil rights movement, previously a response to America's oppression of African Americans, to Asian Americans (Chu, 1986). The Eurocentric-originated label *Oriental*, used to refer to any person of Asian ancestry, was replaced by the current term *Asian American* as the term *Black* replaced the term *Negro*. This label recognized the similar historical treatment of Asian Americans in America, at that time Japanese, Chinese and Filipinos. Determining how one wished to be referred to was also an act of empowerment.

Loo (1988) observed that the historical strike catalyzed Asian America into an adolescent phase of development, and clearly a search for identity. However, Asian American identity has been largely masculine, defined within both a larger societal and cultural patriarchy. U.S. immigration laws reinforced its patriarchal cultural organization. These laws and their effects on the establishment of Asian America resulted in gross sex ratio imbalances that undoubtedly bolstered male determination and definition of

Asian America until approximate equalization of sex ratios was attained only in the 1970s.

Within 5 years of the strike, two students wrote the first chapter on the psychology of Asian American women (Fujitomi & Wong, 1973), which stood alone for almost 20 years.

Asian America

The meaning of Asian American must be qualified by cultural group, generation in this country, immigration status, age, political experiences, and self-proclaimed identity to begin to understand the personal meaning of this identity. Thus, in this chapter, although there are similarities drawn between and among groups of Asian Americans, there are also specific qualifiers to observe the limitations of researchers' knowledge of differences between groups.

Contemporarily, the term *Asian American* refers to the hybidrization of specific Asian ways of thinking with mainstream American ways of thinking (Bradshaw, 1994; L. C. Lee, 1992; Omi, 1992; Root, 1992b; Thornton, 1992b). As an umbrella term, it can obscure the diversity that exists among Asians and Pacific Islanders along the lines of history, religion, matriarchal versus patriarchal organization, language, culture, and race. For example, the majority of women from Cambodia, Laos, and Vietnam are from rural and working-class backgrounds, but some women from Hong Kong come from materially privileged, large-city backgrounds (Homma-True, 1991). Bradshaw (1994) outlined the differences in religious and philosophical influences in the construction of culture and gender. For example, Filipino culture is not rooted in Confucionism. Asian Americans also differ in their origins in patriarchy. For example, Filipino folklore has creation legends in which men and women are equal; unlike in most other Asian groups, there is bilateral recognition of maternal and paternal heritage.

The Asian American Women's Movement

The representative voice and agenda of the Asian American movement was male. Women were in secondary roles as support persons rather than leaders, a status that paralleled the issues of oppression by gender that the mainstream women's movement was fighting.

The mainstream women's movement required a singular loyalty to gender over other affiliations and did not recognize, at that time, that Women of Color had competing "mothers" of race and culture that were not prominent on the agenda of White women (Chow, 1989; Fong, 1978). Unfortunately, skin color and the issues it embodied—classism, racism, ethnocentrism—posed an inherent schism between many White women and Women of Color. Given the history of racism in this country, many Women of Color placed in the position of "having to choose" between sexism and racism (Fong, 1978) chose family and culture.

Fujitomi and Wong (1973) observed that the leadership role was often elusive to Asian American women because their energies were dissipated in the struggle to integrate two cultures, acts that required the violation of proscriptions for female modesty, invisibility, passivity, and support of men. Furthermore, political activism posed contradictions between a Western as opposed to an Asian set of core values. Chow (1989) outlined four such contradictions: "(1) obedience vs. independence; (2) collective (or familial) vs. individual interest; (3) fatalism vs. change; and (4) self-control vs. self-expression or spontaneity" (p. 368).

Participation in the feminist movement by Chinese and Japanese American women was often internally perceived as rejection of the Asian American community and a failure to uphold implicit responsibilities to male–female relationships. It is possible that Asian American lesbians moved more freely between the White women's community and the Asian American community as "revolutionaries" to get needs met and to bolster their self-esteem in a lifestyle orientation that would threaten family values. C. S. Chan (1987b) reflected that feminism and lesbianism were a double rejection of male-oriented Asian culture.

Chow (1989) also suggested that class and economic issues prevented the Asian American women's movement from being stronger. Largely constituted of Chinese and Japanese American women, groups with the longest history in the United States, they had access to resources and education that some other Asian groups did not yet have. Most of the working class of Asian American women—the garment workers, the domestics, and the service industry workers—chose economic survival over direct political participation (Glenn, 1991; Loo, 1991; Loo & Ong, 1982).

J. L. Chin (personal communication, 1992) suggested that additional factors contributed to a delayed emergence of the Asian American women's movement. Asian American groups were isolated from one another and were afraid to openly challenge oppression because of historical responses that threatened safety and survival. Finally, pressure to assimilate, a survival strategy, conflicted with the separatism of the movement.

By the mid-1970s many of the activists of the 1970s were tired. Personal and professional priorities were changing, such as starting a family, caring for aging parents, and so on. There were not enough replacements to continue the growth of the Asian American women's movement at the momentum with which it started.

A political analysis might suggest that the presence of a "culture and racial" hierarchy among Asian groups also may have contributed to the lack of involvement of Filipinos and Koreans, newer immigrants, who had less status in this hierarchical system; the movement also might have failed, as did the mainstream women's movement, to make the movement more relevant to the lives of women in the Asian American community who had less power.

Despite the personal conflicts faced by the Asian woman of the 1960s and 1970s, they laid an amazing political groundwork for future generations. The first courses on Asian American women originated at the University of California, Berkeley, San Francisco State University, and University of California, Los Angeles (UCLA; Chu, 1986). The first chapter on the psychology of the Asian American woman appeared in 1973 (Fujitomi & Wong, 1973). Also, the first special issues and publications on Asian American women's experiences were published in *Gidra* (1971) and *Counterpoint* (Gee, 1976).

ASIAN AMERICAN WOMEN IN THE 1990s

C. S. Chan (1987b) so aptly observed that "when Asian-American women speak of their conflicts they frequently focus first upon their familial relationships, then their work relationships, and only later upon their relationship with the rest of American society" (p. 13). To understand the contemporary psychology of Asian American women, one cannot separate it from their role in society. All of the issues discussed subsequently in this chapter derive from power inequities related to sexism, racism, ethnocentrism, and classism. These issues are deeply ingrained in the stereotypes of Asian American women, which are highly correlated with their history and political experience.

Stereotypes

Stereotypes serve several different dangerous purposes. First, they limit the behavior to which the observer will attend. As Chow (1989) asserted, this is dangerous because "all stereotypes, whether positive or negative, serve as self-fulfilling prophecies when contending with them gradually leads to internalizing them as part of an illusionary reality" (p. 367). Second, stereotypes depersonalize a person or group, which subsequently allows those in power to disregard them as individuals with rights.

Five broad and dangerous stereotypes exist. The first stereotype derives from cultural proscriptions of subservience of women to men on the basis of women's lower status in China and Japan. The Japanese American Citizens' League (1985) suggested that this stereotype has driven a male fantasy in the United States, Australia, and Germany in the form of a growing correspondence bride business.

The second stereotype suggests that Asian American women have a "special sexuality" or "exoticness." The tendency for women in general to be treated as sex objects, combined with racism, contributes to some men's fantasies that Asian American women have different genital anatomy and a different ability to sexually please men. Tajima (1989) specifically observed these stereotypes in the popular culture as a geisha girl.

The media has capitalized on a third stereotype: the Asian American woman as a diabolical, aggressive, manipulative sorceress. Tajima (1989) noted that this stereotype appears in language references to Asian American women as "Dragon Lady" and Fu Manchu's various female relations, prostitutes, and devious madames. This stereotype conveys a moral teaching to prohibit miscegenation, revitalizes the good girl–bad girl dichotomy, may reflect the inability of media moguls to interpret differences outside of the European-derived context, and indirectly makes judgments about non-Christians as somehow being possessed and evil. This stereotype is attributed to Asian American women who do not fit the docile, subservient stereotype and are assertive and demand their rights.

A fourth stereotype, that of the sexless worker or "busy worker bee," reflects the limited employment opportunities available to recent immigrants and older Asian women as garment workers (*Gidra*, 1971) and domestics (Glenn, 1991). This person has been largely invisible to middle America, seldom regarded as a person, and is not currently perceived as a threat. The position of these women and their poor working conditions (Glenn, 1991; Loo, 1991; Loo & Ong, 1982) replicate the initial importation of male Asian labor during the 1800s to boost the economic power of America.

The last stereotype, that of an innocent, fragile, and childlike "creature" (e.g., the "lotus blossom baby," "China doll," or "Asian Thumbelina" in the reptilian monster movies), also becomes the subject of pornography. This stereotype is now being extended to the Amerasian woman (Root, in press). C. S. Chan (1987a) suggested that "Suzie Wong," the "hooker with a heart of gold," is actually a synthesis of several stereotypes.

Stereotypes may not only become part of a proscription for behavior and roles, but even the slightest internalization compromises self-esteem and opportunities for self-determination. Because conventional Asian values have had restrictive roles for girls and women, moving outside of the cultural and familial system might place young Asian American women (who are isolated from their communities) more at risk for assuming these roles in a culture that still offers few positive role models and abounds with racist projections onto Asian American women.

Education and Employment

Compared with any other group of women, Asian American women tend to have completed college twice as often as White women. However, on average, they earned only slightly greater incomes than did White women. S. Chan (1991) noted that the education figures for Asians are inflated because many highly educated Asians are immigrants. For example, although Filipinas are the most highly educated group compared with both men and women in some samples (Carino, Fawcett, Gardner, & Arnold, 1990; Chu, 1988), many of these women obtained their schooling in the Philippines and have since immigrated. Some anecdotal data suggest that this level of education does not hold for second-generation Filipinas in America.

Initial participation in the workforce for immigrant women was shaped by institutional racism and language barriers. For example, Glenn (1991) observed that although Japanese American women, like many European immigrant women, initially worked in domestic service, for years racism prevented them from moving on to other occupations. She noted that institutional racism had to subside to allow other opportunities for *nisei*. Glenn (1991) stated that "involvement in domestic service was thus an important shared experience for Japanese women in the prewar years, serving as one basis for ethnic and gender solidarity" (p. 345). Currently, institutional and language barriers have relegated many recent immigrant Chinese and Southeast Asian women to the garment and factory industries with poor wages and poor hours.

Asian American women, compared with any other group of women, tend to be employed outside the home because they need a second income; Asian men earn less than do White men (S. Chan, 1991). Chu (1988) specifically looked at employment for Asian American women in Los Angeles County from 1980 U.S. Census data and found that Asian women had the highest rates of labor force participation. Their participation usually is part of at least two-income households, as the rates of divorce are lower than the population average. Like other women, they tend to receive less pay for their educational and experience level than men.

Chu (1988) observed the diversity of employment within Asian America by group: Filipina women are employed at a higher rate than men because of their high educational levels, whereas Vietnamese women are employed at the lowest rates in part because of lack of skills relevant to the type of employment that can be obtained in this country. Interestingly, Vietnamese women tended to work more frequently than any other group of women in the United States in nontraditional jobs such as precision and crafts. Chu (1988) also reported on the diversity of jobs Asian American women held. She noted that within Los Angeles County, Korean and Vietnamese women were overrepresented in the lower paying jobs and underrepresented in managerial and professional jobs. By contrast, more than 25% of the employed Filipina and Asian Indian women were in managerial and professional roles and, conversely, there were fewer women in lower paying jobs. More than half of Japanese women were in white-collar occupations (e.g., sales, administrative support, and technical positions).

Chinese women appeared to be present both in managerial and professional positions and in low-mobility occupations.

As Chu (1988) observed, these data cannot simply by explained by relative immigration status. The data obtained from Los Angeles County may be different from Honolulu County in Hawaii or in New York City.

A special issue relevant to immigrant women affects identity and self-esteem. Many Asian women who received specialized training, including professional training, in their countries-of-origin are not able to transfer their credentials to this country. Subsequently, many women with graduate educations are working at jobs that require little or no schooling. Because their skills are not transferable, the women suffer psychologically for having a lower status, often with a loss of self-esteem.

Interracial Dating and Intermarriage

Several variables correlate with higher rates of intermarriage: skin color, socioeconomic status (SES), degree of acculturation, higher education, generation, occupation, income, proximity to different groups, small numbers of one group, and sex ratios (Adams, 1937; Miller, 1992; Sung, 1990). The strict anti-miscegenation laws and racism were the major deterrents to interracial marriages for Asian American men because the imbalanced sex ratios would drive higher rates of interracial marriage. Anti-miscegenation laws were repealed only in the last 14 states in 1967 (Root, 1992a).

The early theories of interracial marriage hypothesized individual pathology as an explanation for partner selection; therefore, these theories also suggested that these marriages would not last. In contemporary times, both M. K. Ho (1984) and Sung (1990) suggested that interracial marriages for Asian Americans would be difficult; however, difficulty does not necessarily mean more divorce or that the marriages are unsuccessful. In fact, recent research shows the opposite.

F. C. Ho and Johnson (1990) explored the question of the longevity of interracial marriages among residents in Hawaii. The divorce rate was proportionately lower for between-group marriages (which included some interethnic marriages among Asians and Hawaiians) compared with within-group marriages. Sung's (1990) study of 50 interracially married New York Chinese showed that the divorce rate was relatively low, 12–18%, compared with 40% for the general population in 1982. When she compared intra- versus intergroup Chinese marriages, the rates were highly similar.

Current theories have moved away from the individual pathology notion. Fujino (1992) conducted several different studies on interracial dating among UCLA students. She suggested that rather than pathology, interracial dating is partly a response to trading status by gender and race. Her research suggests that the pathology rests in the culture that supports stereotypes suggesting that Asian American women and men are viewed as being less physically attractive than their White counterparts. Although women are viewed as less attractive than their White female peers, they are seen as more obedient, more willing to do chores, and more willing to take care of men than their White female peers (Fujino, 1993), which may be viewed as attractive in a relationship but not necessarily reality based.

Ahern, Cole, Johnson, and Wong (1981) studied interracial and interethnic marriage in Hawaii and found that neither partner displayed psychopathology, although the study participants were less traditional, particularly the women, who were largely the Asian American partner. Their findings make sense. In the time frame in which the individuals in their study married, the women would have had to be more unusual to resist their respective families' expectations of whom they would marry.

Several researchers have observed that second marriages have higher rates of intermarriage for Asian Americans because fear of parental and public disapproval affects choices less as one gets older (Jedlicka, 1975; Johnson & Nagoshi, 1990; Sung, 1990). Sung also hypothesized that for Asian American women marrying for a second time, the stigma of divorce in the Chinese American community, particularly for earlier generations, may propel a woman to seek a marital partner outside of her own ethnic group.

Rates of intermarriage also differ by gender, generation, and geographic region of the country. For example, the rates of intermarriage are extremely high in Hawaii (Kitano et al., 1984). Sung (1990) noted that Chinese American intermarriage is highest in Hawaii (more than 75% combining men and women), high in Los Angeles, and relatively low in New York. Generation explains some of these differences, moving from longest established in Hawaii associated with high rates of intermarriage, to a large population of first-generation Chinese in New York City with the lowest rates of intermarriage, similar to studies conducted in the 1930s. In contrast to other studies, which show that the women had higher rates of intermarriage than men, the rates for New York Chinese men and women are similar.

Based on data from Los Angeles County, Kitano and Fujino (in press) reported that generation in this country, acculturation, time in this country, and proximity to other groups play significant roles in determining rates of interracial marriage. Thus, each successive generation generates higher rates of intermarriage. They found that women across ethnic groups in Los Angeles County intermarry more frequently than men.

Leonetti and Newell-Morris (1982) found practically no intermarriage of first-generation Japanese in Seattle, although they now have very high rates of intermarriage (Kitano & Fujino, in press). It has been suggested that the internment of Japanese Americans during World War II, and the subsequent geographic dispersal of internees, accelerated Japanese American intermarriage. Intermarriage as a response to this experience has been viewed as the attempt to assimilate as quickly as possible to protect subsequent generations of Japanese Americans.

Combined with the recently amended Immigration Act of 1965, except for Mexicans, the major source of non-European immigrant spouses have been of Asian origin and female (Thornton, 1992a). This is not surprising given the steady U.S. military presence in the Pacific starting during World War II and continuing with the Korean (B.-L. C. Kim, 1977) and Vietnam wars. Many of the recent marriages are arranged through a correspondence relationship.

Correspondence marriages also have been controversial. Serita (1984) noted that the "mail order" bride business is a transformation of colonization and imperialism of Asian women through sexual, racial, and economic oppression. These brides come predominantly from the Philippines, Malaysia, and Singapore and are using the marriage to escape the economic hardship in their respective countries. Villapando (1989) suggested that the mail order business capitalizes on the economic conditions in many of the countries from which the international brides come; many of the men seeking wives through this means are buying into racial stereotypes of Asian women as obedient, subservient, and agreeable. Two extensive studies that have been conducted showed that, despite the initial concerns of exploitation of these women, the women generally report being happy (Lin, 1991; Yung, 1991). Skeptics suggest that those who participate are the ones for whom these marriages are working well. Villapando (1989) reported preliminary findings from a University of Texas study that showed that many of the women were subsequently in bitter divorces.

CURRENT MENTAL HEALTH CONCERNS FOR ASIAN AMERICAN WOMEN

Female voices in Asian American literature and ethnic studies (Asian American Women United of California, 1989; Kono & Song, 1991; J. F. J. Lee, 1991; Watanabe & Bruchac, 1990) have documented the very human problems within Asian American communites that challenge their "most favored minority" status. Collectively, these authors exposed addiction, sexual and domestic violence, compromised self-esteem, second-class status, triple oppression (race, gender, and culture), depression, suicide, homophobia, and racism within Asian America. Recently, empirically based literature has developed to accompany these voices.

Identity, Self-Esteem, and Attractiveness

Self-esteem, identity and attractiveness are sometimes inseparable for women. Self-esteem might be viewed as a gradual process of identity development that in contemporary Asian America is a delicate balance between assimilation to an individualistic philosophy and simultaneous respect for identity being derived from the family. Self-esteem is partly derived from the reflection of one's value and acceptance in important others' eyes; in the Asian woman's case, identity has been derived from the family identity or name. Her valuation of self as a woman unfortunately includes her sense of physical attractiveness in a country that has denigrated her racial features.

Racism and sexism contribute to the Asian American woman being sexually objectified in stereotypes. C. S. Chan (1987a) suggested that her self-esteem and identity might interact significantly with the degree to which she is sexually objectified. This may cause many young Asian American women to be uncertain about whether they are liked for who they are rather than what they represent in the minds or imaginations of men in particular (C. S. Chan, personal communication, 1991). Valverde (1992) noted that a confluence of oppressive factors in the lives of Vietnamese Amerasian women relegate them to living as prostitutes valued for what they can sell.

The desire for approval from the mainstream culture leads many young people to attempt to divest themselves of cultural values and an Asian identity. For Asian American women, the lower value placed on their lives may contribute to the development of low self-esteem and depression, which may manifest themselves in eating disorders, depression, anxiety, and suicide.

For immigrant women, changes in class status, gender privileges, and a cultural shift from collective to individualistic identity may threaten self-esteem and require a reflection on identity. For Southeast Asian refugee women, most of whom have experienced traumatic losses and violence, their identity and understanding of meaning in life has been severely shaken (Chung, 1991; Leong & Johnson, 1992; Rozee & van Boemel, 1989; Tien, 1994). Their task is to reconstruct their lives, somehow incorporating their experiences into their sense of who they are.

Bradshaw (1994) noted that conventional ethnic identity models are not sufficient to explain how Asian American women accomplish a positive ethnic identity that asserts equal social value with Asian American men. According to her critique, the response of minorities to retreat to the ethnic community as young adults or teenagers when they discover their second-class status suggests that Asian American women must attain a positive sense of self by maintaining contact with a majority culture that supports her personal achievements and increased freedom.

Asian lesbians face further jeopardy in their attempts to declare a lesbian identity, which steps out of the bounds for a "woman's place" and threatens the assumed male privilege (C. S. Chan, 1987b). Chan observed that declaring a lesbian identity is a "revolutionary" act in the Asian American community. She must confront the likelihood of giving up her role in perpetuating a family, does not derive her identity from her male partners, and instead identifies herself by her relationships with women. Without intention to conventionally marry, it is hard for her to achieve full adult status (C. S. Chan, 1987b). Thus, Chan observed that the coming out process is one fraught with challenges and anticipation of loss of benefits associated with her role in the family.

Kanuha (1989) discussed the triple jeopardy faced by lesbians: sexism, racism, and homophobia. Until recently, there have been few places for lesbians to retreat for recognition of all three significant aspects of their being (H., 1989). H. (1989) suggested that "an Asian American lesbian must first strive to develop a basic sense of self-identity before taking the next step of developing a sexual identity" (p. 285).

In the face of preserving family honor, many Asian American lesbians end up socializing outside of the Asian community and come in contact with few other Asian lesbians. It is only in the past decade that organizations have been created by Asian lesbians to support the unique status of this identity that allows both cultural reinforcement and celebration as well as role models for sexual orientation.

A combination of racism and sexism contributes to negative feelings many Asian American women have about their racial features (C. S. Chan, 1985; Hall, in press), such as small breasts, eye and nose shape, skin color, straight hair, and short stature. Fujino (1993) found that young Asian American women were indeed rated as significantly less attractive by both White men and Asian men. Although women of color have suffered from being compared with the European-based standard of attractiveness, perhaps no other group has attempted to change its racial features as much and by as drastic measures as Asian American women. They have subjected themselves to eyefold surgery, nose construction, and breast implants (Kaw, 1993).

Asian Americans have adopted an internalized judgment against darker skin, valuing light skin (Hall, in press). Not only is this based on the European likeness, but on the association of darker skin with manual labor and lower social caste across Asian cultures. In many ways, skin color traditionally was as much a ticket for upward social mobility as thinness has been in Western cultures. Among Filipinos who have been colonized by lighter skinned people (i.e., by the Spanish, then the Americans), the valuation of lighter skin reflects an internalized oppression (Santos, 1983).

Yoshimura (1992) observed that a history of greater body image dissatisfaction among Japanese American children and adolescents poses a risk factor for developing eating disorders. Both Yi (1989) and Yoshimura (1992) found, surprisingly, that acculturation was not associated with greater eating disorder symptomatology among young Asian American women. Root (1990a) conceptualized eating disorders as reflecting conflicts with identity, powerlessness, role conflicts, and devalued esteem, all issues that appear to be tougher for women of color. She suggested that the striving for thinness, associated with eating disorders, is equated with attractiveness. Ironically, the petiteness of many Asian American women, although seen as physically attractive, is also a physique that contradicts social perceptions of powerfulness. Many Asian American women find that a slight build combined with short stature leads to being treated like a child. Asian American women's eating disorders are more likely to include dissatisfaction or loathing of specific racial features not related to body weight and fatness but that are projected onto a feeling of general body dissatisfaction, reflecting the struggles with identity, empowerment, and self-esteem.

Some of the social origins of alcohol and drug abuse are similar to those of eating disorders. Sue, Zane, and Ito (1979) found that patterns of Asian American drinking are associated with assimilation. However, Sun (1991) found that the importance of family identity, restrictiveness of the female role, importance of moderation, and lack of emphasis on drinking contribute to the Asian woman drinking less, as has been found among Koreans in Los Angeles (Lubben, Chi, & Kitano, 1989) and Chinese and Japanese Americans (Sue et al., 1979).

Amerasian Ethnic Identity

Amerasian is the most inclusive term referring to people of Asian heritage who are also of African, Indian, Latino, and White European heritages. It is a term that refers to a subset of the Asian American experience rather than to a distinct ethnic identity (Root, in press-a). Unfortunately, biracial people also experience oppression (Root, 1992a, in press-b); they must repeatedly assert their right to claim an Asian identity in situations in which people define ethnicity synonymously with race.

The term *Amerasian* refers to individuals with at least one parent of Asian heritage and at least one parent of American nationality and includes some people who are still in their "mother's country" or have recently arrived in search of a new life (Root, in press-b). This is particularly true of Vietnamese Amerasians (Chao, in press; Felsman, Johnson, Leong, & Felsman, 1989; Tien, 1994; Tien & Hunthausen, 1990; Valverde, 1992). Chew, Eggebeen, and Uhlenberg (1989) found that the vast majority of multiracial households in the United States are Asian White households in which the majority of women are Asian; these households include White families who have transracially adopted Asian children.

Attitudes about Asians, particularly in the past, made the accomplishment of a positive ethnic and racial identity difficult. Furthermore, the belief in racial purity made it difficult for racially mixed people to be anything but marginal. Kich (1992) observed that "the assertion of the self as biracial requires both the personal organizing structure of a biracial self-label and the interpersonal and social recognition of the individual as biracial. The assertion creates and fosters a coherent, whole sense of self" (p. 317).

Several clinicians have highlighted the importance of providing access and respect for multiple heritages to Amerasians (Chao, in press; Hall, 1992; Murphy-Shigematsu, 1988; Nakashima, 1988, 1992; Root, 1990b; Valverde, 1992; Williams, 1992), providing a multiracial label (Kich, 1992), openly talking about race (Kich, 1992; Root, in press), and providing the child with tools for growing up as a minority in America (Miller & Miller, 1990; Root, in press). In a similar vein, the parents' choice of community becomes significant for role models, orientation to being Asian, and attitude toward multiracial Asians (Mass, 1992; Williams, 1992).

Some researchers are concerned that interracial marriages will result in a loss of culture, as the offspring will be less exposed to Asian American culture. This is not necessarily true, as a variety of researchers across the nation have found (Grove, 1991; Hall, 1992; Kich, 1992; Murphy-Shigematsu, 1988; Stephan, 1992; Thornton, 1983; Williams, 1992). However, race becomes a less significant issue in the proclamation of this identity, and the identity becomes more complex. Stephan (1992) found that in her sample of multiracial Asians in Hawaii, "cultural exposure is extremely important to ethnic identity, although it is neither a necessary nor a sufficient condition for ethnic identity to occur" (p. 62). Researchers find that aspects of identity are situationally and environmentally determined (Stephan, 1992), vary according to how ethnicity is assessed (Nakashima, 1988), and vary according to the researchers' biases about racially mixed individuals (Root, 1992a).

Stereotypes of racially mixed women leave them vulnerable to harassment and objectification (Root, 1994). However, the racial ambiguity of the racially mixed person leads many people to also treat Amerasian men as exotic objects. Particularly without role models and socialization for coping, many will assume the identity projected onto them by society. Valverde (1992) observed this to be the case for some Vietnamese Amerasians who are seen on the streets of San Jose, California, as prostitutes. Other multiracial women may play on their "exoticness" or search for acceptance in the sexuality that has been cast on the multiracial female. Other women in reaction to this stereotype may be particularly cautious about their expression of sexuality.

Sexuality

Although there is a history of erotica in Asian countries, there is little information on the sexuality of Asian Americans. Tsui (1985), however, noted that it would be erroneous to think that Asian cultures are Victorian in the expression of sexuality. Rather, she suggested that certain notions of propriety preclude certain types of written information on this topic. C. S. Chan (1994) suggested that the lack of information reflects the split between public and private selves and may make sexuality a conflicted subject for young Asian Americans who are influenced both by familial rules and peer behavior. Hirayama and Hirayama (1986) further suggested that sexuality may be hard to study because it is both a private behavior and associated with emotion, which is often more controlled.

A summary of the literature suggests that, in general, Asian Americans tend to be sexually conservative in outward expressions of sexuality, which maintains social order within the family and community (C. S. Chan, 1994). As such, many Asian Americans may not explicitly declare their sexual identity, which makes confirmation of a gay or lesbian identity more difficult in the Asian American community (C. S. Chan, 1994). Sexual conservatism would also predict lower rates of sexually active young adults, as Cochran, Mays, and Leung (1991) found in their comparison of Asian American college students and other ethnic and racial groups.

The relative absence of written material on Asian American women's sexuality has far-reaching implications. It makes the declaration of a sexual identity other than heterosexual particularly difficult (H., 1989), may contribute to some abused women staying with a partner for sexual compansionship (Rimonte, 1989), and makes asking for help regarding sexual information and sexual functioning particularly difficult. We hypothesized that the lack of information on the topic of sexuality also may make it particularly difficult to disclose information about extrafamilial rape or sexual molestation.

This is of particular concern in a time of AIDS and HIV. Cochran et al. found that (1991) unsafe sex practices occur at similar frequencies in both their Asian and non-Asian American samples. Homma-True (1991) summarized the research that points to the dramatic increase in AIDS and HIV infection in the Asian American community. She believed that the non-English speaking immigrant population may be particularly at risk for lack of information. Also, given the role of women in sexuality, this may be an extremely difficult topic to address openly, particularly with immigrant women. Aggressive reaching out may be necessary to prevent the spread of AIDS and HIV infection in the Asian American community, particularly because the next risk group worldwide may be women (Homma-True, 1991).

Violence Against Women and Children

Although little has been written or documented about violence against Asian American girls and women, this is not to say that there is truly a lower incidence of these events. Traditional Japanese, Chinese, Korean, and Southeast Asian cultures are at particular risk for the reinforcement of power differentials based on gender (C. K. Ho, 1990, in press; Song, 1994; Rimonte, 1989).

It is likely that a multitude of variables conspire to keep this evidence from public record. The insular nature of the family and cultural imperatives to protect the honor of the family make it particularly difficult to report sexual abuse and domestic violence (Tsui, 1985). To make such a disclosure may amplify the shame and humiliation survivors often feel. Also, some Asian cultures ascribe a positive trait to the ability to endure suffering (C. K. Ho, 1990) and even to consider suffering as one's fate (Rimonte, 1989). Rimonte (1989) further noted that the disruption of extended family systems due to immigration may leave a woman with fewer people to turn to in the insular system. She also observed that, unfortunately, even if elderly parents are part of the family system, they are often dependents of their adult children and thus may no longer have the status to intervene. Furthermore, in some cultural systems, the woman might be abused by other male relatives, and the abuse is accepted, either tacitly or overtly.

Mollica, Wyshak, and Lavelle (1987), working with refugee women in Boston, found that the prevalence of rape and sexual abuse experienced by the women in conjucntion with war atrocities in camp, prison, and encounters with "officials" was horrific, approaching 100%. Subsequently, some Southeast Asian Women may have a particular fear of calling authorities, because in their country-of-origin, the authorities committed many of the war atrocities (e.g., murder, pillage, rape; Rozee & van Boemel, 1989; Tien, 1994). Nevertheless, some literature is beginning to delineate the very real and significant problem of violence within the Asian American communities and against women and girls.

In one of the few studies of child maltreatment, Ima and Hohm (1991) studied Southeast Asians, Filipinos, Koreans, and Pacific Islanders, who were part of the database for a San Deigo agency serving immigrants and refugees. They examined abuse in terms of ethnicity and gender. They found that there were differences in maltreatment of children by ethnic group that were most likely attributable to cultural differences in their life experiences, family structure, and child-rearing patterns. Samoans and Vietnamese reported high rates of child sexual abuse. Sexual abuse was not frequently reported except in the Filipino sample, in which the abuser was often a non-Filipino, military-enlisted stepfather. Comparing their sample with general statistics for the U.S. population, rates of physical abuse were similar and sexual abuse was either lower or underreported.

Domestic violence is a significant, unexposed problem in Asian American communities. Rimonte (1989) reported on the presence of a shelter agency to help Pacific Asian women and their children subjected to violence in Los Angeles County. She emphasized diversity by group, income, and education. She noted that 3,000 individuals were served by this Los Angeles center between 1978 and 1985: One third were Korean; another third were Vietnamese and other Southeast Asians; and the rest were Chinese, Filipinos, Japanese, South Asians, Thai, and Pacific Islanders. Between 1982 and 1985, the majority of these women were Pacific Asian immigrant women, 90% of whom had been battered and 10% were seeking services for rape. Rimonte also offered observations of why immigrant women have a hard time leaving their abusers: because of economic hardship, the need for sexual companionship, and fear of being deported (i.e., losing their immigrant status).

It is important that researchers again recognize and explore the diversity present among Asian and Pacific Americans (C. K. Ho, 1990, in press; Ima & Hohm, 1991). C. K. Ho (1990) started this process with a focus-group methodology in her study of attitudes toward phsyical violence in four Southeast Asian American communities in Seattle, Washington: Khmer, Laotian, Vietnamese, and Southeast Asian Chinese. She found that although similarities existed on the basis of Confucion assertions that men are superior to women and have the authority to dominate, there also were differences between the groups in their attitudes toward violence.

Generational differences also must be considered in drawing conclusions from these data. C. K. Ho (1990) observed that breaking the silence that keeps women and children prisoners of domestic violence is particularly difficult for first-generation individuals because of language facility and lack of familiarity with the system and the resources. Leaving the family home for safety, although a seemingly logical conclusion, confronts the value of honor and name associated with the family hearth (Luu, 1989) and is an "extraordinary gesture of self-assertion" (Rimonte, 1989, p. 332).

Luu (1989) pointed out that the economic realities in the United States of Vietnamese American women are such that many are moving away from traditional roles through employment. Contributing financially to the family threatens the very foundation on which order was established. She noted that the men have had tremendous difficulty with this. Luu suggested that spousal abuse will be present under extreme duress, dislocation, gender role changes that threaten authority, and the distribution of power that determines the hierarchy; some men will attempt to assert their authority through spousal abuse. Song (1994) offered a similar explanation in her survey of 150 Korean immigrant women, 60% of whom reported being battered by their spouses; the battering often started once they were in the United States or intensified thereafter. Agbayani-Siewert (1991), in a study of immigrant Filipinos, also found a similar pattern of marital role strain related to changes in gender role expectations of spouses and increased rates of domestic violence.

In specifically addressing issues relevant to Southeast Asian American refugee women, researchers and therapists must have an informed, broad contextual framework for understanding domestic problems that include a consideration of the traumas incurred before resettlement, expectations of marriage, and power challengers such as women being employed before offering a more formulaic approach to domestic problems (Tien, 1994).

In an increasing atmosphere of Asian-bashing reminiscent of the hostility toward Asian Americans preceding the internment of Japanese Americans in World War II, my colleagues and I have conjectured that the form it takes is different depending on gender. Violence toward men may take place in street violence; violence toward women may occur as sexual assault, which is often not reported to the police and when it is reported, it is not included in racial statistics but in crimes against women (C. S. Chan, 1991, personal communication; B. Lui, 1991, personal communication). This hypothesis remains to be tested.

Marriage and Family

Among Japanese Americans, a significant move away from arranged marriages came with the internment of Japanese Americans when utilitarian reasons for marriage were replaced by marrying for love (Takagi, 1988). The assimilation of mainstream values has also been the basis of conflicts of daughters with parents and women with spouses (Fujitomi & Wong, 1973). Whereas a woman may operate with responsibility at work, with several people having to answer to her, she may have to figure out how to make a transition at home, particularly if married to an Asian American male raised to have similar gender expectations (Homma-True, 1987). Thus, there may be a distinction between public and private lives. Pressures from mothers to conform to more service-oriented roles toward partners may pose further conflicts between mothers and daughters and, in more traditional families, between mother-in-laws and daughter-in-laws. Few social role models exist with whom Asian American women might identify. Homma-True (1990) suggested that self-disclosure may be appropriate and necessary when working with Asian American women when the therapist is Asian American.

Few studies have examined Asian American marital relationships. In her study of Chinese American couples, Ying (1991) found that 42% of the variance in marital satisfaction for women, compared with 30% for men, was accounted for by subjective ratings of life aims, friendships, and communication. The best predictor for marital satisfaction was sharing of goals with partners. This information is important because role delineations among many Asian American couples require neither sharing nor agreement on goals. Marital dissatisfaction, in fact, is primarily related to gender role strains. Agbayani-Siewert (1991) found that shifts in sex role behavior that conflicted with gender role expectations of spouses was correlated with increased marital conflict and dissatisfaction among Filipinos in Los Angeles County. Family life for Southeast Asian refugee families has many conflicts inherent in changes in class status, language barriers, and incomes that will sustain a family. Many women must work, something perceived as a "necessary evil" (Tien, 1994), but this changes the roles of women in relationship to men. Luu (1989) observed that the changing role of women in these communities was correlated with divorce, particularly among Vietnamese.

Divorce is not strictly correlated with marital dissatisfaction or generation in United States. Homma-True (1990) suggested that initiating a divorce may carry greater stigma for many Asian American women than other American women; a divorce is a significant failure of obligation not only to one's partner but to the families involved. Thus, one might expect such a stigma to yield lower divorce rates, which indeed was found in one study (Chu, 1988).

In a study using Los Angeles County data from the 1980 Census, Chu (1988) found that the divorce rate for Asian Americans was much lower than for other women in the United States. With lower divorce rates, proportionally fewer Asian women are single heads of households than other groups of women. However, differences exist between and among Asian groups. For example, she found that the divorce rate was higher among Japanese Americans compared with Vietnamese Americans, a more recent immigrant group; the divorce rate for Korean women was relatively high, although they, too, are a more recently immigrated group. Chu found that generation in this country could not account for the data and reflected on the possibility of assimilation of American values, familiarity of divorce in country-of-origin (e.g., Korea) may have an influence. It is also possible that the importance of children, the belief in staying together for the children's sake, and the orientation toward the collective versus the individual influence decisions to divorce.

Communication, an agreed-on ingredient to a successful relationship, may have different definitions and requirements by ethnic group. For example, Card (1978) found that styles of communication between Filipino American spouses varied situationally. Couples tended not to confront problems between themselves, but they would discuss problems regarding the children. Agbayani-Siewert (1991) suggested that as couples become more assimilated and have fewer sources of support, conventional styles of communication may be less effective. Homma-True (1990) suggested that family therapy may be an effective intervention for adjusting to changes in gender expectations and general social stress.

Within families, conflict may arise over value differences, which create generation gaps between Asian parents and Asian American children (Nguyen, 1992; Shon & Ja, 1982). Homma-True (1991) found that mothers bear the brunt of much of this conflict because, throughout their child's lifetime, the mother adjusts to the child's wish to move toward the American middle-class values of autonomy and independence, and she tries to instill the closeness and dependency that have value in Asian families (Bradshaw, 1990). These conflicts are particularly intense between immigrant generations and their children raised in America (Nguyen, 1992). However, Lui (1990) noted that despite changes in child-rearing practices, there are still distinctions in some of the child-rearing practices of Asian American women compared with White women—several generations later. Thus, despite the acquisition of many mainstream values, many culturally derived values persist, although perhaps in evolved, adaptive forms.

Whereas in traditional families it has been assumed that elderly parents will be cared for by their children (Shon & Ja, 1982), value conflicts are increasingly apparent regarding this responsibility. Like women in many cultures, Asian American women have still been socialized to put family first; in the philosophy of operating more from a collective philosophy than an individualistic one, not only is caretaking of elderly parents assumed, not to do it would violate implicit or explicit role expectations. Mar (personal communication, 1991) noted that caretaking of elderly parents has become an issue, particularly because most Asian American women work. Additionally, fewer daughters live close to their parents.

Most recently, a new family constellation has evolved, and distress has arisen over immigrating Hong Kong families in which the wives and children reside in America and the husband frequently travels between countries. These men have been called "astronauts" because of the frequency and distance of travel. Subsequently, many of these women have been thrust into roles of essentially heading up the household, making unilateral decisions, disciplining the children, and acquainting themselves with American culture. When husbands return home, their wives have changed and conflicts ensue over role expectations and conflicts.

General Mental Health

Perhaps one of the widest assertions about the expression of emotional distress among Asians is the tendency to somatize psychological problems and view this as pathological. This is a very ethnocentric view of health. Rozee and van Boemel (1989) stated "somatization is probably a universal phenomenon with varying degrees of acceptability in different cultures, and that an understanding of the client's cultural background may help us to understand the significance and meaning of the symptom" (p. 36).

Psychotherapy is not among the first interventions sought for emotional distress by most Asian Americans because it does not make sense (Chao, 1992; Loo & Ong, 1982). There are several reasons for this, including fear of bringing shame on one's family, conceptualization of problems in ways that would not lead to seeking psychotherapy, language barriers, scheduling conflicts, and some degree of fatalism (Root, 1985). Finally, formalized psychotherapy is a European invention that splits mind and body.

Many immigrants and refugees have their own beliefs about who and what can help them that are consistent with their personal theories about the origins of their distress. Even when a problem might be conceptualized psychologically, Ying (1990) found that Chinese Americans turned to themselves, family, and friends for assistance. Immigrant Chinese Americans who conceptualized their distress along a physical dimension sought medical assistance. That immigrant women in Ying's sample tended toward relational strategies to address problems of a psychological nature is not aberrant but likely to be grounded in the explanatory model of illness (Kleinman, 1980). Given that "harmony in one's relationships as well as within onself (e.g., balance of mind and body) are paramount in the (mental) health of the Chinese person" (Ying, 1990, p. 394), it makes sense that the solution sought is relational in nature.

Besides this pattern of help seeking being culturally consistent for many Asian American groups, it may also be a protective strategy. Many refugees distrust seeking help from government agencies because of the government's role in the past war traumas they sustained in their country of origin (Chao, 1992; Rozee & van Boemel, 1989).

When some of these obstacles are removed, Asian Americans do seek mental health services (Homma-True, 1990). Homma-True found that approximately half of the clients using San Francisco Bay area public mental health services were Asian American women. And, like studies of American women in general, these women seem to struggle with depression moreso than Asian American men. She attributed these differences largely to role strain, the stress of living biculturally and unappreciated in both cultures, and often denying one's needs. Risk factors for depression such as low self-esteem, devalued social status, and poverty are simultaneously relevant variables describing much, but not all, of Asian America, and particularly Asian American women. On the other hand, women had lower rates of schizophrenia than did Asian American men based on service utilization. Homma-True (1991) suggested the possibility that Schizophrenia and psychotic disorders may impinge on men's ability to work within their gender role proscriptions moreso than women, which would subsequently bring them to the attention of the mental health service systems.

Fujino and Chung (1991) suggested that despite the information about the presence or absence of certain forms of distress in the Asian American population, the rates do not speak to the origins of the distress (e.g., "biological underpinnings," "differential access to structural power," and "diagnostic system biases"; p. 3). Using Los Angeles County Department of Mental Health records comparing rates of mental disorders for Asian Americans, African Americans, Latinos, and Whites, their results were similar to Homma-True's (1989) findings by gender using San Francisco County mental health data. There were no gender differences for Asian Americans for depression. However, Asian American men had higher rates of depression than men in other ethnic groups. Asians and African Americans had higher rates of schizophrenia across gender; men had higher rates across groups than women. The first observation might be attributable to error variance in help-seeking behavior and the second observation to the fact that more schizophrenic men than women use the public mental health system for various reasons. Asian American women had significantly more adjustment disorders than did Asian American men, but they were not significantly different from other groups of women.

Several studies have documented that there are psychosocial stressors particularly faced by immigrants and refugees (Chao, 1992; Gong-Guy, 1987; Felsman, Leong, Johnson, Felsman, 1990; Leong & Johnson, 1992; Tien, 1994) that increase their risk for continued psychological distress and need for mental health services after they have fled their countries. Depression among women appears to be particularly salient in some reports, whether on the West Coast (Homma-True, 1989) or East Coast (Yu, Liu, & Wong, 1987). However, if SES or birth place and length of residence in the United States are controlled for, the differences between genders disappears in a San Francisco immigrant Chinese sample (Ying, 1988). In this same study, if SES is controlled for and education and occupation are allowed to vary, age is correlated with depression, with younger respondents reporting more depressive symptoms.

Immigration poses many stresses to immigrant women, who may have less support and help from extended family who are not present, may feel alienated by customs of interaction, and feel constrained in the environment for language, social, or knowledge of resources (Homma-True, 1991). As discussed earlier, many women work in the United States, which upsets traditional gender role proscriptions, adding to the immigrants' stress. Furthermore, immigrant women and men may end up taking lower status and lower paying jobs because certification or credentialing procedures in this country differ from their country of origin. This lends itself to depression, low self-esteem, and alienation even from oneself.

Mental health concerns are particularly salient for Southeast Asian refugees, Vietnamese, Laotian, and Khmer (Cambodian), who have migrated involuntarily, have not necessarily preferred to reside in the United

States and have most likely sustained a significant number of war atrocities (Kinzie, Fredrickson, Ben, Fleck, & Karls, 1984). (Again, not all people from these countries are refugees, and this term is a political status reserved for the groups who have fled persecution and have not had time to psychologically prepare to leave as emigrants do; Tien, 1994.) Powerlessness, grief, displacement, separation from larger family networks, and loss of status from country of origin predict high rates of psychological distress. Felsman et al. (1990) emphasized that resettlement involves four phases in which traumas unique to these phases might be sustained: politically based trauma in home country, fleeing, refugee camp experience, and postarrival. Many refugees are still adolescents experiencing distress (Chao, 1992); the mothers of these adolescents are distressed themselves and are unable to provide the psychological caregiving their children might need because they themselves are traumatized (Leong & Johnson, 1992).

In addition to the war atrocities witnessed and experienced by both genders, a significant number of the women witnessed the murder, rape and torture of their spouses, children, and other family members. Rozee and van Boemel's (1989) study of female Cambodian refugees documented that 90% of the participants had lost 1–10 relatives, many of the deaths they witnessed. Tien (1994) suggested that if one is treating a Southeast Asian woman who came to the United States as a refugee, assume that she at least witnessed murder. She also pointed out the diversity in experiences by group and by date of flight from the country of origin. For example, the Vietnamese women who left before 1975 tended to have money and did not go through the resettlement camp experience.

Chung (1991) used data from one of the first statewide needs assessment studies that used a nonclinical, representative sample to study the well-being of Southeast Asian refugees in California. These differences between groups and by gender were explained by pre- and postmigration variables, such that Cambodians were the most distressed group, followed by Lao and Vietnamese, with the women in all groups more distressed than the men. Chung explained these results as follows: Cambodians reported more and multiple traumas compared with the other two groups, the women more than the men had lost their partners and other family members; Cambodians had resided in camps much longer than the other groups, and Vietnamese the least. Cambodian and Laotian women had less facility with English, and the decision to leave their country was more frequently made by someone else. Cambodian and Laotian women, compared with Vietnamese women, tended to be unemployed (this likely contributed to anxiety when many of these women were the main wage earners), and had low family income. Cambodian men and women did not show gender differences on postmigration variables because they were still concerned with premigration issues, having been in the United States a shorter time than people from either of the other two groups. Across groups and gender, the premigration trauma experiences were a consistent predictor of distress, as measured by depression and anxiety; in general, men's distress, more than women's, could be predicted in part by postmigration issues that involved employment and income. Kinzie et al. (1984) noted that 1–4 million people died under the Khmer Rouge regime from 1974–1979.

SUMMARY

The question of what defines Asian American and Asian American identity is currently being studied in Asian American studies and in psychology. It is no longer as simple as defining Asian American by the country of origin or traditions that are practiced in the home. Asian Americans are not a single "race," nor are they uniformly of patriarchal custom. Today, several different generations of Asian American women represent different religions, values, and orientations toward family and society (Bradshaw, 1994).

No single characterization exists to portray the Asian American woman. This may be a particularly important finding because a generation ago, it might have been easier to point out very salient similarities among Asian American women. Even then, Asian American women were complex, perhaps with less discrepancy between public- and private-life roles than Asian American women experience now. Perhaps the largest single change in defining the Asian American woman from even 20 years ago is that she is less defined by the men she is in relationship to (i.e., her father, her partner, and her sons) or by traditional familial roles.

The increasing size and variability of Asian America underscores the importance of studying the differential impact that specific cultural and political legacies exert on behavior, identity, and mental health. Researchers must study the differences between Asian American groups to understand the origins of behavior, attitudes, and mental health. Furthermore, the consideration of specific political and cultural legacies must become the domain of psychology if psychologists are to move away from stereotypes to understand the psychology of the Asian American woman in context. Declaring and knowing oneself as an Asian American woman requires knowing one's personal, familial, and ethnic histories that connect the past with the present.

REFERENCES

Adams, R. (1937). Chinese familialism and interracial marriage. In R. Adams (Ed.), *Interracial marriage in Hawaii*. New York: Macmillan.

Agbayani-Siewert, P. (1991). *Filipino American social role strain, self-esteem, locus of control, social networks, coping, stress and mental health outcome.* Unpublished doctoral dissertation, University of California, Los Angeles.

Ahern, F. M., Cole, R. E., Johnson, R. C., & Wong, B. (1981). Personality attributes of males and females marrying within vs. across racial/ethnic groups. *Behavior Genetics, 11,* 181–194.

Allen, P. G. (1988). Who is your mother? Red roots of white feminism. In R. Simonson & S. Walker (Eds.), *The Graywolf annual five: Multicultural literacy.* Saint Paul, MN: Graywolf Press.

Asian Women United of California. (1989). *Making waves: An anthology of writings by and about Asian American women.* Boston: Beacon Press.

Bradshaw, C. (1990). A Japanese view of dependency: What can amae psychology contribute to feminist theory and therapy? In L. S. Brown & M. P. P. Root (Eds.), *Diversity and complexity in feminist therapy* (pp. 67–86). New York: Haworth Press.

Bradshaw, C. (1994). Asian American women. In L. Comas Díaz & B. Greene (Eds.), *Women of color: Integrating ethnic and gender identities in psychotherapy* (pp. 72–113). New York: Guilford Press.

Card, J. (1978). Correspondence of data gathered from husband and wife: Implications for family planning studies. *Social Biology, 25,* 196–204.

Carino, B. V., Fawcett, J. T., Gardner, R. W., & Arnold, F. (1990). *The new Filipino immigrants to the United States: Increasing diversity and change* (No. 15). Honolulu, HI: East-West Population Institute.

Chan, C. S. (1985). Self-esteem and body-image of Asian American adolescent girls. *Journal of the Asian American Psychological Association, 4,* 24–25.

Chan, C. S. (1987a). Asian-American women: Psychological responses to sexual exploitation and cultural stereotypes. *Asian American Psychological Association Journal,* 11–15.

Chan, C. S. (1987b). Asian lesbians: Psychological issues in the "coming out" process. *Asian American Psychological Association Journal,* 16–18.

Chan, C. S. (1994). Asian American adolescents: Issues of sexuality. In J. Irvine (Ed.), *Sexual cultures: Adolescence, communities, and the constructions of identities* (pp. 88–99). Philadelphia: Temple University Press.

Chan, S. (1991). *Asian Americans: An interpretive history.* Boston: Twayne.

Chao, C. M. (1992). The inner heart: Therapy with Southeast Asian families (pp. 157–181). In L. A. Vargas & J. D. Koss-Chioino (Eds.), *Working with culture: Psychotherapeutic interventions with ethnic minority children and adolescents.* San Francisco: Jossey-Bass.

Chao, C. A. (in press). A bridge over troubled waters: Being Eurasian in the U.S. of A. In J. Adleman & G. Enguidanos-Clark (Eds.), *Racism in the lives of women: Testimony, theory, and guides to antiracist practice* (pp. 33–43). New York: Haworth Press.

Chen, M. Y. (1976). Teaching a course on Asian American women. In E. Gee (Ed.), *Counterpoint* (pp. 234–239). Los Angeles: University of California Asian American Students Center.

Chew, K., Eggebeen, D., & Uhlenberg, P. (1989). American children in multiracial households. *Sociological Perspectives, 32,* 65–85.

Chow, E. N.-L. (1989). The feminist movement: Where are all the Asian American women? In Asian Women United of California (Eds.), *Making waves: An anthology of writings by and about Asian American women* (pp. 362–377). Boston: Beacon Press.

Chu, J. (1986). Asian American women's studies courses: A look back at our beginnings. *Frontiers, 8,* 96–101.

Chu, J. (1988). Social and economic profile of Asian Pacific American women: Los Angeles County. In G. Y. Okihiro, S. Hune, A. A. Hansen, & J. M. Liu (Eds.), *Reflections on shattered windows: Promises and prospects for Asian American studies* (pp. 193–205). Pullman: Washington State University Press.

Chung, R. C. (1991, August). *Predictors of distress among Southeast Asian refugees: Group and gender differences.* Paper presented at the Asian American Psychological Association Conference, San Francisco.

Cochran, S., Mays, V., & Leung, L. (1991). Sexual practices of heterosexual Asian-American young adults: Implications for risk of HIV infection. *Archives of Sexual Behavior, 20,* 381–391.

Felsman, J. K., Johnson, M. C., Leong, F. T. L., & Felsman, I. C. (1989). *Vietnamese Amerasians: Practical implications of current research.* Washington, DC: U.S. Department of Health and Human Services, Office of Refugee Resettlement.

Felsman, J. K., Leong, F. T. L., Johnson, M. C., & Felsman, I. C. (1990). Estimates of psychological distress among Vietnamese refugees: Adolescents, unaccompanied minors and young adults. *Social Science Medicine, 31,* 1251–1256.

Fong, K. M. (1978, Winter). Feminism is fine, but what's it done for Asia America? *Bridge: An Asian American perspective.* Winter, 21–22.

Fujino, D. (1992). *Extending exchange theory: Effects of ethnicity and gender on Asian American heterosexual relationships.* Doctoral dissertation, University of California, Los Angeles.

Fujino, D. (1993, August). *Cultural standards of beauty, power, and interracial relationships.* Paper presented at the Annual Asian American Psychological Association Convention, Toronto, Ontario, Canada.

Fujino, D. C., & Chung, R. C.-Y. (1991, August). *Asian American mental health: An examination of gender issues.* Paper presented at the Asian American Psychological Association Convention, San Francisco.

Fujitomi, I., & Wong, D. (1973). The New Asian-American woman. In S. Sue & N. N. Wagner (Eds.), *Asian Americans: Psychological perspectives* (pp. 252–263). Ben Lomond, CA: Science and Behavior Books.

Gee, E. (Ed.). (1976). *Counterpoint: Perspectives on Asian America.* Los Angeles: University of California, Asian American Studies Center.

Gidra. (1971, January). Women's issue.

Glenn, E. N. (1991). The dialectics of wage work: Japanese-American women and domestic service, 1905–1940. In C. DuBois & V. L. Ruiz (Eds.), *Unequal sisters: A multicultural reader in U.S. women's history* (pp. 345–372). New York: Routledge & Kegan Paul.

Gong-Guy, E. (1987). *The California Southeast Asian Mental Health Needs Assessment.* Oakland, CA: Asian Community Mental Health Services.

Grove, K. J. (1991). Identity development in interracial, Asian/White late adolescents: Must it be so problematic? *Journal of Youth and Adolescence, 20,* 617–628.

H., P. (1989). Asian American lesbians: An emerging voice in the Asian American community. In Asian Women United of California (Eds.), *Making waves: An anthology of writings by and about Asian American women* (pp. 282–290). Boston: Beacon Press.

Hall, C. I. (1992). Please choose one: Ethnic identity choices for biracial individuals. In M. P. P. Root (Ed.), *Racially mixed people in America* (pp. 239–249). Newbury Park, CA: Sage.

Hall, C. I. (in press). Asian eyes: Body image and eating disorders of Asian American women. *Eating Disorders: Journal of Prevention and Treatment.*

Hirayama, H., & Hirayama, K. (1986). The sexuality of Japanese Americans. *Journal of Social Work and Human Sexuality, 4,* 81–98.

Ho, C. K. (1990). An analysis of domestic violence in Asian American communities: A multicultural approach to counseling. In L. Brown & M. P. P. Root (Eds.), *Diversity and complexity in feminist therapy* (pp. 129–150). New York: Haworth Press.

Ho, C. K. (in press). Wife abuse in Asian America. In L. C. Lee & N. Zane (Ed.), *Handbook of Asian American mental health.* Newbury Park, CA: Sage.

Ho, F. C., & Johnson, R. C. (1990). Intraethnic and interethnic marriage and divorce in Hawaii. *Social Biology, 37,* 44–51.

Ho, M. K. (1984). *Building a successful intermarriage.* St. Meinrad, IN: St. Meinrad Archabbey.

Homma-True, R. (1987, August). *Psychotherapeutic issues with Asian American women.* Paper presented at the annual convention of the Asian American Psychological Association, New York.

Homma-True, R. (1989, August). *Mental health service utilization by Asian American women in San Francisco.* Paper presented at the annual convention of the Asian American Psychological Association, New York.

Homma-True, R. (1990). Psychotherapeutic issues with Asian American women. *Sex Roles, 22,* 477–486.

Homma-True, R. (1991, August). *Psychological impact of immigration on Asian women.* Paper presented at the 99th Annual Convention of the American Psychological Association, San Francisco.

Ichioka, Y. (1977). Ameyuki-san: Japanese prostitutes in nineteenth-century America. *Amerasia Journal, 4,* 1–21.

Ima, K., & Hohm, C. F. (1991). Child maltreatment among Asian and Pacific Islander refugees and immigrants: The San Diego case. *Journal of Interpersonal Violence, 6,* 267–285.

Japanese American Citizen's League. (1985). *Mail order Asian Women catalogues.* Los Angeles: Author.

Jedlicka, D. (1975). *Ethnic serial marriage in Hawaii: Application of a sequential preference pattern.* Doctoral dissertation, University of Hawaii, Honolulu, Hawaii.

Johnson, R. C., & Nagoshi, C. T. (1990). *Intergroup marriage in Hawaii.* Unpublished manuscript.

Kanuha, V. (1990). Compounding the triple jeopardy: Battering in lesbian of color relationships. In L. S. Brown & M. P. P. Root (Eds.), *Diversity and complexity in feminist therapy* (pp. 169–184). New York: Haworth Press.

Kaw, E. (1993). Medicalization of racial features: Asian American women and cosmetic surgery. *Medical Anthropology Quarterly, 7,* 74–89.

Kich, G. K. (1992). The developmental process of asserting a biracial, bicultural identity. In M. P. P. Root (Ed.), *Racially mixed people in America* (pp. 304–320). Newbury Park, CA: Sage.

Kim, B.-L. C. (1977). Asian wives of U.S. servicemen: Women in shadows. *Amerasia, 4,* 91–115.

Kim, E. H., & Otani, J. (1983). *With silk wings: Asian American women at work.* Oakland: Asian Women United of California.

Kinzie, J. D., Fredrickson, R. H., Ben, R., Fleck, J., & Karls, W. (1984). Posttraumatic stress disorder among survivors of Cambodian concentration camps. *American Journal of Psychiatry, 141,* 645–650.

Kitano, H. L. L., & Fujino, D. (in press). Interracial marriage: Where are the Asian Americans and where are they going? In L. C. Lee & N. Zane (Eds.). *Handbook of Asian American mental health.* Newbury Park, CA: Sage.

Kitano, H., Yeung, W.-T., Chai, L., & Hatanaka, H. (1984). Asian American interracial marriage. *Journal of Marriage and the Family, 46,* 179–190.

Kleinman, A. M. (1980). *Patients and healers in the context of culture: An exploration of the borderland between anthropology, medicine and psychiatry.* Berkeley: University of California Press.

Kono, J. S., & Song, C. (Ed.). (1991). *Sister stew.* Honolulu, HI: Bamboo Ridge Press.

Lee, J. F. J. (1991). *Asian American experiences in the United States: Oral histories of first to fourth generation Americans from China, the Philippines, Japan, India, the Pacific Islands, Vietnam and Cambodia.* Jefferson, NC: McFarland & Company.

Lee, L. C. (Ed.). (1992). *Asian Americans: Collages of identities* (Monograph No. 1). Ithaca, NY: Cornell University, Asian American Studies.

Leonetti, D. L., & Newell-Morris, L. (1982). Exogamy and change in the biosocial structure of a modern urban population. *American Anthropologist, 84,* 19–36.

Leong, F. T. L., & Johnson, M. C. (1992). *Vietnamese Amerasian mothers: Psychological distress and high-risk factors.* Washington, DC: Department of Health and Human Services, Office of Refugee Resettlement.

Lin, J. (1991). *Marital satisfaction and conflict in intercultural correspondence marriage.* Doctoral dissertation, University of Washington, Seattle.

Loo, C. (1988). The "middle-aging" of Asian American studies. In G. Y. Okihiro, S. Hune, A. A. Hansen, & J. M. Liu (Eds.), *Reflections on shattered windows: Promises and prospects for Asian American studies* (pp. 16–23). Pullman: Washington State University Press.

Loo, C. (1991). *Most time, hard time Chinatown.* New York: Praeger.

Loo, C., & Ong, P. (1982). Slaying demons with a sewing needle: Feminist issues for Chinatown women. *Berkeley Journal of Sociology, 27,* 77–88.

Lubben, J. E., Chi, I., & Kitano, H. (1989). The relative influence of selected social factors on Korean drinking behavior in Los Angeles. *Advances in Alcohol and Substance Abuse, 8,* 1–17.

Lui, B. (1990). *Asian American childrearing practices and acculturation: A cross-cultural examination.* Doctoral dissertation, University of Washington, Seattle, WA.

Luu, V. (1989). The hardships of escape for Vietnamese women. In Asian Women United of California (Eds.), *Making waves: An anthology of writings by and about Asian American Women* (pp. 60–72). Boston: Beacon Press.

Mass, A. I. (1992). Interracial Japanese Americans: The best of both worlds or the end of the Japanese American community? In M. P. P. Root (Ed.), *Racially mixed people in America* (pp. 265–279). Newbury Park, CA: Sage.

Miller, R. L. (1992). The human ecology of multiracial identity. In M. P. P. Root (Ed.), *Racially mixed people in America* (pp. 24–36). Newbury Park, CA: Sage.

Miller, R. L., & Miller, B. (1990). Mothering the biracial child: Bridging the gaps between African-American and White parenting styles. *Women and Therapy, 10,* 169–180.

Mollica, R., Wyshak, G., & Lavelle, J. (1987). The psychological impact of war trauma and torture on Southeast Asian refugees. *American Journal of Psychiatry, 144,* 1567–1571.

Murphy-Shigematsu, S. (1988). Addressing issues of biracial/bicultural Asian Americans. In G. Y. Okihiro, S. Hune, A. A. Hansen, & J. M. Liu (Eds.), *Reflections on shattered windows: Promises and prospects for Asian American studies* (pp. 111–116). Pullman: Washington State University Press.

Nagata, D. K. (in press). Understanding the training experiences of Asian-American women. In J. Adleman & G. Enguidanos-Clark (Eds.), *Racism in the lives of women: Testimony, theory, and guides to antiracist practice.* New York: Haworth Press.

Nakashima, C. L. (1988). Research notes on Nikkei Happa identity. In G. Y. Okihiro, S. Hune, A. A. Hansen, & J. M. Liu (Eds.), *Reflection on shattered windows: Promises and prospects for Asian American studies* (pp. 206–213). Pullman: Washington State University Press.

Nakashima, C. L. (1992). An invisible monster: The creation and denial of mixed-race people in America. In M. P. P. Root (Ed.), *Racially mixed people in America* (pp. 162–178). Newbury Park, CA: Sage.

Nguyen, N. A. (1992). Living between two cultures: Treating first-generation Asian Americans. In L. A. Vargas and J. D. Koss-Chioino (Eds.), *Working with culture: Psychotherapeutic interventions with ethnic minority children and adolescents* (pp. 204–224). San Francisco: Jossey-Bass.

Omi, M. (1988). It just ain't the sixties no more: The contemporary dilemmas of Asian American studies. In G. Y. Okihiro, S. Hune, A. A. Hansen, & J. M. Liu (Eds.), *Reflections on shattered windows: Promises and prospects for Asian American studies* (pp. 31–36). Pullman: Washington State University Press.

Omi, M. (1992). Elegant chaos: Postmodern Asian American Identity. In L. C. Lee (Ed.), Asian Americans: Collages of identities (pp. 143–154). Ithaca, NY: Cornell University.

Rimonte, N. (1989). Domestic violence among Pacific Asians. In Asian Women United (Eds.), *Making waves: An anthology of writings by and about Asian American women* (pp. 327–337). Boston: Beacon Press.

Root, M. P. P. (1985). Guidelines for facilitating therapy with Asian American Clients. *Psychotherapy: Theory, Research, and Practice, 22,* 349–356.

Root, M. P. P. (1990a). Disordered eating in women of color. *Sex Roles, 22,* 525–536.

Root, M. P. P. (1990b). Resolving "other" status: Biracial identity development. In L. Brown & M. P. P. Root (Eds.), *Complexity and diversity in feminist theory and therapy* (pp. 191–211). New York: Haworth Press.

Root, M. P. P. (Ed.). (1992a). *Racially mixed people in America.* Newbury Park, CA: Sage.

Root, M. P. P. (1992b). Loyalty, rootedness and belonging: The quest for defining Asian American identity. In L. C. Lee (Ed.), *Asian Americans: Collages of identities* (Monograph No. 1). Ithaca, NY: Cornell University, Asian American Studies.

Root, M. P. P. (1994). Mixed race women. In L. Comas Díaz & B. Greene (Eds.), *Women of color: Integrating ethnic and gender identities in psychotherapy* (pp. 455–478). New York: Guilford Press.

Root, M. P. P. (in press-a). Amerasians and the evolving face of the Asian American community. In L. C. Lee & N. Zane (Ed.), *Handbook of Asian American psychology.* Newbury Park, CA: Sage.

Root, M. P. P. (Ed.). (in press-b). *Racially mixed people in the new millenium.* Newbury Park: Sage.

Rozee, P. D., & van Boemel, G. (1989). The psychological effects of war trauma and abuse on older Cambodian refugee women. *Women and Therapy, 8,* 23–50.

Santos, R. A. (1983). The social and emotional development of Filipino-American children. In G. J. Powell, J. Yamamoto, A. Romero, & A. Morales (Eds.),

The psychosocial development of minority group children (pp. 131–146). New York: Brunner/Mazel.

Serita, T. (1984). Mail order sexploitation. *Bridge, 9,* 39–41.

Shon, S. P., & Ja, D. (1982). Asian families. In M. McGoldrick, J. K. Pearce, & J. Giordano (Eds.), *Ethnicity and family therapy* (pp. 208–228). New York: Guilford Press.

Song, Y. (1994). *Battered women in Korean immigrant families.* Hamden, CT: Garland.

Stephan, C. W. (1992). Mixed-heritage individuals: Ethnic identity and trait characteristics. In M. P. P. Root (Ed.), *Racially mixed people in America* (pp. 50–63). Newbury Park, CA: Sage.

Sue, S., Zane, N., & Ito, J. (1979). Alcohol drinking patterns among Asian and Caucasian Americans. *Journal of Cross-Cultural Psychology, 10,* 41–56.

Sun, A.-P. (1991). Issues for Asian American women. In P. Roth (Ed.), *Alcohol and drugs are women's issues* (Vol. 1, pp. 125–129). Metuchen, MJ: Women's Action Alliance/Scarecrow Press.

Sung, B. L. (1990). *Chinese American intermarriage.* New York: Center for Migration Studies.

Tajima, R. E. (1989). Lotus blossoms don't bleed: Images of Asian women. In Asian Women United of California (Eds.), *Making waves: An anthology of writings by and about Asian American women* (pp. 308–317). Boston: Beacon Press.

Takagi, D. Y. (1988). Personality and history: Hostile Nisei women. In G. Y. Okihiro, S. Hune, A. A. Hansen, & J. M. Liu (Eds.), *Reflections on shattered windows: Promises and prospects for Asian American studies* (pp. 184–192). Pullman: Washington State University Press.

Thornton, M. C. (1983). *A social history of a multiethnic identity: The case of black Japanese Americans.* Unpublished doctoral dissertation, University of Michigan, Ann Arbor.

Thornton, M. C. (1992a). The quiet immigration: Foreign spouses of U.S. citizens, 1945–1985. In M. P. P. Root (Ed.), *Racially mixed people in America* (pp. 64–76). Newbury Park, CA: Sage.

Thornton, M. C. (1992b). Finding a way home: Race, nation and sex in (Asian) American identity. In L. C. Lee (Ed.), *Asian Americans: Collages of identities* (Monograph No. 1). Ithaca, NY: Cornell University, Asian American Studies.

Tien, L. (1994). Southeast Asian women. In L. Comas Díaz & B. Greene (Eds.), *Women of color: Integrating ethnic and gender identities in psychotherapy* (pp. 479–503). New York: Guilford Press.

Tien, L., & Hunthausen, D. (1990). The Vietnamese Amerasian resettlement experience: From initial application to the first six months in the United States. In K. Tal (Ed.), *Vietnam generation* (pp. 16–30). Silver Spring, MD: Vietnam Generations.

Tsui, A. M. (1985). Psychotherapeutic considerations in sexual counseling for Asian immigrants. *Psychotherapy: Theory, Research, and Practice, 22,* 357–362.

Valverde, K. C. (1992). From dust to gold: The Vietnamese Amerasian experience. In M. P. P. Root (Ed.), *Racially mixed people in America* (pp. 144–161). Newbury Park, CA: Sage.

Villapando, V. (1989). The business of selling mail-order brides. In Asian Women United (Eds.), *Making waves: An anthology of writings by and about Asian American women* (pp. 318–326). Boston: Beacon Press.

Watanabe, S., & Bruchac, C. (Ed.). (1990). *Home to stay: Asian American women's fiction.* Greenfield Center, NY: Greenfield Review Press.

Williams, T. K. (1992). Prism lives: Identity of binational Amerasians. In M. P. P. Root (Ed.), *Racially mixed people in America* (pp. 280–303). Newbury Park, CA: Sage.

Yi, K. Y. (1989). *Symptoms of eating disorders among Asian-American college female students as a function of acculturation.* Unpublished doctoral dissertation, California School of Professional Psychology, Los Angeles.

Ying, Y. W. (1988). Depressive symptomatology among Chinese-Americans as measured by the CES-D. *Journal of Clinical Psychology, 44,* 739–746.

Ying, Y. W. (1990). Explanatory models of major depression and implications for help-seeking among immigrant Chinese-American women. *Culture, Medicine, and Psychiatry, 14,* 393–408.

Ying, Y. W. (1991). Marital satisfaction among San Francisco Chinese-Americans. *International Journal of Social Psychiatry, 37,* 201–213.

Yoshimura, K. K (1992). *Acculturative and sociocultural influences on the development of eating disorders in Asian-American females.* Unpublished doctoral dissertation, California School of Professional Psychology, Los Angeles.

Yu, W. S. H., Liu, W. T., & Wong, S. C. (1987). Measurement of depression in a Chinatown health clinic. In W. T. Liu (Ed.), *A decade review of mental health research, training, and services.* Chicago: Pacific/Asian American Mental Health Research Center, University of Illinois.

Yung, J. (1991). The social awakening of Chinese American women as reported in *Chung Sai Yat Po,* 1900–1911. In C. DuBois & V. L. Ruiz (Eds.), *Unequal sisters: A multicultural reader in U.S. women's history* (pp. 195–207). New York: Routledge & Kegan Paul.

13

PSYCHOLOGY OF BLACK WOMEN: PAST, PRESENT, AND FUTURE

VERONICA G. THOMAS and SHARI E. MILES

In this chapter we critically examine the study of Black women in the field of psychology, as well as Black women as psychologists, in terms of where they have been, where they are, and where they are going. Various theoretical, methodological, and practical concerns are highlighted with the goal of offering recommendations for further development.

A number of factors inhibit scholarship in the psychology of Black women. These range from too few Black female psychologists available to challenge and expand existing knowledge to a sociopolitical climate that continues to ignore or devalue the study of Black women. Despite these obstacles, some scholars within psychology continue to ask new questions, formulate and test new (and old) hypotheses, and develop alternative perspectives. These researchers recognize that there are some universalities in women's experiences irrespective of race and social class. Simultaneously, they emphasize that the social and economic conditions under which Black women live facilitate significant differences from their White female counterparts. Black women also share some commonalities with Black men, yet Black women have unique experiences related to the interaction of their race and gender. Description and explanation of the complexity of this diversity within a contextual and interactive framework are the essence of the psychology of Black women.

HISTORICAL PERSPECTIVES

In the late 1960s, a group of female psychologists critically examined the field of psychology and challenged the validity of nearly every aspect of the field, from conceptual issues and models of intervention and treatment to specific research methodologies. As an outgrowth of their efforts and the work of their many successors, a new research area, "the psychology of women," emerged. During the 1970s, various institutional changes occurred that reflected the underlying philosophy of the new field. These changes included the establishment of the Association for Women in Psychology in 1969 and of a new division (Division 35, Psychology of Women) of the American Psychological Association (APA) in 1973. Consequently, psychology was radically transformed from a profession that, in Naomi Weisstein's words (cited in Walsh, 1987), "had nothing to say about women to one that has a great deal to say" (p. 4). To date, feminist scholars have taken the discipline to new levels of theory and research about women. And, at the core of the philosophy of the psychology of women has been the dilemma of combining feminism—a value orientation with action implications—with the tradition of psychology as an empirical science striving for objectivity and value neutrality (Peplau & Conrad, 1989).

Parallel with a critical look at the field by feminist psychologists in the late 1960s and early 1970s, many Black scholars proposed the development of a "Black psychology." These scholars believed that the racism inherent in Western psychological models fostered a need for the creation of an area that would be methodologically sound yet sensitive to and supportive of the cultural and adaptive experiences of Black people. Thus, the major objective of the Association of Black Psychologists (ABPsi), established in 1968, was the eradication of myths regarding the psychological reality of Black people, the countering of negative images and formulations about Black people, and the reversal of the severe underrepresentation of and exclusion of Black individuals from the field of psychology.

On the whole, the psychological realities and impact of the victimization of Black women by both sexist and racist forms of oppression were essentially ignored by both Black psychology and, to a slightly lesser degree, by the psychology of women. hooks (1981) noted that "no other group in America has had their identity so socialized out of existence as Black women" (p. 7). It is often mistakenly taken for granted, according to King (1988), that being Black and a female does not differ from being "generically" Black (i.e., male) or "generically" a woman (i.e., White). Within this context, some Black female psychologists have taken a serious look at the psychology of women and at Black psychology to determine their relevance to Black women.

Black Women's Perspectives Within the Psychology of Women

Many of the criticisms that White feminist psychologists lodged against the discipline in the 1960s and 1970s are still being raised by Black female psychologists. Most prominent among these is the paucity of theoretical and empirical work devoted to Black women. On the basis of a review of psychology of women textbooks, A. Brown, Goodwin, Hall, and Jackson-Lowman (1985) concluded that these texts most often made either token or no references to Black women. In addition, a survey of instructors of psychology of women courses revealed that the average instructor gave herself a rating of only "moderate" on the item regarding the extent to which she presented materials on Women of Color in their courses; one Black instructor stated explicitly that she "has to stretch to find material (on minority women) . . . so I all too often have to generalize from my experience, unfortunately" (Matlin, 1989). Reid and Kelly (1994) pointed out that research paradigms directed at the study of the "universal woman" have in actuality focused on White middle-class populations and, thus, researchers must break from the mainstream paradigms in order to invest the study of women with a sense of cultural diversity.

Various scholars (e.g., Hare-Mustin & Marecek, 1988; Kahn & Yoder, 1989; M. S. Mednick, 1991) argue that much of the research in the psychology of women has examined women and men without regard to the social, historical, and political contexts surrounding gender. This observation is particularly relevant to Black women. King (1988) depicted Black women as conceptually invisible, interpersonally misunderstood and insulted, and strategically marginal. Black female psychologists often have found that the psychology of women denied significant aspects of their history and experiences such as enslavement, physical and mental abuse, economic marginality, and the chronic low social position of Black women within American society. Despite these concerns, many nonetheless continue their involvement in the field and emphasize the need for feminist psychology to integrate the often unique experiences of Black women into its theoretical frameworks. Only recently have enlightened White feminist psychologists acknowledged that when "Blacks" were studied, they were most often "Black men," and when "women" were studied, the women were invariably "White women." Hyde (1991), in the fourth edition of *Half of the Human Experience: The Psychology of Women*, pointed out that "we must confront a serious problem: much of the scholarship on the psychology of women is, in reality, a psychology of white middle-class American women" (p. 194). Other feminist psychologists (e.g., L. S. Brown,

1990; P. S. Reid, 1993; Yoder & Kahn, 1993) have suggested that the psychology of women is guilty of adopting a privileged White female norm.

A number of feminist psychologists within the APA embraced the notion of the need for more critical attention to the psychology of Black women. This developed from recognizing that human experience is complex, diverse, and significantly modified by social, historical, and political forces. Consequently, Martha Mednick, then president of Division 35 of the APA, appointed Saundra (Murray) Nettles to form the Task Force on Black Women's Concerns in 1976. This task force eventually evolved into a standing committee of Division 35. Members of this committee sought the evolution of a subspecialty of psychology that would increase scientific understanding of the roles of ethnicity, class, culture, and gender in the lives of Black women. Black feminist psychologists called for the development of methods of research and models and treatment and intervention that were ethnic, culture, and gender appropriate for Black women.

As an outgrowth of the Committee on Black Women's Concerns, a Section on the Psychology of Black Women was established. The goals of the Section were threefold: (a) to encourage theory, research, and practice that seeks an understanding of the psychology of Black women coupled with action implications for the elimination of sexism, racism, and classism; (b) to provide a structure enabling its members to better organize, promote, and advance the subspecialty of the psychology of Black women; and (c) to advocate policies and issues critical to the growth and survival of Black women in psychology. Its members are committed to understanding the interactive effects of racism and sexism in the psychology of Black women and to significantly affect the field of psychology in general and the psychology of women in particular.

Black Women's Perspectives Within Black Psychology

Within the parameters of Black psychology, there have been few critical analyses of the psychological impact of the dual stigmas of being a woman and being Black in a society that devalues both. Beale (1970) noted that there was no recognition of the fact that Black women suffer the burdens of racial prejudice, in addition to having to cope with White and Black men. More recently, P. T. Reid (1989) made reference to two texts that discuss the Black experience from a psychological perspective. She noted that issues related to gender were essentially excluded.

Black women's concerns that are distinct and separate from the general concerns of Black men have not been a priority in Black psychology. There may be four reasons for this. First, Blacks in general and Black men in particular historically have been leery of identification with "feminist" concerns. In the early years of the women's movement of the late 1960s, many White feminists defined the term *liberation* as access to the status and acquisitions of White men. Many Blacks perceived this as a desire to acquire positions in an establishment that supports racism. A 1979 *Newsweek* article noted that Black women and men tended to agree that their problems are rooted in racism; they did not agree, however, on the issues of sexism or the women's movement (Weathers, Camper, Smith, Russel, & Moore, cited in Schaffer, 1981). Thus, forming an alliance between Blacks and feminists was difficult, and, subsequently, an enrichment of each perspective by the other did not emerge for the psychology of women or for Black psychology.

Second, although both women and Blacks face discrimination and stereotyping that limit their access to prestige, power, and fulfillment of their potential, the "skin privilege" afforded White women has often served as a significant barrier that divided White feminists and Blacks. Although recognizing that women from various White ethnic groups have shared the consequences of exploitation by White men in American society, it is undeniable that White women's immediate experiences were not as victims of the extreme and brutal forms of racism that continue to play a major role in the lives of Blacks (Joseph & Lewis, 1981). Thus, many Black male psychologists refused to identify with "feminist" concerns even though the issues entailed were relevant to Black women. Moreover, it was generally felt that White women "could not" or "would not" offer any relief by addressing the causes and consequences of institutional racism.

In addition to these reasons, Black psychology also may have viewed a concentration on Black women's experiences as being too restrictive given the larger maze of issues that the area chose to place at the forefront of its agenda (e.g., the misuse of standardized psychological instruments to label Black youth; the inadequacies of clinical and counseling psychology training programs in terms of their relevance to social problems; and the underrepresentation of Black psychologists, Black graduate students, and Black students in undergraduate programs). Even most recently, it seems that Black psychology continues not to vigorously address theoretical and research issues concerning Black women at what may be perceived the expense of more general concerns affecting the larger Black population. This strategy is consistent with the philosophy of many Black scholars (i.e., to attack racism first and afterward consider what to do about the problem of sexism; Staples, 1981).

Furthermore, much of the work emanating from the discipline of Black psychology emphasizes collectivism and unity. In this view, addressing concerns of women may be perceived as divisive. Finally, Black psychology's failure to deal seriously with women's issues may simply reflect the view that Black women need only be considered as a reflection of Black men, thus being unworthy of serious empirical investigation apart from the study of Black men's world. In other words, just as psychology has overlooked the theoretical and empirical needs and perspectives of White women, Black psychology has responded similarly with regard to Black women.

CURRENT PERSPECTIVES

The current state of the psychology of Black women can be assessed by examining three indicators. First, because it is Black women who are taking the lead in theory and research about Black women, assessing their representation in the profession provides an important gauge. Second, data on the membership of Black women in the APA and the ABPsi are also significant because this cadre of Black women, through their various institutional networks, are the social and political advocates who voice Black women's concerns. Finally, because published research is the major vehicle through which psychological knowledge is shared, assessing the incidence of psychological research on or about Black women is another important indicator of the current state of the psychology of Black women.

Black Women in Psychology

The proportion of women in psychology has increased dramatically in the past 20 years, leading some to debate the consequences of the increasing "feminization of psychology" (e.g., Howard et al., 1986; Kendel, 1991; Walker, 1991). A report from the APA Committee on Employment and Human Resources (Howard et al., 1986) indicated that by 1984, certain subfields (e.g., clinical, counseling, and school psychology) experienced parity between men and women in terms of the number of PhDs. Data reported by the National Center of Education Statistics (NCES, 1994) indicated that in 1992, women earned 72.6% of the bachelor's degrees awarded in psychology, 70% of all master's degrees awarded in psychology, and 59.7% of all doctorate degrees awarded in psychology.

Black women's participation in psychology, however, has not increased substantially. Table 1 reveals that the percentage of Black women receiving bachelor's degrees in psychology has remained between 4.3% and 5.6% of total degrees awarded between 1977 and 1992. Master's degrees in psychology awarded to Black women increased slightly from 3.6% in 1977 to 3.7 in 1990 but dropped to 3.5% in 1991 and rose to 4.1% in 1992. Although the proportion of Black women earning doctorates in psychology rose slightly between 1977 and 1992 from 1.9% to 2.5%, there is still a paucity of PhDs awarded to Black women. Given that the Black female population is approximately 6.5% of the total U.S. population, the proportion of Black women earning graduate degrees in psychology is extraordinarily low. Although psychology is rapidly "changing its face" from a predominantly White male profession to one in which half of all doctorates

TABLE 1
Psychology Degrees Earned by Black Women: 1977–1991

Year	Bachelor's		Master's		Doctorate	
	n	% Total	n	% Total	n	% Total
1976–1977	2,124	4.5	300	3.6	53	1.9
1978–1979	2,164	5.1	301	3.8	61	2.3
1980–1981	2,268	5.6	260	3.3	54	1.8
1984–1985	1,916	4.8	280	3.3	62	2.1
1986–1987	1,852	4.3	275	3.4	64	2.1
1988–1989	2,154	4.4	288	3.4	73	2.2
1989–1990	2,451	4.1	342	3.7	78	2.3
1990–1991	2,883	4.9	341	3.5	82	2.4
1991–1992	2,890	4.9	416	4.1	82	2.5

Note. These data were taken from the *Digest of Education Statistics*, National Center for Education Statistics, U.S. Department of Education.

are awarded to White women, the continued scarcity of Black women in the discipline fosters a perception that Black women are outsiders.

Areas of Concentration of Black Women in Psychology

Between 1975 and 1984, the number of Blacks earning doctorates in clinical psychology more than doubled, and in counseling psychology it more than quadrupled. Simultaneously, the traditional research subfields evidenced some decline in absolute numbers of Black doctoral recipients (National Research Council, Office of Scientific and Engineering Personnel; National Science Foundation, 1983; cited in Howard et al., 1986). More recent data suggest that this picture has not changed and is unlikely to change in the near future. For example, in 1993, the vast majority (69%) of all Black doctoral students enrolled full time in psychology departments were in program specialties in health service-provider fields. Of the Black women doctoral students, an overwhelming proportion (73%) were in health service-provider fields (compared with 59.6% of Black male doctoral students). Consequently, a large segment (72.4%) of Black women in psychology are employed full time in a service occupation.[1] Research in the psychology of Black women is disheartening because there are few Black female psychologists available to conduct research on and to promote the empirical study of Black women. However, a number of the women who are employed in practice fields do have some link to an academic institution, and this may allow them to develop and promote Black feminist

---

[1] These 1993 data, compiled by the American Psychological Association's Office of Demographic, Employment, and Educational Research, are based on women who were members of the American Psychological Association.

research agendas and to engage in scholarship and curriculum development.

Black Women in APA and ABPsi

With the dramatic increase of women in the field of psychology, their membership within the APA has been increasing. In 1991, women represented 53.2% of APA associates, 40% of APA members, and 18.9% of APA fellows. Black women, on the other hand, represented a relatively small proportion of the APA's membership (see Table 2). Specifically, in 1993, only 551 Black women held membership in the APA, representing 2.1% of the total APA female membership and less than 1% of the APA total membership. Even more startling is the fact that only 15 Black women (7 of whom were Division 35 fellows) were fellows in the APA in that same year.

Examination of 1993 statistics on the composition of Division 35 indicated that of its 2,543 members, 2.1% ($n = 53$) were Black. The Section on the Psychology of Black Women had approximately 110 members in 1993. Members of this Section, however, may be APA or non-APA members. Although the Section is open to anyone, regardless of race, ethnicity, and sex, roughly 98% of its members are Black women.

The only other segment of the APA that is likely to have a cluster of Black women is Division 45 (Society for the Psychological Study of Ethnic Minority Issues). However, this does not appear to be the case. Although the data were not presented as Gender × Ethnicity, available statistics indicated that in 1993 27.3% ($n = 221$) of its 810 members were Black, and 48.6% were women. Within the ABPsi, not surprisingly, a relatively large proportion of the members were Black women. An examination of the 1988–1989 *Expert Directory of the Association of Black Psy-*

TABLE 2
Membership of Black Women in the American Psychological Association:
1993

Type of member	% of Female APA members	% of Total APA membership	n
Associate	1.4	0.74	54
Member	2.1	0.90	551
Fellow	1.8	0.36	15
Total	2.0	0.85	620

Note. These data were taken from the 1993 *APA Directory*, Office of Demographic, Employment, and Educational Research.

chologists revealed that 52% of the individuals listed were women,[2] in contrast to White women, who made up only 40.6% of the total APA 73,268 membership in 1993.

The issue of APA membership among Black women is worth some consideration. A census survey by Stapp, Tucker, and VandenBos (1985) indicated that APA membership includes individuals engaged in health service provision or in research, but is poorly representative for psychologists involved in education-related issues. Because many Black female psychologists are in health service-provider fields, documentation of the number of Black women in the psychology profession from the APA membership data is encouraging. However, because there are also many Black women working in the psychological fields of school and educational psychology (and who may have received their degrees in education), there should not be a complete reliance on the APA data for documentation of the total numbers of Black women in psychology.

Of course, the small numbers of Black women in the APA result from several factors. On the one hand, the absolute numbers are small because of Black women's sparse representation in the discipline. On the other hand, there are Black female psychologists who choose not to become part of the APA for varied reasons (e.g., cost, perceptions of elitism, racism, and various forms of discrimination within the structure of the APA). Finally, although some Black female psychologists hold dual membership, there may be a number of Black women who permanently resigned from the APA when the ABPsi was formed. The two latter groups of Black female psychologists are not reflected in the APA data. Therefore, the numbers of Black women in psychology may be somewhat higher than statistics suggest.

Black Women's Participation in Governance

Although the participation of women (primarily White women) in the APA governance structure (e.g., boards and committees, Board of Directors, and Council of Representatives) has steadily risen over the past 15 years, this increase has not reached parity with that of men. According to 1990–1991 data, women represent less than 25% of individuals in key policymaking positions in APA governance. They represent only 7 of the past presidents of the APA; 16.7% of the 12 members of the APA Board

---

[2] Because a recent membership directory of the Association of Black Psychologists (ABPsi) was unavailable, a decision was made to use their latest *Expert Directory* to obtain relevant data; a personal communication from ABPsi's Program Office indicated that the listing in the *Expert Directory* is fairly reflective of its membership; the statistics reported were determined by examination of the directory and constructing estimates on the basis of the assumptions about the gender of the member as a function of that person's name.

of Directors; 28% of presidents of state psychological associations, and less than 20% (18.2%) of APA journal editors. Not surprising is the fact that Black women are virtually invisible in APA governance. Division 35 has attempted to remedy this by the designation of one of its Council of Representatives to a Woman of Color (not necessarily a Black woman). Particularly encouraging is that fact that the (elected) Division 35 president, Pamela Reid (1991–1992 program year), was a Black woman. Additionally, the establishment of a division, the Society of the Psychological Study of Ethnic Minority Issues (Division 45), may result in more Black women moving into the APA governance structure.

In terms of Black women's involvement in the governance of the ABPsi, the picture is somewhat more encouraging. Black women have been more visible in the leadership structure of ABPsi than in the APA, probably due in large part to the absolute numbers of women in the association. An examination of past-presidents of ABPsi indicates that 17% ($n = 5$) of the association's 23 presidents were Black women.[3] It also appears that Black women more often serve as state and regional representatives of the ABPsi, compared with their White female counterparts in the APA. Although the picture is more encouraging, it is also evident that there is not parity within the ABPsi in terms of Black women's representation as high-ranking officers relative to their proportion within the organization.

Black Women's Participation on Editorial Boards

Data reported by the APA Journals Office revealed that the proportion of female editors and associate editors of APA journals increased from 0 in 1971 to 32.8% in 1976, declined to 12.9% in 1981, and then rose to 23.6% in 1990. Although White women have made some strides toward increasing their numbers among publishing decision makers in the field of psychology, the success of Blacks, both men and women, in gaining access to the publication network through serving on editorial boards and as reviewers has been minimal. For example, no Black woman has ever served as editor of *Psychology of Women Quarterly* (PWQ) or *Sex Roles*, the two feminist journals in psychology, since their inception in 1975 and 1977, respectively.[4] The PWQ's 1982 special issue on Black women did have two Black women, Saundra (Murray) Nettles and Patricia Bell Scott, serve as special guest editors; also, a 1994 special issue of PWQ on gender and culture had one Black woman, Janis Sanchez, serve as a special guest editor. Additionally, the PWQ has had only three Black female associate editors, Vickie Mays, Pamela Reid, and Gail Wyatt.

---

[3] The women who were presidents of the Association of Black Psychologists included Ruth E. King (who served two terms), M. Bennett, Suzanne Randolph, Lynda James Myers, and Anna Jackson.
[4] It should be noted that *Sex Roles* has had only two editors since its inception in 1975 and that *Psychology of Women Quarterly* has had six editors since its publication in 1977.

To date, *Sex Roles* has not had any Black women serve as either editor or associate editor. In 1995, two Black women, Sherryl Graves and Veronica G. Thomas, served on the 31-member editorial board of *Sex Roles*.[5] The current editor of *Sex Roles* is continually seeking Women of Color to serve on the editorial review board in an effort to encourage more submissions addressing diverse racial and ethnic populations (S. Zalk, personal communication, January 25, 1993).

Journal of Black Psychology (*JBP*), the official publication of the ABPsi, has a more equitable distribution of Black women, relative to Black men, serving on their editorial board, in contrast to White women's representation on APA journal editorial boards. Since the inception of the *JBP* in 1975, two of the four editors have been Black women. These individuals are Ruth E. King and Ann Kathleen Burlew. Furthermore, two Black women, Anna M. Jackson and Lynda James Myers, have served as associate editors. In 1990, three Black women, Faye Z. Belgrave, Harriette P. McAdoo, and Vonnie McLloyd, made up 27.3% of the 11 members of the *JBP*'s editorial board.

Black Women in the Teaching of Psychology

According to NCES (1993) data, Blacks accounted for only 4.7% of full-time faculty at institutions of higher learning in 1991.[6] Black women, in particular, accounted for 2.2% of all full-time faculty, 47% of all Black faculty at institutions of higher learning, and 7% of the female faculty (see Table 3 for more details). Women represented only 27% of faculty in doctoral and master's programs of psychology in 1990–1991 (ODEER, 1992). Minorities accounted for 6% of the total doctoral faculty and 7% of master's faculty. Black women, in particular, made up only 8% of total graduate faculty. They represented 6% of the total female faculty in doctoral programs of psychology and 49% of the total Black faculty, compared with White women, who represented 90% of female full-time faculty and only 26% of White faculty. In terms of master's programs in psychology, Black women represented 1.8% of total faculty, 7% of the total female faculty, and 60% of the total Black faculty. On the other hand, in master's programs, White women represented only 26% of the total White faculty and 89% of female faculty.

Black women faculty, like minorities in general, hold lower faculty rank, are less likely to be tenured, and are more likely to be in non-tenure-track positions than their White counterparts. In fact, data from the APA

---

[5] Pamela Reid also serves as *Sex Roles*' book review editor.
[6] The data in this section were taken from the American Psychological Association's Office of Demographic, Employment, and Educational Research. It was based on information provided by departments that responded to the 1989–1990 Survey of Graduate Department of Psychology. Thus, the sample sizes reported underestimated the total population of psychology faculty.

TABLE 3
Black Female Faculty at Universities and Colleges: Fall 1991

Faculty	% of Total faculty	% of Female faculty	% of Black faculty
Professor	0.21	0.66	4.51
Associate professor	0.38	1.22	8.23
Assistant professor	0.69	2.20	14.84
Instructor	0.56	1.75	11.80
Lecturer	0.08	0.24	1.68
Other	0.26	0.84	5.66
Total	**2.2**	**7.0**	**47.0**

Note. These data were taken from the National Center for Education Statistics, *Digest of Education Statistics*, 1993.

Office of Demographic, Employment, and Educational Research indicate that as minority representation on the faculty increases, faculty rank decreases. Overall, the incidence of minority representation on graduate faculty has not increased substantially over the past decade. In 1980–1981, minorities were 2% of full professors, 4% of associate professors, 8% of assistant professors, and 13% of lecturers/instructors. By 1990–1991, the corresponding figures were 3%, 7%, 10%, and 11%, respectively. Thus, although there has been some modest increase of Black women in the teaching of psychology, they often still are the only Black female psychology faculty members at their institution.

PUBLISHED RESEARCH ON BLACK WOMEN

Theoretically, publication of research is a major indicator of what a profession views as the important and substantive issues of a particular field. In practice, however, biases emerge, resulting in the neglect of significant topics in need of critical analyses. Such biases can occur at several levels, including what is studied, who is studied, how it is studied, and the conclusions drawn. Three decades ago, Nagel (1961) stated the following: "The things a social scientist selects for study are determined by his [sic] concept of what are socially important values. The student of human affairs deals only with material to which he [sic] attributes 'cultural significance' " (p. 485). He further added that "it is not easy in most areas of inquiry to prevent our likes, aversions, hopes, and fears from coloring our conclusions" (p. 488).

Given the impact of attitudes and values on social science research in general, it is not surprising to find an effect in the field of psychology. More than three decades ago, Kuhn (1962) pointed out that people's formal laws and theories are explanations based on a set of social connections. More recently, Marecek (1989) noted that "psychology, like all sciences, is a cultural institution and a social activity subject to external influences as well as internal regulation" (p. 369). In this view, historically there has been a dearth of psychological research on Black women. Unfortunately, however, this continues to be the case. Research conducted is frequently ignored or devalued by the "insiders" (i.e., established White male and selected White female scholars) in the field. This is evident by the virtual absence of Whites and men at sessions focusing on the psychology of Black women at the APA annual conventions.

The paucity of psychological research on Black women may result from four major factors: (a) the research is not conducted because Black women may be viewed not only as outsiders within the profession but also as outside the boundaries of appropriate research topics; (b) because the majority of the individuals (namely, Black women) who are most committed to the psychology of Black women are in service fields rather than in academia, they are not available to conduct the research; (c) scholars may not seriously pursue a program of research on Black women because psychology does not appear to reward such research; and (d) because funding opportunities for research on Black women are limited, such research may not be feasible. Yet, more social science published literature exists on Black women than on other ethnic minority women. The sources of this literature, however, are primarily sociology, history, and anthropology.

To gauge the nature of research on Black women in the field of psychology, we conducted a content analysis of the *PWQ*, *Sex Roles*, and the *JBP* since their inception. This review reinforces what is already well-known: that little psychological research on Black women exists (see Table 4). The content analysis of the *PWQ* revealed that from 1977 through 1990, only 5.3% (*n* = 23) of the 435 articles identified Black

TABLE 4
Articles With Black Female Research Participants in Selected Psychological Journals

Journal	1975–1979		1980–1984		1985–1989		1990	
	n	% Total	*n*	% Total	*n*	% Total	*n*	% Total
PWQ	3	3.1	9[a]	5.3	3	2.2	8	25.0
Sex Roles	9	4.1	16	3.0	20[b]	3.7	7[c]	7.4
JPB	11	26.0	19	63.0	12	44.0	4	57.0

Note. The *Psychology of Women Quarterly (PWQ)* was first published in 1977; *Sex Roles* and the *Journal of Black Psychology (JBP)* were first published in 1975.
[a]Six of these seven articles appeared in a spring 1982 special issue on Black women.
[b]Nine of these 20 articles appeared in a 1989 special issue on Black women.
[c]Volume 22 (December) is not included in this *n* and %.

girls or women as research participants. Six of these 23 articles appeared in the *PWQ*'s 1982 special issue on Black women. A content analysis of articles in *Sex Roles* showed a similar pattern. Of articles published between 1975 and 1990, only 3.8% ($n = 52$) of the total 1,381 articles identified Black women as part of their samples, with 9 of these articles appearing in the 1989 special issue on Black women.[7] It is noteworthy that the *Journal of Social Issues*, a publication of Division 9 of the APA, the Society for the Psychological Study of Social Issues (SPSSI), devoted one of its 1983 issues to Black women. In the *JBP*, slightly more than one half (57%) of their articles published in 1990 indicated that Black girls or women were included as research participants (see Table 4 for more details).

Research Themes and Trends of Published Work on Black Women

An examination of the published psychological literature on Black women reveals that the topics studied are highly restrictive.[8] This may be the case for several reasons: (a) a legitimate social need and political push to focus on certain areas of research; (b) a bandwagon effect (M. T. Mednick, 1989), that is, studying concepts (e.g., fear of success, impostor phenomenon, androgyny) that gained prominence and popularity; (c) a broader societal and more specific scientific bias of viewing certain topics (e.g., leadership styles, decision making, power motivation) as irrelevant to Black women; and (d) limited funding opportunities to support certain kinds of research on Black women because of this societal and scientific bias. Campbell (1983) noted that "bias in topic selection has contributed to gaps in our knowledge base. It has also allowed us to close our minds to testing alternative hypotheses or explanations for behaviors that fall outside our expectations" (p. 201).

Despite this scientific bias, some research on Black women has been done over the years. A review of the published work prior to 1980 that either focused on Black women or included them as a target group in their analyses indicates that much of the literature, both theoretical and empirical, centered around the family, the Black matriarchy, and work (e.g., Allen, 1979; Axelson, 1970; Harrison & Minor, 1978; Landry & Jendrek, 1978; Lewis, 1975; Mack, 1974; Scanzoni, 1975; Staples, 1970, 1973; Steinman & Fox, 1970); androgyny, sex role identity and attitudes, and sex role stereotyping (e.g., Gackenbach, 1978; Gump, 1975, 1978; Hershey, 1978; O'Leary & Harrison, 1975); self-esteem and fear of success (e.g., Dansby, 1975; Fleming, 1978; M. Mednick & Puryear, 1975; Myers, 1975;

---

[7] The December 1990 issue (Vol. 22) of *Sex Roles* is not included in this figure.
[8] Although there was a concerted effort to focus only on the psychological literature, a number of studies cited in this section were taken from other disciplines such as sociology and history.

Owens, 1975; Puryear & Mednick, 1974; Rushing, 1978; Savage, Stearns, & Friedman, 1979; Weston & Mednick, 1970); occupational aspirations, career orientation, and achievement (e.g., Epstein, 1978; Gurin & Gaylord, 1976; Kelly & Wingrove, 1975; M. Mednick & Puryear, 1975; Murray & Mednick, 1977; Schroth, 1976; Scott, 1977; Turner & McCaffrey, 1974); and mental health outcomes (e.g., Steele, 1978).

Although more research on Black women has been conducted since 1980, there still does not appear to be a significant expansion of knowledge, particularly that based on empirical work on Black women. There continued to be published work, both theoretical and empirical, on family and work (e.g., Ganrose & Cunningham, 1988; McCray, 1980; Moses, 1985), sex role identity (e.g., Brown-Collins & Sussewell, 1986; Harris, 1992), sex roles (e.g., Dugger, 1988; Landrine, 1985; Lyson, 1986; Malson, 1983), career aspirations and achievement (e.g., Bailey & Mednick, 1988; Burlew, 1982; Chester, 1983; Dillard & Campbell, 1982; Gilkes, 1983; Murrell, Frieze, & Frost, 1991; Thomas, 1983), mental health (e.g., Gray & Jones, 1987; Jones & Gray, 1984; McGrath, Keita, Strickland, & Russo, 1990), and sexual assault (e.g., Hines, 1989; Wyatt, 1985, 1992). The literature indicates that some other areas of research involving Black women have emerged. These include, for example, studies on dual-career Black couples (e.g., Thomas, 1990a, 1990b), social support networks and psychological well-being (e.g., D. R. Brown & Gary, 1985; McAdoo, 1980), coping strategies (e.g., Myers, 1980), and body image satisfaction (e.g., Thomas, 1989; Thomas & James, 1988). No longitudinal work on Black women was found in the psychological literature, although such a study was initiated in 1989.[9]

There has been little instrument development particularly suitable for Black women. One notable exception is the African-American Women's Stress Scale (AWSS) developed by Watts-Jones (1990). Her major premise in the development of this measure was that Black women and their communities are distressed, largely as a result of ongoing undesirable situations (e.g., poverty, economic marginality, inadequate housing, unemployment, crime) and the duality of African and American identity. Watts-Jones further noted that the more widely used stress scales such as the Social Readjustment Rating Scale (Holmes & Rahe, 1967) and the Peri Life Events Scale (Dohrenwend, Krasnoff, Askenasy, & Dohrenwend, 1978), do not reflect many of the stressors frequently confronting Black women. Although further refinement and validation of the AWSS are needed, Watts-Jones's philosophy of using a within-cultural context for assessing this construct is encouraging.

---

[9] This National Institute of Mental Health funded study, being conducted by Sandra S. Tangri, Martha T. Mednick, and Veronica G. Thomas, is a longitudinal study of Howard University female graduates of the classes of 1959, 1964, and 1967.

Racial Comparative Research in the Psychology of Women

In psychology, as in other scientific disciplines, research focusing on Black populations is usually comparative. That is, the data for Blacks are compared with those for Whites. The problem presented by comparative research is that it is conducted within a biased framework (i.e., the behavior of Whites is assumed to be the norm from which Blacks deviate). Much comparative research measures and demonstrates deviations of Blacks from White norms and so suggests pathological conditions among Black Americans. Of White researchers studying the Black community, Williams (1980) observed that in many studies, researchers looked for and found pathology, while ignoring strengths and adaptive capacities. The limitations of racial comparative research are complex and involve conceptual, theoretical, methodological, and political concerns that are beyond the scope of this chapter. Discussions of these issues have been offered by others (e.g., Azibo, 1988; Banks, McQuarter, & Ross, 1979). In this section we briefly discuss racial comparative research in the psychology of women.

Much of the theoretical and empirical literature on Black women, particularly work authored by White investigators, is structured in a racial comparative framework. In psychological studies focusing on Black women, a question most often asked by journal editors and other White scholars, both women and men, is, How do or would the data for Black women differ from those of White women? Unfortunately, this question arises even if a racial comparative framework was not conceptually justified, an objective of the research, or even a point of interest in the investigation. If no White female comparison group had been used, the journal editor may suggest that the research include such a group, analyze the results, make racial comparisons, then resubmit the manuscript for publication.[10] Here, the underlying assumption is that research on Black women is valid, important, and publishable if White women are included. In some respects, comparative studies have been detrimental to a complete and accurate understanding of Black women. Although comparative work can be useful if conducted within the proper framework, it certainly should not represent the only conditions in which research on Black women is seen as "scholarly" and of value.

SUMMARY

This examination of the psychology of Black women highlights the need for an increase in scholarship as well as in the number of scholars in

---

[10]This observation is based on a personal experience of Veronica G. Thomas and discussion of the experiences of other Black female psychologists who have undergone this review process.

this subspecialty. Several questions are crucial in this area of work: Is it more appropriate for the psychology of Black women to be part of the psychology of women or of Black psychology? Should the psychology of Black women attempt to fully integrate with both of these other subspecialties? Or, should the psychyology of Black women seek its own identity apart from the psychology of women and from Black psychology? Has the area met the challenges set forth by the original Task Force on the Psychology of Black Women that was formed in 1976? Has the psychology of Black women had a significant impact on the psychology of women or on Black psychology? Have those who study the psychology of Black women developed theories, perspectives, and methodologies relevant to the life experiences of Black women? Who should conduct the needed research on Black women? Should it be Black women, Black and White women, or Black men and Black women?

Although these questions are difficult to answer, as the field of the psychology of Black women matures, the answers (and other questions) may become evident. It is undeniable that the psychology of Black women has had an impact on the psychology of women. Because of the concerns raised by the Section on the Psychology of Black Women, feminist psychologists are indeed more sensitive to the issues of diversity as well as to the need to integrate the interactive impact of race, class, and ethnicity into research on the psychology of women. Although there is an increased awareness of the need for research on Black women, unfortunately such an awareness has not yet been translated into a major increase in research proposals, research funding, and published work within the area. The impact of the psychology of Black women on Black psychology, however, is less easily discernible. In an effort to avoid conflict, many Black female psychologists have not challenged Black psychology to integrate a feminist agenda within its perspective.

The psychology of Black women has yet to develop sophisticated theories, perspectives, and methodologies relevant to Black women. This is not to negate some significant work underway. A cadre of Black female psychologists (sometimes in collaboration with White feminist psychologists and Black male psychologists) are increasingly charting new frontiers in theory and research. This core group is working to ensure that the psychological research of tomorrow is more accurate and inclusive than that of yesterday and today. In particular, the members of the Section on the Psychology of Black Women have been the major advocates for research on Black women and recruiting Black women as members of Division 35, thereby meeting much of the challenge of the original Division 35 Task Force on the Psychology of Black Women.

The issue of "who" should conduct research on the psychology of Black women echoes concerns raised earlier by feminist psychologists and scholars of Black psychology. If, in fact, the scientific method is value free, the question of who conducts research would not need to be asked. However, because it is clear that the scientific method is not value free (e.g., Campbell, 1983; Lott, 1985; Unger, 1983; Unger, Draper, & Pendergrass, 1986), this issue represents a critical concern. If we believe that a racist and sexist society engenders (unwitting but nonetheless) racist and sexist science and scientists, then empirical research in the psychology of Black women must be conducted by Black female psychologists. Furthermore, because Black women may have values and concerns that differ from those of both White women and Black men, Black women may be more appropriate investigators of the life experiences of Black women. Thus, Black women can bring to feminist psychology another "consciousness," one specific to their own social, cultural, and historical experiences.

RECOMMENDATIONS

Currently, considerable attention is being devoted to examining the "crisis" in the Black male population. Once again, Black women's concerns are essentially ignored. On the whole, and particularly among Black scholars, there tends to be more sympathy for the plight of Black men and boys than for Black women and girls. Nonetheless, a number of Black women psychologists are still actively voicing their concerns regarding the often "forgotten" minority group, Black girls and women. Thus, the psychology of Black women today remains devoted to the issues of 15 years ago (i.e., the absence of concern for Black women in psychological theory, the absence of empirical research on Black girls and women, and the virtual absence of grant support for research on Black women).

The Need for Theory

At the most basic level, traditional theory in psychology needs to be challenged for its lack of relevance to Black women (see chapter 7 in this book). Just as feminist psychology and Black psychology have aggressively moved toward developing appropriate theory and research for women and Blacks, the psychology of Black women needs to follow their model. Older perspectives need to be transformed into newer ones that reflect Black women's life experiences. There is a need to question the theories from which the discipline derives its questions.

Black female psychologists must critically examine the philosophical foundations of traditional psychological theory and research commensurate with such an analysis. In particular, Black female psychologists must now scrutinize and evaluate the different approaches within the psychology of women and question the appropriateness of the philosophy of science entailed therein. The two prevailing approaches in research on the psychology of women are the "gender differences" and the "gender analysis" perspectives. The gender differences approach focuses on person-based causes of gender differences between women and men. Kahn and Yoder (1989) noted that too many psychologists (consciously or not) assume that women and men are basically different and subsequently attempt to verify those differences. The gender difference approach, or "alpha bias" as Hare-Mustin and Marecek (1988) called it, permeates Gilligan's work on gender differences in morality (Gilligan, 1982; Gilligan, Ward, Taylor, & Bardige, 1989), Belenky, Clinchy, Goldberger, and Tarule's (1986) work on cognitive development and women's ways of knowing, and most of the work on women and achievement (e.g., Clance & Imes, 1978; Horner, 1970). The alternative approach, a gender analysis or social constructionist approach, views gender as a social construct whose nature is unknowable. Within this framework, the issue is not the extent to which gender differences actually exist but an analysis of the social forces (not biology or socialization) that elicit ostensible gender differences. This position characterizes the work of scholars such as Hare-Mustin and Marecek (1988), Kahn and Yoder (1988), and Unger (1983, 1989).

The gender difference and gender analysis approaches have different implications for feminist research on women in general and on Black women in particular. Hare-Mustin and Marecek (1988) emphasized that the question of gender differences has been a divisive one for feminist scholars. Some feminists argue that such differences affirm women's value and special nature, and others argue that focusing on differences reinforces ideology and supports inequality as long as the power to define remains in the hands of (White) men.

Within the context of the psychology of Black women, it is most appropriate for theoretical and empirical analysis to take a social constructivist, gender analysis approach. Just as psychology has accepted the social meaning of gender as difference (Hare-Mustin & Marecek, 1988), the same has been the case for the social meaning of race. Race has often been understood as race differences, and these differences are, in turn, understood as Black deficits. The focus of the psychology of Black women should not be the extent to which Black women differ from White women. Rather, the focus should be on the specific historical, social, political, and other forces that elicit and maintain ostensible race and gender differences. In addition, analyses of the benefits White feminists may reap by constructing Black women as different also may be beneficial.

With the recognition of the multiple jeopardy of Black women's experiences, there was growing support for the notion that the relationships among sexism, racism, and classism are additive. Currently, however, many scholars believe that perspectives that support this approach are oversimplistic. Rather, it has been more recently theorized that an interactive model is essential in explaining Black women's experiences. King (1988) noted that the modifier "multiple" (taken from concept *multiple jeopardy*) refers not only to several simultaneous oppressions but to the multiplicative relationship among them as well. Although nonadditive models have long been considered by sociologists, they have been gaining support only recently in the psychological literature (e.g., A. Smith & Stewart, 1983). This interactive model has been detailed by King (1988) and A. Smith and Stewart (1983).

The Need for Research

The kind of research needed on Black women can be summarized as "more, more; better, better." More empirical research needs to be conducted. Just as feminist psychologists have developed guidelines for avoiding sexism in psychological research (Denmark, Russo, Frieze, & Sechzer, 1988), it may be useful to develop parallel guidelines for conducting nonracist, nonsexist research. These efforts should be spearheaded by Black female psychologists who are committed to feminist and Black agendas. There also needs to be review and evaluation of previous research on Black women that examine the topics studied, methodologies used, findings reported and conclusions drawn.

More instruments need to be constructed and validated for use with Black women and girls. Scales, tests, and other instruments are, to a large extent, the major tools used by psychologists to collect data. It is imperative that these tools appropriately reflect the life experiences of those individuals for whom the measures are to be used to generate data. Nonsexist and nonracist measurement is not simply a concern of special interest groups but is a matter of good empirical research.

More empirical research needs to be conducted in areas that traditionally have not targeted Black women but are nonetheless relevant to their lives. Denmark et al. (1988) pointed out that it is assumed that topics relevant to White men are important and more "basic," whereas topics related to White women, people of color, and Women of Color are "specialized" or applied. They stressed that construing topics as basic or specialized should not be made on the basis of the ethnicity of the research participants or on the topic's relevance to a particular group. When such classification occurs, important and relevant topics on Black women may not be researched. Some notable examples include the absence of empirical work on Black women and leadership styles, conformity, aggression, interpersonal perception, cognitive styles, and life stages.

Not only is more research needed, but "better" research is needed. Researchers must do more than simply include Black women in their samples. Rather, researchers also must then critically examine their data from a Black woman's perspective. Similarly, research involving Black women does not have to be comparative. When comparative research is conducted, however, it must frame questions and discuss outcomes in terms of "apparent" differences within the theory under consideration. Comparative research needs to be carefully designed and conducted to account for gender, race, or Gender × Race differences in a nonsexist and nonracist manner. As Washington and McLoyd (1982) noted, race-comparative research must demonstrate its population, ecological, and construct validity, as well as its cultural and interpretative validity. Interpretation of apparent differences must begin with the assumption that such differences may well be an artifact of social inequities and power differences among the groups studied.

Better research also would involve studies that focus only on Black women. Park and Rothbart (1982) noted that out-groups (such as Blacks and women) are often viewed as being more homogeneous than the dominant group (i.e., White men). Consequently, psychological research has treated Whites as individuals but regarded Blacks as "Blacks" and as a homogeneous group. There is significant diversity among Black women that needs to be addressed. All Black women are not poor, uneducated, single parents. The goal of feminist research on Black women should be to illuminate the lives of Black women of different ages, social classes, and educational levels. Such analyses would be particularly enlightening given the fact that class, ethnicity, gender, and age are the four primary axes used by most societies to establish hierarchies.

Conducting more and better research on Black women is not sufficient to bring diversity to feminist psychology. In addition, such research must be published. Unfortunately, research on Black women by Black female psychologists often is not published or is published in nonfeminist journals. Editors of feminist journals must actively solicit such manuscripts and ensure their publication if feminist psychology is to be a psychology of all women.

The Need for Practice

There is a continued need for the development of clinical theories and interventions focusing on Black women. There is little information on how gender role stereotypes and expectations may result in different diagnoses and treatment of specific psychopathologies among women of diverse ethnic groups (e.g., McGrath et al., 1990). Likewise, practicing therapists need to critically examine their own ethnic, gender, and racial biases and assess their impact on the Black women patients. A detailed discussion of clinical diagnoses and treatment relevant to Black women (and other minority women) is beyond the scope of this chapter; however, excellent discussions in this area are available (e.g., Mays & Comas-Díaz, 1989; McGrath et al., 1990).

CONCLUDING REMARKS

Before feminist psychology can become culturally diverse and the psychology of Black women can be considered a specialty in the discipline, a number of changes are needed. There must be a genuine acknowledgment of Black female populations as an integral part of society, thereby worthy of a serious scientific attention. Black female psychologists may need to lobby to have these and other concerns heard within the discipline. Likewise, although more research is needed, such research cannot be conducted in the absence of federal and private funding for psychological research on Black women. The absence of grant support for such research reflects and reinforces the view that Black women are not worthy of scientific attention and further ensures their continued neglect by the discipline. Various divisions (e.g., Divisions 35, 9, 45) and the ABPsi could establish a small grant fund for such research as a demonstration of the commitment to the issues of diversity and inclusiveness that all espouse. Finally, because Black women are the most likely researchers of Black women, psychology departments must establish better recruiting and mentoring programs for them. Special attention must be given to attracting Black women to research and academic careers in particular. Although service professions are in urgent demand given the many concerns that are deleteriously affecting the Black community, it is also important to have a cadre of Black female scholars that can take the research on the psychology of Black women to broader dimensions in years to come.

REFERENCES

Allen, W. R. (1979). Family roles, occupational statuses and achievement orientation among black women in the United States. *Signs, 4,* 670–686.

Axelson, L. J. (1970). The working wife: Differences in the perception among Negro and white males. *Journal of Marriage and the Family, 32,* 457–467.

Azibo, D. (1988). Understanding the proper and improper usage of the comparative framework. *Journal of Black Psychology, 15,* 81–91.

Bailey, C., & Mednick, M. (1988). Career aspiration in black college women: An examination of performance and social esteem. *Women in Therapy, 6,* 65–75.

Banks, W. C., McQuarter, G., & Ross, J. (1979). On the importance of white preference and the comparative differences of blacks and others: Reply to Williams and Moreland. *Psychological Bulletin, 86,* 33–36.

Beale, F. (1970). Double jeopardy: To be black and female. In T. Cade (Ed.), *The black woman: An anthology* (pp. 90–100). New York: New American Library.

Belenky, M. F., Clinchy, B. M., Goldberger, N. R., & Tarule, J. M. (1986). *Women ways of knowing: The development of self, voice, and mind.* New York: Basic Books.

Brown, A., Goodwin, B. J., Hall, B. A., & Jackson-Lowman, H. (1985). A review of psychology of women textbooks: Focus on Afro-American women. *Psychology of Women Quarterly, 9,* 29–38.

Brown, D. R., & Gary, L. E. (1985). Social support network differentials among married and nonmarried black females. *Psychology of Women Quarterly, 9,* 229–241.

Brown-Collins, A. R., & Sussewell, D. R. (1986). The Afro-American women's emerging selves. *Journal of Black Psychology, 13,* 1–11.

Brown, L. S. (1990). The naming of a multicultural perspective for theory-building in feminist therapy. *Women and Therapy, 9,* 1–21.

Burlew, A. K. (1982). The experience of black females in traditional and non-traditional professions. *Psychology of Women Quarterly, 6,* 312–326.

Campbell, P. B. (1983). The impact of societal biases on research methods. In B. L. Richardson & J. Wirtenberg (Eds.), *Sex role research: Measuring social change* (pp. 197–213). New York: Praeger.

Chester, N. L. (1983). Sex differences in high school environments: Implications for career development among black adolescent females. *Journal of Social Issues, 39,* 29–40.

Clance, P. R., & Imes, S. A. (1978). The imposter phenomenon is high achieving women: Dynamics and therapeutic intervention. *Psychotherapy: Theory, Research and Practice, 15,* 241–247.

Dansby, P. G. (1975). Perceptions of role and status of black females. *Journal of Social and Behavioral Sciences, 21,* 31–47.

Denmark, F., Russo, N. F., Frieze, L. H., & Sechzer, J. A. (1988). Guidelines for avoiding sexism in psychological research. *American Psychologist, 43,* 582–585.

Dillard, J. M., & Campbell, N. J. (1982). Career values and aspirations of Puerto Rican, black and Anglo adolescents' career aspirations, expectations, and maturity. *Vocations Guidance Quarterly, 28,* 313–321.

Dohrenwend, B., Kransnoff, L., Askenasy, A., & Dohrenwend, B. (1978). Exemplification of a method for scaling life events: The Peri Life Events Scale. *Journal of Health and Social Behavior, 19,* 205–229.

Dugger, K. (1988). Social location and gender role attitudes: A comparison of black and white women. *Gender and Society, 2,* 425–448.

Epstein, C. (1978). Positive effects of the multiple negative: Explaining the success of black professional women. *American Journal of Sociology, 78,* 912–935.

Fleming, J. (1978). Fear of success: Achievement related motives and behavior in black college women. *Journal of Personality, 46,* 694–716.

Gackenbach, J. (1978). The effect of race, sex, and career goal differences at home and at work. *Journal of Vocational Behavior, 12,* 93–101.

Gilkes, C. T. (1983). Going up for the oppressed: The career mobility of black women community workers. *Journal of Social Issues, 39,* 114–140.

Gilligan, C., Ward, J. V., Taylor, J. M., & Bardige, B. (Eds.). (1989). *Mapping the moral domain: A contribution of women's thinking to psychological theory and education.* Cambridge, MA: Harvard University Press.

Gilligan, C. (1982). *In a different voice: Psychological theory and women's development.* Cambridge, MA: Harvard University Press.

Ganrose, C. S., & Cunningham, E. A. (1988). Post-partum work intentions among black and white college women. *Career Development Quarterly, 37,* 149–164.

Gray, B. A., & Jones, B. E. (1987). Psychotherapy and black women: A survey. *Journal of National Medical Association, 79,* 177–181.

Gump, J. P. (1975). Comparative analysis of black women's and white women's sex role attitudes. *Journal of Consulting and Clinical Psychology, 43,* 858–863.

Gump, J. P. (1978). Reality and myth: Employment and sex-role identity in black women. In J. Sherman & F. L. Denmark (Eds.), *The psychology of women: Directions in research* (pp. 349–380). New York: Psychological Dimensions.

Gurin, P., & Gaylord, C. (1976). Educational and occupational goals of men and women at black colleges. *Monthly Labor Review, 99,* 10–16.

Hare-Mustin, R. T., & Marecek, J. (1988). The meaning of difference: Gender theory, postmodernism, and psychology. *American Psychologist, 43,* 455–464.

Harris, D. (1992). A cultural model for assessing the growth and development of the African American female. *Journal of Multicultural Counseling and Development, 20,* 158–167.

Harrison, A. O., & Minor, J. H. (1978). Interrole conflict, coping strategies, and satisfaction among black working wives. *Journal of Marriage and the Family, 40,* 799–805.

Hershey, M. R. (1978). Racial differences in sex-identities and sex stereotyping: Evidence against a common assumption. *Social Science Quarterly, 58,* 583–596.

Hines, D. C. (1989). Rape and the inner lives of black women in the Middle West. *Signs, 14,* 912–920.

Holmes, T., & Rahe, R. (1967). The Social Readjustment Rating Scale. *Journal of Psychosomatic Research, 11,* 213–218.

hooks, b. (1981). *Ain't I a woman: Black women and feminism.* Boston: South End Press.

Horner, M. J. (1970). Femininity and successful achievement: A basic inconsistency. In J. M. Bardwick, E. Douvan, M. S. Horner, & D. Gutman (Eds.), *Feminine personality and conflict.* Belmont, CA: Brooks/Cole.

Howard, A., Pion, G. M., Gottfredson, G. D., Oskamp, S., Phafflin, S. M., Bray, D. W., & Burnstein, A. G. (1986). The changing face of American psychology. *American Psychologist, 41,* 1311–1327.

Hyde, J. S. (1991). *Half the human experience: The psychology of women* (4th ed.). Lexington, MA: Heath.

Jones, B. E., & Gray, B. A. (1984). Similarities and differences in black men and women in psychotherapy. *Journal of the National Medical Association, 76,* 21–27.

Joseph, G. I., & Lewis, J. (1981). *Common differences: Conflicts in black and white feminist perspectives.* New York: Anchor Books.

Kahn, A. S., & Yoder, J. D. (1989). The psychology of women and conservatism: Rediscovering social change. *Psychology of Women Quarterly, 13,* 417–432.

Kelly, P. E., & Wingrove, C. R. (1975). Educational and occupational choices of black and white female students in a rural Georgia community. *Journal of Research and Development and Education, 9,* 45–46.

Kendel, M. B. (1991). The feminization of psychology. In G. E. Edwall (Ed.), *Above the glass ceiling: Raising the roof.* Tucson, AZ: National Council of Schools of Professional Psychology.

King, D. K. (1988). Multiple jeopardy, multiple consciousness: The context of a black feminist ideology. *Signs, 14,* 42–72.

Kuhn, T. S. (1962). *The structure of scientific revolutions.* Chicago: University of Chicago Press.

Landrine, H. (1985). Race × class stereotype of women. *Sex Roles, 13,* 65–75.

Landry, B., & Jendrek, M. P. (1978). The employment of wives in middle-class black families. *Journal of Marriage and the Family, 40,* 787–797.

Lewis, D. K. (1975). A response to inequality: Black women, racism, and sexism. *Signs, 3,* 339–361.

Lott, B. (1985). The potential enrichment of social/personality through feminist research and vice versa. *American Psychologist, 40,* 155–164.

Lyson, T. A. (1986). Race and sex differences in sex role attitudes of Southern college students. *Psychology of Women Quarterly, 10,* 421–428.

Mack, D. E. (1974). The power relationship in black families and white families. *Journal of Personality and Social Psychology, 30,* 409–413.

Malson, M. R. (1983). Black women's sex roles: The social context for a new ideology. *Journal of Social Issues, 39,* 101–113.

Marecek, J. (1989). Introduction. *Psychology of Women Quarterly, 13,* 367–377.

Matlin, M. W. (1989). Teaching psychology of women: A survey of instructors. *Psychology of Women Quarterly, 13,* 245–261.

Mays, V. M., & Comas-Díaz, L. (1989). Feminist therapy with ethnic minority populations: A closer look at blacks and Hispanics. In M. A. Dutton-Douglas & L. E. A. Walker (Eds.), *Feminist psychotherapies: Integration of therapeutic and feminist systems.* New York: Springer.

McAdoo, H. P. (1980). Black mothers and the extended family support network. In L. Rodgers-Rose (Ed.), *The black woman* (pp. 125–144). Beverly Hills, CA: Sage.

McCray, C. A. (1980). The black woman and family roles. In L. Rodgers-Rose (Ed.), *The black woman* (pp. 67–78). Beverly Hills, CA: Sage.

McGrath, E., Keita, G. P., Strickland, B., & Russo, N. (1990). *Women and depression: Risk factors and treatment issues*. Washington, DC: American Psychological Association.

Mednick, M. S. (1991). Current and future in American feminist psychology. *Psychology of Women Quarterly, 15*, 611–621.

Mednick, M., & Puryear, G. (1975). Motivational and personality factors related to career goals of black women. *Journal of Social and Behavioral Sciences, 2*, 1–30.

Mednick, M. T. (1989). On the politics of psychological constructs: Stop the bandwagon, I want to get off. *American Psychologist, 44*, 1118–1123.

Moses, Y. T. (1985). Black American women and work: Historical and contemporary strategies for empowerment. *Women's Studies International Forum, 8*, 351–359.

Murray, S. R., & Mednick, M. (1977). Black women's achievement orientation: Motivation and cognitive factors. *Psychology of Women's Quarterly, 1*, 259–274.

Murrell, A. J., Frieze, I. H., & Frost, J. L. (1991). Aspiring to careers in male- and female-dominated professions: A study of black and white college women. *Psychology of Women Quarterly, 15*, 103–126.

Myers, L. W. (1975). Black women and self-esteem. In M. Millman & R. Kantor (Eds.), *Another voice* (pp. 240–250). New York: Anchor Books.

Myers, L. W. (1980). *Black women: Do they cope better?* Englewood Cliffs, NJ: Prentice Hall.

Nagel, E. (1961). *The structure of science*. New York: Harcourt Brace & World.

National Center for Education Statistics. (1994). *Digest of education statistics* (NCES 94-115). Washington, DC: U.S. Department of Education, Office of Educational Research and Improvement.

Office of Demographic, Employment and Educational Research. (1992). *1990–1991 Characteristics of graduate departments of psychology*. Washington, DC: American Psychological Association.

O'Leary, V. C., & Harrison, A. O. (1975, August). *Sex role stereotypes as a function of race and sex*. Paper presented at the 83rd Annual Convention of the American Psychological Association, Chicago.

Owens, S. (1975). Self-esteem of Black women in a comparative perspective. In W. D. Johnson & T. L. Green (Eds.), *Perspectives on Afro-American Women*. Washington, DC: ECCA Publications.

Park, B., & Rothbart, M. (1982). Perception of out-group homogeneity and levels of social categorization: Memory for the subordinate attributes of in-group and out-group members. *Journal of Personality and Social Psychology, 42*, 1051–1068.

Peplau, L. A., & Conrad, E. (1989). Beyond sexist research: The perils of feminist methods in psychology. *Psychology of Women Quarterly, 13*, 379–400.

Puryear, G. R., & Mednick, M. S. (1974). Black militancy, affective attachment, and the fear of success in black college women. *Journal of Counseling and Clinical Psychology, 42,* 263–266.

Reid, P. S. (1993). Poor women in psychological research: Shut up and shut out. *Psychology of Women Quarterly, 17,* 133–150.

Reid, P. T., & Kelly, E. (1994). Research on women of color: From ignorance to awareness. *Psychology of Women Quarterly, 18,* 477–486.

Rushing, A. B. (1978). Images of black women in Afro-American poetry. In S. Harley & R. Terborg-Penn (Eds.), *The Afro-American woman: Struggles and images.* Port Washington, NY: Kennikat Press.

Savage, J. E., Sterns, A. P., & Friedman, P. (1979). Relationship of internal-external locus of control, self-concept, and masculinity-femininity to fear of success in black freshman and senior college women. *Sex Roles, 5,* 373–383.

Scanzoni, J. (1975). Sex roles, economic factors and marital solidarity in black and white marriages. *Journal of Marriage and the Family, 37,* 130–144.

Schroth, M. L. (1976). Sex and grade-level differences in need achievement among black college students. *Perceptual and Motor Skills, 43,* 135–140.

Schaffer, K. F. (1981). *Sex roles and human behavior.* Cambridge, MA: Winthrop.

Scott, P. B. (1977, Summer). Preparing black women for nontraditional professions. *Journal of the National Association for Women Dean, Administrators, and Counselors,* 135–139.

Smith, A., & Stewart, A. J. (1983). Approaches to studying racism and sexism in black women's lives. *Journal of Social Issues, 39,* 1–15.

Staples, R. (1970). The myth of the black matriarchy. *The Black Scholar, 1,* 8–16.

Staples, R. (1973). *The black woman in America: Sex, marriage, and the family.* Chicago: Nelson-Hall.

Staples, R. (1981). Race and marital status: An overview. In H. P. McAdoo (Ed.), *Black families.* Beverly Hills, CA: Sage.

Stapp, J., Tucker, A. M., & VandenBos, G. R. (1985). Census of psychological personnel: 1983. *American Psychologist, 42,* 1317–1351.

Steele, R. E. (1978). Relationship of race, sex, and social mobility to depression in normal adults. *Journal of Social Psychology, 104,* 34–47.

Steinman, A., & Fox, P. J. (1970). Attitudes toward women's family roles among black and white undergrads. *The Family Coordinator, 19,* 363–367.

Thomas, V. G. (1983). Perceived traditionality and non-traditionality of career aspirations of black college women. *Perceptual and Motor Skills, 57,* 979–982.

Thomas, V. G. (1989). Body image satisfaction among black women. *Journal of Social Psychology, 129,* 107–112.

Thomas, V. G. (1990a). Determinants of global life happiness and marital happiness in dual-career black couples. *Family Relations: Journal of Applied Family and Child Studies, 30,* 174–178.

Thomas, V. G. (1990b). Problems of dual-career black couples: Identification and implications for family intervention. *Journal of Multicultural Counseling and Development, 18*, 58–67.

Thomas, V. G., & James, M. D. (1988). Body image, dieting tendencies and sex role traits in Black women. *Sex Roles, 18*, 523–529.

Turner, B. F., & McCaffrey, J. H. (1974). Socialization and career orientation among black and white college women. *Journal of Vocational Behavior, 5*, 307–319.

Unger, R. K. (1983). Through the looking glass: No wonderland yet! (The reciprocal relationship between methodology and models of reality.) *Psychology of Women Quarterly, 8*, 9–32.

Unger, R. K. (1989). Psychological, feminist, and personal epistemology: Transcending contradiction. In M. M. Green (Ed.), *Feminist thought and the structure of knowledge* (pp. 124–141). New York: New York University Press.

Unger, R. K., Draper, R. D., & Pendergrass, M. L. (1986). Personal epistemology and personal experience. *Journal of Social Issues, 42*, 67–79.

Walker, L. E. (1991). The feminization of psychology. *Psychology of Women Quarterly Newsletter, 18*(2), pp. 1, 4.

Walsh, M. R. (1987). (Ed.). *The psychology of women: Ongoing debates.* New Haven, CT: Yale University Press.

Washington, E. D., & McLoyd, V. C. (1982). The external validity of research involving American minorities. *Human Development, 25*, 324–339.

Watts-Jones, D. (1990). Toward a stress scale for African-American women. *Psychology of Women Quarterly, 14*, 271–275.

Weston, P. J., & Mednick, T. (1970). Race, social class, and motive to avoid success in women. *Journal of Cross-Cultural Psychology, 1*, 285–291.

Williams, R. L. (1980). The death of white research in the black community. In R. L. Jones (Ed.), *Black psychology* (2nd ed.), New York: Harper & Row.

Wyatt, G. E. (1985). The sexual abuse of Afro-American and white women in childhood. *Child Abuse and Neglect, 9*, 507–519.

Wyatt, G. E. (1992). The sociocultural context of African American and white women's rape. *Journal of Social Issues, 48*, 77–91.

Yoder, J. D., & Kahn, A. S. (1993). Working toward an inclusive psychology of women. *American Psychologist, 48*, 846–850.

IV

ETHNICITY AND SELECTED RESEARCH TOPICS IN FEMINIST PSYCHOLOGY

INTRODUCTION

In this section, Ethnicity and Selected Research Topics in Feminist Psychology, three of the many important research areas in feminist psychology are examined from a multicultural perspective: women's health, women's ostensible language (i.e., gender differences in language use), and pornography. As noted in the preface, many other major topics in feminist research (e.g., rape, domestic violence, psychopathology, etc.) could not be addressed in this volume but hopefully will be addressed in future, broader editions. The three areas included here, however, are broad and important ones; the analyses that they entail strongly suggest that bringng cultural diversity to other research areas would have equally significant effects and implications.

In chapter 14, "Double Jeopardy: Ethnicity and Gender in Health Research," Elizabeth Klonoff, Hope Landrine, and Judy Scott analyze the topics covered in articles on health in feminist as well as nonfeminist psychological journals. They demonstrate that health research published in nonfeminist journals ignores women, people of color, and Women of Color, even when the disease being studied is more prevalent among these groups. Likewise, they demonstrate that health research published in feminist journals also ignores Women of Color. In addition, feminist health research neglects serious health problems among women of all ethnic groups and instead focuses on the reproductive issues (e.g., pregnancy and abortion) of concern to relatively healthy, wealthy European American feminists. The major health problems that Women of Color face (e.g., high rates of debilitating hypertension, diabetes, cancer, sarcoidosis, thyroid disorders, as well as lack of access to adequate care) have not been addressed by researchers in women's health, are rarely mentioned in women's health textbooks, and never have been included in feminist efforts to empower women through self-help groups, educational campaigns, or political action. They then present suggestions for a culturally diverse women's health research program.

In chapter 15, "Ethnicity and Gender in American English Use," Nancy Henley demonstrates that bringing cultural diversity to studies of "women's language" challenges the concept itself. She demonstrates that when Women of Color are included in analyses, researchers do not find that their speech is overly polite, weak, uncertain, conservative, and thereby highly differentiated from men's. Indeed, Henley indicates that when the diversity of languages and linguistic communities of people of color are included in the analysis of gender and language use, complex issues ranging from bilingualism to code switching must be addressed. These issues and corresponding data challenge the validity of findings regarding gender differences in language use and strongly suggest that such differences (to the extent that they exist at all) are manufactured by a middle-class, European American context and exist only for middle-class, European American speakers.

In chapter 16, "Black and White (and Blue): A Feminist Analysis of Ethnicity and Pornography," Gloria Cowan addresses the limitations of feminist analyses of pornography to date. These analyses have ignored the extent to which pornography also serves racist agendas and seeks to degrade Women of Color because they are women *and* because they are minorities. Cowan also presents an empirical analysis of ethnicity in pornographic videos, with particular attention given to interracial pornography. She suggests that racism and misogyny cannot readily be disentangled in pornography or in the lives of Women of Color and that research and political action regarding pornography must begin to address racism.

These three chapters differ in their approach, perspective, and analyses but have in common the conclusion that feminist psychology's knowledge (of women's health, language use, and of representations of women in pornography) has been structured by a European American cultural context; consequently, feminist psychology's knowledge is not simply limited to a small portion of the world's women but is mistaken to the extent that gender, rather than implicit culture, is posited as the major explanatory factor.

The book ends with a concluding chapter by Rhoda Unger on the meaning of cultural diversity for the future of feminist psychology.

14

DOUBLE JEOPARDY: ETHNICITY AND GENDER IN HEALTH RESEARCH

ELIZABETH A. KLONOFF, HOPE LANDRINE, and JUDYTH SCOTT

In the past several years, both the lay and the scientific press have noted the virtual absence of women participants in medical research that is not concerned specifically with obstetrics, gynecology, or breast and gynecological cancers (Meyerowitz, cited in McCarthy, 1993). Consequently, government funding agencies have recently increased their efforts to encourage researchers to address issues of gender and ethnicity. The 1991 revision of the standard Application for Public Health Service Grant, for example, requires potential applicants either to include women and people of color or to justify why a specific group is excluded (U.S. Department of Health and Human Services [DHHS], p. 21). A number of explanations have been offered for the relative absence of women research participants in medical studies, particularly studies involving pharmacological agents. These explanations center around concerns about the potential effects of pharmacologic agents on a developing fetus, potential threats to the reproductive ability of women of child-bearing age, the impact of cyclic hormonal changes and menstruation on findings, hormonal differences between men and women, and so forth.

Psychological research on health issues, on the other hand, with its emphasis on lifestyle and behavioral changes that may affect health status, should be immune to these concerns. Because research in health psychology relies not on biochemistry or pharmacology but on understanding, predicting, and changing behavior, women and ethnic minorities should be adequately represented in its research. In addition, because psychological research has a long history of focusing on high-risk populations, published studies should reflect those populations that have been demonstrated to have high incidences of the problems being studied. Thus, the purpose of the current chapter is to explore the extent to which psychological research in the area of health includes women, minorities, and Women of Color as participants, and adequately addresses issues of importance to ethnic minority women. We attempt to accomplish this in three parts. First, we present national epidemiological data on the ethnic and gender distribution of a number of serious, life-threatening illnesses, with emphasis on the diseases and conditions that appear frequently in psychological research. These data provide a background on the kinds of health problems that Women of Color face and consequently on their health concerns. Second, empirical articles published in the journal *Health Psychology* are reviewed to assess the kinds of topics covered, their relevance to the health problems of Women of Color, and the extent to which Women of Color were included in the research. As the official journal of Division 38 (Health Psychology) of the American Psychological Association (APA) and as the only APA journal devoted exclusively to issues of health, we believe that any deficiencies found in this journal are likely to reflect more global problems in health psychology research. Other journals covering health psychology topics are no doubt similar. Finally, a similar review of ethnicity and gender in studies on health-related topics published in two major feminist psychology journals (*Psychology of Women Quarterly* and *Sex Roles*) is presented.

EPIDEMIOLOGY OF DISEASES WITH BEHAVIORAL COMPONENTS

To determine the extent to which psychological research has attended adequately to the health concerns of ethnic minority women, baseline data on the incidence of a number of diseases and various lifestyle practices were obtained from *Health United States: 1990*, a DHHS (1991a) publication that reviews the health status of U.S. citizens. These data are presented by topic.

Topics Addressing Lifestyle Issues

Smoking

Figure 1 shows DHHS statistics on deaths from pulmonary causes between 1950 and 1988 by gender and ethnicity. As can be seen, more men than women die from pulmonary causes, presumably because of the (historical) greater rate of smoking among men than women. However, between 1980 and 1988, there was a leveling off in deaths of White men, whereas for both White and African American women and African American men there continued to be an increase. It is estimated that 28.4% of men and 22.8% of women are current smokers (Morbidity and Mortality Weekly Report [MMWR], 1992). Although rates of smoking for both genders have declined in recent years, the decline among women has been less than that among men (DHHS, 1991b), and the rate of initiation of smoking among women has remained fairly consistent (Fiore et al., 1989). Although for all ethnic groups, men smoke more than women, this difference is less pronounced for Whites (men = 27.9%, women = 23.5%) and Native Americans (men = 40.1%, women = 36.2%; MMWR, 1992). Simultaneously, there has been increased effort on the part of tobacco companies to market cigarettes to minorities; more than $5 million per year is spent on tobacco billboards in African American communities and more than $1.4 million for tobacco advertising in Latino communities (Davis,

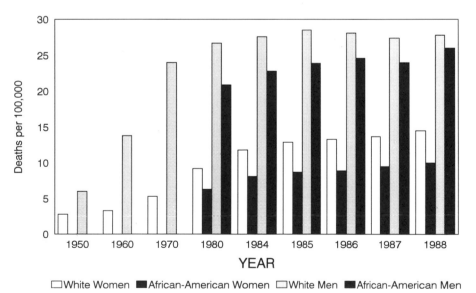

□White Women ■African-American Women □White Men ■African-American Men

Figure 1. Pulmonary disease: Death rates in selected years, 1950–1988. Data are from U.S. Department of Health and Human Services (1991a).

1987). Given these data, one should expect psychological literature on smoking prevention and cessation programs to target women and minorities.

Obesity and Exercise

Figure 2 shows the percentage of people classified as overweight on the basis of physical examinations performed during three time periods. These data are presented by ethnic group and gender. As can be seen, the percentage of African American women who are overweight is greater than any other Ethnic × Gender combination at all time periods; Latino women, for whom data are available for only the most recent time period, represent the next largest group classified as overweight. Thus, one should expect the psychological literature on programs to treat obesity and to increase exercise and exercise adherence to include substantial numbers of African American and Latino women.

Epidemiology of Specific Diseases

Hypertension

Figure 3 shows the percentage of patients exhibiting high blood pressure during physical examination by gender and ethnicity. Again, the percentage of African Americans is greater than the percentage of Whites at each time period; the percentage of African American women with high

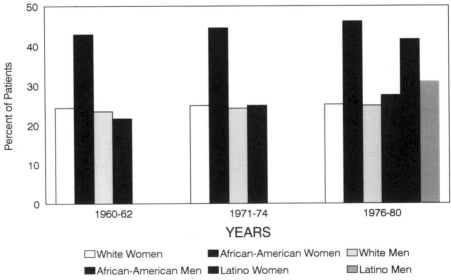

Figure 2. Overweight persons based on physical examination. Data are from U.S. Department of Health and Human Services (1991a).

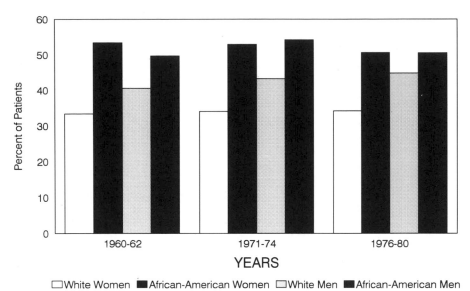

Figure 3. Hypertension based on physical examination. Data are from U.S. Department of Health and Human Services (1991a).

blood pressure is almost equivalent to the percentage of African American men, and it is greater than the percentage of White men at every time period. Thus, one should expect that research and interventions related to hypertension would include significant numbers of African American men and African American women as well in their samples.

Cerebrovascular Disease

Figure 4 shows the deaths from cerebrovascular disease for the years 1950 through 1988 by gender and ethnicity. Although the deaths have decreased dramatically over that time period, deaths of African Americans are greater than those of Whites, and deaths of African American women are greater than those of White men. Again, one would expect that psychological research on cerebrovascular disease would include a large number of African American women participants.

Heart Disease

Figure 5 shows deaths from heart disease by gender and ethnicity for the years 1950–1988. Deaths of men are greater than of women at every time period; deaths of African Americans are greater than deaths of Whites for each gender. One should expect, then, that the majority of the studies would focus on men. However, when studies include women, African American women should make up the majority of the women participants.

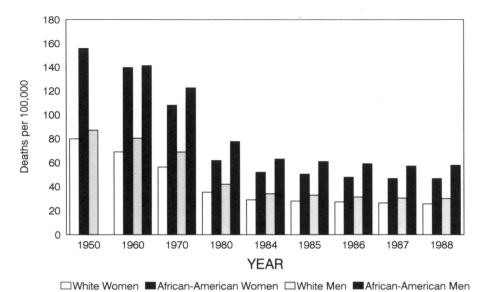

□White Women ■African-American Women □White Men ■African-American Men

Figure 4. Cardiovascular disease: Deaths in selected years, 1950–1988. Data are from U.S. Department of Health and Human Services (1991a).

Diabetes

Figure 6 depicts deaths from diabetes from 1950 to 1988 by gender and ethnicity. As can be seen, African Americans die more often than Whites, and African American women die more frequently than all other

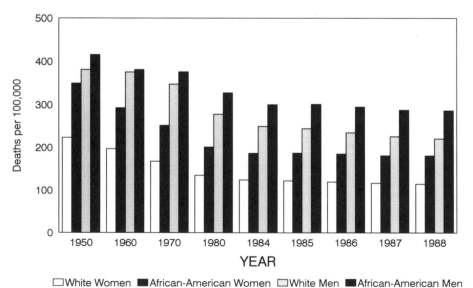

□White Women ■African-American Women □White Men ■African-American Men

Figure 5. Heart disease: Death rates in selected years, 1950–1988. Data are from U.S. Department of Health and Human Services (1991a).

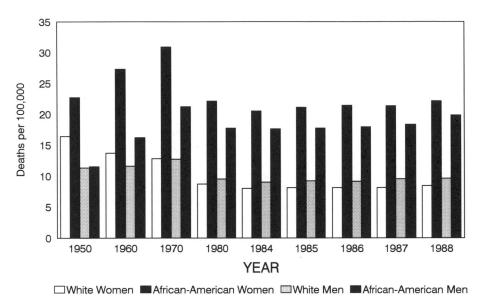

Figure 6. Diabetes mellitus: Death rates in selected years, 1950–1988. Data are from U.S. Department of Health and Human Services (1991a).

groups at every time period. Thus, psychological research on diabetes should include, if not focus on, African American women participants.

Cancer

Figure 7 depicts deaths from cancer for the years 1950–1988 by ethnicity and gender. Again, men die more often than women, but African

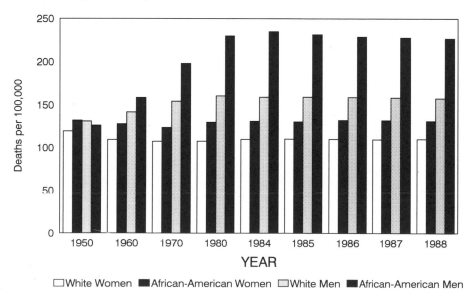

Figure 7. Cancer: Death rates in selected years, 1950–1988. Data are from U.S. Department of Health and Human Services (1991a).

Americans of both genders die more frequently than Whites. Figure 8 shows the percentage of patients surviving 5 years after the diagnosis of cancer. White women have the highest 5-year survival rates, and African American men have the lowest. Although African American women and White men have similar five-year survival rates, there is a consistently decreasing trend for African American women over the time periods reported. With respect to breast cancer specifically, the data suggest dramatically differing survival rates by ethnicity, even when access to health care is controlled (Richardson, Landrine, & Marks, 1994).

Thus, the major health problems of minority women include tobacco use, obesity, high blood pressure, cardiovascular disease, diabetes, and cancer. Epidemiologically, these problems and death as a result of them are more frequent among minority women than among White women and, in many cases, are more prevalent among minority women than among White men. Thus, one should expect that psychological literature on these topics should include minority women participants.

HEALTH PSYCHOLOGY'S RESEARCH ON MINORITY WOMEN'S HEALTH

To assess the extent to which research in health psychology reflects the health problems and concerns of minority women, as detailed earlier,

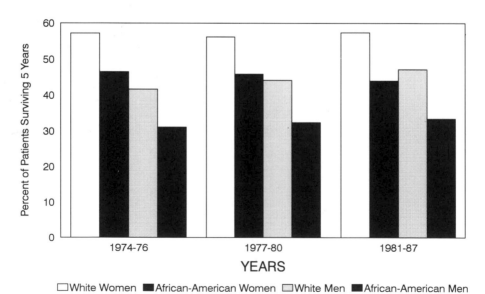

Figure 8. Cancer 5-year survival rates: Selected sites. Data are from U.S. Department of Health and Human Services (1991a).

we reviewed all issues of *Health Psychology* published from 1982 through 1994 (Number 3). Each empirical article published was coded for topic (broadly defined as the major theme of the article); age, gender, and ethnicity of participants; whether gender differences were tested statistically and, if tested, whether significant differences were found; and whether ethnic differences were tested and, if tested, whether there were significant differences. A total of 444 articles were reviewed. Seven of these articles were animal studies, and were therefore not included in any of the subsequent analyses.

Table 1 shows the results of this analysis by topic for gender of the participants. A study was categorized as having an equal number of men and women if 45–55% of the total number of participants represented each gender. Studies in which both genders were represented but more than 55% of the participants were men or women were categorized as both—predominantly men or as both—predominantly women, respectively. Studies in which the gender of the participants was not given were classified as gender unspecified. As can be seen, 63 (14.4%) of the articles included only women; 55 (12.6%) included only men; 97 (22.2%) included equal numbers of men and women; 113 (25.9%) included both genders with the majority being women; 63 (14.4%) included both genders with the majority men; and 46 (10.5%) failed to report the gender of the sample. Tests to determine gender differences were reported in 146 (33.4%) studies. When tests for gender differences were performed, 94 (64.4%) studies reported significant gender differences for at least one test conducted.

Thus, 62.5% of the articles published in *Health Psychology* included a representative proportion of women in their samples, with 40.3% of the articles including either all or a majority of women participants, and 22.2% including equal numbers of men and women. However, the publication of 46 articles that did not provide the gender of their participants suggests that concerns remain about potential unexplored gender effects, which may limit the generalizability of previous findings in health psychology research.

Table 2 shows a similar analysis for ethnicity of the participants. As can be seen, 255 articles (or 58.4% of the total) failed to report *any* information on the ethnicity of their participants; in 94 (21.5%) of the articles, the participants were either all White or more than 80% White; in only seven (1.6%) of the articles were participants all members of a minority group; 34 studies (7.8%) included Whites and one other minority group; and 47 (10.8%) included samples of at least one ethnic minority group that better approximated that group's representation in the population as a whole (e.g., the sample was less than 80% White and the authors specifically addressed the ethnic composition of the sample in the article). Tests for ethnic differences were performed in only 49 (11.2%) of the articles; of these, 35 (71.4%) studies reported significant differences for at least one test conducted. Thus, 58.4% of the articles published in *Health*

TABLE 1
Gender of Participants by Topic of Article in *Health Psychology*

Topic	N	All women	All men	Equal	Both—more women	Both—more men	Gender unspecified
					Gender		
AIDS	16	1 (6.3)	6 (37.5)	2 (12.5)	3 (18.8)	3 (18.8)	1 (6.3)
Alcohol/drugs	3	0	0	2 (66.7)	0	0	1 (33.3)
Arthritis	12	4 (33.3)	0	0	6 (50)	0	2 (16.7)
Breast cancer	14	14 (100)	0	0	0	0	0
Cardiovascular disease	14	2 (14.3)	4 (28.6)	2 (14.3)	2 (14.3)	2 (14.3)	2 (14.3)
Cancer	12	1 (8.3)	0	1 (8.3)	6 (50)	2 (16.7)	2 (16.7)
Diabetes	31	2 (6.5)	1 (3.2)	10 (32.3)	16 (51.6)	1 (3.2)	1 (3.2)
Gynecology	10	8 (80)	0	0	0	2 (20)	0
Health behaviors	42	8 (19)	2 (4.8)	12 (28.6)	11 (26.2)	4 (9.5)	5 (11.9)
Health schema	16	0	0	2 (12.5)	7 (43.8)	5 (31.3)	2 (12.5)
Hypertension/ blood pressure	45	2 (4.4)	17 (37.8)	11 (24.4)	8 (17.8)	7 (15.6)	0
Immunology	5	0	1 (20)	0	3 (60)	0	1 (20)
Obesity/exercise	31	6 (19.4)	0	8 (25.8)	8 (25.8)	4 (12.9)	5 (16.1)
Pain	12	0	1 (8.3)	2 (16.7)	5 (41.7)	2 (16.7)	2 (16.7)
Personality types	25	2 (8)	9 (36)	5 (20)	5 (20)	1 (4)	3 (12)
Physician visits	7	2 (28.6)	0	3 (42.9)	2 (28.6)	0	0
Procedures	11	0	0	2 (18.2)	3 (27.3)	6 (54.5)	0
Renal disease	10	0	1 (10)	2 (20)	1 (10)	4 (40)	2 (20)
Respiratory disorder	6	0	0	2 (33.3)	1 (16.7)	2 (33.3)	1 (16.7)
Smoking	43	4 (9.3)	2 (4.7)	15 (34.9)	11 (25.6)	4 (9.3)	7 (16.3)
Stress	28	4 (14.3)	6 (21.4)	7 (25)	4 (14.3)	4 (14.3)	3 (10.7)
Surgery	5	0	2 (40)	0	2 (40)	1 (20)	0
Other	39	3 (7.7)	3 (7.7)	9 (23.1)	7 (17.9)	11 (28.2)	6 (15.4)
Total	437	63 (14.4)	55 (12.6)	97 (22.2)	113 (25.9)	63 (14.4)	46 (10.5)

Note. Numbers in parentheses are percentages.

TABLE 2
Ethnicity of Participants by Topic of Article in *Health Psychology*

Topic	N	Ethnicity				
		Ethnicity unspecified	All or >80% White	All minority	White and one other minority	Ethnicity considered
AIDS	16	4 (25)	5 (31.3)	1 (6.3)	0	6 (37.5)
Alcohol/drugs	3	3 (33.3)	1 (33.3)	0	0	1 (33.3)
Arthritis	12	8 (66.7)	2 (16.7)	0	0	2 (16.7)
Breast cancer	14	5 (35.7)	7 (50)	0	1 (7.1)	1 (7.1)
Cardiovascular disease	14	11 (78.6)	3 (21.4)	0	0	0
Cancer	12	7 (58.3)	2 (16.7)	1 (8.3)	0	2 (16.7)
Diabetes	31	24 (77.4)	5 (16.1)	0	2 (6.5)	0
Gynecology	10	4 (40)	4 (40)	1 (10)	0	1 (10)
Health behaviors	42	17 (40.5)	13 (30.9)	1 (2.4)	5 (11.9)	6 (14.4)
Health schema	16	10 (62.5)	4 (25)	0	1 (6.3)	1 (6.3)
Hypertension/ blood pressure	45	17 (37.8)	8 (17.8)	1 (2.2)	14 (31.1)	5 (11.1)
Immunology	5	5 (100)	0	0	0	0
Obesity/exercise	31	23 (74.2)	3 (9.7)	0	2 (6.4)	3 (9.7)
Pain	12	8 (66.7)	3 (25)	0	0	1 (8.3)
Personality types	25	18 (72)	3 (12)	1 (4)	0	3 (12)
Physician visits	7	2 (28.6)	2 (28.6)	0	2 (28.6)	1 (14.3)
Procedures	11	7 (63.6)	1 (9.1)	0	1 (9.1)	2 (18.2)
Renal disease	10	8 (80)	0	0	1 (10)	1 (10)
Respiratory disorder	6	6 (100)	0	0	0	0
Smoking	43	25 (58.1)	9 (20.9)	0	4 (9.3)	5 (11.6)
Stress	28	15 (53.6)	10 (35.7)	0	1 (3.6)	2 (7.1)
Surgery	5	1 (20)	4 (80)	0	0	0
Other	39	29 (74.4)	5 (12.8)	1 (2.6)	0	4 (10.3)
Total	437	255 (58.4)	94 (21.5)	7 (1.6)	33 (7.6)	48 (11)

Note. Numbers in parentheses are percentages.

Psychology did not even report the ethnicity of the participants, and in 79.9% of the articles the participants were either all White, predominantly White, or the ethnicity of the participants was not given. These data alone suggest that ethnicity has not been adequately addressed in health psychology.

Topics Specifically Addressing Lifestyles

Smoking

Forty-three articles focused on smoking. Seven of these (16.3%) did not provide information about the gender of the participants, and 25 (58.1%) did not specify the ethnicity. Of the 15 articles that included equal numbers of men and women, only three (20%) clearly included minority participants; two of these compared African Americans with Whites. Three of the four studies involving only women did not indicate the ethnicity of their participants; the fourth adequately addressed ethnicity. Of the 11 studies that involved predominantly women participants, four (36.4%) did not identify ethnicity, and three (27.3%) included predominantly Whites; however, one study compared Latinos with Whites and three used an ethnic distribution that more closely matches the population as a whole. Thus, despite evidence that smoking rates among women are not decreasing as rapidly as those of men (Fiore et al., 1989), only 35.2% of the articles on smoking focused primarily on women. Similarly, although the tobacco industry's advertising campaign entails efforts to sustain and increase the number of minority smokers (Davis, 1987), only 20.9% of the articles clearly included people of color as participants.

Obesity and Exercise

There were 31 articles on obesity or exercise. Although gender was unspecified in five (16.1%) of these, the majority of the articles (71%) focused either solely on women, predominantly on women, or on equal numbers of women and men. However, 23 (74.2%) of the studies did not include information regarding the ethnicity of their participants. Of the remaining eight studies, three involved only White or predominantly White participants; three involved participants whose ethnicity was more representative of the population; and one study compared African Americans with Whites and another compared Latinos with Whites. Thus, minorities were identified as participants in only 16.1% of the articles, albeit African American and Latino women have the highest rates of obesity (DHHS, 1991a).

Preventive Health Behaviors

The 42 articles in this category focused on encouraging preventive health behaviors such as colorectal cancer screening, mammography, and condom use. Five articles (11.9%) did not report data on gender, and 17 (40.5%) did not report participants' ethnicity. Ethnicity was appropriately represented in six articles (14.3%); however, in two of these, gender was not provided. Nine of the 19 articles focusing predominantly on women included only or predominantly White participants, and six did not report ethnicity. Of the four remaining articles focusing primarily on women, two compared African Americans with Whites, one compared Latinos with Whites, and one used a representative sample of minorities. Thus, women were represented in of 63.8% of the articles and minorities in only 28.6%.

Articles on Specific Diseases

Hypertension

Forty-five of the articles reviewed concerned hypertension or blood pressure response. Although all of these studies reported the gender of participants, 17 (37.8%) did not provide any information regarding their ethnicity. Of the 14 (31.1%) studies comparing African Americans with Whites, five (35.7%) involved only men, seven (50%) had equal numbers of men and women, 1 (7.1%) involved predominantly men, and one (7.1%) involved predominantly women. Of the two studies that included only female participants, one did not report their ethnicity and the other used only Whites. Of the eight (17.8%) studies that included a majority of women as respondents, four (50%) did not report ethnicity, one (12.5%) was more than 80% White, one (12.5%) compared African American with White subjects, and only two (25%) adequately accounted for ethnicity in their sample. Thus, despite the well-known prevalence of hypertension in the African American community (DHHS, 1991a), more than half of the articles focusing on blood pressure (55.6%) either did not identify the ethnicity of their respondents or involved primarily White respondents. Only 15 articles focused solely on African Americans or compared responses of African American participants with those of Whites. Of these, eight (53.3%) were in a single special issue devoted to race, reactivity, and blood pressure regulation (1989, Vol. 8, No. 5).

Cardiovascular Disease

Fourteen articles focused on cardiovascular disease or responses. Six studies (42.9%) used predominantly men, four (28.6%) used predominantly women, two (14.3%) used equal numbers of men and women, and two (14.3%) did not specify the gender of their participants. The overwhelming majority of articles (11, or 78.6% of the total) did not report the respondents' ethnicity; the remaining three articles all involved predominantly White participants. Thus, despite the clear evidence of increased risk of cardiovascular disease among people of color and Women of Color (DHHS, 1991a), these groups are not the focus of current research.

Diabetes

There were 31 articles on this topic. The gender of the participants in these studies more closely matched the epidemiological distribution of diabetes, that is, 58.1% (18 articles), included all or predominantly women participants. Only two (6.4%) articles included all or predominantly men, and 10 (32.3%) involved an equal number of each gender; only one article (3.2%) did not provide gender information. By contrast, ethnicity was ignored in the vast majority (77.4%, or 24) of articles; of the remaining seven articles, five included predominantly White participants, and two compared African Americans with Whites. The Ethnicity × Gender distribution of the participants in these studies does not match the epidemiological data on diabetes (DHHS, 1991a), which suggests that African American women are most likely to die from diabetes.

Cancer

There were 12 articles on cancer. The majority involved predominantly women respondents (7 articles, or 58.3%). Ethnicity, however, tended to be ignored: Seven articles (58.6%) did not report it, whereas two (16.7%) included predominantly White participants. The remaining three studies included one that examined Latino women and two that included a representative distribution of minorities. Thus, despite the relatively poor cancer survival rates of people of color and of Women of Color (DHHS, 1991a), ethnicity seems to be ignored in much of the research.

Traditional Women's Health Topics

A variety of topics have long been considered to be the mainstay of women's health issues (i.e., pregnancy, gynecological concerns, and breast cancer). Twenty-four articles focused on these topics. Of the three articles on pregnancy, one included only Whites, one included only Latinas, and one included a representative ethnic distribution. Seven articles dealt primarily with gynecological issues; of these, four (57.1%) did not report ethnicity, whereas the remaining three used predominantly White participants. Interestingly, two of the seven articles included men, but these were among the four that did not report ethnicity. A total of 14 articles were on breast cancer. Of these, five (35.7%) did not specify the ethnicity of their sample, whereas seven (50%) included either all White or predominantly White participants. Of the remaining two articles, one compared Whites with African Americans and one included a representative number of minorities. Given the clear differential survival rates from breast cancer by ethnicity (Richardson et al., 1994), the lack of attention to Women of Color is striking. Thus, of the 24 articles addressing traditional topics in women's health, 37.5% did not report ethnicity, whereas 45.8% involved all or predominantly White participants. Only 16.6% of the articles considered ethnicity as a possible factor.

Summary of Findings for *Health Psychology*

Although there has been increased discussion of the possible role of ethnicity in health beliefs and behavior (Landrine & Klonoff, 1992) and increased attention paid to ethnicity over time (see Table 3), the majority of articles nonetheless fail to report the ethnicity of their participants or include predominantly Whites. More than 10% of the articles reviewed did not report the gender of the sample, whereas almost 60% did not report the ethnicity of the participants. Amazingly, 37 articles (8.5%) reported neither the gender nor the ethnicity of their respondents. Who were these respondents? What do these results mean in the absence of information regarding from whom they were obtained? To whom should one generalize these results? From our review of articles published in *Health Psychology*, we conclude the following:

1. Health psychology has ignored the problems of people of color in general and of Women of Color specifically. Reporting such basic information as the ethnicity of the participants does not seem to be a necessary criterion for publication, given that 58.4% of the articles published in the journal in a 12-year period did not provide this information.
2. Although certain topic areas (e.g., hypertension) are more likely to include people of color as participants, people of color nonetheless do not make up the majority of participants in these studies despite clear ethnic differences in illness prevalences.
3. Although certain topic areas (e.g., obesity and exercise) are more likely to include women as participants, the majority of these women tend to be White; Women of Color appear to be excluded from research despite clear ethnic differences among women.
4. Even when a topic area includes people of color, respondents tend to be men of color rather than Women of Color. Thus, Women of Color tend to be the most neglected group.
5. In studies of traditional women's health topics, the majority of the participants studied are White. Obstetrical and gynecological (OB/GYN) concerns of Women of Color have been virtually ignored.

TABLE 3
Health Psychology: Year of Publication by Ethnicity of Participants in Study

Year	Total	Ethnicity				
		Ethnicity unspecified	All or >80% White	All minority	White and one other minority	Ethnicity considered
1982	8	4 (50)	1 (12.5)	0	1 (12.5)	2 (25)
1983	11	10 (90.9)	0	0	1 (9.1)	0
1984	24	14 (58.3)	6 (25)	0	2 (8.3)	2 (8.3)
1985	23	20 (87)	2 (8.7)	0	1 (4.3)	0
1986	33	21 (63.6)	7 (21.2)	1 (3)	1 (3)	3 (9.10)
1987	45	30 (66.7)	7 (15.6)	0	1 (2.2)	7 (15.6)
1988	26	20 (76.9)	2 (7.7)	0	0	4 (15.4)
1989	35	17 (48.6)	5 (14.3)	1 (2.9)	12 (34.3)	0
1990	44	32 (72.7)	10 (22.7)	0	1 (2.3)	1 (2.3)
1991	49	27 (55.1)	11 (22.4)	0	4 (8.2)	7 (14.3)
1992	40	21 (52.5)	12 (30)	0	2 (5)	5 (12.5)
1993	33	9 (27.3)	12 (36.4)	3 (9.1)	2 (6.1)	7 (21.2)

Note. Numbers in parentheses are percentages.

FEMINIST PSYCHOLOGY'S RESEARCH ON WOMEN'S HEALTH

It is clear from our review that health psychology research has virtually ignored the unique problems of ethnic minority women. We next assessed the extent to which feminist psychological research on women's health has addressed the health problems and concerns of Women of Color. We analyzed the content of articles published in *Psychology of Women Quarterly* (*PWQ*; 1980–1992) and in *Sex Roles* (1982–1992). Specifically, we sought to determine (a) how frequently the major feminist psychological journals address women's health, (b) the types of health issues of focus, and (c) the extent to which Women of Color have been included in studies or review articles on women's health.

The topics covered in *PWQ* from 1980 to 1992 are summarized in Table 4. As indicated in column 1 of Table 4, 442 articles were published in the journal over the 12-year period. Of these, only 37 articles (8.4%) addressed women's health (column 2), with nine of the articles (24.3%) published in a special issue on women's health (1988, Vol. 12, No. 4). Twenty-five of the 37 articles on women's health (67.6%) focused on OB/GYN issues such as menstruation (eight articles), pregnancy (six articles), menopause (three articles), abortion (two articles), fertility (two articles), and contraception (two articles), with no articles addressing the types of health problems of Women of Color as outlined earlier. In addition, of the 37 articles on women's health, only nine (24.3%) included Women of Color in their samples or, in the case of a review article, devoted attention to the health of Women of Color. A similar analysis of articles published in *Sex Roles* is shown in Table 5.

As indicated in column 1 in Table 5, 1,170 articles were published in this journal over the 10-year period. Of these, only 19 articles (1.6%) focused on women's health (column 2). Of the 19 articles on women's health, 10 (52.6%) focused on OB/GYN issues such as menstruation (five articles), pregnancy (two articles), fertility (two articles), or menopause (one article), with no articles focusing on the health problems or concerns of Women of Color. Of the 19 articles on women's health, only three included Women of Color in their samples; two of the three articles focused on women in other countries (i.e., a 1987 article on female circumcision in Nigeria and a 1992 article on menstrual taboos among Brahmin women).

Summary of Findings for PWQ and Sex Roles

Thus, 1,612 articles were published in *PWQ* and *Sex Roles* from 1980 to 1992, with only 3.5% of these focusing on women's health; of these health articles, only 21% included Women of Color in their samples. Finally, the majority (62.5%) of these health articles focused on OB/GYN topics such as menstruation, menopause, or pregnancy, and none focused

TABLE 4
Articles Published in *Psychology of Women Quarterly* (1980–1992)

Year	Total no. of articles	No. on women's health	No. including minority women	Topic of article
1980	27	0	N/A	N/A
1981	58	5	2	Menstruation (2), pregnancy (1), pregnancy in African American women (1), reproductive symptoms (1)
1982	28	1	0	Menstrual cycle (1)
1983	33	1	0	Absence from work (1)
1984	15	1	0	Abortion (1)
1985	43	3	0	Menopausal symptoms (1), pain perception (1), fertility (1)
1986	34	2	0	Pregnancy (1), menstruation (1)
1987	37	0	N/A	N/A
1988	32	11[a]	1	Delivery (1), menstruation (1), illness rates (1), disability (1), diabetes (1), AIDS in Hispanic women (1), child bearing (1), abortion (1), breast self-exam (1), sexuality and menopause (1), intro (1)
1989	30	1	1	Japanese perceptions of motherhood (1)
1990	34	5	1	Menstrual symptoms (2), menopause (1), herpes (1), physical activity (1)
1991	39	2	0	Fertility (1), feminist contributions to health psychology (1)
1992	32	5	4	Body shapes (1), breast self-exam (1), contraception (1), condom use (1), menstruation (1)
Total	442	37 (8.4%)	9	Menstruation (8), pregnancy (6), menopause (3), abortion (2), fertility (2), contraception (2), breast self-exam, Other (12). Total gynecologic = 25 (67.6%) of total.

Note. Numbers in parentheses are the number of articles on that topic. N/A = not applicable.
[a]1988 Volume 12, Issue 4, was a special issue on women's health and accounts for nine of the articles.

TABLE 5
Articles Published in *Sex Roles* (1982–1992)

Year	Total no. of articles	No. on women's health	No. including minority women	Topic of article
1982	90	1	0	Menstrual-related excuses (1)
1983	99	1	0	Perceptions of fertility (1)
1984	166	5	0	Psychosomatic symptoms (1), mortality (1), teen pregnancy (1), men's health (1), physician treatment of patients (1)
1985	142	2	0	Fertility (1), neuroendocrine stress response and sex roles (1)
1986	100	1	0	Attitudes about menstrual cycle (1)
1987	98	3	1	Menstrual attitudes (1), menopause (1), female circumcision in Nigeria (1)
1988	108	0	N/A	N/A
1989	101	0	N/A	N/A
1990[a]	96	2	0	Health on a kibbutz (1), postoperative pain (1)
1991	97	1	1	Kidney failure (1)
1992	73	3	1	Menstrual taboos in Brahim women (1), pregnancy (1), menstrual attitudes (1)
Total	1,170	19 (1.6%)	3	

Note. Numbers in parentheses are the number of articles on that topic. N/A = not applicable.
[a]Volume 23, No. 7/8, is missing from this analysis.

on the major health problems or concerns of Women of Color. From these data, we conclude the following.

1. Feminist psychology has devoted almost no attention to women's health, insofar as only 3.5% of publications in the two major journals for the past 12 years have addressed health-related issues. The majority of studies of women's health continue to be conducted by nonfeminist researchers and to be published in nonfeminist journals. The dangers inherent in this situation need not be detailed. Feminist psychologists must devote more attention to women's health, and the two feminist psychological journals must encourage and solicit such research.

2. The little attention that feminist psychology has paid to women's health has been narrowly focused on OB/GYN issues, insofar as 62.5% of the published articles revolve around such topics. This narrow focus might be considered to be sexist because it equates women's health needs and concerns with OB/GYN issues, equates women with reproduction, and "genitalizes" women (Meyerowitz, cited in McCarthy, 1993). A health problem need not involve reproduction or any of the ways in which women differ physically from men to be a "women's health issue" (Meyerowitz, cited in McCarthy, 1993). Rather, the health problem needs merely to be one that the majority of women face, and one that nonfeminist researchers (consequently perhaps) ignore nonetheless.

3. Feminist psychology's tendency to focus on OB/GYN issues is dangerous in that the major health problems that all women face are being neglected. Serious health issues such as women's persistent failure to exercise (Dishman, Sallis, & Orenstein, 1985; Sallis et al., 1986) despite the role of exercise in decreasing osteoporosis (Fiatarone et al., 1990) and cancer (Kohl, LaPorte, & Blair, 1988), and the increase in cigarette smoking and in lung cancer (DHHS, 1991b) among women, are being ignored in favor of studies on perceptions of menstruation. Given that psychology's journals devoted to the study of health (e.g., *Health Psychology*, as we have already demonstrated) also tend to ignore these serious health problems among women and focus instead almost exclusively on these problems among men, many of the life-threatening diseases that women and girls face are ignored by the discipline as a whole. Inevitably, the burden of addressing women's health needs will fall on feminist psychology, because mainstream psychology is likely to continue to ignore these issues

just as it ignores women's issues more generally. Thus, feminist psychology must change its focus from somewhat trivial studies of OB/GYN issues to studies of the life-threatening health problems that women and girls face if the latter are to be addressed at all.

4. In feminist psychology's few studies of women's health, Women of Color have been ignored; Women of Color were included in only 21% of the published articles; in the majority of these articles, only a few Women of Color participated (e.g., 10% of the sample); and analyses for ethnic differences typically were not conducted.

5. Finally, the specific health problems that Women of Color face (outlined previously) have been ignored by researchers in feminist psychology. We found no studies on any of these health problems published in *PWQ* or in *Sex Roles* from 1980 to 1992.

WHY ETHNICITY IS IMPORTANT

Researchers have demonstrated that gender and social roles, employment status, the nature and amount of social support, and other factors, many of which are differentiated by gender, can all affect health status (e.g., Klonoff & Landrine, 1992). It is highly likely that cultural beliefs and schema exert the same type of influence (Klonoff & Landrine, 1994; Landrine & Klonoff, 1992; Landrine & Klonoff, 1994) and that there are Gender × Culture interactions. A few examples of the importance of ethnicity in health are given next. In a recent study, Landrine, Richardson, Klonoff, and Flay (1994) found that for different ethnic groups, different factors predicted smoking among adolescents. Furthermore, different factors predicted smoking in more acculturated Latino adolescents that in less acculturated ones, with the more acculturated ones closely resembling the White population. Similarly, women are more likely than men to cite fear of weight gain as a reason to not stop smoking (Waldron, 1988). To what degree are Latino girls affected by both acculturation and gender concerns? Differences in beliefs, religion, foods, customs, traditional folk remedies, and so forth, all may have significant implications for research with minorities. When ethnicity is ignored, the potential role of these factors is therefore artificially obscured. Culture also affects the recognition and report of symptoms. For example, although most people would agree that menopause is a biological event, to what extent are the experiences of "hot flashes" biologically mediated? The data suggest that cultural, social, or psychological differences in the tendency to focus on internal changes, differences in the thresholds of sensitivity to these changes, and expectations and norms regarding the public expression of bodily symptoms or changes may all alter the extent to which physiological events are perceived, construed, or labeled a *hot flash*. Goodman (1982) compared the report of hot flashes in a group of women from Aberdeen, Texas, to the report from a group of women from Hawaii. Although 74% of the Aberdeen women reported hot flashes, a significant number of the Hawaiian women did not. Beyene (1986) evaluated hot flashes in a group of rural Mayan Indian women on the Yucatan peninsula and a group of rural Greek women on the island of Evia. Although 72.7% of the Greek menopausal and postmenopausal women reported hot flashes, the only symptom of menopause recognized by the Mayan women was the irregularity and eventual cessation of menses. Thus, there may be cultural differences in what constitutes a physical symptom.

Finally, as long as there are ethnic differences in illness prevalence, mortality, and morbidity, the potential role of ethnicity cannot continue to be ignored. Although these ethnic differences have primarily been attributed to socioeconomic differences in the availability and quality of medical care, recent studies suggest that these differences persist despite equal access to health care. Thus, increased attention must be paid to determining what factors, both physiological and psychological, contribute to these differences. In the absence of increased effort devoted to understanding ethnic differences, psychologists will continue to develop a health psychology of White people.

CONCLUSIONS AND RECOMMENDATIONS

Taken together, these data suggest a number of important implications for the way in which biopsychosocial models are implemented in health psychology research and intervention, as follows:

1. Because both gender and ethnicity can potentially affect the outcomes of research, all published articles on health-related topics should be required to routinely report both the gender and ethnicity of the participants being studied. Without this information, it is impossible to know to whom results can be generalized.

2. All researchers should recognize that results obtained primarily from White participants, particularly White men, cannot be generalized to the population as a whole. A statement clearly delineating the limits of the findings should be included in health research that relies on all or predominantly White participants. That is, results from White participants should not be assumed to represent results from the general

population. Similarly, results that demonstrate differences for minority participants should not merely be presented as deviations from "normal" or White. Differences in cultural beliefs and practices (e.g., Landrine & Klonoff, 1992) may result in widely differing outcomes, and the possibility that these outcomes could affect research results needs to be given increased attention.

3. Merely matching sample demographics to the demographics of the geographical area surrounding the research facility should no longer be considered sufficient. Research centers are often located in population areas in which certain groups (e.g., Whites) are overrepresented relative to the population of the country as a whole. Researchers seeking to generalize their results to the population as a whole should match the demographics of their subject pool to the demographics of the population, not of their particular location. This may require researchers to make special efforts to seek out minority participants, particularly minority women. This is particularly important for those diseases and health-compromising behaviors for which minority women are at clear risk.

4. Researchers in all areas of health, and feminist researchers with an interest in health, may need to devote more attention to the epidemiological data on the incidence and prevalence of various diseases by ethnicity and gender. Research can then be directed toward adequately representing those most at risk. "Convenience" samples that do not match the distribution of a given problem should be discouraged in favor of planned attempts to study those populations that actually experience higher rates of illnesses.

5. Methods of subject recruitment that fail to attract adequate numbers of minorities and women should be discarded in favor of those that may be more culturally and gender sensitive. Researchers who have been successful in recruiting a diverse subject population should be encouraged to share their methodologies with other researchers who have been less successful. Journal editors should be more cognizant of the exclusion of minority participants and, if necessary, devote journal space to articles specifically addressing methods and procedures to increase minority subject recruitment. In addition, alternative methods of recruiting participants, some of which may require the assistance and cooperation of local indigenous minority groups and networks, should be developed. Continuing to focus primarily on White participants decreases the potential impact of our research and increases

the likelihood that our medical colleagues, who may be more familiar with who constitutes the at-risk groups, will find our findings trivial or of no use.

6. Finally, the differing incidence of various diseases by different ethnic groups suggests that traditional research methods and interventions are not effectively reaching minority populations. Consultation with and increased involvement of members of individual cultural groups may be necessary to develop new ways of conceptualizing problems, a better understanding of the factors that may be involved, and new interventions that may be of particular benefit to minority women.

In light of the data presented here, we believe that the future direction of health research being conducted by nonfeminists, and especially by feminists, should be along the following lines:

1. The emphasis should shift from health issues that are primarily OB/GYN in nature to *all* health problems that contribute to increases in mortality and morbidity rates among women. This does not mean that important topics such as breast and ovarian cancer should be ignored. Rather, feminist health researchers should expand their spheres of inquiry to include the broader range of illnesses, diseases, and health-related behaviors that may be contributing to early death and disability in women. This may require new research to address questions regarding lifestyles and the various effects gender and gender roles have on health enhancement.

2. Similarly, a feminist perspective on research in areas such as health attitudes, health services utilization, and compliance with medical directives could provide extremely crucial information that could benefit large numbers of women.

3. However, these changes in emphasis must occur simultaneously with an awareness that research should serve all women, including Women of Color. Feminist researchers should actively seek out Women of Color to serve as collaborators and as research participants.

REFERENCES

Beyene, Y. (1986). Cultural significance and physiological manifestations of menopause: A biocultural analysis. *Culture, Medicine, and Psychiatry, 10*, 47–71.

Davis, R. M. (1987). Current trends in cigarette advertising and marketing. *New England Journal of Medicine, 316*, 725–732.

Dishman, R. K., Sallis, J. F., & Orenstein, D. R. (1985). The determinants of physical activity and exercise. *Public Health Reports, 100,* 158–171.

Fiatarone, M. A., Marks, E. C., Ryan, N. D., Meredith, C. N., Lipsitz, L. A., & Evans, W. J. (1990). High-intensity strength training in nonagenarians. *Journal of the American Medical Association, 263,* 3029–3034.

Fiore, M. C., Novotny, T. E., Pierce, J. P., Hatziandreu, E. J., Patel, K. M., & Davis, R. M. (1989). Trends in cigarette smoking in the United States: The changing influence of gender and race. *Journal of the American Medical Association, 261,* 49–55.

Goodman, M. (1982). A critique of menopause research. In A. Voda, M. Dinnerstein, & S. O'Donnell (Eds.), *Changing perspectives on menopause.* Austin: University of Texas Press.

Kohl, H. W., LaPorte, R. E., & Blair, S. N. (1988). Physical activity and cancer. *Sports Medicine, 6,* 222–237.

Klonoff, E. A., & Landrine, H. (1992). Sex-roles, occupational roles, and symptom reporting: A test of competing hypotheses on sex differences. *Journal of Behavioral Medicine, 15,* 355–364.

Klonoff, E. A., & Landrine, H. (1994). Cultural and gender diversity in common-sense beliefs about the causes of six illnesses. *Journal of Behavioral Medicine, 17,* 407–418.

Landrine, H., & Klonoff, E. A. (1992). Culture and health-related schema: A review and proposal for interdisciplinary integration. *Health Psychology, 11,* 267–276.

Landrine, H., & Klonoff, E. A. (1994). Cultural diversity in causal attributions for illness: The role of the supernatural. *Journal of Behavioral Medicine, 17,* 181–193.

Landrine, H., Richardson, J. L., Klonoff, E. A., & Flay, B. (1994). Cultural diversity in the predictors of adolescent smoking: The relative influence of peers. *Journal of Behavioral Medicine, 17,* 331–346.

McCarthy, K. (1993, July). Research on women's health doesn't show whole picture. *APA Monitor,* pp. 14–15.

MMWR. (1992). Cigarette smoking among adults: United States, 1990.41(20), 354–355, 361–367.

Richardson, J. L., Landrine, H., & Marks, G. (1994). Does psychological status influence cancer survival? In C. E. Lewis, C. O. Sullivan, & J. Barraclough (Eds.), *The psychoimmunology of human cancer: Mind and body in the fight for survival* (pp. 228–245). Oxford, England: Oxford University Press.

Sallis, J. F., Haskell, W. L., Fortmann, S. P., Vranizan, K. M., Taylor, C. B., & Solomon, D. S. (1986). Predictors of adoption and maintenance of physical activity in a community sample. *Preventive Medicine, 15,* 331–341.

U.S. Department of Health and Human Services. (1991a). *Health United States 1990* (DHHS Publication No. 91-1232). Hyattsville, MD: U.S. Department of Health and Human Services, Public Health Service, Centers for Disease Control, National Center for Health Statistics.

U.S. Department of Health and Human Services. (1991b). *Strategies to control tobacco use in the United States* (NIH Publication No. 92-3316). Washington, DC: Author.

Waldron, I. (1988). Gender and health related behavior. In D. S. Gochman (Ed.), *Health behavior: Emerging research perspectives* (pp. 193–213). New York: Plenum.

15

ETHNICITY AND GENDER ISSUES IN LANGUAGE

NANCY M. HENLEY

Women of Color note that much writing on the topic of language and gender is founded on the assumptions of White/Anglo (upper) middle-class experience. This writing often incorporates the idea of a "women's language" that is weak, uncertain, trivial, "hypercorrect," linguistically conservative, overpolite, and highly differentiated from that of men. Studies of ethnic variation in language (often conducted by Whites) have, on the other hand, tended to emphasize experience from males' point of view. This research has typically studied Black English forms exclusively among African American males or characterized only males as skilled performers of ritual insult in African American culture. Most studies also confound class with race and ethnicity. Investigations by and of Women and Men

I wish to thank Barrie Thorne, Cheris Kramarae, Joyce Penfield, and Vickie Mays for their references and other support; members of the UCLA (University of California, Los Angeles) Ford Ethnic Women Project, particularly Karen Rowe, Norma Rice, and participants in the fall 1989 and spring 1990 seminars, for their stimulation and assistance; and the UCLA Academic Senate Research Committee for partial financial support of this research. A condensed version of this chapter was presented at the 99th Annual Convention of the American Psychological Association, San Francisco, August 1991.

of Color have not only corrected these biases or shortcomings but have also challenged theory and raised new and important concerns in the area of language and gender. In this chapter I attempt to make these works and issues more widely known and debated. I also wrote it with the hope that examining the links between the racism, ethnocentrism, and sexism that help shape language and language usage will further the development of a psychology of power and oppression and lead to the social change necessary to overturn all forms of prejudice and oppression.

The topic of language, gender, and ethnicity or culture is prohibitively large when the various languages, cultures, and countries of the world are included. I limit this chapter to a discussion of ethnic and racial and gender issues with respect to American English (including Black English and Spanish–English code-switching[1]). Work in this field has come from many disciplines, and I draw on them in this chapter, particularly their empirical research, but with an emphasis on psychological research and implications.

Although I recognize their interconnection, I find it useful to maintain the distinction between two broad types of concern in language and gender: (a) sex *bias* in language (e.g., available and prescribed terms of address, personal pronouns, sex- and gender-marked words) and in language use (individual choice of certain forms from among those available); and (b) sex *difference* in language use (e.g., of color terms, intonational patterns, question types). Finally, I use the term *language and gender* to refer broadly to this field of study.

EARLY WRITINGS ON LANGUAGE, GENDER, AND ETHNICITY

The intersection of language, gender, and ethnicity was a topic within anthropological linguistics as early as 1664, when Breton (cited in Jespersen, 1922/1964) described differences in the words used by women and men among the Carib people. In 1912 Chamberlain reviewed theories proposed to explain various "women's languages." Articles by Furfey (1944), Haas (1944), and Flannery (1946) further demonstrated White anthropologists' interest in the topic of sex differentiation in language. These anthropologists identified sex differentiation in far-off tribal societies, but not in their own. Women's forms were often viewed as "women's language" because the language spoken by men of these societies was seen by these mostly male anthropologists as "the" language.

---

[1]The term *code switching* refers to switching from one language, dialect, or other type of linguistic code to another; this may occur when one goes from one situation to another, or it may take place from sentence to sentence or word to word within the same utterance.

Despite their sex-biased interpretations, some scholars, like laypeople, were aware of gender differences in language usage in the more industrialized countries. The anthropologist Elsie Clews Parsons wrote in 1913 of "sex dialects" in English and other languages in her book, *The Old-Fashioned Woman: Primitive Fancies About the Sex*. The first chapter on gender difference in a book on linguistics seems to have been that titled "The Woman" by the prominent Danish linguist Otto Jespersen (1922/1964), in his classic *Language: Its nature, development and origins*.

Jespersen (1922/1964), despite his underlying model of female deficiency (Henley & Kramarae, 1991), was broad-ranging and often thoughtful. He covered a variety of languages and cultures in which sex differentiation in language has been noted. He wrote not only of the different forms used by women and men in various tribal cultures but also of gender-linked taboo, bilingualism, innovation, vocabulary, and grammar (see Exhibit 1 for a summary of his contentions). Jespersen's data sources cited for illustrations of women's speech in English and European languages were often characters in novels and dramas by European men rather than actual speech collected from life; thus, his ideas are presented only for illustrative purposes.

WHITE AMERICAN FEMINIST LINGUISTICS

American feminist scholarship on language and gender has burgeoned since the 1960s, but without the prominence of the early interest in cultural difference.

Lakoff

In the late 1960s and early 1970s, White feminist writers began calling attention to the sexism in the English language, and, by the mid-1970s, recognition of sex differences in language usage was added to (White) feminist concerns. The linguist Robin Lakoff published the most comprehensive and widely read scholarly article from this time, "Language and Woman's Place" in 1973 (see Exhibit 2). That and other scholarly articles and books (e.g., Key, 1972, 1975; Kramer, 1974; Lakoff, 1975; Miller & Swift, 1976; Thorne & Henley, 1975) ignited a field of interest and research that continues to grow even now.

Lakoff's thesis was that women experience discrimination in language in two ways: (a) by being taught a weaker form of language than that used by men (rife with markers of uncertainty [e.g., tag questions]; of weakness [e.g., mild expletives]; and of triviality [e.g., fine color distinctions]); and (b) from the sexism found in the structure and usage of the language (e.g.,

EXHIBIT 1
Jespersen (1922/1964): Features Claimed for Women's Language

Women are more conservative linguistically than men ("it is generally said")
- women as keepers or transmitters of culture and language
- men as innovators of slang and new technical words

Women show excessive use of emphasis (Japanese, French, and English women)
- more intensive words
- exaggerated stress
- exaggerated tone or accent

Some women's speech is more polite and "refined"
- Japanese women use politeness prefixes more than men
- French women's speech is more "delicate" than men's

Women instinctively shrink from coarse and gross expressions and object to swearing
- true in all countries
- exercises a great influence on language
- not a taboo but ordained by (older) women themselves
- young do not always comply; feminists begin to imitate men

Women's vocabulary is less extensive than men's
- not due to limited education or mental or linguistic slowness
- women's and men's topical vocabularies differ
- men care more about language, words, and puns than women

Women have special adverb and adjective uses
- women use the words *pretty* and *nice*, and use *quite* to mean "very"
- adverbs of intensity are used hyperbolically, without regard to proper meaning (e.g., vastly, horribly)
- intensive *so*, *such*, to a degree unanchored, unfinished

Women leave sentences unfinished
- do not complete thought before beginning sentence
- men build long sentences with intricate clausal relationships, whereas women use coordinate (not subordinate) clauses
- women mark relationship between ideas emotionally (by stress and intonation) rather than grammatically

Volubility is women's

euphemisms for *woman*, nonparallel terms such as *master/mistress, bachelor /spinster*, address titles). Echoing (but not citing) many of Jespersen's (1922/1964) points, Lakoff claimed the existence of gender differences in American upper-middle-class English speakers, summarized in Exhibit 2 (from Lakoff, 1975, pp. 53 ff.).

Lakoff clearly described her sources:

> The data on which I am basing my claims have been gathered mainly by introspection: I have examined my own speech and that of my acquaintances and have used my own intuitions in analyzing it. I have

EXHIBIT 2
Lakoff (1975): Features Claimed for "Women's Language"

Many special-interest words
- relating to "women's work" and color terms (considered trivial)

Weaker particles (expletives)
- "oh, fudge!" versus "oh, shit!"

"Empty" adjectives (e.g., *divine*, *charming*, *cute*)

Question intonation in declarative context
- tag questions
- rising intonation in statement contexts
- shows lack of full commitment to one's statement

Hedging
- "well, y'know, kinda, sorta, I guess"
- show uncertainty

Intensive *so*
- hedges one's feelings

Hypercorrect grammar
- pronounce end (ng) sound in "singing," "going"
- women generally viewed as preservers of literacy and culture

Superpolite forms
- includes euphemism, eschewing of off-color and indelicacy
- "men carelessly blurt out whatever they are thinking"

Don't tell jokes (women can't tell jokes and don't get jokes)
- just an elaboration of preceding two points
- "women have no sense of humor"

Speak in italics
- shows uncertainty and the belief that one is not being listened to

Other devices
- wider intonational range than in men's speech (may also show uncertainty)
- more prone to gesturing while speaking than men

also made use of the media . . . is the educated, white, middle-class group that the writer of the book identifies with less worthy of study than any other? (pp. 4–5)

Thus Lakoff's ideas too are presented primarily for illustrative purposes, and are not to be taken as well-supported empirically. (Although numerous empirical studies based on these ideas have been conducted, some of which are cited later in this chapter, evaluating the ideas is not the main purpose of the chapter.)

Lakoff's (1973) presentation and discussion of these ideas, although questioned by some (e.g., Kramer, 1974; O'Barr & Atkins, 1980; Stanback, 1986; Thorne & Henley, 1975; Valian, 1977), have been highly influential in the field of language and gender and have stimulated valuable research by psychologists (e.g., Crosby & Nyquist, 1977; McMillan, Clifton, McGrath, & Gale, 1977) and others.

Studies of White Conversational Interaction

The study of gender in conversational interaction, mostly by sociologists (e.g., Fishman, 1978, 1983; West & Zimmerman, 1983; Zimmerman & West, 1975), has documented White men's conversational dominance. Strategies such as interruption and low involvement in conversational maintenance are used to control topics and turn-taking.

Related to conversational control but developed mostly in an independent literature is the topic of silencing (Houston & Kramarae, 1991; Kramarae, 1981; Spender, 1980; Rich, 1979). Kramarae (1981) delineated the "muted group" framework (E. Ardener, 1975; S. Ardener, 1975) as it applies to gender:

1. Women perceive the world differently from men because of women's and men's different experiences and activities rooted in the division of labor.
2. Because of their political dominance, the men's system of perception is dominant, impeding the free expression of the women's alternative models of the world.
3. In order to participate in society women must transform their own models in terms of the received male system of expression. (p. 3)

Ethnicity has been addressed rarely in the approximately 60 books and innumerable published articles on language and gender. Only a few seriously examine issues of importance to ethnic minority populations. In this regard, the convocation of the conference on the Sociology of the Languages of American Women at New Mexico State University in 1976[2] is a landmark in the history of language and gender study in the United States. Papers were presented (and later published) on, among other things, code-switching by Puerto Rican (Boricaña) and by Chicana women, on conservatism and innovation in the speech of Black women and men, and on Chicana mothers' speech to their children. The diverse spectrum of this conference has rarely been copied in most of the conferences and books on language and gender since then. Notable exceptions are the excellent collections by Penfield (1987) and Philips, Steel, and Tanz (1987; cross-nationally diverse); exceptions in review articles include those of Parlee (1979) and Kramarae (1990).

---

[2]The papers of the conference were published by Trinity University (Dubois & Crouch, 1976), and seven were subsequently published in a special issue of the *International Journal of the Sociology of Language* (Vol. 17, 1978). Neither is currently in print.

CURRENT WRITINGS ON LANGUAGE, GENDER, AND ETHNICITY

Studies of racial and ethnic variation in English, especially those of the Black English vernacular (BEV), tend to focus on male speakers. As Folb (1980) wrote,

> Most accounts of black expressive behavior have not only focused on males but have made the assumption—implicitly or expressly—that vernacular expressive forms, such as shooting the dozens or toasts, are the male's exclusive domains. This is not especially surprising, given the fact that most contemporary studies of black expressive behavior have been done by males, from a male perspective. (pp. 193–194)[3]

More than a decade later, Morgan (1991b) noted that

> Though the study of African American English (AAE) has resulted in detailed descriptions of the dialect, most of the data which contributed to its analysis were gathered from young African American males, at a time when the center of their participation in the community was in the urban street sub-culture. Although Mitchell-Kernan (1971) included women in the body of her work on African American culture and communication style, it was nearly twenty years . . . before intergenerational data and women's speech were again systematically collected and included in the study of urban language behavior. (pp. 421–422)

Gender Bias

Little has been written specifically to link race or ethnicity with sex bias in American English. Scott (1974) pointed out the racism and sexism of English and the interaction of the two in lexical terms by which Black women (e.g., in BEV dictionaries, in films and literature) are defined by the names of animals (fox, mink, filly, etc.), by physical attractiveness (hammer, stone fox, little mama), and by complexion (redbone, banana, high yaller, pinky). Bruner and Kelso (1980) reported that an examination of graffiti in restrooms at a (presumably White-dominant) university revealed a major gender difference in the use of sexually and racially and ethnically biased language: Fifty-four percent of men's, but only 15% of women's inscriptions were derogatory—of women, of homosexuals, and of specific racial and ethnic groups. Their interpretation, from a semiotic perspective, is that men's restroom inscriptions reaffirm White, Anglo, gentile

---

[3]Folb admitted that she, too, operated on this assumption for the first years of her field work but later began to seek out female informants (who still constituted only one sixth of those interviewed).

male dominance and reinforce the power structure over Blacks, Jews, gays, women, and any other group that threatens their homogenous hegemony. Stanley (1974) noted the same racism and sexism in (White) gay men's sexual slang as those among White heterosexual men.

Medicine (1987) illustrated the introduction of sex bias through imposition of language:

> The introduction of the majority language—English—placed and continues to place a heavy burden on Indian women because adopting the English language often has meant losing linguistic symbols of culture and gaining male bias carried by the semantic system of English. . . .
>
> Aside from the more obvious linguistic markers which exist in American Indian ancestral languages and which do not in English, there are also an entire set of kinship terms serving to depict social and familial relationships in American Indian culture. Again, these do not exist in their English translation. . . . As a result, one can understand the confusion a superimposed kinship system, such as English, brought to social structures and reciprocal relationships in this particular American Indian culture and to others. In those cases where the ancestral language has literally died or barely continues to exist, often even linguistic marking of female-female relationships, feminine bonds, and responsive relationships have been obliterated. (pp. 160–161)

Unfortunately, there is little written touching on sex bias and ethnicity together in English. Accounts of sex bias in languages of other countries that are spoken by people of color in the United States have been written, such as those of Cherry (1987), Hampares (1976), Lee (1976), Meseguer (1977), and Tan (1990). However, because these are not written specifically about U.S. usage and U.S. usage cannot be reliably inferred from them, they do not fall within the purview of this chapter.

The dearth of material on sex bias and ethnicity echoes the dearth of material on sex bias in White language and gender studies. Much more has been written on sex difference (and perceptions thereof) in language usage than on sex bias. Therefore, most of this chapter considers this latter topic.

Gender Differences

What are the language and gender difference issues of concern to Women and Men of Color in the United States? The topics include some of those already mentioned, such as the issues of conservatism versus innovation in language usage, politeness, weakness, assertiveness, and language skills, as well as others that have been raised in writings by Native, Latina, Asian, and African American women, such as bilingualism, code-switching, gender and generational differences in usage; ethnic and gender identity issues associated with language choice and cultural preservation;

and ultimately who are to be counted as "women" in studies of language and gender.

Anthropological studies of various American Indian languages, beginning in 1903, have noted differentiation of forms for females and males, but interpretation has been sparse; Bodine (1975) offered a comprehensive and integrative survey of the studies to that point. Because this chapter is limited to American English dialects (a term that includes "standard" English), I do not review Native American languages here (e.g., Flannery, 1946; Haas, 1944; see also Bodine, 1975, for more references to early studies, and Medicine, 1987). As with sex bias, there is material on language sex differences in other countries whose languages are spoken by people of color in U.S. communities (e.g., Cheung, 1991; Ochs, 1987; Reynolds, 1985; Saint-Jacques, 1973; Shibamoto, 1987), but much less on the sex differences in usage in those languages in the United States. As in many other fields of psychology, African Americans and Latin Americans have been more widely studied than have the various Asian American and Native American ethnic groups; hence, African American and Latino groups receive the most coverage in this chapter.

CONSERVATISM VERSUS INNOVATION IN LANGUAGE USAGE

Jespersen (1922/1964) noted that to the question of which sex is more linguistically conservative (i.e., tends to retain old forms rather than introduce new ones),

> an answer . . . often given is that as a rule women are more conservative than men, and that they do nothing more than keep to the traditional language which they have learnt from their parents and hand on to their children, while innovations are due to the initiative of men. (p. 242)

The evidence that has been used to support the claim that women are conservative linguistically is mainly based on three sources: (a) the traditional role of woman as child caregiver and hence as conservator and transmitter of culture; (b) studies of slang, which have been carried out mostly on males; and (c) sociolinguistic surveys of language use, in which women have repeatedly been found to use more "prestige standard"[4] forms than men of the same class. However, see Coates's (1986, pp. 41–44) discussion

---

[4]What is called "standard" is, of course, determined by the group that dominates U.S. scholarship and society (i.e., White/Anglo speakers of English). References to "standard" and "nonstandard" forms, when used in this chapter, will be enclosed in quotes to remind the reader of this fact. Also note that the terms *African American* and *Black* are used interchangeably, as are *Mexican American* and *Chicano*.

of opposing beliefs in women's or men's greater conservatism among dialectologists and Graddol and Swann's (1989, pp. 51–58) critique of social stratification studies.

Social Role

Jespersen (1922/1964) showed that the social role explanation of women's conservatism dates back to antiquity:

> Thus Cicero in an often-quoted passage says that when he hears his mother-in-law Lælia, it is to him as if he heard Plautus or Nævius [Romans of an earlier age], for it is more natural for women to keep the old language uncorrupted, as they do not hear many people's way of speaking and thus retain what they have first learnt. (p. 242)

Medicine (1987) gave a similar interpretation to the importance of Native American women's language:

> American Indian women perform at least three distinctive social roles through their patterns of language use in their communities. They maintain cultural values through the socialization of children; they serve as evaluators of language use by setting the normative standards of the native or ancestral tongue and English; and they are effective as agents of change through mediation strategies with the White society. . . .
>
> The historical pattern of English language domination has been especially significant for Indian women—the primary socializers of children. (p. 160)

Morgan (1991a) likewise argued for the importance of studying African American women's language "because women have historically been responsible for the language development of their children and therefore their community" (pp. 7, 13).

The argument based on social role, which might be considered restricted by sexist assumptions, is not however unlike the "feminist standpoint" arguments made by feminist scholars (e.g., Smith, 1987). These scholars claim that there is a gender difference in perception of the world, based on the sexes' differential involvement with its everyday tasks, such as cooking, cleaning, sick care, typing, and filing. In any case, for psychologists, argument that is based on assumptions about roles is acceptable only as a stimulus for empirically directed research and theory. It also should be noted that although Medicine (1987) argued from women's traditional role as conservators of language, she also argued for their role in fostering successful change through language in Native American communities.

Slang and Street Talk

Slang, colorful and creative and the source of vitalization for a language, has been a subject of long-standing interest to language scholars (Dumas & Lighter, 1978; Farmer & Henley, 1890/1966; Partridge, 1984). The study of slang frequently assumes that slang, with its underworld and street-life associations and frequently misogynist content, is created and used mostly by males. Jespersen (1922/1964), for example, stated the following:[5]

> Women move preferably in the central field of language, avoiding everything that is out of the way or bizarre, while men will often either coin new words or expressions or take up old-fashioned ones, if by that means they are enabled, or think they are enabled, to find a more adequate or precise expression for their thoughts. (p. 248)

This assumption that slang and innovation are masculine has been held for both people of color and Whites; as previously noted, the study of BEV by a host of linguists in the 1960s and 1970s (e.g., Hannerz, 1969; Labov, 1972a; Wolfram, 1969) concentrated on Black males. Extensive descriptions of "sounding," "the dozens," and so forth, are limited to their use by males. There are a few exceptions to this rule, such as Folb (1980), Mitchell-Kernan (1972, 1973) and Galindo (cited in Penfield & Ornstein-Galicia, 1985),[6] but, overall, innovation and creativity in language have been seen to be the province not of women and girls but of men and boys. Obviously, researchers' common limitation of their studies to male samples has not allowed adequate determination of the extent of female innovation.

Social Stratification

The third argument for female linguistic conservativeness is based on class-stratified studies of the use of particular language forms, such as pronouncing the final sound of words such as *looking* and *going* as "ng," considered more standard and prestigious, rather than as "n," or pronouncing the initial sound of words such as *that* and *this* as "th" rather than "d." In studies around the United States (e.g., Fischer, 1964; Hartford, 1976; Labov, 1972b; Wolfram, 1969) as well as in England (Trudgill, 1972, 1975),

---

[5]To be fair, it should be noted that Jespersen (1922/1964, pp. 242–243) also cited a South American culture in which women coined new words adopted by all and said that Japanese women are less conservative than men, because they are not as influenced by written language.

[6]There have been sex-comparative studies, for example, of the use of obscenities or taboo words (e.g., Bailey & Timm, 1976; Gallahorn, 1970; Jay, 1980; Johnson & Fine, 1985; Kutner & Brogan, 1974; Nelson & Rosenbaum, 1972; Sanders & Robinson, 1979; Walsh & Leonard, 1974; Wilson, 1975) and studies of some females' slang in particular occupations or domains, such as menstrual terms (e.g., Boone, 1954; Ernster, 1975; Joffe, 1948; Larsen, 1963), but, to my knowledge ethnic and racial factors have not been much considered in either of these areas.

Scotland (Macauley, 1978) and elsewhere, female speakers of English tend to use the prestige "standard" forms more often and males tend to use the nonprestige, "nonstandard" forms more often.

Explanations for this sex difference have varied. Trudgill (1975, pp. 91–92) speculated on two psychological, interconnected explanatory factors, one of them to explain women's use of more prestigious forms and one to explain men's use of less prestigious ones: (a) Women are more status conscious than men and more aware of the social significance of linguistic variables. This may be because women's social position is less secure than and subordinate to that of men, so women may need to secure and signal their social status linguistically and in other ways, and because although men can be rated socially by what they do, women may be rated more on how they appear. Because they are not rated by occupation or success, other signals of status, such as speech, become more important. (b) Men of all classes associate masculinity with working-class men and adopt working-class men's nonstandard speech as a symbolic means to represent virility.

Challenges to Claims of Women's Linguistic Conservatism: African American Women

Two types of challenges have been put forward to the universalistic claim of women's linguistic conservatism, both of which are based on the experience of African American women. Both make clear that African American women can be as innovative as, or more so than, African American men (although that is not their primary aim).

The first challenge comes from studies of slang, of BEV street talk. As previously noted, nowhere has the study of "nonstandard" speech been so intensive as in the study of African American males, with the implicit and sometimes explicit assumption that males are the creators and users of this slang. However, Marjorie Goodwin and Marsha Stanback have questioned the implications and claims that Black women do not use "signifying" speech, the aggressive, witty performance talk that has been so extensively studied in young Black men.

Goodwin (1980a, 1988, 1990) studied speech sequences of directives (e.g., imperatives and requests) and responses to them among Black working-class 8- to 13-year-old boys and girls in play and task activities. She found extensive speech differences that reflected and themselves constituted different social organizations. Boys' speech was more hierarchical, competitive, and direct, and less backbiting, than that of girls.

Goodwin examined the use of *aggravated directives* in particular. Aggravated directives are those that, if they give any justification, justify directing another by reference to the rights of the speaker or obligation of the hearer ("Gimme the pliers!" "Get off my steps"). *Mitigated directives* do so by referring to the activity or abilities of the hearer ("Come on Maria, can't you show us the steps?") and are more indirect and respecting of the hearer's rights. Girls were less likely to use aggravated directives or to use them asymmetrically than were boys. Still, girls had full competence with aggravated forms and used them in appropriate circumstances. Furthermore, in mixed-sex situations, girls were as skillful as boys at countering another's (boy's or girl's) comment and showed themselves to be able, like boys, to engage in an extended sequence of ritual insult. Goodwin noted that the Black females she studied were neither more polite, as claimed by Lakoff (1975), nor dominated by men, as claimed by West (1979). Goodwin (1980b, 1982a, 1982b, 1985, 1987, 1989, 1990/1991) has dealt with a wide range of female speech genres in her studies, including (in addition to directives), storytelling, arguing, and gossip and has made use of an extensive ethnographic record of Black female speech.

Stanback (1986), too, found Black females to be proficient in the full range of BEV forms. Their conversation included various forms of "smart talk," such as "signifying," loud talking, braggadocio, and "sweet sarcasm." However, like Folb (1980), Stanback believed that there were more situational constraints on Black women's BEV speech than Black men's; thus, women did not use it to the same extent that men did.

Another source of female innovation that has emerged in recent years is the new generation of (Black) female rap musicians, who explicitly demonstrate their prowess in this formerly male-dominated form derived from African American culture and speech styles.

The second challenge to female conservatism based on Black women comes from sociolinguistic studies. Nichols (1976, 1980, 1983) argued that a generalized "women's language" is a myth: "When we ask questions about women's use of language, we must ask also, *which* women as members of *which* social groups" (1983, p. 54). Nichols conducted research on three generations of women in an all-Black speech community of coastal South Carolina, where the traditional Creole language Gullah (Geechee) had long been spoken but had largely given way to a form of BEV and "standard" English. In this community, standard forms would be considered innovative and Gullah and other "nonstandard" forms conservative. Nichols found age, gender, and class effects: The older, poorer women of the mainland were more conservative (used more Creole) than the older men or the older women of a nearby river island community. The latter group of women used nonstandard forms to an equal extent with the men of the community. Among the middle and younger adults of the island, however, the women used Creole forms far less than men of their cohort.

Nichols (similarly to Hannerz, 1970) traced these differences to different work opportunities for men and women at different historical periods in the region. Older women had few occupational choices outside of farm and domestic labor, which entailed little language interaction with speakers of standard English. Younger and middle-aged women had access to the jobs of sales clerk, mail carrier, nurse, and elementary school teacher, which brought them into such interaction. In fact, to qualify for these jobs (which pay less than the blue-collar jobs the Black men in the area could obtain), the women had to learn the new forms and often get higher education as well. Both younger and older men had lumber camp and construction work. Their interaction was mainly within their own groups, and there was little incentive or opportunity to adopt new forms.

The Importance of Situational Variables

Nichols's (1983) conclusion was that universalistic assumptions and flawed research that lead to beliefs in women's linguistic conservatism must be abandoned and more attention given to specific situational variables:

> Women use language in ways that reflect the options available to them within their particular speech communities. In some circumstances they exhibit linguistically innovative behavior; in others, conservative. They make choices in the contexts of particular social networks rather than as some generalized response to the universal condition of women. (p. 54)

These examinations of African American women's and men's speech illustrate the point that innovation in language is not the prerogative of any one gender. Language use for both sexes is strongly influenced by the social context, including the occupations and workplaces differentially available to women and men and to specific ethnic groups. The idea of a universalistic female linguistic conservatism and male innovativeness is refuted by actual empirical studies that look carefully at the social circumstances affecting people's behavior.

BILINGUALISM AND CODE-SWITCHING

Bilingualism and code-switching (or style-shifting) are important factors in the lives of many Americans of color, whether as people from immigrant families, people whose lands were invaded, or people who were brought as slaves. They are large, well-studied topics, but less well studied relative to gender. A few studies of more psychological interest or implications are discussed here. There has been particular psycholinguistic interest in gender factors in bilingualism and code-switching among Spanish-speaking people, especially Chicana/Chicanos and Puerto Ricans (Boricaña/Boricaños). Zentella (1987), for example, noted that "differences in bilingual language behavior and proficiency can be accounted for by many variables . . . , but the socialization of Puerto Rican children into appropriate female and male roles is particularly significant" (p. 172).

Questions of interest include, Which sex speaks Spanish more, and which English, and why? To which sex is Spanish or English spoken more and why? What circumstances may interact with gender to influence whether one speaks one language or another or a mixture and what pattern of code-switching one uses? How does the interplay of gender and language choice affect identity, life variables, and so forth?

Bilingual Abilities and Behaviors

Mexican Americans

Patella and Kuvlesky (1973) in a study of Mexican American high school students and dropouts, found that girls tended to use Spanish less and English more than boys. They suggested several possible reasons for these significant differences: (a) girls' greater obedience to authority because of sex role training resulted in their learning English better than boys; (b) teachers' stereotypes of docile Mexican American females and resistant Mexican American males may lead, through self-fulfilling expectations (Rosenthal & Jacobson, 1968) to more proficient English in girls; (c) boys may learn English as well as girls (they read more English printed materials than girls), but because of unknown factors may use it selectively in interaction.

Betancourt (1976), working with Mexican American third- and fourth-grade pupils, tested boys and girls on oral proficiency and vocabulary in Spanish and English and obtained their scores for reading in English. He found girls to score higher in English oral proficiency and reading but boys to score higher in Spanish oral proficiency and vocabulary. Differences for English vocabulary were nonsignificant. Betancourt interpreted the girls' lower performance in Spanish to be due to culturally and sex-role-induced passivity and caution. It is interesting that he saw no need to explain boys' lower performance in English, apparently because he was operating within a context of expecting greater language proficiency in general in females (which had been widely reported).

Solé (1978) studied Mexican American university students' self-reported language use in different relationships and contexts. Solé found a consistent pattern in which females "tend to claim mostly and only English more often than do males, who, by and large, favor code-switching, that is, Spanish and English with equal frequency" (p. 34). She suggested the females' greater use of English may be affected by

> (1) the greater proneness to identification among girls and their readier access to outgroup ego-models; (2) their greater affiliative needs and

greater tendency to be externally controlled; (3) the prevalence of integrative learning styles among them; and (4) their differential elaboration of the achievement motive in self-realization. (p. 38)

Finding greater use of English among females is counter to traditional expectations of more "conservative" adherence to original language among women (e.g., Diebold, 1961; Hughes, 1971; Jespersen, 1922/1964; Lieberson, 1971; Loo, 1991, p. 193), which has also been found in Latinas. Penfield and Ornstein-Galicia (1985), for example, noted that in middle-class Anglo–Chicano/Chicana marriages,

> in those marriages where the female is Chicano, there is perhaps more maintenance of various varieties of Spanish since society easily accepts the use of Spanish in the home, especially by the mother. According to Ornstein et al. (1976) lower middle-class mothers tend to maintain Spanish more often than the more mobile and higher middle-class mothers. (p. 27)

These differences in findings serve to remind us again that language use is socially situated, tied to gender mainly through specific activity patterns, not through universalistic biology or even "social roles."

Puerto Ricans

Studying a different ethnic group, Puerto Ricans of three generations in New York's East Harlem barrio, Zentella (1987) found a pattern in which females were more likely to speak Spanish than males. She attributed this finding to several factors: (a) Females' activities were more likely than males' to be restricted to the home, with closer ties to their Spanish-speaking mothers and other older females; (b) they may be more bound by the norm of "speak the language that is spoken to you"; (c) they were expected to maintain greater contact with family members in Puerto Rico; (d) as adolescents they may become more adept than males at code-switching "to maneuver in public and private domains and to accomplish varied discourse objectives" (Zentella, 1987, p. 173); and (e) they seem to have more loyalty to Spanish and more sensitivity to nuances of social class in language.

Zentella (1987) addressed questions of identity conflicts for Puerto Ricans, brought about by confusing national, racial, and linguistic categorizations. Gender and language are two core pillars of one's identity; these Puerto Rican women's ability to move adeptly in both languages and cultures serves as a source of strength, enabling them to navigate varied situations. The research and writing of Black women similarly shows the importance to them of demonstrating their expertise in BEV as well as in "standard" English. These strengths of bilingual adaptivity contrast with

Lakoff's implication that women's required bidialectism in "women's language" and "neutral language" is a burden.[7]

Code-Switching Patterns and Relationships

Valdés-Fallis's (1978) study of code-switching by Mexican American women in interaction with males or females, although limited by a small sample, has interesting implications for the study of power and dominance in female–male relationships. Valdés-Fallis studied transcriptions of four female university students in 11 female–male and 13 female–female conversations. Particular attention was given to sequential and associative forms of code-switching. These forms are related to speakers' perceptions of their own role and status relative to that of their interlocuters. *Sequential code-switching* is the term applied to using the last language used by the preceding speaker. *Associative code-switching* describes code-switching having a blend and proportion of language alternation resembling that of the other speaker.

Valdés-Fallis (1978) found Mexican American females to use more sequential switches when speaking to males than when speaking to females and to associate more noticeably to the code-switching styles of male interlocutors than to those of female ones. She interpreted these findings as reflecting females' social conditioning and self-concepts of having lower status than males.

CONVERSATIONAL INTERACTION

The topic of code-switching, especially as reflecting male dominance, leads well into the discussion of other features of conversational interaction. Conversation is often studied as a means of understanding other subjects, such as topics of discussion or social dominance.[8] Prominent examinations of gender issues in conversational interaction include those of male conversational dominance, male inexpressiveness, and male–female street interaction.

---

[7]Lakoff most often contrasted "women's language" not with "men's language" but with what she called "neutral language." It is also interesting that despite her intriguing suggestion that young boys first learn "women's language" and later must switch to men's or neutral language (while women do not necessarily do so), she did not posit a bidialectalism in men.

[8]Robins and Adenika (1987), for example, obtained retrospective self-reports of conversational topics among urban African American women across three time periods as a means of ascertaining their values and belief structures from their own perspectives.

Male Conversational Dominance

Males' dominance of mixed-sex conversations through a variety of strategies (presumably unconscious) has been demonstrated among primarily White samples, in both field and laboratory studies, through analysis of recorded interchanges. Some of these stategies are greater amount of talk; interruptions and overlaps; inhibiting or delayed minimal responses; unilateral topic shifts; ignoring of new topics introduced by women; and general failure to participate in the "interactional work" of conversations (for references on the amount of speech, see Kramarae, Thorne, & Henley, 1983, pp. 279–281; for other strategies, see DeFrancisco, 1991; Fishman, 1978, 1983; Leet-Pellegrini, 1980; West & Garcia, 1988; West & Zimmerman, 1983; Zimmerman & West, 1975).

The differential use of interruption has been studied in U.S. White-dominant populations, in which males' greater tendency to interrupt, and females' greater likelihood of being interrupted, are well documented (e.g., DeFrancisco, 1991; Eakins & Eakins, 1978; McMillan et al., 1977; Natale, Entin, & Jaffe, 1979; Octigan & Niederman, 1979; Willis & Williams, 1976). However, the patterns of European American conversational interaction may not be those of other U.S. ethnic communities.

Conversational Parity Between Black Women and Men

Black women have challenged the idea that they are conversationally subordinate. Stanback (1986) argued that Lakoff's (1973) ideas of a "women's language" are based on the division of labor within the White middle class and that they do hold up in the different structure and situation of the Black middle class. Black women have always been active in both "public" and "private" spheres—are expected to work outside the home and be strong within the family—and have more nearly equal relationships with Black men than White women do with White men. At the same time, Black women have, like Black men, the "double consciousness" of their own culture and the White culture—awareness of the sometimes-conflicting values of both and of the dominance of the latter, which may compel nonpreferred behaviors from Blacks. These forces create ambivalence and, she said, shape Black women's speech and conversational styles.

Stanback (1986) found that Black women's use of the features Lakoff (1973) described varied according to context, as does White women's. She studied college-educated middle-class Black and White women's speech with others of three different groups: same sex, same ethnicity; same sex, different ethnicity; and different sex, same ethnicity. Black women were more outspoken and assertive than White women, and, being bidialectal, their repertoire also included varied use of BEV. As noted earlier, Stanback found Black women to be adept at BEV and all kinds of "smart talk," which is simultaneously outspoken and indirect, humorous and serious.

This equality of communicative competence, however, did not mean that Black women had total communicative parity with Black men: Black women had lower total speaking turn times and fewer backchannel utterances (non-interruptive comments such as "uh-huh") than did Black men and spoke approximately half as much as in their conversations with women. Stanback (1986) described Black women as retreating to the background in cross-gender conversation and quoted one of the women as saying that the men often did not seem to include the women in their talk. However, Stanback emphasized that the genesis of communicative gender asymmetry in the Black and White communities is different:

> White women are often described in the literature as unskilled in using certain features of mainstream speech because of their confinement to domestic roles. Black women are described as proficient in using the full range of black communicative features, but as experiencing situational constraints which black men do not experience. (p. 188)

Another way in which gender and ethnicity interact in language dominance is observed in interruption patterns within racial, sexual, and occupational hierarchies. West (1984) found that in doctor–patient interaction, White male physicians' interruption rate varied with patients' race and gender: The doctors made the fewest interruptions of other White males and the most interruptions of Black females. Conversely, White female physicians' rate of *being interrupted* varied differently with gender and race: both White and Black male patients interrupted female doctors more than the physicians interrupted them, but interruptions of female patients, both Black and White, by female doctors were approximately evenly balanced with those patients' interruptions of the physicians.

Male Inexpressiveness

The claim that men's speech style is taciturn, especially in the expression of emotion, is based mostly on studies of White men, and often specifically associated with working-class men (e.g., Balswick, 1981; Balswick & Peek, 1971; DeFrancisco, 1991; Komarovsky, 1962; Lewis, 1978; Rubin, 1976; Tannen, 1990). Studies of African American men's speech, on the other hand, have emphasized their adeptness with language and their formation and maintenance of identity and reputation through skillful, competitive use of BEV forms (e.g., Abrahams, 1974; also see the citations in the section on slang). Obviously, the White and Black men studied are from different cultures, sometimes different classes, and one may not be surprised that different claims are made for each. However, in the case of Black men, the claims of their language use are specific to their ethnic group. In the case of White men, claims about their speech are often attributed to "men" in general.

Such universalistic claims, besides treating Black men and other men of color as nonexistent, make it difficult to see all men in the full spectrum of their language use. Attending to specific ethnic, class, and situational factors of men's speech will allow for a finer understanding of how it is determined and how and why it differs from women's. As one example from White male speech, Philipsen (1975) wrote of the situational factors affecting the amount of speech used by the working-class men he studied: It was appropriate to talk a lot in symmetrical social identity situations (i.e., with other males of one's group), but not in asymmetrical situations, such as with one's wife or child, boss, or outsider.[9]

Similarly, Abrahams (1974) made distinctions between public and private, informational and performative, and serious and nonserious contexts for Black men's amount and types of speech (focusing on street speech). In fact, Black men are said to yield to women's authority in their speech inside the home, observing silence or other verbal restrictions (Abrahams, 1974, 1975). Here, there might be another example of similar behavior patterns in two groups but a different genesis. That is, the domestic silence of both Black and White males may look similar, but White men's silence may be attributable to feeling that speech is inappropriate because of their wives' lower social status, whereas Black men's silence may be attributable to respect for female authority in the home. At present, researchers cannot be sure of such explanations without further research on men's speech in a variety of populations, settings, and relationships.

Rather than emphasizing men's silence in the home, hooks (1989) wrote more positively of women's linguistic performance within what is seen as their domain:

> To speak then when one was not spoken to was a courageous act—an act of risk and daring. And yet it was hard not to speak in warm rooms where heated discussions began at the crack of dawn, women's voices filling the air, giving orders, making threats, fussing. Black men may have excelled in the art of poetic preaching in the male-dominated church, but in the church of the home, where the everyday rules of how to live and how to act were established, it was black women who preached. There, black women spoke in a language so rich, so poetic, that it felt to me like being shut off from life, smothered to death if one were not allowed to participate. (p. 5)

---

[9]Sattel (1976, 1983) further questioned the traditional understanding of (White) male inexpressiveness as a "tragedy" by putting it in the context of these males' social power and sexual politics.

This lyrical description brings home the point that researchers have little studied, and rarely celebrated, women's in-home speech[10] and speech in all-women's groups, especially that of Women of Color. One can, for example, imagine a whole book on the different forms of Chicanas' linguistic interactions, similar to those analyzing in detail African American men's street forms.

Male–Female Street Interaction

White feminists have been particularly critical of men's street remarks. Gardner (1981) pointed out the double bind women are put in when men make remarks. Women are required by politeness rules to respond, but by the norm of "civil inattention" not to respond. They are aware of being baited by sexual innuendoes of double-entendre remarks but dare not respond to them because men will claim nonsexual meaning and innocent intentions. Such harassment reinforces male bonding and men's territorial claims on public spaces and threatens women and restricts their mobility. Kissling (1991) and Wise and Stanley (1987) provided evidence of similar phenomena in various societies around the world, for example, in Australia, France, Guyana, Iran, Lebanon, Malaysia, Mexico, Pakistan, Singapore, Syria, Taiwan, the United Kingdom, and West Germany.

Although Gardner's (1981) description and interpretation may be apt for many White American women's experience, others have described a much different interpretation for African American male–female street interaction.[11] Smitherman (1977), for example, wrote,

> the existence of love rappin in the oral tradition allows a strange black man to approach a strange black woman without fear of strong reprisal. Black women are accustomed to—and many even expect—this kind of verbal aggressiveness from black men. Black culture thus provides a socially approved verbal mechanism with which the man can initiate conversation aimed at deepening the acquaintance. (p. 85)

Kochman (1981, especially pp. 74–88) detailed Black–White cultural differences that make for cross-gender, cross-race misunderstandings. He claimed that in Black culture, unlike White, women are not dichotomized into good or bad, may display sexual interest without implying sexual availability, and are expected to respond actively to men's remarks. Thus, Black men's street remarks are not taken as harassment by Black women but as part of normal interchange and playful verbal interaction.

---

[10]Note that one form of women's in-home speech, mothers' language to children, has been widely studied.

[11]Gardner was explicit that her analysis was not meant to apply to interactions within specific urban cultures such as Black or Italian.

However, Kochman (1981) took for granted and did not discuss the asymmetrical norms determining who can initiate these encounters, within both Black and White cultures. Although claiming that Black culture allows equal interest and assertiveness of sexuality on the part of Black women and men, he provided no examples of Black females' initiation of sexual comments, as he did of Black men's. Kochman elsewhere cited McCarty's statement that "black women are beginning to just be up front and tell men that if they can't come to them better in the street than in the obviously sexual manner, they can just shut up" (pp. 85–86).

Different Black female authors (e.g., Joseph & Lewis, 1981; Smitherman, 1977) have presented different perspectives on this issue, but there seems to be no question that Blacks do not feel the extent of male–female division, threat, and animosity that is found among Whites. Thus, a broader analysis of male–female street interaction would distinguish and recognize the experiences of people of different ethnicities, including experiences of other racial and ethnic groups, classes, and so on, as well as those of Black and White.

Silencing and Indirectness

Double Silencing

Women of Color face silencing both as women and as members of ethnic groups oppressed by European Americans. Long denied literacy and not admitted to public discourse, their speech styles belittled, their accounts (e.g., slave narratives, women's letters and diaries) denied status as literature, and trapped in language that expresses European American and male realities more than their own, they have been increasingly studying and confronting this suppression in recent years (e.g., hooks, 1989; Moraga & Anzaldúa, 1981). Etter-Lewis (1991), for example, studied elderly African American women's oral narratives, analyzing the ways they both suppress and speak out about racism and sexism in their lives. Such discourse was previously suppressed but is now released through the mechanism of narration.

Women of Color may be silenced not only by men but by White women. Houston and Kramarae (1991) discussed ways women are silenced and how they are breaking out of silence. They described Houston's (unpublished) list of communication practices she has observed, titled "Why the Dialogues Are Difficult or 15 Ways a Black Woman Knows When a White Woman's Not Listening" (Houston & Kramarae, 1991, p. 389). For example, White women's pejorative use of the term *confrontational* when referring to Black women's speech style attempts to shape and control, if not silence, Black women's speech.

Indirectness and Responsibility

Morgan (1990, 1991b) also studied African American women's narratives, demonstrating their use of indirectness (related to silencing) in describing even central events. She noted that in the United States, unlike in Africa and the Caribbean, indirect communication has historically been reserved for the counterlanguage, a communication system evolved by slaves and their descendants to communicate without their oppressors' understanding. In the counterlanguage, as in African and Caribbean societies, the notion of speaker responsibility for what is said is essential (i.e., interpreting after the speech act that that is not what one meant is not as legitimate as it is in European American culture).

Morgan's (1991b) data show that African American and European American women have much different perceptions regarding the meanings of silence and indirectness in narratives and an underlying divergence in assumption of speaker responsibility for others' interpretations. African American women are more prone to take the speaker at her word and hold her responsible for what others understand her to say, whereas European American women tended more to reinterpret the utterance. Morgan also found striking generational differences in the degree to which African American women held to the principle of speaker responsibility. The youngest generation's responses were more like European American women's, whereas the two older generation groups held the speaker more responsible.

CONCLUSION

Attention to issues of ethnicity makes us revise earlier conclusions and conceptualizations having to do with the intersection of language and gender. Studies of African American women show both innovative and conservative speech, rather than testifying to women's basic linguistic conservatism, "hypercorrection," or lesser expertise with the vernacular. Conversational dominance among Blacks does not appear in the same ways as has been apparent in studies of Whites, suggesting either less sexual inequality among Blacks or different patterns by which inequality is manifest, or both. Bringing in bilingual code-switching among Chicanos, moreover, gives a new perspective on conversational dominance and its subtleties. Common beliefs about male inexpressiveness must fall in the face of Black males' performative expressiveness and verbal games. Writings on African American male–female interaction raise questions about the generalizability of White feminist interpretations of men's street harassment of women.

Silencing and indirectness, although apparently common to women of different ethnicities, may have different meanings for them.

In addition to these reassessments of existing topics, studies of and by people of color also bring completely new themes to the forefront of language and gender concerns: the meaning of bilingual language choice and code-switching; the interaction of generation with gender in language use (including the various meanings that generational difference carries within different cultures); the experience of being doubly silenced; the complex psychological issues involved in the interactions of gender and ethnic identity; sexual and cultural dominance; double minority status; personal development; and cultural preservation.

The issues that arise for Women of Color are much different from those that were initially identified as the major issues in language and gender for White middle-class women; indeed, they raise the question of just who are to be counted as women. Clearly, African Americans, Asian Americans, Latina/Latinos, and Native Americans are frequently not included when sweeping statements are made about women's language forms. Rather than a list of characteristics of "women's language," studying ethnicity, language, and gender led to the drawing up of a list of central themes (see Exhibit 3), some of which have come up in White/Anglo language and gender studies, but others of which have not. Common experiences of racism and ethnocentrism, sexism, and marginalization are obviously major factors creating similarity in the issues that arise in different studies and

EXHIBIT 3
Central Themes in the Study of Ethnicity, Gender, and Language

Language conservatism versus innovation
Language proficiency versus deficiency
- in "standard" forms
- in "nonstandard" forms
Bilingualism and bidialectalism
- competence
- performance
- generational change, acculturation, and family and work roles
Code-switching
- extent
- patterns and relationship contexts
Pressures to assimilate versus loss of cultural identity
- alienation and ambivalence regarding "standard" English
- issues of identity and self-worth
Self-labeling, group-labeling, and other-labeling
Status, power, and silencing

across ethnicities.[12] At the same time, although the issues of importance may be similar, the responses within different ethnic groups will not be the same: Diversity of cultures, of histories, of gender inequalities and relationships, of religion, of geographical distribution, of acculturation, and so forth, create diverse approaches and solutions.

A repeated lesson is that researchers must conceive of communication as socially and culturally situated action that is not universally determined by simplistically conceived gender, socialization, role, or personality. Just as gender is continually being re-created through social interaction (West & Zimmerman, 1987), so is ethnicity: People "do" both gender and ethnicity, and we do gender differently according to which ethnicity we are also doing (and we do ethnicity differently according to which gender we are also doing). Intimately tied to this dynamic interpretation of social and linguistic interaction must be a recognition of the dimension of *power* as being critical to an understanding of language in women's lives—in both women's speech and speech about women. Power is a prime dimension of social interaction, determining subtle differences that result in great effect, such as whose reality gets encoded in a language, whose voice is heard in public discourse, whose speech is deemed "standard."

Problems that have clouded the understanding of language, ethnicity, and gender include inattention to or poor understanding of class. Class and ethnicity are correlated, so that studies of people of color are often studies of people of lower and lower-middle class and those of Whites, of people of middle- and upper-middle class—even when the subjects are ostensibly from the same group, such as students of the same college or university. However, just because ethnicity and class are correlated does not mean they must be confounded: Careful selection of samples, holding class constant when wishing to compare only gender and ethnicity, and describing class as well as ethnic background of subject samples will go a long way toward improving the knowledge of ethnicity and gender factors as well as those of class.

Needless to say, much research needs to be done and redone. First, little is known about the interaction of language and gender within Chinese American, Japanese American, and other Asian American communities, and little is known about this interaction among Native Americans, regardless of whether they are speakers of indigenous languages or of English (or both). Second, although there are more studies of gender and language interaction among Latina/Latinos and Blacks, these studies are mostly at a beginning stage. The questions already raised by Women of

---

[12]It is interesting to note that many of the same issues, such as cultural alienation, self-labeling, code-switching, and identity, were identified by Hayes (1981) as language issues for gay men and lesbians.

Color need further elaboration and exploration. One interesting question is that of possibly disparate genesis for similar elements found in different American cultures (e.g., communicative nonparity of the sexes or male nontalkativeness); further study is needed to verify these claims. Also, questions raised by White/Anglo writers about "standard" English, such as the extent and types of sex bias in language and sex difference in usage, may fruitfully be explored among other American-language communities and ethnicities.

Other questions arise from studies of the frequency of female and male bilingual speakers' use of Spanish or English. An obvious factor in the studies in which females were more likely to use English is age. High school or college students were the participants in these studies, whereas older married women were the subject of the comment on females' tendency to speak Spanish more. Age-related findings suggest either a developmental factor (as Latinas age, they tend to speak Spanish more than when they were younger) or a cohort factor (Latinas born in the 1930s and 1940s typically speak Spanish more than those born in the 1960s and 1970s). A third factor, which links development at a group level with age cohorts, is that of generation, a concept of importance in the study of varied ethnic populations. One would expect that, regardless of year of arrival in the United States, new arrivals would tend to speak Spanish more than second- and third-generation descendants. However, social factors acting differentially on females and males (e.g., jobs requiring English-language skills, traditional woman-at-home family arrangements) can also act to create differences in English- and Spanish-language use. Further study could better separate how these factors operate in different circumstances.

The various explanations offered for language choice and code-switching patterns, making use of psychological variables such as cultural and gender identity, stereotypes and sex roles, expectation effects, and dominance, need much more exploration and testing. Another question of interest is that of the interplay of gender attitudes, ethnic identity, and bilingualism attitudes (on the latter two factors, see Hurtado & Gurin, 1987).

Some of the most important and intriguing thinking being done on language and gender involves the cognitive processing of language, particularly the hearer or reader's task of constructing meaning from discourse when that discourse embodies sexist assumptions; the hearer is obliged to engage in sexist assumptions and engage in sexist reasoning as well (Crawford & Chaffin, 1986; Graddol & Swann, 1989; McConnell-Ginet, 1984; Penelope, 1990). Articulating the pieces of the jigsaw puzzle that links linguistic processing, gender and ethnic differences, and ethnic and gender bias will be a massive undertaking but one well worth the price for the advance of psychological knowledge. It is my opinion that until social information is more thoroughly integrated into psycholinguistic study (and the study of cognition more broadly), little worthwhile progress can be made in cognitive studies.

Clearly, experimental as well as observational studies will be helpful in broadening knowledge of language and gender. However, this comment is not meant to suggest limiting the methods and concepts researchers use in pursuing research in language, gender, and ethnicity. Psychologists of race and ethnicity and psychologists of gender alike have learned that they must not limit themselves to psychological sources and concepts in conducting research, but must search in various disciplines and genres for the answers they seek.

Fortunately, various scholars have begun to research these issues. Goodwin's (1980a, 1980b, 1982a, 1982b, 1985, 1987, 1989, 1990/1991) extensive ethnographic fieldwork analyzing a number of diverse speech events among both female and male African American children has been the major program of research documenting Black female speech and is ongoing. Newer research programs include those of Houston, currently completing a book on middle-class African American women as a speech community (Houston & Kramarae, 1991, p. 398); Etter-Lewis (1991), part of whose study of elderly African American women's oral narratives was previously cited; Morgan (1991a), among whose goals are to develop a large linguistic sample of African American women's speech to "analyze discourse and styles from women in urban and Southern communities" and to "describe the women's language behaviors as a linguistic and communication system independent of male speech patterns" (p. 7); and Eberhardt (1991), who has begun a study of perceptions of attitudes toward BEV and "standard" English as spoken by Black females and males. Although this list promises riches to come, it also underscores the need for language and gender studies by and of a broader variety of U.S. ethnicities.

Future directions for research on ethnicity, language, and gender beckon from a broad network of paths, but their limitations may be not only those of scholarly imagination but of racism, ethnocentrism, classism, and sexism as they apply to all facets of research, including funding and publication decisions. Gender manifests itself differently in different cultures, but understanding it is crucial to the creation of an equal world for women and men. As Women of Color insist, such a world is not possible in the context of racial and cultural inequality that affects both men and women. The study of ethnicity, language, and gender, properly done, may help to lead to such a world.

REFERENCES

Abrahams, R. D. (1974). Black talking on the streets. In R. Bauman & J. Sherzer (Eds.), *Explorations in the ethnography of speaking* (pp. 240–262). New York: Cambridge University Press.

Abrahams, R. D. (1975). Negotiating respect: Patterns of presentation among Black women. *Journal of American Folklore, 88,* 58–80.

Ardener, E. (1975). The "problem" revisited. In S. Ardener (Ed.), *Perceiving women* (pp. 19–27). London: Malaby Press.

Ardener, S. (1975). *Perceiving women.* London: Malaby Press.

Bailey, L. A., & Timm, L. A. (1976). More on women's—and men's—expletives. *Anthropological Linguistics, 18,* 438–449.

Balswick, J. O. (1981). Types of inexpressive male roles. In R. A. Lewis (Eds.), *Men in difficult times* (pp. 111–119). Englewood Cliffs, NJ: Prentice Hall.

Balswick, J. O., & Peek, C. W. (1971). The inexpressive male: A tragedy of American society. *Family Coordinator, 20,* 363–368.

Betancourt, R. (1976). Sex differences in language proficiency of Mexican-American third and fourth graders. *Journal of Education, 158*(2), 55–65.

Bodine, A. (1975). Sex differentiation in language. In B. Thorne & N. Henley (Eds.), *Language and sex: Difference and dominance* (pp. 130–151). Rowley, MA: Newbury House.

Boone, L. P. (1954). Vernacular of menstruation. *American Speech, 29,* 297–298.

Bruner, E. M., & Kelso, J. P. (1980). Gender differences in graffiti: A semiotic perspective. *Women's Studies International Quarterly, 3,* 239–252.

Chamberlain, A. (1912). Women's language. *American Anthropologist, 14,* 579–581.

Cherry, K. (1987). *Womansword: What Japanese words say about women.* Tokyo: Kodansha International.

Cheung, K-K. (1991). Double-telling: Intertextual silence in Hisaye Yamamoto's fiction. *American Literary History, 3,* 277–293.

Coates, J. (1986). *Women, men and language: A sociolinguistic account of sex differences in language.* London: Longman.

Crawford, M., & Chaffin, R. (1986). The reader's construction of meaning: Cognitive research on gender and comprehension. In E. Flynn & P. Schweikart (Eds.), *Gender and reading: Essays on reader, text and context* (pp. 3–30). Baltimore: Johns Hopkins University Press.

Crosby, F., & Nyquist, L. (1977). The female register: An empirical study of Lakoff's hypotheses. *Language in Society, 6,* 313–322.

DeFrancisco, V. L. (1991). The sounds of silence: How men silence women in marital relations. *Discourse & Society, 2,* 413–423.

Diebold, A. R. (1961). Incipient bilingualism. *Language, 37,* 97–112.

Dubois, B. L., & Crouch, I. (Eds.). (1976). *The sociology of the languages of American women.* San Antonio, TX: Trinity University.

Dumas, B. K., & Lighter, J. (1978). Is slang a word for linguists? *American Speech, 53,* 5–17.

Eakins, B. W., & Eakins, R. G. (1978). *Sex differences in human communication.* Boston: Houghton Mifflin.

Eberhardt, J. L. (1991, August). *Perceptions of Black English vernacular: An investigation of the linguistic ramifications of race, gender, and class.* Paper presented at the Fourth International Conference on Language and Social Psychology, Santa Barbara, CA.

Ernster, V. L. (1975). American menstrual expressions. *Sex Roles, 1,* 3–13.

Etter-Lewis, G. (1991). Standing up and speaking out: African American women's narrative legacy. *Discourse & Society, 2,* 425–437.

Farmer, J. S., & Henley, W. E. (1966). *Dictionary of slang and its analogues, past and present.* New Hyde Park, NY: University Books. (Original work published 1890)

Fischer, J. L. (1964). Social influences on the choice of a linguistic variant. In D. Hymes (Ed.), *Language in culture and society* (pp. 483–488). New York: Harper & Row.

Fishman, P. M. (1978). Interaction: The work women do. *Social Problems, 25,* 397–406.

Fishman, P. M. (1983) Interaction: The work women do. In B. Thorne, C. Kramarae, & N. Henley (Eds.), *Language, gender and society* (pp. 89–101). Rowley, MA: Newbury House (now Harper & Row).

Flannery, R. (1946). Men's and women's speech in Gros Ventre. *International Journal of American Linguistics, 12,* 133–135.

Folb, E. A. (1980). *Runnin' down some lines: The language and culture of Black teenagers.* Cambridge, MA: Harvard University Press, 1980.

Furfey, P. H. (1944). Men's and women's language. *American Catholic Sociological Review, 5,* 218–223.

Gallahorn, G. E. (1970). The use of taboo words by psychiatric ward personnel. *Psychiatry, 34,* 309–321.

Gardner, C. B. (1981). Passing by: Street remarks, address rights, and the urban female. *Sociological Inquiry, 50,* 328–356.

Goodwin, M. H. (1980a). Directive-response speech sequences in girls' and boys' task activities. In S. McConnell-Ginet, R. Borker, & N. Furman (Eds.), *Women and language in literature and society* (pp. 93–110). New York: Praeger.

Goodwin, M. H. (1980b). "He-said-she-said": Formal cultural procedures for the construction of a gossip dispute activity. *American Ethnologist, 7,* 674–695.

Goodwin, M. H. (1982a). "Instigating": Storytelling as social process. *American Ethnologist, 9,* 799–819.

Goodwin, M. H. (1982b). Processes of dispute management among urban Black children. *American Ethnologist, 9,* 76–96.

Goodwin, M. H. (1985). The serious side of jump rope: Conversational practices and social organization in the frame of play. *Journal of American Folklore, 98,* 315–330.

Goodwin, M. H. (1987). Children's arguing. In S. U. Philips, S. Steele, & C. Tanz (Eds.), *Language, gender, and sex in comparative perspective* (pp. 200–248). Cambridge, England: Cambridge University Press.

Goodwin, M. H. (1988). Cooperation and competition across girls' play activities. In S. Fisher & A. Todd (Eds.), *Gender and discourse: The power of talk* (pp. 55–94). Norwood, NJ: Ablex.

Goodwin, M. H. (1989). Tactical uses of stories: Participation frameworks within girls' and boys' disputes. *Discourse Processes, 13,* 33–71.

Goodwin, M. H. (1990). *He-said-she-said: Talk as social organization among black children.* Bloomington: Indiana University Press.

Goodwin, M. H. (1990/1991). Retellings, pretellings and hypothetical stories. *Research in Language and Social Interaction, 24,* 263–276.

Graddol, D., & Swann, J. (1989). *Gender voices.* Oxford, England: Basil Blackwell.

Haas, M. R. (1944). Men's and women's speech in Koasati. *Language, 20,* 142–149.

Hampares, K. J. (1976). Sexism in Spanish lexicography? *Hispania, 59,* 100–109.

Hannerz, U. (1969). *Soulside.* New York: Columbia University Press.

Hannerz, U. (1970). Language variation and social relationships. *Studia Linguistica, 24,* 128–151.

Hartford, B. S. (1976). Phonological differences in the English of adolescent Chicanas and Chicanos. In B. L. Dubois & I. Crouch (Eds.), *The sociology of the languages of American women* (pp. 73–80). San Antonio, TX: Trinity University.

Hayes, J. J. (1981). Lesbians, gay men, and their "languages." In J. W. Chesebro (Ed.), *Gayspeak: Gay male and lesbian communication* (pp. 28–42, 317–319). New York: Pilgrim Press.

Henley, N. M., & Kramarae, C. (1991). Gender, power, and miscommunication. In N. Coupland, H. Giles, & J. M. Wiemann (Eds.), *"Miscommunication" and problematic talk* (pp. 18–43). Newbury Park, CA: Sage.

hooks, b. (1989). *Talking back: Thinking feminist, thinking black.* Boston, MA: South End Press.

Houston, M., & Kramarae, C. (1991). Speaking from silence: Methods of silencing and of resistance. *Discourse & Society, 2,* 387–399.

Hughes, E. C. (1971). The linguistic division of labor in industrial and urban societies. In J. A. Fishman (Ed.), *Advances in the sociology of language II* (pp. 296–309). The Hague: Mouton.

Hurtado, A., & Gurin, P. (1987). Ethnic identity and bilingualism attitudes. *Hispanic Journal of Behavioral Sciences, 9,* 1–18.

Jay, T. B. (1980). Sex roles and dirty word usage: A review of the literaure and a reply to Haas. *Psychological Bulletin, 88,* 614–621.

Jespersen, O. (1964). The woman. In *Language: Its nature, development, and origin* (pp. 237–254). New York: Norton. (Original work published 1922)

Joffe, N. F. (1948). Vernacular of menstruation. *Word, 4,* 181–186.

Johnson, F. L., & Fine, M. G. (1985). Sex differences in uses and perceptions of obscenity. *Women's Studies in Communication, 8,* 11–24.

Joseph, G. I., & Lewis, J. (1981). *Common differences: Conflicts in black and white feminist perspectives*. New York: Doubleday.

Key, M. R. (1972). Linguistic behavior of male and female. *Linguistics, 88*, 15–31.

Key, M. R. (1975). *Male/female language*. Metuchen, NJ: Scarecrow Press.

Kissling, E. A. (1991). Street harassment: The language of sexual terrorism. *Discourse & Society, 2*, 451–460.

Kochman, T. (1981). Male and female interaction: The first phase. In *Black and white styles in conflict* (pp. 74–88). Chicago: University of Chicago Press.

Komarovsky, M. (1962). *Blue-collar marriage*. New York: Random House.

Kramarae, C. (1981). *Women and men speaking*. Rowley, MA: Newbury House.

Kramarae, C. (1990). Changing the complexion of gender in language research. In H. Giles & P. Robinson (Eds.), *Handbook of language and social psychology* (pp. 345–361). New York: Wiley

Kramarae, C., Thorne, B., & Henley, N. (1983). Sex similarities and differences in language, speech, and nonverbal communication: An annotated bibliography. In B. Thorne, C. Kramarae, & N. Henley (Eds.), *Language, gender and society* (pp. 151–342). Rowley, MA: Newbury House.

Kramer, C. (1974). Women's speech: Separate but unequal? *Quarterly Journal of Speech, 60*, 14–24.

Kutner, N. G., & Brogan, D. (1974). An investigation of sex-related slang vocabulary and sex-role orientation among male and female university students. *Journal of Marriage and the Family, 36*, 474–484.

Labov, W. (1972a). *Language in the inner city: Studies in the black english vernacular*. Philadelphia: University of Pennsylvania Press.

Labov, W. (1972b). *Sociolinguistic patterns*. Philadelphia: University of Pennsylvania Press.

Lakoff, R. (1973). Language and woman's place. *Language in Society, 2*, 45–80.

Lakoff, R. (1975). *Language and woman's place*. Harper & Row.

Larsen, V. L. (1963). Psychological study of colloquial menstrual expressions. *Northwest Medicine, 62*, 874–877.

Lee, M. Y. (1976). The married women's status and role as reflected in Japanese: An exploratory sociolinguistic study. *Signs, 1*, 991–999.

Leet-Pellegrini, H. M. (1980). Conversational dominance as a function of gender and expertise. In H. Giles, W. P. Robinson, & P. M. Smith (Eds.), *Language: Social psychological perspectives* (pp. 97–104). Elmsford, NY: Pergamon Press.

Lewis, R. A. (1978). Emotional intimacy among men. *Journal of Social Issues, 34*, 108–121.

Lieberson, S. (1971). Bilingualism in Montreal: A demographic analysis. In J. A. Fishman (Ed.), *Advances in the sociology of language II* (pp. 231–254). The Hague: Mouton.

Loo, C. M. (1991). *Chinatown: Most time, hard time*. New York: Praeger.

Macauley, R. K. S. (1978). Variation and consistency in Glaswegian English. In P. Trudgill (Ed.), *Sociolinguistic patterns in British English* (pp. 132–143). London: Edward Arnold.

McConnell-Ginet, S. (1984). The origins of sexist language in discourse. Annals of the New York Academy of Sciences, 433, 123–135.

McMillan, J. R., Clifton, A. K., McGrath, D., & Gale, W. S. (1977). Women's language: Uncertainty or interpersonal sensitivity and emotionality? *Sex Roles, 3,* 545–559.

Medicine, B. (1987). The role of American Indian women in cultural continuity and transition. In J. Penfield (Ed.), *Women and language in transition* (pp. 159–166). Albany: State University of New York Press.

Meseguer, A. G. (1977). *Lenguaje y discriminacion sexual.* Madrid: Editorial Cuadernos Para el Dialogo.

Miller, C., & Swift, K. (1976). *Words and women: New language in new times.* Garden City, NY: Doubleday.

Mitchell-Kernan, C. (1971). Language behavior in a black urban community. *Monographs of the Language-Behavior Research Laboratory* (No. 2). Berkeley: University of California Language.

Mitchell-Kernan, C. (1972). Signifying and marking: Two Afro-American speech acts. In J. J. Gumperz & D. Hymes (Eds.), *Directions in sociolinguistics* (pp. 161–179). New York: Holt, Rinehart & Winston.

Mitchell-Kernan, C. (1973). Signifying. In A. Dundes (Ed.), *Mother wit from the laughing barrel* (pp. 310–328). Englewood Cliffs, NJ: Prentice Hall.

Moraga, C., & Anzaldúa, G. (1981). *This bridge called my back: Writings by radical women of color.* Watertown, MA: Persephone Press.

Morgan, M. (1990). From down south to up south: The language behavior of three generations of black women residing in Chicago (Doctoral dissertation, University of Pennsylvania, 1989). *Dissertation Abstracts International, 51,* 154A.

Morgan, M. (1991a, Spring). Language and communication style among African American women. *Center for the Study of Women Newsletter,* pp. 7, 13.

Morgan, M. (1991b). Indirectness and interpretation in African American women's discourse. *Pragmatics, 1,* 421–451.

Natale, M., Entin, E., & Jaffe, J. (1979). Vocal interruptions in dyadic communication as a function of speech and social anxiety. *Journal of Personality and Social Psychology, 37,* 865–878.

Nelson, E. A., & Rosenbaum, E. (1972). Language patterns within the youth subculture: Development of slang vocabularies. *Merrill-Palmer Quarterly, 18,* 273–285.

Nichols, P. C. (1976). Black women in the rural south: Conservative and innovative. In B. L. Dubois & I. Crouch (Eds.), *The sociology of the languages of American women* (pp. 103–114). San Antonio, TX: Trinity University.

Nichols, P. C. (1980). Women in their speech communities. In S. McConnell-Ginet, R. Borker, & N. Furman (Eds.), *Women and language in literature and society* (pp. 140–149). New York: Praeger.

Nichols, P. C. (1983). Linguistic options and choices for black women in the rural South. In B. Thorne, C. Kramarae, & N. Henley (Eds.), *Language, gender and society* (pp. 54–68). Rowley, MA: Newbury House.

O'Barr, W. M., & Atkins, B. K. (1980). "Women's language" or "powerless language"? In S. McConnell-Ginet, R. Borker, & N. Furman (Eds.), *Women and language in literature and society* (pp. 93–110). New York: Praeger.

Ochs, E. (1987). The impact of stratification and socialization on men's and women's speech in western Samoa. In S. U. Philips, S. Steele, & C. Tanz (Eds.), *Language, gender, and sex in comparative perspective* (pp. 50–70). Cambridge, England: Cambridge University Press.

Octigan, M., & Niederman, S. (1979). Male dominance in conversations. *Frontiers*, 4, 50–54.

Ornstein, J., Valdés-Fallis, G., & Dubois, B. L. (1976). Bilingual child-language acquisition along the United/States-Mexico border: The El Paso-Ciudad Juarez-Las Cruces triangle. In W. von Raffler-Engel (Ed.), *Child language: 1975* (pp. 386–404). New York: International Linguistic Association.

Parlee, M. (1979, May). Conversational politics. *Psychology Today*, pp. 48–56.

Parsons, E. C. (1913). *The old-fashioned woman: Primitive fancies about the sex*. New York: Putnam.

Partridge, E. (1984). *A dictionary of slang and unconventional English* (8th ed.). New York: Macmillan.

Patella, V., & Kuvlesky, W. P. (1973). Situational variation in language patterns of Mexican American boys and girls. *Social Science Quarterly*, 53, 855–864.

Penelope, J. (1990). *Speaking freely: Unlearning the lies of the fathers' tongues*. Elmsford, NY: Pergamon Press.

Penfield, J. (Ed.) (1987). *Women and language in transition*. Albany: State University of New York Press.

Penfield, J., & Ornstein-Galicia, J. L. (1985). *Chicano English: An ethnic contact dialect*. Amsterdam: John Benjamins.

Philips, S. U., Steele, S., & Tanz, C. (1987). *Language, gender, and sex in comparative perspective*. Cambridge, England: Cambridge University Press.

Philipsen, G. (1975). Speaking "like a man" in Teamsterville: Culture patterns of role enactment in an urban neighborhood. *Quarterly Journal of Speech*, 61, 13–22.

Reynolds, K. A. (1985). Female speakers of Japanese. *Feminist Issues*, 5(2), 13–46.

Rich, A. (1979). *On lies, secrets, and silence: Selected prose, 1966–1978*. New York: Norton.

Robins, K. N., & Adenika, T. J. (1987). Informal conversation topics among urban Afro-American women. In J. Penfield (Ed.), *Women and language in transition* (pp. 180–195). Albany: State University of New York Press.

Rosenthal, R., & Jacobson, L. (1968). *Pygmalion in the classroom: Teacher expectation and pupils' intellectual development*. New York: Holt, Rinehart & Winston.

Rubin, L. B. (1976). *Worlds of pain: Life in the working-class family.* New York: Basic Books.

Saint-Jacques, B. (1973). Sex, dependency and language. *La Linguistique, 9,* 89–96.

Sanders, J. S., & Robinson, W. L. (1979). Talking and not talking about sex: Male and female vocabularies. *Journal of Communication, 29,* 22–30.

Sattel, J. (1976). The inexpressive male: Tragedy or sexual politics? *Social Problems, 23,* 469–477.

Sattel, J. (1983). Men, inexpressiveness, and power. In B. Thorne, C. Kramarae, & N. Henley (Eds.), *Language, gender and society* (pp. 118–124). Rowley, MA: Newbury House.

Scott, P. B. (1974). The English language and black womanhood: A low blow at self-esteem. *Journal of Afro-American Issues, 2,* 218–224.

Shibamoto, J. S. (1987). The womanly woman: Manipulation of stereotypical and nonstereotypical features of Japanese female speech. In S. U. Philips, S. Steele, & C. Tanz (Eds.), *Language, gender, and sex in comparative perspective* (pp. 26–49). Cambridge, England: Cambridge University Press.

Smith, D. E. (1987). Women's perspective as a radical critique of sociology. In S. Harding (Ed.), *Feminism and methodology* (pp. 84–96). Bloomington: Indiana University Press.

Smitherman, G. (1977). *Talkin and testifyin: The language of black America.* Boston: Houghton Mifflin.

Solé, Y. (1978). Sociocultural and sociopsychological factors in differential language retentiveness by sex. *International Journal of the Sociology of Language, 17,* 29–44.

Spender, D. (1980). *Man made language.* London: Routledge & Kegan Paul.

Stanback, M. H. (1986). Language and black woman's place: Evidence from the black middle class. In P. A. Treichler, C. Kramarae, & B. Stafford (Eds.), *For alma mater* (pp. 177–196). Urbana: University of Illinois Press.

Stanley, J. P. (1974). When we say "Out of the closets!" *College English, 36,* 385–391.

Tan, D. (1990). Sexism in the Chinese language. *NWSA Journal, 2,* 635–639.

Tannen, D. (1990). *You just don't understand: Women and men in conversation.* New York: Morrow.

Thorne, B., & Henley, N. (1975). *Language and sex: Difference and dominance.* Rowley, MA: Newbury House.

Trudgill, P. (1972). Sex covert prestige, and linguistic change in the urban British English of Norwich. *Language in Society, 1,* 179–195.

Trudgill, P. (1975). Sex covert prestige, and linguistic change in the urban British English of Norwich. In B. Thorne & N. Henley (Eds.), *Language and sex: Difference and dominance* (pp. 88–104). Rowley, MA: Newbury House.

Valdés-Fallis, G. (1978). Code-switching among bilingual Mexican-American women: Towards an understanding of sex-related language alteration. *International Journal of the Sociology of Language, 17,* 65–72.

Valian, V. (1977). Linguistics and feminism. In M. Vetterling-Braggin, F. A. Elliston, & J. English (Eds.), *Feminism and philosophy* (pp. 154–166). Totowa, NJ: Littlefield, Adams.

Walsh, R., & Leonard, W. (1974). Usage of terms for sexual intercourse by men and women. *Archives of Sexual Behavior, 3,* 373–376.

West, C. (1979). Against our will: Male interruptions of females in cross-sex conversations. In J. Orasanu, M. K. Slater, & L. L. Adler (Eds.), *Language, sex and gender* (pp. 81–97). New York: New York Academy of Sciences.

West, C. (1984). *Routine complications: Troubles with talk between doctors and patients.* Bloomington: Indiana University Press.

West, C., & Garcia, A. (1988). Conversational shiftwork: A study of topical transitions between women and men. *Social Problems, 35,* 551–575.

West, C., & Zimmerman, D. (1983). Small insults: A study of interruptions in cross-sex conversations between unacquainted persons. In B. Thorne, C. Kramarae, & N. Henley (Eds.), *Language, gender and society* (pp. 102–117). Rowley, MA: Newbury House.

West, C., & Zimmerman, D. (1987). Doing gender. *Gender and Society, 1,* 125–151.

Willis, F. N., & Williams, S. J. (1976). Simultaneous talking in conversation and sex of speakers. *Perceptual and Motor Skills, 43,* 1067–1070.

Wilson, W. (1975). Sex differences in response to obscenities and bawdy humor. *Psychological Reports, 37,* 1074.

Wise, S., & Stanley, L. (1987). *Georgie Porgie: Sexual harassment in everyday life.* London: Pandora.

Wolfram, W. A. (1969). *A sociolinguistic description of Detroit Negro speech.* Washington, DC: Center for Applied Linguistics.

Zentella, A. C. (1987). Language and female identity in the Puerto Rican community. In J. Penfield (Ed.), *Women and language in transition* (pp. 167–179). Albany: State University of New York Press.

Zimmerman, D. H., & West, C. (1975). Sex roles, interruptions and silences in conversation. In B. Thorne & N. Henley (Eds.), *Language and sex: Difference and dominance* (pp. 105–129). Rowley, MA: Newbury House.

16

BLACK AND WHITE (AND BLUE): ETHNICITY AND PORNOGRAPHY

GLORIA COWAN

PORNOGRAPHY AS A FEMINIST ISSUE

Pornography has been a significant area of feminist analysis and protest and a subject of civil legislation. In the late 1970s, feminists staged demonstrations against media violence toward women, including films and billboards. In 1978, Women Against Violence in Pornography and Media held a national conference, during which a "Take Back the Night March" was staged in San Francisco's pornography district. An edited set of articles containing feminist anti-pornography analyses, *Take Back the Night* (Lederer, 1980), soon followed. During the next 10 years, pornography became a salient public issue and a mainstream topic of social psychological research. Public awareness of pornography and its effects were magnified by media attention to the 1986 Attorney General's Commission on Pornography.

The 1980s also saw civil legislation to redress victims of pornography proposed by attorney Catherine MacKinnon and writer Andrea Dworkin (Dworkin, 1985; MacKinnon, 1985). They argued the case that pornography discriminates against women by sanctioning and contributing to inequality. Dworkin and MacKinnon's anti-discrimination civil legislation was initiated and passed in Indianapolis and Minneapolis. It was subsequently vetoed by Minneapolis' mayor and declared an unconstitutional violation by the U.S. Court of Appeals for the Seventh Circuit on the basis of the First Amendment (*American Booksellers v. Hudnut*, 1986). In 1992, the Canadian Supreme Court, under its *Charter* rights of equality, redefined *obscenity* in terms of inequality, based on the harm of pornography to women and to society. A conference held at the University of Chicago's Law School in 1993 titled "Speech, Equality, and Harm: Feminist Legal Perspectives on Pornography and Hate Propaganda" brought together legal scholars, feminists, and activists in recognition of the commonalities between racial hate speech and pornography.[1]

From a scientific vantage point, social psychological researchers published books on pornography and its effects in the 1980s (Donnerstein, Linz, & Penrod, 1987; Malamuth & Donnerstein, 1984; Zillmann & Bryant, 1989). Psychology of women texts (e.g., Hyde, 1991; Lott, 1994; Walsh, 1987) briefly discuss pornography. Despite the resurgence of interest in pornography and the recognition that pornography may be part of the propaganda and "text" of sexual violence (Morgan, 1980), little attention has been given in theoretical discussions to ethnicity, and almost no empirical attention has been devoted to ethnic issues related to pornography. It is for this reason that much of the material in this chapter focuses on how feminists in disciplines other than psychology have examined pornography from an ethnic perspective.

PORNOGRAPHY CONTROVERSIES

The issue of pornography has been colored by intense controversy and mutual accusations—among politicians, theorists, researchers, and feminists. Among researchers and theorists, there are those who reflect the conservative anti-pornography position that pornography takes women off their pedestal and renders them vulnerable to a host of devaluating perceptions and attitudes (e.g., Zillman & Weaver, 1989). There are the pro-pornography researchers who emphasize the prosocial and educational benefits of sexually explicit material (e.g., Kelley, Dawson, & Musialowski,

---

[1]Pornography can be regarded as "hate speech"—hatred of women. Where to draw the line on hate speech has become an important issue in connection with political correctness and freedom of expression. In an article on racist speech, Matsuda (1989) argued against an absolutist First Amendment position on the basis of harm experienced by victims of hate speech individually and the harm of perpetuating racism in general. The same argument can be made, and has been done in Canada, regarding pornography and harm.

1989). Finally, there are the researchers who believe that only violent pornography is harmful (e.g., Donnerstein et al., 1987).

In the political world, there are the right-wing religious groups who are against pornography on moral bases; liberals who are concerned about the possibility of censorship and abridgement of freedom of expression; and feminists, some of whom dislike the liberals as much as the conservatives. Among the feminists, most of whom are not psychologists or researchers, three groups can be found: anti-pornography feminists, pro-pornography feminists, and liberal feminists who are concerned more about the effects of censorship on women's as well as on men's freedom of expression. The anti-pornography feminists (e.g., Dworkin and MacKinnon) take the position that pornography is about power, not morality. The feminist critique of pornography has as its standpoint the subordination of women. From this perspective, pornography eroticizes dominance, submission, and gender inequality (MacKinnon, 1989). The "pro-pornography" or "anti-anti-porn" feminists (e.g., Rubin, 1984; Vance, 1984; Willis, 1983) argue that patriarchal culture represses women's sexual expression and that pornography challenges the traditional construction of female sexuality as monogamous, romantic, tied to procreation, and expressed only in committed relationships. Pro-pornography feminists call anti-pornography feminists "prudes," and anti-pornography feminists suggest that pro-pornography and liberal feminists have "sold out" to the pornographers. Some feminists believe that the harm caused by pornography warrants its control, whereas others argue that censorship is more harmful than any harmful effects of pornography. Although anti-pornography feminists and religious conservatives find themselves on the same side of the pornography issue, they do so for different reasons. Conservatives are concerned that pornography erodes the moral climate of society and traditional values, whereas the anti-pornography feminists are concerned that pornography promotes misogynist attitudes and violence against women. Civil libertarian feminists also find themselves in sometimes-hostile company, defending pornographers and the voices of misogyny to preserve freedom of expression. Liberalism should not be equated with approval of pornography, nor should anti-pornography feminists be grouped with religious conservatives as anti-sex.

DEFINITIONS AND CATEGORIES OF PORNOGRAPHY

The definitions of pornography are as variable as the theories about it. Because religious conservatives view the portrayal of sexuality itself as immoral, they label an extremely broad range of material as pornographic, including the exposure of female breasts. By contrast, anti-pornography feminists tend to reserve the term *pornography* for sexually explicit material that degrades or dehumanizes women or presents women as physically abused in a sexual context. Longino's (1980) definition of pornography as "material that explicitly represents or describes degrading or abusive sexual behavior so as to endorse and/or recommend that behavior as described" (p. 44) excludes sexual material intended to educate. By contrast, erotica among feminists refers to sexual material that is intended to be sexually arousing but is not degrading or violent, as sexual images that are mutually pleasurable and freely chosen (Steinem, 1980).

Social science researchers (Donnerstein et al., 1987) and the Meese Commission (Attorney General's Commission on Pornography, 1986) have divided pornography into four primary categories: (a) nudity without force, coercion, sexual activity, or degradation; (b) sexually explicit material (sexual activity) without violence, degradation, submission, domination, or humiliation; (c) sexually explicit material or activity without violence but with degradation, submission, domination, or humiliation; and (d) sexually violent material, including rape and sadomasochistic themes. Traditional research on the effects of pornography has focused mainly on sexually violent material. However, some researchers have examined differential responses to erotica, degrading pornography, and violent pornography (Check & Guloien, 1989). Additionally, Zillmann (1989) examined the effects of prolonged exposure to "common" (nonviolent) pornography.

BLACK WOMEN AND PORNOGRAPHY

Black feminist literature rarely deals with pornography. Collins (1993) noted the neglect of theoretical work explaining patterns of Black women's inclusions in the international pornography industry and, in a larger sense, the absence of Black feminist analysis on a number of issues of sexual politics. Davis (1981) suggested that the absence of Black women in the anti-violence movement (and, consequently, the anti-pornography movement) may be attributable to the movement's indifference toward the historical use of the false rape charge as a component of racism. Also, Black women may perceive pornography and sexual violence as issues that foster divisiveness among Black women and Black men.

Some feminist writers have discussed the connection between racism and sexism in pornography. The novelist, Alice Walker (1981), in her fictional essay, *Coming Apart*, provided a historical analysis of treatment of the Black woman during slavery as the root of modern pornography. She noted the inhumane and completely objectified use of the slave woman by White men who bred, raped, and profited from Black women. According to hooks (1981) and Teich (1980), the sexual assaults on Black women during slavery and after slavery by White men led to a devaluation of Black womanhood that continues even now. One consequence is the designation of "all black women as sexually depraved, immoral, and loose . . . as sexual savages" (hooks, 1981, p. 52) and whores. hooks believed that the continued devaluation of the Black female after slavery was conscious and a deliberate form of social control.

Political scientist and feminist theorist Patricia Collins (1993) drew a parallel between contemporary pornography and the rape of African women during slavery. For example, she noted that the use of Black women as sex objects for the pleasure of White men parallels the portrayal of women in pornography as objects for male pleasure. Collins related the economic exploitation of Black women by White men to the treatment of women in pornography. To Collins, pornography is grounded in racism as much as in sexism. She believed that it is inaccurate to say that racism is secondary in the understanding of pornography. To her, pornography should be reconceptualized as an example of the interlocking nature of race, gender, and class oppression in which African American women are placed within a gender hierarchy in which race and social class inequalities have been sexualized and cast as deviant.

Dworkin (1989) described the sexualization of the Jewish woman in Jew-hating cultures as the "paradigm for the sexualization of all racially or ethnically degraded women" (p. 143). Like hooks and Collins, both anti-pornography feminists Brownmiller (1975) and Dworkin (1989) believed that male projection of sexual fantasies on Women of Color originated with forcible rape. To Dworkin (1989), "every racially hated group is invested with a bestial sexual nature" (p. 147). Dworkin and hooks suggested that Women of Color are not seen as raped or forced because they are thought to elicit and desire their assaults and are more completely sexually personified than are White women.

Walker (1981) and Collins (1993) suggested that the pornography industry's presentation of the Black woman's body is qualitatively different from that of White women. Collins proposed that White women are seen as objects and Black women as animals. The portrayal of Black women in pornography can be described as "savage, wild and primitive, exotic . . . and less than human" (Forna, 1992, p. 104). According to Walker, Black women are depicted as lower, if possible, than White women. Collins believed that the understanding of the role of pornography in the broader political and economic systems awaits an Afrocentric feminist analysis.

BLACK MEN AND PORNOGRAPHY

The treatment of Black men is also part of the historical relationship between racism and pornography. White men have projected unacceptable acts of aggression and sex on Black men and have cast them as their rivals in the sense that Black men are seen by White men as phallic symbols with "monster" penises and inordinate sexual power (Gardner, 1980). While raping and exploiting Black women, White men were "protecting" White women from the Black man. Thus, according to Gardner, during slavery, the White man projected his own savagery onto the Black man and invented the Black rapist of White women to justify lynchings of Black men. During the years 1889–1899, more than 2,000 Black men were lynched, and more than 50% of these men were accused of raping White women. Between 1945 and 1985, 455 men were executed for the crime of rape; 405 were Black, and 398 of the executions took place in the South (Benjamin, 1985).

The interconnection of racial sexual imagery and cultural models of masculinity has a long history. Hoch (1979) described the use of the archetype of the black beast/White goddess theme throughout literary history. Locked in battle with the dark villain or black beast, the White (male) hero's quest for the White feminine goddess is a constant theme. According to Graves (cited in Hoch, 1979), this interracial competition is central to almost all Western mythology and literary works. Here, the black beast figure is the "dark" side of White civilization, embodying all the unacceptable and bestial, or satanic, forces in contrast to the White hero figure. This polarity between the black beast and the White hero is found in the oldest stories in Western civilization dating back 3,000 years and continuing into the present: Egyptian and Greek mythology, Shakespeare's plays, classic literature and films (e.g., *King Kong*), fairy tales (*Beauty and the Beast*), and modern science fiction (*Star Wars*).

Hoch (1979) attributed the projection of animal lust to the dark man to the repression of sexuality. The morally superior White female goddess is in constant sexual danger from the dark beast, thus justifying White males' superiority. At the core of the projection of Black male sexuality is not the protection of the White woman but the control of White male sexuality. Similarly, inside the pure and chaste White woman lurks the sexual whore projected onto Black women.

Feminist analysis would suggest that repressed sexuality cannot account for this mythologized theme. Despite the projection of sexual lust to the dark figure, at the core of this story is the woman as sexual prey. The chauvinistic mind projects itself on both the black beast and the woman (Griffin, 1981): "In the black man, the force of desire, of appetite, of wanting is played out, and in the White woman an awareness of vulnerability, weakness, mortality, fear can be lived" (p. 166). To Griffin, the chauvinistic and the racist mind are the same, both projecting the dark, feminine self. Thus, it is not the repression of sexuality per se; rather, it may be the repression of the feminine.

GENDER AND RACE POLITICS IN PORNOGRAPHY

Interracial pornographic imagery is not only symbolically and historically important but also is of current political significance. The critique of Black (and White) masculinity inherent in the feminist analysis of pornography may be thought to divert attention from racism and, in a sense, blame the oppressed Black man. In her analysis of Spike Lee's film, *She's Gotta Have It*, hooks (1989) noted the interconnection of racism and sexism and did not hesitate to confront sexism. According to hooks, both Black men and White men have aspired to a model of masculinity that includes in its display an entitlement to women's bodies. The wounds of racism do not justify the oppression of Black women. hooks (1990) noted the use of sexualized metaphors of masculinity in the Black power movement in the 1960s and 1970s, the sexual images of "castration," "impotence," and "emasculinization." hooks insisted that Black people—men and women—must reject the sexualization of Black liberation because this model feeds into racist stereotyped images of Black men as rapists and in turn feeds both sexism and racism.

Likewise, Dworkin (1989), in her discussion of force in pornography, also linked racism and sexism and described the means by which the sexual depiction of the Black man as beast gives license to his oppression. The masculine identification offered the Black man in collaboration with White men in the conquest of women is used as justification for his colonialization and ultimately his destruction. The exploitation and abuse of women in pornography creates a male–male collusion in which men can bond, interracial conflict may be prevented, but the Black man ultimately loses.

Walker (1981) expressed concern with the use of pornography by Black men because pornography makes the White woman available to Black men (making him "White"). By sexual association with the White woman, the Black man raises his own status and dignity and bonds White and Black men as men. Gardner (1980) regarded some Black men as buying into the White man's ideology, consequently destroying relationships between Black men and Black women. She noted that Black as well as White men are buying pornography and beating and raping women but White men are producing pornography and profiting by it.

In her fictional account interwoven with analysis, Walker (1981) described a Black man who uses pornographic images of White women to masturbate: "She pauses, looks at her husband: 'So, how does a black woman feel when her black man leaves *Playboy* on the coffee table?' " (p. 52). As his wife begins to understand the meaning of his act and becomes aware of the objectification of women, he withdraws from her and their relationship becomes strained.

The critique of interracial sexual relationships between Black men and White women by Spike Lee in his film, *Jungle Fever*, draws on the

White projection of the Black man's phallus-centered sexuality. In this film, White women are portrayed as sexually desiring Black men for their sexual prowess and large penises. Interracial sex, according to Lee's work, is cast in cultural mythology rather than individual preference. Lincoln (1970), in a chapter titled "Who Will Revere the Black Woman?," poignantly stated the following:

> We are the women whose bars and recreation halls are invaded by flagrantly disrespectful, bigoted, simpering, amoral, emotionally unstable, outcast, maladjusted, nymphomaniacal, condescending white women in desperate and untiring search of the "frothing-at-the-mouth-for-a-white-woman, strongbacked, sixty-minute hot black." Our men. (p. 84)

This quote castigates the pornographically constructed White woman, making her the enemy. When sexism and racism are intertwined, it is difficult to know the enemy.

RESEARCH ON ETHNICITY AND PORNOGRAPHY

One important issue, linking this historical and mythological treatment of Black men and women to current pornography, is the actual images of Women and Men of Color in contemporary pornography. Statements have been made about the treatment of Black women and men in pornography, yet these statements have not been subject to empirical verification through content analyses.

Are different ethnic groups interchangeable in pornography, or does racism get expressed with sexism? In pornography with White actors, a majority of the sexual scenes in X-rated pornography videos contain themes of domination and exploitation (Cowan, Lee, Levy, & Snyder, 1988). To determine whether these themes of domination and exploitation characterize Black women and men in interracial pornography, Cowan and Campbell (1994) analyzed images of Women and Men of Color in interracial X-rated videocassettes. These films were selected from local video shops on the basis of evidence of interracial themes as portrayed in either the title or when interracial couples were displayed on the videocassette box.[2] Five coders analyzed 476 characters in the sex scenes of 54 interracial films. Characters were coded on aggregate indexes of physical and verbal aggression, inequality cues, racial cues, and intimacy cues, as well as other specific indexes. Analyses were conducted comparing themes associated with gen-

---

[2]Black and interracial pornography was introduced in 1983 and is produced and marketed for a White male audience. Interracial pornography is readily available in the pornography sections of video rental stores. The use of Women and Men of Color is typically indicated on the cover and sometimes in the title of the film (e.g., *Bet Black, Black to the Future, Hot Chocolate, Jungle Juice*).

der and ethnicity. Additional analyses considered the ethnicity of each character's partner (i.e., cross-race vs. same-race [heterosexual] partner).

Sexism was demonstrated by the unidirectional aggression by men toward women. Racism was demonstrated in the lower status of Black characters and the presence of racial stereotypes. Racism was expressed somewhat differently by sex and sexism somewhat differently by race. For example, Black women received a significantly greater number of acts of verbal and physical aggression than did White women. Black men performed fewer intimate behaviors (e.g., kissing, having face-to-face intercourse, talking during sex) than did White men. One interpretation is that race exaggerates gender roles in pornography. Women are dominated, but Black women more so than White women. Men are shown as sex machines, but Black men more so than White men. A cross-race interaction was found, with White men being more physically and verbally aggressive to Black women than to White women and Black men more physically and verbally aggressive to White women than to Black women. Interpretations for the cross-race effects include the idea that the images of White men subjugating Black women implements the fantasy for White men of acting out both sexism and racism simultaneously. And, the Black man may serve vicariously, as he has through mythology and literature, as the punisher of the sexual White woman.

One memorable scene was in a video titled *Let Me Tell Ya 'Bout Black Chicks* in which two White men wearing Klu Klux Klan hoods enter a Black woman's bedroom, where she is masturbating to a background of gospel music, and engage in sex with her. She barely protests and appears to respond positively (paradigmatic rape myth). They say "Let's f_____ the s_____ out of this darky." The degradingness of this image has little to do with the particular sex acts performed. Rather, it is the context provided by our knowledge of the Klu Klux Klan and the lie that the oppressed wants to engage in sex with her oppressor that is degrading to African Americans.

Another study examined the covers and titles of interracial pornography (Mayall & Russell, 1993), including magazines, books, films, and videos, in seven pornography stores, as well as analyzing the content of seven pornography books about people of color and Jews. African American women were disproportionately used in magazine covers relative to other Women of Color. Mayall and Russell (1993) concluded from their analysis of the seven books that this genre of pornography portrayed African Americans in derogatory and stereotypic ways—"as animalistic, incapable of self-control, sexually depraved, impulsive, unclean, and so forth" (p. 176).

A second question relevant to the examination of ethnic images and racism in pornography is the perception of the actor depending on her or his ethnicity (i.e., ethnicity as a stimulus variable). In his doctoral dissertation, Johnson (1984) examined the effects of level of enjoyment of the woman in the pornographic written passage, the race of the woman in the passage (Black or White), and the race of the rape victim in a simulated rape trial used to measure the dependent variable. First, he exposed White male college students to the rape depiction, varying the race of the female in the script and the level of enjoyment of the female. After exposure to the passage, ratings of either a Black or White victim in a simulated rape trial were obtained. The race of the victim in the simulated trial had no effect on the ratings. However, after reading the pornographic material in which the White female resisted the attack, was unwilling throughout the entire passage, and never appeared to enjoy her rape, the participants perceived a greater probability of the rape victim in the simulated trial enjoying the act than when the pornographic female stimulus person was Black. In the enjoyment condition, when the female in the pornographic scenario was Black, the rape victim in the simulated trial was seen as enjoying the act more than when the female stimulus person was White. These findings, not predicted by the author, are understandable. When Black women resist, they may be believed more than White women.

Muehlenhard (1988) suggested that the double standard, which implies that it is less acceptable for a woman than a man to be sexually active outside a committed relationship, can contribute to the idea that a woman wants to have sex when she offers resistance. This belief may be moderated by the ethnicity of the woman. Because the sexual double standard has been applied more to Whites than Blacks, a Black woman's resistance may be more likely to be taken at face value. Thus, White women may be seen as more likely than Black women to offer what is perceived as "token resistance" or "scripted refusal," saying no when they mean yes. Conversely, if the Black woman is seen as inherently more sexual than the White woman, generalization to the rape victim would be in the direction of greater enjoyment when participants have been exposed previously to a nonresisting Black than White woman.

AREAS IN NEED OF RESEARCH

Areas in need of research are ethnic attitudes toward pornography, attitudes toward the relationship between pornography and violence toward women, and attitudes toward pornography control. Sociologist Robert Staples (1991) purported that most Blacks think that pornography is a trivial White man's problem. In the context of social issues such as poverty and hunger, pornography is inconsequential. Of course, Staples was treating pornography as a medium of sexual expression rather than as a medium in which the sexual and racial hierarchy is sexualized. Furthermore, he reinforced racial sexual stereotypes by suggesting that Blacks have traditionally had a more naturalistic (read "animalistic") attitude toward human sexuality.

In contrast to Staples's (1991) presumptions about Black attitudes toward pornography, Timberlake and Carpenter's (1990) study on the sexual attitudes of 124 Black adults indicated that respondents were strongly against pornography. In this primarily middle-class and 75% female sample, 82% thought pornography was harmful to society; 57% believed it was a major cause of incest, rape, and child molestation; and 65% felt that it should not be protected by law. No gender, educational, or income differences were found in attitudes toward pornography, but this sample did not have broad representations of social class. Similar to studies primarily of Whites, one might expect to find that Blacks and other ethnic groups would be divided on the issue of pornography and pornography control. Studies done on the general population show a lack of agreement on whether pornography should be legally controlled (Roper Center for Public Opinion Research, 1986). Samples of college students and feminists (Cowan, 1992; Cowan, Chase, & Stahly, 1989; Cowan & Stahly, 1992) also are divided about the issue of pornography control. Within the past 15 years, feminist theorists have become less unanimously against pornography and pornography control (Russo, 1987), although surveys of feminists (Cowan, 1992) indicate that feminists appear to have strong negative feelings about pornography itself, see it as harmful to women, but are split on the control issue.

A number of questions about people of color's attitudes toward pornography and its control should be addressed by investigating the correlates of attitudes toward pornography control among Blacks, Latinos, and Asians. Here, the religiosity of the sample may be a factor in ethnic samples, as well as among Whites. Does fundamentalism have the same force among Black and Latina samples as it does among White samples? Are censorship concerns and harm to women as important predictors of attitudes toward pornography control among various ethnic groups as they are among Whites? Are socioeconomic indicators within ethnic groups predictive of attitudes toward pornography and pornography control? Do members of various ethnic groups avail themselves of pornography, renting it or viewing it in pornography shops? These are some of the issues surrounding attitudes toward and exposure to pornography unanswered at the present time.

Controversy exists among researchers who have examined the effects of pornography. In criticizing the recommendations of the Attorney General's Commission on Pornography (1986), Linz et al. (1987) believed that it is the violence, not the sex, that is harmful. Zillmann (1989) and Check and Guloien (1989) provided research showing that exposure to "common" pornography (typically material that degrades and dehumanizes women) is harmful in its attitudinal and value effects. For example, prolonged consumption of pornography leads to discontent with the physical appearance and the sexual performance of the viewer's partner, promotes insensitivity toward victims of sexual violence, trivializes rape as a criminal offense, and increases men's reported likelihood of rape if not caught or punished (Zillmann, 1989). Most of the research on the effects of pornography has studied the responses of White male undergraduates. The effects of pornography on members of ethnic groups has been virtually ignored.

Are the effects demonstrated on White participants in pornography relevant to people of color? Zillmann (1989) showed that White college men are less satisfied with their partners following prolonged exposure to pornography. Do Black men experience similar devaluations of their partners, as described in Walker's (1981) fiction?

Also, does desensitization to victims of violence occur among Black men exposed to pornography? The desensitization effect of pornography and violent films, such that rape victims and battering victims are seen as less injured and more responsible for their victimization, is a great concern for Women of Color who have been raped or battered. A battered or raped woman who is depending on a jury to convict her attacker may be at a disadvantage if the jury consists of media consumers of sexual violence or pornography that "merely" degrades women. Given the treatment of Black women in the history of the legal justice system, the exposure of potential jurors to interracial pornography in which Black women are "fair game," ready and willing for any sexual encounter and subject to sexual violence, probably hurts Black victims of violence. Future research needs to address the implications of the desensitization effect for Black women who have been victims of violence.

Last, as little as researchers know about African Americans in relation to pornography, less is known about other ethnic groups. An image often used in anti-pornography media is the picture of Asian women bound and hanging from trees from the cover of *Penthouse* (1985, December). Third World women are economically and sexually exploited by the international pornography market (Forna, 1992). In Thailand and throughout Southeast Asia, prostitution and pornography are part of a large slave trade. Collins (1993) cited Bell (1987) in contrasting the images of Black women and Asian women in pornography. Black women are portrayed in situations of bondage and slavery, breaking away from their chains, whereas the images of Asian women are those of torture. These distinctions are not empirically based and should be examined in content analyses.

In short, women (and men) of color are present in pornography, are probably exposed to pornography, but have not been visible in pornography research. And, Women of Color are at least as likely as White women to be victims of violence. Although researchers are debating the effects of pornography and White feminists are debating issues of freedom of expression, censorship, and civil legislation, they need to recognize that pornography is not just a White person's issue. With this awareness, research on pornography should include people of color.

REFERENCES

American Booksellers v. Hudnut, 598 F.Supp 1319 (S.D. Ind. 1984), aff'd 771 F.2nd 323 (7th Cir. 1985), aff'd 475 U.S. 1001 (1986).

Attorney General's Commission on Pornography: Final report. (1986). Washington, DC: U.S. Department of Justice.

Bell, L. (Ed.). (1987). *Good girls/bad girls: Feminists and sex trade workers face to face.* Toronto: Seal.

Benjamin, L. (1985). Pornography as racial and sexual violence. In G. E. McCuen (Ed.), *Pornography and sexual violence* (pp. 15–19). Beverly Hills, CA: Sage.

Brownmiller, S. (1975). *Against our will: Men, women and rape.* New York: Bantam Books.

Check, J. M. V., & Guloien, T. H. (1989). Reported proclivity for coercive sex following repeated exposure to sexually violent pornography, nonviolent dehumanizing pornography, and erotica. In D. Zillman & J. Bryant (Eds.), *Pornography: Research advances and policy considerations* (pp. 159–184). Hillsdale, NJ: Erlbaum.

Collins, P. H. (1993). The sexual politics of black womanhood. In P. B. Bart & E. G. Moran (Eds.), *Violence against women: The bloody footprints* (pp. 85–104). Newbury Park, CA: Sage.

Cowan, G. (1992). Feminist attitudes toward pornography control. *Psychology of Women Quarterly, 16,* 166–177.

Cowan, G., & Campbell, R. R. (1994). Racism and sexism in interracial pornography. *Psychology of Women Quarterly, 18,* 323–338.

Cowan, G., Chase, C. J., & Stahly, G. B. (1989). Feminist and fundamentalist women's attitudes toward pornography control. *Psychology of Women Quarterly, 13,* 97–112.

Cowan, G., Lee, C., Levy, D., & Snyder, D. (1988). Dominance and inequality in X-rated videocassettes. *Psychology of Women Quarterly, 12,* 299–312.

Cowan, G., & Stahly, G. (1992). Attitudes toward pornography control. In J. C. Chrisler & D. Howard (Eds.), *New directions in feminist psychology: Practice, theory, and research* (pp. 200–214). New York: Springer.

Davis, A. (1981). *Women, race, and sex.* New York: Random House.

Donnerstein, E., Linz, D., & Penrod, S. (1987). *The question of pornography: Research findings and policy implications.* New York: Free Press.

Dworkin, A. (1985). Against the male flood: Censorship, pornography, and equality. *Harvard Women's Law Journal, 8,* 1–29.

Dworkin, A. (1989). *Pornography: Men possessing women.* New York: Dutton.

Forna, A. (1992). Pornography and racism: Sexualizing oppression and inciting hatred. In C. Itzen (Ed.), *Pornography: Women, violence and civil liberties. A radical new view* (pp. 102–112). New York: Oxford University Press.

Gardner, T. A. (1980). Racism in pornography and the women's movement. In L. Lederer (Ed.), *Take back the night* (pp. 105–114). New York: Morrow.

Griffin, S. (1981). *Pornography and silence.* New York: Harper & Row.

Hoch, P. (1979). *White hero, black beast: Racism, sexism and the mask of masculinity.* London: Pluto Press.

hooks, b. (1981). *Ain't I a woman: Black women and feminism* (pp. 51–86). Boston: South End Press.

hooks, b. (1989). "Whose pussy is this": A feminist comment. In b. hooks (Ed.), *Talking back* (pp. 134–141). Boston: South End Press.

hooks, b. (1990). Reflections on race and sex. In b. hooks (Ed.), *Yearning: Race, gender, and cultural politics* (pp. 57–64). Boston: South End Press.

Hyde, J. S. (1991). *Half the human experience: The psychology of women* (4th ed.). Lexington, MA: Heath.

Johnson, J. D. (1984). *The differential racial effects of exposure to erotica.* Unpublished doctoral dissertation, Indiana University, Bloomington.

Kelley, K., Dawson, L., & Musialowski, D. M. (1989). Three faces of sexual explicitness: The good, the bad, and the useful. In D. Zillman & J. Bryant (Eds.), *Pornography: Research advances and policy considerations* (pp. 57–91). Hillsdale, NJ: Erlbaum.

Lederer, L. (Ed.). (1980). *Take back the night.* New York: Morrow.

Lincoln, A. (1970). Who will revere the Black woman? In T. Cade (Ed.), *The black woman: An anthology* (pp. 80–84). New York: New American Library.

Linz, D., Donnerstein, E., & Penrod, S. (1987). The findings and recommendations of the Attorney General's Commission on Pornography: Do the psychological "facts" fit the political fury? *American Psychologist, 42,* 946–953.

Longino, H. (1980). Pornography, oppression, and freedom. In L. Lederer (Ed.), *Take back the night* (pp. 40–54). New York: Morrow.

Lott, B. (1994). *Women's lives: Themes and variations in gender learning* (2nd ed.). Pacific Grove, CA: Brooks/Cole.

MacKinnon, C. A. (1985). Pornography, civil rights, and speech. *Harvard Civil Rights-Civil Liberties Law Review, 20,* 1–70.

MacKinnon, C. A. (1989). *Toward a feminist theory of the state.* Cambridge, MA: Harvard University Press.

Malamuth, N. M., & Donnerstein, E. (Eds.). (1984). *Pornography and sexual aggression.* San Diego, CA: Academic Press.

Matsuda, M. J. (1989). Public response to racist speech: Considering the victim's story. *Michigan Law Review, 87,* 2320–2381.

Mayall, A., & Russell, D. E. H. (1993). Racism in pornography. In D. E. H. Russell (Ed.), *Making violence sexy: Feminist views on pornography* (pp. 167–178). New York: Teacher's College Press.

Morgan, R. (1980). Theory and practice: Pornography and rape. In L. Lederer (Ed.), *Take back the night* (pp. 134–140). New York: Morrow.

Muehlenhard, C. L. (1988). "Nice women" don't say yes and "real men" don't say no: How miscommunication and the double standard can cause sexual problems. *Women and Therapy: A Feminist Quarterly, 7,* 95–108.

Roper Center for Public Opinion Research. (1986). *General social survey, 1972–1986: Cumulative codebook July, 1985.* Storrs: University of Connecticut Press.

Staples, R. (1991). Blacks and pornography: A different response. In M. Kimmel (Ed.), *Men confront pornography* (pp. 111–114). New York: Meridian.

Rubin, G. (1984). Thinking sex. In C. Vance (Ed.), *Pleasure and danger: Exploring female sexuality* (pp. 267–319). London: Routledge and Kegan Paul.

Russo, A. (1987). Conflicts and contradictions among feminists over issues of pornography and sexual freedom. *Women's Studies International Forum, 10,* 103–112.

Steinem, G. (1980). Erotica and pornography: A clear and present difference. In L. Lederer (Ed.), *Take back the night* (pp. 35–39). New York: Morrow.

Teich, L. (1980). A quiet subversion. In L. Lederer (Ed.), *Take back the night* (pp. 115–118). New York: Morrow.

Timberlake, C. A., & Carpenter, W. D. (1990). Sexuality attitudes of black adults. *Family Relations, 39,* 87–91.

Vance, C. (1984). *Pleasure and danger: Exploring female sexuality.* London: Routledge & Kegan Paul.

Walker, A. (1981). Coming apart. In A. Walker (Ed.), *You can't keep a good woman down* (pp. 40–53). San Diego, CA: Harcourt Brace Jovanovich.

Walsh, M. R. (1987). *The psychology of women: Ongoing debates.* New Haven, CT: Yale University Press.

Willis, E. (1983). Feminism, moralism, and pornography. In A. Smitow, C. Stansell, & S. Thompson (Eds.), *Powers of desire: The politics of sexuality* (pp. 460–467). New York: Monthly Review Press.

Zillmann, D. (1989). Effects of prolonged consumption of pornography. In D. Zillman & J. Bryant (Eds.), *Pornography: Research advances and policy considerations* (pp. 127–157). Hillsdale, NJ: Erlbaum.

Zillman, D., & Bryant, J. (1989). *Pornography: Research advances and policy considerations.* Hillsdale, NJ: Erlbaum.

Zillmann, D., & Weaver, J. B. (1989). Pornography and men's sexual callousness toward women. In D. Zillmann & J. Bryant (Eds.), *Pornography: Research advances and policy considerations* (pp. 95–125). Hillsdale, NJ: Erlbaum.

CONCLUSION: CULTURAL DIVERSITY AND THE FUTURE OF FEMINIST PSYCHOLOGY

RHODA K. UNGER

When I was first asked to do the concluding chapter for this book on the question of what cultural diversity means for the future of feminist psychology, I thought the answer was obvious. Recently, a number of feminist scholars have eloquently stated the case for moving psychology away from its emphasis on the middle-class White male (and his sisters; cf. Brown, 1990; Reid, 1993). The wealth of information provided by this book amply demonstrates how much psychology is enriched when ethnically diverse women are moved from margin to center (hooks, 1984).

Nevertheless, many unresolved issues remain. It is important not to reproduce the history of the psychology of White women, in which assumptions about essential qualities of femaleness and femininity have only recently been replaced by social constructionist perspectives (Unger & Crawford, 1993). In this chapter, I focus on social context and social processes to show how they question essentialist conceptions of race as well as gender. A rigorous analysis of race and ethnicity can assist psychologists in working through the often thorny issues involving "difference." Paradoxically, difference can then be used as a vehicle for a renewed and inclusive feminist activism.

413

EPISTEMOLOGICAL AND METHODOLOGICAL CAVEATS

The history of the psychology of women demonstrates that researchers should be cautious about adding groups to their studies without any theoretical justification for doing so. This practice of "add women and stir" has led to an emphasis on the differences between women and men and can lead to a devaluation of those traits and behaviors considered to be characteristic of females. Ethnocentric biases similar to androcentric ones persist in both psychology as a discipline and in society as a whole. Such biases make it easy to predict which populations will be considered deficient when "perfidious comparisons" are made between groups that differ from the dominant one in ethnicity, class, and gender (Yoder & Kahn, 1993).

Many feminist psychologists are becoming aware that consideration of any single group in isolation can be divisive. The dominant discourse has tended to view the characteristics of subordinate groups in society as deficient, deviant, or both. Psychologists incorporate societal ideology and focus their research on such deviance. Angela Ginorio and her colleagues (chapter 11 in this book) point out, for example, that Latinas are more likely to be studied in terms of their reproductive roles (particularly as teenage mothers) than as workers. There also is a disproportionate number of studies of teenage child bearing among African Americans even though the majority of teenagers who have children are White (Graham, 1992; Unger & Crawford, 1992).

Methodological biases within psychology also help frame Women of Color as victims. When Women of Color are studied by psychologists, they are more likely to be found as case histories or anecdotal data than in experimental designs (Unger & Saundra, 1993). These kinds of "data" reinforce stereotypes about women in various groups (see Cowan, chapter 16 in this book, for particularly vicious examples of such stereotypes).

By contrast, the strengths of marginalized populations are likely to be ignored. For example, despite their economic disadvantage, Blacks actually report greater life satisfaction than Whites during their late middle years (Carlson & Videka-Sherman, 1990). Their positive responses appear to be related to the greater social support African Americans and other ethnic groups who live in poverty give each other as well as to the greater importance of organized religion in their lives. Social scientists from the dominant culture, with its more autonomous and secular values, have tended to neglect these variables.

The lack of comparability between studies of White men and non-White "others" obviously limits the conclusions that can be drawn in any review. Moreover, because of the differences between the methodologies used, the inclusion of Women of Color as "exceptions" to dominant paradigms may be perceived as tokenism. Thus, the data may be ignored rather than used to provide an effective challenge to such paradigms.

There has been even less research on what happens when gender, ethnicity, and class are combined rather than studied as separate variables (Landrine, Klonoff, & Brown-Collins, 1992; Reid, 1988; Unger & Saundra, 1993). To paraphrase the title of a book on Black women's studies (Hull, Scott, & Smith, 1982), all the Blacks have been men and all the women have been White in most empirical studies.

Reid (1988) suggested that the consequences of combining gender, ethnicity, and class are likely to be multiplicative rather than additive. The problem for those who are interested in the relationship between cultural diversity and gender is how to develop a theoretical framework for analyzing such multiplicative processes. In this chapter I discuss some problems that arise when ethnicity and race and class become part of the gender equation.

Some of these problems are caused as well as ameliorated by postmodernist and deconstructionist critiques of traditional scholarship. Unfortunately, postmodernist theory is complex, and its language is sometimes inaccessible to psychologists. Some feminist psychologists have, however, begun to decode its tenets and apply them to psychological research (cf. Bohan, 1993; Hare-Mustin & Marecek, 1988; Morawski & Bayer, chapter 6 in this book). In this chapter, I focus on those issues that I believe are important for psychologists who, like myself, would prefer to integrate some aspects of empirical work with culturally diverse populations into the discipline as a whole.

NEGLECTED ISSUES IN THE STUDY OF ALL WOMEN

The Challenge of the Socially Constructed Self

One of the challenges posed by postmodernist theory for feminist psychologists is how to deal with the proposition that a stable self does not exist but is continually constructed as a function of social forces (see Landrine, chapter 1 in this book). Social construction would seem to say that there is no such thing as stable personality or individuality. If this view is correct, one cannot generalize, neither about any one woman nor about groups of women. One is left with the individual's life experiences and the meaning she extracts from them. However, these meanings, too, are transient. They are subject to constant reconstruction by the individual as her circumstances change.

These assumptions pose a particular dilemma for empiricists interested in cultural diversity because research in this area involves looking at collective as well as individual responses. If one accepts them in toto, many of the chapters in this book that generalize about women from particular ethnic groups could be viewed as problematic because group categorization is seen as problematic. Similar to so-called differences between women and men, differences within ethnic groups may be larger than the differences between them.

If one cannot generalize about women within a particular group, it is even more problematic to generalize between groups of women. This is a basic dilemma that confronts feminist psychology as a whole. It can be partially resolved by moving away from comparisons that are based only on gender to comparisons between many kinds of women (e.g., women who vary in ethnicity, religion, class, age, etc.). Paradoxically, increasing the number of such variables that researchers examine both limits their ability to make universalist assumptions on the basis of gender and sharpens their understanding of how gender works (Unger, 1992). It makes gender both more and less important.

Group Processes and the Study of Identity

When researchers study ethnicity as well as gender, they need to move beyond a psychology of groups to a psychology of group processes. They must look at psychological processes in terms of a variety of levels: intrapsychic, interpersonal, institutional and structural, and sociocultural in nature (Unger & Saundra, 1993). This kind of analysis may allow researchers to differentiate between those traits and behaviors that are unique to an individual, those that are characteristic of her group, those that are characteristic of women in a particular role or setting, or, perhaps those characteristic of women in general. This kind of analysis will also help researchers to move beyond description toward an understanding of the complex nature of the processes involved.

Identity, for example, can be explored at several different levels. One's sense of oneself is an intrapsychic phenomenon, but it is influenced both by interactions with others and by the social context. The meaning of individuality is also defined differently by various subcultural groups. Identity appears to be viewed more collectively among many ethnic populations than it is in mainstream culture as a whole. The devaluation of collective concerns by the dominant culture can produce enormous burdens for women from ethnicities that stress the importance of group needs over individual autonomy. When they have the luxury of choice, these women may be able to choose only between personal accomplishments and collective needs (see chapters 10 and 11 in this book). Thus, autonomy may not have the same unambiguously high value for Women of Color that it does for White women.

Psychologists need to determine which aspects of identity are transient and unique to the individual and which are generalizable across culturally diverse groups. They need both innovative theory and methodology to do so. As usual for psychology, the methodology appears to be in advance of the theory here.

For example, Hope Landrine and her colleagues (Landrine, et al., 1992; see also chapter 3 in this book) developed a methodology that permitted them to look at women's responses at both an intrapsychic and between-groups level. They examined several groups of undergraduate women who differed in ethnicity using a number of gender-stereotypic adjectives as cues. They found that although there were few differences between ethnic groups in self-evaluations, women from the various groups differed in terms of the meaning they attached to the adjectives. In other words, they appeared to be more similar than they actually were because they were using the same words with differing meanings. Dion and Dion (1993) found similar differences between ethnically diverse populations in what they mean by the term *love*.

The Meaning of Meaning

The challenge for psychologists is to find variables which are related to differences in the construction of meaning across groups. Besides requiring a combination of emic and etic strategies, this task also requires a theoretical framework for determining a priori which ethnic and cultural groups should be examined in a given study. This strategy moves beyond a description of group differences toward the beginnings of theoretical explanations for some of these differences.

The values of a culture may, for example, provide one clue to the determination of meaning. Gibbons et al. (1993) used anthropological data on cultural values to select national groups that varied on an individualist–collectivist dimension. They found that adolescents' attitudes about women's work and family roles varied in the direction predicted by these culturally based distinctions (e.g., even employment was viewed more communally in collectivist societies).

Meaning may also be determined by causal attributions that are indirectly derived only from cultural ideology. For example, Kauppinen-Toropainen and Gruber (1993) found cultural differences in the impact of sexual harassment between Russian, Scandinavian, and U.S. women. With the same level of harassment, Russian women were more severely affected because they believed that they were more personally responsible for it than women from other national groups.

Cohort Effects and Changes in Meaning

What all of these studies have in common is the provision of another source of variation besides a group label such as gender or ethnicity. Thus, phenomenological experience as a carrier of subjective meaning may be studied not only for itself but also as an indicator of a collective reality in the lives of some groups of women. Of course, reality and its meaning change over time. Another source of variation that has been relatively neglected by feminist psychologists (for some exceptions, see Franz & Stewart, 1994) are cohort effects. Cohorts reflect changes in critical circumstances so that apparently similar experiences generate differing meanings at different times.

One example of such effects can be found in a recent study by Apfelbaum (1993) on female political leaders. Although all Western European democracies may "look alike," Apfelbaum found that female leaders in Norway and France differed greatly in their views of themselves and their accomplishments. French female leaders tended to see themselves as more illegitimate, more alienated from their male companions, and less representative of the feminist movement than did their Norwegian counterparts. Apfelbaum attributed part of this effect to culturally bound ideology about sexual relationships. She also noted, however, that attitudes among the French women have begun to change in the Norwegian direction among the younger cohort of leaders. Such differences in the meaning of similar experiences cannot be explored without taking into account these women's historical and situational contexts.

Physical Setting and Cultural Variables

Although none of the chapters in this book directly address the issue of historical and situational context, several authors (LaFromboise et al.; Root; Ginorio, et al.) have indicated the importance of physical setting. Physical setting can carry with it important information that psychologists may not see if they look at demography alone.

For example, mobility, in one form or another, appears to produce greater and more complex problems for women than for men. Its impact has been relatively ignored by psychologists. Only the consequences of job mobility have been studied extensively. This neglect is an example of racist and classist biases in traditional psychology. Forced migration or immigration is not the same thing as changing jobs. These events have a much greater impact on individuals and their families because cultural continuity is disrupted and no improvement in economic conditions is assured after such a move.

Teresa LaFromboise and her associates (chapter 10 in this book) point out that American Indians often face the difficult decision of remaining on reservations or rural farms in poverty or leaving their communities in search of employment. Because American Indian women tend to be better educated than men from their tribal group, family stress is exacerbated by increased opportunities for women while their partners' options decline. Increasing opportunities through mobility also come at the cost of cultural alienation.

Similar stress-related effects can be found in other groups of women who migrate voluntarily or are forced to flee their countries as refugees (Espin, 1987; Lykes, 1994). Angela Ginorio and her colleagues (chapter 11 in this book) have suggested some variables that need to be explored for all ethnic groups. These include migration history, acculturation, adherence to culturally determined gender roles, dominant language, acceptance of cultural values, and family position. Each of these may affect women and men differently and thus be confounded with gender.

Feminist psychologists have begun to recognize that war and other forms of state-sponsored violence produce sex-specific effects in addition to the horrific costs to everyone who is caught up in them (Lykes, Brabeck, Ferns, & Radan, 1993). As custodians of culture, women typically pass on the dress, language, and customs of their group. Refugee women (and to a lesser extent those who migrate voluntarily) lose significant ties to their culture. These losses can have a serious impact on their sense of self (Melville & Lykes, 1992).

As noted in a number of chapters in this book (cf. LaFromboise et al., chapter 11; Porter, chapter 8), ethnic women appear to underuse the psychological support services available to them. They may be reluctant to discuss losses of identity with individuals who do not share their culture. Such disclosures are particularly difficult when aspects of that culture are regarded as "primitive" and devalued by members of the dominant group.

Unfortunately, those aspects of culture (e.g., language, dress, forms of interpersonal behavior, etc.) that lend richness to particular ethnic groups are often also those that are denigrated by others. Ethnic differences, like gender differences, are "not separate but equal." Difference, qua difference, is a problematic term.

CONCEPTUAL ISSUES IN THE STUDY OF ETHNIC DIFFERENCES

The Dilemma of Difference (Again)

Psychologists have tended to treat ethnicity (if they deal with it at all) as a descriptive variable defined by the selection of particular populations. Although I applaud attempts to understand neglected populations for their own sake, ethnicity suffers from the same problems as gender when it is used only as a way of describing differences between groups (Unger, 1979). It does not indicate what underlies such differences, and the situational context remains unexplored.

Many of the constructions of difference are ideologically and historically situated and are not easily accessible to conscious awareness. Their invisibility may be more harmful than negative images to which people may react. Thus, cross-cultural and cross-ethnic analyses are particularly valuable because they make the invisible visible (Unger & Sanchez-Hucles, 1993). However, culture cannot be examined merely as another divisional category. Psychologists must develop methodological techniques for interrogating cultural differences in meaning.

Unexamined Confounds and Group Differences in Meaning

A number of alternative explanations are possible for findings indicating differences in meaning between groups. Differences could be attributable to variations in linguistic usage among different ethnic groups (Henley, chapter 15 in this book); they could be attributable to differences in the way people perceive the testing situation and how they should respond; or they could be attributable to differences in the way people from different groups construct reality.

Of course, none of these explanations are limited to ethnicity but may prove to be confounded with it. In a recent study, Smith-Brinton and Unger (1993) found that people who were positivist in their explanations about how the world works used significantly different synonyms for defining some words than did those with a more constructionist orientation. Positivists tend to believe that "facts" are discovered rather than created; that determinist cause–effect relationships are important in human affairs; and that one or another source of authority defines "truth" (Unger, Draper, & Pendergrass, 1986). Differences in belief structure and language use could lead positivists to deny evidence that others see as self-evident.

Attitudes about reality have been found to vary between some ethnic groups in the United States as well as between individuals within these groups (Unger & Jones, 1988). They also have been found to vary between groups of women who differ in their degree of religiosity (Unger, 1992). Religious and secular women in Israel, for example, are more different from each other than religious women are from religious men. Such findings should make psychologists wary of reifying attitudes or behaviors as characteristic of any one ethnicity or gender.

Integrating Disciplines

Examining the meaning and condition of particular women's lives blurs traditional distinctions between subdisciplines of psychology. It is sometimes difficult reading chapters in this book to determine whether the author was trained as an experimental, a developmental, or a clinical psychologist. As psychologists begin to explore neglected areas within psychology, it becomes clear that they cannot explore people's experience without taking into account its situated context. Feminist therapists have been aware of this for many years. As Laura Brown (chapter 7 in this book) eloquently states, "feminist therapy theory always has been one part sociology (a description of the external reality and social context) and one part phenomenology (the description of lived and felt internal reality as experienced from within the social context)."

Ethnicity, like other culture-bound variables, should be explored empirically by using both frames of reference: internal and external reality. Ethnic identity represents one kind of filter, as does gender, class, age, and other yet unexplored variables. However, in their concern for subjectivity, psychologists must not neglect objective circumstances. Many of the chapters in this book point out that one of the things that women in many ethnic groups have in common is poverty. As I discuss later in this chapter, poverty may explain many of the behaviors that psychologists tend to attribute to ethnicity.

It is particularly important not to overpathologize ethnic women's responses to stress. These responses must be viewed in terms of the woman's cultural context (cf. Fine, 1983). Lykes et al. (1993) made this point dramatically in their analysis of women's responses to conditions of state-supported violence. They underscored the importance of not privatizing psychic trauma under conditions in which the broader society has gone crazy. Some clinical symptomatology would be highly predictable under such circumstances. Their work illustrates the importance of focusing on the social process at a variety of levels rather than on particular individuals or groups.

HOW ETHNICITY IS CONSTRUCTED

How Group Identities Help to Translate Common Experiences

The task of psychologists interested in gender and cultural diversity is to explain the processes through which particular traits and behaviors are produced and maintained. Naming the process as social construction is no longer sufficient. It is especially important that psychologists recognize that social construction is not the same thing as socialization, just as it is certainly not the same thing as biology. Instead, psychologists must look at how interpersonal transactions, sociostructural beliefs, and values, as well as their internalization, cause people to "do ethnicity" in a manner similar to the ways they "do gender" (West & Zimmerman, 1987).

This is an enormous task. Where should psychologists begin? First, they must emphasize that ethnicity, like gender, is not simply an issue for subordinate or marginalized groups. For example, White women are largely unaware of the importance of Whiteness in their own lives (cf. Frankenberg, 1993). Racial identity is considered an issue only for others and the awareness of White skin privilege is submerged. Because it is invisible to them, Whites may even be unaware of how visible it is to others (hooks, 1992).

It may be impossible to view different groups without taking into account their relationship to each other. As Glenn (1992) pointed out, categories such as male–female and Anglo–Latino are positioned and gain meaning from each other. The experiences of White women and Women of Color are not just different but are connected in systematic ways. Privileged women's lives are often purchased at the cost of the exploited labor of women (and men) in subordinated race and class locations (Zinn, 1994).

Ethnicity and Social Perception

A social constructionist view of ethnicity or race also requires that psychologists explore the bases for "ethnicizing" individuals. This is an area in which psychologists who have been studying social perception can be valuable. I have argued elsewhere that external appearance is a potent mediator for the creation of gender-related characteristics (Unger, 1985, 1993). Such cues are used as a basis for how one is to relate to others. Behavioral mechanisms such as the self-fulfilling prophecy have even been found to produce gender-stereotypic behaviors in people who are not of the "correct" sexual category (Skrypnek & Snyder, 1982).

Obviously, this kind of analysis must apply to "Whiteness" as a form of ethnicity as well. By ignoring Whiteness, psychologists have obscured both differences and similarities between groups of women who differ in social class, age, and religiosity. Investigations of groups of White women who are denied (or deny themselves) some forms of White privilege may be particularly useful for challenging the bases of ethnic categorization, particularly the relationship between Women of Color and marginality.

For example, battered women's shelters are usually seen primarily as resources for ethnic minority families. However, Jewish women from some ultraorthodox groups also need the support of battered women's shelters. They cannot, however, "go local." An unpublicized underground network of shelters for them has grown up throughout the United States that includes the need for an "underground railroad" to transport them and their 8–10 children (Fine, personal communication, April 15, 1994).

An analysis of diversity may be particularly illuminating when examined within such an all-White context. Although all Whites sometimes "look alike," traditional religious groups often use attire as one method for setting themselves apart. Feminists scholars have begun to analyze the meaning of traditional attire for women in these groups. Its meaning must be viewed in terms of its context and appears to serve several purposes at the same time.

For example, Orthodox Jewish and Moslem women are frequently admonished by their male religious leaders to maintain traditional garb. This attire is often seen as a mark of their subordination by secular feminists. However, traditional attire also may provide them with a means to engage in public activity within their communities without difficulty. It also provides them with a symbol of rebellion against the perceived cultural annihilation that modernization has brought (El-Or, 1993). Psychologists need to recognize that these meanings—both that of the "observer" and those of the "participants"—are equally valid.

The Importance of Physical Appearance

Attire as a cue for interpersonal behaviors has been neglected as a serious area of study. Differences in physical appearance have received more attention from psychologists. Recent studies have indicated that physical attractiveness is a cue that is recognized and used in attributional processes at least as quickly as physical sex (Locher, Unger, Sociedad, & Wahl, 1993). However, the stimulus aspects of race and ethnicity have rarely been explored. This is probably because researchers have lacked a good theoretical justification for such studies and because they are unwilling to recognize that people do indeed judge others by their appearance. The unwillingness to examine these effects is part of the invisible nature of sexism and racism in American society.

Social construction provides a theoretical justification for feminist research on appearance as a mediator of gender and ethnicity. Studies that examine variations in appearance within a particular group allow researchers to control for alleged differences between groups in terms of biology, long-term socialization, and so on. Popular culture may be less willing to accept the idea of "physical attractiveness centers" in the brain than the idea of neural differences that are based on gender or race.

The use of variations in appearance within a particular group to predict variations in traits considered indicative of differences between that group and others is a powerful demonstration of social construction. This usage turns the tables on the usual practices of psychology by using within-group variation to explain cross-group differences. It contrasts with psychology's usual practice of using cross-group variation in areas such as mathematics ability or IQ to predict the characteristics of individuals within groups.

Skin Color as a Cue for Behavior

One aspect of physical appearance that has been underexamined in terms of the construction of ethnicity is skin color. A recent book by Russell, Wilson, and Hall (1992) documents both the consequences of differences in skin color for African Americans and their unwillingness to discuss it publicly. Studies by sociologists (Hughes & Hertel, 1990) have shown, however, that lighter skinned Blacks fared better both educationally and economically than their darker peers even when the socioeconomic status of their families was taken into account.

Yet, unpublished research by Midge Wilson and her students (reported in Russell et al., 1992) indicates that skin color has a greater impact on Black women than on Black men. She found that both Black and White college students rated photographs of darker skinned women as being less successful, less happy in love, less popular, less physically attractive, less physically and emotionally healthy, and less intelligent than their light-skinned counterparts. The only quality in which the dark-skinned women were not rated lower was sense of humor, a phenomenon they labeled the "Whoopi Goldberg effect." African American girls as young as 6 years of age have been found to be twice as sensitive as boys to the social importance of skin color (Porter, 1991).

The preference for lighter skin tones among Blacks (as well as a preference for more White features) may be seen as a form of internalized racism. Similar skin preferences can be found in other ethnic groups such as some Latino populations and Asian Indians. In part, they are a response to media pronouncements that define female beauty as White (Unger & Crawford, 1992). However, they are also influenced by social relationships within ethnic communities. For example, Bond and Cash (1992) reported that regardless of their own satisfaction with their skin coloring, 70% of the Black women in their study believed that Black men preferred women whose skin was very light.

Although these studies are interesting in their own right, they also are interesting because they document the extent of variation possible within a group that has been portrayed monolithically within the mainstream discipline. This variability is particularly important because it based on an external cue that provokes differing social reactions. As I have argued earlier (Unger, 1985), this kind of information makes it more difficult for researchers to argue for the primacy of biology as a cause of differences between groups.

Distinguishing Between Biological and Sociocultural Variables

Of course, skin color is not the only variable that can and should be examined to clarify the relationship between biology and social variables.

Maria Root (chapter 12 in this book) points to studies that show that some biracial individuals may have a stronger ethnic identity than some monoracial individuals from the same ethnic group. Such studies demonstrate that biological and social "race" are not co-terminus. They may help to explain points such as that made by Diane Halpern (chapter 4 in this book) that gender differences in mathematical performance similar to those found among Asian and White populations are not found in Latino or African American populations.

Just as feminist scholars have tried to make a distinction between sex and gender in order to differentiate between biological and sociocultural aspects of being a male or a female, a similar distinction between race and ethnicity needs to be drawn. Evidence for the need for such a distinction is provided by studies of women's health as well as of their identity and cognitive abilities. For example, "hot flashes" during menopause are considered to be clearly a consequence of estrogen depletion. However, a number of studies have shown that Greek, Mayan, and Hawaiian women have many fewer episodes than do White women from the mainland United States (Klonoff et al., chapter 14 in this book). If such phenomena are primarily biological in origin, it is difficult to understand why they should be found in some ethnic groups but not in others.

Social Processes in a Developmental Context

An emphasis on social construction does not mean that researchers should ignore socialization completely. Perceptual and attributional processes affect individuals throughout their life span. Those that occur during childhood may be particularly important in the development of how individuals view themselves. Pamela Reid et al. (chapter 5 in this book) point out that researchers do not know much about gender differences in the socialization of ethnic minority children.

Both Reid's chapter and the one by Angela Ginorio et al. (chapter 11) illustrate how racism and sexism combine to the detriment of both Latina and African American girls. These girls are seen as less able than comparably gifted White girls. Subtle social processes within elementary schools probably stem from these beliefs. For example, Black girls, more than other students, are encouraged to assume roles as helper, enforcer, or go-between (Grant, 1994). Although such roles bring approval from teachers, they facilitate the development of social rather than academic skills.

Young women from ethnic minority groups also are more likely to be harassed in an academic setting than are young women from the dominant culture (Paludi et al., chapter 9 in this book). It is therefore not surprising that many ethnic minority women do not strive for formal academic credentials in American society (cf. chapters 10, 11, and 13 in this book). This double burden of racism and sexism helps explain findings that Black men of high professional stature were likely to come from diverse socio-economic backgrounds, whereas Black women who were high achievers typically came from a middle-class background (Reid and Robinson, 1985).

Confounds Between Ethnicity and Power

It is easy to confuse ethnicity (like gender) and power. Many of the effects discussed in various chapters in this book are not the consequences of a particular subcultural identity in itself but are attributable to the practices of a society that devalues ethnicity. Covert societal ideologies help maintain structural inequality between various groups. Such ideologies often take the form of stereotypes. The truth of these stereotypes often goes unchallenged even when they appear to be contradictory. For example, Ginorio and her colleagues (chapter 11) note the popular belief that Latino husbands provide protection and support for their families despite findings that 44% of Puerto Rican families are headed by women.

One of the few conclusions that can be drawn across marginalized ethnic groups is that they live disproportionately in poverty. Poverty affects not only access to external resources, but it also constrains people's choices, perceptions of choices, and their sense of entitlement to choose. Sometimes, there are no "right" choices. In fact, liberal feminism's emphasis on personal choice may be a consequence of the privileged position of many feminist scholars.

The Relation Between Cultural Categories and Social Processes

Poor women are often put into double binds not of their choosing. For example, mothers on public assistance may be excoriated for their "lack of the work ethic." However, when they work outside of the home, they are blamed for "latchkey children" and a lack of nurturance. Because there is little state-supported childcare available, no one has yet explained how these mothers can both spend more hours in employment and take better care of their children.

Marginalized populations appear to be more susceptible to double binds than other groups (Unger, 1988). The term *double bind* refers to situations in which the individual is confronted with two contradictory definitions of appropriate behavior. The individual may not be aware of these culturally based definitions and, in any case, has little power to change them without some form of collective action.

Women of Color have little power to define themselves or to challenge contradictions in others' definitions. Moreover, they may be subject to competing definitions both from the dominant society and the ideology of their own ethnic group. Assertiveness, for example, may be particularly problematic for women from groups that value feminine modesty and submissiveness even more than the dominant culture does. For them, assertiveness may be perceived not only as unfeminine but also as an abandonment of traditional cultural values.

Categorization processes affect everyone, not just members of marginalized groups. Although every individual belongs to at least one sexual, racial, and social class category simultaneously, such categories do not have an equal cultural meaning. Although individuals of one group are disadvantaged by a social label, others are privileged by not being subject to that label. It is society rather than the individual that decides whether a particular label will be imposed. This aspect of the categorization process tends to be ignored by social psychologists who work only within a laboratory context.

These issues are relevant for clinical psychologists too. They need to distinguish between labels, identities, and contexts. Psychologists can help individuals who suffer stress from conflicting views of the self by viewing identities as situated rather than essential parts of the individual. From this viewpoint, individuals are free to choose which aspect of themselves is most salient at the time without feeling that they have to abandon other aspects of their identity. This insight may be helpful to Women of Color who are frequently put in the difficult position of either reacting to the racism of White society or reacting to the sexism of White society and the men of their own group. They often feel that they must choose which form of oppression is more meaningful to them.

SUGGESTIONS FOR INTEGRATING DIFFERENCE

Integrating gender, race and ethnicity, and class is not easy. I challenge the field to determine when it is important to focus on particularities and when it is possible to look at commonalities without sacrificing values important to each group. To accomplish such aims, we as psychologists need to be innovative in both theory and methodology. As a preliminary step, I offer a few modest proposals.

1. We need to move away from sex and gender as our only major explanatory tool.
2. We need to operationalize what feminist psychologists mean by social construction and not view it simply as everything that biology is not.
3. We need to interrogate both ourselves and our discipline in terms of the biases with which we examine the world.
4. We need to explore the empiricist feminist dilemma of how to be social constructionist and still use "data." This process includes the obvious technique of redefining what we mean

by data as well as deconstructing our customary categories of analysis.

5. We need to begin to develop a "moral" basis for feminist psychology and its concern with diversity. To do so, we will need to move beyond our laboratory context, where issues of poverty and power are irrelevant. We will also need to leave our comfortable surroundings for much less pleasant realities so that we can better understand healthy coping in dire circumstances.

6. We may have to recognize that some dilemmas are not absolutely resolvable and that "solutions" need to be constantly redefined. Certainty is possible only in a homogeneous and unchanging world.

7. We should not let our preoccupation with scholarship that asks what is really true stop us from doing activist, challenging feminist psychology. As Weisstein (1993) eloquently stated,

> it has been my experience that, in times of no movement, reality itself falls into question. In times of dynamism, change and movement, people abandon doubts about reality, properly seeing them as part of the conservative past which they are rejecting. The fog lifts. The fact of movement gives us a clearer picture of what is really out there—what we are fighting against, and what we are fighting for. We need a feminist scholarship which will, once again, be infused, revitalized, and renewed, by movement. (p. 244)

REFERENCES

Apfelbaum, E. (1993). Norwegian and French women in high leadership positions: The importance of cultural contexts upon gendered relations. *Psychology of Women Quarterly, 17,* 409–430.

Bohan, J. S. (1993). Regarding gender: Essentialism, constructionism, and feminist psychology. *Psychology of Women Quarterly, 17,* 5–21.

Bond, S., & Cash, T. F. (1992). Black beauty: Skin color and body images among African-American college women. *Journal of Applied Social Psychology, 22,* 874–888.

Brown, L. S. (1990). The meaning of a multicultural perspective for theory-building in feminist therapy. *Women and Therapy, 9,* 1–23.

Carlson, B. E., & Videka-Sherman, L. (1990). An empirical test of androgyny in the middle years: Evidence from a national survey. *Sex Roles, 23,* 305–324.

Dion, K. L., & Dion, K. K. (1993). Gender and ethnocultural comparisons of styles of love. *Psychology of Women Quarterly, 17,* 463–474.

El-Or, T. (1993). The length of the slits and the spread of luxury: Reconstructing the subordination of ultra-orthodox Jewish women through the patriarchy of men scholars. *Sex Roles, 29,* 585–598.

Espin, O. M. (1987). Psychological impact of migration on Latinas: Implications of psychotherapeutic practice. *Psychology of Women Quarterly, 11,* 489–503.

Fine, M. (1983). Coping with rape: Critical perspectives on consciousness. *Imagination, Cognition, and Personality, 3,* 249–267.

Frankenberg, R. (1993). *White women, race matters: The social construction of whiteness.* Minneapolis: University of Minnesota Press.

Franz, C. E., & Stewart, A. J. (Eds.). (1994). *Women creating lives: Identities, resilience, and resistance.* Boulder, CO: Westview Press.

Gibbons, J. L., Lynn, M., Stiles, D. A., de Berducido, E. J., Richter, R., Walker, K., & Wiley, D. (1993). Guatemalan, Filipino, and U. S. adolescents' images of women as office workers and homemakers. *Psychology of Women Quarterly, 17,* 373–388.

Glenn, E. N. (1992). From servitude to service work: Historical continuities in the racial division of paid reproductive labor. *Signs, 18,* 1–43.

Graham, S. (1992). Most of the subjects were white and middle class. *American Psychologist, 47,* 629–639.

Grant, L. (1994). Helpers, enforcers, and go-betweens: Black females in elementary school classrooms. In M. B. Zinn & B. T. Dill (Eds.), *Women of color in U.S. society.* (pp. 43–63). Philadelphia: Temple University Press.

Hare-Mustin, R. T., & Marecek, J. (1988). The meaning of difference: Gender theory, postmodernism, and psychology. *American Psychologist, 43,* 455–464.

hooks, b. (1984). *Feminist theory: From margin to center.* Boston: South End Press.

hooks, b. (1992). *Black looks: Race and representation.* Boston: South End Press.

Hughes, M. G., & Hertel, B. R. (1990). The significance of color remains: A study of life chances, mate selection, and ethnic consciousness among black Americans. *Social Forces, 68,* 1–16.

Hull, A., Scott, P., & Smith, B. (1982). *All the women are white, all the blacks are men, but some of us are brave: Black women's studies.* Westbury, NY: Feminist Press.

Kauppinen-Toropainen, K., & Gruber, J. E. (1993). Antecedents and outcomes of women-unfriendly experiences: A study of Scandinavian, formerly Soviet, and American women. *Psychology of Women Quarterly, 17,* 431–456.

Landrine, H., Klonoff, E. A., & Brown-Collins, A. (1992). Cultural diversity and methodology in feminist psychology: Critique, proposal, empirical example. *Psychology of Women Quarterly, 16,* 145–163.

Locher, P., Unger, R. K., Sociedad, P., & Wahl, J. (1993). At first glance: Accessibility of the physical attractiveness stereotype. *Sex Roles, 28,* 729–743.

Lykes, M. B. (1994). Speaking against the silence: One Maya woman's exile and return. In C. E. Franz & A. J. Stewart (Eds.), *Women creating lives: Identities, resilience, and resistance* (pp. 97–114). Boulder, CO: Westview Press.

Lykes, M. B., Brabeck, M. M., Ferns, T., & Radan, A. (1993). Human rights and mental health among Latin American women in situations of state-sponsored violence: Bibliographic resources. *Psychology of Women Quarterly, 17*, 525–544.

Melville, M. B., & Lykes, M. B. (1992). Guatemalan Indian children and the sociocultural effects of government sponsored terrorism. *Social Science and Medicine, 34*, 533–548.

Porter, C. (1991). Social reasons for skin tone preferences of black school-age children. *American Journal of Orthopsychiatry, 61*, 149–154.

Reid, P. T. (1988). Racism and sexism: Comparisons and conflicts. In P. A. Katz & D. A. Taylor (Eds.), *Eliminating racism: Profiles in controversy* (pp. 203–221). New York: Plenum.

Reid, P. T. (1993). Poor women in psychological research: Shut up and shut out. *Psychology of Women Quarterly, 17*, 133–150.

Reid, P. T., & Robinson, W. L. (1985). Professional black men and women: Attainment of terminal academic degrees. *Psychological Reports, 56*, 547–549.

Russell, K., Wilson, M., & Hall, R. (1992). *The color complex: The politics of skin color among African Americans.* New York: Harcourt Brace Jovanovich.

Skrypnek, B. J., & Snyder, M. (1982). On the self-perpetuating nature of stereotypes about women and men. *Journal of Experimental Social Psychology, 18*, 277–291.

Smith-Brinton, M., & Unger, R. K. (1993). Ideological differences in the construction of meaning. *Imagination, Cognition, and Personality, 12*, 395–412.

Unger, R. K. (1979). Toward a redefinition of sex and gender. *American Psychologist, 34*, 1085–1094.

Unger, R. K. (1985). Personal appearance and social control. In M. Safir, M. Mednick, D. Izraeli, & J. Bernard (Eds.), *Women's worlds: The new scholarship* (pp. 142–151). New York: Praeger.

Unger, R. K. (1988). Psychological, feminist, and personal epistemology: Transcending contradiction. In M. Gergen (Ed.), *Feminist thought and the structure of knowledge* (pp. 124–141). New York: New York University Press.

Unger, R. K. (1989). Sex, gender, and epistemology. In M. Crawford & M. Gentry (Eds.), *Gender and thought* (pp. 17–35). New York: Springer-Verlag.

Unger, R. K. (1992). Will the real sex difference please stand up? *Feminism and Psychology, 2*, 231–238.

Unger, R. K. (1993). Alternative conceptions of sex (and sex differences). In M. Haug, R. Whalen, C. Aron, & K. L. Olsen (Eds.), *The development of sex differences and similarities in behavior* (pp. 457–476). Dordrecht, The Netherlands: Kluwer Academic.

Unger, R. K., & Crawford, M. (1992). *Women and gender: A feminist psychology.* New York: McGraw-Hill.

Unger, R. K., & Crawford, M. (1993). Sex and gender: The troubled relationship between terms and concepts. *Psychological Science, 4*, 122–124.

Unger, R. K., Draper, R. D., & Pendergrass, M. L. (1986). Personal epistemology and personal experience. *Journal of Social Issues, 42,* 67–79.

Unger, R. K., & Jones, J. (1988). *Personal epistemology and its correlates: The subjective nature of sex and race.* International Society of Political Psychology, Meadowlands, NJ.

Unger, R. K., & Sanchez-Hucles, J. (1993). Integrating gender: Implications for the psychology of women. *Psychology of Women Quarterly, 17,* 365–372.

Unger, R. K., & Saundra (1993). Sexism: An integrated perspective. In F. L. Denmark & M. Paludi (Eds.), *Psychology of women: A handbook of issues and theories* (pp. 141–188). Westport, CT: Greenwood Press.

Weisstein, N. (1993). Power, resistance, and science: A call for a revitalized feminist psychology. *Feminism and Psychology, 3,* 239–245.

West, C., & Zimmerman, D. H. (1987). Doing gender. *Gender and Society, 1,* 125–151.

Yoder, J. D., & Kahn, A. S. (1993). Working toward an inclusive psychology of women. *American Psychologist, 48,* 846–850.

Zinn, M. B. (1994). Feminist rethinking from racial-ethnic families. In M. B. Zinn & B. T. Dill (Eds.), *Women of color in U.S. society* (pp. 303–314). Philadelphia: Temple University Press.

APPENDIX

Goals and Accomplishments of the APA Division 35 Cultural Diversity Task Force, 1990–1991

The Cultural Diversity Task Force of the American Psychological Association's (APA's) Division 35 (Psychology of Women) convened in 1990. Bernice Lott, PhD, president of Division 35 for 1990–1991, was determined that leadership positions in the division reflect the ethnic diversity of the membership that is so vital to the continued development of theory, research, and practice in the field. Therefore, the first task force she formed was on cultural diversity in feminist psychology, and the person she chose to head the task force was Hope Landrine, PhD, editor of this volume. Dr. Landrine was able to enlist the energies and skills of a large number of already overextended psychologists to participate in a number of tasks, including the creation of this book.

The task force set out to do and accomplished the following:

1. We addressed issues of the education, training, recruitment, and mentoring of women of color graduate students in psychology and made specific, viable suggestions (Mary Kay Biaggio & Michele C. Boyer).
2. We suggested guidelines for teachers of psychology of women courses on integrating data on women of color into their syllabi (Alice Brown-Collins).
3. We outlined procedures for increasing communication and networking among feminist and ethnic minority psychol-

433

ogi-pfjcal organizations, committees, boards, divisions, and directorates (Martha Banks).

4. We suggested changes in the publication policies of *Psychology of Women Quarterly*, *Sex Roles*, and *Women and Therapy* to increase cultural diversity in published articles as well as among journal editors and reviewers (the task force as a whole).

5. We presented a symposium at the APA convention in 1991 on cultural diversity in feminist psychology to an audience of more than 500 (Elizabeth Klonoff, Nancy Henley, Diane Halpern, Veronica Thomas, Lula Beatty, Michele Paludi, Ellen Kimmel, and Hope Landrine) and highlighted the importance of diversity.

6. We wrote this book in an effort to gather some of the data and theory on women of color into a single volume that could serve as a resource for students and scholars alike.

Accomplishments 1–4 were presented to Division 35's Executive Committee (1990–1991), and all were accepted, approved unanimously, and adopted. Item 4 (changing the publication policies of the major feminist psychological journals), however, could be implemented only for *Psychology of Women Quarterly*, a Division 35 journal. The remaining journals were contacted by Division 35's Executive Committee, and the recommendations of the task force were communicated to them.

Changing the publication policies of the major feminist psychological journals was a primary objective of the task force, because publication policies demarcate legitimate knowledge and reflect and permit a culturally specific epistemology, ontology, and politics. We recommended, and gained, unanimous Division 35 Executive Committee approval for the following: (a) Feminist psychological journals will increase the number of women of color who serve as reviewers and consulting editors; (b) will publish a "special issue" on women of color or cultural diversity every 1–2 years; (c) will draft a statement regarding ethnocentric or racist language that is analogous to the statement on sexist language; (d) will include a sentence encouraging papers on cultural diversity in their statement regarding the topics of interest to the journal; (e) will instruct authors to include the available literature on people of color in their literature review or to indicate that no such data are available; and (f) will request that authors whose samples include no people of color indicate in their discussion section that the absence of people of color is a limitation of the study and that the results cannot be generalized to people of color.

This accomplishment is an important step in changing the face of feminist psychology. It could not have been achieved without the enthusiastic participation and support of *Psychology of Women Quarterly*'s editor (1989–1994) Judith Worell, who made a strong commitment to assuring these changes in that journal.

The many individuals who were responsible for these and other accomplishments have been listed in the Acknowledgments of this book.

AUTHOR INDEX

Numbers in italics refer to listings in reference sections.

McDiarmid, G., 200, *234*
McGlone, J., 84, *91*
McGoldrick, M., 164, *174*
McGrath, D., 365, 378, *392*
McGrath, E., 317, 323, *328*
McHugh, M. D., 56, *74*
McKay, S., 201, *237*
McKinnell, T., *236*
McLloyd, V. C., 116, *136*, 323, *330*
McMillan, J. R., 365, 378, *392*
McQuarter, G., 318, *324*
McShane, D. A., 220, *237*
Mead, M., 186, *190*
Medicine, B., 198, 200, 226, *234*, 368, 369, 370, *392*
Mednick, M., 6, *19*, 317, *324*, *328*
Mednick, M. S., 305, 317, *328*, *329*
Mednick, M. T., 316, *328*
Mednick, T., 317, *330*
Meinhardt, K., 253, 254, *263*
Melville, M., 244, *261*
Melville, M. E., 419, *430*
Meredith, C. N., 354, *359*
Meseguer, A. G., 368, *392*
Metcalf, A., *234*
Metoyer, C., 198, *234*
Meyer, B., 105, *109*
Miller, B., 283, *298*
Miller, C., 363, *392*
Miller, D., 164, *174*
Miller, J. B., 145, 151, *160*
Miller, J. G., 72, *75*
Miller, M. J., 105, *109*
Miller, N. K., 131, 132, 133, *136*
Miller, R. L., 277, 283, *298*
Miller, S. I., 202, *234*
Minor, J. H., 316, *326*
Mirabla, K., 221, *236*
Miramontez, A., 222, *226*
Misiak, H., 30n1, *53*
Mitchell-Kernan, C., 367, 371, *392*
Mittlefehldt, P. K., *234*
Modesto, R., 212, *234*
Mohatt, G., 200, 210, *232*, *234*
Mollica, R., 285, *298*
Monelli, C., 256, *259*
Montalvo, B., 172, *175*
Montgomery, P., 242, *260*
Montoya, V., 200, *234*
Moore, C. I., *234*
Moore, H. A., 251, *261*
Moore, J., 242, 243, 244, 249, *261*

Moore, K., 188, *190*
Moraga, C., 153, *160*, 166, *175*, 382, *392*
Moran, B., 210, *234*
Morawski, J. G., 56, *75*, 114, 116, 123, 130, *136*
Morey, S. M., 213, *234*
Morgan, M., 367, 370, 383, 387, *392*
Morgan, R., 398, *411*
Morris, E. K., 3, 6, *19*
Morrison, T., 155, *160*
Moschkovich, J., 156, *160*
Moses, Y., 188, *190*
Moses, Y. T., 317, *328*
Mount, G., 212, *234*
Muehlenhard, C. L., 406, *411*
Mummendey, A., 8, *19*
Murphy, M. N., 213, *234*
Murphy-Shigematsu, S., 283, *298*
Murray, S. R., 317, *328*
Murrell, A. J., 317, *328*
Musialowski, D. M., 398, *410*
Myers, L. W., 317, *328*

Nadelman, L., 105, *109*
Nagata, D. K., 266, *298*
Nagel, E., 314, *328*
Nagel, J. K., 202, *235*
Nagoshi, C. T., 278, *297*
Nakashima, C. L., 283, *298*, *299*
Natale, M., 378, *392*
National Center for Education Statistics, 308, 313, 314, *328*
National Education Association, 85, *91*
National Institute on Alcohol Abuse and Alcoholism Newsletter, 203, *235*
National Research Council, 87, *91*
National Science Foundation, 212, *235*
"Native Americans Gaining," 199, *235*
"Natives Cheer Clinton Choice," 199, *235*
Neligh, G., 201, *235*
Nelson, C., 243, 244, *261*
Nelson, E. A., 371n6, *392*
Nelson, S. H., 210, *235*
Nelson-LeGall, S., 94, 104, *109*
Neumann, A. K., 199, *235*
Newell-Morris, L., 278, *297*
Nguyen, N. A., 289, *299*
Nicholls, J. G., 104, *109*
Nichols, P. C., 373, 374, *392*, *393*
Nicholson, L. J., 123, 124, *134*

Wahl, J., 423, *429*
Waldron, I., 355, *360*
Walker, A., 153, 155, *161*, 400, 401, 403, 408, *411*
Walker, K., 417, *429*
Walker, L. A., 145, *160*
Walker, L. E., 308, *330*
Walker, L. E. A., 144, 145, *159*, 164, *175*
Walker, R. D., 201, 219, *234*
Wallace, M., 166, *175*
Wallston, B., 56, *75*
Wallston, B. S., 30, 51, *53*
Walsh, M. R., 304, *330*, 398, *411*
Walsh, R., 371n6, *395*
Ward, J. V., 321, *326*
Warheit, G. J., 253, 254, *263*
Warshaw, J., 149, *160*
Washington, E. D., 323, *330*
Watanabe, S., 279, *301*
Watkins, F. E., *238*
Watts, D., 184, *189*
Watts-Jones, D., 317, *330*
Wax, R. H., 213, *238*
Weaver, J. B., 398, *411*
Webb-Watson, L., 220, *238*
Weiner, L., 181, 182, *189*
Weisstein, N., 428, *431*
Weitzman, L., 183, *190*
Welch, D., 198, *238*
Welch, D. S., *238*
West, C., 366, 373, 378, 379, 385, *395*, 421, *431*
Weston, P. J., 317, *330*
Whitehead, H., *238*
Whitely, R., 72, *74*
Wiley, D., 417, *429*
Williams, N., 246, *263*
Williams, R. L., 318, *330*
Williams, S. J., 378, *395*
Williams, T. K., 283, *301*
Williams-McCoy, J., 147, *161*, 167, 173, *175*
Willis, D. J., 204, *238*
Willis, E., 399, *411*
Willis, F. N., 378, *395*
Wills, T. A., 248, *259*
Wilson, K., 181, *191*
Wilson, M., 424, *430*

Wilson, M. N., 95, *108*, 110, *111*
Wilson, S., 219, *239*
Wilson, W., 371n6, *395*
Wingrove, C. R., 317, *327*
Winter, M., 258, *262*
Wise, S., 381, *395*
Witmer, J. M., 213, *237*
Witt, S. H., 198, *238*
Wittig, M. A., 56, *75*
Wittstock, L. W., *238*
Wolchik, S. A., 105, *107*
Wolfram, W. A., 371, *395*
Wolman, C., 222, *238*
Wong, B., 278, *294*
Wong, D., 266, 272, 273, 274, 287, *295*
Wong, S. C., 291, *301*
Woolgar, S., 72, *74*, 125, 126, 129, 130, *137*
Wyatt, G., 147, *161*
Wyatt, G. E., 317, *330*
Wyshak, G., 285, *298*

Yang, D., 247, *259*
Ybarra, L., 249, *263*
Yeung, W.-T., 266, 278, *297*
Yi, K. Y., 282, *301*
Ying, Y. W., 99, 103, *108*, 287, 290, 291, *301*
Yinger, I. M., 99, *110*
Yoder, J. D., 114, *135*, 305, 306, 321, *327*, *330*, 414, *431*
Yoshimura, K. K., 281, 282, *301*
Young, T. J., 200, *239*
Yu, W. S. H., 291, *301*
Yung, J., 269, 279, *301*

Zak, N., *239*
Zalk, S., 313
Zalk, S. R., 98, *111*, 180, 181, *191*
Zane, N., 164, 167, 171, *175*, 214, *237*, 282, *300*
Zeff, S. B., 252, *263*
Zentella, A. C., 374, 376, *395*
Zillmann, D., 398, 400, 407, 408, *411*
Zimmerman, D., 366, 378, 385, *395*
Zimmerman, D. H., 366, 378, *395*, 421, *431*
Zimmerman, M., 219, *239*
Zinn, M. B., 118, *137*, 172, *175*, 422, *431*

SUBJECT INDEX

Education (*continued*)
    American Indian women, 208–209
    Asian American women, 277–279
    and gender role attitudes, 249
    Latinas, 250–252
Effect-size statistic, 81
Elderly
    American Indian women, 198–199,
      203
    Asian Americans, caretaking, 289
Emic method, 61–73
    definition, 62
    in feminist research, 63–73
    in self-ratings study, 64–71
Empiricist epistemology
    alternatives to, 123
    feminists' violation of, 122–123
    social and political influences, 117
Employment
    American Indian women, 200–201
    Asian American women, 275–277
    feminists' experience, 41–43
    Latinas, 253
Empowerment, and Latina therapy, 257
Endogamy, and Latina education, 252
Enmeshment, 165
Ethics, research subjects, 58
Ethnic groups. *See also specific groups*
    academic sexual harassment,
      182–184
    conceptual issues, 419–428
    contextualism, 1–14
    cultural influences, research
      implications, 64–73
    emic research methods advantage,
      64–73
    gender socialization, 93–106
    psychotherapy limitations, 164–165
    and research methodology
      differences, 57–58
Ethnic identity
    Amerasians, 282–283
    Asian American women, 280–282
    cultural context importance, 421
    Latina college students, 252
Ethnic validity model, 173
Etic method, 61–73
    definition, 62
    in self-ratings study, 64–71
Eurocentrism, 148–152
European American women. *See* White
    women

"Eventing," 215–216
Exercise
    Health Psychology articles, 346
    minority women need for, 338
Experimental methods. *See* Research
    methods
*Expert Directory of the Association of Black
    Psychologists*, 310–311
Extended family, Latinos, 246
Eye contact, American Indians, 217
Eyefold surgery, 281

Familiarismo, 256
Family relationships
    American Indian women, 200
    Asian American women, 287–289
    feminists' experience of, 42–44
    Latinas, 244–248
Family therapy
    American Indians, 220–221
    and Latina beliefs, 257
Femininity, emic data, 65–71
Feminist therapy, 143–158
    culture and class-bound norms,
      151–152
    Eurocentrism, 148–152
    inadequacies for women of color,
      166
    personality theory in, 154–155
    psychodynamic theory in, 150–151
    racism in training programs,
      146–147
    theoretical considerations, 144
    White women biases, 145–146
Fertility rates, Latinas, 250
Fetal alcohol syndrome, 203
Filipina Americans
    education, 276
    immigration history, 269–270
    marital relationships, 288–289
    violence against, 287
Friendships, feminists' experience, 43–45

Geisha girl stereotype, 275
Gender analysis approach, 321
Gender differences
    bias in research on, 321
    in cognition, 77–90
    contextualism, 1–14
    in conversational interactions, 366
    in language use, 361–387

Interruption patterns, conversations, 378–379
Inventory to Diagnose Depression, 219

Japanese American women
    divorce rate, 288
    employment, 276
    immigration history, 269–270
    intermarriage, 278–279
    stereotypes, 274–275
    women's movement participation, 273
Japanese families, 165
Jespersen, Otto, 363
Jewish women, sexualization paradigm, 401
Johnson O'Malley counselor, 211
Journal of Black Psychology
    Black women editors, 313
    publications on Black women, 315–316
Journal of Social Issues, 316
Jungian theory, 155

Korean American women
    divorce rate, 288
    employment, 276
    immigration history, 270
    violence against, 286–287

Lakoff, Robin, 363–365
Language, 361–387
    African American use of, 377–383
    code switching in, 374–377
    conservatism in women, 369–374
    in conversational interaction, 377–383
    gender bias, 361–387
    gender differences in usage, 361–387
    social role influences, 370
    social stratification, 371–372, 385
Laotian refugees, 291–292
Latinas, 241–258
    cultural influences, research implications, 64–73
    double standards, 251
    education, 250–252
    emic method advantages with, 64–71
    family issues, 244–248
    gender role behavior, 248–250
    gender socialization, 100, 103

labor force participation, 253
    mental health, 253–257
    overweight data, 338
    psychological issues, 241–258
    psychotherapy, 256–257
    salary discrimination, 253
    self-ratings of, cultural influences, 64–71
    smoking, 355
    stereotypes, 245–247
    unprotected anal intercourse motivation, 9–11
    work issues, 253
Latinos
    gender role attitudes, 248–250
    gender socialization, families, 100, 245–247
    historical context, 242–243
    racial discrimination, 242
Leadership ability, emic data, 65–71
Lesbians
    American Indian tribal acceptance, 198
    Asian Americans, 281
Lighter skinned Blacks, 424
Linguistic conservatism, women, 369–374

Mail-order brides, 279
Male inexpressiveness, 379–380
Marianismo, 246–247, 256–257
Marital relationships
    Asian Americans, 287–289
    feminists' experience, 43–44
    Filipinos, 288–289
Marriage statistics, Latinos, 245
Master's degrees in psychology, 308–309
Mathematical ability
    gender differences, biological, 84–85, 425
    gender expectations, 104
Mecegenation, Asian Americans, 277–279
Mechanistic behaviorism, 3–6
Media influences, gender socialization, 102
Medical research, 335–358
Medicine women, 209–210
Menopausal symptoms, 356, 425
Menstruation, language of, 371n6
Mental health
    American Indians, 201–203
    Asian American women, 279–293

Peri Life Events Scale, 317
Person-centered approaches. *See also*
    Emic method
    in feminist research, 61–73
Personal Attributes Questionnaire, 102
Personalismo, 246, 256
Personality theory, 154–155
Phenomenology, feminist therapy,
    148–150
Physical abuse, Asian Americans,
    285–287
Physical appearance
    Asian American women, 280–282
    social constructions, 423
Plastic surgery, Asian Americans, 281
Political activism, 273
Pornography, 397–409
    attitudes toward, research needs,
      406–408
    Black attitudes toward, 407
    and Black men, 401–402
    and Black women, 400–406
    civil legislation, 397–398
    controversies, 398–399
    definitions and categories, 399
    desensitizing effects, 408
    as hate speech, 398
    interracial themes, 404–405
    political and racist aspects, 403–404
    racism in, 400–406
    research, 404–409
    sexism in, 401–406
Positivism, 420–421
Postmenopausal symptoms, 356
Postmodern feminism, 123–124, 415–416
Posttraumatic stress disorder
    American Indian women, 219
    Latina immigrants, 256
Poverty
    American Indians, 200
    ethnic groups pervasive effect, 426
    Latino families, 245
    and scholastic achievement test
      scores, 87
Power issues
    in academic sexual harassment,
      180–181, 183
    ethnicity confounds, 426
    in mentor–protégé relationships,
      187–188
Pregnancy
    American Indians, 202

Health Psychology articles, 348
Premigration stress
    Latinas, 255–256
    Southeast Asians, 291–293
Psychiatric problems
    American Indians, 201–203
    Asian American women, 290–291
Psychiatrist's role, 215
Psychoanalytic theory
    in feminist therapy, 150–151
    gender socialization, 95–96
Psychoeducational approaches, 220
Psychological assessment
    American Indian women, 219–220
    cultural influences, 64–73
Psychological research, 117–118. *See also*
    Research methods
Psychological tests, 64–73
Psychology degrees
    African American women, 308–309
    American Indian women, 211–212
Psychology of Women Quarterly
    Black women editors, 312
    health psychology articles, 351–355
    publications on Black women,
      315–316
Psychology training programs. *See*
    Training programs
Psychotherapy. *See also* Feminist therapy
    American Indian women, 220–224
    Asian Americans, 290
    ethnic minority inadequacies,
      164–165
    Latinas, cultural considerations,
      256–257
    limitations for women, 164
Psychotherapy supervision
    components, 171–173
    principles, 166
    process of, 166–171
Psychotherapy training programs, 148
Puberty rites, 198
Puerto Ricans
    bilingual code switching, 376–377
    ethnic discrimination history, 243
    labor force participation, 253
    sex-role traditionalism, 249
Pulmonary disease, and smoking, 337

Qualitative approaches, 61–73. *See also*
    Emic method
Questionnaires

Violence against women
    Asian Americans, 285–287
    in pornography, 407–408
Virgin Mary model, 257
Vocabulary, gender differences, 82

War Brides Act, 267, 270
When and Where I Enter (Gidding), 155
White Buffalo Calf Woman, 210
White women
    career expectations, 105
    cultural influences, research
        implications of, 64–73
    feminism experience, 50–51

health problem epidemiology,
    336–342
Health Psychology research articles,
    342–355
language, 363–366
life satisfaction, middle years, 414
self-ratings, 64–71
social perception, 422–423
Wise women, 209–210, 225
Womanism, 30, 35–52
Women's language, 362–365
Work. *See* Employment
Work ethic, double bind, 426
Work relationships, feminists, 40–43

X-rated videos, 404–405

ABOUT THE EDITOR

Hope Landrine received her PhD in clinical psychology from the University of Rhode Island (1983), completed her postdoctoral training in social psychology at Stanford University (1984–1986), and received additional training in preventive medicine in the Department of Preventive Medicine, University of Southern California Medical School (1992–1993). She is currently a research scientist at the Public Health Foundation of Los Angeles County, where she conducts full-time, grant-supported research and preventive interventions to improve the health of African American and Latino children and adults, and of women and girls of all ethnic groups. She has published numerous articles on cultural diversity. Her other books include *The Politics of Madness* (1992, Peter Lang); *African-American Acculturation: Deconstructing Race and Reviving Culture*, with Elizabeth Klonoff (1995, Sage); and *Preventing Misdiagnosis of Women: A Therapist's Guide to Physical Disorders With Psychiatric Symptoms* (in press, Sage). Dr. Landrine received the 1994 American Psychological Association Minority Fellowship Program Achievement Award for Research for outstanding contributions to research on cultural diversity in feminist, clinical, and health psychology.